OSGi Service Platform, Enterprise Specification Release 4, Version 4.2

January 25, 2010 9:42 pm

OSGi Service Platform
Enterprise Specification

The OSGi Alliance

Release 4, Version 4.2
March 2010

Trademarks

OSGi™ is a trademark, registered trademark, or service mark of the OSGi Alliance in the US and other countries. Java™, JRE™, JDBC™, and JMX™ are trademarks, registered trademarks, or service marks of Sun Microsystems, Inc. in the US and other countries. All other trademarks, registered trademarks, or service marks used in this document are the property of their respective owners and are hereby recognized.

Feedback

This specification can be downloaded from the OSGi Alliance web site:

    http://www.osgi.org

Comments about this specification can be raised at:

    http://www.osgi.org/bugzilla/

Book Publication

Publisher	aQute Publishing
	9c, Avenue St. Drezery, Beaulieu, FRANCE
	+33467542167 / books@aQute.biz
	http://www.aQute.biz
ISBN	978-90-79350-06-3

Table Of Contents

105   Metatype Service Specification   83

107   User Admin Service Specification   103

110   Initial Provisioning Specification   123

112   Declarative Services Specification   141

113   Event Admin Service Specification   177

121   Blueprint Container Specification   193

1   Introduction

The OSGi Service Platform Specifications have now been released in their fourth edition. While the original focus of the specifications was geared towards embedded systems, the latest 4.2 version added framework core functionality and new services that make the OSGi Service Platform more appealing to the enterprise world.

The OSGi Enterprise Expert Group (EEG) is chartered to define the technical requirements and specifications to tailor and extend the OSGi Service Platform to address information technology software infrastructure use cases found in enterprise scenarios.

The EEG technical areas of concern include:

- Scaling, including multi-container and multi-process environments
- Distributed and/or federated service model for:
    - Multiple Service Platforms
    - External, heterogeneous systems
- Requirements for extensions to the OSGi publish/find/bind service model
- Enterprise-class life cycle and configuration management
- Integration of established Java EE technology into OSGi

This specification is based on [2] *OSGi Service Platform Core Specification,Release 4, Version 4.2.* The specification combines previously published, as well as new, OSGi services that address the common use cases of enterprise application and application server developers. It serves as a first reference point for the suggested audience when considering the use of OSGi in their environment to fulfill their own needs or to better serve the needs of their customers. This collection of services is taken from the complete set of available specifications and narrowed down to what can be relevant to the enterprise domain.

The services of the Enterprise Specification have been designed to integrate with OSGi and cooperate with each other. None of the listed service specifications is mandatory; all service specifications are optional. However, services provided must follow their specification completely.

It is not suggested, or expected, that an enterprise solution will incorporate support for all listed specifications, instead a customized subset to satisfy the requirements at hand is recommended. A solution can further include other core and compendium services that are not listed as part of the Enterprise Specification. The selection of appropriate services should be driven by requirements and use cases.

The Enterprise Specification includes the recommended specifications for a number of areas. The services of the Enterprise Specification have been designed to guarantee integration with OSGi and cooperation among each other. These Enterprise Specification areas are described in the following sections.

1.1   Overview of Services

1.1.1   Component Models

While the OSGi framework API is relatively simple to use, it is still considered infrastructure that can bleed into the application code of a bundle. This Enterprise Specification therefore provides multiple, interoperable, Dependency Injection based component models. These DI models ensure decoupling of the application code from the OSGi APIs; they provide an OSGi bundle programming model with minimal implementation dependencies and virtually no accidental complexity in the Java code. Both models provide support for handling the life cycle of services, albeit in different ways. These component models are the Declarative Services Specification and the Blueprint Container Specification:

- *Declarative Services Specification* – The Declarative Services specification provides dependency injection for services. It handles the service life cycle dynamics by notifying the component or managing the component's life cycle. See chapter *112 Declarative Services Specification.*
- *Blueprint Container Specification* – The Blueprint Container is derived from the Spring Dynamic Module project. It provides a general DI framework; services are supported by proxying them and damping their life cycle. See chapter *121 Blueprint Container Specification.*

1.1.2   Distributed Services

The OSGi framework provides a local service registry for bundles to communicate through service objects, where a service is an object that one bundle registers and another bundle looks up. The Enterprise Specification enhances this model by defining endpoints that represent services hosted in a remote systems. It allows for seamless access to remote services within the OSGi Service Platform without changing the service layer. The remote system may or may not be based on OSGi.

The Enterprise Specification includes the specifications of:

- *Remote Services* - The Remote Services specification defines a number of service properties that participating bundles can use to convey information to a distribution provider.The distribution provider creates endpoints that are accessible to remote clients or registers proxies that access services hosted external to the OSGi framework. See chapter *13 Remote Services.*
- *Remote Service Admin Specification* - The Remote Services Admin Service Specification defines an API for the distribution provider and discovery of services in a network. A management agent can use this API to provide an actual distribution policy. This management agent can export and import services as well as discovering services in the network. See *122 Remote Service Admin Service Specification.*
- *SCA Configuration Type* – Distribution providers support a number of communication protocols configured by specific configuration types. The SCA Remote Services Configuration Specification defines such a configuration type. See *129 SCA Configuration Type Specification.*

1.1.3   Web Applications and HTTP Servlets

Current Java EE architectures almost always require support for web technologies in the form of Java Servlets or Web Applications. The Enterprise Specification includes two complementary service specifications in support:

- *Web Application Specification* - The Web Application specification provides support for web applications written to the Servlet 2.5 specification as well as the JSP 2.1 specification. This specification details how web applications packaged as a WAR or as bundles (WABs) can be installed into an OSGi Service Platform, as well as how this application can use OSGi services. See *128 Web Applications Specification.*
- *Http Service Specification* - Bundle developers typically need to develop communication and user interface solutions for standard technologies such as HTTP, HTML, XML, and servlets. The Http Service supports two standard techniques for this purpose: registering servlets and registering resources. See *102 Http Service Specification.*

1.1.4   Event models

The OSGi service model is based on synchronous APIs. Support for asynchronous invocations and event driven interactions usually involves the definition of listeners. However, this model does not scale well for fine grained events that must be dispatched to many different handlers. The Enterprise Specification therefore contains the:

- *Event Admin Service Specification* - The Event Admin service provides an inter-bundle communication mechanism. It is based on a event publish and subscribe model, popular in many message based systems. See *113 Event Admin Service Specification.*

1.1.5 Management and Configuration services

Support for managing the servers and their applications is essential to all enterprise systems. The Enterprise Specification includes several services addressing the need to manage the framework from the outside as well as configuring individual bundles and applications from within the OSGi Service Platform.

- *JMX™ Management Model Specification* - The Java Management Extensions (JMX) is the standard API specification for providing a management interface to Java SE and Java EE applications. The JMX Management Model specification provides an MBean interface adaptation of the existing OSGi framework artifacts; these can then be used to expose an OSGi Framework manipulation API over JMX. See *124 JMX™ Management Model Specification*.
- *User Admin Service Specification* – The User Admin Service Specification provides authorization for OSGi Service Platform actions based on authenticated users, instead of using the Java code-based permission model. See *107 User Admin Service Specification*.
- *Initial Provisioning Specification* - This specification defines how the Management Agent can make its way into the Service Platform, and gives a structured view of the problems and their corresponding resolution methods. The purpose of this specification is to enable the management of a Service Platform by an operator, and (optionally) to hand over the management of the Service Platform later to another operator. See *110 Initial Provisioning Specification*.
- *Configuration Admin Service Specification* - The Configuration Admin service allows an operator to set the configuration information of bundles. See *104 Configuration Admin Service Specification*.
- *Metatype Service Specification* - The Metatype specification defines interfaces that allow bundle developers to describe attribute types in a computer readable form using metadata. It is mostly used in conjunction with the Configuration Admin Service. See *105 Metatype Service Specification*.

1.1.6 Naming and Directory services

Naming and directory services are well established and useful tools in enterprise applications. The Enterprise Specification includes the:

- *JNDI Services Specification* – The Java Naming and Directory Interface (JNDI) is a registry technology in Java applications, both in the Java SE and Java EE space. JNDI provides a vendor-neutral set of APIs that allow clients to interact with a naming service. See *126 JNDI Services Specification*.

1.1.7 Database Access

There are multiple approaches available to model and persist data in databases. The Enterprise Specification includes support for the common technologies:

- *JDBC™ Service Specification* – provides an API for applications to interact with relational database systems from different vendors. See *125 JDBC™ Service Specification*.
- *JPA Service Specification* – The Java Persistence API (JPA) is a specification that sets a standard for persistence in enterprise and non-enterprise JRE™-based environments. The JPA Service Specification defines how bundles may access and use JPA persistence units in applications, as well as how a JPA implementation can become available and be invoked within an OSGi framework. See *127 JPA Service Specification*.

1.1.8 Transaction Support

The support for transactions in Java is well defined outside of the OSGi specification. The Enterprise Specification includes the:

- *JTA Transaction Services Specification* – This specification provides the User Transaction, Transaction Manager, and Synchronization Registry services, which are based on their counterparts in the Java EE™ JTA Specifications. These services can be used to demarcate transaction boundaries, enlists durable and volatile resources, and provides transactional aware code to influence the outcome of a transaction and synchronize with the ending of a transaction. See *123 JTA Transaction Services Specification*.

1.1.9   Miscellaneous Supporting Services

Services providing solutions to common infrastructure requirements include:

*   *Log Service Specification* – Provides a general purpose message logger for the OSGi Service Platform. See *101 Log Service Specification*.
*   *XML Parser Service Specification* – Addresses how the classes defined in JAXP can be used in an OSGi Service Platform. See *702 XML Parser Service Specification*.
*   *Tracker Specification* – Simplifies tracking the life cycle of bundles and services. See *701 Tracker Specification*.

1.2   Reader Level

This specification is written for the following audiences:

*   Application developers
*   Framework and system service developers (system developers)
*   Architects

This specification assumes that the reader has at least one year of practical experience in writing Java programs. Experience with enterprise systems and server-environments is a plus. Application developers must be aware that the OSGi environment is significantly more dynamic than traditional desktop or server environments.

System developers require a very deep understanding of Java. At least three years of Java coding experience in a system environment is recommended. A Framework implementation will use areas of Java that are not normally encountered in traditional applications. Detailed understanding is required of class loaders, garbage collection, Java 2 security, and Java native library loading.

Architects should focus on the introduction of each subject. This introduction contains a general overview of the subject, the requirements that influenced its design, and a short description of its operation as well as the entities that are used. The introductory sections require knowledge of Java concepts like classes and interfaces, but should not require coding experience.

Most of these specifications are equally applicable to application developers and system developers.

1.3   Version Information

This document is the Enterprise Specification for the OSGi Service Platform Release 4, Version 4.2.

Components in this specification have their own specification version, independent of the OSGi Service Platform, Release 4, Version 4.2 specification. The following table summarizes the packages and specification versions for the different subjects.

Table 1.1   *Packages and versions*

Item	Package(s)	Version
101 Log Service Specification	org.osgi.service.log	Version 1.3
102 Http Service Specification	org.osgi.service.http	Version 1.2
104 Configuration Admin Service Specification	org.osgi.service.cm	Version 1.3
105 Metatype Service Specification	org.osgi.service.metatype	Version 1.1
107 User Admin Service Specification	org.osgi.service.useradmin	Version 1.1
110 Initial Provisioning Specification	org.osgi.service.provisioning	Version 1.2
112 Declarative Services Specification	org.osgi.service.component	Version 1.1
113 Event Admin Service Specification	org.osgi.service.event	Version 1.2
115 Auto Configuration Specification	–	Version 1.2

Table 1.1   *Packages and versions*

Item	Package(s)	Version
116 Application Admin Specification	org.osgi.service.application	Version 1.1
121 Blueprint Container Specification	org.osgi.blueprint.container org.osgi.blueprint.reflect	Version 1.0
122 Remote Service Admin Service Specification	org.osgi.service. remoteserviceadmin	Version 1.0
123 JTA Transaction Services Specification	-	Version 1.0
124 JMX™ Management Model Specification	org.osgi.jmx[1]	Version 1.0
125 JDBC™ Service Specification	org.osgi.service.jdbc	Version 1.0
126 JNDI Services Specification	org.osgi.service.jndi	Version 1.0
127 JPA Service Specification	org.osgi.service.jpa	Version 1.0
128 Web Applications Specification	-	Version 1.0
129 SCA Configuration Type Specification	-	Version 1.0
701 Tracker Specification	org.osgi.util.tracker	Version 1.4
702 XML Parser Service Specification	org.osgi.util.xml	Version 1.0

When a component is represented in a bundle, a version attribute is needed in the declaration of the Import-Package or Export-Package manifest headers.

1.3.1   Note

1 The org.osgi.jmx sub-packages are individually versioned to be aligned with the service they manage.

1.4   References

[1]   *Bradner, S., Key words for use in RFCs to Indicate Requirement Levels*
http://www.ietf.org/rfc/rfc2119.txt, March 1997.

[2]   *OSGi Service Platform Core Specification,Release 4, Version 4.2*
http://www.osgi.org/Specifications/HomePage

13 **Remote Services**

Version 1.0

The OSGi framework provides a *local* service registry for bundles to communicate through service objects, where a service is an object that one bundle registers and another bundle gets. A *distribution provider* can use this loose coupling between bundles to *export* a registered service by creating an *endpoint*. Vice versa, the distribution provider can create a *proxy* that accesses an endpoint and then registers this proxy as an *imported* service. A Framework can contain multiple distribution providers simultaneously, each independently importing and exporting services.

An endpoint is a communications access mechanisms to a service in another framework, a (web) service, another process, or a queue or topic destination, etc., requiring some protocol for communications. The constellation of the mapping between services and endpoints as well as their communication characteristics is called the *topology*. A common case for distribution providers is to be present on multiple frameworks importing and exporting services; effectively distributing the service registry.

The local architecture for remote services is depicted in Figure 13.1 on page 7.

Figure 13.1   *Remote Services Architecture*

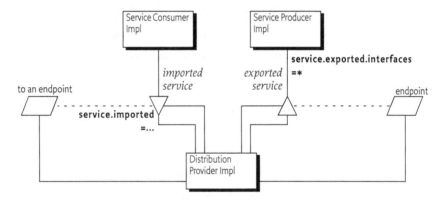

Local services imply in-VM call semantics. Many of these semantics cannot be supported over a communications connection, or require special configuration of the communications connection. It is therefore necessary to define a mechanism for bundles to convey their assumptions and requirements to the distribution provider. This chapter defines a number of service properties that a distribution provider can use to establish a topology while adhering to the given constraints.

13.1 **The Fallacies**

General abstractions for distributed systems have been tried before and often failed. Well known are the fallacies described in [2] *The Fallacies of Distributed Computing Explained*:

- The network is reliable
- Latency is zero
- Bandwidth is infinite
- The network is secure
- Topology doesn't change

- There is one administrator
- Transport cost is zero
- The network is homogeneous

Most fallacies represent non-functional trade-offs that should be considered by administrators, their decisions can then be reflected in the topology. For example, in certain cases limited bandwidth is acceptable and the latency in a datacenter is near zero. However, the reliability fallacy is the hardest because it intrudes into the application code. If a communication channel is lost, the application code needs to take specific actions to recover from this failure.

This reliability aspect is also addressed with OSGi services because services are dynamic. Failures in the communications layer can be mapped to the unregistration of the imported service. OSGi bundles are already well aware of these dynamics, and a number of programming models have been developed to minimize the complexity of writing these dynamic applications.

13.2   Remote Service Properties

This section introduces a number of properties that participating bundles can use to convey information to the distribution provider according to this Remote Service specification. These properties are listed alphabetically in Table 13.1. The scenarios that these properties are used in are discussed in later sections.

Table 13.1   *Remote Service Properties*

Service Property Name	Type	Description
remote.configs.supported	String+	Registered by the distribution provider on one of its services to indicate the supported configuration types. See *Configuration Types* on page 14 and *Dependencies* on page 16.
remote.intents.supported	String+	Registered by the distribution provider on one of its services to indicate the vocabulary of implemented intents. See *Dependencies* on page 16.
service.exported.configs	String+	A list of configuration types that should be used to export the service. Each configuration type represents the configuration parameters for one or more Endpoints. A distribution provider should create endpoints for each configuration type that it supports. See *Configuration Types* on page 14 for more details.
service.exported.intents	String+	A list of *intents* that the distribution provider must implement to distribute the service. Intents listed in this property are reserved for intents that are critical for the code to function correctly, for example, ordering of messages. These intents should not be configurable. For more information about intents, see *Intents* on page 12.

Table 13.1 *Remote Service Properties*

Service Property Name	Type	Description
service.exported.intents.extra	String+	This property is merged with the service.exported.intents property before the distribution provider interprets the listed intents; it has therefore the same semantics but the property should be configurable so the administrator can choose the intents based on the topology. Bundles should therefore make this property configurable, for example through the Configuration Admin service. See *Intents* on page 12.
service.exported.interfaces	String+	Setting this property marks this service for export. It defines the interfaces under which this service can be exported. This list must be a subset of the types listed in the objectClass service property. The single value of an asterisk ('*', \u002A) indicates all interfaces in the registration's objectClass property and ignore the classes. It is strongly recommended to only export interfaces and not concrete classes due to the complexity of creating proxies for some type of concrete classes. See *Registering a Service for Export* on page 11.
service.imported	*	Must be set by a distribution provider to any value when it registers the endpoint proxy as an imported service. A bundle can use this property to filter out imported services.
service.imported.configs	String+	The configuration information used to import this service, as described in service.exported.configs. Any associated properties for this configuration types must be properly mapped to the importing system. For example, a URL in these properties must point to a valid resource when used in the importing framework.
		If multiple configuration types are listed in this property, then they must be synonyms for exactly the same remote endpoint that is used to export this service.

Table 13.1   *Remote Service Properties*

Service Property Name	Type	Description

service.intents	String+	A list of intents that this service implements. This property has a dual purpose:
		
		• A bundle can use this service property to notify the distribution provider that these intents are already implemented by the exported service object.
		• A distribution provider must use this property to convey the combined intents of:
		  • The exporting service, and
		  • The intents that the exporting distribution provider adds.
		  • The intents that the importing distribution provider adds.
		
		To export a service, a distribution provider must expand any qualified intents to include those supported by the endpoint. This can be a subset of all known qualified intents. See *Intents* on page 12.

service.pid	String+	Services that are exported should have a service.pid property. The service.pid (PID) is a unique persistent identity for the service, the PID is defined in *Persistent Identifier (PID)* on page 129 of the Core specification. This property enables a distribution provider to associate persistent proprietary data with a service registration.

The properties and their treatment by the distribution provider is depicted in *Distribution Service Properties* on page 10.

Figure 13.2   *Distribution Service Properties*

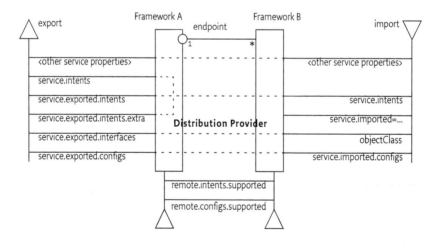

13.2.1   Registering a Service for Export

A distribution provider should create one or more endpoints for an exported service when the following conditions are met:

- The service has the service property service.exported.interfaces set.
- All intents listed in service.exported.intents, service.exported.intents.extra and service.intents are part of the distributed provider's vocabulary
- None of the intents are mutually exclusive.
- The distribution provider can use the configuration types in service.exported.configs to create one or more endpoints.

The endpoint must at least implement all the intents that are listed in the service.exported.intents and service.exported.intents.extra properties.

The configuration types listed in the service.exported.configs can contain *alternatives* and/or *synonyms*. Alternatives describe different endpoints for the same service while a synonym describes a different configuration type for the same endpoint.

A distribution provider should create endpoints for each of the configuration types it supports; these configuration types should be alternatives. Synonyms are allowed.

If no configuration types are recognized, the distribution provider should create an endpoint with a default configuration type except when one of the listed configuration types is <<nodefault>>.

For more information about the configuration types, see further *Configuration Types* on page 14.

13.2.2   Getting an Imported Service

An imported service must be a normal service, there are therefore no special rules for getting it. An imported service has a number of additional properties that must be set by the distribution provider.

If the endpoint for an exported service is imported as an OSGi service in another framework, then the following properties must be treated as special.

- service.imported – Must be set to some value.
- service.intents – This must be the combination of the following:
  - The service.intents property on the exported service
  - The service.exported.intents and service.exported.intents.extra properties on the exported service
  - Any additional intents implemented by the distribution providers on both sides.
- service.imported.configs – Contains the configuration types that can be used to import this service. The types listed in this property must be *synonymous*, that is, they must refer to exactly the same endpoint that is exporting the service. See *Configuration Types* on page 14.
- service.exported.* – Properties starting with service.exported. must not be set on the imported service.
- service.exported.interfaces – This property must not be set, its content is reflected in the objectClass property.

All other *public* service properties (not starting with a dot ('.' \u002E)) must be listed on the imported service if they use the basic service property types. If the service property cannot be communicated because, for example, it uses a type that can not be marshalled by the distribution provider then the distribution provider must ignore this property.

The service.imported property indicates that a service is an imported service. If this service property is set to any value, then the imported service is a proxy for an endpoint. If a bundle wants to filter out imported services, then it can add the following filter:

```
(&(! (service. imported=*))  <previous filter>)
```

Distribution providers can also use the *Service Hooks Specification* on page 315 of the core specification to hide services from specific bundles.

13.2.3   **On Demand Import**

The Service Hooks specification, see *Service Hooks Specification* on page 315 of the core specification, allows a distribution provider to detect when a bundle is listening for specific services. Bundles can request imported services with specific intents by building an appropriate filter. The distribution provider can use this information to import a service on demand.

The following example creates a Service Tracker that is interested in an imported service.

```
Filter f = context.createFilter(
    "(&(objectClasss=com.acme.Foo)"
  +    "(service.intents=confidentiality))"
);
ServiceTracker tracker =
  new ServiceTracker(context, f, null );
tracker.open();
```

Such a Service Tracker will inform the Listener Hook and will give it the filter expression. If the distribution provider has registered such a hook, it will be informed about the need for an imported com.acme.Foo service that has a confidentiality intent. It can then use some proprietary means to find a service to import that matches the given object class and intent.

How the distribution provider finds an appropriate endpoint is out of scope for this specification.

13.3   Intents

An intent is a name for an abstract distribution capability. An intent can be *implemented* by a service; this can then be reflected in the service.intents property. An intent can also *constrain* the possible communication mechanisms that a distribution provider can choose to distribute a service. This is reflected in the service.export.intents and service.exported.intents.extra properties.

The purpose of the intents is to have a *vocabulary* that is shared between distribution aware bundles and the distribution provider. This vocabulary allows the bundles to express constraints on the export of their services as well as providing information on what intents are implemented by a service.

Intents have the following syntax

```
intent    ::= token ( '.' token )?
```

Qualified intents use a dot ('.' \u002E) to separate the intent from the qualifier. A qualifier provides additional details, however, it implies its prefix. For example:

```
confidentiality.message
```

This example, can be *expanded* into confidentiality and confidentiality.message. Qualified intents can be used to provide additional details how an intent is achieved. However, a Distribution Provider must expand any qualified intents to include those supported by the endpoint. This can be a subset of all known qualified intents.

The concept of intents is derived from the [4] *SCA Policy Framework specification*. When designing a vocabulary for a distribution provider it is recommended to closely follow the vocabulary of intents defined in the SCA Policy Framework.

13.4 General Usage

13.4.1 Call by Value

Normal service semantics are call-by-reference. An object passed as an argument in a service call is a direct reference to that object. Any changes to this object will be shared on both sides of the service registry.

Distributed services are different. Arguments are normally passed by value, which means that a copy is sent to the remote system, changes to this value are not reflected in the originating framework. When using distributed services, call-by-value should always be assumed by all participants in the distribution chain.

13.4.2 Data Fencing

Services are syntactically defined by their Java interfaces. When exposing a service over a remote protocol, typically such an interface is mapped to a protocol-specific interface definition. For example, in CORBA the Java interfaces would be converted to a corresponding IDL definition. This mapping does not always result in a complete solution.

Therefore, for many practical distributed applications it will be necessary to constrain the possible usage of data types in service interfaces. A distribution provider must at least support interfaces (not classes) that only use the basic types as defined for the service properties. These are the primitive types and their wrappers as well as arrays and collections. See *Filter Syntax* on page 33 of the Core Specification for a list of service property types.

Distribution providers will in general provide a richer set of types that can be distributed.

13.4.3 Remote Services Life Cycle

If a distribution provider has distributed a service, it must closely track any modifications on the exported service. If there is a corresponding imported service, it must closely match any modified service properties in the way that was specified for the registration. If the exported service is unregistered, the endpoint must be withdrawn as soon as possible. If there is a corresponding imported service, then this imported service must also be unregistered expediently.

13.4.4 Runtime

An imported service is just like any other service and can be used as such. However, certain non-functional characteristics of this service can differ significantly from what is normal for an in-VM object call. Many of these characteristics can be mapped to the normal service operations. That is, if the connection fails in any way, the service can be unregistered. According to the standard OSGi contract, this means that the users of that service must perform the appropriate cleanup to prevent stale references.

13.4.5 Exceptions

It is impossible to guarantee that a service is not used when it is no longer valid. Even with the synchronous callbacks from the Service Listeners, there is always a finite window where a service can be used while the underlying implementation has failed. In a distributed environment, this window can actually be quite large for an imported service.

Such failure situations must be exposed to the application code that uses a failing imported service. In these occasions, the distribution provider must notify the application by throwing a Service Exception, or subclass thereof, with the reason REMOTE. The Service Exception is a Runtime Exception, it can be handled higher up in the call chain. The cause of this Service Exception must be the Exception that caused the problem.

A distribution provider should log any problems with the communications layer to the Log Service, if available.

13.5 Configuration Types

An exported service can have a service.exported.configs service property. This property lists configuration types for endpoints that are provided for this service. Each type provides a specification that defines how the configuration data for one or more endpoints is provided. For example, a hypothetical configuration type could use a service property to hold a URL for the RMI naming registry.

Configuration types that are not defined by the OSGi Alliance should use a name that follows the reverse internet domain name scheme defined in [5] *Java Language Specification* for Java packages. For example, com.acme.wsdl would be the proprietary way for the ACME company to specify a WSDL configuration type.

13.5.1 Configuration Type Properties

The service.exported.configs and service.imported.configs use the configuration types in very different ways. That is, the service.imported.configs property is not a copy of the service.exported.configs as the name might seem to imply.

An exporting service can list its desired configuration types in the service.exported.configs property. This property is potentially seen and interpreted by multiple distribution providers. Each of these providers can independently create endpoints from the configuration types. In principle, the service.exported.configs lists *alternatives* for a single distribution provider and can list *synonyms* to support alternative distribution providers. If only one of the synonyms is useful, there is an implicit assumption that when the service is exported, only one of the synonyms should be supported by the installed distribution providers. If it is detected that this assumption is violated, then an error should be logged and the conflicting configuration is further ignored.

The interplay of synonyms and alternatives is depicted in Table 13.2. In this table, the first columns on the left list different combinations of the configuration types in the service.exported.configs property. The next two columns list two distribution providers that each support an overlapping set of configuration types. The x's in this table indicate if a configuration type or distribution provider is active in a line. The description then outlines the issues, if any. It is assumed in this table that hypothetical configuration types net.rmi and com.rmix map to an identical endpoint, just like net.soap and net.soapx..

Table 13.2   Synonyms and Alternatives in Exported Configurations

service.exported.configs					Distribution Provider A	Distribution Provider B	Description
net.rmi	com.rmix	net.soap	com.soapx	<<no default>>	Supports: net.rmi com.rmix com.soapx	Supports net.rmi net.soap	
x	x				x		*Ok*, A will create an endpoint for the RMI and SOAP alternatives.
x					x	x	*Configuration error.* There is a clash for net.rmi because A and B can both create an endpoint for the same configuration. It is likely that one will fail.
		x	x		x		*Ok*, exported on com.soapx by A, the net.soap is ignored.

Table 13.2   *Synonyms and Alternatives in Exported Configurations*

service.exported.configs	Distribution Provider A	Distribution Provider B	Description
x x	x	x	*Synonym error* because A and B export to same SOAP endpoint, it is likely that one will fail.
x x	x	x	*Ok*, two alternative endpoints over RMI (by A) and SOAP (by B) are created. This is a typical use case.
x x	x		*Ok*. Synonyms are used to allow frameworks that have either A or B installed. In this case A exports over SOAP.
x x		x	*Ok*. Synonyms are used to allow frameworks that have either A or B installed. In this case B exports.
	x		*Ok*. A creates an endpoint with default configuration type.
	x	x	*Ok*. Both A and B each create an endpoint with their default configuration type.
x	x		*Ok*. No endpoint is created.
x x		x	Provider B does not recognize the configuration types it should therefore use a default configuration type.

To summarize, the following rules apply for a single distribution provider:

- Only configuration types that are supported by this distribution provider must be used. All other configuration types must be ignored.
- All of the supported configuration types must be *alternatives*, that is, they must map to different endpoints. Synonyms for the same distribution provider should be logged as errors.
- If a configuration type results in an endpoint that is already in use, then an error should be logged. It is likely then that another distribution provider already had created that endpoint.

An export of a service can therefore result in multiple endpoints being created. For example, a service can be exported over RMI as well as SOAP. Creating an endpoint can fail, in that case the distribution provider must log this information in the Log Service, if available, and not export the service to that endpoint. Such a failure can, for example, occur when two configuration types are synonym and multiple distribution providers are installed that supporting this type.

On the importing side, the service.imported.configs property lists configuration types that must refer to the same endpoint. That is, it can list alternative configuration types for this endpoint but all configuration types must result in the same endpoint.

For example, there are two distribution providers installed at the exporting and importing frameworks. Distribution provider A supports the hypothetical configuration type net.rmi and net.soap. Distribution provider B supports the hypothetical configuration type net.smart. A service is registered that list all three of those configuration types.

Distribution provider A will create two endpoints, one for RMI and one for SOAP. Distribution provider B will create one endpoint for the smart protocol. The distribution provider A knows how to create the configuration data for the com.acme.rmi configuration type as well and can therefore create a synonymous description of the endpoint in that configuration type. It will therefore set the imported configuration type for the RMI endpoint to:

```
service.imported.configs = net.rmi, com.acme.rmi
net.rmi.url = rmi://172.25.25.109:1099/service-id/24
com.acme.rmi.address = 172.25.25.109
com.acme.rmi.port = 1099
```

```
com.acme.rmi.path = service-id/24
```

Figure 13.3   *Relation between imported and exported configuration types*

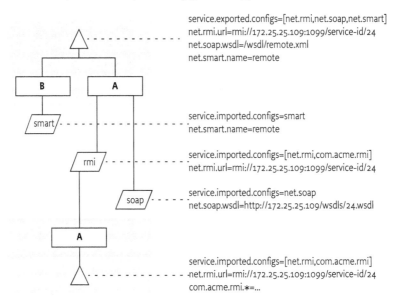

service.exported.configs=[net.rmi,net.soap,net.smart]
net.rmi.url=rmi://172.25.25.109:1099/service-id/24
net.soap.wsdl=/wsdl/remote.xml
net.smart.name=remote

service.imported.configs=smart
net.smart.name=remote

service.imported.configs=[net.rmi,com.acme.rmi]
net.rmi.url=rmi://172.25.25.109:1099/service-id/24

service.imported.configs=net.soap
net.soap.wsdl=http://172.25.25.109/wsdls/24.wsdl

service.imported.configs=[net.rmi,com.acme.rmi]
net.rmi.url=rmi://172.25.25.109:1099/service-id/24
com.acme.rmi.*=...

13.5.2   Dependencies

A bundle that uses a configuration type has an implicit dependency on the distribution provider. To make this dependency explicit, the distribution provider must register a service with the following properties:

- remote.intents.supported – (String+) The vocabulary of the given distribution provider.
- remote.configs.supported – (String+) The configuration types that are implemented by the distribution provider.

A bundle that depends on the availability of specific intents or configuration types can create a service dependency on an anonymous service with the given properties. The following filter is an example of depending on a hypothetical net.rmi configuration type:

```
(remote.configs.supported=net.rmi)
```

13.6   Security

The distribution provider will be required to invoke methods on any exported service. This implies that it must have the combined set of permissions of all methods it can call. It also implies that the distribution provider is responsible for ensuring that a bundle that calls an imported service is not granted additional permissions through the fact that the distribution provider will call the exported service, not the original invoker.

The actual mechanism to ensure that bundles can get additional permissions through the distribution is out of scope for this specification. However, distribution providers should provide mechanisms to limit the set of available permissions for a remote invocation, preferably on a small granularity basis.

One possible means is to use the getAccessControlContext method on the Conditional Permission Admin service to get an Access Control Context that is used in a doPrivileged block where the invocation takes place. The getAccessControlContext method takes a list of signers which could represent the remote bundles that cause an invocation. How these are authenticated is up to the distribution provider.

A distribution provider is a potential attack point for intruders. Great care should be taken to properly setup the permissions or topology in an environment that requires security.

13.6.1 Limiting Exports and Imports

Service registration and getting services is controlled through the ServicePermission class. This permission supports a filter based constructor that can assert service properties. This facility can be used to limit bundles from being able to register exported services or get imported services if they are combined with Conditional Permission Admin's ALLOW facility. The following example shows how all bundles except from www.acme.com are denied the registration and getting of distributed services.

```
DENY {
    [...BundleLocationCondition("http://www.acme.com/*" "!")]
    (...ServicePermission "(service.imported=*)" "GET" )
    (...ServicePermission "(service.exported.interfaces=*)"
                                      "REGISTER" )
}
```

13.7 Changes

- Any number of levels of qualifier intents could be used, this was not possible in SCA. This is now aligned with the SCA specification so that now only one level of qualifiers is supported.

13.8 References

[1] *OSGi Core Specifications*
     http://www.osgi.org/Specifications/HomePage

[2] *The Fallacies of Distributed Computing Explained*
     http://www.rgoarchitects.com/Files/fallacies.pdf

[3] *Service Component Architecture (SCA)*
     http://www.oasis-opencsa.org/

[4] *SCA Policy Framework specification*
     http://www.oasis-open.org/committees/sca-policy/

[5] *Java Language Specification*
     http://java.sun.com/docs/books/jls/

101   Log Service Specification

Version 1.3

101.1   Introduction

The Log Service provides a general purpose message logger for the OSGi Service Platform. It consists of two services, one for logging information and another for retrieving current or previously recorded log information.

This specification defines the methods and semantics of interfaces which bundle developers can use to log entries and to retrieve log entries.

Bundles can use the Log Service to log information for the Operator. Other bundles, oriented toward management of the environment, can use the Log Reader Service to retrieve Log Entry objects that were recorded recently or to receive Log Entry objects as they are logged by other bundles.

101.1.1   Entities

- *LogService* – The service interface that allows a bundle to log information, including a message, a level, an exception, a ServiceReference object, and a Bundle object.
- *LogEntry* - An interface that allows access to a log entry in the log. It includes all the information that can be logged through the Log Service and a time stamp.
- *LogReaderService* - A service interface that allows access to a list of recent LogEntry objects, and allows the registration of a LogListener object that receives LogEntry objects as they are created.
- *LogListener* - The interface for the listener to LogEntry objects. Must be registered with the Log Reader Service.

Figure 101.1   *Log Service Class Diagram org.osgi.service.log package*

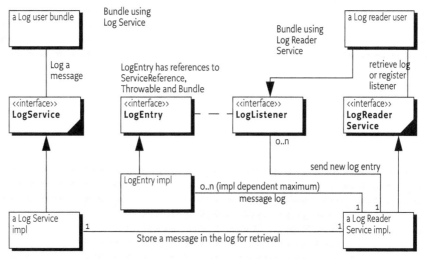

101.2   The Log Service Interface

The LogService interface allows bundle developers to log messages that can be distributed to other bundles, which in turn can forward the logged entries to a file system, remote system, or some other destination.

The LogService interface allows the bundle developer to:

- Specify a message and/or exception to be logged.
- Supply a log level representing the severity of the message being logged. This should be one of the levels defined in the LogService interface but it may be any integer that is interpreted in a user-defined way.
- Specify the Service associated with the log requests.

By obtaining a LogService object from the Framework service registry, a bundle can start logging messages to the LogService object by calling one of the LogService methods. A Log Service object can log any message, but it is primarily intended for reporting events and error conditions.

The LogService interface defines these methods for logging messages:

- log(int, String) – This method logs a simple message at a given log level.
- log(int, String, Throwable) – This method logs a message with an exception at a given log level.
- log(ServiceReference, int, String) – This method logs a message associated with a specific service.
- log(ServiceReference, int, String, Throwable) – This method logs a message with an exception associated with a specific service.

While it is possible for a bundle to call one of the log methods without providing a ServiceReference object, it is recommended that the caller supply the ServiceReference argument whenever appropriate, because it provides important context information to the operator in the event of problems.

The following example demonstrates the use of a log method to write a message into the log.

```
logService.log(
    myServiceReference,
    LogService.LOG_INFO,
    "myService is up and running"
);
```

In the example, the myServiceReference parameter identifies the service associated with the log request. The specified level, LogService.LOG_INFO, indicates that this message is informational.

The following example code records error conditions as log messages.

```
try {
    FileInputStream fis = new FileInputStream("myFile");
    int b;
    while ( (b = fis.read()) != -1 ) {
        ...
    }
    fis.close();
}
catch ( IOException exception ) {
    logService.log(
        myServiceReference,
        LogService.LOG_ERROR,
        "Cannot access file",
        exception );
}
```

Notice that in addition to the error message, the exception itself is also logged. Providing this information can significantly simplify problem determination by the Operator.

101.3   Log Level and Error Severity

The log methods expect a log level indicating error severity, which can be used to filter log messages when they are retrieved. The severity levels are defined in the LogService interface.

Callers must supply the log levels that they deem appropriate when making log requests. The following table lists the log levels.

Table 101.1   *Log Levels*

Level	Descriptions
LOG_DEBUG	Used for problem determination and may be irrelevant to anyone but the bundle developer.
LOG_ERROR	Indicates the bundle or service may not be functional. Action should be taken to correct this situation.
LOG_INFO	May be the result of any change in the bundle or service and does not indicate a problem.
LOG_WARNING	Indicates a bundle or service is still functioning but may experience problems in the future because of the warning condition.

101.4   Log Reader Service

The Log Reader Service maintains a list of LogEntry objects called the *log*. The Log Reader Service is a service that bundle developers can use to retrieve information contained in this log, and receive notifications about LogEntry objects when they are created through the Log Service.

The size of the log is implementation-specific, and it determines how far into the past the log entries go. Additionally, some log entries may not be recorded in the log in order to save space. In particular, LOG_DEBUG log entries may not be recorded. Note that this rule is implementation-dependent. Some implementations may allow a configurable policy to ignore certain LogEntry object types.

The LogReaderService interface defines these methods for retrieving log entries.

- getLog() – This method retrieves past log entries as an enumeration with the most recent entry first.
- addLogListener(LogListener) – This method is used to subscribe to the Log Reader Service in order to receive log messages as they occur. Unlike the previously recorded log entries, all log messages must be sent to subscribers of the Log Reader Service as they are recorded.
  A subscriber to the Log Reader Service must implement the LogListener interface.
  After a subscription to the Log Reader Service has been started, the subscriber's LogListener.logged method must be called with a LogEntry object for the message each time a message is logged.

The LogListener interface defines the following method:

- logged(LogEntry) – This method is called for each LogEntry object created. A Log Reader Service implementation must not filter entries to the LogListener interface as it is allowed to do for its log. A LogListener object should see all LogEntry objects that are created.

The delivery of LogEntry objects to the LogListener object should be done asynchronously.

101.5   Log Entry Interface

The LogEntry interface abstracts a log entry. It is a record of the information that was passed when an event was logged, and consists of a superset of information which can be passed through the LogService methods. The LogEntry interface defines these methods to retrieve information related to Log Entry objects:

- getBundle() – This method returns the Bundle object related to a LogEntry object.
- getException() – This method returns the exception related to a LogEntry object. In some implementations, the returned exception may not be the original exception. To avoid references to a bundle defined exception class, thus preventing an uninstalled bundle from being garbage collected, the Log Service may return an exception object of an implementation defined Throwable subclass. This object will attempt to return as much information as possible, such as the message and stack trace, from the original exception object .
- getLevel() – This method returns the severity level related to a LogEntry object.
- getMessage() – This method returns the message related to a LogEntry object.
- getServiceReference() –This method returns the ServiceReference object of the service related to a Log Entry object.
- getTime() – This method returns the time that the log entry was created.

101.6   Mapping of Events

Implementations of a Log Service must log Framework-generated events and map the information to LogEntry objects in a consistent way. Framework events must be treated exactly the same as other logged events and distributed to all LogListener objects that are associated with the Log Reader Service. The following sections define the mapping for the three different event types: Bundle, Service, and Framework.

101.6.1   Bundle Events Mapping

A Bundle Event is mapped to a LogEntry object according to Table 101.2, "Mapping of Bundle Events to Log Entries," on page 22.

Table 101.2   Mapping of Bundle Events to Log Entries

Log Entry method	Information about Bundle Event
getLevel()	LOG_INFO
getBundle()	Identifies the bundle to which the event happened. In other words, it identifies the bundle that was installed, started, stopped, updated, or uninstalled. This identification is obtained by calling getBundle() on the BundleEvent object.
getException()	null
getServiceReference()	null
getMessage()	The message depends on the event type:

- INSTALLED – "BundleEvent INSTALLED"
- STARTED – "BundleEvent STARTED"
- STOPPED – "BundleEvent STOPPED"
- UPDATED – "BundleEvent UPDATED"
- UNINSTALLED – "BundleEvent UNINSTALLED"
- RESOLVED – "BundleEvent RESOLVED"
- UNRESOLVED – "BundleEvent UNRESOLVED"

101.6.2 Service Events Mapping

A Service Event is mapped to a LogEntry object according to Table 101.3, "Mapping of Service Events to Log Entries," on page 23.

Table 101.3 *Mapping of Service Events to Log Entries*

Log Entry method	Information about Service Event
getLevel()	LOG_INFO, except for the ServiceEvent.MODIFIED event. This event can happen frequently and contains relatively little information. It must be logged with a level of LOG_DEBUG.
getBundle()	Identifies the bundle that registered the service associated with this event. It is obtained by calling getServiceReference().getBundle() on the ServiceEvent object.
getException()	null
getServiceReference()	Identifies a reference to the service associated with the event. It is obtained by calling getServiceReference() on the ServiceEvent object.
getMessage()	This message depends on the actual event type. The messages are mapped as follows: • REGISTERED – "ServiceEvent REGISTERED" • MODIFIED – "ServiceEvent MODIFIED" • UNREGISTERING – "ServiceEvent UNREGISTERING"

101.6.3 Framework Events Mapping

A Framework Event is mapped to a LogEntry object according to Table 101.4, "Mapping of Framework Event to Log Entries," on page 23.

Table 101.4 *Mapping of Framework Event to Log Entries*

Log Entry method	Information about Framework Event
getLevel()	LOG_INFO, except for the FrameworkEvent.ERROR event. This event represents an error and is logged with a level of LOG_ERROR.
getBundle()	Identifies the bundle associated with the event. This may be the system bundle. It is obtained by calling getBundle() on the FrameworkEvent object.
getException()	Identifies the exception associated with the error. This will be null for event types other than ERROR. It is obtained by calling getThrowable() on the FrameworkEvent object.
getServiceReference()	null
getMessage()	This message depends on the actual event type. The messages are mapped as follows: • STARTED – "FrameworkEvent STARTED" • ERROR – "FrameworkEvent ERROR" • PACKAGES_REFRESHED – "FrameworkEvent PACKAGES REFRESHED" • STARTLEVEL_CHANGED – "FrameworkEvent STARTLEVEL CHANGED" • WARNING – "FrameworkEvent WARNING" • INFO – "FrameworkEvent INFO"

101.6.4 Log Events

Log events must be delivered by the Log Service implementation to the Event Admin service (if present) asynchronously under the topic:

```
org/osgi/service/log/LogEntry/<event type>
```

The logging level is used as event type:

```
LOG_ERROR
LOG_WARNING
LOG_INFO
LOG_DEBUG
LOG_OTHER (when event is not recognized)
```

The properties of a log event are:

- bundle.id – (Long) The source bundle's id.
- bundle.symbolicName – (String) The source bundle's symbolic name. Only set if not null.
- bundle – (Bundle) The source bundle.
- log.level – (Integer) The log level.
- message – (String) The log message.
- timestamp – (Long) The log entry's timestamp.
- log.entry – (LogEntry) The LogEntry object.

If the log entry has an associated Exception:

- exception.class – (String) The fully-qualified class name of the attached exception. Only set if the getExceptionmethod returns a non-null value.
- exception.message – (String) The message of the attached Exception. Only set if the Exception message is not null.
- exception – (Throwable) The Exception returned by the getException method.

If the getServiceReference method returns a non-null value:

- service – (ServiceReference) The result of the getServiceReference method.
- service.id – (Long) The id of the service.
- service.pid – (String) The service's persistent identity. Only set if the service.pid service property is not null.
- service.objectClass – (String[]) The object class of the service object.

101.7 Security

The Log Service should only be implemented by trusted bundles. This bundle requires ServicePermission[LogService|LogReaderService, REGISTER]. Virtually all bundles should get ServicePermission[LogService, GET]. The ServicePermission[LogReaderService, GET] should only be assigned to trusted bundles.

101.8 org.osgi.service.log

Log Service Package Version 1.3.

Bundles wishing to use this package must list the package in the Import-Package header of the bundle's manifest. For example:

```
Import-Package: org.osgi.service.log; version="[1.3,2.0)"
```

101.8.1 Summary

- *LogEntry* - Provides methods to access the information contained in an individual Log Service log entry.
- *LogListener* - Subscribes to LogEntry objects from the LogReaderService.
- *LogReaderService* - Provides methods to retrieve LogEntry objects from the log.
- *LogService* - Provides methods for bundles to write messages to the log.

101.8.2 public interface LogEntry

Provides methods to access the information contained in an individual Log Service log entry.

A LogEntry object may be acquired from the LogReaderService.getLog method or by registering a LogListener object.

See Also LogReaderService.getLog, LogListener

Concurrency Thread-safe

101.8.2.1 public Bundle getBundle( )

❑ Returns the bundle that created this LogEntry object.

Returns The bundle that created this LogEntry object; null if no bundle is associated with this LogEntry object.

101.8.2.2 public Throwable getException( )

❑ Returns the exception object associated with this LogEntry object.

In some implementations, the returned exception may not be the original exception. To avoid references to a bundle defined exception class, thus preventing an uninstalled bundle from being garbage collected, the Log Service may return an exception object of an implementation defined Throwable subclass. The returned object will attempt to provide as much information as possible from the original exception object such as the message and stack trace.

Returns Throwable object of the exception associated with this LogEntry;null if no exception is associated with this LogEntry object.

101.8.2.3 public int getLevel( )

❑ Returns the severity level of this LogEntry object.

This is one of the severity levels defined by the LogService interface.

Returns Severity level of this LogEntry object.

See Also LogService.LOG_ERROR, LogService.LOG_WARNING, LogService.LOG_INFO, LogService.LOG_DEBUG

101.8.2.4 public String getMessage( )

❑ Returns the human readable message associated with this LogEntry object.

Returns String containing the message associated with this LogEntry object.

101.8.2.5 public ServiceReference getServiceReference( )

❑ Returns the ServiceReference object for the service associated with this LogEntry object.

Returns ServiceReference object for the service associated with this LogEntry object; null if no ServiceReference object was provided.

101.8.2.6 public long getTime( )

❑ Returns the value of currentTimeMillis() at the time this LogEntry object was created.

Returns The system time in milliseconds when this LogEntry object was created.

See Also System.currentTimeMillis()

101.8.3 public interface LogListener
extends EventListener

Subscribes to LogEntry objects from the LogReaderService.

A LogListener object may be registered with the Log Reader Service using the LogReaderService.addLogListener method. After the listener is registered, the logged method will be called for each LogEntry object created. The LogListener object may be unregistered by calling the LogReaderService.removeLogListener method.

See Also   LogReaderService, LogEntry, LogReaderService.addLogListener(LogListener), LogReaderService.removeLogListener(LogListener)

Concurrency   Thread-safe

101.8.3.1   **public void logged(LogEntry entry)**

entry   A LogEntry object containing log information.

□   Listener method called for each LogEntry object created.

As with all event listeners, this method should return to its caller as soon as possible.

See Also   LogEntry

101.8.4   public interface LogReaderService

Provides methods to retrieve LogEntry objects from the log.

There are two ways to retrieve LogEntry objects:

- The primary way to retrieve LogEntry objects is to register a LogListener object whose LogListener.logged method will be called for each entry added to the log.
- To retrieve past LogEntry objects, the getLog method can be called which will return an Enumeration of all LogEntry objects in the log.

See Also   LogEntry, LogListener, LogListener.logged(LogEntry)

Concurrency   Thread-safe

101.8.4.1   **public void addLogListener(LogListener listener)**

listener   A LogListener object to register; the LogListener object is used to receive LogEntry objects.

□   Subscribes to LogEntry objects.

This method registers a LogListener object with the Log Reader Service. The LogListener.logged(LogEntry) method will be called for each LogEntry object placed into the log.

When a bundle which registers a LogListener object is stopped or otherwise releases the Log Reader Service, the Log Reader Service must remove all of the bundle's listeners.

If this Log Reader Service's list of listeners already contains a listener l such that (l==listener), this method does nothing.

See Also   LogListener, LogEntry, LogListener.logged(LogEntry)

101.8.4.2   **public Enumeration getLog( )**

□   Returns an Enumeration of all LogEntry objects in the log.

Each element of the enumeration is a LogEntry object, ordered with the most recent entry first. Whether the enumeration is of all LogEntry objects since the Log Service was started or some recent past is implementation-specific. Also implementation-specific is whether informational and debug LogEntry objects are included in the enumeration.

Returns   An Enumeration of all LogEntry objects in the log.

101.8.4.3   **public void removeLogListener(LogListener listener)**

listener   A LogListener object to unregister.

□   Unsubscribes to LogEntry objects.

This method unregisters a LogListener object from the Log Reader Service.

If listener is not contained in this Log Reader Service's list of listeners, this method does nothing.

See Also LogListener

101.8.5   public interface LogService

Provides methods for bundles to write messages to the log.

LogService methods are provided to log messages; optionally with a ServiceReference object or an exception.

Bundles must log messages in the OSGi environment with a severity level according to the following hierarchy:

1 LOG_ERROR
2 LOG_WARNING
3 LOG_INFO
4 LOG_DEBUG

Concurrency Thread-safe

101.8.5.1   public static final int LOG_DEBUG = 4

A debugging message (Value 4).

This log entry is used for problem determination and may be irrelevant to anyone but the bundle developer.

101.8.5.2   public static final int LOG_ERROR = 1

An error message (Value 1).

This log entry indicates the bundle or service may not be functional.

101.8.5.3   public static final int LOG_INFO = 3

An informational message (Value 3).

This log entry may be the result of any change in the bundle or service and does not indicate a problem.

101.8.5.4   public static final int LOG_WARNING = 2

A warning message (Value 2).

This log entry indicates a bundle or service is still functioning but may experience problems in the future because of the warning condition.

101.8.5.5   public void log(int level, String message)

level The severity of the message. This should be one of the defined log levels but may be any integer that is interpreted in a user defined way.

message Human readable string describing the condition or null.

☐ Logs a message.

The ServiceReference field and the Throwable field of the LogEntry object will be set to null.

See Also LOG_ERROR, LOG_WARNING, LOG_INFO, LOG_DEBUG

101.8.5.6   public void log(int level, String message, Throwable exception)

level The severity of the message. This should be one of the defined log levels but may be any integer that is interpreted in a user defined way.

message The human readable string describing the condition or null.

exception The exception that reflects the condition or null.

   ☐ Logs a message with an exception.

The ServiceReference field of the LogEntry object will be set to null.

See Also LOG_ERROR, LOG_WARNING, LOG_INFO, LOG_DEBUG

101.8.5.7 **public void log(ServiceReference sr, int level, String message)**

sr The ServiceReference object of the service that this message is associated with or null.

level The severity of the message. This should be one of the defined log levels but may be any integer that is interpreted in a user defined way.

message Human readable string describing the condition or null.

   ☐ Logs a message associated with a specific ServiceReference object.

The Throwable field of the LogEntry will be set to null.

See Also LOG_ERROR, LOG_WARNING, LOG_INFO, LOG_DEBUG

101.8.5.8 **public void log(ServiceReference sr, int level, String message, Throwable exception)**

sr The ServiceReference object of the service that this message is associated with.

level The severity of the message. This should be one of the defined log levels but may be any integer that is interpreted in a user defined way.

message Human readable string describing the condition or null.

exception The exception that reflects the condition or null.

   ☐ Logs a message with an exception associated and a ServiceReference object.

See Also LOG_ERROR, LOG_WARNING, LOG_INFO, LOG_DEBUG

102   **Http Service Specification**

Version 1.2

102.1   **Introduction**

An OSGi Service Platform normally provides users with access to services on the Internet and other networks. This access allows users to remotely retrieve information from, and send control to, services in an OSGi Service Platform using a standard web browser.

Bundle developers typically need to develop communication and user interface solutions for standard technologies such as HTTP, HTML, XML, and servlets.

The Http Service supports two standard techniques for this purpose:

- *Registering servlets* – A servlet is a Java object which implements the Java Servlet API. Registering a servlet in the Framework gives it control over some part of the Http Service URI name-space.
- *Registering resources* – Registering a resource allows HTML files, image files, and other static resources to be made visible in the Http Service URI name-space by the requesting bundle.

Implementations of the Http Service can be based on:

- [1] *HTTP 1.0 Specification RFC-1945*
- [2] *HTTP 1.1 Specification RFC-2616*

Alternatively, implementations of this service can support other protocols if these protocols can conform to the semantics of the javax.servlet API. This additional support is necessary because the Http Service is closely related to [3] *Java Servlet Technology*. Http Service implementations must support at least version 2.1 of the Java Servlet API.

102.1.1   **Entities**

This specification defines the following interfaces which a bundle developer can implement collectively as an Http Service or use individually:

- HttpContext – Allows bundles to provide information for a servlet or resource registration.
- HttpService – Allows other bundles in the Framework to dynamically register and unregister resources and servlets into the Http Service URI name-space.
- NamespaceException – Is thrown to indicate an error with the caller's request to register a servlet or resource into the Http Service URI name-space.

Figure 102.1   *Http Service Overview Diagram*

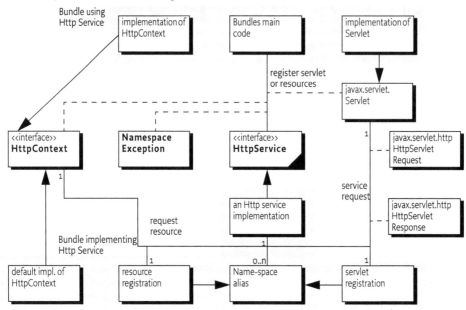

102.2   **Registering Servlets**

javax.servlet.Servlet objects can be registered with the Http Service by using the HttpService interface. For this purpose, the HttpService interface defines the method registerServlet(String, javax.servlet.Servlet,Dictionary,HttpContext).

For example, if the Http Service implementation is listening to port 80 on the machine www.acme.com and the Servlet object is registered with the name "/servlet", then the Servlet object's service method is called when the following URL is used from a web browser:

```
http://www.acme.com/servletname=bugs
```

All Servlet objects and resource registrations share the same name-space. If an attempt is made to register a resource or Servlet object under the same name as a currently registered resource or Servlet object, a NamespaceException is thrown. See *Mapping HTTP Requests to Servlet and Resource Registrations* on page 33 for more information about the handling of the Http Service name-space.

Each Servlet registration must be accompanied with an HttpContext object. This object provides the handling of resources, media typing, and a method to handle authentication of remote requests. See *Authentication* on page 36.

For convenience, a default HttpContext object is provided by the Http Service and can be obtained with createDefaultHttpContext(). Passing a null parameter to the registration method achieves the same effect.

Servlet objects require a ServletContext object. This object provides a number of functions to access the Http Service Java Servlet environment. It is created by the implementation of the Http Service for each unique HttpContext object with which a Servlet object is registered. Thus, Servlet objects registered with the same HttpContext object must also share the same ServletContext object.

Servlet objects are initialized by the Http Service when they are registered and bound to that specific Http Service. The initialization is done by calling the Servlet object's Servlet.init(ServletConfig) method. The ServletConfig parameter provides access to the initialization parameters specified when the Servlet object was registered.

Therefore, the same Servlet instance must not be reused for registration with another Http Service, nor can it be registered under multiple names. Unique instances are required for each registration.

The following example code demonstrates the use of the registerServlet method:

```
Hashtable initparams = new Hashtable();
initparams.put( "name", "value" );

Servlet myServlet = new HttpServlet() {
   String    name = "<not set>";

   public void init( ServletConfig config ) {
      this.name = (String)
         config.getInitParameter( "name" );
   }

   public void doGet(
      HttpServletRequest req,
      HttpServletResponse rsp
   ) throws IOException {
      rsp.setContentType( "text/plain" );
      req.getWriter().println( this.name );
   }
};

getHttpService().registerServlet(
   "/servletAlias",
   myServlet,
   initparams,
   null // use default context
);
// myServlet has been registered
// and its init method has been called. Remote
// requests are now handled and forwarded to
// the servlet.
...
getHttpService().unregister("/servletAlias");
// myServlet has been unregistered and its
// destroy method has been called
```

This example registers the servlet, myServlet, at alias: /servletAlias. Future requests for http://www.acme.com/servletAlias maps to the servlet, myServlet, whose service method is called to process the request. (The service method is called in the HttpServlet base class and dispatched to a doGet, doPut, doPost, doOptions, doTrace, or doDelete call depending on the HTTP request method used.)

102.3 Registering Resources

A resource is a file containing images, static HTML pages, sounds, movies, applets, etc. Resources do not require any handling from the bundle. They are transferred directly from their source--usually the JAR file that contains the code for the bundle--to the requestor using HTTP.

Resources could be handled by Servlet objects as explained in *Registering Servlets* on page 30. Transferring a resource over HTTP, however, would require very similar Servlet objects for each bundle. To prevent this redundancy, resources can be registered directly with the Http Service via the HttpService interface. This HttpService interface defines the registerResources(String,String,HttpContext) method for registering a resource into the Http Service URI name-space.

The first parameter is the external alias under which the resource is registered with the Http Service. The second parameter is an internal prefix to map this resource to the bundle's name-space. When a request is received, the HttpService object must remove the external alias from the URI, replace it with the internal prefix, and call the getResource(String) method with this new name on the associated HttpContext object. The HttpContext object is further used to get the MIME type of the resource and to authenticate the request.

Resources are returned as a java.net.URL object. The Http Service must read from this URL object and transfer the content to the initiator of the HTTP request.

This return type was chosen because it matches the return type of the java.lang.Class.getResource(String resource) method. This method can retrieve resources directly from the same place as the one from which the class was loaded – often a package directory in the JAR file of the bundle. This method makes it very convenient to retrieve resources from the bundle that are contained in the package.

The following example code demonstrates the use of the register Resources method:

```
package com.acme;
...
HttpContext context = new HttpContext() {
   public boolean handleSecurity(
      HttpServletRequest request,
      HttpServletResponse response
   ) throws IOException {
      return true;
   }

   public URL getResource(String name) {
      return getClass().getResource(name);
   }

   public String getMimeType(String name) {
      return null;
   }
};

getHttpService().registerResources (
   "/files",
   "www",
   context
);
...
getHttpService().unregister("/files");
```

This example registers the alias /files on the Http Service. Requests for resources below this name-space are transferred to the HttpContext object with an internal name of www/<name>. This example uses the Class.get Resource(String) method. Because the internal name does not start with a

"/", it must map to a resource in the "com/acme/www" directory of the JAR file. If the internal name did start with a "/", the package name would not have to be prefixed and the JAR file would be searched from the root. Consult the java.lang.Class.getResource(String) method for more information.

In the example, a request for http://www.acme.com/files/myfile.html must map to the name "com/acme/www/myfile.html" which is in the bundle's JAR file.

More sophisticated implementations of the getResource(String) method could filter the input name, restricting the resources that may be returned or map the input name onto the file system (if the security implications of this action are acceptable).

Alternatively, the resource registration could have used a default HttpContext object, as demonstrated in the following call to registerResources:

```
getHttpService().registerResources(
    "/files",
    "/com/acme/www",
    null
);
```

In this case, the Http Service implementation would call the createDefaultHttpContext() method and use its return value as the HttpContext argument for the registerResources method. The default implementation must map the resource request to the bundle's resource, using Bundle.getResource(String). In the case of the previous example, however, the internal name must now specify the full path to the directory containing the resource files in the JAR file. No automatic prefixing of the package name is done.

The getMimeType(String) implementation of the default HttpContext object should rely on the default mapping provided by the Http Service by returning null. Its handleSecurity(HttpServletRequest,HttpServletResponse) may implement an authentication mechanism that is implementation-dependent.

102.4   Mapping HTTP Requests to Servlet and Resource Registrations

When an HTTP request comes in from a client, the Http Service checks to see if the requested URI matches any registered aliases. A URI matches only if the path part of the URI is exactly the same string. Matching is case sensitive.

If it does match, a matching registration takes place, which is processed as follows:

1. If the registration corresponds to a servlet, the authorization is verified by calling the handleSecurity method of the associated HttpContext object. See *Authentication* on page 36. If the request is authorized, the servlet must be called by its service method to complete the HTTP request.

2. If the registration corresponds to a resource, the authorization is verified by calling the handleSecurity method of the associated HttpContext object. See *Authentication* on page 36. If the request is authorized, a target resource name is constructed from the requested URI by substituting the alias from the registration with the internal name from the registration if the alias is not "/". If the alias is "/", then the target resource name is constructed by prefixing the requested URI with the internal name. An internal name of "/" is considered to have the value of the empty string ("") during this process.

3. The target resource name must be passed to the getResource method of the associated HttpContext object.

4. If the returned URL object is not null, the Http Service must return the contents of the URL to the client completing the HTTP request. The translated target name, as opposed to the original requested URI, must also be used as the argument to HttpContext.getMimeType.

5. If the returned URL object is null, the Http Service continues as if there was no match.

6. If there is no match, the Http Service must attempt to match sub-strings of the requested URI to registered aliases. The sub-strings of the requested URI are selected by removing the last "/" and everything to the right of the last "/".

The Http Service must repeat this process until either a match is found or the sub-string is an empty string. If the sub-string is empty and the alias "/" is registered, the request is considered to match the alias "/". Otherwise, the Http Service must return HttpServletResponse.SC_NOT_FOUND(404) to the client.

For example, an HTTP request comes in with a request URI of "/fudd/bugs/foo.txt", and the only registered alias is "/fudd". A search for "/fudd/bugs/foo.txt" will not match an alias. Therefore, the Http Service will search for the alias "/fudd/bugs" and the alias "/fudd". The latter search will result in a match and the matched alias registration must be used.

Registrations for identical aliases are not allowed. If a bundle registers the alias "/fudd", and another bundle tries to register the exactly the same alias, the second caller must receive a NamespaceException and its resource or servlet must *not* be registered. It could, however, register a similar alias – for example, "/fudd/bugs", as long as no other registration for this alias already exists.

The following table shows some examples of the usage of the name-space.

Table 102.1　　　*Examples of Name-space Mapping*

Alias	Internal Name	URI	getResource Parameter
/	(empty string)	/fudd/bugs	/fudd/bugs
/	/	/fudd/bugs	/fudd/bugs
/	/tmp	/fudd/bugs	/tmp/fudd/bugs
/fudd	(empty string)	/fudd/bugs	/bugs
/fudd	/	/fudd/bugs	/bugs
/fudd	/tmp	/fudd/bugs	/tmp/bugs
/fudd	tmp	/fudd/bugs/x.gif	tmp/bugs/x.gif
/fudd/bugs/x.gif	tmp/y.gif	/fudd/bugs/x.gif	tmp/y.gif

102.5　The Default Http Context Object

The HttpContext object in the first example demonstrates simple implementations of the HttpContext interface methods. Alternatively, the example could have used a default HttpContext object, as demonstrated in the following call to registerServlet:

```
getHttpService().registerServlet(
    "/servletAlias",
    myServlet,
    initparams,
    null
);
```

In this case, the Http Service implementation must call createDefault HttpContext and use the return value as the HttpContext argument.

If the default HttpContext object, and thus the ServletContext object, is to be shared by multiple servlet registrations, the previous servlet registration example code needs to be changed to use the same default HttpContext object. This change is demonstrated in the next example:

```
HttpContext defaultContext =
    getHttpService().createDefaultHttpContext();

getHttpService().registerServlet(
    "/servletAlias",
    myServlet,
    initparams,
    defaultContext
);

// defaultContext can be reused
// for further servlet registrations
```

102.6   Multipurpose Internet Mail Extension (MIME) Types

MIME defines an extensive set of headers and procedures to encode binary messages in US-ASCII mails. For an overview of all the related RFCs, consult [4] *MIME Multipurpose Internet Mail Extension*.

An important aspect of this extension is the type (file format) mechanism of the binary messages. The type is defined by a string containing a general category (text, application, image, audio and video, multipart, and message) followed by a "/" and a specific media type, as in the example, "text/html" for HTML formatted text files. A MIME type string can be followed by additional specifiers by separating key=value pairs with a ';'. These specifiers can be used, for example, to define character sets as follows:

```
text/plain ; charset=iso-8859-1
```

The Internet Assigned Number Authority (IANA) maintains a set of defined MIME media types. This list can be found at [5] *Assigned MIME Media Types*. MIME media types are extendable, and when any part of the type starts with the prefix "x-", it is assumed to be vendor-specific and can be used for testing. New types can be registered as described in [6] *Registration Procedures for new MIME media types*.

HTTP bases its media typing on the MIME RFCs. The "Content-Type" header should contain a MIME media type so that the browser can recognize the type and format the content correctly.

The source of the data must define the MIME media type for each transfer. Most operating systems do not support types for files, but use conventions based on file names, such as the last part of the file name after the last ".". This extension is then mapped to a media type.

Implementations of the Http Service should have a reasonable default of mapping common extensions to media types based on file extensions.

Table 102.2   Sample Extension to MIME Media Mapping

Extension	MIME media type	Description
.jpg .jpeg	image/jpeg	JPEG Files
.gif	image/gif	GIF Files
.css	text/css	Cascading Style Sheet Files
.txt	text/plain	Text Files
.wml	text/vnd.wap.wml	Wireless Access Protocol (WAP) Mark Language

Table 102.2   *Sample Extension to MIME Media Mapping*

Extension	MIME media type	Description
.htm .html	text/html	Hyper Text Markup Language
.wbmp	image/vnd.wap.wbmp	Bitmaps for WAP

Only the bundle developer, however, knows exactly which files have what media type. The HttpContext interface can therefore be used to map this knowledge to the media type. The HttpContext class has the following method for this: getMimeType(String).

The implementation of this method should inspect the file name and use its internal knowledge to map this name to a MIME media type.

Simple implementations can extract the extension and look up this extension in a table.

Returning null from this method allows the Http Service implementation to use its default mapping mechanism.

102.7 Authentication

The Http Service has separated the authentication and authorization of a request from the execution of the request. This separation allows bundles to use available Servlet sub-classes while still providing bundle specific authentication and authorization of the requests.

Prior to servicing each incoming request, the Http Service calls the handleSecurity(javax.servlet.http.HttpServletRequest,javax.servlet.http.HttpServletResponse) method on the HttpContext object that is associated with the request URI. This method controls whether the request is processed in the normal manner or an authentication error is returned.

If an implementation wants to authenticate the request, it can use the authentication mechanisms of HTTP. See [7] *RFC 2617: HTTP Authentication: Basic and Digest Access Authentication.* These mechanisms normally interpret the headers and decide if the user identity is available, and if it is, whether that user has authenticated itself correctly.

There are many different ways of authenticating users, and the handleSecurity method on the HttpContext object can use whatever method it requires. If the method returns true, the request must continue to be processed using the potentially modified HttpServletRequest and HttpServletResponse objects. If the method returns false, the request must *not* be processed.

A common standard for HTTP is the basic authentication scheme that is not secure when used with HTTP. Basic authentication passes the password in base 64 encoded strings that are trivial to decode into clear text. Secure transport protocols like HTTPS use SSL to hide this information. With these protocols basic authentication is secure.

Using basic authentication requires the following steps:

1. If no Authorization header is set in the request, the method should set the WWW-Authenticate header in the response. This header indicates the desired authentication mechanism and the realm. For example, WWW-Authenticate: Basic realm="ACME".
   The header should be set with the response object that is given as a parameter to the handleSecurity method. The handleSecurity method should set the status to HttpServletResponse.SC_UNAUTHORIZED (401) and return false.

2. Secure connections can be verified with the ServletRequest.getScheme() method. This method returns, for example, "https" for an SSL connection; the handleSecurity method can use this and other information to decide if the connection's security level is acceptable. If not, the handleSecurity method should set the status to HttpServletResponse.SC_FORBIDDEN (403) and return false.

3. Next, the request must be authenticated. When basic authentication is used, the Authorization header is available in the request and should be parsed to find the user and password. See [7] *RFC 2617: HTTP Authentication: Basic and Digest Access Authentication* for more information. If the user cannot be authenticated, the status of the response object should be set to HttpServletResponse.SC_UNAUTHORIZED (401) and return false.

4. The authentication mechanism that is actually used and the identity of the authenticated user can be of interest to the Servlet object. Therefore, the implementation of the handleSecurity method should set this information in the request object using the ServletRequest.setAttribute method. This specification has defined a number of OSGi-specific attribute names for this purpose:

   • AUTHENTICATION_TYPE - Specifies the scheme used in authentication. A Servlet may retrieve the value of this attribute by calling the HttpServletRequest.getAuthType method. This attribute name is org.osgi.service.http.authentication.type.

   • REMOTE_USER - Specifies the name of the authenticated user. A Servlet may retrieve the value of this attribute by calling the HttpServletRequest.getRemoteUser method. This attribute name is org.osgi.service.http.authentication.remote.user.

   • AUTHORIZATION - If a User Admin service is available in the environment, then the handleSecurity method should set this attribute with the Authorization object obtained from the User Admin service. Such an object encapsulates the authentication of its remote user. A Servlet may retrieve the value of this attribute by calling ServletRequest.getAttribute(HttpContext.AUTHORIZATION). This header name is org.osgi.service.useradmin.authorization.

5. Once the request is authenticated and any attributes are set, the handleSecurity method should return true. This return indicates to the Http Service that the request is authorized and processing may continue. If the request is for a Servlet, the Http Service must then call the service method on the Servlet object.

102.8 Security

This section only applies when executing in an OSGi environment which is enforcing Java permissions.

102.8.1 Accessing Resources in Bundles

The Http Service must be granted AdminPermission[*,RESOURCE] so that bundles may use a default HttpContext object. This is necessary because the implementation of the default HttpContext object must call Bundle.getResource to access the resources of a bundle and this method requires the caller to have AdminPermission[bundle,RESOURCE].

Any bundle may access resources in its own bundle by calling Class.getResource. This operation is privileged. The resulting URL object may then be passed to the Http Service as the result of a HttpContext.getResource call. No further permission checks are performed when accessing bundle resource URL objects, so the Http Service does not need to be granted any additional permissions.

102.8.2 Accessing Other Types of Resources

In order to access resources that were not registered using the default HttpContext object, the Http Service must be granted sufficient privileges to access these resources. For example, if the getResource method of the registered HttpContext object returns a file URL, the Http Service requires the corresponding FilePermission to read the file. Similarly, if the getResource method of the registered HttpContext object returns an HTTP URL, the Http Service requires the corresponding SocketPermission to connect to the resource.

Therefore, in most cases, the Http Service should be a privileged service that is granted sufficient permission to serve any bundle's resources, no matter where these resources are located. Therefore, the Http Service must capture the AccessControlContext object of the bundle registering resources or a servlet, and then use the captured AccessControlContext object when accessing resources returned by the registered HttpContext object. This situation prevents a bundle from registering resources that it does not have permission to access.

Therefore, the Http Service should follow a scheme like the following example. When a resource or servlet is registered, it should capture the context.

```
AccessControlContext acc =
    AccessController.getContext();
```

When a URL returned by the getResource method of the associated HttpContext object is called, the Http Service must call the getResource method in a doPrivileged construct using the AccessControlContext object of the registering bundle:

```
AccessController.doPrivileged(
    new PrivilegedExceptionAction() {
        public Object run() throws Exception {
            ...
        }
    }, acc);
```

The Http Service must only use the captured AccessControlContext when accessing resource URL objects. Servlet and HttpContext objects must use a doPrivileged construct in their implementations when performing privileged operations.

102.9 Configuration Properties

If the Http Service does not have its port values configured through some other means, the Http Service implementation should use the following properties to determine the port values upon which to listen.

The following OSGi environment properties are used to specify default HTTP ports:

- org.osgi.service.http.port – This property specifies the port used for servlets and resources accessible via HTTP. The default value for this property is 80.
- org.osgi.service.http.port.secure – This property specifies the port used for servlets and resources accessible via HTTPS. The default value for this property is 443.

102.10 org.osgi.service.http

Http Service Package Version 1.2.

Bundles wishing to use this package must list the package in the Import-Package header of the bundle's manifest. For example:

```
Import-Package: org.osgi.service.http; version="[1.2,2.0)"
```

102.10.1 Summary

- *HttpContext* - This interface defines methods that the Http Service may call to get information about a registration.
- *HttpService* - The Http Service allows other bundles in the OSGi environment to dynamically register resources and servlets into the URI namespace of Http Service.
- *NamespaceException* - A NamespaceException is thrown to indicate an error with the caller's request to register a servlet or resources into the URI namespace of the Http Service.

102.10.2   public interface HttpContext

This interface defines methods that the Http Service may call to get information about a registration.

Servlets and resources may be registered with an HttpContext object; if no HttpContext object is specified, a default HttpContext object is used. Servlets that are registered using the same HttpContext object will share the same ServletContext object.

This interface is implemented by users of the HttpService.

102.10.2.1   public static final String AUTHENTICATION_TYPE = "org.osgi.service.http.authentication.type"

HttpServletRequest attribute specifying the scheme used in authentication. The value of the attribute can be retrieved by HttpServletRequest.getAuthType. This attribute name is org.osgi.service.http.authentication.type.

Since 1.1

102.10.2.2   public static final String AUTHORIZATION = "org.osgi.service.useradmin.authorization"

HttpServletRequest attribute specifying the Authorization object obtained from the org.osgi.service.useradmin.UserAdmin service. The value of the attribute can be retrieved by HttpServletRequest.getAttribute(HttpContext.AUTHORIZATION). This attribute name is org.osgi.service.useradmin.authorization.

Since 1.1

102.10.2.3   public static final String REMOTE_USER = "org.osgi.service.http.authentication.remote.user"

HttpServletRequest attribute specifying the name of the authenticated user. The value of the attribute can be retrieved by HttpServletRequest.getRemoteUser. This attribute name is org.osgi.service.http.authentication.remote.user.

Since 1.1

102.10.2.4   public String getMimeType(String name)

name determine the MIME type for this name.

□ Maps a name to a MIME type. Called by the Http Service to determine the MIME type for the name. For servlet registrations, the Http Service will call this method to support the ServletContext method getMimeType. For resource registrations, the Http Service will call this method to determine the MIME type for the Content-Type header in the response.

Returns MIME type (e.g. text/html) of the name or null to indicate that the Http Service should determine the MIME type itself.

102.10.2.5   public URL getResource(String name)

name the name of the requested resource

□ Maps a resource name to a URL.

Called by the Http Service to map a resource name to a URL. For servlet registrations, Http Service will call this method to support the ServletContext methods getResource and getResourceAsStream. For resource registrations, Http Service will call this method to locate the named resource. The context can control from where resources come. For example, the resource can be mapped to a file in the bundle's persistent storage area via bundleContext.getDataFile(name).toURL() or to a resource in the context's bundle via getClass().getResource(name)

Returns URL that Http Service can use to read the resource or null if the resource does not exist.

102.10.2.6   public boolean handleSecurity(HttpServletRequest request, HttpServletResponse response) throws IOException

request the HTTP request

response   the HTTP response

□ Handles security for the specified request.

The Http Service calls this method prior to servicing the specified request. This method controls whether the request is processed in the normal manner or an error is returned.

If the request requires authentication and the Authorization header in the request is missing or not acceptable, then this method should set the WWW-Authenticate header in the response object, set the status in the response object to Unauthorized(401) and return false. See also RFC 2617: *HTTP Authentication: Basic and Digest Access Authentication* (available at http://www.ietf.org/rfc/rfc2617.txt).

If the request requires a secure connection and the getScheme method in the request does not return 'https' or some other acceptable secure protocol, then this method should set the status in the response object to Forbidden(403) and return false.

When this method returns false, the Http Service will send the response back to the client, thereby completing the request. When this method returns true, the Http Service will proceed with servicing the request.

If the specified request has been authenticated, this method must set the AUTHENTICATION_TYPE request attribute to the type of authentication used, and the REMOTE_USER request attribute to the remote user (request attributes are set using the setAttribute method on the request). If this method does not perform any authentication, it must not set these attributes.

If the authenticated user is also authorized to access certain resources, this method must set the AUTHORIZATION request attribute to the Authorization object obtained from the org.osgi.service.useradmin.UserAdmin service.

The servlet responsible for servicing the specified request determines the authentication type and remote user by calling the getAuthType and getRemoteUser methods, respectively, on the request.

Returns   true if the request should be serviced, false if the request should not be serviced and Http Service will send the response back to the client.

Throws   IOException – may be thrown by this method. If this occurs, the Http Service will terminate the request and close the socket.

102.10.3   public interface HttpService

The Http Service allows other bundles in the OSGi environment to dynamically register resources and servlets into the URI namespace of Http Service. A bundle may later unregister its resources or servlets.

See Also   HttpContext

102.10.3.1   public HttpContext createDefaultHttpContext( )

□ Creates a default HttpContext for registering servlets or resources with the HttpService, a new HttpContext object is created each time this method is called.

The behavior of the methods on the default HttpContext is defined as follows:

- getMimeType- Does not define any customized MIME types for the Content-Type header in the response, and always returns null.
- handleSecurity- Performs implementation-defined authentication on the request.
- getResource- Assumes the named resource is in the context bundle; this method calls the context bundle's Bundle.getResource method, and returns the appropriate URL to access the resource. On a Java runtime environment that supports permissions, the Http Service needs to be granted org.osgi.framework.AdminPermission[*,RESOURCE].

Returns   a default HttpContext object.

Since   1.1

102.10.3.2   **public void registerResources(String alias, String name, HttpContext context) throws NamespaceException**

> *alias* name in the URI namespace at which the resources are registered
>
> *name* the base name of the resources that will be registered
>
> *context* the HttpContext object for the registered resources, or null if a default HttpContext is to be created and used.

> ☐ Registers resources into the URI namespace.
>
> The alias is the name in the URI namespace of the Http Service at which the registration will be mapped. An alias must begin with slash ('/') and must not end with slash ('/'), with the exception that an alias of the form "/" is used to denote the root alias. The name parameter must also not end with slash ('/') with the exception that a name of the form "/" is used to denote the root of the bundle. See the specification text for details on how HTTP requests are mapped to servlet and resource registrations.
>
> For example, suppose the resource name /tmp is registered to the alias /files. A request for /files/foo.txt will map to the resource name /tmp/foo.txt.
>
> ```
> httpservice.registerResources("/files", "/tmp", context);
> ```
>
> The Http Service will call the HttpContext argument to map resource names to URLs and MIME types and to handle security for requests. If the HttpContext argument is null, a default HttpContext is used (see createDefaultHttpContext).

> *Throws* NamespaceException – if the registration fails because the alias is already in use.
>
> IllegalArgumentException – if any of the parameters are invalid

102.10.3.3   **public void registerServlet(String alias, Servlet servlet, Dictionary initparams, HttpContext context) throws ServletException, NamespaceException**

> *alias* name in the URI namespace at which the servlet is registered
>
> *servlet* the servlet object to register
>
> *initparams* initialization arguments for the servlet or null if there are none. This argument is used by the servlet's ServletConfig object.
>
> *context* the HttpContext object for the registered servlet, or null if a default HttpContext is to be created and used.

> ☐ Registers a servlet into the URI namespace.
>
> The alias is the name in the URI namespace of the Http Service at which the registration will be mapped.
>
> An alias must begin with slash ('/') and must not end with slash ('/'), with the exception that an alias of the form "/" is used to denote the root alias. See the specification text for details on how HTTP requests are mapped to servlet and resource registrations.
>
> The Http Service will call the servlet's init method before returning.
>
> ```
> httpService.registerServlet("/myservlet", servlet, initparams, context);
> ```
>
> Servlets registered with the same HttpContext object will share the same ServletContext. The Http Service will call the context argument to support the ServletContext methods getResource, getResourceAsStream and getMimeType, and to handle security for requests. If the context argument is null, a default HttpContext object is used (see createDefaultHttpContext).

> *Throws* NamespaceException – if the registration fails because the alias is already in use.
>
> javax.servlet.ServletException – if the servlet's init method throws an exception, or the given servlet object has already been registered at a different alias.

IllegalArgumentException – if any of the arguments are invalid

102.10.3.4   **public void unregister(String alias)**

alias name in the URI name-space of the registration to unregister

☐ Unregisters a previous registration done by registerServlet or registerResources methods.

After this call, the registered alias in the URI name-space will no longer be available. If the registration was for a servlet, the Http Service must call the destroy method of the servlet before returning.

If the bundle which performed the registration is stopped or otherwise "unget"s the Http Service without calling unregister then Http Service must automatically unregister the registration. However, if the registration was for a servlet, the destroy method of the servlet will not be called in this case since the bundle may be stopped. unregister must be explicitly called to cause the destroy method of the servlet to be called. This can be done in the BundleActivator.stop method of the bundle registering the servlet.

Throws IllegalArgumentException – if there is no registration for the alias or the calling bundle was not the bundle which registered the alias.

102.10.4   **public class NamespaceException**
extends Exception

A NamespaceException is thrown to indicate an error with the caller's request to register a servlet or resources into the URI namespace of the Http Service. This exception indicates that the requested alias already is in use.

102.10.4.1   **public NamespaceException(String message)**

message the detail message

☐ Construct a NamespaceException object with a detail message.

102.10.4.2   **public NamespaceException(String message, Throwable cause)**

message The detail message.

cause The nested exception.

☐ Construct a NamespaceException object with a detail message and a nested exception.

102.10.4.3   **public Throwable getCause( )**

☐ Returns the cause of this exception or null if no cause was set.

Returns The cause of this exception or null if no cause was set.

Since 1.2

102.10.4.4   **public Throwable getException( )**

☐ Returns the nested exception.

This method predates the general purpose exception chaining mechanism. The getCause() method is now the preferred means of obtaining this information.

Returns The result of calling getCause().

102.10.4.5   **public Throwable initCause(Throwable cause)**

cause The cause of this exception.

☐ Initializes the cause of this exception to the specified value.

Returns This exception.

Throws IllegalArgumentException – If the specified cause is this exception.

IllegalStateException – If the cause of this exception has already been set.

Since 1.2

102.11   References

[1]   *HTTP 1.0 Specification RFC-1945*
       http://www.ietf.org/rfc/rfc1945.txt, May 1996

[2]   *HTTP 1.1 Specification RFC-2616*
       http://www.ietf.org/rfc/rfc2616.txt, June 1999

[3]   *Java Servlet Technology*
       http://java.sun.com/products/servlet/index.html

[4]   *MIME Multipurpose Internet Mail Extension*
       http://www.mhonarc.org/~ehood/MIME/MIME.html

[5]   *Assigned MIME Media Types*
       http://www.iana.org/assignments/media-types

[6]   *Registration Procedures for new MIME media types*
       http://www.ietf.org/rfc/rfc2048.txt

[7]   *RFC 2617: HTTP Authentication: Basic and Digest Access Authentication*
       http://www.ietf.org/rfc/rfc2617.txt

104   Configuration Admin Service Specification

Version 1.3

104.1   Introduction

The Configuration Admin service is an important aspect of the deployment of an OSGi Service Platform. It allows an Operator to set the configuration information of deployed bundles.

Configuration is the process of defining the configuration data of bundles and assuring that those bundles receive that data when they are active in the OSGi Service Platform.

Figure 104.1   *Configuration Admin Service Overview*

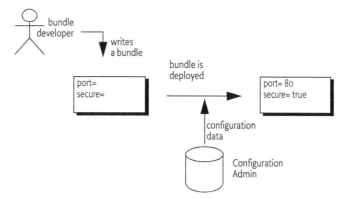

104.1.1   Essentials

The following requirements and patterns are associated with the Configuration Admin service specification:

- *Local Configuration* – The Configuration Admin service must support bundles that have their own user interface to change their configurations.
- *Reflection* – The Configuration Admin service must be able to deduce the names and types of the needed configuration data.
- *Legacy* – The Configuration Admin service must support configuration data of existing entities (such as devices).
- *Object Oriented* – The Configuration Admin service must support the creation and deletion of instances of configuration information so that a bundle can create the appropriate number of services under the control of the Configuration Admin service.
- *Embedded Devices* – The Configuration Admin service must be deployable on a wide range of platforms. This requirement means that the interface should not assume file storage on the platform. The choice to use file storage should be left to the implementation of the Configuration Admin service.
- *Remote versus Local Management* – The Configuration Admin service must allow for a remotely managed OSGi Service Platform, and must not assume that configuration information is stored

locally. Nor should it assume that the Configuration Admin service is always done remotely. Both implementation approaches should be viable.

- *Availability* – The OSGi environment is a dynamic environment that must run continuously (24/7/365). Configuration updates must happen dynamically and should not require restarting of the system or bundles.
- *Immediate Response* – Changes in configuration should be reflected immediately.
- *Execution Environment* – The Configuration Admin service will not require more than an environment that fulfills the minimal execution requirements.
- *Communications* – The Configuration Admin service should not assume "always-on" connectivity, so the API is also applicable for mobile applications in cars, phones, or boats.
- *Extendability* – The Configuration Admin service should expose the process of configuration to other bundles. This exposure should at a minimum encompass initiating an update, removing certain configuration properties, adding properties, and modifying the value of properties potentially based on existing property or service values.
- *Complexity Trade-offs* – Bundles in need of configuration data should have a simple way of obtaining it. Most bundles have this need and the code to accept this data. Additionally, updates should be simple from the perspective of the receiver.
  Trade-offs in simplicity should be made at the expense of the bundle implementing the Configuration Admin service and in favor of bundles that need configuration information. The reason for this choice is that normal bundles will outnumber Configuration Admin bundles.

104.1.2 Operation

This specification is based on the concept of a Configuration Admin service that manages the configuration of an OSGi Service Platform. It maintains a database of Configuration objects, locally or remote. This service monitors the service registry and provides configuration information to services that are registered with a service.pid property, the Persistent IDentity (PID), and implement one of the following interfaces:

- *Managed Service* – A service registered with this interface receives its *configuration dictionary* from the database or receives null when no such configuration exists or when an existing configuration has never been updated.
- *Managed Service Factory* – Services registered with this interface receive several configuration dictionaries when registered. The database contains zero or more configuration dictionaries for this service. Each configuration dictionary is given sequentially to the service.

The database can be manipulated either by the Management Agent or bundles that configure themselves.

Other parties can provide Configuration Plugin services. Such services participate in the configuration process. They can inspect the configuration dictionary and modify it before it reaches the target service.

104.1.3 Entities

- *Configuration information* – The information needed by a bundle before it can provide its intended functionality.
- *Configuration dictionary* – The configuration information when it is passed to the target service. It consists of a Dictionary object with a number of properties and identifiers.
- *Configuring Bundle* – A bundle that modifies the configuration information through the Configuration Admin service. This bundle is either a management bundle or the bundle for which the configuration information is intended.
- *Configuration Target* – The target (bundle or service) that will receive the configuration information. For services, there are two types of targets: ManagedServiceFactory or ManagedService objects.
- *Configuration Admin Service* – This service is responsible for supplying configuration target bundles with their configuration information. It maintains a database with configuration infor-

mation, keyed on the service.pid of configuration target services. These services receive their configuration dictionary or dictionaries when they are registered with the Framework. Configurations can be modified or extended using Configuration Plugin services before they reach the target bundle.

- *Managed Service* – A Managed Service represents a client of the Configuration Admin service, and is thus a configuration target. Bundles should register a Managed Service to receive the configuration data from the Configuration Admin service. A Managed Service adds one or more unique service.pid service registration properties as a primary key for the configuration information.

- *Managed Service Factory* – A Managed Service Factory can receive a number of configuration dictionaries from the Configuration Admin service, and is thus also a configuration target service. It should register with one or more service.pid strings and receives zero or more configuration dictionaries. Each dictionary has its own PID.

- *Configuration Object* – Implements the Configuration interface and contains the configuration dictionary for a Managed Service or one of the configuration dictionaries for a Managed Service Factory. These objects are manipulated by configuring bundles.

- *Configuration Plugin* Services – Configuration Plugin services are called before the configuration dictionary is given to the configuration targets. The plug-in can modify the configuration dictionary, which is passed to the Configuration Target.

Figure 104.2   Configuration Admin Class Diagram org.osgi.service.cm

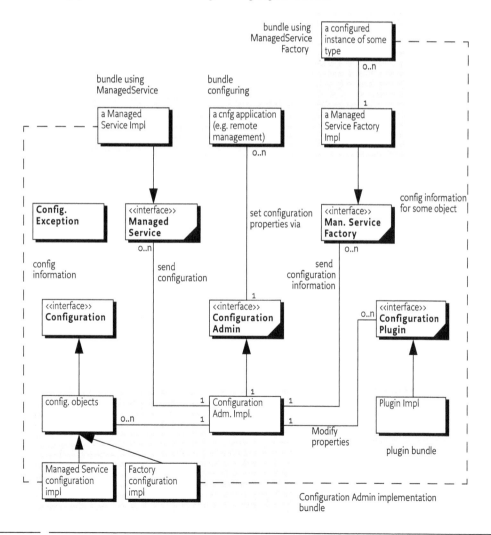

104.2   Configuration Targets

One of the more complicated aspects of this specification is the subtle distinction between the ManagedService and ManagedServiceFactory classes.

Both receive configuration information from the Configuration Admin service and are treated similarly in most respects. Therefore, this specification refers to *configuration targets* when the distinction is irrelevant.

The difference between these types is related to the cardinality of the configuration dictionary. A Managed Service is used when an existing entity needs a configuration dictionary. Thus, a one-to-one relationship always exists between the configuration dictionary and the entity.

A Managed Service Factory is used when part of the configuration is to define *how many instances are required*. A management bundle can create, modify, and delete any number of instances for a Managed Service Factory through the Configuration Admin service. Each instance is configured by a single Configuration object. Therefore, a Managed Service Factory can have multiple associated Configuration objects.

Figure 104.3   *Differentiation of ManagedService and ManagedServiceFactory Classes*

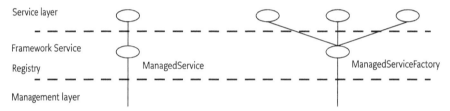

To summarize:

- A *Managed Service* must receive a single configuration dictionary when it is registered or when its configuration is modified.
- A *Managed Service Factory* must receive from zero to *n* configuration dictionaries when it registers, depending on the current configuration. The Managed Service Factory is informed of configuration dictionary changes: modifications, creations, and deletions.

104.3   The Persistent Identity

A crucial concept in the Configuration Admin service specification is the Persistent IDentity (PID) as defined in the Framework's service layer. Its purpose is to act as a primary key for objects that need a configuration dictionary. The name of the service property for PID is defined in the Framework in org.osgi.framework.Constants.SERVICE.PID.

The Configuration Admin service requires the use of PIDs with Managed Service and Managed Service Factory registrations because it associates its configuration data with PIDs.

PIDs must be unique for each service, though a service can register with multiple PIDs. A bundle must not register multiple configuration target services with the same PID. If that should occur, the Configuration Admin service must:

- Send the appropriate configuration data to all services registered under that PID from that bundle only.
- Report an error in the log.
- Ignore duplicate PIDs from other bundles and report them to the log.

104.3.1   **PID Syntax**

PIDs are intended for use by other bundles, not by people, but sometimes the user is confronted with a PID. For example, when installing an alarm system, the user needs to identify the different components to a wiring application. This type of application exposes the PID to end users.

PIDs should follow the symbolic-name syntax, which uses a very restricted character set. The following sections, define some schemes for common cases. These schemes are not required, but bundle developers are urged to use them to achieve consistency.

104.3.1.1   **Local Bundle PIDs**

As a convention, descriptions starting with the bundle identity and a dot (.) are reserved for a bundle. As an example, a PID of "65.536" would belong to the bundle with a bundle identity of 65.

104.3.1.2   **Software PIDs**

Configuration target services that are singletons can use a Java package name they own as the PID (the reverse domain name scheme) as long as they do not use characters outside the basic ASCII set. As an example, the PID named com.acme.watchdog would represent a Watchdog service from the ACME company.

104.3.1.3   **Devices**

Devices are usually organized on buses or networks. The identity of a device, such as a unique serial number or an address, is a good component of a PID. The format of the serial number should be the same as that printed on the housing or box, to aid in recognition.

Table 104.1   Schemes for Device-Oriented PID Names

Bus	Example	Format	Description
USB	USB.0123-0002-9909873	idVendor (hex 4) idProduct (hex 4) iSerialNumber (decimal)	Universal Serial Bus. Use the standard device descriptor.
IP	IP.172.16.28.21	IP nr (dotted decimal)	Internet Protocol
802	802-00:60:97:00:9A:56	MAC address with: separators	IEEE 802 MAC address (Token Ring, Ethernet, ...)
ONE	ONE.06-00000021E461	Family (hex 2) and serial number including CRC (hex 6)	1-wire bus of Dallas Semiconductor
COM	COM.krups-brewer-12323	serial number or type name of device	Serial ports

104.4   The Configuration Object

A Configuration object contains the configuration dictionary, which is a set of properties that configure an aspect of a bundle. A bundle can receive Configuration objects by registering a configuration target service with a PID service property. See *The Persistent Identity* on page 48 for more information about PIDs.

During registration, the Configuration Admin service must detect these configuration target services and hand over their configuration dictionary via a callback. If this configuration dictionary is subsequently modified, the modified dictionary is handed over to the configuration target again with the same callback.

The Configuration object is primarily a set of properties that can be updated by a Management Agent, user interfaces on the OSGi Service Platform, or other applications. Configuration changes are first made persistent, and then passed to the target service via a call to the updated method in the ManagedServiceFactory or ManagedService class.

A Configuration object must be uniquely bound to a Managed Service or Managed Service Factory. This implies that a bundle must not register a Managed Service Factory with a PID that is the same as the PID given to a Managed Service.

104.4.1 Location Binding

When a Configuration object is created by either getConfiguration or createFactoryConfiguration, it becomes bound to the location of the calling bundle. This location is obtained with the associated bundle's getLocation method.

Location binding is a security feature that assures that only management bundles can modify configuration data, and other bundles can only modify their own configuration data. A SecurityException is thrown if a bundle other than a Management Agent bundle attempts to modify the configuration information of another bundle.

If a Managed Service is registered with a PID that is already bound to another location, the normal callback to ManagedService.updated must not take place.

The two argument versions of getConfiguration and createFactoryConfiguration take a location String as their second argument. These methods require the correct permission, and they create Configuration objects bound to the specified location, instead of the location of the calling bundle. These methods are intended for management bundles.

The creation of a Configuration object does not in itself initiate a callback to the target.

A null location parameter may be used to create Configuration objects that are not bound. In this case, the objects become bound to a specific location the first time that they are used by a bundle. When this dynamically bound bundle is subsequently uninstalled, the Configuration object's bundle location must be set to null again so it can be bound again later.

A management bundle may create a Configuration object before the associated Managed Service is registered. It may use a null location to avoid any dependency on the actual location of the bundle which registers this service. When the Managed Service is registered later, the Configuration object must be bound to the location of the registering bundle, and its configuration dictionary must then be passed to ManagedService.updated.

104.4.2 Configuration Properties

A configuration dictionary contains a set of properties in a Dictionary object. The value of the property must be the same type as the set of types specified in the OSGi Core Specification in *Figure 3.8 Primary property types*.

The name or key of a property must always be a String object, and is not case-sensitive during look up, but must preserve the original case. The format of a property name should be:

```
property-name ::= public | private
public       ::= symbolic-name // See 1.3.2
private      ::= '.' symbolic-name
```

Properties can be used in other subsystems that have restrictions on the character set that can be used. The symbolic-name production uses a very minimal character set.

Bundles must not use nested vectors or arrays, nor must they use mixed types. Using mixed types or nesting makes it impossible to use the meta typing specification. See *Metatype Service Specification* on page 83.

104.4.3 Property Propagation

A configuration target should copy the public configuration properties (properties whose name does not start with a '.' or \u002E) of the Dictionary object argument in updated(Dictionary) into the service properties on any resulting service registration.

This propagation allows the development of applications that leverage the Framework service registry more extensively, so compliance with this mechanism is advised.

A configuration target may ignore any configuration properties it does not recognize, or it may change the values of the configuration properties before these properties are registered as service properties. Configuration properties in the Framework service registry are not strictly related to the configuration information.

Bundles that follow this recommendation to propagate public configuration properties can participate in horizontal applications. For example, an application that maintains physical location information in the Framework service registry could find out where a particular device is located in the house or car. This service could use a property dedicated to the physical location and provide functions that leverage this property, such as a graphic user interface that displays these locations.

Bundles performing service registrations on behalf of other bundles (e.g. OSGi Declarative Services) should propagate all public configuration properties and not propagate private configuration properties.

104.4.4 Automatic Properties

The Configuration Admin service must automatically add a number of properties to the configuration dictionary. If these properties are also set by a configuring bundle or a plug-in, they must always be overridden before they are given to the target service. See *Configuration Plugin* on page 62, Therefore, the receiving bundle or plug-in can assume that the following properties are defined by the Configuration Admin service and not by the configuring bundle:

- service.pid – Set to the PID of the associated Configuration object.
- service.factoryPid – Only set for a Managed Service Factory. It is then set to the PID of the associated Managed Service Factory.
- service.bundleLocation – Set to the location of the bundle that can use this Configuration object. This property can only be used for searching, it may not appear in the configuration dictionary returned from the getProperties method due to security reasons, nor may it be used when the target is updated.

Constants for some of these properties can be found in org.osgi.framework.Constants. These system properties are all of type String.

104.4.5 Equality

Two different Configuration objects can actually represent the same underlying configuration. This means that a Configuration object must implement the equals and hashCode methods in such a way that two Configuration objects are equal when their PID is equal.

104.5 Managed Service

A Managed Service is used by a bundle that needs one configuration dictionary and is thus associated with one Configuration object in the Configuration Admin service.

A bundle can register any number of ManagedService objects, but each must be identified with its own PID or PIDs.

A bundle should use a Managed Service when it needs configuration information for the following:

- *A Singleton* – A single entity in the bundle that needs to be configured.

- *Externally Detected Devices* – Each device that is detected causes a registration of an associated ManagedService object. The PID of this object is related to the identity of the device, such as the address or serial number.

104.5.1 Singletons

When an object must be instantiated only once, it is called a *singleton*. A singleton requires a single configuration dictionary. Bundles may implement several different types of singletons if necessary.

For example, a Watchdog service could watch the registry for the status and presence of services in the Framework service registry. Only one instance of a Watchdog service is needed, so only a single configuration dictionary is required that contains the polling time and the list of services to watch.

104.5.2 Networks

When a device in the external world needs to be represented in the OSGi Environment, it must be detected in some manner. The Configuration Admin service cannot know the identity and the number of instances of the device without assistance. When a device is detected, it still needs configuration information in order to play a useful role.

For example, a 1-Wire network can automatically detect devices that are attached and removed. When it detects a temperature sensor, it could register a Sensor service with the Framework service registry. This Sensor service needs configuration information specifically for that sensor, such as which lamps should be turned on, at what temperature the sensor is triggered, what timer should be started, in what zone it resides, and so on. One bundle could potentially have hundreds of these sensors and actuators, and each needs its own configuration information.

Each of these Sensor services should be registered as a Managed Service with a PID related to the physical sensor (such as the address) to receive configuration information.

Other examples are services discovered on networks with protocols like Jini, UPnP, and Salutation. They can usually be represented in the Framework service registry. A network printer, for example, could be detected via UPnP. Once in the service registry, these services usually require local configuration information. A Printer service needs to be configured for its local role: location, access list, and so on.

This information needs to be available in the Framework service registry whenever that particular Printer service is registered. Therefore, the Configuration Admin service must remember the configuration information for this Printer service.

This type of service should register with the Framework as a Managed Service in order to receive appropriate configuration information.

104.5.3 Configuring Managed Services

A bundle that needs configuration information should register one or more ManagedService objects with a PID service property. If it has a default set of properties for its configuration, it may include them as service properties of the Managed Service. These properties may be used as a configuration template when a Configuration object is created for the first time. A Managed Service optionally implements the MetaTypeProvider interface to provide information about the property types. See *Meta Typing* on page 65.

When this registration is detected by the Configuration Admin service, the following steps must occur:

- The configuration stored for the registered PID must be retrieved. If there is a Configuration object for this PID, it is sent to the Managed Service with updated(Dictionary).
- If a Managed Service is registered and no configuration information is available, the Configuration Admin service must call updated(Dictionary) with a null parameter.

- If the Configuration Admin service starts *after* a Managed Service is registered, it must call updated(Dictionary) on this service as soon as possible. For this reason, a Managed Service must always get a callback when it registers *and* the Configuration Admin service is started.

The updated(Dictionary) callback from the Configuration Admin service to the Managed Service must take place asynchronously. This requirement allows the Managed Service to finish its initialization in a synchronized method without interference from the Configuration Admin service callback.

Care should be taken not to cause deadlocks by calling the Framework within a synchronized method.

Figure 104.4   Managed Service Configuration Action Diagram

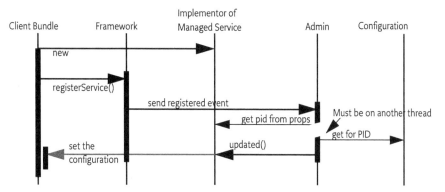

The updated method may throw a ConfigurationException. This object must describe the problem and what property caused the exception.

104.5.4   Race Conditions

When a Managed Service is registered, the default properties may be visible in the service registry for a short period before they are replaced by the properties of the actual configuration dictionary. Care should be taken that this visibility does not cause race conditions for other bundles.

In cases where race conditions could be harmful, the Managed Service must be split into two pieces: an object performing the actual service and a Managed Service. First, the Managed Service is registered, the configuration is received, and the actual service object is registered. In such cases, the use of a Managed Service Factory that performs this function should be considered.

104.5.5   Examples of Managed Service

Figure 104.5 shows a Managed Service configuration example. Two services are registered under the ManagedService interface, each with a different PID.

Figure 104.5   *PIDs and External Associations*

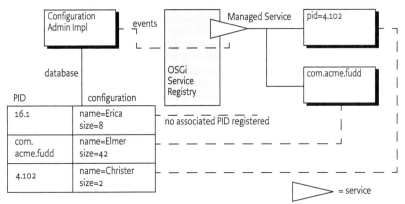

The Configuration Admin service has a database containing a configuration record for each PID. When the Managed Service with service.pid = com.acme.fudd is registered, the Configuration Admin service will retrieve the properties name=Elmer and size=42 from its database. The properties are stored in a Dictionary object and then given to the Managed Service with the updated(Dictionary) method.

104.5.5.1   Configuring A Console Bundle

In this example, a bundle can run a single debugging console over a Telnet connection. It is a singleton, so it uses a ManagedService object to get its configuration information: the port and the network name on which it should register.

```
class SampleManagedService implements ManagedService {
    Dictionary              properties;
    ServiceRegistration     registration;
    Console                 console;

    public synchronized void start(
        BundleContext context ) throws Exception {
        properties = new Hashtable();
        properties.put( Constants.SERVICE_PID,
            "com.acme.console" );
        properties.put( "port",   new Integer(2011) );

        registration = context.registerService(
            ManagedService.class.getName(),
            this,
            properties
        );
    }

    public synchronized void updated( Dictionary np ) {
        if ( np != null ) {
            properties = np;
            properties.put(
                Constants.SERVICE_PID, "com.acme.console" );
        }

        if (console == null)
            console = new Console();
```

```
                    int port = ((Integer)properties.get("port"))
                       .intValue();

                    String network = (String) properties.get("network");
                    console.setPort(port, network);
                    registration.setProperties(properties);
                }
                ... further methods
            }
```

104.5.6 Deletion

When a Configuration object for a Managed Service is deleted, the Configuration Admin service must call updated(Dictionary) with a null argument on a thread that is different from that on which the Configuration.delete was executed. This deletion must send out a Configuration Event CM_DELETED to any registered Configuration Listener services after the updated method is called with a null.

104.6 Managed Service Factory

A Managed Service Factory is used when configuration information is needed for a service that can be instantiated multiple times. When a Managed Service Factory is registered with the Framework, the Configuration Admin service consults its database and calls updated(String,Dictionary) for each associated Configuration object. It passes the identifier of the instance, which can be used as a PID, as well as a Dictionary object with the configuration properties.

A Managed Service Factory is useful when the bundle can provide functionality a number of times, each time with different configuration dictionaries. In this situation, the Managed Service Factory acts like a *class* and the Configuration Admin service can use this Managed Service Factory to *instantiate instances* for that *class*.

In the next section, the word *factory* refers to this concept of creating *instances* of a function defined by a bundle that registers a Managed Service Factory.

104.6.1 When to Use a Managed Service Factory

A Managed Service Factory should be used when a bundle does not have an internal or external entity associated with the configuration information but can potentially be instantiated multiple times.

104.6.1.1 Example Email Fetcher

An email fetcher program displays the number of emails that a user has – a function likely to be required for different users. This function could be viewed as a *class* that needs to be *instantiated* for each user. Each instance requires different parameters, including password, host, protocol, user id, and so on.

An implementation of the Email Fetcher service should register a ManagedServiceFactory object. In this way, the Configuration Admin service can define the configuration information for each user separately. The Email Fetcher service will only receive a configuration dictionary for each required instance (user).

104.6.1.2 Example Temperature Conversion Service

Assume a bundle has the code to implement a conversion service that receives a temperature and, depending on settings, can turn an actuator on and off. This service would need to be instantiated many times depending on where it is needed. Each instance would require its own configuration information for the following:

- Upper value
- Lower value
- Switch Identification
- ...

Such a conversion service should register a service object under a ManagedServiceFactory interface. A configuration program can then use this Managed Service Factory to create instances as needed. For example, this program could use a Graphic User Interface (GUI) to create such a component and configure it.

104.6.1.3   Serial Ports

Serial ports cannot always be used by the OSGi Device Access specification implementations. Some environments have no means to identify available serial ports, and a device on a serial port cannot always provide information about its type.

Therefore, each serial port requires a description of the device that is connected. The bundle managing the serial ports would need to instantiate a number of serial ports under the control of the Configuration Admin service, with the appropriate DEVICE_CATEGORY property to allow it to participate in the Device Access implementation.

If the bundle cannot detect the available serial ports automatically, it should register a Managed Service Factory. The Configuration Admin service can then, with the help of a configuration program, define configuration information for each available serial port.

104.6.2   Registration

Similar to the Managed Service configuration dictionary, the configuration dictionary for a Managed Service Factory is identified by a PID. The Managed Service Factory, however, also has a *factory* PID, which is the PID of the associated Managed Service Factory. It is used to group all Managed Service Factory configuration dictionaries together.

When a Configuration object for a Managed Service Factory is created (ConfigurationAdmin.createFactoryConfiguration), a new unique PID is created for this object by the Configuration Admin service. The scheme used for this PID is defined by the Configuration Admin service and is unrelated to the factory PID.

When the Configuration Admin service detects the registration of a Managed Service Factory, it must find all configuration dictionaries for this factory and must then sequentially call ManagedServiceFactory.updated(String,Dictionary) for each configuration dictionary. The first argument is the PID of the Configuration object (the one created by the Configuration Admin service) and the second argument contains the configuration properties.

The Managed Service Factory should then create any artifacts associated with that factory. Using the PID given in the Configuration object, the bundle may register new services (other than a Managed Service) with the Framework, but this is not required. This may be necessary when the PID is useful in contexts other than the Configuration Admin service.

The receiver must *not* register a Managed Service with this PID because this would force two Configuration objects to have the same PID. If a bundle attempts to do this, the Configuration Admin service should log an error and must ignore the registration of the Managed Service.

The Configuration Admin service must guarantee that no race conditions exist between initialization, updates, and deletions.

Figure 104.6   *Managed Service Factory Action Diagram*

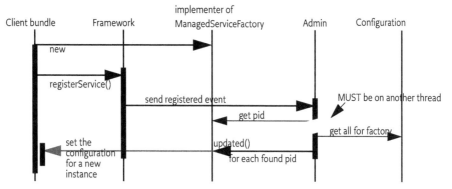

A Managed Service Factory has only one update method: updated(String,Dictionary). This method can be called any number of times as Configuration objects are created or updated.

The Managed Service Factory must detect whether a PID is being used for the first time, in which case it should create a new *instance*, or a subsequent time, in which case it should update an existing instance.

The Configuration Admin service must call updated(String,Dictionary) on a thread that is different from the one that executed the registration. This requirement allows an implementation of a Managed Service Factory to use a synchronized method to assure that the callbacks do not interfere with the Managed Service Factory registration.

The updated(String,Dictionary) method may throw a ConfigurationException object. This object describes the problem and what property caused the problem. These exceptions should be logged by a Configuration Admin service.

104.6.3   Deletion

If a configuring bundle deletes an instance of a Managed Service Factory, the deleted(String) method is called. The argument is the PID for this instance. The implementation of the Managed Service Factory must remove all information and stop any behavior associated with that PID. If a service was registered for this PID, it should be unregistered.

Deletion will asynchronously send out a Configuration Event CM_DELETED to all registered Configuration Listener services.

104.6.4   Managed Service Factory Example

Figure 104.7 highlights the differences between a Managed Service and a Managed Service Factory. It shows how a Managed Service Factory implementation receives configuration information that was created before it was registered.

- A bundle implements an EMail Fetcher service. It registers a ManagedServiceFactory object with PID=com.acme.email.
- The Configuration Admin service notices the registration and consults its database. It finds three Configuration objects for which the factory PID is equal to com.acme.email. It must call updated(String,Dictionary) for each of these Configuration objects on the newly registered ManagedServiceFactory object.
- For each configuration dictionary received, the factory should create a new instance of a EMailFetcher object, one for erica (PID=16.1), one for anna (PID=16.3), and one for elmer (PID=16.2).
- The EMailFetcher objects are registered under the Topic interface so their results can be viewed by an online display.
  If the EMailFetcher object is registered, it may safely use the PID of the Configuration object because the Configuration Admin service must guarantee its suitability for this purpose.

Figure 104.7   *Managed Service Factory Example*

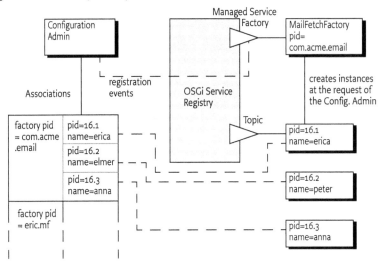

104.6.5   Multiple Consoles Example

This example illustrates how multiple consoles, each of which has its own port and interface can run simultaneously. This approach is very similar to the example for the Managed Service, but highlights the difference by allowing multiple consoles to be created.

```
class ExampleFactory implements ManagedServiceFactory {
  Hashtable consoles = new Hashtable();
  BundleContext context;
  public void start( BundleContext context )
    throws Exception {
    this.context = context;
    Hashtable local = new Hashtable();
    local.put(Constants.SERVICE_PID, "com.acme.console");
    context.registerService(
      ManagedServiceFactory.class.getName(),
      this,
      local );
  }

  public void updated( String pid, Dictionary config ){
    Console console = (Console) consoles.get(pid);
    if (console == null) {
      console = new Console(context);
      consoles.put(pid, console);
    }

    int port = getInt(config, "port", 2011);
    String network = getString(
      config,
      "network",
      null /*all*/
    );
    console.setPort(port, network);
  }
```

```
        public void deleted(String pid) {
          Console console = (Console) consoles.get(pid);
          if (console != null) {
            consoles.remove(pid);
            console.close();
          }
        }
      }
```

104.7   Configuration Admin Service

The ConfigurationAdmin interface provides methods to maintain configuration data in an OSGi environment. This configuration information is defined by a number of Configuration objects associated with specific configuration targets. Configuration objects can be created, listed, modified, and deleted through this interface. Either a remote management system or the bundles configuring their own configuration information may perform these operations.

The ConfigurationAdmin interface has methods for creating and accessing Configuration objects for a Managed Service, as well as methods for managing new Configuration objects for a Managed Service Factory.

104.7.1   Creating a Managed Service Configuration Object

A bundle can create a new Managed Service Configuration object with ConfigurationAdmin.getConfiguration. No create method is offered because doing so could introduce race conditions between different bundles trying to create a Configuration object for the same Managed Service. The getConfiguration method must atomically create and persistently store an object if it does not yet exist.

Two variants of this method are:

- getConfiguration(String) – This method is used by a bundle with a given location to configure its *own* ManagedService objects. The argument specifies the PID of the targeted service.
- getConfiguration(String,String) – This method is used by a management bundle to configure *another* bundle. Therefore, this management bundle needs the right permission. The first argument is the PID and the second argument is the location identifier of the targeted ManagedService object.

All Configuration objects have a method, getFactoryPid(), which in this case must return null because the Configuration object is associated with a Managed Service.

Creating a new Configuration object must *not* initiate a callback to the Managed Service updated method.

104.7.2   Creating a Managed Service Factory Configuration Object

The ConfigurationAdmin class provides two methods to create a new instance of a Managed Service Factory:

- createFactoryConfiguration(String) – This method is used by a bundle with a given location to configure its own ManagedServiceFactory objects. The argument specifies the PID of the targeted ManagedServiceFactory object. This *factory PID* can be obtained from the returned Configuration object with the getFactoryPid() method.
- createFactoryConfiguration(String,String)– This method is used by a management bundle to configure another bundle's ManagedServiceFactory object. The first argument is the PID and the second is the location identifier of the targeted ManagedServiceFactory object. The *factory PID* can be obtained from the returned Configuration object with getFactoryPid method.

Creating a new factory configuration must *not* initiate a callback to the Managed Service Factory updated method until the properties are set in the Configuration object with the update method.

104.7.3   Accessing Existing Configurations

The existing set of Configuration objects can be listed with listConfigurations(String). The argument is a String object with a filter expression. This filter expression has the same syntax as the Framework Filter class. For example:

```
(&(size=42)(service.factoryPid=*osgi*))
```

The filter function must use the properties of the Configuration objects and only return the ones that match the filter expression.

A single Configuration object is identified with a PID and can be obtained with getConfiguration(String).

If the caller has the right permission, then all Configuration objects are eligible for search. In other cases, only Configuration objects bound to the calling bundle's location must be returned.

null is returned in both cases when an appropriate Configuration object cannot be found.

104.7.3.1   Updating a Configuration

The process of updating a Configuration object is the same for Managed Services and Managed Service Factories. First, listConfigurations(String) or getConfiguration(String) should be used to get a Configuration object. The properties can be obtained with Configuration.getProperties. When no update has occurred since this object was created, getProperties returns null.

New properties can be set by calling Configuration.update. The Configuration Admin service must first store the configuration information and then call a configuration target's updated method: either the ManagedService.updated or ManagedServiceFactory.updated method. If this target service is not registered, the fresh configuration information must be given to the target when the configuration target service registers.

The update method calls in Configuration objects are not executed synchronously with the related target service updated method. This method must be called asynchronously. The Configuration Admin service, however, must have updated the persistent storage before the update method returns.

The update method must also asynchronously send out a Configuration Event CM_UPDATED to all registered Configuration Listeners.

104.7.4   Deletion

A Configuration object that is no longer needed can be deleted with Configuration.delete, which removes the Configuration object from the database. The database must be updated before the target service updated method is called.

If the target service is a Managed Service Factory, the factory is informed of the deleted Configuration object by a call to ManagedServiceFactory.deleted. It should then remove the associated *instance*. The ManagedServiceFactory.deleted call must be done asynchronously with respect to Configuration.delete.

When a Configuration object of a Managed Service is deleted, ManagedService.updated is called with null for the properties argument. This method may be used for clean-up, to revert to default values, or to unregister a service.

The update method must also asynchronously send out a Configuration Event CM_DELETED to all registered Configuration Listeners.

104.7.5   Updating a Bundle's Own Configuration

The Configuration Admin service specification does not distinguish between updates via a Management Agent and a bundle updating its own configuration information (as defined by its location). Even if a bundle updates its own configuration information, the Configuration Admin service must callback the associated target service updated method.

As a rule, to update its own configuration, a bundle's user interface should *only* update the configuration information and never its internal structures directly. This rule has the advantage that the events, from the bundle implementation's perspective, appear similar for internal updates, remote management updates, and initialization.

104.8   Configuration Events

Configuration Admin can update interested parties of changes in its repository. The model is based on the white board pattern where a Configuration Listener service is registered with the service registry. The Configuration Listener service will receive ConfigurationEvent objects if important changes take place. The Configuration Admin service must call the ConfigurationListener. configuration-Event(ConfigurationEvent) method with such an event. This method should be called asynchronously, and on another thread, than the call that caused the event. Configuration Events must be delivered in order for each listener as they are generated. The way events must be delivered is the same as described in *Delivering Events* on page 116 of the Core specification.

The ConfigurationEvent object carries a factory PID (getFactoryPid()) and a PID (getPid()). If the factory PID is null, the event is related to a Managed Service Configuration object, else the event is related to a Managed Service Factory Configuration object.

The ConfigurationEvent object can deliver the following events from the getType() method:

- CM_DELETED – The Configuration object is deleted.
- CM_UPDATED – The Configuration object is updated.

The Configuration Event also carries the ServiceReference object of the Configuration Admin service that generated the event.

104.8.1   Event Admin Service and Configuration Change Events

Configuration events must delivered asynchronously by the Configuration Admin implementation, if present. The topic of a configuration event must be:

```
org/osgi/service/cm/ConfigurationEvent/<event type>
```

Event type can be any of the following:

```
CM_UPDATED
CM_DELETED
```

The properties of a configuration event are:

- cm.factoryPid – (String) The factory PID of the associated Configuration object, if the target is a Managed Service Factory. Otherwise not set.
- cm.pid – (String) The PID of the associated Configuration object.
- service – (ServiceReference) The Service Reference of the Configuration Admin service.
- service.id – (Long) The Configuration Admin service's ID.
- service.objectClass – (String[]) The Configuration Admin service's object class (which must include org.osgi.service.cm.ConfigurationAdmin)
- service.pid – (String) The Configuration Admin service's persistent identity

104.9   Configuration Plugin

The Configuration Admin service allows third-party applications to participate in the configuration process. Bundles that register a service object under a ConfigurationPlugin interface can process the configuration dictionary just before it reaches the configuration target service.

Plug-ins allow sufficiently privileged bundles to intercept configuration dictionaries just *before* they must be passed to the intended Managed Service or Managed Service Factory but *after* the properties are stored. The changes the plug-in makes are dynamic and must not be stored. The plug-in must only be called when an update takes place while it is registered and there is a valid dictionary. The plugin is not called when a configuration is deleted.

The ConfigurationPlugin interface has only one method: modifyConfiguration(ServiceReference, Dictionary). This method inspects or modifies configuration data.

All plug-ins in the service registry must be traversed and called before the properties are passed to the configuration target service. Each Configuration Plugin object gets a chance to inspect the existing data, look at the target object, which can be a ManagedService object or a ManagedServiceFactory object, and modify the properties of the configuration dictionary. The changes made by a plug-in must be visible to plugins that are called later.

ConfigurationPlugin objects should not modify properties that belong to the configuration properties of the target service unless the implications are understood. This functionality is mainly intended to provide functions that leverage the Framework service registry. The changes made by the plugin should normally not be validated. However, the Configuration Admin must ignore changes to the automatic properties as described in *Automatic Properties* on page 51.

For example, a Configuration Plugin service may add a physical location property to a service. This property can be leveraged by applications that want to know where a service is physically located. This scenario could be carried out without any further support of the service itself, except for the general requirement that the service should propagate the public properties it receives from the Configuration Admin service to the service registry.

Figure 104.8   *Order of Configuration Plugin Services*

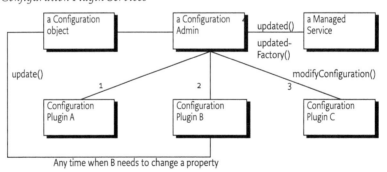

104.9.1   Limiting The Targets

A ConfigurationPlugin object may optionally specify a cm.target registration property. This value is the PID of the configuration target whose configuration updates the ConfigurationPlugin object wants to intercept.

The ConfigurationPlugin object must then only be called with updates for the configuration target service with the specified PID. For a factory target service, the factory PID is used and the plugin will see all instances of the factory. Omitting the cm.target registration property means that it is called for *all* configuration updates.

104.9.2   Example of Property Expansion

Consider a Managed Service that has a configuration property service.to with the value (objectclass=com.acme.Alarm). When the Configuration Admin service sets this property on the target service, a ConfigurationPlugin object may replace the (objectclass=com.acme.Alarm) filter with an array of existing alarm systems' PIDs as follows:

> ID "service.to=[32434,232,12421,1212]"

A new Alarm Service with service.pid=343 is registered, requiring that the list of the target service be updated. The bundle which registered the Configuration Plugin service, therefore, wants to set the to registration property on the target service. It does *not* do this by calling ManagedService.updated directly for several reasons:

- In a securely configured system, it should not have the permission to make this call or even obtain the target service.
- It could get into race conditions with the Configuration Admin service if it had the permissions in the previous bullet. Both services would compete for access simultaneously.

Instead, it must get the Configuration object from the Configuration Admin service and call the update method on it.

The Configuration Admin service must schedule a new update cycle on another thread, and sometime in the future must call ConfigurationPlugin.modifyProperties. The ConfigurationPlugin object could then set the service.to property to [32434,232,12421,1212, 343]. After that, the Configuration Admin service must call updated on the target service with the new service.to list.

104.9.3   Configuration Data Modifications

Modifications to the configuration dictionary are still under the control of the Configuration Admin service, which must determine whether to accept the changes, hide critical variables, or deny the changes for other reasons.

The ConfigurationPlugin interface must also allow plugins to detect configuration updates to the service via the callback. This ability allows them to synchronize the configuration updates with transient information.

104.9.4   Forcing a Callback

If a bundle needs to force a Configuration Plugin service to be called again, it must fetch the appropriate Configuration object from the Configuration Admin service and call the update() method (the no parameter version) on this object. This call forces an update with the current configuration dictionary so that all applicable plug-ins get called again.

104.9.5   Calling Order

The order in which the ConfigurationPlugin objects are called must depend on the service.cmRanking configuration property of the ConfigurationPlugin object. Table 104.2 shows the usage of the service.cmRanking property for the order of calling the Configuration Plugin services.

Table 104.2   service.cmRanking *Usage For Ordering*

service.cmRanking value	Description
< 0	The Configuration Plugin service should not modify properties and must be called before any modifications are made.

Table 104.2   service.cmRanking *Usage For Ordering*

service.cmRanking value	Description
>= 0 && <= 1000	The Configuration Plugin service modifies the configuration data. The calling order should be based on the value of the service.cmRanking property.
> 1000	The Configuration Plugin service should not modify data and is called after all modifications are made.

104.10 Remote Management

This specification does not attempt to define a remote management interface for the Framework. The purpose of this specification is to define a minimal interface for bundles that is complete enough for testing.

The Configuration Admin service is a primary aspect of remote management, however, and this specification must be compatible with common remote management standards. This section discusses some of the issues of using this specification with [1] *DMTF Common Information Model* (CIM) and [2] *Simple Network Management Protocol* (SNMP), the most likely candidates for remote management today.

These discussions are not complete, comprehensive, or normative. They are intended to point the bundle developer in relevant directions. Further specifications are needed to make a more concrete mapping.

104.10.1 Common Information Model

Common Information Model (CIM) defines the managed objects in [4] *Interface Definition Language* (IDL) language, which was developed for the Common Object Request Broker Architecture (CORBA).

The data types and the data values have a syntax. Additionally, these syntaxes can be mapped to XML. Unfortunately, this XML mapping is very different from the very applicable [3] *XSchema* XML data type definition language. The Framework service registry property types are a proper subset of the CIM data types.

In this specification, a Managed Service Factory maps to a CIM class definition. The primitives create, delete, and set are supported in this specification via the ManagedServiceFactory interface. The possible data types in CIM are richer than those the Framework supports and should thus be limited to cases when CIM classes for bundles are defined.

An important conceptual difference between this specification and CIM is the naming of properties. CIM properties are defined within the scope of a class. In this specification, properties are primarily defined within the scope of the Managed Service Factory, but are then placed in the registry, where they have global scope. This mechanism is similar to LDAP, see [5] *Understanding and Deploying LDAP Directory services*, in which the semantics of the properties are defined globally and a class is a collection of globally defined properties.

This specification does not address the non-Configuration Admin service primitives such as notifications and method calls.

104.10.2 Simple Network Management Protocol

The Simple Network Management Protocol (SNMP) defines the data model in ASN.1. SNMP is a rich data typing language that supports many types that are difficult to map to the data types supported in this specification. A large overlap exists, however, and it should be possible to design a data type that is applicable in this context.

The PID of a Managed Service should map to the SNMP Object IDentifier (OID). Managed Service Factories are mapped to tables in SNMP, although this mapping creates an obvious restriction in data types because tables can only contain scalar values. Therefore, the property values of the Configuration object would have to be limited to scalar values.

Similar scope issues as seen in CIM arise for SNMP because properties have a global scope in the service registry.

SNMP does not support the concept of method calls or function calls. All information is conveyed as the setting of values. The SNMP paradigm maps closely to this specification.

This specification does not address non-Configuration Admin primitives such as traps.

104.11 Meta Typing

This section discusses how the Metatype specification is used in the context of a Configuration Admin service.

When a Managed Service or Managed Service Factory is registered, the service object may also implement the MetaTypeProvider interface.

If the Managed Service or Managed Service Factory object implements the MetaTypeProvider interface, a management bundle may assume that the associated ObjectClassDefinition object can be used to configure the service.

The ObjectClassDefinition and AttributeDefinition objects contain sufficient information to automatically build simple user interfaces. They can also be used to augment dedicated interfaces with accurate validations.

When the Metatype specification is used, care should be taken to match the capabilities of the metatype package to the capabilities of the Configuration Admin service specification. Specifically:

- The metatype specification must describe nested arrays and vectors or arrays/vectors of mixed type.

This specification does not address how the metatype is made available to a management system due to the many open issues regarding remote management.

104.12 Security

104.12.1 Configuration Permission

The Configuration Permission provides a bundle with the authority to configure other bundles. All bundles implicitly have the permission to manage configurations that are bound to their own location.

The Configure Permission has only a single action and the target must always be ∗. The action is:

- CONFIGURE – This action grants a bundle the authority to manage configurations for any other bundle.

The ∗ wildcard for the actions parameter is supported.

104.12.2 Permissions Summary

Configuration Admin service security is implemented using Service Permission and Configuration Permission. The following table summarizes the permissions needed by the Configuration Admin bundle itself, as well as the typical permissions needed by the bundles with which it interacts.

Configuration Admin:

```
ServicePermission[ ..ConfigurationAdmin, REGISTER ]
ServicePermission[ ..ManagedService, GET ]
ServicePermission[ ..ManagedServiceFactory, GET ]
ServicePermission[ ..ConfigurationPlugin, GET ]
ConfigurationPermission[ *, CONFIGURE ]
AdminPermission[ *, METADATA ]
```

Managed Service:

```
ServicePermission[ ..ConfigurationAdmin, GET ]
ServicePermission[ ..ManagedService, REGISTER ]
```

Managed Service Factory:

```
ServicePermission[ ..ConfigurationAdmin, GET ]
ServicePermission[ ..ManagedServiceFactory, REGISTER ]
```

Configuration Plugin:

```
ServicePermission[ ..ConfigurationPlugin, REGISTER ]
```

Configuration Listener:

```
ServicePermission[ ..ConfigurationListener, REGISTER ]
```

The Configuration Admin service must have ServicePermission[ConfigurationAdmin, REGISTER]. It will also be the only bundle that needs the ServicePermission[ManagedService | ManagedServiceFactory |Configur ationPlugin, GET]. No other bundle should be allowed to have GET permission for these interfaces. The Configuration Admin bundle must also hold ConfigurationPermission[*,CONFIGURE].

Bundles that can be configured must have the ServicePermission[ManagedService | ManagedServiceFactory, REGISTER]. Bundles registering ConfigurationPlugin objects must have ServicePermission[ConfigurationPlugin, REGISTER]. The Configuration Admin service must trust all services registered with the ConfigurationPlugin interface. Only the Configuration Admin service should have ServicePermission[Configur ationPlugin, GET].

If a Managed Service or Managed Service Factory is implemented by an object that is also registered under another interface, it is possible, although inappropriate, for a bundle other than the Configuration Admin service implementation to call the updated method. Security-aware bundles can avoid this problem by having their updated methods check that the caller has ConfigurationPermission[*, CONFIGURE].

Bundles that want to change their own configuration need ServicePermission[ConfigurationAdmin, GET]. A bundle with ConfigurationPermission[*,CONFIGURE]is allowed to access and modify any Configuration object.

Pre-configuration of bundles requires ConfigurationPermission[*,CONFIGURE] because the methods that specify a location require this permission.

104.12.3   Forging PIDs

A risk exists of an unauthorized bundle forging a PID in order to obtain and possibly modify the configuration information of another bundle. To mitigate this risk, Configuration objects are generally *bound* to a specific bundle location, and are not passed to any Managed Service or Managed Service Factory registered by a different bundle.

Bundles with the required permission can create Configuration objects that are not bound. In other words, they have their location set to null. This can be useful for pre-configuring bundles before they are installed without having to know their actual locations.

In this scenario, the Configuration object must become bound to the first bundle that registers a Managed Service (or Managed Service Factory) with the right PID.

A bundle could still possibly obtain another bundle's configuration by registering a Managed Service with the right PID before the victim bundle does so. This situation can be regarded as a denial-of-service attack, because the victim bundle would never receive its configuration information. Such an attack can be avoided by always binding Configuration objects to the right locations. It can also be detected by the Configuration Admin service when the victim bundle registers the correct PID and two equal PIDs are then registered. This violation of this specification should be logged.

104.12.4   Configuration and Permission Administration

Configuration information has a direct influence on the permissions needed by a bundle. For example, when the Configuration Admin Bundle orders a bundle to use port 2011 for a console, that bundle also needs permission for listening to incoming connections on that port.

Both a simple and a complex solution exist for this situation.

The simple solution for this situation provides the bundle with a set of permissions that do not define specific values but allow a range of values. For example, a bundle could listen to ports above 1024 freely. All these ports could then be used for configuration.

The other solution is more complicated. In an environment where there is very strong security, the bundle would only be allowed access to a specific port. This situation requires an atomic update of both the configuration data and the permissions. If this update was not atomic, a potential security hole would exist during the period of time that the set of permissions did not match the configuration.

The following scenario can be used to update a configuration and the security permissions:

1   Stop the bundle.
2   Update the appropriate Configuration object via the Configuration Admin service.
3   Update the permissions in the Framework.
4   Start the bundle.

This scenario would achieve atomicity from the point of view of the bundle.

104.13   Configurable Service

Both the Configuration Admin service and the org.osgi.framework.Configurable interface address configuration management issues. It is the intention of this specification to replace the Framework interface for configuration management.

The Framework Configurable mechanism works as follows. A registered service object implements the Configurable interface to allow a management bundle to configure that service. The Configurable interface has only one method: getConfigurationObject(). This method returns a Java Bean. Beans can be examined and modified with the java.reflect or java.bean packages.

This scheme has the following disadvantages:

- *No factory* – Only registered services can be configured, unlike the Managed Service Factory that configures any number of services.
- *Atomicity* – The beans or reflection API can only modify one property at a time and there is no way to tell the bean that no more modifications to the properties will follow. This limitation complicates updates of configurations that have dependencies between properties.
  This specification passes a Dictionary object that sets all the configuration properties atomically.
- *Profile* – The Java beans API is linked to many packages that are not likely to be present in OSGi environments. The reflection API may be present but is not simple to use.
  This specification has no required libraries.
- *User Interface support* – UI support in beans is very rudimentary when no AWT is present.
  The associated Metatyping specification does not require any external libraries, and has extensive support for UIs including localization.

104.14   org.osgi.service.cm

Configuration Admin Package Version 1.3.

Bundles wishing to use this package must list the package in the Import-Package header of the bundle's manifest. For example:

```
Import-Package: org.osgi.service.cm; version="[1.3,2.0)"
```

104.14.1   Summary

- *Configuration* - The configuration information for a ManagedService or ManagedServiceFactory object.
- *ConfigurationAdmin* - Service for administering configuration data.
- *ConfigurationEvent* - A Configuration Event.
- *ConfigurationException* - An Exception class to inform the Configuration Admin service of problems with configuration data.
- *ConfigurationListener* - Listener for Configuration Events.
- *ConfigurationPermission* - Indicates a bundle's authority to configure bundles.
- *ConfigurationPlugin* - A service interface for processing configuration dictionary before the update.
- *ManagedService* - A service that can receive configuration data from a Configuration Admin service.
- *ManagedServiceFactory* - Manage multiple service instances.

104.14.2   public interface Configuration

The configuration information for a ManagedService or ManagedServiceFactory object. The Configuration Admin service uses this interface to represent the configuration information for a ManagedService or for a service instance of a ManagedServiceFactory.

A Configuration object contains a configuration dictionary and allows the properties to be updated via this object. Bundles wishing to receive configuration dictionaries do not need to use this class - they register a ManagedService or ManagedServiceFactory. Only administrative bundles, and bundles wishing to update their own configurations need to use this class.

The properties handled in this configuration have case insensitive String objects as keys. However, case is preserved from the last set key/value.

A configuration can be *bound* to a bundle location (Bundle.getLocation()). The purpose of binding a Configuration object to a location is to make it impossible for another bundle to forge a PID that would match this configuration. When a configuration is bound to a specific location, and a bundle with a different location registers a corresponding ManagedService object or ManagedServiceFactory object, then the configuration is not passed to the updated method of that object.

If a configuration's location is null, it is not yet bound to a location. It will become bound to the location of the first bundle that registers a ManagedService or ManagedServiceFactory object with the corresponding PID.

The same Configuration object is used for configuring both a Managed Service Factory and a Managed Service. When it is important to differentiate between these two the term "factory configuration" is used.

104.14.2.1   public void delete( ) throws IOException

☐   Delete this Configuration object. Removes this configuration object from the persistent store. Notify asynchronously the corresponding Managed Service or Managed Service Factory. A ManagedService object is notified by a call to its updated method with a null properties argument. A ManagedServiceFactory object is notified by a call to its deleted method.

Also initiates an asynchronous call to all ConfigurationListeners with a ConfigurationEvent.CM_DELETED event.

Throws IOException – If delete fails

IllegalStateException – if this configuration has been deleted

104.14.2.2   **public boolean equals(Object other)**

other Configuration object to compare against

☐ Equality is defined to have equal PIDs Two Configuration objects are equal when their PIDs are equal.

Returns true if equal, false if not a Configuration object or one with a different PID.

104.14.2.3   **public String getBundleLocation( )**

☐ Get the bundle location. Returns the bundle location to which this configuration is bound, or null if it is not yet bound to a bundle location.

Returns location to which this configuration is bound, or null.

Throws IllegalStateException – If this Configuration object has been deleted.

SecurityException – If the caller does not have ConfigurationPermission[*,CONFIGURE].

104.14.2.4   **public String getFactoryPid( )**

☐ For a factory configuration return the PID of the corresponding Managed Service Factory, else return null.

Returns factory PID or null

Throws IllegalStateException – if this configuration has been deleted

104.14.2.5   **public String getPid( )**

☐ Get the PID for this Configuration object.

Returns the PID for this Configuration object.

Throws IllegalStateException – if this configuration has been deleted

104.14.2.6   **public Dictionary getProperties( )**

☐ Return the properties of this Configuration object. The Dictionary object returned is a private copy for the caller and may be changed without influencing the stored configuration. The keys in the returned dictionary are case insensitive and are always of type String.

If called just after the configuration is created and before update has been called, this method returns null.

Returns A private copy of the properties for the caller or null. These properties must not contain the "service.bundleLocation" property. The value of this property may be obtained from the getBundleLocation method.

Throws IllegalStateException – if this configuration has been deleted

104.14.2.7   **public int hashCode( )**

☐ Hash code is based on PID. The hashcode for two Configuration objects must be the same when the Configuration PID's are the same.

Returns hash code for this Configuration object

104.14.2.8   **public void setBundleLocation(String bundleLocation)**

bundleLocation a bundle location or null

❑ Bind this Configuration object to the specified bundle location. If the bundleLocation parameter is null then the Configuration object will not be bound to a location. It will be set to the bundle's location before the first time a Managed Service/Managed Service Factory receives this Configuration object via the updated method and before any plugins are called. The bundle location will be set persistently.

Throws IllegalStateException – If this configuration has been deleted.

SecurityException – If the caller does not have ConfigurationPermission[*,CONFIGURE].

104.14.2.9   **public void update(Dictionary properties) throws IOException**

properties the new set of properties for this configuration

❑ Update the properties of this Configuration object. Stores the properties in persistent storage after adding or overwriting the following properties:

- "service.pid" : is set to be the PID of this configuration.
- "service.factoryPid" : if this is a factory configuration it is set to the factory PID else it is not set.

These system properties are all of type String.

If the corresponding Managed Service/Managed Service Factory is registered, its updated method must be called asynchronously. Else, this callback is delayed until aforementioned registration occurs.

Also initiates an asynchronous call to all ConfigurationListeners with a ConfigurationEvent.CM_UPDATED event.

Throws IOException – if update cannot be made persistent

IllegalArgumentException – if the Dictionary object contains invalid configuration types or contains case variants of the same key name.

IllegalStateException – if this configuration has been deleted

104.14.2.10   **public void update( ) throws IOException**

❑ Update the Configuration object with the current properties. Initiate the updated callback to the Managed Service or Managed Service Factory with the current properties asynchronously.

This is the only way for a bundle that uses a Configuration Plugin service to initiate a callback. For example, when that bundle detects a change that requires an update of the Managed Service or Managed Service Factory via its ConfigurationPlugin object.

Throws IOException – if update cannot access the properties in persistent storage

IllegalStateException – if this configuration has been deleted

See Also ConfigurationPlugin

104.14.3   **public interface ConfigurationAdmin**

Service for administering configuration data.

The main purpose of this interface is to store bundle configuration data persistently. This information is represented in Configuration objects. The actual configuration data is a Dictionary of properties inside a Configuration object.

There are two principally different ways to manage configurations. First there is the concept of a Managed Service, where configuration data is uniquely associated with an object registered with the service registry.

Next, there is the concept of a factory where the Configuration Admin service will maintain 0 or more Configuration objects for a Managed Service Factory that is registered with the Framework.

The first concept is intended for configuration data about "things/services" whose existence is defined externally, e.g. a specific printer. Factories are intended for "things/services" that can be created any number of times, e.g. a configuration for a DHCP server for different networks.

Bundles that require configuration should register a Managed Service or a Managed Service Factory in the service registry. A registration property named service.pid (persistent identifier or PID) must be used to identify this Managed Service or Managed Service Factory to the Configuration Admin service.

When the ConfigurationAdmin detects the registration of a Managed Service, it checks its persistent storage for a configuration object whose service.pid property matches the PID service property (service.pid) of the Managed Service. If found, it calls ManagedService.updated method with the new properties. The implementation of a Configuration Admin service must run these call-backs asynchronously to allow proper synchronization.

When the Configuration Admin service detects a Managed Service Factory registration, it checks its storage for configuration objects whose service.factoryPid property matches the PID service property of the Managed Service Factory. For each such Configuration objects, it calls the ManagedServiceFactory.updated method asynchronously with the new properties. The calls to the updated method of a ManagedServiceFactory must be executed sequentially and not overlap in time.

In general, bundles having permission to use the Configuration Admin service can only access and modify their own configuration information. Accessing or modifying the configuration of another bundle requires ConfigurationPermission[*,CONFIGURE].

Configuration objects can be *bound* to a specified bundle location. In this case, if a matching Managed Service or Managed Service Factory is registered by a bundle with a different location, then the Configuration Admin service must not do the normal callback, and it should log an error. In the case where a Configuration object is not bound, its location field is null, the Configuration Admin service will bind it to the location of the bundle that registers the first Managed Service or Managed Service Factory that has a corresponding PID property. When a Configuration object is bound to a bundle location in this manner, the Configuration Admin service must detect if the bundle corresponding to the location is uninstalled. If this occurs, the Configuration object is unbound, that is its location field is set back to null.

The method descriptions of this class refer to a concept of "the calling bundle". This is a loose way of referring to the bundle which obtained the Configuration Admin service from the service registry. Implementations of ConfigurationAdmin must use a org.osgi.framework.ServiceFactory to support this concept.

104.14.3.1   **public static final String SERVICE_BUNDLELOCATION = "service.bundleLocation"**

Configuration property naming the location of the bundle that is associated with a a Configuration object. This property can be searched for but must not appear in the configuration dictionary for security reason. The property's value is of type String.

Since   1.1

104.14.3.2   **public static final String SERVICE_FACTORYPID = "service.factoryPid"**

Configuration property naming the Factory PID in the configuration dictionary. The property's value is of type String.

Since   1.1

104.14.3.3   **public Configuration createFactoryConfiguration(String factoryPid) throws IOException**

factoryPid   PID of factory (not null).

□   Create a new factory Configuration object with a new PID. The properties of the new Configuration object are null until the first time that its Configuration.update(Dictionary) method is called.

It is not required that the factoryPid maps to a registered Managed Service Factory.

The Configuration object is bound to the location of the calling bundle.

Returns A new Configuration object.

Throws IOException – if access to persistent storage fails.

SecurityException – if caller does not have ConfigurationPermission[*,CONFIGURE] and factoryPid is bound to another bundle.

104.14.3.4 **public Configuration createFactoryConfiguration(String factoryPid, String location) throws IOException**

factoryPid PID of factory (not null).

location A bundle location string, or null.

☐ Create a new factory Configuration object with a new PID. The properties of the new Configuration object are null until the first time that its Configuration.update(Dictionary) method is called.

It is not required that the factoryPid maps to a registered Managed Service Factory.

The Configuration is bound to the location specified. If this location is null it will be bound to the location of the first bundle that registers a Managed Service Factory with a corresponding PID.

Returns a new Configuration object.

Throws IOException – if access to persistent storage fails.

SecurityException – if caller does not have ConfigurationPermission[*,CONFIGURE].

104.14.3.5 **public Configuration getConfiguration(String pid, String location) throws IOException**

pid Persistent identifier.

location The bundle location string, or null.

☐ Get an existing Configuration object from the persistent store, or create a new Configuration object.

If a Configuration with this PID already exists in Configuration Admin service return it. The location parameter is ignored in this case.

Else, return a new Configuration object. This new object is bound to the location and the properties are set to null. If the location parameter is null, it will be set when a Managed Service with the corresponding PID is registered for the first time.

Returns An existing or new Configuration object.

Throws IOException – if access to persistent storage fails.

SecurityException – if the caller does not have ConfigurationPermission[*,CONFIGURE].

104.14.3.6 **public Configuration getConfiguration(String pid) throws IOException**

pid persistent identifier.

☐ Get an existing or new Configuration object from the persistent store. If the Configuration object for this PID does not exist, create a new Configuration object for that PID, where properties are null. Bind its location to the calling bundle's location.

Otherwise, if the location of the existing Configuration object is null, set it to the calling bundle's location.

Returns an existing or new Configuration matching the PID.

Throws IOException – if access to persistent storage fails.

SecurityException – if the Configuration object is bound to a location different from that of the calling bundle and it has no ConfigurationPermission[*,CONFIGURE].

104.14.3.7 **public Configuration[] listConfigurations(String filter) throws IOException,**
InvalidSyntaxException

filter A filter string, or null to retrieve all Configuration objects.

☐ List the current Configuration objects which match the filter.

Only Configuration objects with non- null properties are considered current. That is,
Configuration.getProperties() is guaranteed not to return null for each of the returned
Configuration objects.

Normally only Configuration objects that are bound to the location of the calling bundle are
returned, or all if the caller has ConfigurationPermission[*,CONFIGURE].

The syntax of the filter string is as defined in the org.osgi.framework.Filter class. The filter can test
any configuration properties including the following:

- service.pid-String- the PID under which this is registered
- service.factoryPid-String- the factory if applicable
- service.bundleLocation-String- the bundle location

The filter can also be null, meaning that all Configuration objects should be returned.

Returns All matching Configuration objects, or null if there aren't any.

Throws IOException – if access to persistent storage fails

InvalidSyntaxException – if the filter string is invalid

104.14.4 public class ConfigurationEvent

A Configuration Event.

ConfigurationEvent objects are delivered to all registered ConfigurationListener service objects. Con-
figurationEvents must be asynchronously delivered in chronological order with respect to each listener.

A type code is used to identify the type of event. The following event types are defined:

- CM_UPDATED
- CM_DELETED

Security Considerations. ConfigurationEvent objects do not provide Configuration objects, so no sensitive configuration information is available from the event. If the listener wants to locate the
Configuration object for the specified pid, it must use ConfigurationAdmin.

See Also ConfigurationListener

Since 1.2

104.14.4.1 **public static final int CM_DELETED = 2**

A Configuration has been deleted.

This ConfigurationEvent type that indicates that a Configuration object has been deleted. An event
is fired when a call to Configuration.delete() successfully deletes a configuration.

The value of CM_DELETED is 2.

104.14.4.2 **public static final int CM_UPDATED = 1**

A Configuration has been updated.

This ConfigurationEvent type that indicates that a Configuration object has been updated with new
properties. An event is fired when a call to Configuration.update(Dictionary) successfully changes a
configuration.

The value of CM_UPDATED is 1.

104.14.4.3   **public ConfigurationEvent(ServiceReference reference, int type, String factoryPid, String pid)**

reference   The ServiceReference object of the Configuration Admin service that created this event.

type   The event type. See getType.

factoryPid   The factory pid of the associated configuration if the target of the configuration is a ManagedService-Factory. Otherwise null if the target of the configuration is a ManagedService.

pid   The pid of the associated configuration.

☐ Constructs a ConfigurationEvent object from the given ServiceReference object, event type, and pids.

104.14.4.4   **public String getFactoryPid( )**

☐ Returns the factory pid of the associated configuration.

Returns   Returns the factory pid of the associated configuration if the target of the configuration is a Managed-ServiceFactory. Otherwise null if the target of the configuration is a ManagedService.

104.14.4.5   **public String getPid( )**

☐ Returns the pid of the associated configuration.

Returns   Returns the pid of the associated configuration.

104.14.4.6   **public ServiceReference getReference( )**

☐ Return the ServiceReference object of the Configuration Admin service that created this event.

Returns   The ServiceReference object for the Configuration Admin service that created this event.

104.14.4.7   **public int getType( )**

☐ Return the type of this event.

The type values are:

- CM_UPDATED
- CM_DELETED

Returns   The type of this event.

104.14.5   **public class ConfigurationException
extends Exception**

An Exception class to inform the Configuration Admin service of problems with configuration data.

104.14.5.1   **public ConfigurationException(String property, String reason)**

property   name of the property that caused the problem, null if no specific property was the cause

reason   reason for failure

☐ Create a ConfigurationException object.

104.14.5.2   **public ConfigurationException(String property, String reason, Throwable cause)**

property   name of the property that caused the problem, null if no specific property was the cause

reason   reason for failure

cause   The cause of this exception.

☐ Create a ConfigurationException object.

Since   1.2

104.14.5.3   **public Throwable getCause( )**

◻ Returns the cause of this exception or null if no cause was set.

Returns The cause of this exception or null if no cause was set.

Since 1.2

104.14.5.4   **public String getProperty( )**

◻ Return the property name that caused the failure or null.

Returns name of property or null if no specific property caused the problem

104.14.5.5   **public String getReason( )**

◻ Return the reason for this exception.

Returns reason of the failure

104.14.5.6   **public Throwable initCause(Throwable cause)**

cause The cause of this exception.

◻ Initializes the cause of this exception to the specified value.

Returns This exception.

Throws IllegalArgumentException – If the specified cause is this exception.

IllegalStateException – If the cause of this exception has already been set.

Since 1.2

104.14.6   public interface ConfigurationListener

Listener for Configuration Events. When a ConfigurationEvent is fired, it is asynchronously delivered to a ConfigurationListener.

ConfigurationListener objects are registered with the Framework service registry and are notified with a ConfigurationEvent object when an event is fired.

ConfigurationListener objects can inspect the received ConfigurationEvent object to determine its type, the pid of the Configuration object with which it is associated, and the Configuration Admin service that fired the event.

Security Considerations. Bundles wishing to monitor configuration events will require ServicePermission[ConfigurationListener,REGISTER] to register a ConfigurationListener service.

Since 1.2

104.14.6.1   **public void configurationEvent(ConfigurationEvent event)**

event The ConfigurationEvent.

◻ Receives notification of a Configuration that has changed.

104.14.7   public final class ConfigurationPermission
extends BasicPermission

Indicates a bundle's authority to configure bundles. This permission has only a single action: CONFIGURE.

Since 1.2

Concurrency Thread-safe

104.14.7.1   **public static final String CONFIGURE = "configure"**

The action string configure.

104.14.7.2 **public ConfigurationPermission(String name, String actions)**

name Name must be "∗".

actions configure (canonical order).

☐ Create a new ConfigurationPermission.

104.14.7.3 **public boolean equals(Object obj)**

obj The object being compared for equality with this object.

☐ Determines the equality of two ConfigurationPermission objects.

Two ConfigurationPermission objects are equal.

Returns true if obj is equivalent to this ConfigurationPermission; false otherwise.

104.14.7.4 **public String getActions( )**

☐ Returns the canonical string representation of the ConfigurationPermission actions.

Always returns present ConfigurationPermission actions in the following order: CONFIGURE

Returns Canonical string representation of the ConfigurationPermission actions.

104.14.7.5 **public int hashCode( )**

☐ Returns the hash code value for this object.

Returns Hash code value for this object.

104.14.7.6 **public boolean implies(Permission p)**

p The target permission to check.

☐ Determines if a ConfigurationPermission object "implies" the specified permission.

Returns true if the specified permission is implied by this object; false otherwise.

104.14.7.7 **public PermissionCollection newPermissionCollection( )**

☐ Returns a new PermissionCollection object suitable for storing ConfigurationPermissions.

Returns A new PermissionCollection object.

104.14.8 public interface ConfigurationPlugin

A service interface for processing configuration dictionary before the update.

A bundle registers a ConfigurationPlugin object in order to process configuration updates before they reach the Managed Service or Managed Service Factory. The Configuration Admin service will detect registrations of Configuration Plugin services and must call these services every time before it calls the ManagedService or ManagedServiceFactoryupdated method. The Configuration Plugin service thus has the opportunity to view and modify the properties before they are passed to the Managed Service or Managed Service Factory.

Configuration Plugin (plugin) services have full read/write access to all configuration information. Therefore, bundles using this facility should be trusted. Access to this facility should be limited with ServicePermission[ConfigurationPlugin,REGISTER]. Implementations of a Configuration Plugin service should assure that they only act on appropriate configurations.

The Integerservice.cmRanking registration property may be specified. Not specifying this registration property, or setting it to something other than an Integer, is the same as setting it to the Integer zero. The service.cmRanking property determines the order in which plugins are invoked. Lower ranked plugins are called before higher ranked ones. In the event of more than one plugin having the same value of service.cmRanking, then the Configuration Admin service arbitrarily chooses the order in which they are called.

By convention, plugins with service.cmRanking< 0 or service.cmRanking > 1000 should not make modifications to the properties.

The Configuration Admin service has the right to hide properties from plugins, or to ignore some or all the changes that they make. This might be done for security reasons. Any such behavior is entirely implementation defined.

A plugin may optionally specify a cm.target registration property whose value is the PID of the Managed Service or Managed Service Factory whose configuration updates the plugin is intended to intercept. The plugin will then only be called with configuration updates that are targeted at the Managed Service or Managed Service Factory with the specified PID. Omitting the cm.target registration property means that the plugin is called for all configuration updates.

104.14.8.1   **public static final String CM_RANKING = "service.cmRanking"**

A service property to specify the order in which plugins are invoked. This property contains an Integer ranking of the plugin. Not specifying this registration property, or setting it to something other than an Integer, is the same as setting it to the Integer zero. This property determines the order in which plugins are invoked. Lower ranked plugins are called before higher ranked ones.

Since 1.2

104.14.8.2   **public static final String CM_TARGET = "cm.target"**

A service property to limit the Managed Service or Managed Service Factory configuration dictionaries a Configuration Plugin service receives. This property contains a String[] of PIDs. A Configuration Admin service must call a Configuration Plugin service only when this property is not set, or the target service's PID is listed in this property.

104.14.8.3   **public void modifyConfiguration(ServiceReference reference, Dictionary properties)**

reference reference to the Managed Service or Managed Service Factory

properties The configuration properties. This argument must not contain the "service.bundleLocation" property. The value of this property may be obtained from the Configuration.getBundleLocation method.

☐ View and possibly modify the a set of configuration properties before they are sent to the Managed Service or the Managed Service Factory. The Configuration Plugin services are called in increasing order of their service.cmRanking property. If this property is undefined or is a non-Integer type, 0 is used.

This method should not modify the properties unless the service.cmRanking of this plugin is in the range 0 <= service.cmRanking <= 1000.

If this method throws any Exception, the Configuration Admin service must catch it and should log it.

104.14.9   **public interface ManagedService**

A service that can receive configuration data from a Configuration Admin service.

A Managed Service is a service that needs configuration data. Such an object should be registered with the Framework registry with the service.pid property set to some unique identifier called a PID.

If the Configuration Admin service has a Configuration object corresponding to this PID, it will callback the updated() method of the ManagedService object, passing the properties of that Configuration object.

If it has no such Configuration object, then it calls back with a null properties argument. Registering a Managed Service will always result in a callback to the updated() method provided the Configuration Admin service is, or becomes active. This callback must always be done asynchronously.

Else, every time that either of the updated() methods is called on that Configuration object, the ManagedService.updated() method with the new properties is called. If the delete() method is called on that Configuration object, ManagedService.updated() is called with a null for the properties parameter. All these callbacks must be done asynchronously.

The following example shows the code of a serial port that will create a port depending on configuration information.

```
class SerialPort implements ManagedService {

    ServiceRegistration registration;
    Hashtable configuration;
    CommPortIdentifier id;

    synchronized void open(CommPortIdentifier id,
    BundleContext context) {
        this.id = id;
        registration = context.registerService(
            ManagedService.class.getName(),
            this,
            getDefaults()
        );
    }

    Hashtable getDefaults() {
        Hashtable defaults = new Hashtable();
        defaults.put( "port", id.getName() );
        defaults.put( "product", "unknown" );
        defaults.put( "baud", "9600" );
        defaults.put( Constants.SERVICE_PID,
            "com.acme.serialport." + id.getName() );
        return defaults;
    }

    public synchronized void updated(
        Dictionary configuration  ) {
        if ( configuration ==
  null
  )
            registration.setProperties( getDefaults() );
        else {
            setSpeed( configuration.get("baud") );
            registration.setProperties( configuration );
        }
    }
    ...
}
```

As a convention, it is recommended that when a Managed Service is updated, it should copy all the properties it does not recognize into the service registration properties. This will allow the Configuration Admin service to set properties on services which can then be used by other applications.

104.14.9.1   **public void updated(Dictionary properties) throws ConfigurationException**

properties A copy of the Configuration properties, or null. This argument must not contain the "service.bundle-Location" property. The value of this property may be obtained from the Configuration.getBundleLocation method.

☐ Update the configuration for a Managed Service.

When the implementation of updated(Dictionary) detects any kind of error in the configuration properties, it should create a new ConfigurationException which describes the problem. This can allow a management system to provide useful information to a human administrator.

If this method throws any other Exception, the Configuration Admin service must catch it and should log it.

The Configuration Admin service must call this method asynchronously which initiated the callback. This implies that implementors of Managed Service can be assured that the callback will not take place during registration when they execute the registration in a synchronized method.

Throws ConfigurationException – when the update fails

104.14.10   public interface ManagedServiceFactory

Manage multiple service instances. Bundles registering this interface are giving the Configuration Admin service the ability to create and configure a number of instances of a service that the implementing bundle can provide. For example, a bundle implementing a DHCP server could be instantiated multiple times for different interfaces using a factory.

Each of these *service instances* is represented, in the persistent storage of the Configuration Admin service, by a factory Configuration object that has a PID. When such a Configuration is updated, the Configuration Admin service calls the ManagedServiceFactory updated method with the new properties. When updated is called with a new PID, the Managed Service Factory should create a new factory instance based on these configuration properties. When called with a PID that it has seen before, it should update that existing service instance with the new configuration information.

In general it is expected that the implementation of this interface will maintain a data structure that maps PIDs to the factory instances that it has created. The semantics of a factory instance are defined by the Managed Service Factory. However, if the factory instance is registered as a service object with the service registry, its PID should match the PID of the corresponding Configuration object (but it should **not** be registered as a Managed Service!).

An example that demonstrates the use of a factory. It will create serial ports under command of the Configuration Admin service.

```
class SerialPortFactory
  implements ManagedServiceFactory {
  ServiceRegistration registration;
  Hashtable ports;
  void start(BundleContext context) {
    Hashtable properties = new Hashtable();
    properties.put( Constants.SERVICE_PID,
      "com.acme.serialportfactory" );
    registration = context.registerService(
      ManagedServiceFactory.class.getName(),
      this,
      properties
    );
  }
  public void updated( String pid,
    Dictionary properties  ) {
```

```
         String portName = (String) properties.get("port");
         SerialPortService port =
           (SerialPort) ports.get( pid );
         if ( port == null ) {
           port = new SerialPortService();
           ports.put( pid, port );
           port.open();
         }
         if ( port.getPortName().equals(portName) )
           return;
         port.setPortName( portName );
      }
      public void deleted( String pid ) {
         SerialPortService port =
           (SerialPort) ports.get( pid );
         port.close();
         ports.remove( pid );
      }
      ...
   }
```

104.14.10.1 **public void deleted(String pid)**

pid the PID of the service to be removed

☐ Remove a factory instance. Remove the factory instance associated with the PID. If the instance was registered with the service registry, it should be unregistered.

If this method throws any Exception, the Configuration Admin service must catch it and should log it.

The Configuration Admin service must call this method asynchronously.

104.14.10.2 **public String getName( )**

☐ Return a descriptive name of this factory.

Returns the name for the factory, which might be localized

104.14.10.3 **public void updated(String pid, Dictionary properties) throws ConfigurationException**

pid The PID for this configuration.

properties A copy of the configuration properties. This argument must not contain the service.bundleLocation" property. The value of this property may be obtained from the Configuration.getBundleLocation method.

☐ Create a new instance, or update the configuration of an existing instance. If the PID of the Configuration object is new for the Managed Service Factory, then create a new factory instance, using the configuration properties provided. Else, update the service instance with the provided properties.

If the factory instance is registered with the Framework, then the configuration properties should be copied to its registry properties. This is not mandatory and security sensitive properties should obviously not be copied.

If this method throws any Exception, the Configuration Admin service must catch it and should log it.

When the implementation of updated detects any kind of error in the configuration properties, it should create a new ConfigurationException which describes the problem.

The Configuration Admin service must call this method asynchronously. This implies that implementors of the ManagedServiceFactory class can be assured that the callback will not take place during registration when they execute the registration in a synchronized method.

Throws ConfigurationException – when the configuration properties are invalid.

104.15 References

[1] *DMTF Common Information Model*
http://www.dmtf.org

[2] *Simple Network Management Protocol*
RFCs http://directory.google.com/Top/Computers/Internet/Protocols/SNMP/RFCs

[3] *XSchema*
http://www.w3.org/TR/xmlschema-0/

[4] *Interface Definition Language*
http://www.omg.org

[5] *Understanding and Deploying LDAP Directory services*
Timothy Howes et. al. ISBN 1-57870-070-1, MacMillan Technical publishing.

105   Metatype Service Specification

Version 1.1

105.1   Introduction

The Metatype specification defines interfaces that allow bundle developers to describe attribute types in a computer readable form using so-called *metadata*.

The purpose of this specification is to allow services to specify the type information of data that they can use as arguments. The data is based on *attributes*, which are key/value pairs like properties.

A designer in a type-safe language like Java is often confronted with the choice of using the language constructs to exchange data or using a technique based on attributes/properties that are based on key/value pairs. Attributes provide an escape from the rigid type-safety requirements of modern programming languages.

Type-safety works very well for software development environments in which multiple programmers work together on large applications or systems, but often lacks the flexibility needed to receive structured data from the outside world.

The attribute paradigm has several characteristics that make this approach suitable when data needs to be communicated between different entities which "speak" different languages. Attributes are uncomplicated, resilient to change, and allow the receiver to dynamically adapt to different types of data.

As an example, the OSGi Service Platform Specifications define several attribute types which are used in a Framework implementation, but which are also used and referenced by other OSGi specifications such as the *Configuration Admin Service Specification* on page 45. A Configuration Admin service implementation deploys attributes (key/value pairs) as configuration properties.

The Meta Type Service provides a unified access point to the Meta Type information that is associated with bundles. This Meta Type information can be defined by an XML resource in a bundle (OSGI-INF/metatype directories must be scanned for any XML resources), or it can be obtained from Managed Service or Managed Service Factory services that are implemented by a bundle.

105.1.1   Essentials

- *Conceptual model* – The specification must have a conceptual model for how classes and attributes are organized.
- *Standards* – The specification should be aligned with appropriate standards, and explained in situations where the specification is not aligned with, or cannot be mapped to, standards.
- *Remote Management* – Remote management should be taken into account.
- *Size* – Minimal overhead in size for a bundle using this specification is required.
- *Localization* – It must be possible to use this specification with different languages at the same time. This ability allows servlets to serve information in the language selected in the browser.
- *Type information* – The definition of an attribution should contain the name (if it is required), the cardinality, a label, a description, labels for enumerated values, and the Java class that should be used for the values.
- *Validation* – It should be possible to validate the values of the attributes.

105.1.2   Entities

- *Meta Type Service* – A service that provides a unified access point for meta type information.
- *Attribute* – A key/value pair.

- *PID* – A unique persistent ID, defined in configuration management.
- *Attribute Definition* – Defines a description, name, help text, and type information of an attribute.
- *Object Class Definition* – Defines the type of a datum. It contains a description and name of the type plus a set of AttributeDefinition objects.
- *Meta Type Provider* – Provides access to the object classes that are available for this object. Access uses the PID and a locale to find the best ObjectClassDefinition object.
- *Meta Type Information* – Provides meta type information for a bundle.

Figure 105.1   Class Diagram Meta Type Service, org.osgi.service.metatype

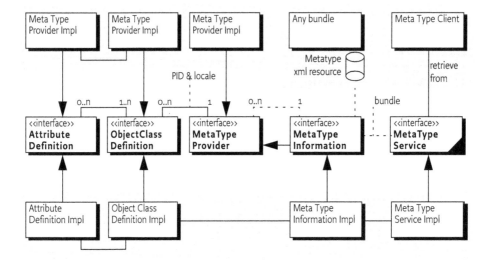

105.1.3   Operation

The Meta Type service defines a rich dynamic typing system for properties. The purpose of the type system is to allow reasonable User Interfaces to be constructed dynamically.

The type information is normally carried by the bundles themselves. Either by implementing the MetaTypeProvider interface or by carrying one or more XML resources in that define a number of Meta Types in the OSGI-INF/metatype directories. Additionally, a Meta Type service could have other sources.

The Meta Type Service provides unified access to Meta Types that are carried by the resident bundles. The Meta Type Service collects this information from the bundles and provides uniform access to it. A client can requests the Meta Type Information associated with a particular bundle. The MetaTypeInformation object provides a list of ObjectClassDefinition objects for a bundle. These objects define all the information for a specific *object class*. An object class is a some descriptive information and a set of named attributes (which are key/value pairs).

Access to Object Class Definitions is qualified by a locale and a Persistent IDentity (PID). This specification does not specify what the PID means. One application is OSGi Configuration Management where a PID is used by the Managed Service and Managed Service Factory services. In general, a PID should be regarded as the name of a variable where an Object Class Definition defines its type.

105.2   Attributes Model

The Framework uses the LDAP filter syntax for searching the Framework registry. The usage of the attributes in this specification and the Framework specification closely resemble the LDAP attribute model. Therefore, the names used in this specification have been aligned with LDAP. Consequently, the interfaces which are defined by this Specification are:

- AttributeDefinition
- ObjectClassDefinition
- MetaTypeProvider

These names correspond to the LDAP attribute model. For further information on ASN.1-defined attributes and X.500 object classes and attributes, see [2] *Understanding and Deploying LDAP Directory services*.

The LDAP attribute model assumes a global name-space for attributes, and object classes consist of a number of attributes. So, if an object class inherits the same attribute from different parents, only one copy of the attribute must become part of the object class definition. This name-space implies that a given attribute, for example cn, should *always* be the common name and the type must always be a String. An attribute cn cannot be an Integer in another object class definition. In this respect, the OSGi approach towards attribute definitions is comparable with the LDAP attribute model.

105.3   Object Class Definition

The ObjectClassDefinition interface is used to group the attributes which are defined in AttributeDefinition objects.

An ObjectClassDefinition object contains the information about the overall set of attributes and has the following elements:

- A name which can be returned in different locales.
- A global name-space in the registry, which is the same condition as LDAP/X.500 object classes. In these standards the OSI Object Identifier (OID) is used to uniquely identify object classes. If such an OID exists, (which can be requested at several standard organizations, and many companies already have a node in the tree) it can be returned here. Otherwise, a unique id should be returned. This id can be a Java class name (reverse domain name) or can be generated with a GUID algorithm. All LDAP-defined object classes already have an associated OID. It is strongly advised to define the object classes from existing LDAP schemes which provide many preexisting OIDs. Many such schemes exist ranging from postal addresses to DHCP parameters.
- A human-readable description of the class.
- A list of attribute definitions which can be filtered as required, or optional. Note that in X.500 the mandatory or required status of an attribute is part of the object class definition and not of the attribute definition.
- An icon, in different sizes.

105.4   Attribute Definition

The AttributeDefinition interface provides the means to describe the data type of attributes.

The AttributeDefinition interface defines the following elements:

- Defined names (final ints) for the data types as restricted in the Framework for the attributes, called the syntax in OSI terms, which can be obtained with the getType() method.
- AttributeDefinition objects should use and ID that is similar to the OID as described in the ID field for ObjectClassDefinition.
- A localized name intended to be used in user interfaces.

- A localized description that defines the semantics of the attribute and possible constraints, which should be usable for tooltips.
- An indication if this attribute should be stored as a unique value, a Vector, or an array of values, as well as the maximum cardinality of the type.
- The data type, as limited by the Framework service registry attribute types.
- A validation function to verify if a possible value is correct.
- A list of values and a list of localized labels. Intended for popup menus in GUIs, allowing the user to choose from a set.
- A default value. The return type of this is a String[ ]. For cardinality = zero, this return type must be an array of one String object. For other cardinalities, the array must not contain more than the absolute value of *cardinality* String objects. In that case, it may contain 0 objects.

105.5   Meta Type Service

The Meta Type Service provides unified access to Meta Type information that is associated with a Bundle. It can get this information through the following means:

- *Meta Type Resource* – A bundle can provide one ore more XML resources that are contained in its JAR file. These resources contain and XML definition of meta types as well as to what PIDs these Meta Types apply. These XML resources must reside in the OSGI-INF/metatype directories of the bundle (including any fragments).
- *ManagedService[Factory] objects* – As defined in the configuration management specification, ManagedService and ManagedServiceFactory service objects can optionally implement the MetaTypeProvider interface. The Meta Type Service will only search for MetaTypeProvider objects if no meta type resources are found in the bundle.

Figure 105.2   *Sources for Meta Types*

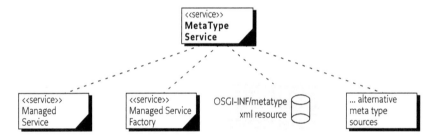

This model is depicted in Figure 105.2.

The Meta Type Service can therefore be used to retrieve meta type information for bundles which contain Meta Type resources or which provide their own MetaTypeProvider objects. The MetaTypeService interface has a single method:

- getMetaTypeInformation(Bundle) – Given a bundle, it must return the Meta Type Information for that bundle, even if there is no meta type information available at the moment of the call.

The returned MetaTypeInformation object maintains a map of PID to ObjectClassDefinition objects. The map is keyed by locale and PID. The list of maintained PIDs is available from the MetaTypeInformation object with the following methods:

- getPids() – PIDs for which Meta Types are available.
- getFactoryPids() – PIDs associated with Managed Service Factory services.

These methods and their interaction with the Meta Type resource are described in *Use of the Designate Element* on page 92.

The MetaTypeInformation interface extends the MetaTypeProvider interface. The MetaTypeProvider interface is used to access meta type information.It supports locale dependent information so that the text used in AttributeDefinition and ObjectClassDefinition objects can be adapted to different locales.

Which locales are supported by the MetaTypeProvider object are defined by the implementer or the meta type resources.The list of available locales can be obtained from the MetaTypeProvider object.

The MetaTypeProvider interface provides the following methods:

- getObjectClassDefinition(String,String) – Get access to an ObjectClassDefinition object for the given PID. The second parameter defines the locale.
- getLocales() – List the locales.that are available.

Locale objects are represented in String objects because not all profiles support Locale. The String holds the standard Locale presentation of:

```
locale = language ( '_' country ( '_' variation) )
language ::= < defined by ISO 3166 >
country  ::= < defined by ISO 639 >
```

For example, en, nl_BE, en_CA_posix are valid locales. The use of null for locale indicates that java.util.Locale.getDefault() must be used.

The Meta Type Service implementation class is the main class. It registers the org.osgi.service.metatype.MetaTypeService service and has a method to get a MetaTypeInformation object for a bundle.

Following is some sample code demonstrating how to print out all the Object Class Definitions and Attribute Definitions contained in a bundle:

```
void printMetaTypes( MetaTypeService mts, Bundle b ) {
    MetaTypeInformation mti =
        mts.getMetaTypeInformation(b);
    String [] pids = mti.getPids();
    String [] locales = mti.getLocales();

    for ( int locale = 0; locale<locales.length; locale++ ) {
        System.out.println("Locale " + locales[locale] );
        for (int i=0; i< pids.length; i++) {
            ObjectClassDefinition ocd =
                mti.getObjectClassDefinition(pids[i], null);
            AttributeDefinition[] ads =
                ocd.getAttributeDefinitions(
                    ObjectClassDefinition.ALL);
            for (int j=0; j< ads.length; j++) {
                System.out.println("OCD="+ocd.getName()
                    + "AD="+ads[j].getName());
            }
        }
    }
}
```

105.6 Using the Meta Type Resources

A bundle that wants to provide meta type resources must place these resources in the OSGI-INF/ metatype directory. The name of the resource must be a valid JAR path. All resources in that directory must be meta type documents. Fragments can contain additional meta type resources in the same directory and they must be taken into account when the meta type resources are searched. A meta type resources must be encoded in UTF-8.

The MetaType Service must support localization of the

- name
- icon
- description
- label attributes

The localization mechanism must be identical using the same mechanism as described in the Core module layer, section *Localization* on page 69, using the same property resource. However, it is possible to override the property resource in the meta type definition resources with the localization attribute of the MetaData element.

The Meta Type Service must examine the bundle and its fragments to locate all localization resources for the localization base name. From that list, the Meta Type Service derives the list of locales which are available for the meta type information. This list can then be returned by MetaTypeInformation.getLocales method. This list can change at any time because the bundle could be refreshed. Clients should be prepared that this list changes after they received it.

105.6.1 XML Schema of a Meta Type Resource

This section describes the schema of the meta type resource. This schema is not intended to be used during runtime for validating meta type resources. The schema is intended to be used by tools and external management systems.

The XML namespace for meta type documents must be:

```
http://www.osgi.org/xmlns/metatype/v1.1.0
```

The namespace abbreviation should be metatype. I.e. the following header should be:

```
<metatype:MetaData
    xmlns:metatype=
        "http://www.osgi.org/xmlns/metatype/v1.1.0"
    xmlns:xsi="http://www.w3.org/2001/XMLSchema-instance"
    >
```

The file can be found in the osgi.jar file that can be downloaded from the www.osgi.org web site.

Figure 105.3   *XML Schema Instance Structure (Type name = Element name)*

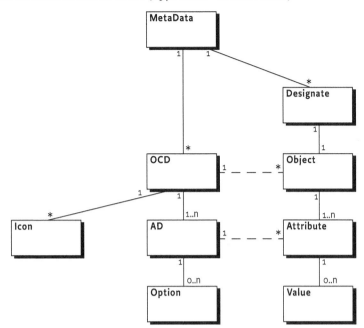

The element structure of the XML file is:

```
MetaData   ::= OCD* Designate*

OCD        ::= AD+  Icon
AD         ::= Option*

Designate  ::= Object
Object     ::= Attribute *

Attribute  ::= Value *
```

The different elements are described in Table 105.1.

Table 105.1   *XML Schema for Meta Type resources*

Attribute	Deflt	Type	Method	Description
MetaData				Top Element
localization		string		Points to the Properties file that can localize this XML. See *Localization* on page 69 of the Core book.
OCD				Object Class Definition
name	<>	string	getName()	A human readable name that can be localized.
description			getDescription()	A human readable description of the Object Class Definition that can be localized.
id	<>		getID()	A unique id, cannot be localized.

Table 105.1   *XML Schema for Meta Type resources*

Attribute	Deflt	Type	Method	Description
Designate				An association between one PID and an Object Class Definition. This element *designates* a PID to be of a certain *type*.
pid	<>	string		The PID that is associated with an OCD. This can be a reference to a factory or singleton configuration object. See *Use of the Designate Element* on page 92.
factoryPid		string		If the factoryPid attribute is set, this Designate element defines a factory configuration for the given factory, if it is not set or empty, it designates a singleton configuration. See *Use of the Designate Element* on page 92.
bundle		string		Location of the bundle that implements the PID. This binds the PID to the bundle. I.e. no other bundle using the same PID may use this designation. In a Meta Type resource this field may be set to an wildcard (\u002A, "∗") to indicate the bundle where the resource comes from. This is an optional attribute but can be mandatory in certain usage schemes, for example the Autoconf Resource Processor.
optional	false	boolean		If true, then this Designate element is optional, errors during processing must be ignored.
merge	false	boolean		If the PID refers to an existing variable, then merge the properties with the existing properties if this attribute is true. Otherwise, replace the properties.
AD				Attribute Definition
name		string	getName()	A localizable name for the Attribute Definition. description
description		string	getDescription()	A localizable description for the Attribute Definition.
id			getID()	The unique ID of the Attribute Definition.

Table 105.1   *XML Schema for Meta Type resources*

Attribute	Deflt	Type	Method	Description
type		string	getType()	The type of an attribute is an enumeration of the different scalar types. The string is mapped to one of the constants on the AttributeDefinition interface. Valid values, which are defined in the Scalar type, are:

```
String   ↔   STRING
Long     ↔   LONG
Double   ↔   DOUBLE
Float    ↔   FLOAT
Integer  ↔   INTEGER
Byte     ↔   BYTE
Char     ↔   CHARACTER
Boolean  ↔   BOOLEAN
Short    ↔   SHORT
```

Attribute	Deflt	Type	Method	Description
cardinality	0		getCardinality()	The number of elements an instance can take. Positive numbers describe an array ([]) and negative numbers describe a Vector object.
min		string	validate(String)	A validation value. This value is not directly available from the AttributeDefinition interface. However, the validate(String) method must verify this. The semantics of this field depend on the type of this Attribute Definition.
max		string	validate(String)	A validation value. Similar to the min field.
default		string	getDefaultValue()	The default value. A default is an array of String objects. The XML attribute must contain a comma delimited list. If the comma must be represented, it must be escaped with a back slash ('\' \u005c). A back slash can be included with two backslashes. White spaces around the command and after/before an XML element must be ignored. For example: dflt="a\,b,b\,c, c\\,d" => ["a,b", "b,c", "c\", "d"]
required	true	boolean		Required attributes
Option				One option label/value for the options in an AD.
label	<>	string	getOptionLabels()	The label
value	<>	string	getOptionValues()	The value
Icon				An icon definition.

Table 105.1   *XML Schema for Meta Type resources*

Attribute	Deflt	Type	Method	Description
resource	<>	string	getIcon(int)	The resource is a URL. The base URL is assumed to be the XML file with the definition. I.e. if the XML is a resource in the JAR file, then this URL can reference another resource in that JAR file using a relative URL.
size	<>	string	getIcon(int)	The number of pixels of the icon, maps to the size parameter of the getIcon(int) method.
Object				A definition of an instance.
ocdref	<>	string		A reference to the id attribute of an OCD element. I.e. this attribute defines the OCD type of this object.
Attribute				A value for an attribute of an object.
adref	<>	string		A reference to the id of the AD in the OCD as referenced by the parent Object.
content		string		The content of the attributes. If this is an array, the content must be separated by commas (',' \u002C). Commas must be escaped as described at the default attribute of the AD element. See default on page 91.
Value				Holds a single value. This element can be repeated multiple times under an Attribute

105.6.2   Use of the Designate Element

For the MetaType Service, the Designate definition is used to declare the available PIDs and factory PIDs; the Attribute elements are never used by the MetaType service.

The getPids() method returns an array of PIDs that were specified in the pid attribute of the Object elements. The getFactoryPids() method returns an array of the factoryPid attributes. For factories, the related pid attribute is ignored because all instances of a factory must share the same meta type.

The following example shows a metatype reference to a singleton configuration and a factory configuration.

```
<Designate pid="com.acme.designate.1">
  <Object ocdref="com.acme.designate". />
</Designate>
<Designate factoryPid="com.acme.designate.factory"
  bundle="*">
  <Object ocdref="com.acme.designate"/>
</Designate>
```

Other schemes can embed the Object element in the Designate element to define actual instances for the Configuration Admin service. In that case the pid attribute must be used together with the factoryPid attribute. However, in that case an aliasing model is required because the Configuration Admin service does not allow the creator to choose the Configuration object's PID.

105.6.3   Example Metadata File

This example defines a meta type file for a Person record, based on ISO attribute types. The ids that are used are derived from ISO attributes.

```
<xml version="1.0" encoding="UTF-8">
<MetaData
  xmlns=
    "http://www.osgi.org/xmlns/metatype/v1.1.0"
  localization="person">
  <OCD name="%person" id="2.5.6.6"
      description="%Person Record">
    <AD name="%sex" id="2.5.4.12" type="Integer">
      <Option label="%male" value="1"/>
      <Option label="%female" value="0"/>
    </AD>
    <AD name="%sn" id="2.5.4.4" type="String"/>
    <AD name="%cn" id="2.5.4.3" type="String"/>
    <AD name="%seeAlso" id="2.5.4.34" type="String"
        cardinality="8" default="http://www.google.com,
            http://www.yahoo.com"/>
    <AD name="%telNumber" id="2.5.4.20" type="String"/>
  </OCD>

  <Designate pid="com.acme.addressbook">
   <Object ocdref="2.5.6.6"/>
  </Designate>
</MetaData>
```

Translations for this file, as indicated by the localization attribute must be stored in the root directory (e.g. person_du_NL.properties). The default localization base name for the properties is OSGI-INF/ l10n/bundle, but can be overridden by the manifest Bundle-Localization header and the localization attribute of the Meta Data element. The property files have the base name of person. The Dutch, French and English translations could look like:

```
person_du_NL.properties:
person=Persoon
person\ record=Persoons beschrijving
cn=Naam
sn=Voornaam
seeAlso=Zie ook
telNumber=Tel. Nummer
sex=Geslacht
male=Mannelijk
female=Vrouwelijk

person_fr.properties
person=Personne
person\ record=Description de la personne
cn=Nom
sn=Surnom
seeAlso=Reference
telNumber=Tel.
sex=Sexe
male=Homme
female=Femme
```

```
person_en_US.properties
person=Person
person\ record=Person Record
cn=Name
sn=Sur Name
seeAlso=See Also
telNumber=Tel.
sex=Sex
male=Male
female=Female
```

105.7   Object

The OCD element can be used to describe the possible contents of a Dictionary object. In this case, the attribute name is the key. The Object element can be used to assign a value to a Dictionary object.

For example:

```
<Designate pid="com.acme.b">
  <Object ocdref="b">
      <Attribute adref="foo" content="Zaphod Beeblebrox"/>
      <Attribute adref="bar">
         <Value>1</Value>
         <Value>2</Value>
         <Value>3</Value>
         <Value>4</Value>
         <Value>5</Value>
      </Attribute>
  </Object>
</Designate>
```

105.8   XML Schema

```
<xml version="1.0" encoding="UTF-8">
<schema xmlns="http://www.w3.org/2001/XMLSchema"
   xmlns:metatype="http://www.osgi.org/xmlns/metatype/v1.1.0"
   targetNamespace="http://www.osgi.org/xmlns/metatype/v1.1.0"
   version="1.1.0">

   <element name="MetaData" type="metatype:Tmetadata" />

   <complexType name="Tmetadata">
      <sequence>
         <element name="OCD" type="metatype:Tocd" minOccurs="0"
            maxOccurs="unbounded" />
         <element name="Designate" type="metatype:Tdesignate"
            minOccurs="0" maxOccurs="unbounded" />
         <any namespace="##other" processContents="lax" minOccurs="0"
            maxOccurs="unbounded" />
      </sequence>
      <attribute name="localization" type="string" use="optional" />
      <anyAttribute />
   </complexType>

   <complexType name="Tocd">
      <sequence>
         <element name="AD" type="metatype:Tad" minOccurs="1"
            maxOccurs="unbounded" />
         <element name="Icon" type="metatype:Ticon" minOccurs="0"
            maxOccurs="1" />
         <any namespace="##other" processContents="lax" minOccurs="0"
            maxOccurs="unbounded" />
```

```
                </sequence>
                <attribute name="name" type="string" use="required" />
                <attribute name="description" type="string" use="optional" />
                <attribute name="id" type="string" use="required" />
                <anyAttribute />
        </complexType>

        <complexType name="Tad">
                <sequence>
                        <element name="Option" type="metatype:Toption" minOccurs="0"
                                maxOccurs="unbounded" />
                        <any namespace="##other" processContents="lax" minOccurs="0"
                                maxOccurs="unbounded" />
                </sequence>
                <attribute name="name" type="string" use="optional" />
                <attribute name="description" type="string" use="optional" />
                <attribute name="id" type="string" use="required" />
                <attribute name="type" type="metatype:Tscalar" use="required" />
                <attribute name="cardinality" type="int" use="optional"
                        default="0" />
                <attribute name="min" type="string" use="optional" />
                <attribute name="max" type="string" use="optional" />
                <attribute name="default" type="string" use="optional" />
                <attribute name="required" type="boolean" use="optional"
                        default="true" />
                <anyAttribute />
        </complexType>

        <complexType name="Tobject">
                <sequence>
                        <element name="Attribute" type="metatype:Tattribute"
                                minOccurs="0" maxOccurs="unbounded" />
                        <any namespace="##other" processContents="lax" minOccurs="0"
                                maxOccurs="unbounded" />
                </sequence>
                <attribute name="ocdref" type="string" use="required" />
                <anyAttribute />
        </complexType>

        <complexType name="Tattribute">
                <sequence>
                        <element name="Value" type="string" minOccurs="0"
                                maxOccurs="unbounded" />
                        <any namespace="##other" processContents="lax" minOccurs="0"
                                maxOccurs="unbounded" />
                </sequence>
                <attribute name="adref" type="string" use="required" />
                <attribute name="content" type="string" use="optional" />
                <anyAttribute />
        </complexType>

        <complexType name="Tdesignate">
                <sequence>
                        <element name="Object" type="metatype:Tobject" minOccurs="1"
                                maxOccurs="1" />
                        <any namespace="##any" processContents="lax" minOccurs="0"
                                maxOccurs="unbounded" />
                </sequence>
                <attribute name="pid" type="string" use="required" />
                <attribute name="factoryPid" type="string" use="optional" />
                <attribute name="bundle" type="string" use="optional" />
                <attribute name="optional" type="boolean" default="false"
                        use="optional" />
                <attribute name="merge" type="boolean" default="false"
                        use="optional" />
                <anyAttribute />
        </complexType>

        <simpleType name="Tscalar">
                <restriction base="string">
                        <enumeration value="String" />
                        <enumeration value="Long" />
                        <enumeration value="Double" />
                        <enumeration value="Float" />
                        <enumeration value="Integer" />
```

```
            <enumeration value="Byte" />
            <enumeration value="Char" />
            <enumeration value="Boolean" />
            <enumeration value="Short" />
        </restriction>
    </simpleType>

    <complexType name="Toption">
        <sequence>
            <any namespace="##any" processContents="lax" minOccurs="0"
                maxOccurs="unbounded" />
        </sequence>
        <attribute name="label" type="string" use="required" />
        <attribute name="value" type="string" use="required" />
        <anyAttribute />
    </complexType>

    <complexType name="Ticon">
        <sequence>
            <any namespace="##any" processContents="lax" minOccurs="0"
                maxOccurs="unbounded" />
        </sequence>
        <attribute name="resource" type="string" use="required" />
        <attribute name="size" type="positiveInteger" use="required" />
        <anyAttribute />
    </complexType>

    <attribute name="must-understand" type="boolean">
        <annotation>
            <documentation xml:lang="en">
                This attribute should be used by extensions to documents
                to require that the document consumer understand the
                extension.
            </documentation>
        </annotation>
    </attribute>
</schema>
```

105.9 Limitations

The OSGi MetaType specification is intended to be used for simple applications. It does not, therefore, support recursive data types, mixed types in arrays/vectors, or nested arrays/vectors.

105.10 Related Standards

One of the primary goals of this specification is to make metatype information available at run-time with minimal overhead. Many related standards are applicable to metatypes; except for Java beans, however, all other metatype standards are based on document formats (e.g. XML). In the OSGi Service Platform, document format standards are deemed unsuitable due to the overhead required in the execution environment (they require a parser during run-time).

Another consideration is the applicability of these standards. Most of these standards were developed for management systems on platforms where resources are not necessarily a concern. In this case, a metatype standard is normally used to describe the data structures needed to control some other computer via a network. This other computer, however, does not require the metatype information as it is *implementing* this information.

In some traditional cases, a management system uses the metatype information to control objects in an OSGi Service Platform. Therefore, the concepts and the syntax of the metatype information must be mappable to these popular standards. Clearly, then, these standards must be able to describe objects in an OSGi Service Platform. This ability is usually not a problem, because the metatype languages used by current management systems are very powerful.

105.11   Security Considerations

Special security issues are not applicable for this specification.

105.12   org.osgi.service.metatype

Metatype Package Version 1.1.

Bundles wishing to use this package must list the package in the Import-Package header of the bundle's manifest. For example:

```
Import-Package: org.osgi.service.metatype; version="[1.1,2.0)"
```

105.12.1   Summary

- *AttributeDefinition* - An interface to describe an attribute.
- *MetaTypeInformation* - A MetaType Information object is created by the MetaTypeService to return meta type information for a specific bundle.
- *MetaTypeProvider* - Provides access to metatypes.
- *MetaTypeService* - The MetaType Service can be used to obtain meta type information for a bundle.
- *ObjectClassDefinition* - Description for the data type information of an objectclass.

105.12.2   public interface AttributeDefinition

An interface to describe an attribute.

An AttributeDefinition object defines a description of the data type of a property/attribute.

105.12.2.1   public static final int BIGDECIMAL = 10

The BIGDECIMAL (10) type. Attributes of this type should be stored as BigDecimal, Vector with BigDecimal or BigDecimal[] objects depending on getCardinality().

Deprecated As of 1.1.

105.12.2.2   public static final int BIGINTEGER = 9

The BIGINTEGER (9) type. Attributes of this type should be stored as BigInteger, Vector with BigInteger or BigInteger[] objects, depending on the getCardinality() value.

Deprecated As of 1.1.

105.12.2.3   public static final int BOOLEAN = 11

The BOOLEAN (11) type. Attributes of this type should be stored as Boolean, Vector with Boolean or boolean[] objects depending on getCardinality().

105.12.2.4   public static final int BYTE = 6

The BYTE (6) type. Attributes of this type should be stored as Byte, Vector with Byte or byte[] objects, depending on the getCardinality() value.

105.12.2.5   public static final int CHARACTER = 5

The CHARACTER (5) type. Attributes of this type should be stored as Character, Vector with Character or char[] objects, depending on the getCardinality() value.

105.12.2.6   public static final int DOUBLE = 7

The DOUBLE (7) type. Attributes of this type should be stored as Double, Vector with Double or double[] objects, depending on the getCardinality() value.

105.12.2.7   **public static final int FLOAT = 8**

The FLOAT (8) type. Attributes of this type should be stored as Float, Vector with Float or float[] objects, depending on the getCardinality() value.

105.12.2.8   **public static final int INTEGER = 3**

The INTEGER (3) type. Attributes of this type should be stored as Integer, Vector with Integer or int[] objects, depending on the getCardinality() value.

105.12.2.9   **public static final int LONG = 2**

The LONG (2) type. Attributes of this type should be stored as Long, Vector with Long or long[] objects, depending on the getCardinality() value.

105.12.2.10   **public static final int SHORT = 4**

The SHORT (4) type. Attributes of this type should be stored as Short, Vector with Short or short[] objects, depending on the getCardinality() value.

105.12.2.11   **public static final int STRING = 1**

The STRING (1) type.

Attributes of this type should be stored as String, Vector with String or String[] objects, depending on the getCardinality() value.

105.12.2.12   **public int getCardinality( )**

☐ Return the cardinality of this attribute. The OSGi environment handles multi valued attributes in arrays ([]) or in Vector objects. The return value is defined as follows:

```
x = Integer.MIN_VALUE    no limit, but use Vector
x < 0                    -x = max occurrences, store in Vector
x > 0                     x = max occurrences, store in array []
x = Integer.MAX_VALUE    no limit, but use array []
x = 0                    1 occurrence required
```

Returns The cardinality of this attribute.

105.12.2.13   **public String[] getDefaultValue( )**

☐ Return a default for this attribute. The object must be of the appropriate type as defined by the cardinality and getType(). The return type is a list of String objects that can be converted to the appropriate type. The cardinality of the return array must follow the absolute cardinality of this type. E.g. if the cardinality = 0, the array must contain 1 element. If the cardinality is 1, it must contain 0 or 1 elements. If it is -5, it must contain from 0 to max 5 elements. Note that the special case of a 0 cardinality, meaning a single value, does not allow arrays or vectors of 0 elements.

Returns Return a default value or null if no default exists.

105.12.2.14   **public String getDescription( )**

☐ Return a description of this attribute. The description may be localized and must describe the semantics of this type and any constraints.

Returns The localized description of the definition.

105.12.2.15   **public String getID( )**

□ Unique identity for this attribute. Attributes share a global namespace in the registry. E.g. an attribute cn or commonName must always be a String and the semantics are always a name of some object. They share this aspect with LDAP/X.500 attributes. In these standards the OSI Object Identifier (OID) is used to uniquely identify an attribute. If such an OID exists, (which can be requested at several standard organisations and many companies already have a node in the tree) it can be returned here. Otherwise, a unique id should be returned which can be a Java class name (reverse domain name) or generated with a GUID algorithm. Note that all LDAP defined attributes already have an OID. It is strongly advised to define the attributes from existing LDAP schemes which will give the OID. Many such schemes exist ranging from postal addresses to DHCP parameters.

Returns The id or oid

105.12.2.16   **public String getName( )**

□ Get the name of the attribute. This name may be localized.

Returns The localized name of the definition.

105.12.2.17   **public String[] getOptionLabels( )**

□ Return a list of labels of option values.

The purpose of this method is to allow menus with localized labels. It is associated with getOptionValues. The labels returned here are ordered in the same way as the values in that method.

If the function returns null, there are no option labels available.

This list must be in the same sequence as the getOptionValues() method. I.e. for each index i in getOptionLabels, i in getOptionValues() should be the associated value.

For example, if an attribute can have the value male, female, unknown, this list can return (for dutch) new String[] { "Man", "Vrouw", "Onbekend" }.

Returns A list values

105.12.2.18   **public String[] getOptionValues( )**

□ Return a list of option values that this attribute can take.

If the function returns null, there are no option values available.

Each value must be acceptable to validate() (return "") and must be a String object that can be converted to the data type defined by getType() for this attribute.

This list must be in the same sequence as getOptionLabels(). I.e. for each index i in getOptionValues, i in getOptionLabels() should be the label.

For example, if an attribute can have the value male, female, unknown, this list can return new String[] { "male", "female", "unknown" }.

Returns A list values

105.12.2.19   **public int getType( )**

□ Return the type for this attribute.

Defined in the following constants which map to the appropriate Java type. STRING,LONG,INTEGER, CHAR,BYTE,DOUBLE,FLOAT, BOOLEAN.

Returns The type for this attribute.

105.12.2.20   **public String validate(String value)**

value The value before turning it into the basic data type

❑ Validate an attribute in String form. An attribute might be further constrained in value. This method will attempt to validate the attribute according to these constraints. It can return three different values:

```
null          No validation present
" "           No problems detected
"..."         A localized description of why the value is wrong
```

Returns null, "", or another string

105.12.3   public interface MetaTypeInformation
extends MetaTypeProvider

A MetaType Information object is created by the MetaTypeService to return meta type information for a specific bundle.

Since 1.1

105.12.3.1   public Bundle getBundle( )

❑ Return the bundle for which this object provides meta type information.

Returns Bundle for which this object provides meta type information.

105.12.3.2   public String[] getFactoryPids( )

❑ Return the Factory PIDs (for ManagedServiceFactories) for which ObjectClassDefinition information is available.

Returns Array of Factory PIDs.

105.12.3.3   public String[] getPids( )

❑ Return the PIDs (for ManagedServices) for which ObjectClassDefinition information is available.

Returns Array of PIDs.

105.12.4   public interface MetaTypeProvider

Provides access to metatypes.

105.12.4.1   public String[] getLocales( )

❑ Return a list of available locales. The results must be names that consists of language [_ country [_ variation]] as is customary in the Locale class.

Returns An array of locale strings or null if there is no locale specific localization can be found.

105.12.4.2   public ObjectClassDefinition getObjectClassDefinition(String id, String locale)

id The ID of the requested object class. This can be a pid or factory pid returned by getPids or getFactoryPids.

locale The locale of the definition or null for default locale.

❑ Returns an object class definition for the specified id localized to the specified locale.

The locale parameter must be a name that consists of language["_" country["_" variation]] as is customary in the Locale class. This Locale class is not used because certain profiles do not contain it.

Returns A ObjectClassDefinition object.

Throws IllegalArgumentException – If the id or locale arguments are not valid

105.12.5   public interface MetaTypeService

The MetaType Service can be used to obtain meta type information for a bundle. The MetaType Service will examine the specified bundle for meta type documents to create the returned MetaTypeInformation object.

If the specified bundle does not contain any meta type documents, then a MetaTypeInformation object will be returned that wrappers any ManagedService or ManagedServiceFactory services registered by the specified bundle that implement MetaTypeProvider. Thus the MetaType Service can be used to retrieve meta type information for bundles which contain a meta type documents or which provide their own MetaTypeProvider objects.

Since 1.1

105.12.5.1   public static final String METATYPE_DOCUMENTS_LOCATION = "OSGI-INF/metatype"

Location of meta type documents. The MetaType Service will process each entry in the meta type documents directory.

105.12.5.2   public MetaTypeInformation getMetaTypeInformation(Bundle bundle)

bundle The bundle for which meta type information is requested.

☐ Return the MetaType information for the specified bundle.

Returns A MetaTypeInformation object for the specified bundle.

105.12.6   public interface ObjectClassDefinition

Description for the data type information of an objectclass.

105.12.6.1   public static final int ALL = -1

Argument for getAttributeDefinitions(int).

ALL indicates that all the definitions are returned. The value is -1.

105.12.6.2   public static final int OPTIONAL = 2

Argument for getAttributeDefinitions(int).

OPTIONAL indicates that only the optional definitions are returned. The value is 2.

105.12.6.3   public static final int REQUIRED = 1

Argument for getAttributeDefinitions(int).

REQUIRED indicates that only the required definitions are returned. The value is 1.

105.12.6.4   public AttributeDefinition[] getAttributeDefinitions(int filter)

filter ALL,REQUIRED,OPTIONAL

☐ Return the attribute definitions for this object class.

Return a set of attributes. The filter parameter can distinguish between ALL,REQUIRED or the OPTIONAL attributes.

Returns An array of attribute definitions or null if no attributes are selected

105.12.6.5   public String getDescription( )

☐ Return a description of this object class. The description may be localized.

Returns The description of this object class.

105.12.6.6   **public InputStream getIcon(int size) throws IOException**

    size Requested size of an icon, e.g. a 16x16 pixels icon then size = 16

       □ Return an InputStream object that can be used to create an icon from.

        Indicate the size and return an InputStream object containing an icon. The returned icon maybe larger or smaller than the indicated size.

        The icon may depend on the localization.

    Returns An InputStream representing an icon or null

    Throws IOException – If the InputStream cannot be returned.

105.12.6.7   **public String getID( )**

       □ Return the id of this object class.

        ObjectDefintion objects share a global namespace in the registry. They share this aspect with LDAP/X.500 attributes. In these standards the OSI Object Identifier (OID) is used to uniquely identify object classes. If such an OID exists, (which can be requested at several standard organisations and many companies already have a node in the tree) it can be returned here. Otherwise, a unique id should be returned which can be a java class name (reverse domain name) or generated with a GUID algorithm. Note that all LDAP defined object classes already have an OID associated. It is strongly advised to define the object classes from existing LDAP schemes which will give the OID for free. Many such schemes exist ranging from postal addresses to DHCP parameters.

    Returns The id of this object class.

105.12.6.8   **public String getName( )**

       □ Return the name of this object class. The name may be localized.

    Returns The name of this object class.

105.13   References

    [1] *LDAP.*
        http://en.wikipedia.org/wiki/Lightweight_Directory_Access_Protocol

    [2] *Understanding and Deploying LDAP Directory services*
        Timothy Howes et. al. ISBN 1-57870-070-1, MacMillan Technical publishing.

107 User Admin Service Specification

Version 1.1

107.1 Introduction

OSGi Service Platforms are often used in places where end users or devices initiate actions. These kinds of actions inevitably create a need for authenticating the initiator. Authenticating can be done in many different ways, including with passwords, one-time token cards, bio-metrics, and certificates.

Once the initiator is authenticated, it is necessary to verify that this principal is authorized to perform the requested action. This authorization can only be decided by the operator of the OSGi environment, and thus requires administration.

The User Admin service provides this type of functionality. Bundles can use the User Admin service to authenticate an initiator and represent this authentication as an Authorization object. Bundles that execute actions on behalf of this user can use the Authorization object to verify if that user is authorized.

The User Admin service provides authorization based on who runs the code, instead of using the Java code-based permission model. See [1] *The Java Security Architecture for JDK 1.2*. It performs a role similar to [2] *Java Authentication and Authorization Service*.

107.1.1 Essentials

- *Authentication* – A large number of authentication schemes already exist, and more will be developed. The User Admin service must be flexible enough to adapt to the many different authentication schemes that can be run on a computer system.
- *Authorization* – All bundles should use the User Admin service to authenticate users and to find out if those users are authorized. It is therefore paramount that a bundle can find out authorization information with little effort.
- *Security* – Detailed security, based on the Framework security model, is needed to provide safe access to the User Admin service. It should allow limited access to the credentials and other properties.
- *Extensibility* – Other bundles should be able to build on the User Admin service. It should be possible to examine the information from this service and get real-time notifications of changes.
- *Properties* – The User Admin service must maintain a persistent database of users. It must be possible to use this database to hold more information about this user.
- *Administration* – Administering authorizations for each possible action and initiator is time-consuming and error-prone. It is therefore necessary to have mechanisms to group end users and make it simple to assign authorizations to all members of a group at one time.

107.1.2 Entities

This Specification defines the following User Admin service entities:

- *UserAdmin* – This interface manages a database of named roles which can be used for authorization and authentication purposes.
- *Role* – This interface exposes the characteristics shared by all roles: a name, a type, and a set of properties.

- *User* – This interface (which extends Role) is used to represent any entity which may have credentials associated with it. These credentials can be used to authenticate an initiator.
- *Group* – This interface (which extends User) is used to contain an aggregation of named Role objects (Group or User objects).
- *Authorization* – This interface encapsulates an authorization context on which bundles can base authorization decisions.
- *UserAdminEvent* – This class is used to represent a role change event.
- *UserAdminListener* – This interface provides a listener for events of type UserAdminEvent that can be registered as a service.
- *UserAdminPermission* – This permission is needed to configure and access the roles managed by a User Admin service.
- *Role.USER_ANYONE* – This is a special User object that represents *any* user, it implies all other User objects. It is also used when a Group is used with only basic members. The Role.USER_ANYONE is then the only required member.

Figure 107.1   *User Admin Service*, org.osgi.service.useradmin

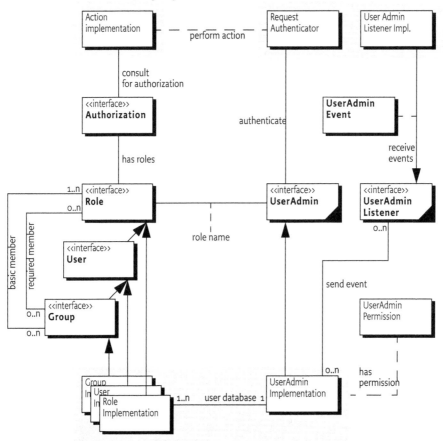

107.1.3   Operation

An Operator uses the User Admin service to define OSGi Service Platform users and configure them with properties, credentials, and *roles*.

A Role object represents the initiator of a request (human or otherwise). This specification defines two types of roles:

- *User* – A User object can be configured with credentials, such as a password, and properties, such as address, telephone number, and so on.
- *Group* – A Group object is an aggregation of *basic* and *required* roles. Basic and required roles are used in the authorization phase.

An OSGi Service Platform can have several entry points, each of which will be responsible for authenticating incoming requests. An example of an entry point is the Http Service, which delegates authentication of incoming requests to the handleSecurity method of the HttpContext object that was specified when the target servlet or resource of the request was registered.

The OSGi Service Platform entry points should use the information in the User Admin service to authenticate incoming requests, such as a password stored in the private credentials or the use of a certificate.

A bundle can determine if a request for an action is authorized by looking for a Role object that has the name of the requested action.

The bundle may execute the action if the Role object representing the initiator *implies* the Role object representing the requested action.

For example, an initiator Role object X implies an action Group object A if:

- X implies at least one of A's basic members, and
- X implies all of A's required members.

An initiator Role object X implies an action User object A if:

- A and X are equal.

The Authorization class handles this non-trivial logic. The User Admin service can capture the privileges of an authenticated User object into an Authorization object. The Authorization.hasRole method checks if the authenticate User object has (or implies) a specified action Role object.

For example, in the case of the Http Service, the HttpContext object can authenticate the initiator and place an Authorization object in the request header. The servlet calls the hasRole method on this Authorization object to verify that the initiator has the authority to perform a certain action. See *Authentication* on page 36.

107.2 **Authentication**

The authentication phase determines if the initiator is actually the one it says it is. Mechanisms to authenticate always need some information related to the user or the OSGi Service Platform to authenticate an external user. This information can consist of the following:

- A secret known only to the initiator.
- Knowledge about cards that can generate a unique token.
- Public information like certificates of trusted signers.
- Information about the user that can be measured in a trusted way.
- Other specific information.

107.2.1 **Repository**

The User Admin service offers a repository of Role objects. Each Role object has a unique name and a set of properties that are readable by anyone, and are changeable when the changer has the UserAdminPermission. Additionally, User objects, a sub-interface of Role, also have a set of private protected properties called credentials. Credentials are an extra set of properties that are used to authenticate users and that are protected by UserAdminPermission.

Properties are accessed with the Role.getProperties() method and credentials with the User.getCredentials()method. Both methods return a Dictionary object containing key/value pairs. The keys are String objects and the values of the Dictionary object are limited to String or byte[ ] objects.

This specification does not define any standard keys for the properties or credentials. The keys depend on the implementation of the authentication mechanism and are not formally defined by OSGi specifications.

The repository can be searched for objects that have a unique property (key/value pair) with the method UserAdmin.getUser(String,String). This makes it easy to find a specific user related to a specific authentication mechanism. For example, a secure card mechanism that generates unique tokens could have a serial number identifying the user. The owner of the card could be found with the method

```
User owner = useradmin.getUser(
    "secure-card-serial", "132456712-1212" );
```

If multiple User objects have the same property (key *and* value), a null is returned.

There is a convenience method to verify that a user has a credential without actually getting the credential. This is the User.hasCredential(String,Object) method.

Access to credentials is protected on a name basis by UserAdminPermission. Because properties can be read by anyone with access to a User object, UserAdminPermission only protects change access to properties.

107.2.2   Basic Authentication

The following example shows a very simple authentication algorithm based on passwords.

The vendor of the authentication bundle uses the property "com.acme.basic-id" to contain the name of a user as it logs in. This property is used to locate the User object in the repository. Next, the credential "com.acme.password" contains the password and is compared to the entered password. If the password is correct, the User object is returned. In all other cases a SecurityException is thrown.

```
public User authenticate(
      UserAdmin ua, String name, String pwd )
    throws SecurityException {
    User user = ua.getUser("com.acme.basicid",
      username);
    if (user == null)
      throw new SecurityException( "No such user" );

    if (!user.hasCredential("com.acme.password", pwd))
      throw new SecurityException(
        "Invalid password" );
    return user;
}
```

107.2.3   Certificates

Authentication based on certificates does not require a shared secret. Instead, a certificate contains a name, a public key, and the signature of one or more signers.

The name in the certificate can be used to locate a User object in the repository. Locating a User object, however, only identifies the initiator and does not authenticate it.

1. The first step to authenticate the initiator is to verify that it has the private key of the certificate.

2. Next, the User Admin service must verify that it has a User object with the right property, for example "com.acme.certificate"="Fudd".

3. The next step is to see if the certificate is signed by a trusted source. The bundle could use a central list of trusted signers and only accept certificates signed by those sources. Alternatively, it could require that the certificate itself is already stored in the repository under a unique key as a byte[] in the credentials.

4. In any case, once the certificate is verified, the associated User object is authenticated.

107.3 Authorization

The User Admin service authorization architecture is a *role-based model*. In this model, every action that can be performed by a bundle is associated with a *role*. Such a role is a Group object (called group from now on) from the User Admin service repository. For example, if a servlet could be used to activate the alarm system, there should be a group named AlarmSystemActivation.

The operator can administrate authorizations by populating the group with User objects (users) and other groups. Groups are used to minimize the amount of administration required. For example, it is easier to create one Administrators group and add administrative roles to it rather than individually administer all users for each role. Such a group requires only one action to remove or add a user as an administrator.

The authorization decision can now be made in two fundamentally different ways:

An initiator could be allowed to carry out an action (represented by a Group object) if it implied any of the Group object's members. For example, the AlarmSystemActivation Group object contains an Administrators and a Family Group object:

```
Administrators          = { Elmer, Pepe, Bugs }
Family                  = { Elmer, Pepe, Daffy }

AlarmSystemActivation   = { Administrators, Family }
```

Any of the four members Elmer, Pepe, Daffy, or Bugs can activate the alarm system.

Alternatively, an initiator could be allowed to perform an action (represented by a Group object) if it implied *all* the Group object's members. In this case, using the same AlarmSystemActivation group, only Elmer and Pepe would be authorized to activate the alarm system, since Daffy and Bugs are *not* members of *both* the Administrators and Family Group objects.

The User Admin service supports a combination of both strategies by defining both a set of *basic members* (any) and a set of *required members* (all).

```
Administrators  = { Elmer, Pepe, Bugs }
Family          = { Elmer, Pepe, Daffy }

AlarmSystemActivation
    required    = { Administrators }
    basic       = { Family }
```

The difference is made when Role objects are added to the Group object. To add a basic member, use the Group.addMember(Role) method. To add a required member, use the Group.addRequiredMember(Role) method.

Basic members define the set of members that can get access and required members reduce this set by requiring the initiator to *imply* each required member.

A User object implies a Group object if it implies the following:

- *All* of the Group's required members, and
- At *least* one of the Group's basic members

A User object always implies itself.

If only required members are used to qualify the implication, then the standard user Role.USER_ANYONE can be obtained from the User Admin service and added to the Group object. This Role object is implied by anybody and therefore does not affect the required members.

107.3.1   The Authorization Object

The complexity of authorization is hidden in an Authorization class. Normally, the authenticator should retrieve an Authorization object from the User Admin service by passing the authenticated User object as an argument. This Authorization object is then passed to the bundle that performs the action. This bundle checks the authorization with the Authorization.hasRole(String) method. The performing bundle must pass the name of the action as an argument. The Authorization object checks whether the authenticated user implies the Role object, specifically a Group object, with the given name. This is shown in the following example.

```
public void activateAlarm(Authorization auth) {
    if ( auth.hasRole( "AlarmSystemActivation" ) ) {
        // activate the alarm
        ...
    }
    else throw new SecurityException(
        "Not authorized to activate alarm" );
}
```

107.3.2   Authorization Example

This section demonstrates a possible use of the User Admin service. The service has a flexible model and many other schemes are possible.

Assume an Operator installs an OSGi Service Platform. Bundles in this environment have defined the following action groups:

```
AlarmSystemControl
InternetAccess
TemperatureControl
PhotoAlbumEdit
PhotoAlbumView
PortForwarding
```

Installing and uninstalling bundles could potentially extend this set. Therefore, the Operator also defines a number of groups that can be used to contain the different types of system users.

```
Administrators
Buddies
Children
Adults
Residents
```

In a particular instance, the Operator installs it in a household with the following residents and buddies:

```
Residents:        Elmer, Fudd, Marvin, Pepe
Buddies:          Daffy, Foghorn
```

First, the residents and buddies are assigned to the system user groups. Second, the user groups need to be assigned to the action groups.

The following tables show how the groups could be assigned.

Table 107.1　　　*Example Groups with Basic and Required Members*

Groups	Elmer	Fudd	Marvin	Pepe	Daffy	Foghorn
Residents	Basic	Basic	Basic	Basic	-	-
Buddies	-	-	-	-	Basic	Basic
Children	-	-	Basic	Basic	-	-
Adults	Basic	Basic	-	-	-	-
Administrators	Basic	-	-	-	-	-

Table 107.2　　　*Example Action Groups with their Basic and Required Members*

Groups	Residents	Buddies	Children	Adults	Admin
AlarmSystemControl	Basic	-	-	-	Required
InternetAccess	Basic	-	-	Required	-
TemperatureControl	Basic	-	-	Required	-
PhotoAlbumEdit	Basic	-	Basic	Basic	-
PhotoAlbumView	Basic	Basic	-	-	-
PortForwarding	Basic	-	-	-	Required

107.4　Repository Maintenance

The UserAdmin interface is a straightforward API to maintain a repository of User and Group objects. It contains methods to create new Group and User objects with the createRole(String,int) method. The method is prepared so that the same signature can be used to create new types of roles in the future. The interface also contains a method to remove a Role object.

The existing configuration can be obtained with methods that list all Role objects using a filter argument. This filter, which has the same syntax as the Framework filter, must only return the Role objects for which the filter matches the properties.

Several utility methods simplify getting User objects depending on their properties.

107.5　User Admin Events

Changes in the User Admin service can be determined in real time. Each User Admin service implementation must send a UserAdminEvent object to any service in the Framework service registry that is registered under the UserAdminListener interface. This event must be send asynchronously from the cause of the event. The way events must be delivered is the same as described in *Delivering Events* on page 116 of the Core specification.

This procedure is demonstrated in the following code sample.

```
class Listener implements UserAdminListener {
  public void roleChanged( UserAdminEvent event ) {
    ...
  }
}
public class MyActivator
  implements BundleActivator {
  public void start( BundleContext context ) {
    context.registerService(
```

```
                    UserAdminListener.class.getName(),
                    new Listener(), null );
            }
            public void stop( BundleContext context ) {}
        }
```

It is not necessary to unregister the listener object when the bundle is stopped because the Framework automatically unregisters it. Once registered, the UserAdminListener object must be notified of all changes to the role repository.

107.5.1 Event Admin and User Admin Change Events

User admin events must be delivered asynchronously to the Event Admin service by the implementation, if present. The topic of a User Admin Event is:

```
org/osgi/service/useradmin/UserAdmin/<event type>
```

The following event types are supported:

```
ROLE_CREATED
ROLE_CHANGED
ROLE_REMOVED
```

All User Admin Events must have the following properties:

- event – (UserAdminEvent) The event that was broadcast by the User Admin service.
- role – (Role) The Role object that was created, modified or removed.
- role.name – (String) The name of the role.
- role.type – (Integer) One of ROLE, USER or GROUP.
- service – (ServiceReference) The Service Reference of the User Admin service.
- service.id – (Long) The User Admin service's ID.
- service.objectClass – (String[]) The User Admin service's object class (which must include org.osgi.service.useradmin.UserAdmin)
- service.pid – (String) The User Admin service's persistent identity

107.6   Security

The User Admin service is related to the security model of the OSGi Service Platform, but is complementary to the [1] *The Java Security Architecture for JDK 1.2*. The final permission of most code should be the intersection of the Java 2 Permissions, which are based on the code that is executing, and the User Admin service authorization, which is based on the user for whom the code runs.

107.6.1 UserAdminPermission

The User Admin service defines the UserAdminPermission class that can be used to restrict bundles in accessing credentials. This permission class has the following actions:

- changeProperty – This permission is required to modify properties. The name of the permission is the prefix of the property name.
- changeCredential – This action permits changing credentials. The name of the permission is the prefix of the name of the credential.
- getCredential – This action permits getting credentials. The name of the permission is the prefix of the credential.

If the name of the permission is "admin", it allows the owner to administer the repository. No action is associated with the permission in that case.

Otherwise, the permission name is used to match the property name. This name may end with a ".*" string to indicate a wildcard. For example, com.acme.* matches com.acme.fudd.elmer and com.acme.bugs.

107.7 Relation to JAAS

At a glance, the Java Authorization and Authentication Service (JAAS) seems to be a very suitable model for user administration. The OSGi organization, however, decided to develop an independent User Admin service because JAAS was not deemed applicable. The reasons for this include dependency on Java SE version 1.3 ("JDK 1.3") and existing mechanisms in the previous OSGi Service Gateway 1.0 specification.

107.7.1 JDK 1.3 Dependencies

The authorization component of JAAS relies on the java.security.DomainCombiner interface, which provides a means to dynamically update the ProtectionDomain objects affiliated with an AccessControlContext object.

This interface was added in JDK 1.3. In the context of JAAS, the SubjectDomainCombiner object, which implements the DomainCombiner interface, is used to update ProtectionDomain objects. The permissions of ProtectionDomain objects depend on where code came from and who signed it, with permissions based on who is running the code.

Leveraging JAAS would have resulted in user-based access control on the OSGi Service Platform being available only with JDK 1.3, which was not deemed acceptable.

107.7.2 Existing OSGi Mechanism

JAAS provides a pluggable authentication architecture, which enables applications and their underlying authentication services to remain independent from each other.

The Http Service already provides a similar feature by allowing servlet and resource registrations to be supported by an HttpContext object, which uses a callback mechanism to perform any required authentication checks before granting access to the servlet or resource. This way, the registering bundle has complete control on a per-servlet and per-resource basis over which authentication protocol to use, how the credentials presented by the remote requestor are to be validated, and who should be granted access to the servlet or resource.

107.7.3 Future Road Map

In the future, the main barrier of 1.3 compatibility will be removed. JAAS could then be implemented in an OSGi environment. At that time, the User Admin service will still be needed and will provide complementary services in the following ways:

- The authorization component relies on group membership information to be stored and managed outside JAAS. JAAS does not manage persistent information, so the User Admin service can be a provider of group information when principals are assigned to a Subject object.
- The authorization component allows for credentials to be collected and verified, but a repository is needed to actually validate the credentials.

In the future, the User Admin service can act as the back-end database to JAAS. The only aspect JAAS will remove from the User Admin service is the need for the Authorization interface.

107.8 org.osgi.service.useradmin

User Admin Package Version 1.1.

Bundles wishing to use this package must list the package in the Import-Package header of the bundle's manifest. For example:

```
Import-Package: org.osgi.service.useradmin; version="[1.1,2.0)"
```

107.8.1   Summary

- *Authorization* - The Authorization interface encapsulates an authorization context on which bundles can base authorization decisions, where appropriate.
- *Group* - A named grouping of roles (Role objects).
- *Role* - The base interface for Role objects managed by the User Admin service.
- *User* - A User role managed by a User Admin service.
- *UserAdmin* - This interface is used to manage a database of named Role objects, which can be used for authentication and authorization purposes.
- *UserAdminEvent* - Role change event.
- *UserAdminListener* - Listener for UserAdminEvents.
- *UserAdminPermission* - Permission to configure and access the Role objects managed by a User Admin service.

107.8.2   public interface Authorization

The Authorization interface encapsulates an authorization context on which bundles can base authorization decisions, where appropriate.

Bundles associate the privilege to access restricted resources or operations with roles. Before granting access to a restricted resource or operation, a bundle will check if the Authorization object passed to it possess the required role, by calling its hasRole method.

Authorization contexts are instantiated by calling the UserAdmin.getAuthorization method.

Trusting Authorization objects

There are no restrictions regarding the creation of Authorization objects. Hence, a service must only accept Authorization objects from bundles that has been authorized to use the service using code based (or Java 2) permissions.

In some cases it is useful to use ServicePermission to do the code based access control. A service basing user access control on Authorization objects passed to it, will then require that a calling bundle has the ServicePermission to get the service in question. This is the most convenient way. The OSGi environment will do the code based permission check when the calling bundle attempts to get the service from the service registry.

Example: A servlet using a service on a user's behalf. The bundle with the servlet must be given the ServicePermission to get the Http Service.

However, in some cases the code based permission checks need to be more fine-grained. A service might allow all bundles to get it, but require certain code based permissions for some of its methods.

Example: A servlet using a service on a user's behalf, where some service functionality is open to anyone, and some is restricted by code based permissions. When a restricted method is called (e.g., one handing over an Authorization object), the service explicitly checks that the calling bundle has permission to make the call.

107.8.2.1   public String getName( )

☐ Gets the name of the User that this Authorization context was created for.

Returns The name of the User object that this Authorization context was created for, or null if no user was specified when this Authorization context was created.

107.8.2.2   public String[] getRoles( )

☐ Gets the names of all roles implied by this Authorization context.

Returns The names of all roles implied by this Authorization context, or null if no roles are in the context. The predefined role user.anyone will not be included in this list.

107.8.2.3   **public boolean hasRole(String name)**

name The name of the role to check for.

☐ Checks if the role with the specified name is implied by this Authorization context.

Bundles must define globally unique role names that are associated with the privilege of accessing restricted resources or operations. Operators will grant users access to these resources, by creating a Group object for each role and adding User objects to it.

Returns true if this Authorization context implies the specified role, otherwise false.

107.8.3   public interface Group
extends User

A named grouping of roles (Role objects).

Whether or not a given Authorization context implies a Group object depends on the members of that Group object.

A Group object can have two kinds of members: *basic* and *required*. A Group object is implied by an Authorization context if all of its required members are implied and at least one of its basic members is implied.

A Group object must contain at least one basic member in order to be implied. In other words, a Group object without any basic member roles is never implied by any Authorization context.

A User object always implies itself.

No loop detection is performed when adding members to Group objects, which means that it is possible to create circular implications. Loop detection is instead done when roles are checked. The semantics is that if a role depends on itself (i.e., there is an implication loop), the role is not implied.

The rule that a Group object must have at least one basic member to be implied is motivated by the following example:

```
group foo
  required members: marketing
  basic members: alice, bob
```

Privileged operations that require membership in "foo" can be performed only by "alice" and "bob", who are in marketing.

If "alice" and "bob" ever transfer to a different department, anybody in marketing will be able to assume the "foo" role, which certainly must be prevented. Requiring that "foo" (or any Group object for that matter) must have at least one basic member accomplishes that.

However, this would make it impossible for a Group object to be implied by just its required members. An example where this implication might be useful is the following declaration: "Any citizen who is an adult is allowed to vote." An intuitive configuration of "voter" would be:

```
group voter
  required members: citizen, adult
    basic members:
```

However, according to the above rule, the "voter" role could never be assumed by anybody, since it lacks any basic members. In order to address this issue a predefined role named "user.anyone" can be specified, which is always implied. The desired implication of the "voter" group can then be achieved by specifying "user.anyone" as its basic member, as follows:

```
group voter
```

```
required members: citizen, adult
   basic members: user.anyone
```

107.8.3.1   **public boolean addMember(Role role)**

role   The role to add as a basic member.

  ☐ Adds the specified Role object as a basic member to this Group object.

Returns   true if the given role could be added as a basic member, and false if this Group object already contains a Role object whose name matches that of the specified role.

Throws   SecurityException – If a security manager exists and the caller does not have the UserAdminPermission with name admin.

107.8.3.2   **public boolean addRequiredMember(Role role)**

role   The Role object to add as a required member.

  ☐ Adds the specified Role object as a required member to this Group object.

Returns   true if the given Role object could be added as a required member, and false if this Group object already contains a Role object whose name matches that of the specified role.

Throws   SecurityException – If a security manager exists and the caller does not have the UserAdminPermission with name admin.

107.8.3.3   **public Role[] getMembers( )**

  ☐ Gets the basic members of this Group object.

Returns   The basic members of this Group object, or null if this Group object does not contain any basic members.

107.8.3.4   **public Role[] getRequiredMembers( )**

  ☐ Gets the required members of this Group object.

Returns   The required members of this Group object, or null if this Group object does not contain any required members.

107.8.3.5   **public boolean removeMember(Role role)**

role   The Role object to remove from this Group object.

  ☐ Removes the specified Role object from this Group object.

Returns   true if the Role object could be removed, otherwise false.

Throws   SecurityException – If a security manager exists and the caller does not have the UserAdminPermission with name admin.

107.8.4   public interface Role

The base interface for Role objects managed by the User Admin service.

This interface exposes the characteristics shared by all Role classes: a name, a type, and a set of properties.

Properties represent public information about the Role object that can be read by anyone. Specific UserAdminPermission objects are required to change a Role object's properties.

Role object properties are Dictionary objects. Changes to these objects are propagated to the User Admin service and made persistent.

Every User Admin service contains a set of predefined Role objects that are always present and cannot be removed. All predefined Role objects are of type ROLE. This version of the org.osgi.service.useradmin package defines a single predefined role named "user.anyone", which is inherited by any other role. Other predefined roles may be added in the future. Since "user.anyone" is a Role object that has properties associated with it that can be read and modified. Access to these properties and their use is application specific and is controlled using UserAdminPermission in the same way that properties for other Role objects are.

107.8.4.1   **public static final int GROUP = 2**

The type of a Group role.

The value of GROUP is 2.

107.8.4.2   **public static final int ROLE = 0**

The type of a predefined role.

The value of ROLE is 0.

107.8.4.3   **public static final int USER = 1**

The type of a User role.

The value of USER is 1.

107.8.4.4   **public static final String USER_ANYONE = "user.anyone"**

The name of the predefined role, user.anyone, that all users and groups belong to.

Since 1.1

107.8.4.5   **public String getName( )**

☐ Returns the name of this role.

Returns The role's name.

107.8.4.6   **public Dictionary getProperties( )**

☐ Returns a Dictionary of the (public) properties of this Role object. Any changes to the returned Dictionary will change the properties of this Role object. This will cause a UserAdminEvent object of type UserAdminEvent.ROLE_CHANGED to be broadcast to any UserAdminListener objects.

Only objects of type String may be used as property keys, and only objects of type String or byte[] may be used as property values. Any other types will cause an exception of type IllegalArgumentException to be raised.

In order to add, change, or remove a property in the returned Dictionary, a UserAdminPermission named after the property name (or a prefix of it) with action changeProperty is required.

Returns Dictionary containing the properties of this Role object.

107.8.4.7   **public int getType( )**

☐ Returns the type of this role.

Returns The role's type.

107.8.5   public interface User
extends Role

A User role managed by a User Admin service.

In this context, the term "user" is not limited to just human beings. Instead, it refers to any entity that may have any number of credentials associated with it that it may use to authenticate itself.

In general, User objects are associated with a specific User Admin service (namely the one that created them), and cannot be used with other User Admin services.

A User object may have credentials (and properties, inherited from the Role class) associated with it. Specific UserAdminPermission objects are required to read or change a User object's credentials.

Credentials are Dictionary objects and have semantics that are similar to the properties in the Role class.

107.8.5.1   **public Dictionary getCredentials( )**

☐ Returns a Dictionary of the credentials of this User object. Any changes to the returned Dictionary object will change the credentials of this User object. This will cause a UserAdminEvent object of type UserAdminEvent.ROLE_CHANGED to be broadcast to any UserAdminListeners objects.

Only objects of type String may be used as credential keys, and only objects of type String or of type byte[] may be used as credential values. Any other types will cause an exception of type IllegalArgumentException to be raised.

In order to retrieve a credential from the returned Dictionary object, a UserAdminPermission named after the credential name (or a prefix of it) with action getCredential is required.

In order to add or remove a credential from the returned Dictionary object, a UserAdminPermission named after the credential name (or a prefix of it) with action changeCredential is required.

Returns   Dictionary object containing the credentials of this User object.

107.8.5.2   **public boolean hasCredential(String key, Object value)**

key   The credential key.

value   The credential value.

☐ Checks to see if this User object has a credential with the specified key set to the specified value.

If the specified credential value is not of type String or byte[], it is ignored, that is, false is returned (as opposed to an IllegalArgumentException being raised).

Returns   true if this user has the specified credential; false otherwise.

Throws   SecurityException – If a security manager exists and the caller does not have the UserAdminPermission named after the credential key (or a prefix of it) with action getCredential.

107.8.6   public interface UserAdmin

This interface is used to manage a database of named Role objects, which can be used for authentication and authorization purposes.

This version of the User Admin service defines two types of Role objects: "User" and "Group". Each type of role is represented by an int constant and an interface. The range of positive integers is reserved for new types of roles that may be added in the future. When defining proprietary role types, negative constant values must be used.

Every role has a name and a type.

A User object can be configured with credentials (e.g., a password) and properties (e.g., a street address, phone number, etc.).

A Group object represents an aggregation of User and Group objects. In other words, the members of a Group object are roles themselves.

Every User Admin service manages and maintains its own namespace of Role objects, in which each Role object has a unique name.

107.8.6.1   **public Role createRole(String name, int type)**

name The name of the Role object to create.

type The type of the Role object to create. Must be either a Role.USER type or Role.GROUP type.

☐ Creates a Role object with the given name and of the given type.

If a Role object was created, a UserAdminEvent object of type UserAdminEvent.ROLE_CREATED is broadcast to any UserAdminListener object.

Returns The newly created Role object, or null if a role with the given name already exists.

Throws IllegalArgumentException – if type is invalid.

SecurityException – If a security manager exists and the caller does not have the UserAdminPermission with name admin.

107.8.6.2   **public Authorization getAuthorization(User user)**

user The User object to create an Authorization object for, or null for the anonymous user.

☐ Creates an Authorization object that encapsulates the specified User object and the Role objects it possesses. The null user is interpreted as the anonymous user. The anonymous user represents a user that has not been authenticated. An Authorization object for an anonymous user will be unnamed, and will only imply groups that user.anyone implies.

Returns the Authorization object for the specified User object.

107.8.6.3   **public Role getRole(String name)**

name The name of the Role object to get.

☐ Gets the Role object with the given name from this User Admin service.

Returns The requested Role object, or null if this User Admin service does not have a Role object with the given name.

107.8.6.4   **public Role[] getRoles(String filter) throws InvalidSyntaxException**

filter The filter criteria to match.

☐ Gets the Role objects managed by this User Admin service that have properties matching the specified LDAP filter criteria. See org.osgi.framework.Filter for a description of the filter syntax. If a null filter is specified, all Role objects managed by this User Admin service are returned.

Returns The Role objects managed by this User Admin service whose properties match the specified filter criteria, or all Role objects if a null filter is specified. If no roles match the filter, null will be returned.

Throws InvalidSyntaxException – If the filter is not well formed.

107.8.6.5   **public User getUser(String key, String value)**

key The property key to look for.

value The property value to compare with.

☐ Gets the user with the given property key-value pair from the User Admin service database. This is a convenience method for retrieving a User object based on a property for which every User object is supposed to have a unique value (within the scope of this User Admin service), such as for example a X.500 distinguished name.

Returns A matching user, if *exactly* one is found. If zero or more than one matching users are found, null is returned.

107.8.6.6   **public boolean removeRole(String name)**

name The name of the Role object to remove.

    □ Removes the Role object with the given name from this User Admin service and all groups it is a member of.

    If the Role object was removed, a UserAdminEvent object of type UserAdminEvent.ROLE_REMOVED is broadcast to any UserAdminListener object.

Returns true If a Role object with the given name is present in this User Admin service and could be removed, otherwise false.

Throws SecurityException – If a security manager exists and the caller does not have the UserAdminPermission with name admin.

107.8.7   public class UserAdminEvent

Role change event.

UserAdminEvent objects are delivered asynchronously to any UserAdminListener objects when a change occurs in any of the Role objects managed by a User Admin service.

A type code is used to identify the event. The following event types are defined: ROLE_CREATED type, ROLE_CHANGED type, and ROLE_REMOVED type. Additional event types may be defined in the future.

See Also UserAdmin, UserAdminListener

107.8.7.1   public static final int ROLE_CHANGED = 2

A Role object has been modified.

The value of ROLE_CHANGED is 0x00000002.

107.8.7.2   public static final int ROLE_CREATED = 1

A Role object has been created.

The value of ROLE_CREATED is 0x00000001.

107.8.7.3   public static final int ROLE_REMOVED = 4

A Role object has been removed.

The value of ROLE_REMOVED is 0x00000004.

107.8.7.4   public UserAdminEvent(ServiceReference ref, int type, Role role)

ref The ServiceReference object of the User Admin service that generated this event.

type The event type.

role The Role object on which this event occurred.

    □ Constructs a UserAdminEvent object from the given ServiceReference object, event type, and Role object.

107.8.7.5   public Role getRole( )

    □ Gets the Role object this event was generated for.

Returns The Role object this event was generated for.

107.8.7.6   public ServiceReference getServiceReference( )

    □ Gets the ServiceReference object of the User Admin service that generated this event.

Returns The User Admin service's ServiceReference object.

107.8.7.7   **public int getType( )**

     ☐ Returns the type of this event.

     The type values are ROLE_CREATED type, ROLE_CHANGED type, and ROLE_REMOVED type.

Returns The event type.

107.8.8   public interface UserAdminListener

Listener for UserAdminEvents.

UserAdminListener objects are registered with the Framework service registry and notified with a UserAdminEvent object when a Role object has been created, removed, or modified.

UserAdminListener objects can further inspect the received UserAdminEvent object to determine its type, the Role object it occurred on, and the User Admin service that generated it.

See Also UserAdmin, UserAdminEvent

107.8.8.1   **public void roleChanged(UserAdminEvent event)**

event The UserAdminEvent object.

     ☐ Receives notification that a Role object has been created, removed, or modified.

107.8.9   public final class UserAdminPermission extends BasicPermission

Permission to configure and access the Role objects managed by a User Admin service.

This class represents access to the Role objects managed by a User Admin service and their properties and credentials (in the case of User objects).

The permission name is the name (or name prefix) of a property or credential. The naming convention follows the hierarchical property naming convention. Also, an asterisk may appear at the end of the name, following a ".", or by itself, to signify a wildcard match. For example: "org.osgi.security.protocol.*" or "*" is valid, but "*protocol" or "a*b" are not valid.

The UserAdminPermission with the reserved name "admin" represents the permission required for creating and removing Role objects in the User Admin service, as well as adding and removing members in a Group object. This UserAdminPermission does not have any actions associated with it.

The actions to be granted are passed to the constructor in a string containing a list of one or more comma-separated keywords. The possible keywords are: changeProperty, changeCredential, and getCredential. Their meaning is defined as follows:

```
action
changeProperty     Permission to change (i.e., add and remove)
                   Role object properties whose names start with
                   the name argument specified in the constructor.
changeCredential   Permission to change (i.e., add and remove)
                   User object credentials whose names start
                   with the name argument specified in the constructor.
getCredential      Permission to retrieve and check for the
                   existence of User object credentials whose names
                   start with the name argument specified in the
                   constructor.
```

The action string is converted to lowercase before processing.

Following is a PermissionInfo style policy entry which grants a user administration bundle a number of UserAdminPermission object:

```
(org.osgi.service.useradmin.UserAdminPermission "admin")
    (org.osgi.service.useradmin.UserAdminPermission "com.foo.*" "changeProperty,get-
Credential,changeCredential")
    (org.osgi.service.useradmin.UserAdminPermission "user.*", "changeProperty,
changeCredential")
```

The first permission statement grants the bundle the permission to perform any User Admin service operations of type "admin", that is, create and remove roles and configure Group objects.

The second permission statement grants the bundle the permission to change any properties as well as get and change any credentials whose names start with com.foo..

The third permission statement grants the bundle the permission to change any properties and credentials whose names start with user.. This means that the bundle is allowed to change, but not retrieve any credentials with the given prefix.

The following policy entry empowers the Http Service bundle to perform user authentication:

```
grant codeBase "${jars}http.jar" {
  permission org.osgi.service.useradmin.UserAdminPermission
    "user.password", "getCredential";
};
```

The permission statement grants the Http Service bundle the permission to validate any password credentials (for authentication purposes), but the bundle is not allowed to change any properties or credentials.

Concurrency Thread-safe

107.8.9.1   **public static final String ADMIN = "admin"**

The permission name "admin".

107.8.9.2   **public static final String CHANGE_CREDENTIAL = "changeCredential"**

The action string "changeCredential".

107.8.9.3   **public static final String CHANGE_PROPERTY = "changeProperty"**

The action string "changeProperty".

107.8.9.4   **public static final String GET_CREDENTIAL = "getCredential"**

The action string "getCredential".

107.8.9.5   **public UserAdminPermission(String name, String actions)**

name   the name of this UserAdminPermission

actions   the action string.

□   Creates a new UserAdminPermission with the specified name and actions. name is either the reserved string "admin" or the name of a credential or property, and actions contains a comma-separated list of the actions granted on the specified name. Valid actions are changeProperty, changeCredential, and getCredential.

Throws   IllegalArgumentException – If name equals "admin" and actions are specified.

107.8.9.6   **public boolean equals(Object obj)**

obj   the object to be compared for equality with this object.

    ☐ Checks two UserAdminPermission objects for equality. Checks that obj is a UserAdminPermission, and has the same name and actions as this object.

Returns true if obj is a UserAdminPermission object, and has the same name and actions as this UserAdminPermission object.

107.8.9.7 **public String getActions( )**

    ☐ Returns the canonical string representation of the actions, separated by comma.

Returns the canonical string representation of the actions.

107.8.9.8 **public int hashCode( )**

    ☐ Returns the hash code value for this object.

Returns A hash code value for this object.

107.8.9.9 **public boolean implies(Permission p)**

  p the permission to check against.

    ☐ Checks if this UserAdminPermission object "implies" the specified permission.

    More specifically, this method returns true if:

- *p* is an instanceof UserAdminPermission,
- *p*'s actions are a proper subset of this object's actions, and
- *p*'s name is implied by this object's name. For example, "java.*" implies "java.home".

Returns true if the specified permission is implied by this object; false otherwise.

107.8.9.10 **public PermissionCollection newPermissionCollection( )**

    ☐ Returns a new PermissionCollection object for storing UserAdminPermission objects.

Returns a new PermissionCollection object suitable for storing UserAdminPermission objects.

107.8.9.11 **public String toString( )**

    ☐ Returns a string describing this UserAdminPermission object. This string must be in PermissionInfo encoded format.

Returns The PermissionInfo encoded string for this UserAdminPermission object.

See Also org.osgi.service.permissionadmin.PermissionInfo.getEncoded

107.9   References

[1] *The Java Security Architecture for JDK 1.2*
Version 1.0, Sun Microsystems, October 1998

[2] *Java Authentication and Authorization Service*
http://java.sun.com/javase/technologies/security/

110 Initial Provisioning Specification

Version 1.2

110.1 Introduction

To allow freedom regarding the choice of management protocol, the OSGi Specifications assumes an architecture to remotely manage a Service Platform with a Management Agent. The Management Agent is implemented with a Management Bundle that can communicate with an unspecified management protocol.

This specification defines how the Management Agent can make its way to the Service Platform, and gives a structured view of the problems and their corresponding resolution methods.

The purpose of this specification is to enable the management of a Service Platform by an Operator, and (optionally) to hand over the management of the Service Platform later to another Operator. This approach is in accordance with the OSGi remote management reference architecture.

This bootstrapping process requires the installation of a Management Agent, with appropriate configuration data, in the Service Platform.

This specification consists of a prologue, in which the principles of the Initial Provisioning are outlined, and a number of mappings to different mechanisms.

110.1.1 Essentials

- *Policy Free* – The proposed solution must be business model agnostic; none of the affected parties (Operators, SPS Manufacturers, etc.) should be forced into any particular business model.
- *Inter-operability* – The Initial Provisioning must permit arbitrary inter-operability between management systems and Service Platforms. Any compliant Remote Manager should be able to manage any compliant Service Platform, even in the absence of a prior business relationship. Adhering to this requirement allows a particular Operator to manage a variety of makes and models of Service Platform Servers using a single management system of the Operator's choice. This rule also gives the consumer the greatest choice when selecting an Operator.
- *Flexible* – The management process should be as open as possible, to allow innovation and specialization while still achieving interoperability.

110.1.2 Entities

- *Provisioning Service* – A service registered with the Framework that provides information about the initial provisioning to the Management Agent.
- *Provisioning Dictionary* – A Dictionary object that is filled with information from the ZIP files that are loaded during initial setup.
- *RSH Protocol* – An OSGi specific secure protocol based on HTTP.
- *Management Agent* – A bundle that is responsible for managing a Service Platform under control of a Remote Manager.

Figure 110.1   *Initial Provisioning*

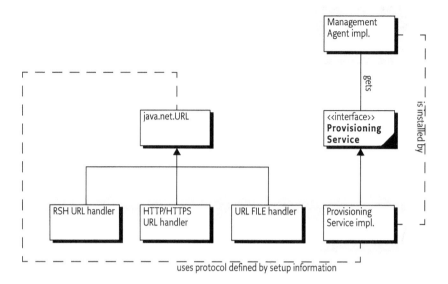

110.2   Procedure

The following procedure should be executed by an OSGi Framework implementation that supports this Initial Provisioning specification.

When the Service Platform is first brought under management control, it must be provided with an initial request URL in order to be provisioned. Either the end user or the manufacturer may provide the initial request URL. How the initial request URL is transferred to the Framework is not specified, but a mechanism might, for example, be a command line parameter when the framework is started.

When asked to start the Initial Provisioning, the Service Platform will send a request to the management system. This request is encoded in a URL, for example:

    http://osgi.acme.com/remote-manager

This URL may use any protocol that is available on the Service Platform Server. Many standard protocols exist, but it is also possible to use a proprietary protocol. For example, software could be present which can communicate with a smart card and could handle, for example, this URL:

    smart-card://com1:0/7F20/6F38

Before the request URL is executed, the Service Platform information is appended to the URL. This information includes at least the Service Platform Identifier, but may also contain proprietary information, as long as the keys for this information do not conflict. Different URL schemes may use different methods of appending parameters; these details are specified in the mappings of this specification to concrete protocols.

The result of the request must be a ZIP file (The content type should be application/zip). It is the responsibility of the underlying protocol to guarantee the integrity and authenticity of this ZIP file.

This ZIP file is unpacked and its entries (except bundle and bundle-url entries, described in Table 110.2) are placed in a Dictionary object. This Dictionary object is called the *Provisioning Dictionary*. It must be made available from the Provisioning Service in the service registry. The names of the entries in the ZIP file must not start with a slash ('/').

The ZIP file may contain only four types of dictionary entries: text, binary, bundle, or bundle-url. The type of an entry can be specified in different ways. An Initial Provisioning service must look in the following places to find the information about an entry's (MIME) type (in the given order):

1   The manifest header InitialProvisioning-Entries of the given ZIP file. This header is defined in *InitialProvisioning-Entries Manifest Header* on page 127. If this header is present, but a given entry's path is not named then try the next step.
2   The ZIP entry's extra field. If this ZIP entry field is present, the Initial Provisioning service should not look further, even if the extra field contains an erroneous value.
3   The extension of the entry path name if one of .txt, .jar, .url extensions. See *Content types of provisioning ZIP file* on page 125 for the mapping of types, MIME types, and extensions.
4   The entry is assumed to be a binary type

The types can optionally be specified as a MIME type as defined in [7] *MIME Types*. The text and bundle-url entries are translated into a String object from an UTF-8 encoded byte array. All other entries must be stored as a byte[].

Table 110.1   *Content types of provisioning ZIP file*

Type	MIME Type	Ext	Description
text	MIME_STRING text/ plain;charset=utf-8	.txt	Must be represented as a String object
binary	MIME_BYTE_ARRAY application/octet-stream	not .txt, .url, or .jar	Must be represented as a byte array (byte[]).
bundle	MIME_BUNDLE application/ vnd.osgi.bundle MIME_BUNDLE_ALT application/ x-osgi-bundle	.jar	Entries must be installed using BundleContext.installBundle(String,InputStream), with the InputStream object constructed from the contents of the ZIP entry. The location must be the name of the ZIP entry without leading slash. This entry must not be stored in the Provisioning Dictionary. If a bundle with this location name is already installed in this system, then this bundle must be updated instead of installed. The MIME_BUNDLE_ALT version is intended for backward compatibility, it specifies the original MIME type for bundles before there was an official IANA MIME type.
bundle-url	MIME_BUNDLE_URL text/ x-osgi-bundle-url; charset=utf-8	.url	The content of this entry is a string coded in utf-8. Entries must be installed using BundleContext.installBundle(String, InputStream), with the InputStream object created from the given URL. The location must be the name of the ZIP entry without leading slash. This entry must not be stored in the Provisioning Dictionary. If a bundle with this location url is already installed in this system, then this bundle must be updated instead of installed.

The Provisioning Service must install (but not start) all entries in the ZIP file that are typed with bundle or bundle-url.

If an entry named PROVISIONING_START_BUNDLE is present in the Provisioning Dictionary, then its content type must be text as defined in Table 110.1. The content of this entry must match the bundle location of a previously loaded bundle. This designated bundle must be given AllPermission and started.

If no PROVISIONING_START_BUNDLE entry is present in the Provisioning Dictionary, the Provisioning Dictionary should contain a reference to another ZIP file under the PROVISIONING_REFERENCE key. If both keys are absent, no further action must take place.

If this PROVISIONING_REFERENCE key is present and holds a String object that can be mapped to a valid URL, then a new ZIP file must be retrieved from this URL. The PROVISIONING_REFERENCE link may be repeated multiple times in successively loaded ZIP files.

Referring to a new ZIP file with such a URL allows a manufacturer to place a fixed reference inside the Service Platform Server (in a file or smart card) that will provide some platform identifying information and then also immediately load the information from the management system. The PROVISIONING_REFERENCE link may be repeated multiple times in successively loaded ZIP files. The entry PROVISIONING_UPDATE_COUNT must be an Integer object that must be incremented on every iteration.

Information retrieved while loading subsequent PROVISIONING_REFERENCE URLs may replace previous key/values in the Provisioning Dictionary, but must not erase unrecognized key/values. For example, if an assignment has assigned the key proprietary-x, with a value '3', then later assignments must not override this value, unless the later loaded ZIP file contains an entry with that name. All these updates to the Provisioning Dictionary must be stored persistently. At the same time, each entry of type bundle or bundle-url (see Table 110.1) must be installed and not started.

Once the Management Agent has been started, the Initial Provisioning service has become operational. In this state, the Initial Provisioning service must react when the Provisioning Dictionary is updated with a new PROVISIONING_REFERENCE property. If this key is set, it should start the cycle again. For example, if the control of a Service Platform needs to be transferred to another Remote Manager, the Management Agent should set the PROVISIONING_REFERENCE to the location of this new Remote Manager's Initial Provisioning ZIP file. This process is called *re-provisioning*.

If errors occur during this process, the Initial Provisioning service should try to notify the Service User of the problem.

The previous description is depicted in Figure 110.2 as a flow chart.

Figure 110.2   *Flow chart installation Management Agent bundle*

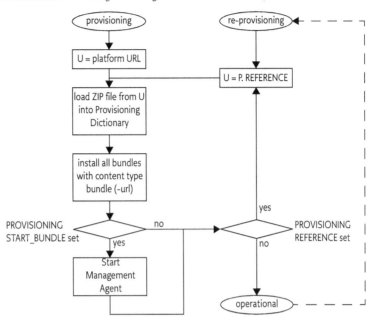

The Management Agent may require configuration data that is specific to the Service Platform instance. If this data is available outside the Management Agent bundle, the merging of this data with the Management Agent may take place in the Service Platform. Transferring the data separately will make it possible to simplify the implementation on the server side, as it is not necessary to create *personalized* Service Platform bundles. The PROVISIONING_AGENT_CONFIG key is reserved for this purpose, but the Management Agent may use another key or mechanisms if so desired.

The PROVISIONING_SPID key must contain the Service Platform Identifier.

110.2.1   InitialProvisioning-Entries Manifest Header

The InitialProvisioning-Entries manifest header optionally specifies the type of the entries in the ZIP file. This header, when present, overrides the extra field for the given entry. The syntax for this header is:

```
InitialProvisioning-Entries ::= ip-entry ( ',' ip-entry ) *
ip-entry                     ::= path ( ';' parameter ) *
```

The entry is the path name of a resource in the ZIP file. This InitialProvisioning-Entries header recognizes the following attribute:

- type – Gives the type of the dictionary entry. The type can have one of the following values: text, binary, bundle, or bundle-url

If the type parameter entry is not specified for an entry, then the type will be inferred from the extension of the entry, as defined in table *Content types of provisioning ZIP file* on page 125.

110.3   Special Configurations

The next section shows some examples of specially configured types of Service Platform Servers and how they are treated with the respect to the specifications in this document.

110.3.1   **Branded Service Platform Server**

If a Service Platform Operator is selling Service Platform Servers branded exclusively for use with their service, the provisioning will most likely be performed prior to shipping the Service Platform Server to the User. Typically the Service Platform is configured with the Dictionary entry PROVISIONING_REFERENCE pointing at a location controlled by the Operator.

Up-to-date bundles and additional configuration data must be loaded from that location at activation time. The Service Platform is probably equipped with necessary security entities, like certificates, to enable secure downloads from the Operator's URL over open networks, if necessary.

110.3.2   **Non-connected Service Platform**

Circumstances might exist in which the Service Platform Server has no WAN connectivity, or prefers not to depend on it for the purposes not covered by this specification.

The non-connected case can be implemented by specifying a file:// URL for the initial ZIP file (PROVISIONING_REFERENCE). That file:// URL would name a local file containing the response that would otherwise be received from a remote server.

The value for the Management Agent PROVISIONING_REFERENCE found in that file will be used as input to the load process. The PROVISIONING_REFERENCE may point to a bundle file stored either locally or remotely. No code changes are necessary for the non-connected scenario. The file:// URLs must be specified, and the appropriate files must be created on the Service Platform.

110.4   The Provisioning Service

Provisioning information is conveyed between bundles using the Provisioning Service, as defined in the ProvisioningService interface. The Provisioning Dictionary is retrieved from the ProvisioningService object using the getInformation() method. This is a read-only Dictionary object, any changes to this Dictionary object must throw an UnsupportedOperationException.

The Provisioning Service provides a number of methods to update the Provisioning Dictionary.

- addInformation(Dictionary) – Add all key/value pairs in the given Dictionary object to the Provisioning Dictionary.
- addInformation(ZipInputStream) – It is also possible to add a ZIP file to the Provisioning Service immediately. This will unpack the ZIP file and add the entries to the Provisioning Dictionary. This method must install the bundles contained in the ZIP file as described in *Procedure* on page 124.
- setInformation(Dictionary) – Set a new Provisioning Dictionary. This will remove all existing entries.

Each of these method will increment the PROVISIONING_UPDATE_COUNT entry.

110.5   Management Agent Environment

The Management Agent should be written with great care to minimize dependencies on other packages and services, as *all* services in OSGi are optional. Some Service Platforms may have other bundles pre-installed, so it is possible that there may be exported packages and services available. Mechanisms outside the current specification, however, must be used to discover these packages and services before the Management Agent is installed.

The Provisioning Service must ensure that the Management Agent is running with AllPermission. The Management Agent should check to see if the Permission Admin service is available, and establish the initial permissions as soon as possible to insure the security of the device when later bundles are installed. As the PermissionAdmin interfaces may not be present (it is an optional service), the Management Agent should export the PermissionAdmin interfaces to ensure they can be resolved.

Once started, the Management Agent may retrieve its configuration data from the Provisioning Service by getting the byte[] object that corresponds to the PROVISIONING_AGENT_CONFIG key in the Provisioning Dictionary. The structure of the configuration data is implementation specific.

The scope of this specification is to provide a mechanism to transmit the raw configuration data to the Management Agent. The Management Agent bundle may alternatively be packaged with its configuration data in the bundle, so it may not be necessary for the Management Agent bundle to use the Provisioning Service at all.

Most likely, the Management Agent bundle will install other bundles to provision the Service Platform. Installing other bundles might even involve downloading a more full featured Management Agent to replace the initial Management Agent.

110.6 Mapping To File Scheme

The file: scheme is the simplest and most completely supported scheme which can be used by the Initial Provisioning specification. It can be used to store the configuration data and Management Agent bundle on the Service Platform Server, and avoids any outside communication.

If the initial request URL has a file scheme, no parameters should be appended, because the file: scheme does not accept parameters.

110.6.1 Example With File Scheme

The manufacturer should prepare a ZIP file containing only one entry named PROVISIONING_START_BUNDLE that contains a location string of an entry of type bundle or bundle-url. For example, the following ZIP file demonstrates this:

```
provisioning.start.bundle  text      agent
agent                      bundle    C0AF0E9B2AB..
```

The bundle may also be specified with a URL:

```
provisioning.start.bundle  text      http://acme.com/a.jar
agent                      bundle-url http://acme.com/a.jar
```

Upon startup, the framework is provided with the URL with the file: scheme that points to this ZIP file:

```
file:/opt/osgi/ma.zip
```

110.7 Mapping To HTTP(S) Scheme

This section defines how HTTP and HTTPS URLs must be used with the Initial Provisioning specification.

- HTTP – May be used when the data exchange takes place over networks that are secured by other means, such as a Virtual Private Network (VPN) or a physically isolated network. Otherwise, HTTP is not a valid scheme because no authentication takes place.
- HTTPS – May be used if the Service Platform is equipped with appropriate certificates.

HTTP and HTTPS share the following qualities:

- Both are well known and widely used
- Numerous implementations of the protocols exist
- Caching of the Management Agent will be desired in many implementations where limited bandwidth is an issue. Both HTTP and HTTPS already contain an accepted protocol for caching.

Both HTTP and HTTPS must be used with the GET method. The response is a ZIP file, implying that the response header Content-Type header must contain application/zip.

110.7.1   HTTPS Certificates

In order to use HTTPS, certificates must be in place. These certificates, that are used to establish trust towards the Operator, may be made available to the Service Platform using the Provisioning Service. The root certificate should be assigned to the Provisioning Dictionary before the HTTPS provider is used. Additionally, the Service Platform should be equipped with a Service Platform certificate that allows the Service Platform to properly authenticate itself towards the Operator. This specification does not state how this certificate gets installed into the Service Platform.

The root certificate is stored in the Provisioning Dictionary under the key:

```
PROVISIONING_ROOTX509
```

The Root X.509 Certificate holds certificates used to represent a handle to a common base for establishing trust. The certificates are typically used when authenticating a Remote Manager to the Service Platform. In this case, a Root X.509 certificate must be part of a certificate chain for the Operator's certificate. The format of the certificate is defined in *Certificate Encoding* on page 130.

110.7.2   Certificate Encoding

Root certificates are X.509 certificates. Each individual certificate is stored as a byte[] object. This byte[] object is encoded in the default Java manner, as follows:

- The original, binary certificate data is DER encoded
- The DER encoded data is encoded into base64 to make it text.
- The base64 encoded data is prefixed with
    ```
    -----BEGIN CERTIFICATE-----
    ```
    and suffixed with:
    ```
    -----END CERTIFICATE-----
    ```
- If a record contains more than one certificate, they are simply appended one after the other, each with a delimiting prefix and suffix.

The decoding of such a certificate may be done with the java.security.cert.CertificateFactory class:

```
InputStream bis = new ByteArrayInputStream(x509); // byte[]
CertificateFactory cf =
   CertificateFactory.getInstance("X.509");
Collection c = cf.generateCertificates(bis);
Iterator i = c.iterator();
while (i.hasNext()) {
   Certificate cert = (Certificate)i.next();
   System.out.println(cert);
}
```

110.7.3   URL Encoding

The URL must contain the Service Platform Identity, and may contain more parameters. These parameters are encoded in the URL according to the HTTP(S) URL scheme. A base URL may be set by an end user but the Provisioning Service must add the Service Platform Identifier.

If the request URL already contains HTTP parameters (if there is a " in the request), the service_platform_id is appended to this URL as an additional parameter. If, on the other hand, the request URL does not contain any HTTP parameters, the service_platform_id will be appended to the URL after a ", becoming the first HTTP parameter. The following two examples show these two variants:

```
http://server.operator.com/service-x «
   foo=bar&service_platform_id=VIN:123456789

http://server.operator.com/service-x «
```

```
service_platform_id=VIN:123456789
```

Proper URL encoding must be applied when the URL contains characters that are not allowed. See [6] *RFC 2396 - Uniform Resource Identifier (URI)*.

110.8   **Mapping To RSH Scheme**

The RSH protocol is an OSGi-specific protocol, and is included in this specification because it is optimized for Initial Provisioning. It requires a shared secret between the management system and the Service Platform that is small enough to be entered by the Service User.

RSH bases authentication and encryption on Message Authentication Codes (MACs) that have been derived from a secret that is shared between the Service Platform and the Operator prior to the start of the protocol execution.

The protocol is based on an ordinary HTTP GET request/response, in which the request must be *signed* and the response must be *encrypted* and *authenticated*. Both the *signature* and *encryption key* are derived from the shared secret using Hashed Message Access Codes (HMAC) functions.

As additional input to the HMAC calculations, one client-generated nonce and one server-generated nonce are used to prevent replay attacks. The nonces are fairly large random numbers that must be generated in relation to each invocation of the protocol, in order to guarantee freshness. These nonces are called clientfg (client-generated freshness guarantee) and serverfg (server-generated freshness guarantee).

In order to separate the HMAC calculations for authentication and encryption, each is based on a different constant value. These constants are called the *authentication constant* and the *encryption constant*.

From an abstract perspective, the protocol may be described as follows.

- δ – Shared secret, 160 bits or more
- s – Server nonce, called servercfg, 128 bits
- c – Client nonce, called clientfg, 128 bits
- K_a – Authentication key, 160 bits
- K_e – Encryption key, 192 bits
- r – Response data
- e – Encrypted data
- E – Encryption constant, a byte[] of 05, 36, 54, 70, 00 (hex)
- A – Authentication constant, a byte[] of 00, 4f, 53, 47, 49 (hex)
- M – Message material, used for K_e calculation.
- m – The calculated message authentication code.
- *3DES* – Triple DES, encryption function, see [8] *3DES*. The bytes of the key must be set to odd parity. CBC mode must be used where the padding method is defined in [9] *RFC 1423 Part III: Algorithms, Modes, and Identifiers*. In [11] *Java Cryptography API (part of Java 1.4)* this is addressed as PKCS5Padding.
- *IV* – Initialization vector for 3DES.
- *SHA1* – Secure Hash Algorithm to generate the Hashed Message Authentication Code, see [12] *SHA-1*. The function takes a single parameter, the block to be worked upon.
- *HMAC* – The function that calculates a message authentication code, which must HMAC-SHA1. HMAC-SHA1 is defined in [1] *HMAC: Keyed-Hashing for Message Authentication*. The HMAC function takes a key and a block to be worked upon as arguments. Note that the lower 16 bytes of the result must be used.
- *{}* – Concatenates its arguments
- *[]* – Indicates access to a sub-part of a variable, in bytes. Index starts at one, not zero.

In each step, the emphasized server or client indicates the context of the calculation. If both are used at the same time, each variable will have server or client as a subscript.

1. The *client* generates a random nonce, stores it and denotes it clientfg

   $c = nonce$

2. The client sends the request with the clientfg to the server.

   $c_{server} \Leftarrow c_{client}$

3. The *server* generates a nonce and denotes it serverfg.

   $s = nonce$

4. The *server* calculates an authentication key based on the SHA1 function, the shared secret, the received clientfg, the serverfg and the authentication constant.

   $K_a \leftarrow SHA1(\{\delta, c, s, A\})$

5. The *server* calculates an encryption key using an SHA-1 function, the shared secret, the received clientfg, the serverfg and the encryption constant. It must first calculate the *key material* M.

   $M[1, 20] \leftarrow SHA1(\{\delta, c, s, E\})$

   $M[21, 40] \leftarrow SHA1(\{\delta, M[1, 20], c, s, E\})$

6. The key for DES consists K_e and IV.

   $K_e \leftarrow M[1, 24]$

   $IV \leftarrow M[25, 32]$

   The *server* encrypts the response data using the encryption key derived in 5. The encryption algorithm that must be used to encrypt/decrypt the response data is 3DES. 24 bytes (192 bits) from M are used to generate K_e, but the low order bit of each byte must be used as an odd parity bit. This means that before using K_e, each byte must be processed to set the low order bit so that the byte has odd parity.

   The encryption/decryption key used is specified by the following:

   $e \leftarrow 3DES(K_e, IV, r)$

7. The *server* calculates a MAC *m* using the HMAC function, the encrypted response data and the authentication key derived in 4.

   $m \leftarrow HMAC(K_a, e)$

8. The *server* sends a response to the *client* containing the serverfg, the MAC *m* and the encrypted response data

   $s_{client} \Leftarrow s_{server}$

   $m_{client} \Leftarrow m_{server}$

   $e_{client} \Leftarrow e_{server}$

   The *client* calculates the encryption key K_e the same way the server did in step 5 and 6, and uses this to decrypt the encrypted response data. The serverfg value received in the response is used in the calculation.

   $r \leftarrow 3DES(K_e, IV, e)$

9. The *client* performs the calculation of the MAC *m'* in the same way the server did, and checks that the results match the received MAC *m*. If they do not match, further processing is discarded. The serverfg value received in the response is used in the calculation.

   $K_a \leftarrow SHA1(\{\delta, c, s, A\})$

   $m' \leftarrow HMAC(K_a, e)$

   $m' = m$

Figure 110.3 *Action Diagram for RSH*

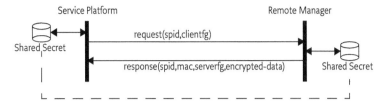

110.8.1   Shared Secret

The *shared secret* should be a key of length 160 bits (20 bytes) or more. The length is selected to match the output of the selected hash algorithm [2] *NIST, FIPS PUB 180-1: Secure Hash Standard, April 1995.*.

In some scenarios, the shared secret is generated by the Operator and communicated to the User, who inserts the secret into the Service Platform through some unspecified means.

The opposite is also possible: the shared secret can be stored within the Service Platform, extracted from it, and then communicated to the Operator. In this scenario, the source of the shared secret could be either the Service Platform or the Operator.

In order for the server to calculate the authentication and encryption keys, it requires the proper shared secret. The server must have access to many different shared secrets, one for each Service Platform it is to support. To be able to resolve this issue, the server must typically also have access to the Service Platform Identifier of the Service Platform. The normal way for the server to know the Service Platform Identifier is through the application protocol, as this value is part of the URL encoded parameters of the HTTP, HTTPS, or RSH mapping of the Initial Provisioning.

In order to be able to switch Operators, a new shared secret must be used. The new secret may be generated by the new Operator and then inserted into the Service Platform device using a mechanism not covered by this specification. Or the device itself may generate the new secret and convey it to the owner of the device using a display device or read-out, which is then communicated to the new operator out-of-band. Additionally, the generation of the new secret may be triggered by some external event, like holding down a button for a specified amount of time.

110.8.2   Request Coding

RSH is mapped to HTTP or HTTPS. Thus, the request parameters are URL encoded as discussed in 110.7.3 *URL Encoding*. RSH requires an additional parameter in the URL: the clientfg parameter. This parameter is a nonce that is used to counter replay attacks. See also *RSH Transport* on page 134.

110.8.3   Response Coding

The server's response to the client is composed of three parts:

- A header containing the protocol version and the serverfg
- The MAC
- The encrypted response

These three items are packaged into a binary container according to Table 110.2.

Table 110.2   *RSH Header description*

Bytes	Description	Value hex
4	Number of bytes in header	2E
1	Major version number	01
1	Minor version number	00
16	serverfg	...

Table 110.2   *RSH Header description*

Bytes	Description	Value hex
4	Number of bytes in MAC	10
16	Message Authentication Code	MAC
4	Number of bytes of encrypted ZIP file	N
N	Encrypted ZIP file	...

The response content type is an RSH-specific encrypted ZIP file, implying that the response header Content-Type must be application/x-rsh for the HTTP request. When the content file is decrypted, the content must be a ZIP file.

110.8.4 RSH URL

The RSH URL must be used internally within the Service Platform to indicate the usage of RSH for initial provisioning. The RSH URL format is identical to the HTTP URL format, except that the scheme is rsh: instead of http:. For example (« means line continues on next line):

```
rsh://server.operator.com/service-x
```

110.8.5 Extensions to the Provisioning Service Dictionary

RSH specifies one additional entry for the Provisioning Dictionary:

```
PROVISIONING_RSH_SECRET
```

The value of this entry is a byte[] containing the shared secret used by the RSH protocol.

110.8.6 RSH Transport

RSH is mapped to HTTP or HTTPS and follows the same URL encoding rules, except that the clientfg is additionally appended to the URL. The key in the URL must be clientfg and the value must be encoded in base 64 format:

The clientfg parameter is transported as an HTTP parameter that is appended after the service_platform_id parameter. The second example above would then be:

```
rsh://server.operator.com/service-x
```

Which, when mapped to HTTP, must become:

```
http://server.operator.com/service-x «
    service_platform_id=VIN:123456789& «
    clientfg=AHPmWcw%2FsiWYC37xZNdKvQ%3D%3D
```

110.9 Exception Handling

The Initial Provisioning process is a a sensitive process that must run without user supervision. There is therefore a need to handle exceptional cases in a well defined way to simplify trouble shooting.

There are only 2 types of problems that halt the provisioning process. They are:

- IOException when reading or writing provisioning information.
- IOException when retrieving or processing a provisioning zip file.

Other exceptions can occur and the Provisioning Service must do any attempt to log these events.

In the cases that the provisioning process stops, it is important that the clients of the provisioning service have a way to find out that the process is stopped. The mechanism that is used for this is a special entry in the provisioning dictionary. The name of the entry must be provisioning.error. The value is a String object with the following format:

- Numeric error code
- Space
- A human readable string describing the error.

Permitted error codes are:

- 0 – Unknown error
- 1 – Couldn't load or save provisioning information
- 2 – MalformedURLException
- 3 – IOException when retrieving document of a URL
- 4 – Corrupted ZipInputStream

The provisioning.update.count will be incremented as normal when a provisioning.error entry is added to the provisioning information. After, the provisioning service will take no further action.

Some examples:

```
0 SIM card removed
2 "http://www.acme.com/secure/blib/ifa.zip"
```

110.10 Security

The security model for the Service Platform is based on the integrity of the Management Agent deployment. If any of the mechanisms used during the deployment of management agents are weak, or can be compromised, the whole security model becomes weak.

From a security perspective, one attractive means of information exchange would be a smart card. This approach enables all relevant information to be stored in a single place. The Operator could then provide the information to the Service Platform by inserting the smart card into the Service Platform.

110.10.1 Concerns

The major security concerns related to the deployment of the Management Agent are:

- The Service Platform is controlled by the intended Operator
- The Operator controls the intended Service Platform(s)
- The integrity and confidentiality of the information exchange that takes place during these processes must be considered

In order to address these concerns, an implementation of the OSGi Remote Management Architecture must assure that:

- The Operator authenticates itself to the Service Platform
- The Service Platform authenticates itself to the Operator
- The integrity and confidentiality of the Management Agent, certificates, and configuration data are fully protected if they are transported over public transports.

Each mapping of the Initial Provisioning specification to a concrete implementation must describe how these goals are met.

110.10.2 Service Platform Long-Term Security

Secrets for long-term use may be exchanged during the Initial Provisioning procedures. This way, one or more secrets may be shared securely, assuming that the Provisioning Dictionary assignments used are implemented with the proper security characteristics.

110.10.3 Permissions

The provisioning information may contain sensitive information. Also, the ability to modify provisioning information can have drastic consequences. Thus, only trusted bundles should be allowed to register, or get the Provisioning Service. This restriction can be enforced using ServicePermission[ProvisioningService, GET].

No Permission classes guard reading or modification of the Provisioning Dictionary, so care must be taken not to leak the Dictionary object received from the Provisioning Service to bundles that are not trusted.

Whether message-based or connection-based, the communications used for Initial Provisioning must support mutual authentication and message integrity checking, at a minimum.

By using both server and client authentication in HTTPS, the problem of establishing identity is solved. In addition, HTTPS will encrypt the transmitted data. HTTPS requires a Public Key Infrastructure implementation in order to retrieve the required certificates.

When RSH is used, it is vital that the shared secret is shared only between the Operator and the Service Platform, and no one else.

110.11 org.osgi.service.provisioning

Provisioning Package Version 1.2.

Bundles wishing to use this package must list the package in the Import-Package header of the bundle's manifest. For example:

```
Import-Package: org.osgi.service.provisioning; version="[1.2,2.0)"
```

110.11.1 public interface ProvisioningService

Service for managing the initial provisioning information.

Initial provisioning of an OSGi device is a multi step process that culminates with the installation and execution of the initial management agent. At each step of the process, information is collected for the next step. Multiple bundles may be involved and this service provides a means for these bundles to exchange information. It also provides a means for the initial Management Bundle to get its initial configuration information.

The provisioning information is collected in a Dictionary object, called the Provisioning Dictionary. Any bundle that can access the service can get a reference to this object and read and update provisioning information. The key of the dictionary is a String object and the value is a String or byte[] object. The single exception is the PROVISIONING_UPDATE_COUNT value which is an Integer. The provisioning prefix is reserved for keys defined by OSGi, other key names may be used for implementation dependent provisioning systems.

Any changes to the provisioning information will be reflected immediately in all the dictionary objects obtained from the Provisioning Service.

Because of the specific application of the Provisioning Service, there should be only one Provisioning Service registered. This restriction will not be enforced by the Framework. Gateway operators or manufactures should ensure that a Provisioning Service bundle is not installed on a device that already has a bundle providing the Provisioning Service.

The provisioning information has the potential to contain sensitive information. Also, the ability to modify provisioning information can have drastic consequences. Thus, only trusted bundles should be allowed to register and get the Provisioning Service. The ServicePermission is used to limit the bundles that can gain access to the Provisioning Service. There is no check of Permission objects to read or modify the provisioning information, so care must be taken not to leak the Provisioning Dictionary received from getInformation method.

110.11.1.1   **public static final String INITIALPROVISIONING_ENTRIES = "InitialProvisioning-Entries"**

Name of the header that specifies the type information for the ZIP file entries.

Since 1.2

110.11.1.2   **public static final String MIME_BUNDLE = "application/vnd.osgi.bundle"**

MIME type to be stored in the extra field of a ZipEntry object for an installable bundle file. Zip entries of this type will be installed in the framework, but not started. The entry will also not be put into the information dictionary.

110.11.1.3   **public static final String MIME_BUNDLE_ALT = "application/x-osgi-bundle"**

Alternative MIME type to be stored in the extra field of a ZipEntry object for an installable bundle file. Zip entries of this type will be installed in the framework, but not started. The entry will also not be put into the information dictionary. This alternative entry is only for backward compatibility, new applications are recommended to use MIME_BUNDLE, which is an official IANA MIME type.

Since 1.2

110.11.1.4   **public static final String MIME_BUNDLE_URL = "text/x-osgi-bundle-url"**

MIME type to be stored in the extra field of a ZipEntry for a String that represents a URL for a bundle. Zip entries of this type will be used to install (but not start) a bundle from the URL. The entry will not be put into the information dictionary.

110.11.1.5   **public static final String MIME_BYTE_ARRAY = "application/octet-stream"**

MIME type to be stored stored in the extra field of a ZipEntry object for byte[] data.

110.11.1.6   **public static final String MIME_STRING = "text/plain;charset=utf-8"**

MIME type to be stored in the extra field of a ZipEntry object for String data.

110.11.1.7   **public static final String PROVISIONING_AGENT_CONFIG = "provisioning.agent.config"**

The key to the provisioning information that contains the initial configuration information of the initial Management Agent. The value will be of type byte[].

110.11.1.8   **public static final String PROVISIONING_REFERENCE = "provisioning.reference"**

The key to the provisioning information that contains the location of the provision data provider. The value must be of type String.

110.11.1.9   **public static final String PROVISIONING_ROOTX509 = "provisioning.rootx509"**

The key to the provisioning information that contains the root X509 certificate used to establish trust with operator when using HTTPS.

110.11.1.10   **public static final String PROVISIONING_RSH_SECRET = "provisioning.rsh.secret"**

The key to the provisioning information that contains the shared secret used in conjunction with the RSH protocol.

110.11.1.11   **public static final String PROVISIONING_SPID = "provisioning.spid"**

The key to the provisioning information that uniquely identifies the Service Platform. The value must be of type String.

110.11.1.12   **public static final String PROVISIONING_START_BUNDLE = "provisioning.start.bundle"**

The key to the provisioning information that contains the location of the bundle to start with AllPermission. The bundle must have be previously installed for this entry to have any effect.

110.11.1.13   **public static final String PROVISIONING_UPDATE_COUNT = "provisioning.update.count"**

The key to the provisioning information that contains the update count of the info data. Each set of changes to the provisioning information must end with this value being incremented. The value must be of type Integer. This key/value pair is also reflected in the properties of the ProvisioningService in the service registry.

110.11.1.14   **public void addInformation(Dictionary info)**

info   the set of Provisioning Information key/value pairs to add to the Provisioning Information dictionary. Any keys are values that are of an invalid type will be silently ignored.

☐   Adds the key/value pairs contained in info to the Provisioning Information dictionary. This method causes the PROVISIONING_UPDATE_COUNT to be incremented.

110.11.1.15   **public void addInformation(ZipInputStream zis) throws IOException**

zis   the ZipInputStream that will be used to add key/value pairs to the Provisioning Information dictionary and install and start bundles. If a ZipEntry does not have an Extra field that corresponds to one of the four defined MIME types (MIME_STRING, MIME_BYTE_ARRAY,MIME_BUNDLE, and MIME_BUNDLE_URL) in will be silently ignored.

☐   Processes the ZipInputStream and extracts information to add to the Provisioning Information dictionary, as well as, install/update and start bundles. This method causes the PROVISIONING_UPDATE_COUNT to be incremented.

Throws   IOException – if an error occurs while processing the ZipInputStream. No additions will be made to the Provisioning Information dictionary and no bundles must be started or installed.

110.11.1.16   **public Dictionary getInformation( )**

☐   Returns a reference to the Provisioning Dictionary. Any change operations (put and remove) to the dictionary will cause an UnsupportedOperationException to be thrown. Changes must be done using the setInformation and addInformation methods of this service.

Returns   A reference to the Provisioning Dictionary.

110.11.1.17   **public void setInformation(Dictionary info)**

info   the new set of Provisioning Information key/value pairs. Any keys are values that are of an invalid type will be silently ignored.

☐   Replaces the Provisioning Information dictionary with the key/value pairs contained in info. Any key/value pairs not in info will be removed from the Provisioning Information dictionary. This method causes the PROVISIONING_UPDATE_COUNT to be incremented.

110.12   References

[1]   *HMAC:* Keyed-Hashing for Message Authentication
      http://www.ietf.org/rfc/rfc2104.txt Krawczyk ,et. al. 1997.

[2] *NIST, FIPS PUB 180-1: Secure Hash Standard, April 1995.*

[3] *Hypertext Transfer Protocol - HTTP/1.1*
http://www.ietf.org/rfc/rfc2616.txt *Fielding, R., et. al.*

[4] *Rescorla, E., HTTP over TLS, IETF RFC 2818, May 2000*
http://www.ietf.org/rfc/rfc2818.txt.

[5] *ZIP Archive format*
ftp://ftp.uu.net/pub/archiving/zip/doc/appnote-970311-iz.zip

[6] *RFC 2396 - Uniform Resource Identifier (URI)*
http://www.ietf.org/rfc/rfc2396.txt

[7] *MIME Types*
http://www.ietf.org/rfc/rfc2046.txt and http://www.iana.org/assignments/media-types

[8] *3DES*
W/ Tuchman, "Hellman Presents No Shortcut Solution to DES," IEEE Spectrum, v. 16, n. 7 July 1979, pp40-41.

[9] *RFC 1423 Part III: Algorithms, Modes, and Identifiers*
http://www.ietf.org/rfc/rfc1423.txt

[10] *PKCS 5*
ftp://ftp.rsasecurity.com/pub/pkcs/pkcs-5v2

[11] *Java Cryptography API (part of Java 1.4)*
http://java.sun.com/javase/technologies/security/

[12] *SHA-1*
U.S. Government, Proposed Federal Information Processing Standard for Secure Hash Standard, January 1992

[13] *Transport Layer Security*
http://www.ietf.org/rfc/rfc2246.txt, January 1999, The TLS Protocol Version 1.0, T. Dierks & C. Allen.

112   Declarative Services Specification

Version 1.1

112.1   Introduction

The OSGi Framework contains a procedural service model which provides a publish/find/bind model for using *services*. This model is elegant and powerful, it enables the building of applications out of bundles that communicate and collaborate using these services.

This specification addresses some of the complications that arise when the OSGi service model is used for larger systems and wider deployments, such as:

- *Startup Time* – The procedural service model requires a bundle to actively register and acquire its services. This is normally done at startup time, requiring all present bundles to be initialized with a Bundle Activator. In larger systems, this quickly results in unacceptably long startup times.
- *Memory Footprint* – A service registered with the Framework implies that the implementation, and related classes and objects, are loaded in memory. If the service is never used, this memory is unnecessarily occupied. The creation of a class loader may therefore cause significant overhead.
- *Complexity* – Service can come and go at any time. This dynamic behavior makes the service programming model more complex than more traditional models. This complexity negatively influences the adoption of the OSGi service model as well as the robustness and reliability of applications because these applications do not always handle the dynamicity correctly.

The *service component* model uses a declarative model for publishing, finding and binding to OSGi services. This model simplifies the task of authoring OSGi services by performing the work of registering the service and handling service dependencies. This minimizes the amount of code a programmer has to write; it also allows service components to be loaded only when they are needed. As a result, bundles need not provide a `BundleActivator` class to collaborate with others through the service registry.

From a system perspective, the service component model means reduced startup time and potentially a reduction of the memory footprint. From a programmer's point of view the service component model provides a simplified programming model.

The Service Component model makes use of concepts described in [1] *Automating Service Dependency Management in a Service-Oriented Component Model*.

112.1.1   Essentials

- *Backward Compatibility* – The service component model must operate seamlessly with the existing service model.
- *Size Constraints* – The service component model must not require memory and performance intensive subsystems. The model must also be applicable on resource constrained devices.
- *Delayed Activation* – The service component model must allow delayed activation of a service component. Delayed activation allows for delayed class loading and object creation until needed, thereby reducing the overall memory footprint.
- *Simplicity* – The programming model for using declarative services must be very simple and not require the programmer to learn a complicated API or XML sub-language.

112.1.2   Entities

- *Service Component* – A service component contains a description that is interpreted at run time to create and dispose objects depending on the availability of other services, the need for such an object, and available configuration data. Such objects can optionally provide a service. This specification also uses the generic term *component* to refer to a service component.
- *Component Description* – The declaration of a service component. It is contained within an XML document in a bundle.
- *Component Properties* – A set of properties which can be specified by the component description, Configuration Admin service and from the component factory.
- *Component Configuration* – A component configuration represents a component description parameterized by component properties. It is the entity that tracks the component dependencies and manages a component instance. An activated component configuration has a component context.
- *Component Instance* – An instance of the component implementation class. A component instance is created when a component configuration is activated and discarded when the component configuration is deactivated. A component instance is associated with exactly one component configuration.
- *Delayed Component* – A component whose component configurations are activated when their service is requested.
- *Immediate Component* – A component whose component configurations are activated immediately upon becoming satisfied.
- *Factory Component* – A component whose component configurations are created and activated through the component's component factory.
- *Reference* – A specified dependency of a component on a set of target services.
- *Service Component Runtime (SCR)* – The actor that manages the components and their life cycle.
- *Target Services* – The set of services that is defined by the reference interface and target property filter.
- *Bound Services* – The set of target services that are bound to a component configuration.

Figure 112.1   *Service Component Runtime, org.osgi.service.component package*

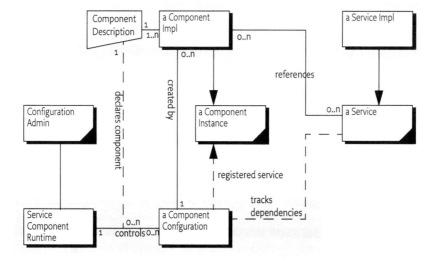

112.1.3   Synopsis

The Service Component Runtime reads component descriptions from started bundles. These descriptions are in the form of XML documents which define a set of components for a bundle. A component can refer to a number of services that must be available before a component configuration becomes satisfied. These dependencies are defined in the descriptions and the specific target services can be influenced by configuration information in the Configuration Admin service. After a component configuration becomes satisfied, a number of different scenarios can take place depending on the component type:

- *Immediate Component* – The component configuration of an immediate component must be activated immediately after becoming satisfied. Immediate components may provide a service.
- *Delayed Component* – When a component configuration of a delayed component becomes satisfied, SCR will register the service specified by the service element without activating the component configuration. If this service is requested, SCR must activate the component configuration creating an instance of the component implementation class that will be returned as the service object. If the servicefactory attribute of the service element is true, then, for each distinct bundle that requests the service, a different component configuration is created and activated and a new instance of the component implementation class is returned as the service object.
- *Factory Component* – If a component's description specifies the factory attribute of the component element, SCR will register a Component Factory service. This service allows client bundles to create and activate multiple component configurations and dispose of them. If the component's description also specifies a service element, then as each component configuration is activated, SCR will register it as a service.

112.1.4   Readers

- *Architects* – The chapter, *Components* on page 143, gives a comprehensive introduction to the capabilities of the component model. It explains the model with a number of examples. The section about *Component Life Cycle* on page 156 provides some deeper insight in the life cycle of components.
- *Service Programmers* – Service programmers should read *Components* on page 143. This chapter should suffice for the most common cases. For the more advanced possibilities, they should consult *Component Description* on page 151 for the details of the XML grammar for component descriptions.
- *Deployers* – Deployers should consult *Deployment* on page 165.

112.2   Components

A component is a normal Java class contained within a bundle. The distinguishing aspect of a component is that it is *declared* in an XML document. Component configurations are activated and deactivated under the full control of SCR. SCR bases its decisions on the information in the component's description. This information consists of basic component information like the name and type, optional services that are implemented by the component, and *references*. References are dependencies that the component has on other services.

SCR must *activate* a component configuration when the component is enabled and the component configuration is satisfied and a component configuration is needed. During the life time of a component configuration, SCR can notify the component of changes in its bound references.

SCR will *deactivate* a previously activated component configuration when the component becomes disabled, the component configuration becomes unsatisfied, or the component configuration is no longer needed.

If an activated component configuration's configuration properties change, SCR must deactivate the component configuration and then attempt to reactivate the component configuration using the new configuration information.

112.2.1 Declaring a Component

A component requires the following artifacts in the bundle:

- An XML document that contains the component description.
- The Service-Component manifest header which names the XML documents that contain the component descriptions.
- An implementation class that is specified in the component description.

The elements in the component's description are defined in *Component Description* on page 151. The XML grammar for the component declaration is defined by the XML Schema, see *Component Description Schema* on page 168.

112.2.2 Immediate Component

An *immediate component* is activated as soon as its dependencies are satisfied. If an immediate component has no dependencies, it is activated immediately. A component is an immediate component if it is not a factory component and either does not specify a service or specifies a service and the immediate attribute of the component element set to true. If an immediate component configuration is satisfied and specifies a service, SCR must register the component configuration as a service in the service registry and then activate the component configuration.

For example, the bundle entry /OSGI-INF/activator.xml contains:

```
<xml version="1.0" encoding="UTF-8">
<scr:component name="example.activator"
   xmlns:scr="http://www.osgi.org/xmlns/scr/v1.1.0">
   <implementation class="com.acme.Activator"/>
</scr:component>
```

The manifest header Service-Component must also be specified in the bundle manifest. For example:

```
Service-Component: OSGI-INF/activator.xml
```

An example class for this component could look like:

```
public class Activator {
   public Activator() {...}
   private void activate(BundleContext context) {...}
   private void deactivate() {...}
}
```

This example component is virtually identical to a Bundle Activator. It has no references to other services so it will be satisfied immediately. It publishes no service so SCR will activate a component configuration immediately.

The activate method is called when SCR activates the component configuration and the deactivate method is called when SCR deactivates the component configuration. If the activate method throws an Exception, then the component configuration is not activated and will be discarded.

112.2.3 Delayed Component

A *delayed component* specifies a service, is not specified to be a factory component and does not have the immediate attribute of the component element set to true. If a delayed component configuration is satisfied, SCR must register the component configuration as a service in the service registry but the activation of the component configuration is delayed until the registered service is requested. The registered service of a delayed component look like on normal registered service but does not incur the overhead of an ordinarily registered service that require a service's bundle to be initialized to register the service.

For example, a bundle needs to see events of a specific topic. The Event Admin uses the white board pattern, receiving the events is therefore as simple as registering a Event Handler service. The example XML for the delayed component looks like:

```
<xml version="1.0" encoding="UTF-8">
<scr:component name="example.handler"
  xmlns:scr="http://www.osgi.org/xmlns/scr/v1.1.0">
  <implementation class="com.acme.HandlerImpl"/>
  <property name="event.topics">some/topic</property>
  <service>
     <provide interface=
        "org.osgi.service.event.EventHandler"/>
  </service>
<scr:component>
```

The associated component class looks like:

```
public class HandlerImpl implements EventHandler {
  public void handleEvent(Event evt ) {
     ...
  }
}
```

The component configuration will only be activated once the Event Admin service requires the service because it has an event to deliver on the topic to which the component subscribed.

112.2.4   Factory Component

Certain software patterns require the creation of component configurations on demand. For example, a component could represent an application that can be launched multiple times and each application instance can then quit independently. Such a pattern requires a factory that creates the instances. This pattern is supported with a *factory component*. A factory component is used if the factory attribute of the component element is set to a *factory identifier*. This identifier can be used by a bundle to associate the factory with externally defined information.

SCR must register a Component Factory service on behalf of the component as soon as the component factory is satisfied. The service properties must be:

- component.name – The name of the component.
- component.factory – The factory identifier.

The service properties of the Component Factory service must not include the component properties.

New configurations of the component can be created and activated by calling the newInstance method on this Component Factory service. The newInstance(Dictionary) method has a Dictionary object as argument. This Dictionary object is merged with the component properties as described in *Component Properties* on page 164. If the component specifies a service, then the service is registered after the created component configuration is satisfied with the component properties. Then the component configuration is activated.

For example, a component can provide a connection to a USB device. Such a connection should normally not be shared and should be created each time such a service is needed. The component description to implement this pattern looks like:

```
<xml version="1.0" encoding="UTF-8">
<scr:component name="example.factory"
  factory="usb.connection"
  xmlns:scr="http://www.osgi.org/xmlns/scr/v1.1.0">
  <implementation class="com.acme.USBConnectionImpl"/>
</scr:component>
```

The component class looks like:

```
public class USBConnectionImpl implements USBConnection {
    private void activate(Map properties) {
        ...
    }
}
```

A factory component can be associated with a service. In that case, such a service is registered for each component configuration. For example, the previous example could provide a USB Connection service.

```
<xml version="1.0" encoding="UTF-8">
<scr:component name="example.factory"
    factory="usb.connection"
    xmlns:scr="http://www.osgi.org/xmlns/scr/v1.1.0">
    <implementation class="com.acme.USBConnectionImpl"/>
    <service>
        <provide interface="com.acme.USBConnection"/>
    </service>
</scr:component>
```

The associated component class looks like:

```
public class USBConnectionImpl implements USBConnection {
    private void activate(Map properties) {...}
    public void connect() { ... }
    ...
    public void close() { ... }
}
```

A new service will be registered each time a new component configuration is created and activated with the newInstance method. This allows a bundle other than the one creating the component configuration to utilize the service. If the component configuration is deactivated, the service must be unregistered.

112.3 References to Services

Most bundles will require access to other services from the service registry. The dynamics of the service registry require care and attention of the programmer because referenced services, once acquired, could be unregistered at any moment. The component model simplifies the handling of these service dependencies significantly.

The services that are selected by a reference are called the *target services*. These are the services selected by the BundleContext.getServiceReferences method where the first argument is the reference's interface and the second argument is the reference's target property, which must be a valid filter.

A component configuration becomes *satisfied* when each specified reference is satisfied. A reference is *satisfied* if it specifies optional cardinality or when the target services contains at least one member. An activated component configuration that becomes *unsatisfied* must be deactivated.

During the activation of a component configuration, SCR must bind some or all of the target services of a reference to the component configuration. Any target service that is bound to the component configuration is called a *bound* service. See *Binding Services* on page 160.

112.3.1   Accessing Services

A component instance must be able to use the services that are referenced by the component configuration, that is, the bound services of the references. There are two strategies for a component instance to acquire these bound services:

- *Event strategy* – SCR calls a method on the component instance when a service becomes bound and another method when a service becomes unbound. These methods are the bind and unbind methods specified by the reference. The event strategy is useful if the component needs to be notified of changes to the bound services for a dynamic reference.
- *Lookup strategy* – A component instance can use one of the locateService methods of Component-Context to locate a bound service. These methods take the name of the reference as a parameter. If the reference has a dynamic policy, it is important to not store the returned service object(s) but look it up every time it is needed.

A component may use either or both strategies to access bound services.

When using the event strategy, the bind and unbind methods must have one of the following prototypes:

```
void <method-name>(ServiceReference);
void <method-name>(<parameter-type>);
void <method-name>(<parameter-type>, Map);
```

If the bind or unbind method has the first prototype, then a Service Reference to the bound service will be passed to the method. This Service Reference may later be passed to the locateService(String, ServiceReference) method to obtain the actual service object. This approach is useful when the service properties need to be examined before accessing the service object. It also allows for the delayed activation of bound services when using the event strategy.

If the bind or unbind method has the second prototype, then the service object of the bound service is passed to the method. The method's parameter type must be assignable from the type specified by the reference's interface attribute. That is, the service object of the bound service must be castable to the method's parameter type.

If the bind or unbind method has the third prototype, then the service object of the bound service is passed to the method as the first argument and an unmodifiable Map containing the service properties of the bound service is passed as the second argument. The method's first parameter type must be assignable from the type specified by the reference's interface attribute. That is, the service object of the bound service must be castable to the method's first parameter type.

The methods must be called once for each bound service. This implies that if the reference has multiple cardinality, then the methods may be called multiple times.

A suitable method is selected using the following priority:

1 The method takes a single argument and the type of the argument is
   org.osgi.framework.ServiceReference.
2 The method takes a single argument and the type of the argument is the type specified by the reference's interface attribute.
3 The method takes a single argument and the type of the argument is assignable from the type specified by the reference's interface attribute. If multiple methods match this rule, this implies the method name is overloaded and SCR may choose any of the methods to call.
4 The method takes two argument and the type of the first argument is the type specified by the reference's interface attribute and the type of the second argument is java.util.Map.
5 The method takes two argument and the type of the first argument is assignable from the type specified by the reference's interface attribute and the type of the second argument is java.util.Map. If multiple methods match this rule, this implies the method name is overloaded and SCR may choose any of the methods to call.

When searching for the bind or unbind method to call, SCR must locate a suitable method as specified in *Locating Component Methods* on page 167. If no suitable method is located, SCR must log an error message with the Log Service, if present, and there will be no bind or unbind notification.

When the service object for a bound service is first provided to a component instance, that is passed to a bind or unbind method or returned by a locate service method, SCR must get the service object from the OSGi Framework's service registry using the getService method on the component's Bundle Context. If the service object for a bound service has been obtained and the service becomes unbound, SCR must unget the service object using the ungetService method on the component's Bundle Context and discard all references to the service object.

For example, a component requires the Log Service and uses the lookup strategy. The reference is declared without any bind and unbind methods:

```
<xml version="1.0" encoding="UTF-8">
<scr:component name="example.listen"
    xmlns:scr="http://www.osgi.org/xmlns/scr/v1.1.0">
    <implementation class="com.acme.LogLookupImpl"/>
    <reference name="LOG"
        interface="org.osgi.service.log.LogService"/>
</scr:component>
```

The component implementation class must now lookup the service. This looks like:

```
public class LogLookupImpl {
    private void activate(ComponentContext ctxt) {
        LogService log = (LogService)
            ctxt.locateService("LOG");
        log.log(LogService.LOG_INFO, "Hello Components!"));
    }
}
```

Alternatively, the component could use the event strategy and ask to be notified with the Log Service by declaring bind and unbind methods.

```
<xml version="1.0" encoding="UTF-8">
<scr:component name="example.listen"
    xmlns:scr="http://www.osgi.org/xmlns/scr/v1.1.0">
    <implementation class="com.acme.LogEventImpl"/>
    <reference name="LOG"
        interface="org.osgi.service.log.LogService"
        bind="setLog"
        unbind="unsetLog"
    />
</scr:component>
```

The component implementation class looks like:

```
public class LogEventImpl {
    private LogService log;
    private void setLog( LogService l ) { log = l; }
    private void unsetLog( LogService l ) { log = null; }
    private void activate() {
        log.log(LogService.LOG_INFO, "Hello Components!"));
    }
}
```

112.3.2   Reference Cardinality

A component implementation is always written with a certain *cardinality* in mind. The cardinality represents two important concepts:

- *Multiplicity* – Does the component implementation assume a single service or does it explicitly handle multiple occurrences For example, when a component uses the Log Service, it only needs to bind to one Log Service to function correctly. Alternatively, when the Configuration Admin uses the Configuration Listener services it needs to bind to all target services present in the service registry to dispatch its events correctly.
- *Optionality* – Can the component function without any bound service present Some components can still perform useful tasks even when no target service is available, other components must bind to at least one target service before they can be useful. For example, the Configuration Admin in the previous example must still provide its functionality even if there are no Configuration Listener services present. Alternatively, an application that solely presents a Servlet page has little to do when the Http Service is not present, it should therefore use a reference with a mandatory cardinality.

The cardinality is expressed with the following syntax:

```
cardinality  ::= optionality '..' multiplicity
optionality  ::= '0' | '1'
multiplicity ::= '1' | 'n'
```

A reference is *satisfied* if the number of target services is equal to or more than the optionality. The multiplicity is irrelevant for the satisfaction of the reference. The multiplicity only specifies if the component implementation is written to handle being bound to multiple services (n) or requires SCR to select and bind to a single service (1).

The cardinality for a reference can be specified as one of four choices:

- 0..1 – Optional and unary.
- 1..1 – Mandatory and unary (Default) .
- 0..n – Optional and multiple.
- 1..n – Mandatory and multiple.

When a satisfied component configuration is activated, there must be at most one bound service for each reference with a unary cardinality and at least one bound service for each reference with a mandatory cardinality. If the cardinality constraints cannot be maintained after a component configuration is activated, that is the reference becomes unsatisfied, the component configuration must be deactivated. If the reference has a unary cardinality and there is more than one target service for the reference, then the bound service must be the target service with the highest service ranking as specified by the service.ranking property. If there are multiple target services with the same service ranking, then the bound service must be the target service with the highest service ranking and the lowest service ID as specified by the service.id property.

For example, a component wants to register a resource with all Http Services that are available. Such a scenario has the cardinality of 0..n. The code must be prepared to handle multiple calls to the bind method for each Http Service in such a case. In this example, the code uses the registerResources method to register a directory for external access.

```
<xml version="1.0" encoding="UTF-8">
<scr:component name="example.listen"
   xmlns:scr="http://www.osgi.org/xmlns/scr/v1.1.0">
   <implementation class="com.acme.HttpResourceImpl"/>
   <reference name="HTTP"
      interface="org.osgi.service.http.HttpService"
      cardinality="0..n"
      bind="setPage"
      unbind="unsetPage"
```

```
      / >
   </scr:component>

   public class HttpResourceImpl {
      private void setPage(HttpService http) {
         http.registerResources("/scr", "scr", null );
      }
      private void unsetPage(HttpService http) {
         http.unregister("/scr");
      }
   }
```

112.3.3 Reference Policy

Once all the references of a component are satisfied, a component configuration can be activated and therefore bound to target services. However, the dynamic nature of the OSGi service registry makes it likely that services are registered, modified and unregistered after target services are bound. These changes in the service registry could make one or more bound services no longer a target service thereby making obsolete any object references that the component has to these service objects. Components therefore must specify a *policy* how to handle these changes in the set of bound services.

The *static policy* is the most simple policy and is the default policy. A component instance never sees any of the dynamics. Component configurations are deactivated before any bound service for a reference having a static policy becomes unavailable. If a target service is available to replace the bound service which became unavailable, the component configuration must be reactivated and bound to the replacement service. A reference with a static policy is called a *static reference.*

The static policy can be very expensive if it depends on services that frequently unregister and re-register or if the cost of activating and deactivating a component configuration is high. Static policy is usually also not applicable if the cardinality specifies multiple bound services.

The *dynamic policy* is slightly more complex since the component implementation must properly handle changes in the set of bound services. With the dynamic policy, SCR can change the set of bound services without deactivating a component configuration. If the component uses the event strategy to access services, then the component instance will be notified of changes in the set of bound services by calls to the bind and unbind methods. A reference with a dynamic policy is called a *dynamic reference.*

The previous example with the registering of a resource directory used a static policy. This implied that the component configurations are deactivated when there is a change in the bound set of Http Services. The code in the example can be seen to easily handle the dynamics of Http Services that come and go. The component description can therefore be updated to:

```
   <xml version="1.0" encoding="UTF-8">
   <scr:component name="example.listen"
      xmlns:scr="http://www.osgi.org/xmlns/scr/v1.1.0">
      <implementation class="com.acme.HttpResourceImpl"/>
      <reference name="HTTP"
         interface="org.osgi.service.http.HttpService"
         cardinality="0..n"
         policy="dynamic"
         bind="setPage"
         unbind="unsetPage"
      / >
   </scr:component>
```

The code is identical to the previous example.

112.3.4 ## Selecting Target Services

The target services for a reference are constrained by the reference's interface name and target property. By specifying a filter in the target property, the programmer and deployer can constrain the set of services that should be part of the target services.

For example, a component wants to track all Component Factory services that have a factory identification of acme.application. The following component description shows how this can be done.

```
<xml version="1.0" encoding="UTF-8">
<scr:component name="example.listen"
   xmlns:scr="http://www.osgi.org/xmlns/scr/v1.1.0">
   <implementation class="com.acme.FactoryTracker"/>
   <reference name="FACTORY"
      interface=
         "org.osgi.service.component.ComponentFactory"
      target="(component.factory=acme.application)"
   />
</scr:component>
```

The filter is manifested as a component property called the *target property*. The target property can also be set by property and properties elements, see *Properties and Property Elements* on page 154. The deployer can also set the target property by establishing a configuration for the component which sets the value of the target property. This allows the deployer to override the target property in the component description. See *Component Properties* on page 164 for more information.

112.3.5 ## Circular References

It is possible for a set of component descriptions to create a circular dependency. For example, if component A references a service provided by component B and component B references a service provided by component A then a component configuration of one component cannot be satisfied without accessing a partially activated component instance of the other component. SCR must ensure that a component instance is never accessible to another component instance or as a service until it has been fully activated, that is it has returned from its activate method if it has one.

Circular references must be detected by SCR when it attempts to satisfy component configurations and SCR must fail to satisfy the references involved in the cycle and log an error message with the Log Service, if present. However, if one of the references in the cycle has optional cardinality SCR must break the cycle. The reference with the optional cardinality can be satisfied and bound to zero target services. Therefore the cycle is broken and the other references may be satisfied.

112.4 Component Description

Component descriptions are defined in XML documents contained in a bundle and any attached fragments.

If SCR detects an error when processing a component description, it must log an error message with the Log Service, if present, and ignore the component description. Errors can include XML parsing errors and ill-formed component descriptions.

112.4.1 ## Service Component Header

XML documents containing component descriptions must be specified by the Service-Component header in the manifest. The value of the header is a comma separated list of paths to XML entries within the bundle.

```
Service-Component ::= header // 3.2.4
```

The Service-Component header has no architected directives or properties.

The last component of each path in the Service-Component header may use wildcards so that `Bundle.findEntries` can be used to locate the XML document within the bundle and its fragments. For example:

```
Service-Component: OSGI-INF/*.xml
```

A Service-Component manifest header specified in a fragment is ignored by SCR. However, XML documents referenced by a bundle's Service-Component manifest header may be contained in attached fragments.

SCR must process each XML document specified in this header. If an XML document specified by the header cannot be located in the bundle and its attached fragments, SCR must log an error message with the Log Service, if present, and continue.

112.4.2　XML Document

A component description must be in a well-formed XML document [4] stored in a UTF-8 encoded bundle entry. The namespace for component descriptions is:

```
http://www.osgi.org/xmlns/scr/v1.1.0
```

The recommended prefix for this namespace is scr. This prefix is used by examples in this specification. XML documents containing component descriptions may contain a single, root component element or one or more component elements embedded in a larger document. Use of the namespace for component descriptions is mandatory. The attributes and sub-elements of a component element are always unqualified.

If an XML document contains a single, root component element which does not specify a namespace, then the http://www.osgi.org/xmlns/scr/v1.0.0 namespace is assumed. Component descriptions using the http://www.osgi.org/xmlns/scr/v1.0.0 namespace must be treated according to version 1.0 of this specification.

SCR must parse all component elements in the namespace. Elements not in this namespace must be ignored. Ignoring elements that are not recognized allows component descriptions to be embedded in any XML document. For example, an entry can provide additional information about components. These additional elements are parsed by another sub-system.

See *Component Description Schema* on page 168 for component description schema.

112.4.3　Component Element

The component element specifies the component description. The following text defines the structure of the XML grammar using a form that is similar to the normal grammar used in OSGi specifications. In this case the grammar should be mapped to XML elements:

```
<component>         ::= <implementation>
                        <properties> *
                        <service>
                        <reference> *
```

SCR must not require component descriptions to specify the elements in the order listed above and as required by the XML schema. SCR must allow other orderings since arbitrary orderings of these elements do not affect the meaning of the component description. Only the relative ordering of property and properties element have meaning.

The component element has the following attributes:

- name – The *name* of a component must be unique within a bundle. The component name is used as a PID to retrieve component properties from the OSGi Configuration Admin service if present. See *Deployment* on page 165 for more information. Since the component name is used as a PID, it should be unique within the framework. The XML schema allows the use of component names which are not valid PIDs. Care must be taken to use a valid PID for a component name if the component should be configured by the Configuration Admin service. This attribute is optional. The default value of this attribute is the value of the class attribute of the nested implementation element. If multiple component elements in a bundle use the same value for the class attribute of their nested implementation element, then using the default value for this attribute will result in duplicate component names. In this case, this attribute must be specified with a unique value.

- enabled – Controls whether the component is *enabled* when the bundle is started. The default value is true. If enabled is set to false, the component is disabled until the method enableComponent is called on the ComponentContext object. This allows some initialization to be performed by some other component in the bundle before this component can become satisfied. See *Enabled* on page 156.

- factory – If set to a non-empty string, it indicates that this component is a *factory component*. SCR must register a Component Factory service for each factory component. See *Factory Component* on page 145.

- immediate – Controls whether component configurations must be immediately activated after becoming satisfied or whether activation should be delayed. The default value is false if the factory attribute or if the service element is specified and true otherwise. If this attribute is specified, its value must be false if the factory attribute is also specified or must be true unless the service element is also specified.

- configuration-policy – Controls whether component configurations must be satisfied depending on the presence of a corresponding Configuration object in the OSGi Configuration Admin service. A corresponding configuration is a Configuration object where the PID is the name of the component.
  - optional – (default) Use the corresponding Configuration object if present but allow the component to be satisfied even if the corresponding Configuration object is not present.
  - require – There must be a corresponding Configuration object for the component configuration to become satisfied.
  - ignore – Always allow the component configuration to be satisfied and do not use the corresponding Configuration object even if it is present.

- activate – Specifies the name of the method to call when a component configuration is activated. The default value of this attribute is activate. See *Activate Method* on page 160 for more information.

- deactivate – Specifies the name of the method to call when a component configuration is deactivated. The default value of this attribute is deactivate. See *Deactivate Method* on page 162 for more information.

- modified – Specifies the name of the method to call when the configuration properties for a component configuration is using a Configuration object from the Configuration Admin service and that Configuration object is modified without causing the component configuration to become unsatisfied. If this attribute is not specified, then the component configuration will become unsatisfied if its configuration properties use a Configuration object that is modified in any way. See *Modified Method* on page 161 for more information.

112.4.4   Implementation Element

The implementation element is required and defines the name of the component implementation class. It has therefore only a single attribute:

- class – The Java fully qualified name of the implementation class.

The class is retrieved with the loadClass method of the component's bundle. The class must be public and have a public constructor without arguments (this is normally the default constructor) so component instances may be created by SCR with the newInstance method on Class.

If the component description specifies a service, the class must implement all interfaces that are provided by the service.

112.4.5   **Properties and Property Elements**

A component description can define a number of properties. There are two different elements for this:

- property – Defines a single property.
- properties – Reads a set of properties from a bundle entry.

The property and properties elements can occur multiple times and they can be interleaved. This interleaving is relevant because the properties are processed from top to bottom. Later properties override earlier properties that have the same name.

Properties can also be overridden by a Configuration Admin service's Configuration object before they are exposed to the component or used as service properties. This is described in *Component Properties* on page 164 and *Deployment* on page 165.

The property element has the following attributes:

- name – The name of the property.
- value – The value of the property. This value is parsed according to the property type. If the value attribute is specified, the body of the element is ignored. If the type of the property is not String, parsing of the value is done by the valueOf(String) method. If this method is not available for the given type, the conversion must be done according to the corresponding method in Java 2 SE. For Character types, the conversion is handled by Integer.valueOf method.
- type – The type of the property. Defines how to interpret the value. The type must be one of the following Java types:
    - String (default)
    - Long
    - Double
    - Float
    - Integer
    - Byte
    - Character
    - Boolean
    - Short
- element body – If the value attribute is not specified, the body of the property element must contain one or more values. The value of the property is then an array of the specified type. Except for String objects, the result will be translated to an array of primitive types. For example, if the type attribute specifies Integer, then the resulting array must be int[].
  Values must be placed one per line and blank lines are ignored. Parsing of the value is done by the parse methods in the class identified by the type, after trimming the line of any beginning and ending white space. String values are also trimmed of beginning and ending white space before being placed in the array.

For example, a component that needs an array of hosts can use the following property definition:

```
<property name="hosts">
    www.acme.com
    backup.acme.com
</property>
```

This property declaration results in the property hosts, with a value of String[] { "www.acme.com", "backup.acme.com" }.

The properties element references an entry in the bundle whose contents conform to a standard [3] *Java Properties File.*

The entry is read and processed to obtain the properties and their values. The properties element has the following attributes:

- entry – The entry path relative to the root of the bundle

For example, to include vendor identification properties that are stored in the OSGI-INF directory, the following definition could be used:

```
<properties entry="OSGI-INF/vendor.properties" />
```

112.4.6   Service Element

The service element is optional. It describes the service information to be used when a component configuration is to be registered as a service.

A service element has the following attribute:

- servicefactory – Controls whether the service uses the ServiceFactory concept of the OSGi Framework. The default value is false. If servicefactory is set to true, a different component configuration is created, activated and its component instance returned as the service object for each distinct bundle that requests the service. Each of these component configurations has the same component properties. Otherwise, the same component instance from the single component configuration is returned as the service object for all bundles that request the service.

The servicefactory attribute must not be true if the component is a factory component or an immediate component. This is because SCR is not free to create component configurations as necessary to support servicefactory. A component description is ill-formed if it specifies that the component is a factory component or an immediate component and servicefactory is set to true.

The service element must have one or more provide elements that define the service interfaces. The provide element has a single attribute:

- interface – The name of the interface that this service is registered under. This name must be the fully qualified name of a Java class. For example, org.osgi.service.log.LogService. The specified Java class should be an interface rather than a class, however specifying a class is supported.

The component implementation class must implement all the specified service interfaces.

For example, a component implements an Event Handler service.

```
<service>
   <provide interface=
      "org.osgi.service.eventadmin.EventHandler"/>
</service>
```

112.4.7   Reference Element

A *reference* declares a dependency that a component has on a set of target services. A component configuration is not satisfied, unless all its references are satisfied. A reference specifies target services by specifying their interface and an optional target filter.

A reference element has the following attributes:

- name – The name of the reference. This name is local to the component and can be used to locate a bound service of this reference with one of the locateService methods of ComponentContext. Each reference element within the component must have a unique name. This name attribute is optional. The default value of this attribute is the value of the interface attribute of this element. If multiple reference elements in the component use the same interface name, then using the default value for this attribute will result in duplicate reference names. In this case, this attribute must be specified with a unique name for the reference to avoid an error.
- interface – Fully qualified name of the class that is used by the component to access the service. The service provided to the component must be type compatible with this class. That is, the component must be able to cast the service object to this class. A service must be registered under this name to be considered for the set of target services.
- cardinality – Specifies if the reference is optional and if the component implementation support a single bound service or multiple bound services. See *Reference Cardinality* on page 149.

- policy – The policy declares the assumption of the component about dynamicity. See *Reference Policy* on page 150.
- target – An optional OSGi Framework filter expression that further constrains the set of target services. The default is no filter, limiting the set of matched services to all service registered under the given reference interface. The value of this attribute is used to set a target property. See *Selecting Target Services* on page 151.
- bind – The name of a method in the component implementation class that is used to notify that a service is bound to the component configuration. For static references, this method is only called before the activate method. For dynamic references, this method can also be called while the component configuration is active. See *Accessing Services* on page 147.
- unbind – Same as bind, but is used to notify the component configuration that the service is unbound. For static references, the method is only called after the deactivate method. For dynamic references, this method can also be called while the component configuration is active. See *Accessing Services* on page 147.

112.5 Component Life Cycle

112.5.1 Enabled

A component must first be *enabled* before it can be used. A component cannot be enabled unless the component's bundle is started. See *Starting Bundles* on page 98 of the Core specification. All components in a bundle become disabled when the bundle is stopped. So the life cycle of a component is contained within the life cycle of its bundle.

Every component can be enabled or disabled. The initial enabled state of a component is specified in the component description via the enabled attribute of the component element. See *Component Element* on page 152. Component configurations can be created, satisfied and activated only when the component is enabled.

The enabled state of a component can be controlled with the Component Context enableComponent(String) and disableComponent(String) methods. The purpose of later enabling a component is to be able to decide programmatically when a component can become enabled. For example, an immediate component can perform some initialization work before other components in the bundle are enabled. The component descriptions of all other components in the bundle can be disabled by having enabled set to false in their component descriptions. After any necessary initialization work is complete, the immediate component can call enableComponent to enable the remaining components.

The enableComponent and disableComponent methods must return after changing the enabled state of the named component. Any actions that result from this, such as activating or deactivating a component configuration, must occur asynchronously to the method call. Therefore a component can disable itself.

All components in a bundle can be enabled by passing a null as the argument to enableComponent.

112.5.2 Satisfied

Component configurations can only be activated when the component configuration is *satisfied*. A component configuration becomes satisfied when the following conditions are all satisfied:

- The component is *enabled*.
- If the component description specifies configuration-policy=required, then a Configuration object for the component is present in the Configuration Admin service.
- Using the component properties of the component configuration, all the component's references are satisfied. A reference is satisfied when the reference specifies optional cardinality or there is at least one target service for the reference.

Once any of the listed conditions are no longer true, the component configuration becomes *unsatis-fied*. An activated component configuration that becomes unsatisfied must be deactivated.

112.5.3 Immediate Component

A component is an immediate component when it must be activated as soon as its dependencies are satisfied. Once the component configuration becomes unsatisfied, the component configuration must be deactivated. If an immediate component configuration is satisfied and specifies a service, SCR must register the component configuration as a service in the service registry and then activate the component configuration. The service properties for this registration consist of the component properties as defined in *Service Properties* on page 165.

The state diagram is shown in Figure 112.2.

Figure 112.2   *Immediate Component Configuration*

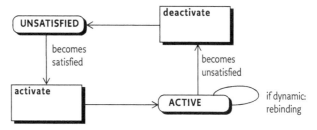

112.5.4 Delayed Component

A key attribute of a delayed component is the delaying of class loading and object creation. Therefore, the activation of a delayed component configuration does not occur until there is an actual request for a service object. A component is a delayed component when it specifies a service but it is not a factory component and does not have the immediate attribute of the component element set to true.

SCR must register a service after the component configuration becomes satisfied. The registration of this service must look to observers of the service registry as if the component's bundle actually registered this service. This strategy makes it possible to register services without creating a class loader for the bundle and loading classes, thereby allowing reduction in initialization time and a delay in memory footprint.

When SCR registers the service on behalf of a component configuration, it must avoid causing a class load to occur from the component's bundle. SCR can ensure this by registering a ServiceFactory object with the Framework for that service. By registering a ServiceFactory object, the actual service object is not needed until the ServiceFactory is called to provide the service object. The service properties for this registration consist of the component properties as defined in *Service Properties* on page 165.

The activation of a component configuration must be delayed until its service is requested. When the service is requested, if the service has the servicefactory attribute set to true, SCR must create and activate a unique component configuration for each bundle requesting the service. Otherwise, SCR must activate a single component configuration which is used by all bundles requesting the service. A component instance can determine the bundle it was activated for by calling the getUsingBundle() method on the Component Context.

The activation of delayed components is depicted in a state diagram in Figure 112.3. Notice that multiple component configurations can be created from the REGISTERED state if a delayed component specifies servicefactory set to true.

If the service registered by a component configuration becomes unused because there are no more bundles using it, then SCR should deactivate that component configuration. This allows SCR implementations to eagerly reclaim activated component configurations.

Figure 112.3   *Delayed Component Configuration*

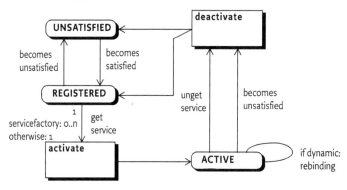

112.5.5   Factory Component

SCR must register a Component Factory service as soon as the *component factory* becomes satisfied. The component factory is satisfied when the following conditions are all satisfied:

- The component is enabled.
- Using the component properties specified by the component description, all the component's references are satisfied. A reference is satisfied when the reference specifies optional cardinality or there is at least one target service for the reference

The component factory, however, does not use any of the target services and does not bind to them.

Once any of the listed conditions are no longer true, the component factory becomes unsatisfied and the Component Factory service must be unregistered. Any component configurations activated via the component factory are unaffected by the unregistration of the Component Factory service, but may themselves become unsatisfied for the same reason.

The Component Factory service must be registered under the name org.osgi.service.component.ComponentFactory with the following service properties:

- component.name – The name of the component.
- component.factory – The value of the factory attribute.

The service properties of the Component Factory service must not include the component properties.

New component configurations are created and activated when the newInstance method of the Component Factory service is called. If the component description specifies a service, the component configuration is registered as a service under the provided interfaces. The service properties for this registration consist of the component properties as defined in *Service Properties* on page 165. The service registration must take place before the component configuration is activated. Service unregistration must take place before the component configuration is deactivated.

Figure 112.4   *Factory Component*

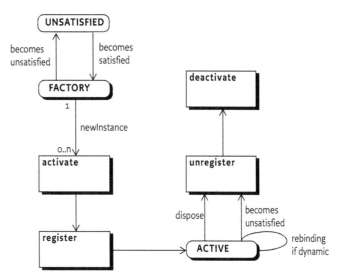

A Component Factory service has a single method: newInstance(Dictionary). This method must create, satisfy and activate a new component configuration and register its component instance as a service if the component description specifies a service. It must then return a ComponentInstance object. This ComponentInstance object can be used to get the component instance with the getInstance() method.

SCR must attempt to satisfy the component configuration created by newInstance before activating it. If SCR is unable to satisfy the component configuration given the component properties and the Dictionary argument to newInstance, the newInstance method must throw a ComponentException.

The client of the Component Factory service can also deactivate a component configuration with the dispose() method on the ComponentInstance object. If the component configuration is already deactivated, or is being deactivated, then this method is ignored. Also, if the component configuration becomes unsatisfied for any reason, it must be deactivated by SCR.

Once a component configuration created by the Component Factory has been deactivated, that component configuration will not be reactivated or used again.

112.5.6   Activation

Activating a component configuration consists of the following steps:

1   Load the component implementation class.
2   Create the component instance and component context.
3   Bind the target services. See *Binding Services* on page 160.
4   Call the activate method, if present. See *Activate Method* on page 160.

Component instances must never be reused. Each time a component configuration is activated, SCR must create a new component instance to use with the activated component configuration. A component instance must complete activation before it can be deactivated. Once the component configuration is deactivated or fails to activate due to an exception, SCR must unbind all the component's bound services and discard all references to the component instance associated with the activation.

112.5.7   Binding Services

When a component configuration's reference is satisfied, there is a set of zero or more target services for that reference. When the component configuration is activated, a subset of the target services for each reference are bound to the component configuration. The subset is chosen by the cardinality of the reference. See *Reference Cardinality* on page 149.

When binding services, the references are processed in the order in which they are specified in the component description. That is, target services from the first specified reference are bound before services from the next specified reference.

For each reference using the event strategy, the bind method must be called for each bound service of that reference. This may result in activating a component configuration of the bound service which could result in an exception. If the loss of the bound service due to the exception causes the reference's cardinality constraint to be violated, then activation of this component configuration will fail. Otherwise the bound service which failed to activate will be considered unbound. If a bind method throws an exception, SCR must log an error message containing the exception with the Log Service, if present, but the activation of the component configuration does not fail.

112.5.8   Activate Method

A component instance can have an activate method. The name of the activate method can be specified by the activate attribute. See *Component Element* on page 152. If the activate attribute is not specified, the default method name of activate is used. The prototype of the activate method is:

```
void <method-name>(<arguments>);
```

The activate method can take zero or more arguments. Each argument must be of one of the following types:

- ComponentContext – The component instance will be passed the Component Context for the component configuration.
- BundleContext – The component instance will be passed the Bundle Context of the component's bundle.
- Map – The component instance will be passed an unmodifiable Map containing the component properties.

A suitable method is selected using the following priority:

1   The method takes a single argument and the type of the argument is org.osgi.service.component.ComponentContext.
2   The method takes a single argument and the type of the argument is org.osgi.framework.BundleContext.
3   The method takes a single argument and the type of the argument is the java.util.Map.
4   The method takes two or more arguments and the type of each argument must be org.osgi.service.component.ComponentContext, org.osgi.framework.BundleContext or java.util.Map. If multiple methods match this rule, this implies the method name is overloaded and SCR may choose any of the methods to call.
5   The method takes zero arguments.

When searching for the activate method to call, SCR must locate a suitable method as specified in *Locating Component Methods* on page 167. If the activate attribute is specified and no suitable method is located, SCR must log an error message with the Log Service, if present, and the component configuration is not activated.

If an activate method is located, SCR must call this method to complete the activation of the component configuration. If the activate method throws an exception, SCR must log an error message containing the exception with the Log Service, if present, and the component configuration is not activated.

112.5.9   Component Context

The Component Context is made available to a component instance via the activate and deactivate methods. It provides the interface to the execution context of the component, much like the Bundle Context provides a bundle the interface to the Framework. A Component Context should therefore be regarded as a capability and not shared with other components or bundles.

Each distinct component instance receives a unique Component Context. Component Contexts are not reused and must be discarded when the component configuration is deactivated.

112.5.10   Bound Service Replacement

If an active component configuration has a dynamic reference with unary cardinality and the bound service is modified or unregistered and ceases to be a target service, SCR must attempt to replace the bound service with a new target service. SCR must first bind a replacement target service and then unbind the outgoing service. If the dynamic reference has a mandatory cardinality and no replacement target service is available, the component configuration must be deactivated because the cardinality constraints will be violated.

If a component configuration has a static reference and a bound service is modified or unregistered and ceases to be a target service, SCR must deactivate the component configuration. Afterwards, SCR must attempt to activate the component configuration again if another target service can be used as a replacement for the outgoing service.

112.5.11   Modification

Modifying a component configuration can occur if the component description specifies the modified attribute and the component properties of the component configuration use a Configuration object from the Configuration Admin service and that Configuration object is modified without causing the component configuration to become unsatisfied. If this occurs, the component instance will be notified of the change in the component properties.

If the modified attribute is not specified, then the component configuration will become unsatisfied if its component properties use a Configuration object and that Configuration object is modified in any way.

Modifying a component configuration consists of the following steps:

1   Update the component context for the component configuration with the modified configuration properties.
2   Call the modified method. See *Modified Method* on page 161.
3   Modify the bound services for the dynamic references if the set of target services changed due to changes in the target properties. See *Bound Service Replacement* on page 161.
4   If the component configuration is registered as a service, modify the service properties.

A component instance must complete activation, or a previous modification, before it can be modified.

See *Modified Configurations* on page 166 for more information.

112.5.12   Modified Method

The name of the modified method is specified by the modified attribute. See *Component Element* on page 152. The prototype and selection priority of the modified method is identical to that of the activate method. See *Activate Method* on page 160.

SCR must locate a suitable method as specified in *Locating Component Methods* on page 167. If the modified attribute is specified and no suitable method is located, SCR must log an error message with the Log Service, if present, and the component configuration becomes unsatisfied and is deactivated as if the modified attribute was not specified.

If a modified method is located, SCR must call this method to notify the component configuration of changes to the component properties. If the modified method throws an exception, SCR must log an error message containing the exception with the Log Service, if present and continue processing the modification.

112.5.13   Deactivation

Deactivating a component configuration consists of the following steps:

1   Call the deactivate method, if present. See *Deactivate Method* on page 162.
2   Unbind any bound services. See *Unbinding* on page 163.
3   Release all references to the component instance and component context.

A component instance must complete activation or modification before it can be deactivated. A component configuration can be deactivated for a variety of reasons. The deactivation reason can be received by the deactivate method. The following reason values are defined:

- 0 – Unspecified.
- 1 – The component was disabled.
- 2 – A reference became unsatisfied.
- 3 – A configuration was changed.
- 4 – A configuration was deleted.
- 5 – The component was disposed.
- 6 – The bundle was stopped.

Once the component configuration is deactivated, SCR must discard all references to the component instance and component context associated with the activation.

112.5.14   Deactivate Method

A component instance can have a deactivate method. The name of the deactivate method can be specified by the deactivate attribute. See *Component Element* on page 152. If the deactivate attribute is not specified, the default method name of deactivate is used. The prototype of the deactivate method is:

```
void <method-name>(<arguments>);
```

The deactivate method can take zero or more arguments. Each argument must be assignable from one of the following types:

- ComponentContext – The component instance will be passed the Component Context for the component.
- BundleContext – The component instance will be passed the Bundle Context of the component's bundle.
- Map – The component instance will be passed an unmodifiable Map containing the component properties.
- int or Integer – The component instance will be passed the reason the component configuration is being deactivated. See *Deactivation* on page 162.

A suitable method is selected using the following priority:

1   The method takes a single argument and the type of the argument is org.osgi.service.component.ComponentContext.
2   The method takes a single argument and the type of the argument is org.osgi.framework.BundleContext.
3   The method takes a single argument and the type of the argument is the java.util.Map.
4   The method takes a single argument and the type of the argument is the int.
5   The method takes a single argument and the type of the argument is the java.lang.Integer.
6   The method takes two or more arguments and the type of each argument must be org.osgi.service.component.ComponentContext, org.osgi.framework.BundleContext,

java.util.Map, int or java.lang.Integer. If multiple methods match this rule, this implies the method name is overloaded and SCR may choose any of the methods to call.

7   The method takes zero arguments.

When searching for the deactivate method to call, SCR must locate a suitable method as specified in *Locating Component Methods* on page 167. If the deactivate attribute is specified and no suitable method is located, SCR must log an error message with the Log Service, if present, and the deactivation of the component configuration will continue.

If a deactivate method is located, SCR must call this method to commence the deactivation of the component configuration. If the deactivate method throws an exception, SCR must log an error message containing the exception with the Log Service, if present, and the deactivation of the component configuration will continue.

112.5.15   Unbinding

When a component configuration is deactivated, the bound services are unbound from the component configuration.

When unbinding services, the references are processed in the reverse order in which they are specified in the component description. That is, target services from the last specified reference are unbound before services from the previous specified reference.

For each reference using the event strategy, the unbind method must be called for each bound service of that reference. If an unbind method throws an exception, SCR must log an error message containing the exception with the Log Service, if present, and the deactivation of the component configuration will continue.

112.5.16   Life Cycle Example

A component could declare a dependency on the Http Service to register some resources.

```xml
<xml version="1.0" encoding="UTF-8">
<scr:component name="example.binding"
   xmlns:scr="http://www.osgi.org/xmlns/scr/v1.1.0">
   <implementation class="example.Binding"/>
   <reference name="LOG"
      interface="org.osgi.service.log.LogService"
      cardinality="1..1"
      policy="static"
   />
   <reference name="HTTP"
      interface="org.osgi.service.http.HttpService"
      cardinality="0..1"
      policy="dynamic"
      bind="setHttp"
      unbind="unsetHttp"
   />
</scr:component>
```

The component implementation code looks like:

```java
public class Binding {
   LogService  log;
   HttpService http;

   private void setHttp(HttpService h) {
      this.http = h;
      // register servlet
   }
```

```
        private void unsetHttp(HttpService h){
           this.h = null;
           // unregister servlet
        }
        private void activate(ComponentContext context ) {.
           log = (LogService) context.locateService("LOG");
        }
        private void deactivate(ComponentContext context ){...}
     }
```

This example is depicted in a sequence diagram in Figure 112.5. with the following scenario:

1   A bundle with the example.Binding component is started. At that time there is a Log Service l1
    and a Http Service h1 registered.
2   The Http Service h1 is unregistered
3   A new Http Service h2 is registered
4   The Log Service h1 is unregistered.

Figure 112.5   *Sequence Diagram for binding*

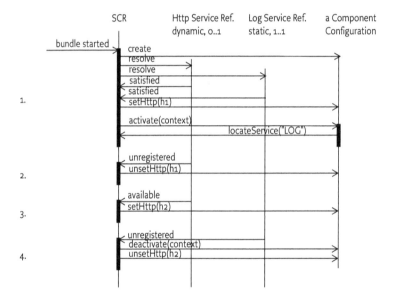

112.6   Component Properties

Each component configuration is associated with a set of component properties. The component
properties are specified in the following places (in order of precedence):

1   Properties specified in the argument of ComponentFactory.newInstance method. This is only
    applicable for factory components.
2   Properties retrieved from the OSGi Configuration Admin service with a Configuration object that
    has a PID equal to the name of the component.
3   Properties specified in the component description. Properties specified later in the component
    description override properties that have the same name specified earlier. Properties can be spec-
    ified in the component description in the following ways:
    •   target attribute of reference elements – Sets a component property called the *target property* of
        the reference. The key of a target property is the name of the reference appended with .target.

The value of a target property is the value of the target attribute. For example, a reference with the name http whose target attribute has the value "(http.port=80)" results in the component property having the name http.target and value "(http.port=80)". See *Selecting Target Services* on page 151. The target property can also be set wherever component properties can be set.

- property and properties elements – See *Properties and Property Elements* on page 154.

The precedence behavior allows certain default values to be specified in the component description while allowing properties to be replaced and extended by:

- A configuration in Configuration Admin
- The argument to ComponentFactory.newInstance method

SCR always adds the following component properties, which cannot be overridden:

- component.name – The component name.

- component.id – A unique value (Long) that is larger than all previously assigned values. These values are not persistent across restarts of SCR.

112.6.1   Service Properties

When SCR registers a service on behalf of a component configuration, SCR must follow the recommendations in *Property Propagation* on page 51 and must not propagate private configuration properties. That is, the service properties of the registered service must be all the component properties of the component configuration whose property names do not start with dot ('.' \u002E).

Component properties whose names start with dot are available to the component instance but are not available as service properties of the registered service.

112.7   Deployment

A component description contains default information to select target services for each reference. However, when a component is deployed, it is often necessary to influence the target service selection in a way that suits the needs of the deployer. Therefore, SCR uses Configuration objects from Configuration Admin to replace and extend the component properties for a component configuration. That is, through Configuration Admin, a deployer can configure component properties.

The name of the component is used as the key for obtaining additional component properties from Configuration Admin. The following situations can arise:

- *No Configuration* – If the component's configuration-policy is set to ignore or there is no Configuration with a PID or factory PID equal to the component name, then component configurations will not obtain component properties from Configuration Admin. Only component properties specified in the component description or via the ComponentFactory.newInstance method will be used.
- *Not Satisfied* – If the component's configuration-policy is set to require and there is no Configuration with a PID or factory PID equal to the component name, then the component configuration is not satisfied and will not be activated.
- *Single Configuration* – If there exists a Configuration with a PID equal to the component name, then component configurations will obtain additional component properties from Configuration Admin.
- *Factory Configuration* – If a factory PID exists, with zero or more Configurations, that is equal to the component name, then for each Configuration, a component configuration must be created that will obtain additional component properties from Configuration Admin.

A factory configuration must not be used if the component is a factory component. This is because SCR is not free to create component configurations as necessary to support multiple Configurations. When SCR detects this condition, it must log an error message with the Log Service, if present, and ignore the component description.

SCR must obtain the Configuration objects from the Configuration Admin service using the Bundle Context of the bundle containing the component.

For example, there is a component named com.acme.client with a reference named HTTP that requires an Http Service which must be bound to a component com.acme.httpserver which provides an Http Service. A deployer can establish the following configuration:

```
[PID=com.acme.client, factoryPID=null]
HTTP.target = (component.name=com.acme.httpserver)
```

112.7.1 Modified Configurations

SCR must track changes in the Configuration objects used in the component properties of a component configuration. If a Configuration object that is used by a component configuration is deleted, then the component configuration will become unsatisfied and SCR must deactivate that component configuration.

If a Configuration object that is used by a component configuration changes, then SCR must take action based upon whether the component configuration has been activated and whether the component description specifies the modified attribute.

If a component configuration has not been activated and it has a service registered, then a Configuration object change that leaves the component configuration satisfied will only cause the service properties of the service to be modified.

If a component description specifies the modified attribute and the changes to the target properties for the component configuration do not cause any references of the component configuration to become unsatisfied, SCR must modify the component properties for the component configuration. See *Modification* on page 161. A reference can become unsatisfied by a target property change if either:

- A bound service of a static reference is no longer a target service, or
- There are no target services for a mandatory dynamic reference.

Otherwise, the component configuration will become unsatisfied and SCR must deactivate that component configuration. SCR must attempt to satisfy the component configuration with the updated component properties.

112.8 Service Component Runtime

112.8.1 Relationship to OSGi Framework

The SCR must have access to the Bundle Context of any bundle that contains a component. The SCR needs access to the Bundle Context for the following reasons:

- To be able to register and get services on behalf of a bundle with components.
- To interact with the Configuration Admin on behalf of a bundle with components.
- To provide a component its Bundle Context when the Component Context getBundleContext method is called.

The SCR should use the Bundle.getBundleContext() method to obtain the Bundle Context reference.

112.8.2 Starting and Stopping SCR

When SCR is implemented as a bundle, any component configurations activated by SCR must be deactivated when the SCR bundle is stopped. When the SCR bundle is started, it must process any components that are declared in bundles that are started. This includes bundles which are started and are awaiting lazy activation.

112.8.3   Logging Error Messages

When SCR must log an error message to the Log Service, it must use a Log Service obtained using the component's Bundle Context so that the resulting Log Entry is associated with the component's bundle.

If SCR is unable to obtain, or use, a Log Service using the component's Bundle Context, then SCR must log the error message to a Log Service obtained using SCR's bundle context to ensure the error message is logged.

112.8.4   Locating Component Methods

SCR will need to locate activate, deactivate, modified, bind and unbind methods for a component instance. These methods will be located, and called, using reflection. The declared methods of each class in the component implementation class' hierarchy are examined for a suitable method. If a suitable method is found in a class, and it is accessible to the component implementation class, then that method must be used. If suitable methods are found in a class but none of the suitable methods are accessible by the component implementation class, then the search for suitable methods terminates with no suitable method having been located. If no suitable methods are found in a class, the search continues in the superclass.

Only methods that are accessible, [5] *Access Control Java Language Specification*, to the component implementation class will be used. If the method has the public or protected access modifier, then access is permitted. Otherwise, if the method has the private access modifier, then access is permitted only if the method is declared in the component implementation class. Otherwise, if the method has default access, also known as package private access, then access is permitted only if the method is declared in the component implementation class or if the method is declared in a superclass and all classes in the hierarchy from the component implementation class to the superclass, inclusive, are in the same package and loaded by the same class loader.

It is recommended that these methods should not be declared with the public access modifier so that they do not appear as public methods on the component instance when it is used as a service object. Having these methods declared public allows any code to call the methods with reflection, even if a Security Manager is installed. These methods are generally intended to only be called by SCR.

112.9   Security

112.9.1   Service Permissions

Declarative services are built upon the existing OSGi service infrastructure. This means that Service Permission applies regarding the ability to publish, find or bind services.

If a component specifies a service, then component configurations for the component cannot be satisfied unless the component's bundle has ServicePermission[<provides>, REGISTER] for each provided interface specified for the service.

If a component's reference does not specify optional cardinality, the reference cannot be satisfied unless the component's bundle has ServicePermission[<interface>, GET] for the specified interface in the reference. If the reference specifies optional cardinality but the component's bundle does not have ServicePermission[<interface>, GET] for the specified interface in the reference, no service must be bound for this reference.

If a component is a factory component, then the above Service Permission checks still apply. But the component's bundle is not required to have ServicePermission[ComponentFactory, REGISTER] as the Component Factory service is registered by SCR.

112.9.2 Required Admin Permission

The SCR requires AdminPermission[*,CONTEXT] because it needs access to the bundle's Bundle Context object with the Bundle.getBundleContext() method.

112.9.3 Using hasPermission

SCR does all publishing, finding and binding of services on behalf of the component using the Bundle Context of the component's bundle. This means that normal stack-based permission checks will check SCR and not the component's bundle. Since SCR is registering and getting services on behalf of a component's bundle, SCR must call the Bundle.hasPermission method to validate that a component's bundle has the necessary permission to register or get a service.

112.10 Component Description Schema

This XML Schema defines the component description grammar.

```
<xml version="1.0" encoding="UTF-8">
<schema xmlns="http://www.w3.org/2001/XMLSchema"
    xmlns:scr="http://www.osgi.org/xmlns/scr/v1.1.0"
    targetNamespace="http://www.osgi.org/xmlns/scr/v1.1.0"
    elementFormDefault="unqualified"
    attributeFormDefault="unqualified"
    version="1.1.0">

    <annotation>
        <documentation xml:lang="en">
            This is the XML Schema for component descriptions used by
            the Service Component Runtime (SCR). Component description
            documents may be embedded in other XML documents. SCR will
            process all XML documents listed in the Service-Component
            manifest header of a bundle. XML documents containing
            component descriptions may contain a single, root component
            element or one or more component elements embedded in a
            larger document. Use of the namespace for component
            descriptions is mandatory. The attributes and subelements
            of a component element are always unqualified.
        </documentation>
    </annotation>
    <element name="component" type="scr:Tcomponent" />
    <complexType name="Tcomponent">
        <sequence>
            <annotation>
                <documentation xml:lang="en">
                    Implementations of SCR must not require component
                    descriptions to specify the subelements of the component
                    element in the order as required by the schema. SCR
                    implementations must allow other orderings since
                    arbitrary orderings do not affect the meaning of the
                    component description. Only the relative ordering of
                    property and properties element have meaning.
                </documentation>
            </annotation>
            <choice minOccurs="0" maxOccurs="unbounded">
                <element name="property" type="scr:Tproperty" />
                <element name="properties" type="scr:Tproperties" />
            </choice>
            <element name="service" type="scr:Tservice" minOccurs="0"
                maxOccurs="1" />
            <element name="reference" type="scr:Treference"
                minOccurs="0" maxOccurs="unbounded" />
            <element name="implementation" type="scr:Timplementation"
                minOccurs="1" maxOccurs="1" />
            <any namespace="##any" processContents="lax" minOccurs="0"
                maxOccurs="unbounded" />
        </sequence>
        <attribute name="enabled" type="boolean" default="true"
            use="optional" />
        <attribute name="name" type="token" use="optional">
```

```
            <annotation>
                <documentation xml:lang="en">
                    The default value of this attribute is the value of
                    the class attribute of the nested implementation
                    element. If multiple component elements use the same
                    value for the class attribute of their nested
                    implementation element, then using the default value
                    for this attribute will result in duplicate names.
                    In this case, this attribute must be specified with
                    a unique value.
                </documentation>
            </annotation>
        </attribute>
        <attribute name="factory" type="string" use="optional" />
        <attribute name="immediate" type="boolean" use="optional" />
        <attribute name="configuration-policy"
            type="scr:Tconfiguration-policy" default="optional" use="optional" />
        <attribute name="activate" type="token" use="optional"
            default="activate" />
        <attribute name="deactivate" type="token" use="optional"
            default="deactivate" />
        <attribute name="modified" type="token" use="optional" />
        <anyAttribute />
    </complexType>
    <complexType name="Timplementation">
        <sequence>
            <any namespace="##any" processContents="lax" minOccurs="0"
                maxOccurs="unbounded" />
        </sequence>
        <attribute name="class" type="token" use="required" />
        <anyAttribute />
    </complexType>
    <complexType name="Tproperty">
        <simpleContent>
            <extension base="string">
                <attribute name="name" type="string" use="required" />
                <attribute name="value" type="string" use="optional" />
                <attribute name="type" type="scr:Tjava-types"
                    default="String" use="optional" />
                <anyAttribute />
            </extension>
        </simpleContent>
    </complexType>
    <complexType name="Tproperties">
        <sequence>
            <any namespace="##any" processContents="lax" minOccurs="0"
                maxOccurs="unbounded" />
        </sequence>
        <attribute name="entry" type="string" use="required" />
        <anyAttribute />
    </complexType>
    <complexType name="Tservice">
        <sequence>
            <element name="provide" type="scr:Tprovide" minOccurs="1"
                maxOccurs="unbounded" />
            <!-- It is non-deterministic, per W3C XML Schema 1.0:
            http://www.w3.org/TR/xmlschema-1/#cos-nonambig
            to use namespace="##any" below. -->
            <any namespace="##other" processContents="lax" minOccurs="0"
                maxOccurs="unbounded" />
        </sequence>
        <attribute name="servicefactory" type="boolean" default="false"
            use="optional" />
        <anyAttribute />
    </complexType>
    <complexType name="Tprovide">
        <sequence>
            <any namespace="##any" processContents="lax" minOccurs="0"
                maxOccurs="unbounded" />
        </sequence>
        <attribute name="interface" type="token" use="required" />
        <anyAttribute />
    </complexType>
    <complexType name="Treference">
        <sequence>
```

```
        <any namespace="##any" processContents="lax" minOccurs="0"
            maxOccurs="unbounded" />
    </sequence>
    <attribute name="name" type="token" use="optional">
        <annotation>
            <documentation xml:lang="en">
                The default value of this attribute is the value of
                the interface attribute of this element. If multiple
                instances of this element within a component element
                use the same value for the interface attribute, then
                using the default value for this attribute will result
                in duplicate names. In this case, this attribute
                must be specified with a unique value.
            </documentation>
        </annotation>
    </attribute>
    <attribute name="interface" type="token" use="required" />
    <attribute name="cardinality" type="scr:Tcardinality"
        default="1..1" use="optional" />
    <attribute name="policy" type="scr:Tpolicy" default="static"
        use="optional" />
    <attribute name="target" type="string" use="optional" />
    <attribute name="bind" type="token" use="optional" />
    <attribute name="unbind" type="token" use="optional" />
    <anyAttribute />
</complexType>
<simpleType name="Tjava-types">
    <restriction base="string">
        <enumeration value="String" />
        <enumeration value="Long" />
        <enumeration value="Double" />
        <enumeration value="Float" />
        <enumeration value="Integer" />
        <enumeration value="Byte" />
        <enumeration value="Character" />
        <enumeration value="Boolean" />
        <enumeration value="Short" />
    </restriction>
</simpleType>
<simpleType name="Tcardinality">
    <restriction base="string">
        <enumeration value="0..1" />
        <enumeration value="0..n" />
        <enumeration value="1..1" />
        <enumeration value="1..n" />
    </restriction>
</simpleType>
<simpleType name="Tpolicy">
    <restriction base="string">
        <enumeration value="static" />
        <enumeration value="dynamic" />
    </restriction>
</simpleType>
<simpleType name="Tconfiguration-policy">
    <restriction base="string">
        <enumeration value="optional" />
        <enumeration value="require" />
        <enumeration value="ignore" />
    </restriction>
</simpleType>
<attribute name="must-understand" type="boolean">
    <annotation>
        <documentation xml:lang="en">
            This attribute should be used by extensions to documents
            to require that the document consumer understand the
            extension. This attribute must be qualified when used.
        </documentation>
    </annotation>
</attribute>
</schema>
```

SCR must not require component descriptions to specify the elements in the order required by the schema. SCR must allow other orderings since arbitrary orderings of these elements do not affect the meaning of the component description. Only the relative ordering of property, properties and reference elements have meaning for overriding previously set property values.

The schema is also available in digital form from [6] *OSGi XML Schemas*.

112.11   org.osgi.service.component

Service Component Package Version 1.1.

Bundles wishing to use this package must list the package in the Import-Package header of the bundle's manifest. For example:

```
Import-Package: org.osgi.service.component; version="[1.1,2.0)"
```

112.11.1   Summary

- *ComponentConstants* - Defines standard names for Service Component constants.
- *ComponentContext* - A Component Context object is used by a component instance to interact with its execution context including locating services by reference name.
- *ComponentException* - Unchecked exception which may be thrown by the Service Component Runtime.
- *ComponentFactory* - When a component is declared with the factory attribute on its component element, the Service Component Runtime will register a Component Factory service to allow new component configurations to be created and activated rather than automatically creating and activating component configuration as necessary.
- *ComponentInstance* - A ComponentInstance encapsulates a component instance of an activated component configuration.

112.11.2   public interface ComponentConstants

Defines standard names for Service Component constants.

112.11.2.1   public static final String COMPONENT_FACTORY = "component.factory"

A service registration property for a Component Factory that contains the value of the factory attribute. The value of this property must be of type String.

112.11.2.2   public static final String COMPONENT_ID = "component.id"

A component property that contains the generated id for a component configuration. The value of this property must be of type Long.

The value of this property is assigned by the Service Component Runtime when a component configuration is created. The Service Component Runtime assigns a unique value that is larger than all previously assigned values since the Service Component Runtime was started. These values are NOT persistent across restarts of the Service Component Runtime.

112.11.2.3   public static final String COMPONENT_NAME = "component.name"

A component property for a component configuration that contains the name of the component as specified in the name attribute of the component element. The value of this property must be of type String.

112.11.2.4   public static final int DEACTIVATION_REASON_BUNDLE_STOPPED = 6

The component configuration was deactivated because the bundle was stopped.

Since 1.1

112.11.2.5 **public static final int DEACTIVATION_REASON_CONFIGURATION_DELETED = 4**

The component configuration was deactivated because its configuration was deleted.

Since 1.1

112.11.2.6 **public static final int DEACTIVATION_REASON_CONFIGURATION_MODIFIED = 3**

The component configuration was deactivated because its configuration was changed.

Since 1.1

112.11.2.7 **public static final int DEACTIVATION_REASON_DISABLED = 1**

The component configuration was deactivated because the component was disabled.

Since 1.1

112.11.2.8 **public static final int DEACTIVATION_REASON_DISPOSED = 5**

The component configuration was deactivated because the component was disposed.

Since 1.1

112.11.2.9 **public static final int DEACTIVATION_REASON_REFERENCE = 2**

The component configuration was deactivated because a reference became unsatisfied.

Since 1.1

112.11.2.10 **public static final int DEACTIVATION_REASON_UNSPECIFIED = 0**

The reason the component configuration was deactivated is unspecified.

Since 1.1

112.11.2.11 **public static final String REFERENCE_TARGET_SUFFIX = ".target"**

The suffix for reference target properties. These properties contain the filter to select the target services for a reference. The value of this property must be of type String.

112.11.2.12 **public static final String SERVICE_COMPONENT = "Service-Component"**

Manifest header specifying the XML documents within a bundle that contain the bundle's Service Component descriptions.

The attribute value may be retrieved from the Dictionary object returned by the Bundle.getHeaders method.

112.11.3   public interface ComponentContext

A Component Context object is used by a component instance to interact with its execution context including locating services by reference name. Each component instance has a unique Component Context.

A component instance may have an activate method. If a component instance has a suitable and accessible activate method, this method will be called when a component configuration is activated. If the activate method takes a ComponentContext argument, it will be passed the component instance's Component Context object. If the activate method takes a BundleContext argument, it will be passed the component instance's Bundle Context object. If the activate method takes a Map argument, it will be passed an unmodifiable Map containing the component properties.

A component instance may have a deactivate method. If a component instance has a suitable and accessible deactivate method, this method will be called when the component configuration is deactivated. If the deactivate method takes a ComponentContext argument, it will be passed the component instance's Component Context object. If the deactivate method takes a BundleContext argument, it will be passed the component instance's Bundle Context object. If the deactivate method takes a Map argument, it will be passed an unmodifiable Map containing the component properties. If the deactivate method takes an int or Integer argument, it will be passed the reason code for the component instance's deactivation.

Concurrency Thread-safe

112.11.3.1 **public void disableComponent(String name)**

name The name of a component.

☐ Disables the specified component name. The specified component name must be in the same bundle as this component.

112.11.3.2 **public void enableComponent(String name)**

name The name of a component or null to indicate all components in the bundle.

☐ Enables the specified component name. The specified component name must be in the same bundle as this component.

112.11.3.3 **public BundleContext getBundleContext( )**

☐ Returns the BundleContext of the bundle which contains this component.

Returns The BundleContext of the bundle containing this component.

112.11.3.4 **public ComponentInstance getComponentInstance( )**

☐ Returns the Component Instance object for the component instance associated with this Component Context.

Returns The Component Instance object for the component instance.

112.11.3.5 **public Dictionary getProperties( )**

☐ Returns the component properties for this Component Context.

Returns The properties for this Component Context. The Dictionary is read only and cannot be modified.

112.11.3.6 **public ServiceReference getServiceReference( )**

☐ If the component instance is registered as a service using the service element, then this method returns the service reference of the service provided by this component instance.

This method will return null if the component instance is not registered as a service.

Returns The ServiceReference object for the component instance or null if the component instance is not registered as a service.

112.11.3.7 **public Bundle getUsingBundle( )**

☐ If the component instance is registered as a service using the servicefactory="true" attribute, then this method returns the bundle using the service provided by the component instance.

This method will return null if:

- The component instance is not a service, then no bundle can be using it as a service.
- The component instance is a service but did not specify the servicefactory="true" attribute, then all bundles using the service provided by the component instance will share the same component instance.
- The service provided by the component instance is not currently being used by any bundle.

Returns The bundle using the component instance as a service or null.

112.11.3.8 **public Object locateService(String name)**

name The name of a reference as specified in a reference element in this component's description.

       ❑ Returns the service object for the specified reference name.

If the cardinality of the reference is 0..n or 1..n and multiple services are bound to the reference, the service with the highest ranking (as specified in its Constants.SERVICE_RANKING property) is returned. If there is a tie in ranking, the service with the lowest service ID (as specified in its Constants.SERVICE_ID property); that is, the service that was registered first is returned.

Returns   A service object for the referenced service or null if the reference cardinality is 0..1 or 0..n and no bound service is available.

Throws   ComponentException – If the Service Component Runtime catches an exception while activating the bound service.

112.11.3.9   **public Object locateService(String name, ServiceReference reference)**

name   The name of a reference as specified in a reference element in this component's description.

reference   The ServiceReference to a bound service. This must be a ServiceReference provided to the component via the bind or unbind method for the specified reference name.

       ❑ Returns the service object for the specified reference name and ServiceReference.

Returns   A service object for the referenced service or null if the specified ServiceReference is not a bound service for the specified reference name.

Throws   ComponentException – If the Service Component Runtime catches an exception while activating the bound service.

112.11.3.10   **public Object[] locateServices(String name)**

name   The name of a reference as specified in a reference element in this component's description.

       ❑ Returns the service objects for the specified reference name.

Returns   An array of service objects for the referenced service or null if the reference cardinality is 0..1 or 0..n and no bound service is available. If the reference cardinality is 0..1 or 1..1 and a bound service is available, the array will have exactly one element.

Throws   ComponentException – If the Service Component Runtime catches an exception while activating a bound service.

112.11.4   public class ComponentException extends RuntimeException

Unchecked exception which may be thrown by the Service Component Runtime.

112.11.4.1   **public ComponentException(String message, Throwable cause)**

message   The message for the exception.

cause   The cause of the exception. May be null.

       ❑ Construct a new ComponentException with the specified message and cause.

112.11.4.2   **public ComponentException(String message)**

message   The message for the exception.

       ❑ Construct a new ComponentException with the specified message.

112.11.4.3   **public ComponentException(Throwable cause)**

cause   The cause of the exception. May be null.

       ❑ Construct a new ComponentException with the specified cause.

112.11.4.4   **public Throwable getCause( )**

☐ Returns the cause of this exception or null if no cause was set.

Returns The cause of this exception or null if no cause was set.

112.11.4.5   **public Throwable initCause(Throwable cause)**

cause The cause of this exception.

☐ Initializes the cause of this exception to the specified value.

Returns This exception.

Throws IllegalArgumentException – If the specified cause is this exception.

IllegalStateException – If the cause of this exception has already been set.

112.11.5   public interface ComponentFactory

When a component is declared with the factory attribute on its component element, the Service Component Runtime will register a Component Factory service to allow new component configurations to be created and activated rather than automatically creating and activating component configuration as necessary.

Concurrency Thread-safe

112.11.5.1   **public ComponentInstance newInstance(Dictionary properties)**

properties Additional properties for the component configuration or null if there are no additional properties.

☐ Create and activate a new component configuration. Additional properties may be provided for the component configuration.

Returns A ComponentInstance object encapsulating the component instance of the component configuration. The component configuration has been activated and, if the component specifies a service element, the component instance has been registered as a service.

Throws ComponentException – If the Service Component Runtime is unable to activate the component configuration.

112.11.6   public interface ComponentInstance

A ComponentInstance encapsulates a component instance of an activated component configuration. ComponentInstances are created whenever a component configuration is activated.

ComponentInstances are never reused. A new ComponentInstance object will be created when the component configuration is activated again.

Concurrency Thread-safe

112.11.6.1   **public void dispose( )**

☐ Dispose of the component configuration for this component instance. The component configuration will be deactivated. If the component configuration has already been deactivated, this method does nothing.

112.11.6.2   **public Object getInstance( )**

☐ Returns the component instance of the activated component configuration.

Returns The component instance or null if the component configuration has been deactivated.

112.12   References

[1]   *Automating Service Dependency Management in a Service-Oriented Component Model*
Humberto Cervantes, Richard S. Hall, Proceedings of the Sixth Component-Based Software
Engineering Workshop, May 2003, pp. 91-96.
http://www-adele.imag.fr/Les.Publications/intConferences/CBSE2003Cer.pdf

[2]   *Service Binder*
Humberto Cervantes, Richard S. Hall, http://gravity.sourceforge.net/servicebinder

[3]   *Java Properties File*
http://java.sun.com/j2se/1.4.2/docs/api/java/util/Properties.html#load(java.io.InputStream)

[4]   *Extensible Markup Language (XML) 1.0*
http://www.w3.org/TR/REC-xml/

[5]   *Access Control Java Language Specification*
http://java.sun.com/docs/books/jls/second_edition/html/names.doc.html#104285

[6]   *OSGi XML Schemas*
http://www.osgi.org/Release4/XMLSchemas

113 Event Admin Service Specification

Version 1.2

113.1 Introduction

Nearly all the bundles in an OSGi framework must deal with events, either as an event publisher or as an event handler. So far, the preferred mechanism to disperse those events have been the service interface mechanism.

Dispatching events for a design related to X, usually involves a service of type XListener. However, this model does not scale well for fine grained events that must be dispatched to many different handlers. Additionally, the dynamic nature of the OSGi environment introduces several complexities because both event publishers and event handlers can appear and disappear at any time.

The Event Admin service provides an inter-bundle communication mechanism. It is based on a event *publish* and *subscribe* model, popular in many message based systems.

This specification defines the details for the participants in this event model.

113.1.1 Essentials

- *Simplifications* – The model must significantly simplify the process of programming an event source and an event handler.
- *Dependencies* – Handle the myriad of dependencies between event sources and event handlers for proper cleanup.
- *Synchronicity* – It must be possible to deliver events asynchronously or synchronously with the caller.
- *Event Window* – Only event handlers that are active when an event is published must receive this event, handlers that register later must not see the event.
- *Performance* – The event mechanism must impose minimal overhead in delivering events.
- *Selectivity* – Event listeners must only receive notifications for the event types for which they are interested
- *Reliability* – The Event Admin must ensure that events continue to be delivered regardless the quality of the event handlers.
- *Security* – Publishing and receiving events are sensitive operations that must be protected per event type.
- *Extensibility* – It must be possible to define new event types with their own data types.
- *Native Code* – Events must be able to be passed to native code or come from native code.
- *OSGi Events* – The OSGi Framework, as well as a number of OSGi services, already have number of its own events defined. For uniformity of processing, these have to be mapped into generic event types.

113.1.2 Entities

- *Event* – An Event object has a topic and a Dictionary object that contains the event properties. It is an immutable object.
- *Event Admin* – The service that provides the publish and subscribe model to Event Handlers and Event Publishers.
- *Event Handler* – A service that receives and handles Event objects.

- *Event Publisher* – A bundle that sends event through the Event Admin service.
- *Event Subscriber* – Another name for an Event Handler.
- *Topic* – The name of an Event type.
- *Event Properties* – The set of properties that is associated with an Event.

Figure 113.1   *The Event Admin service org.osgi.service.event package*

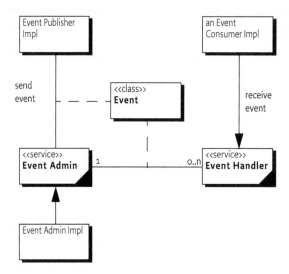

113.1.3   Synopsis

The Event Admin service provides a place for bundles to publish events, regardless of their destination. It is also used by Event Handlers to subscribe to specific types of events.

Events are published under a topic, together with a number of event properties. Event Handlers can specify a filter to control the Events they receive on a very fine grained basis.

113.1.4   What To Read

- *Architects* – The *Event Admin Architecture* on page 178 provides an overview of the Event Admin service.
- *Event Publishers* – The *Event Publisher* on page 181 provides an introduction of how to write an Event Publisher. The *Event Admin Architecture* on page 178 provides a good overview of the design.
- *Event Subscribers/Handlers* – The *Event Handler* on page 180 provides the rules on how to subscribe and handle events.

113.2   Event Admin Architecture

The Event Admin is based on the *Publish-Subscribe* pattern. This pattern decouples sources from their handlers by interposing an *event channel* between them. The publisher posts events to the channel, which identifies which handlers need to be notified and then takes care of the notification process. This model is depicted in Figure 113.2.

Figure 113.2   *Channel Pattern*

In this model, the event source and event handler are completely decoupled because neither has any direct knowledge of the other. The complicated logic of monitoring changes in the event publishers and event handlers is completely contained within the event channel. This is highly advantageous in an OSGi environment because it simplifies the process of both sending and receiving events.

113.3   The Event

Events have the following attributes:

- *Topic* – A topic that defines what happened. For example, when a bundle is started an event is published that has a topic of org/osgi/framework/BundleEvent/STARTED.
- *Properties* – Zero or more properties that contain additional information about the event. For example, the previous example event has a property of bundle.id which is set to a Long object, among other properties.

113.3.1   Topics

The topic of an event defines the *type* of the event. It is fairly granular in order to give handlers the opportunity to register for just the events they are interested in. When a topic is designed, its name should not include any other information, such as the publisher of the event or the data associated with the event, those parts are intended to be stored in the event properties.

The topic is intended to serve as a first-level filter for determining which handlers should receive the event. Event Admin service implementations use the structure of the topic to optimize the dispatching of the events to the handlers.

Topics are arranged in a hierarchical namespace. Each level is defined by a token and levels are separated by slashes. More precisely, the topic must conform to the following grammar:

```
topic ::= token ( '/' token ) *    // See 1.3.2 Core book
```

Topics should be designed to become more specific when going from left to right. Handlers can provide a prefix that matches a topic, using the preferred order allows a handler to minimize the number of prefixes it needs to register.

Topics are case-sensitive. As a convention, topics should follow the reverse domain name scheme used by Java packages to guarantee uniqueness. The separator must be slashes ('/' \u002F) instead of the dot ('.' \u002E).

This specification uses the convention fully/qualified/package/ClassName/ACTION. If necessary, a pseudo-class-name is used.

113.3.2   Properties

Information about the actual event is provided as properties. The property name is a case-sensitive string and the value can be any object. Although any Java object can be used as a property value, only String objects and the eight primitive types (plus their wrappers) should be used. Other types cannot be passed to handlers that reside external from the Java VM.

Another reason that arbitrary classes should not be used is the mutability of objects. If the values are not immutable, then any handler that receives the event could change the value. Any handlers that received the event subsequently would see the altered value and not the value as it was when the event was sent.

The topic of the event is available as a property with the key EVENT_TOPIC. This allows filters to include the topic as a condition if necessary.

113.4 Event Handler

Event handlers must be registered as services with the OSGi framework under the object class org.osgi.service.event.EventHandler.

Event handlers should be registered with a property (constant from the EventConstants class) EVENT_TOPIC. The value being a String or String[] object that describes which *topics* the handler is interested in. A wildcard ('*' \u002A) may be used as the last token of a topic name, for example com/action/*. This matches any topic that shares the same first tokens. For example, com/action/* matches com/action/listen.

Event Handlers which have not specified the EVENT_TOPIC service property must not receive events.

The value of each entry in the EVENT_TOPIC service registration property must conform to the following grammar:

```
topic-scope ::= '*' | ( topic '/*'  )
```

Event handlers can also be registered with a service property named EVENT_FILTER. The value of this property must be a string containing a Framework filter specification. Any of the event's properties can be used in the filter expression.

```
event-filter ::= filter          // 3.2.7 Core book
```

Each Event Handler is notified for any event which belongs to the topics the handler has expressed an interest in. If the handler has defined a EVENT_FILTER service property then the event properties must also match the filter expression. If the filter is an error, then the Event Admin service should log a warning and further ignore the Event Handler.

For example, a bundle wants to see all Log Service events with a level of WARNING or ERROR, but it must ignore the INFO and DEBUG events. Additionally, the only events of interest are when the bundle symbolic name starts with com.acme.

```
public AcmeWatchDog implements BundleActivator,
    EventHandler {
  final static String [] topics = new String[] {
    "org/osgi/service/log/LogEntry/LOG_WARNING",
    "org/osgi/service/log/LogEntry/LOG_ERROR" };

  public void start(BundleContext context) {
    Dictionary d = new Hashtable();
    d.put(EventConstants.EVENT_TOPIC, topics );
    d.put(EventConstants.EVENT_FILTER,
      "(bundle.symbolicName=com.acme.*)" );
    context.registerService( EventHandler.class.getName(),
      this, d );
  }
  public void stop( BundleContext context) {}

  public void handleEvent(Event event ) {
    //...
```

}
}

If there are multiple Event Admin services registered with the Framework then all Event Admin services must send their published events to all registered Event Handlers.

113.5   Event Publisher

To fire an event, the event source must retrieve the Event Admin service from the OSGi service registry. Then it creates the event object and calls one of the Event Admin service's methods to fire the event either synchronously or asynchronously.

The following example is a class that publishes a time event every 60 seconds.

```
public class TimerEvent extends Thread
    implements BundleActivator {
    Hashtable          time = new Hashtable();
    ServiceTracker     tracker;

    public TimerEvent() { super("TimerEvent"); }

    public void start(BundleContext context ) {
        tracker = new ServiceTracker(context,
            EventAdmin.class.getName(), null );
        tracker.open();
        start();
    }

    public void stop( BundleContext context ) {
        interrupt();
        tracker.close();
    }

    public void run() {
        while ( ! Thread.interrupted() ) try {
            Calendar   c = Calendar.getInstance();
            set(c,Calendar.MINUTE, "minutes");
            set(c,Calendar.HOUR, "hours");
            set(c,Calendar.DAY_OF_MONTH, "day");
            set(c,Calendar.MONTH, "month");
            set(c,Calendar.YEAR, "year");

            EventAdmin ea =
                (EventAdmin) tracker.getService();
            if ( ea != null )
                ea.sendEvent(new Event("com/acme/timer",
                    time ));
            Thread.sleep(60000-c.get(Calendar.SECOND)*1000);
        } catch( InterruptedException e ) {
            return;
        }
    }

    void set( Calendar c, int field, String key ) {
        time.put( key, new Integer(c.get(field)) );
    }
```

}

113.6   Specific Events

113.6.1   General Conventions

Some handlers are more interested in the contents of an event rather than what actually happened. For example, a handler wants to be notified whenever an Exception is thrown anywhere in the system. Both Framework Events and Log Entry events may contain an exception that would be of interest to this hypothetical handler. If both Framework Events and Log Entries use the same property names then the handler can access the Exception in exactly the same way. If some future event type follows the same conventions then the handler can receive and process the new event type even though it had no knowledge of it when it was compiled.

The following properties are suggested as conventions. When new event types are defined they should use these names with the corresponding types and values where appropriate. These values should be set only if they are not null

A list of these property names can be found in Table 113.1..

Table 113.1   *General property names for events*

Name	Type	Notes
BUNDLE_SIGNER	String | Collection <String>	A bundle's signers DN
BUNDLE_VERSION	Version	A bundle's version
BUNDLE_SYMBOLICNAME	String	A bundle's symbolic name
EVENT	Object	The actual event object. Used when rebroadcasting an event that was sent via some other event mechanism
EXCEPTION	Throwable	An exception or error
EXCEPTION_MESSAGE	String	Must be equal to exception.getMessage().
EXCEPTION_CLASS	String	Must be equal to the name of the Exception class.
MESSAGE	String	A human-readable message that is usually not localized.
SERVICE	Service Reference	A Service Reference
SERVICE_ID	Long	A service's id
SERVICE_OBJECTCLASS	String[]	A service's objectClass
SERVICE_PID	String | Collection <String>	A service's persistent identity. A PID that is specified with a String[] must be coerced into a Collection<String>.
TIMESTAMP	Long	The time when the event occurred, as reported by System.currentTimeMillis()

The topic of an OSGi event is constructed by taking the fully qualified name of the event class, substituting a slash for every period, and appending a slash followed by the name of the constant that defines the event type. For example, the topic of

```
BundleEvent.STARTED
```

Event becomes

```
org/osgi/framework/BundleEvent/STARTED
```

If a type code for the event is unknown then the event must be ignored.

113.6.2   OSGi Events

In order to present a consistent view of all the events occurring in the system, the existing Framework-level events are mapped to the Event Admin's publish-subscribe model. This allows event subscribers to treat framework events exactly the same as other events.

It is the responsibility of the Event Admin service implementation to map these Framework events to its queue.

The properties associated with the event depends on its class as outlined in the following sections.

113.6.3   Framework Event

Framework Events must be delivered asynchronously with a topic of:

```
org/osgi/framework/FrameworkEvent/<event type>
```

The following event types are supported:

```
STARTED
ERROR
PACKAGES_REFRESHED
STARTLEVEL_CHANGED
WARNING
INFO
```

Other events are ignored, no event will be send by the Event Admin. The following event properties must be set for a Framework Event.

- event – (FrameworkEvent) The original event object.

If the FrameworkEvent getBundle method returns a non-null value, the following fields must be set:

- bundle.id – (Long) The source's bundle id.
- bundle.symbolicName – (String) The source bundle's symbolic name. Only set if the bundle's symbolic name is not null.
- bundle.version – (Version) The version of the bundle, if set.
- bundle.signer – (String|Collection<String>) The DNs of the signers.
- bundle – (Bundle) The source bundle.

If the FrameworkEvent getThrowable method returns a non- null value:

- exception.class – (String) The fully-qualified class name of the attached Exception.
- exception.message –(String) The message of the attached exception. Only set if the Exception message is not null.
- exception – (Throwable) The Exception returned by the getThrowable method.

113.6.4   Bundle Event

Framework Events must be delivered asynchronously with a topic of:

```
org/osgi/framework/BundleEvent/<event type>
```

The following event types are supported:

```
INSTALLED
STARTED
STOPPED
UPDATED
UNINSTALLED
RESOLVED
```

UNRESOLVED

Unknown events must be ignored.

The following event properties must be set for a Bundle Event. If listeners require synchronous delivery then they should register a Synchronous Bundle Listener with the Framework.

- event – (BundleEvent) The original event object.
- bundle.id – (Long) The source's bundle id.
- bundle.symbolicName – (String) The source bundle's symbolic name. Only set if the bundle's symbolic name is not null.
- bundle.version – (Version) The version of the bundle, if set.
- bundle.signer – (String|Collection<String>) The DNs of the signers.
- bundle – (Bundle) The source bundle.

113.6.5 Service Event

Service Events must be delivered asynchronously with the topic:

    org/osgi/framework/ServiceEvent/<event type>

The following event types are supported:

    REGISTERED
    MODIFIED
    UNREGISTERING

Unknown events must be ignored.

- event – (ServiceEvent) The original Service Event object.
- service – (ServiceReference) The result of the getServiceReference method
- service.id – (Long) The service's ID.
- service.pid – (String or Collection<String>) The service's persistent identity. Only set if not null. If the PID is specified as a String[] then it must be coerced into a Collection<String>.
- service.objectClass – (String[]) The service's object class.

113.6.6 Other Event Sources

Several OSGi service specifications define their own event model. It is the responsibility of these services to map their events to Event Admin events. Event Admin is seen as a core service that will be present in most devices. However, if there is no Event Admin service present, applications are not mandated to buffer events.

113.7 Event Admin Service

The Event Admin service must be registered as a service with the object class org.osgi.service.event.EventAdmin. Multiple Event Admin services can be registered. Publishers should publish their event on the Event Admin service with the highest value for the SERVICE_RANKING service property. This is the service selected by the getServiceReference method.

The Event Admin service is responsible for tracking the registered handlers, handling event notifications and providing at least one thread for asynchronous event delivery.

113.7.1 Synchronous Event Delivery

Synchronous event delivery is initiated by the sendEvent method. When this method is invoked, the Event Admin service determines which handlers must be notified of the event and then notifies each one in turn. The handlers can be notified in the caller's thread or in an event-delivery thread, depending on the implementation. In either case, all notifications must be completely handled before the sendEvent method returns to the caller.

Synchronous event delivery is significantly more expensive than asynchronous delivery. All things considered equal, the asynchronous delivery should be preferred over the synchronous delivery.

Callers of this method will need to be coded defensively and assume that synchronous event notifications could be handled in a separate thread. That entails that they must not be holding any monitors when they invoke the sendEvent method. Otherwise they significantly increase the likelihood of deadlocks because Java monitors are not reentrant from another thread by definition. Not holding monitors is good practice even when the event is dispatched in the same thread.

113.7.2 Asynchronous Event Delivery

Asynchronous event delivery is initiated by the postEvent method. When this method is invoked, the Event Admin service must determine which handlers are interested in the event. By collecting this list of handlers during the method invocation, the Event Admin service ensures that only handlers that were registered at the time the event was posted will receive the event notification. This is the same as described in *Delivering Events* on page 116 of the Core specification.

The Event Admin service can use more than one thread to deliver events. If it does then it must guarantee that each handler receives the events in the same order as the events were posted. This ensures that handlers see events in the expected order. For example, it would be an error to see a destroyed event before the corresponding created event.

Before notifying each handler, the event delivery thread must ensure that the handler is still registered in the service registry. If it has been unregistered then the handler must not be notified.

The Event Admin service ensures that events are delivered in a well-defined order. For example, if a thread posts events A and B in the same thread then the handlers should not receive them in the order B, A. if A and B are posted by different threads at about the same time then no guarantees about the order of delivery are made.

113.7.3 Order of Event Delivery

Asynchronous events are delivered in the order in which they arrive in the event queue. Thus if two events are posted by the same thread then they will be delivered in the same order (though other events may come between them). However, if two or more events are posted by different threads then the order in which they arrive in the queue (and therefore the order in which they are delivered) will depend very much on subtle timing issues. The event delivery system cannot make any guarantees in this case.

Synchronous events are delivered as soon as they are sent. If two events are sent by the same thread, one after the other, then they must be guaranteed to be processed serially and in the same order. However, if two events are sent by different threads then no guarantees can be made. The events can be processed in parallel or serially, depending on whether or not the Event Admin service dispatches synchronous events in the caller's thread or in a separate thread.

Note that if the actions of a handler trigger a synchronous event, then the delivery of the first event will be paused and delivery of the second event will begin. Once delivery of the second event has completed, delivery of the first event will resume. Thus some handlers may observe the second event before they observe the first one.

113.8 Reliability

113.8.1 Exceptions in callbacks

If a handler throws an Exception during delivery of an event, it must be caught by the Event Admin service and handled in some implementation specific way. If a Log Service is available the exception should be logged. Once the exception has been caught and dealt with, the event delivery must continue with the next handlers to be notified, if any.

113.8.2 Dealing with Stalled Handlers

Event handlers should not spend too long in the handleEvent method. Doing so will prevent other handlers in the system from being notified. If a handler needs to do something that can take a while, it should do it in a different thread.

An event admin implementation can attempt to detect stalled or deadlocked handlers and deal with them appropriately. Exactly how it deals with this situation is left as implementation specific. One allowed implementation is to mark the current event delivery thread as invalid and spawn a new event delivery thread. Event delivery must resume with the next handler to be notified.

Implementations can choose to blacklist any handlers that they determine are misbehaving. Blacklisted handlers must not be notified of any events. If a handler is blacklisted, the event admin should log a message that explains the reason for it.

113.9   Inter-operability with Native Applications

Implementations of the Event Admin service can support passing events to, and/or receiving events from native applications.

If the implementation supports native inter-operability, it must be able to pass the topic of the event and its properties to/from native code. Implementations must be able to support property values of the following types:

- String objects, including full Unicode support
- Integer, Long, Byte, Short, Float, Double, Boolean, Character objects
- Single-dimension arrays of the above types (including String)
- Single-dimension arrays of Java's eight primitive types (int, long, byte, short, float, double, boolean, char)

Implementations can support additional types. Property values of unsupported types must be silently discarded.

113.10   Security

113.10.1 Topic Permission

The TopicPermission class allows fine-grained control over which bundles may post events to a given topic and which bundles may receive those events.

The target parameter for the permission is the topic name. TopicPermission classes uses a wildcard matching algorithm similar to the BasicPermission class, except that slashes are used as separators instead of periods. For example, a name of a/b/* implies a/b/c but not x/y/z or a/b.

There are two available actions: PUBLISH and SUBSCRIBE. These control a bundle's ability to either publish or receive events, respectively. Neither one implies the other.

113.10.2 Required Permissions

Bundles that need to register an event handler must be granted ServicePermission[org.osgi.service.event.EventHandler, REGISTER]. In addition, handlers require TopicPermission[<topic>, SUBSCRIBE] for each topic they want to be notified about.

Bundles that need to publish an event must be granted ServicePermission[org.osgi.service.event.EventAdmin, GET] so that they may retrieve the Event Admin service and use it. In addition, event sources require TopicPermission[<topic>, PUBLISH] for each topic they want to send events to.

Bundles that need to iterate the handlers registered with the system must be granted ServicePermission[org.osgi.service.event.EventHandler, GET] to retrieve the event handlers from the service registry.

Only a bundle that contains an Event Admin service implementation should be granted ServicePermission[org.osgi.service.event.EventAdmin, REGISTER] to register the event channel admin service.

113.10.3 Security Context During Event Callbacks

During an event notification, the Event Admin service's Protection Domain will be on the stack above the handler's Protection Domain. In the case of a synchronous event, the event publisher's protection domain can also be on the stack.

Therefore, if a handler needs to perform a secure operation using its own privileges, it must invoke the doPrivileged method to isolate its security context from that of its caller.

The event delivery mechanism must not wrap event notifications in a doPrivileged call.

113.11 org.osgi.service.event

Event Admin Package Version 1.2.

Bundles wishing to use this package must list the package in the Import-Package header of the bundle's manifest. For example:

```
Import-Package: org.osgi.service.event; version="[1.2,2.0)"
```

113.11.1 Summary

- *Event* - An event.
- *EventAdmin* - The Event Admin service.
- *EventConstants* - Defines standard names for EventHandler properties.
- *EventHandler* - Listener for Events.
- *TopicPermission* - A bundle's authority to publish or subscribe to event on a topic.

113.11.2 public class Event

An event. Event objects are delivered to EventHandler services which subscribe to the topic of the event.

Concurrency Immutable

113.11.2.1 public Event(String topic, Map properties)

topic The topic of the event.

properties The event's properties (may be null). A property whose key is not of type String will be ignored.

   □ Constructs an event.

Throws IllegalArgumentException – If topic is not a valid topic name.

Since 1.2

113.11.2.2 public Event(String topic, Dictionary properties)

topic The topic of the event.

properties The event's properties (may be null). A property whose key is not of type String will be ignored.

   □ Constructs an event.

Throws IllegalArgumentException – If topic is not a valid topic name.

113.11.2.3   **public boolean equals(Object object)**

object The Event object to be compared.

❑ Compares this Event object to another object.

An event is considered to be **equal to** another event if the topic is equal and the properties are equal. The properties are compared using the java.util.Map.equals() rules which includes identity comparison for array values.

Returns true if object is a Event and is equal to this object; false otherwise.

113.11.2.4   **public final Object getProperty(String name)**

name the name of the property to retrieve

❑ Retrieves a property.

Returns The value of the property, or null if not found.

113.11.2.5   **public final String[] getPropertyNames( )**

❑ Returns a list of this event's property names.

Returns A non-empty array with one element per property.

113.11.2.6   **public final String getTopic( )**

❑ Returns the topic of this event.

Returns The topic of this event.

113.11.2.7   **public int hashCode( )**

❑ Returns a hash code value for the object.

Returns An integer which is a hash code value for this object.

113.11.2.8   **public final boolean matches(Filter filter)**

filter The filter to test.

❑ Tests this event's properties against the given filter using a case sensitive match.

Returns true If this event's properties match the filter, false otherwise.

113.11.2.9   **public String toString( )**

❑ Returns the string representation of this event.

Returns The string representation of this event.

113.11.3   public interface EventAdmin

The Event Admin service. Bundles wishing to publish events must obtain the Event Admin service and call one of the event delivery methods.

Concurrency Thread-safe

113.11.3.1   **public void postEvent(Event event)**

event The event to send to all listeners which subscribe to the topic of the event.

❑ Initiate asynchronous delivery of an event. This method returns to the caller before delivery of the event is completed.

Throws SecurityException – If the caller does not have TopicPermission[topic,PUBLISH] for the topic specified in the event.

113.11.3.2   **public void sendEvent(Event event)**

event The event to send to all listeners which subscribe to the topic of the event.

□ Initiate synchronous delivery of an event. This method does not return to the caller until delivery of the event is completed.

Throws SecurityException – If the caller does not have TopicPermission[topic,PUBLISH] for the topic specified in the event.

113.11.4 public interface EventConstants

Defines standard names for EventHandler properties.

113.11.4.1 public static final String BUNDLE = "bundle"

The Bundle object of the bundle relevant to the event. The type of the value for this event property is Bundle.

Since 1.1

113.11.4.2 public static final String BUNDLE_ID = "bundle.id"

The Bundle id of the bundle relevant to the event. The type of the value for this event property is Long.

Since 1.1

113.11.4.3 public static final String BUNDLE_SIGNER = "bundle.signer"

The Distinguished Names of the signers of the bundle relevant to the event. The type of the value for this event property is String or Collection of String.

113.11.4.4 public static final String BUNDLE_SYMBOLICNAME = "bundle.symbolicName"

The Bundle Symbolic Name of the bundle relevant to the event. The type of the value for this event property is String.

113.11.4.5 public static final String BUNDLE_VERSION = "bundle.version"

The version of the bundle relevant to the event. The type of the value for this event property is Version.

Since 1.2

113.11.4.6 public static final String EVENT = "event"

The forwarded event object. Used when rebroadcasting an event that was sent via some other event mechanism. The type of the value for this event property is Object.

113.11.4.7 public static final String EVENT_FILTER = "event.filter"

Service Registration property (named event.filter) specifying a filter to further select Event s of interest to a Event Handler service.

Event handlers MAY be registered with this property. The value of this property is a string containing an LDAP-style filter specification. Any of the event's properties may be used in the filter expression. Each event handler is notified for any event which belongs to the topics in which the handler has expressed an interest. If the event handler is also registered with this service property, then the properties of the event must also match the filter for the event to be delivered to the event handler.

If the filter syntax is invalid, then the Event Handler must be ignored and a warning should be logged.

See Also Event, Filter

113.11.4.8 public static final String EVENT_TOPIC = "event.topics"

Service registration property (named event.topics) specifying the Event topics of interest to a Event Handler service.

Event handlers SHOULD be registered with this property. The value of the property is a string or an array of strings that describe the topics in which the handler is interested. An asterisk ('*') may be used as a trailing wildcard. Event Handlers which do not have a value for this property must not receive events. More precisely, the value of each string must conform to the following grammar:

```
topic-description := '*' | topic ( '/*' )?
topic := token ( '/' token )*
```

See Also   Event

113.11.4.9   **public static final String EXCEPTION = "exception"**

An exception or error. The type of the value for this event property is Throwable.

113.11.4.10   **public static final String EXCEPTION_CLASS = "exception.class"**

The name of the exception type. Must be equal to the name of the class of the exception in the event property EXCEPTION. The type of the value for this event property is String.

Since   1.1

113.11.4.11   **public static final String EXCEPTION_MESSAGE = "exception.message"**

The exception message. Must be equal to the result of calling getMessage() on the exception in the event property EXCEPTION. The type of the value for this event property is String.

113.11.4.12   **public static final String EXECPTION_CLASS = "exception.class"**

This constant was released with an incorrectly spelled name. It has been replaced by EXCEPTION_CLASS

Deprecated   As of 1.1, replaced by EXCEPTION_CLASS

113.11.4.13   **public static final String MESSAGE = "message"**

A human-readable message that is usually not localized. The type of the value for this event property is String.

113.11.4.14   **public static final String SERVICE = "service"**

A service reference. The type of the value for this event property is ServiceReference.

113.11.4.15   **public static final String SERVICE_ID = "service.id"**

A service's id. The type of the value for this event property is Long.

113.11.4.16   **public static final String SERVICE_OBJECTCLASS = "service.objectClass"**

A service's objectClass. The type of the value for this event property is String[].

113.11.4.17   **public static final String SERVICE_PID = "service.pid"**

A service's persistent identity. The type of the value for this event property is String.

113.11.4.18   **public static final String TIMESTAMP = "timestamp"**

The time when the event occurred, as reported by System.currentTimeMillis(). The type of the value for this event property is Long.

113.11.5   **public interface EventHandler**

Listener for Events.

EventHandler objects are registered with the Framework service registry and are notified with an Event object when an event is sent or posted.

EventHandler objects can inspect the received Event object to determine its topic and properties.

EventHandler objects must be registered with a service property EventConstants.EVENT_TOPIC whose value is the list of topics in which the event handler is interested.

For example:

```
String[] topics = new String[] {"com/isv/*"};
Hashtable ht = new Hashtable();
ht.put(EventConstants.EVENT_TOPIC, topics);
context.registerService(EventHandler.class.getName(), this, ht);
```

Event Handler services can also be registered with an EventConstants.EVENT_FILTER service property to further filter the events. If the syntax of this filter is invalid, then the Event Handler must be ignored by the Event Admin service. The Event Admin service should log a warning.

Security Considerations. Bundles wishing to monitor Event objects will require ServicePermission[EventHandler,REGISTER] to register an EventHandler service. The bundle must also have TopicPermission[topic,SUBSCRIBE] for the topic specified in the event in order to receive the event.

See Also Event

Concurrency Thread-safe

113.11.5.1 **public void handleEvent(Event event)**

event The event that occurred.

□ Called by the EventAdmin service to notify the listener of an event.

113.11.6 public final class TopicPermission extends Permission

A bundle's authority to publish or subscribe to event on a topic.

A topic is a slash-separated string that defines a topic.

For example:

```
org / osgi / service / foo / FooEvent / ACTION
```

TopicPermission has two actions: publish and subscribe.

Concurrency Thread-safe

113.11.6.1 **public static final String PUBLISH = "publish"**

The action string publish.

113.11.6.2 **public static final String SUBSCRIBE = "subscribe"**

The action string subscribe.

113.11.6.3 **public TopicPermission(String name, String actions)**

name Topic name.

actions publish,subscribe (canonical order).

□ Defines the authority to publich and/or subscribe to a topic within the EventAdmin service.

The name is specified as a slash-separated string. Wildcards may be used. For example:

```
org/osgi/service/fooFooEvent/ACTION
com/isv/*
*
```

A bundle that needs to publish events on a topic must have the appropriate TopicPermission for that topic; similarly, a bundle that needs to subscribe to events on a topic must have the appropriate TopicPermssion for that topic.

113.11.6.4	**public boolean equals(Object obj)**

obj	The object to test for equality with this TopicPermission object.

☐	Determines the equality of two TopicPermission objects. This method checks that specified TopicPermission has the same topic name and actions as this TopicPermission object.

Returns	true if obj is a TopicPermission, and has the same topic name and actions as this TopicPermission object; false otherwise.

113.11.6.5	**public String getActions( )**

☐	Returns the canonical string representation of the TopicPermission actions.

Always returns present TopicPermission actions in the following order: publish,subscribe.

Returns	Canonical string representation of the TopicPermission actions.

113.11.6.6	**public int hashCode( )**

☐	Returns the hash code value for this object.

Returns	A hash code value for this object.

113.11.6.7	**public boolean implies(Permission p)**

p	The target permission to interrogate.

☐	Determines if the specified permission is implied by this object.

This method checks that the topic name of the target is implied by the topic name of this object. The list of TopicPermission actions must either match or allow for the list of the target object to imply the target TopicPermission action.

```
x/y/*,"publish" -> x/y/z,"publish" is true
*,"subscribe" -> x/y,"subscribe"   is true
*,"publish" -> x/y,"subscribe"     is false
x/y,"publish" -> x/y/z,"publish"   is false
```

Returns	true if the specified TopicPermission action is implied by this object; false otherwise.

113.11.6.8	**public PermissionCollection newPermissionCollection( )**

☐	Returns a new PermissionCollection object suitable for storing TopicPermission objects.

Returns	A new PermissionCollection object.

121 Blueprint Container Specification

Version 1.0

121.1 Introduction

One of the great promises of object oriented languages was the greater reuse it should enable. However, over time it turned out that reuse was still hard. One of the key reasons was *coupling*. Trying to reuse a few classes usually ended up in dragging in many more classes, that in their turn dragged in even more classes, ad nauseum.

One of the key innovations in the Java language to address this coupling issue were *interfaces*. Interfaces significantly could minimize coupling because they were void of any implementation details. Any class can use an interface, where that interface can be implemented by any other class. However, coupling was still necessary because objects need to be created, and for creating an object its concrete class is necessary.

One of the most successful insights in the software industry of late has been *inversion of control*, or more specific *dependency injection*. With dependency injection, an object is given the collaborators that it needs to work with. By not creating these dependencies itself, the object is not coupled to the concrete type of these implementations and their transitive implementation dependencies. However, these objects are not useful on their own, they can only function when an external party provides these objects with their collaborating objects.

An injection framework creates these objects, and also their concrete dependencies, and wires them together. Injection frameworks can significantly increase reuse and provide increased flexibility. For example, during testing it is possible to inject mocked up objects instead of the actual objects.

There exists a number of these injection frameworks in the market, for example [2] *Spring Framework*, [4] *Guice*, and [5] *Picocontainer*. These containers are configured with XML, Java annotations, or provide automatic configuration based on types.

Decoupling is one of the primary drivers for the OSGi specifications. The module layer provides many mechanisms to hide implementation details and explicitly defines any dependencies. The service layer provides a mechanism to collaborate with other bundles without caring about who that other bundle is. However, using the OSGi APIs to construct an application out of services and objects also implies coupling to these OSGi APIs.

This specification therefore defines a dependency injection framework, specifically for OSGi bundles, that understands the unique dynamic nature of services. It provides an OSGi bundle programming model with minimal implementation dependencies and virtually no accidental complexity in the Java code. Bundles in this programming model contain a number of XML definition resources which are used by the Blueprint Container to wire the application together and start it when the bundle is active.

This Blueprint Container specification is derived from the [3] *Spring Dynamic Modules* project.

121.1.1 Essentials

- *Dependency Injection Framework* – Provide an advanced dependency injection framework for bundles that can create and wire objects and services together into an application.

- *Inversion of Control* – (IOC) A pattern in which a framework/library provides the control over the component instances instead of the other way around. Dependency injection is a form of IOC.
- *Extender Model* – Enable the configuration of components inside a bundle based on configuration data provided by the bundle developer. The life cycle of these components is controlled by the extender based on the extended bundle's state.
- *Unencumbered* – Do not require any special bundle activator or other code to be written inside the bundle in order to have components instantiated and configured.
- *Services* – Enable the usage of OSGi services as injected dependencies.
- *Dependencies* – Allow components to depend on other components like services and beans as well as register as services, with the full breadth of the OSGi capabilities.
- *Dynamicity* – Minimize the complexity of using the dynamicity of services
- *Business Logic* – A focus on writing business logic in regular Java classes that are not required to implement certain framework APIs or contracts in order to integrate with a container.
- *Declarative* – This facilitates independent testing of components and reduces environment dependencies.
- *Familiarity* – Familiar to enterprise Java developers.

121.1.2   Entities

- *Blueprint Extender* – The bundle that creates and injects component instances for a Blueprint bundle as configured in that Blueprint bundle's XML definition resources.
- *Blueprint Container* – Represents the activities of the Blueprint Extender for a specific Blueprint Bundle.
- *Blueprint Bundle* – A bundle that is being constructed by the Blueprint Container because it has a Bundle-Blueprint header or it contains XML resources in the OSGI-INF/blueprint directory.
- *Manager* – A manager is responsible for the life cycle of all *component instances* for one *component definition*. There are the following types of managers. A manager is a *bean manager*, a *service reference manager*, or a *service manager*. A manager can have *explicit* and *implicit* dependencies on other manager. During instantiation and runtime, a manager can *provide* a component instance to be injected or used in other ways.
- *Component* – A loosely defined term for the application building blocks and their infrastructure. Components are instantiated into *component instances* by a *manager* that is configured with a *Component Metadata* subclass that is derived from a *Component Definition*.
- *Component Instance* – An object that is part of the application. Component Instances are created and managed by their component *manager*.
- *Component Definition* – Configuration data used by a manager to construct and manage component instances. This configuration data is represented in Metadata, an interface hierarchy starting with the *Metadata* interface.
- *Bean Manager* – A manager that has metadata for creating Java objects and injecting them with objects and component instances that come from other managers it implicitly depends on.
- *Service Manager* – A manager that handles the registration of a service object that is provided by a component instance.
- *Service Reference Manager* – The general name for the reference and reference-list managers.
- *Reference Manager* – A manager that handles the dependency on a single OSGi service.
- *Reference-list Manager* – A manager that handles the dependency on a list of OSGi services.
- *Environment Manager* – A manager that can provide information from the Bundle's environment. For example, the BlueprintContainer object is made available through an environment manager.
- *Target* – A manager type useful in a callback context. These are the ref (which is an indirection to), a reference, and a bean manager.
- *Property* – A conceptual instance variable of a component instance provided by a bean manager that is set on the component instance with a corresponding set<Name> method.
- *Argument* – Metadata for an argument in a constructor or method.
- *Type Converter* – A component instance defined, or referenced, in the type-converters section implementing the Converter interface.

Figure 121.1   *Blueprint Class and Service Overview*

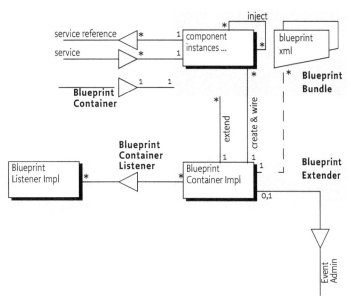

121.1.3   Synopsis

The Blueprint Extender bundle waits for Blueprint bundles. These are bundles that contain Blueprint XML resources called the definitions. These XML resources can be found in a fixed location or pointed to from a manifest header. When a Blueprint extender bundle detects that a Blueprint bundle is ready, it creates a Blueprint Container to manage that Blueprint bundle.

The Blueprint Container then parses the definitions into metadata objects. All top-level elements in the definitions are ComponentMetadata objects and are registered in the Blueprint Container by their id.

For each of the ComponentMetadata objects, the Blueprint Container has a corresponding component manager. For example, a BeanMetadata object relates to a Bean Manager instance. There are the following types of managers:

- *Bean Managers* – Can provide general objects that are properly constructed and configured
- *Service Managers* – Can register services
- *Service Reference Managers* – Provide proxies to one or more services. there are two sub-types: reference-list and reference.
- *Environment Managers* – Holding environment values like the Blueprint Bundle object

After creation, all managers are not yet activated. A manager is activated on demand when it has to provide a component instance for the first time.

All service reference managers track services in the service registry in order to determine if they are satisfied or not. If not, the Blueprint Container can optionally start a *grace* period. During the grace period, the Blueprint Container waits for all mandatory service reference managers to become satisfied. If this does not happen during the grace period, the Blueprint Container must abort the initialization.

From now on, the Blueprint Container is ready to provide component instances. Whenever a manager is asked to provide a component instance for the first time, the manager is activated. This activation will first request all its dependencies to provide a component instance, activating these managers if not already activated, recursively.

However, the activation needs a trigger to start. There are two triggers.

- *Service Request* – All service managers must have a Service Factory registered with the OSGi service registry whenever that service manager is enabled, see *Enabled* on page 225.
- *Eager Managers* – To kick start the application in the bundle, the Blueprint Container must ask all eager managers to provide a component instance, thereby activating these managers, see *Eager Instantiation* on page 208.

Service references must actuate their reference listeners when they are activated.

Bean managers have a scope. This scope can be singleton, where the manager always provides the same object, or prototype, where the manager creates a new object for each request.

Service reference managers provide proxies to the actual service objects and fetch the service object lazily. They provide a constant reference that dampen the dynamics of the underlying service objects.

If the Blueprint Container has successfully activated the eager managers, it will register a Blueprint Container service.

When the Blueprint Container must be destroyed because: the Blueprint bundle has stopped, there is a failure, or the Blueprint extender is stopped, then the Blueprint Container service is unregistered and all managers are deactivated. This will unregister any services and disable listeners, which release the component instances. Then all component instances are destroyed in reverse dependency order. That is, a component instance is destroyed when no other component instances depend on it.

121.2 Managers

The key feature of the Blueprint Container specification is to let the application in the bundle be constructed in the proper order from objects that are not required to be aware of Blueprint, OSGi, or even each other. These objects are called *component instances.* The active entity that orchestrates the life cycle of the bundle application is the *Blueprint Container.* It is configured by XML resources in the Blueprint bundle. The Blueprint Container is responsible for construction and configuration of the component instances as well as the interaction with the service registry.

Inside the Blueprint Container, component instances are managed by a *manager.* A manager is configured with one Component Definition, for example a bean definition, and can then provide one or more component instances. Such a configured manager instance is also loosely called a *component.*

A manager can have additional behavior associated with it. This behavior is controlled by the manager's *type.* This specification defines a number of manager types: bean, service, environment, reference, and reference-list. These types are further defined in the next section.

These managers are conceptual, they are not visible in the API of this specification. That is, an implementation is free to implement the specification without these objects as long as the externally observable behavior is the same.

As an example, a trivial echo service:

```
<blueprint>
   <service id="echoService"
       interface="com.acme.Echo" ref="echo"/>
   <bean id="echo" class="com.acme.EchoImpl">
     <property name="message" value="Echo: "/>
   </bean>
</blueprint>

public interface Echo {
  public String echo(String m);
}
public class EchoImpl implements Echo {
  String message;
```

```
      public void setMessage(String m) {
        this.message= m;
      }
      public void echo(String s) { return message + s; }
   }
```

The example defines two *top-level* managers: echoService and echo. The echoService manager is of type *service*, and the echo manager is of type *bean*. The service manager is responsible for registering an OSGi service, where the service object will be the component instance provided by the echo manager. The echo component instance gets a message injected.

As seen from the example, managers can use component instances from other managers to construct their component instances. The use of other managers creates an *implicit dependency*. Managers can also declare *explicit dependencies*. Dependencies are transitive, see *Manager Dependencies* on page 199 for more information. In the previous example, the echoService service manager depends on the echo manager, this is an implicit dependency.

Managers have their own life cycle. They are conceptually created after the Blueprint Container has decided to run the application, see *Blueprint Life-Cycle* on page 203. However, the intention of this specification is to allow the bundle application to lazily *activate*. That is, no application code is used until there is a trigger like a service request or a service manager has an explicit dependency. A manager must always be atomically activated before it provides its first component instance. During activation, listeners are actuated and notified, service objects are requested, etc. The details are described in the appropriate manager's type description.

Each manager type has an associated *component metadata* type. Component Metadata is used to configure a manager. XML definition resources in the bundle define the source for this Metadata. In the previous example, the service and bean XML element are translated to a ServiceMetadata and BeanMetadata object respectively.

The Blueprint Container maintains a registry of managers by their *id*. These are the managers that are called the *top-level* managers. Top level managers are managers defined as child elements of the top XML blueprint element or bean managers in the type-converters element. Their Metadata is registered under their id (or calculated id) in the Blueprint Container. All top level managers share a single namespace. That is, it is an error if the same id is used multiple times or attempts to override the built-in environment managers.

Top level managers can depend on other top level managers but there are many places where a manager can depend on an *inlined* manager. In these places, a complete manager can be defined inside another manager. Such inlined managers are always *anonymous*: they must not have an id and must not be registered as a top-level manager. Inlined beans are further constrained to always have prototype scope. That is, every time they are asked to provide a component instance, they must return a different object.

When the Blueprint Container must be *destroyed*, all singleton component instances that have been created must be destroyed. This must first *deactivate* all activated managers. All these managers must release their dependencies on any component instances they hold. Then the Blueprint Container must destroy all singleton component instances. The order of this destruction must be such that a component instance is only destroyed if there are no other component instances depending on it. See *Reverse Dependency Order* on page 200.

The relations between manager types, component instances, metadata and the Blueprint Container is schematically depicted in Figure 121.2 on page 198.

Figure 121.2   *Managers and Metadata*

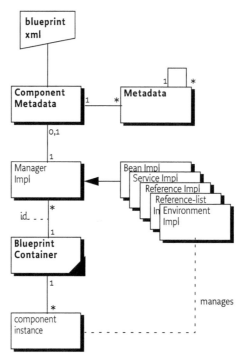

121.2.1   Manager Types

Blueprint only supports a fixed set of the following *manager types*:

- *Bean* – A bean manager provides regular Java objects as component instances. It has the following features:
    - Construction via class name, static factory method, or a factory method on a *target*. A *target* is a reference to a top level manager of type bean or service reference, or a referral to a top level manager of those types.
    - Can have *arguments* for a constructor or factory method.
    - Can have *properties* that are injected.
    - Manages a singleton or creates objects on demand depending on its *scope*.
    - Life cycle callbacks for end of initialization and destruction.

    See *Bean Manager* on page 214 for more details.
- *Reference* – Reference managers track a service in the OSGi service registry. When activated, they provide a proxy to a service object. See *Service Reference Managers* on page 226 for more details. A reference is satisfied when its selection matches a service in the registry.
- *Reference-list* – Reference-list managers track multiple services. A reference-list is satisfied when its selection matches one or more services in the registry. See *Service Reference Managers* on page 226 for more details.
- *Service* – Service managers maintain the registration of an OSGi service object. Service managers provide a proxied ServiceRegistration object so that the application code has a constant reference, even if the service is unregistered and then registered again. A service manager is *enabled* if all the mandatory service references in its dependencies are satisfied. See *Service Manager* on page 219.
- *Environment* – Environment managers provide access to the environment of the Blueprint bundle, for example its Bundle Context. See *Blueprint Container* on page 247 for more details.

121.2.2   ## Metadata Objects

Metadata objects hold the configuration information (from the Component Definition) for the managers. These metadata objects represent the element structure found in the XML definitions in canonical form. Each element in the XML has a corresponding Metadata sub-type that has a name that maps directly to the element. For example, the bean element represents the bean manager that has its configuration data defined in the BeanMetadata interface.

There are Metadata interfaces for all the manager types, except the environment type. Some dependency injections require the construction of arrays, maps, properties, simple objects, etc. For these type of objects, additional Metadata sub-interfaces are defined; these interfaces provide the information to construct the basic programming types. For example, the CollectionMetadata interface contains the information to construct an Array or Collection of a given type, where its member values are defined by other Metadata objects.

The set of Metadata types is fixed in this specification, just like the set of manager types. It is impossible to extend this set with user defined Metadata types. For more information about Metadata, see *Metadata* on page 251.

121.2.3   ## Activation and Deactivation

Managers are created after all the definitions are parsed. Some managers can already show some activity, for example service managers always activate explicit dependencies and register a Service Factory with the OSGi service registry. However, in this state a manager should attempt to not use any resources from the Blueprint bundle until it is activated itself.

A manager must be atomically activated when it has to provide its first component instance. During activation it can perform a manager specific initialization that will actually consume resources from the Blueprint bundle. This activation must be atomic. That is, if a manager is being activated then other threads must block until the activation is completed.

Deactivation only happens during the destruction of the Blueprint Container. During deactivation, a manager must release any dependencies on resources of the Blueprint bundle. No components instances are destroyed during deactivation because the singleton component instance destruction must happen after all managers are deactivated.

Each manager type has a dedicated section that describes what must happen during its activation and deactivation.

121.2.4   ## Manager Dependencies

Managers that refer to other managers depend on these managers transitively. For example, a service manager depends directly on the manager that provides the service object. In its turn, that service object could depend on any provided objects that were used to construct and inject this service object, and so on. This transitive set of dependencies are called *implicit dependencies* because these dependencies are implicitly created by the use of other managers in the Component Definitions.

Managers can also be configured with *explicit dependencies*. The XML definitions for all managers have a depends-on attribute with a whitespace delimited list of manager ids. Each of these depends-on managers must provide an object, that will be ignored. The timing of activation of dependencies depends on the specific managers but in general should happen before any observable behavior.

There is no ordering guarantee between independent sets of dependencies. The dependency graph is based on the managers, not the component instances. For example, the following definition:

```
<blueprint default-activation='eager'>
  <bean id='A'...>  <argument ref='B'> </bean>
  <bean id='B' depends-on='C E'...>
    <argument ref='C'>
  </bean>
  <bean id='C' scope='prototype' ...>
```

```
        <argument ref='D'>
      </bean>
      <bean id='D' .../>
      <bean id='E' ...> <argument ref='C'/> </bean>
      <bean id='F' depends-on='B' activation="lazy"/>
   </blueprint>
```

After initialization, there will be the following component instances: a, b, d, e, and three c's. Lower case names are used for instances, the corresponding upper case is its manager. The ordering guarantee is that manager D is activated before manager C, manager C is activated before manager E and B, manager E is activated before manager B, and manager B is activated before manager A. There will be no component instance f created because F is a lazy manager. There are three c's because manager E and B have an implicit dependency on C and manager B has an additional explicit dependency, totalling 3 dependencies. One of these c's is an orphan and will be garbage collected over time because it is not referred to by any component instance.

The example is depicted in Figure 121.3 on page 200.

Figure 121.3   *Dependency Graph after initialization*

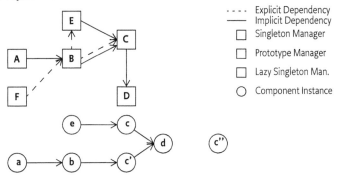

121.2.5   Reverse Dependency Order

The destruction of component instances must be done in *reverse dependency order*. This concept is defined as only destroying a singleton component instance (in a manager specific way) when no other activated singleton component instance has an implicit or explicit dependency on it. That is, a component instance has no more field references to other component instances. A component that never was activated does not have any dependencies.

This strategy will ensure that a component instance cannot have an instance field that refers to an component instance that has been destroyed.

Deactivating the manager will release its dependencies, which then frees up other component instances until all component instances are destroyed, or there are cyclic references. In the case of cyclic dependencies, the order of destruction is undefined.

In the example depicted in Figure 121.3 on page 200, the previous rules imply that component instance a can be immediately destroyed first because it has no clients. After component instance a is destroyed, component instance b becomes free because no other component instances refer to it. The explicit dependency from manager F to manager B was never activated, so it is not taken into account. The destruction of component instance b frees up component instance e and c because now the explicit dependency from manager B to manager E and manager B to manager C have been released. Manager C is deactivated but no component instances are destructed because it has prototype scope; these managers do not destroy their component instances. Then component instance d can be destructed.

121.2.6   Cyclic Dependencies

The implicit and explicit dependencies of a component form a dependency graph. In the ideal case, this graph should be free from *cycles*. A cycle occurs when a set of one or more managers find themselves in their own implicit or explicit dependencies. For example:

```
public class A { public A(B b); }
public class B { public void setA(A a); }

<bean id="a" class="A"> <argument ref="b"/> </bean>
<bean id="b" class="B"> <property name="a" ref="a"/> </bean>
```

In this example, the cycle is the set {a,b}. Managers can be part of multiple cycles.

When a member of a cycle is requested to provide a component instance, the Blueprint Container must break the cycle by finding one *breaking member* in the cycle's members. A breaking member must be a singleton bean and use property injection for the dependency that causes the cycle. The Blueprint Container can pick any suitable member of the cycle for breaking member, if no such member can be found, then initialization fails or the getComponentInstance method must throw a Component Definition Exception.

In the previous example, manager b can be a breaking member because it uses the property injection for the cyclic dependency on manager a. Manager a cannot be a breaking member because the cyclic dependency is caused by a constructor argument, a breaking member must use property injection for the cyclic dependency to be broken.

A breaking member must return a partially initialized component instance when it is asked to provide an object. A partially initialized object has done all possible initialization but has not yet been called with the initMethod (if specified) nor has it been injected any of the properties that causes a cycle. The *finalization* of the partially initialized component instance must be delayed until the breaking member has been injected in all referring members of the cycles. Finalization means injecting any remaining unset properties and calling of the initMethod, if specified.

The consequence of partially initialized component instances is that they can be used before they have all properties set, applications must be aware of this.

All partially initialized component instances must be finalized before the Blueprint Container enters the Runtime phase and before a call to the getComponentInstance method returns a component instance.

All detected cycles should be logged.

Consider the following example:

```
public class A {
 public A(B b) {}
}
public class B {
 public B(A a) {}
}
```

And the configuration:

```
<bean id="a" class="A"> <argument ref="b"/>        </bean>
<bean id="b" class="B"> <argument ref="a"/>        </bean>
```

In this case, the cycle cannot be broken because neither manager qualifies as breaking manager because they have a constructor/factory argument dependency. That is, it is impossible to construct an object without using the dependency. However, consider the following example:

```
public class A {
 public A(B b) {}
}
```

```
public class B {
 public B(C c) {}
}
public class C {
   public void setA(A a) {}
}
```

And the configuration:

```
<bean id="a" class="A"> <argument ref="b"/>          </bean>
<bean id="b" class="B"> <argument ref="c"/>          </bean>
<bean id="c" class="C" init-method="done">
    <property name="a" ref="a"/>
</bean>
```

This configuration is depicted in Figure 121.4 on page 202. This cycle {a,b,c} can be broken by select-ing manager c as the breaking member. If manager a is requested to provide a component instance for the first time, then the following sequence takes place:

```
activate a
  activate b
    activate c
       c = new C()
      b = new B(c)
    a = new A(b)
    c.seta(a)
    c.done()
  return a
```

Figure 121.4   *Cyclic Dependency*

Cycles must be broken, if possible, both for singleton managers as well as prototype beans, although a breaking manager must always be a singleton bean because a prototype bean must always return a new object, making it impossible to break the cycle by returning a partially initialized component instance. That is, the following definition is not allowed to attempt to create an infinite loop:

```
<bean id="a" scope="singleton" class="A">
    <property name="a" ref="a">
</bean>
```

The previous definition must create an A object that refers to itself. However, if the example had used a prototype scope, it would be an unbreakable cycle.

121.2.7   Eager Managers

The Blueprint Container can force the activation of the application in the Blueprint bundle with *eager* managers. An eager manager is a manager that has the activation set to eager. A bean manager can only be eager if it has singleton scope.

Eager managers are explicitly activated by asking them to provide a component instance after all other initialization is done. A bundle that wants to be lazily initialized should not define any eager managers.

121.3   Blueprint Life-Cycle

A bundle is a *Blueprint bundle* if it contains one or more blueprint XML *definition* resources in the OSGI-INF/blueprint directory or it contains the Bundle-Blueprint manifest header referring to existing resources.

A *Blueprint extender* is an implementation of this specification and must track blueprint bundles that are *type compatible* for the Blueprint packages and initialize them appropriately. The timing and ordering of the initialization process is detailed in the following section.

There should be only one Blueprint extender present in an OSGi framework because this specification does not specify a way to resolve the conflicts that arise when two Blueprint extenders extend the same Blueprint bundle.

121.3.1   Class Space Compatibility

A Blueprint extender must not manage a Blueprint bundle if there is a class space incompatibility for the org.osgi.service.blueprint packages. For example, if the Blueprint bundle uses the BlueprintContainer class, then it must import the org.osgi.service.blueprint.container package. The Blueprint extender and the Blueprint bundle must then share the same class space for this package. Type compatibility can be verified by loading a class from the blueprint packages via the Blueprint extender bundle and the Blueprint bundle's loadClass methods. If the Blueprint bundle cannot load the class or the class is identical to the class loaded from the extender, then the two bundles are compatible for the given package. If the Blueprint extender is not class space compatible with the Blueprint bundle, then Blueprint extender must not start to manage the Blueprint bundle.

121.3.2   Initialization of a Blueprint Container

A Blueprint extender manages the application life cycle of Blueprint bundles based on:

- The Blueprint bundle state,
- The Blueprint definitions,
- The Blueprint extender's bundle state
- The class space compatibility

All activities on behalf of the Blueprint bundle must use the Bundle Context of the Blueprint bundle. All dynamic class loads must use the Blueprint bundle's Bundle loadClass method.

The following sections describe a linear process that handles one Blueprint bundle as if it was managed by a special thread, that is, waits are specified if the thread waits. Implementations are likely to use a state machine instead for each managed Blueprint bundle, the linear description is only used for simplicity.

In the following description of the initialization steps, the Blueprint Container will update its state. State changes are broadcast as events, see *Events* on page 248.

If any failure occurs during initialization, or the Blueprint bundle or Blueprint extender bundle is stopped, the Blueprint Container must be destroyed, see *Failure* on page 204. These checks are not indicated in the normal flow for clarity.

121.3.2.1   Initialization Steps

The initialization process of a Blueprint Container is defined in the following steps:

1. Wait until a blueprint bundle is *ready*. A blueprint bundle is ready when it is in the ACTIVE state, and for blueprint bundles that have a lazy activation policy, also in the STARTING state.
2. Prepare, verify if this Blueprint bundle must be managed, see *Preparing* on page 206.
3. State = CREATING
4. Parse the XML definition resources.
5. Service reference managers must start tracking their satisfiablity without actually activating. See *Tracking References* on page 207.

6 If all mandatory service references are satisfied, or the blueprint.graceperiod is false, then go to step 9.
7 State = GRACE_PERIOD
8 Perform the *grace period*. This period waits until all mandatory service references are satisfied. See *Grace Period* on page 207. This step fails if the mandatory dependencies are not satisfied at the end of the grace period.
9 The Blueprint Container is now ready to provide component instances.
10 Service managers must initialize their explicit dependencies and have a Service Factory registered during the periods that they are enabled. See *Service Registration* on page 207.
11 Ask all eager managers to provide a component instance. See *Eager Instantiation* on page 208.
12 State = CREATED
13 Register the Blueprint Container
14 The components are now active and perform their function until the Blueprint bundle or the Blueprint extender bundle are stopped.
15 State = DESTROYING
16 Perform the Destroy phase, see *Destroy the Blueprint Container* on page 208.
17 State = DESTROYED

121.3.2.2   **Failure**

If at any time there is a failure, the Blueprint Container must:

1 State = FAILURE
2 Unregister the Blueprint Container service.
3 Destroy the Blueprint Container.
4 Wait for the Blueprint bundle to be stopped.

121.3.2.3   **Diagram**

This initialization process is depicted in Figure 121.5 on page 205.

Figure 121.5   *Blueprint Bundle Initialization*

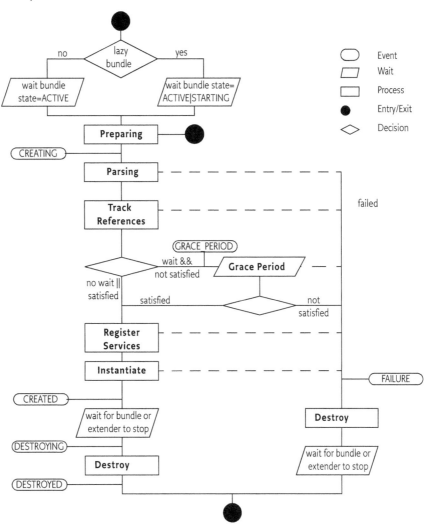

121.3.3 Extensions

A compliant implementation of this specification must follow the rules as outlined. However, implementations can provide functional extensions by including attributes or elements of other namespaces. For example, a Blueprint extender implementation that supports proxying of certain classes and a number of additional type converters could include a http://www.acme.com/extensions namespace that adds an extensions attribute on the blueprint element:

```xml
<xml version="1.0" encoding="UTF-8">
<blueprint
 xmlns="http://www.osgi.org/xmlns/blueprint/v1.0.0"
 xmlns:ext="http://www.acme.com/extensions"

  ext:extensions="proxyClasses"
>
  ...
</blueprint>
```

Blueprint extenders that detect the use of an unrecognized namespace must fail to signal a portability problem.

121.3.4   Preparing

Blueprint definitions are stored as resources in the Blueprint bundle. If a Bundle-Blueprint manifest header is defined, then this header contains a list of paths. The Bundle-Blueprint header has the following syntax:

```
Bundle-Blueprint   ::= header
                       // Core 3.2.4 Common Header Syntax
```

This specification does not define any attributes or directives for this header. Implementations can provide proprietary parameters that should be registered with the OSGi Alliance to prevent name collisions. The non-localized version of the header must be used.

The last component of each path in the Bundle-Blueprint header may use wildcards so that Bundle.findEntries can be used to locate the XML document within the bundle and its fragments. The findEndtries method must always be used in the non-recursive mode. Valid paths in the header have one of the following forms:

- *absolute path* – The path to a resource in the fragment or directory, this resource must exist. For example cnf/start.xml.
- *directory* – The path to directory in a fragment or main bundle, the path must end in a slash ('/'). The pattern used in the findEntries method must then be *.xml. The directory is allowed to be empty.
- *pattern* – The last component of the path specifies a filename with optional wildcards. The part before is the path of directory in the bundle or one of its fragments. These two parts specify the parameter to findEntries. It is allowed to have no matching resources. An example of a pattern is: cnf/*.xml.

If no resources can be found, then the Blueprint bundle will not be managed and the initialization exits.

For example, the following header will read the resources /lib/account.xml, /security.bp, and all resources which path ends in .xml in the /cnf directory:

```
Bundle-Blueprint: lib/account.xml, security.bp, cnf/*.xml
```

If the Bundle-Blueprint header is not defined, then its default value is:

```
OSGI-INF/blueprint/*.xml
```

A Bundle-Blueprint manifest header specified in a fragment is ignored by the Blueprint Container. However, XML documents referenced by a bundle's Bundle-Blueprint manifest header, or its default, may be contained in attached fragments, as defined by the findEntries method.

If the Bundle-Blueprint header is specified but empty, then the Blueprint bundle must not be managed. This can be used to temporarily disable a Blueprint bundle.

121.3.5   Parsing

The Blueprint Container must parse the XML definitions into the Blueprint Container's metadata registry. Parsing fails if:

- A path from the Bundle-Blueprint header cannot be found in the bundle or any of its fragments.
- An XML definition does not validate against its schema.
- The XML elements do not meet one or more of their constraints
- Any errors occur

For failure, see *Failure* on page 209.

121.3.6   Tracking References

Service reference managers must track the service registry to see if they are satisfied or not. These managers must not be activated to register these service listeners nor must they activate any dependencies until they are activated. That is, no component instances for the reference listeners are obtained until the service reference manager is activated.

121.3.7   Grace Period

A Blueprint Container by default will wait for its dependencies in the *grace period*. However, this can be overridden with a directive on the Bundle-SymbolicName header of the Blueprint bundle:

- blueprint.graceperiod (true|false) – If set to true, then the Blueprint Container must enter the grace period and wait for dependencies, this is the default. Otherwise, it must skip the grace period and progress to the next phase regardless if there are any unsatisfied service references.

The purpose of the grace period is to handle the initialization of multiple bundles *gracefully*. The grace period will first wait a configurable time for all mandatory service references to become satisfied, or for the bundle to stop. If these mandatory services are satisfied, then the grace period succeeds, otherwise it will fail. If the bundle is stopped during the grace period, then the Blueprint Container must be destroyed.

During the waiting period services can come and go. Each time such a service event takes place that involves any of the mandatory service references, the Blueprint Container must send out another GRACE_PERIOD event if that event does not result in ending the grace period. The event contains the complete filters of the unsatisfied service references, see *Blueprint Event* on page 248.

The wait time for the grace period is defined in a directive on the Bundle-SymbolicName header of the Blueprint bundle:

- blueprint.timeout (Integer >= 0) – The time to wait in the grace period for dependencies to become satisfied in milliseconds. The default is 300000, which is 5 minutes. If the timeout is 0, an indefinite wait will take place.

OSGi services are dynamic, therefore the grace period does not guarantee that all mandatory service references are still available. It only guarantees that at one moment in time they were available. A mandatory reference can become *unsatisfied* at any moment in time when a service is not available. See the *Service Dynamics* on page 245 for a description of how this is handled.

For example, the following header will make the bundle wait a maximum of 10 seconds for its mandatory service references to be satisfied. These dependencies must be satisfied, or a failure occurs.

```
Bundle-SymbolicName: com.acme.foo;
    blueprint.graceperiod:=true;
    blueprint.timeout:= 10000
```

121.3.8   Service Registration

A service manager must first activate all its explicit dependencies but it must not activate. It must then ensure that a Service Factory object is registered as a service when that service is *enabled*. Enabled means that all of the mandatory service references in its dependencies are satisfied.

Once the Service Factory is registered, any bundle can get the corresponding service object. Such a request must activate the service manager, if it is not already activated. Activation of a service manager must obtain a component instance from the Blueprint Container for the service object and any registration listeners. The registration listeners are then actuated and notified of the initial state.

121.3.9 Eager Instantiation

After all initialization is done, the Blueprint Container is ready. It is now possible to request component instances. If a bundle needs immediate startup because they cannot wait until they are triggered, then it should set the activation of its bean managers to eager. The Blueprint Container must request all eager managers to provide a component instance in this instantiation phase, see also *Lazy and Eager* on page 213.

121.3.10 Runtime Phase

The Blueprint Container must be registered as a service with the following service properties:

- osgi.blueprint.container.symbolicname – The bundle symbolic name of the Blueprint bundle
- osgi.blueprint.container.version – The version of the Blueprint bundle

The Blueprint Container service must only be available during the runtime phase when initialization has succeeded.

As long as the Blueprint extender and the Blueprint bundle are active, the application is in the runtime phase. The component instances perform their requested functionality in collaboration. The Blueprint Container can be used to provide objects from the defined managers, get information about the configuration, and general state information, see *Blueprint Container* on page 247.

121.3.11 Destroy the Blueprint Container

The Blueprint Container must be destroyed when any of the following conditions becomes true:

- The Blueprint bundle is stopped, that is, it is no longer ready.
- The Blueprint extender is stopped
- One of the initialization phases failed.

Destroying the Blueprint Container must occur synchronously with the Bundle STOPPING event if that caused any of the previous conditions. For example, if the Blueprint extender is stopped, it must synchronously destroy all Blueprint Containers it has created.

Destroying the Blueprint Container means:

1　Unregistering the Blueprint Container service
2　Deactivating all managers.
3　Destroying all component instances in reverse dependency order, see *Reverse Dependency Order* on page 200.

A Blueprint Container must continue to follow the destruction even when component instances throw exceptions or other problems occur. These errors should be logged.

If the Blueprint extender is stopped, then all its active Blueprint Containers must be destroyed in an orderly fashion, synchronously with the stopping of the Blueprint extender bundle. Blueprint Containers must use the following algorithm to destroy multiple Blueprint Containers:

1　Destroy Blueprint Containers that do not have any services registered that are in use by other bundles. More recently installed bundles must be destroyed before later installed bundles, that is, reverse bundle id order.
2　The previous step can have released services, therefore, repeat step 1 until no more Blueprint Containers can be destroyed.
3　If there are still Blueprint Containers that are not destroyed, then destroy the Blueprint Container with:
- The registered service that is in use with the lowest ranking number, or if a tie
- The highest registered service id
If there are still Bundle Containers to be destroyed, retry step 1

During the shutting down of an OSGi framework, it is likely that many bundles are stopped near simultaneously. The Blueprint extender should be able to handle this case, without deadlock, when the stop of a Blueprint bundle overlaps with the stop of the Blueprint extender bundle.

121.3.12 Failure

If a failure occurs during the initialization of the Blueprint bundle, then first a FAILURE event must be posted, see *Events* on page 248. Then the Blueprint Container should be destroyed, ensuring that no uninitialized or half initialized objects are destroyed. Failures should be logged if a Log Service is present.

121.3.13 Lazy

The Blueprint Container specification specifically allows lazy initialization of the application in the Blueprint bundle. No component instances are created until an eager manager is activated, or a service request comes in.

If no eager managers are defined and no service has explicit dependencies, then no component instances are provided until an external trigger occurs. This trigger can be a service request or a call to the getComponentInstance method of the Blueprint Container, which is registered as a service. This allows a Blueprint bundle to not create component instances, and thereby load classes, until they are really needed. This can significantly reduce startup time.

Some features of the component definitions can only be verified by inspecting a class. This class loading can break the lazy initialization of a Blueprint bundle. It is therefore allowed to delay this kind of verification until the activation of a manager.

This lazy behavior is independent of the bundle's lazy activation policy. Though the Blueprint extender recognizes this policy to detect when the bundle is ready (for a lazy activated bundle the STARTING state is like the ACTIVE state), it is further ignored. That is, the relation between a Bundle Activator that is lazily activated and the Blueprint Container is not defined.

121.4 Blueprint Definitions

The Blueprint XML resources in a bundle are the *definitions*. Each definition can include multiple namespaces. Implementations of the Blueprint core namespace must strictly follow this specification, if they add additional behavior they must add additional namespaces that are actually used in the definitions to signal the deviation from this specification.

The namespace for the core Blueprint definition resources is:

```
http://www.osgi.org/xmlns/blueprint/v1.0.0
```

Blueprint resources that use this core specification must have as top the blueprint element. The following example shows the body of a Blueprint definition:

```
<xml version="1.0" encoding="UTF-8">
<blueprint
 xmlns="http://www.osgi.org/xmlns/blueprint/v1.0.0">

  ...
</blueprint>
```

The recommended prefix for the Blueprint core namespace is bp.

All elements in the Blueprint namespace are prepared for future extensions and provide a description child element in most positions.

121.4.1   **XML**

In the following sections, the XML is explained using the normal syntax notation used for headers. There is, however, one addition to the normal usage specific to XML, and that is the use of the angled brackets (‹›). A term enclosed in angled brackets, indicates the use of a real element. Without the angled brackets it is the definition of a term that is expanded later to a one or more other terms or elements. For example:

```
people     ::= <person> *
person     ::= <child>* address
address    ::= <fr> | <us> | <nl>
```

Describes for example the following XML:

```
<people>
   <person id="mieke">
      <child name="mischa"/>
      <child name="thomas"/>
      <fr zip="34160"/>
   </person>
</people>
```

Attributes are described in tables that define how they map to their corresponding Metadata. As a rule, the XML elements and attributes are expressed directly in the Metadata.

The text in the following sections is a normative description of the semantics of the schema. However, the structure information is illustrative. For example, all description elements have been ignored for brevity. The exact structure is described by the XML schema, see *Blueprint XML Schema* on page 252.

There are a number of convenient XML types used in the following sections. There schema types are defined here:

- fqn – A fully qualified Java class name in dotted form, for example java.lang.String.
- method – A valid Java method name, for example setFoo.
- NCName – A string syntax for names defined in [9] *XML Schema.*
- ID – A string syntax for ids defined in [9] *XML Schema.*
- type – A name of a Java type including arrays, see the next section *Syntax for Java types* on page 210.
- target – An inline bean, reference, or ref, see *Target* on page 213.
- object – An object value, see *Object Values* on page 232

In several cases, the actual syntax depends on the type conversion. This type of syntax is indicated with ‹‹type›› indicates that the syntax of the string depends on the type conversion, where ten type is usually given as a parameter on the same Metadata.

121.4.2   **Syntax for Java types**

A number of elements can refer to a Java type, for example the value element has a type attribute and a map element has a key-type attribute. The syntax for these types is as follows:

```
type       ::= fqn array
array      ::= '[]' *
```

Where fqn is the fully qualified name of a Java class or interface, or the name of a primitive type.

For example:

```
<value type="java.lang.String[]"/>
```

It is not possible to specify generic information in this syntax.

121.4.3   XML and Metadata

The Blueprint Container parses the XML into Metadata objects, see *Metadata* on page 251. During parsing, the XML parser validates against the detailed Blueprint schema and will therefore catch many errors. However, the XML schema and the Metadata type are not equivalent. The XML contains many conveniences that the Blueprint Container must convert to the canonical type in the Metadata. A number of general rules apply for this conversion:

- An absent attribute will result in null, unless the schema element provides a default value. In that case, the default must be returned from the Metadata object. That is, a default is indistinguishable from a specifically set value.
- Defaults from the blueprint element are filled in the Metadata objects, they are not available in any other way.
- Strings are trimmed from extraneous whitespace, as described in XML normalization.
- Child elements are represented by List objects, in the order of their definition. If no child elements are specified, the list will be empty.

For example, the activation feature reflects the total of default-activation and activation attributes but does not reflect that a prototype scope always makes a bean lazy. That is, even if activation is eager, the bean must still have lazy activation when it has prototype scope.

121.4.4   <blueprint>

The blueprint element is the top element. The definitions consist of two sections: the type-converter section and the managers section.

```
blueprint          ::= <type-converters> manager*
manager            ::= <bean> | <service>
                         | service-reference
service-reference  ::= <reference> | <reference-list>
type-converters    ::= <bean> | <ref>
```

In this specification, the reference and reference-list managers are referred to as *service references* when their differences are irrelevant. The blueprint element structure is visualized in Figure 121.6.

Figure 121.6   *Managers (bold = element name, plain=base type)*

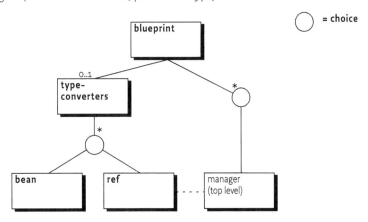

121.4.5   Metadata

The blueprint element has no corresponding Metadata class.

121.4.6   Defaults

The blueprint element supports the setting of the diverse defaults for the current definition resource with the following attributes:

- default-activation – Controls the default for the activation attribute on a manager. See *Lazy and Eager* on page 213. The default for this attribute is eager.
- default-availability – The default availability of the service reference elements, see *Service Reference Managers* on page 226. The default for this attribute is mandatory.
- default-timeout – The default for the reference element timeout attribute, see *Service Reference Managers* on page 226. The default for this attribute is is 30000, or 5 minutes.

These defaults are specific for one definition resource, they apply only to elements enclosed to any depth in the blueprint element. These defaults are not visible in the Metadata.

121.4.7   <type-converters>

The Blueprint definitions are text based but the component instances require actual classes for their construction and dependency injection. Component instances are injected with general objects the target type is not always compatible with the source type. This specification therefore allows for *type conversion*. Type conversion rules are specified in *Type Conversion* on page 240. This section provides beans, or referrals to beans, that can be used in this type conversion process. They are listed in a separate section so they can be registered as a type converter, pre-instantiated, and preventing dependencies that easily become cyclic. Beans defined in the type-converters element must be registered as top-level managers.

The structure of the type-converters element is:

```
type-converters ::= ( <bean> | <ref> )*
```

Type converters defined with the ref element can refer to bean managers or reference managers. Type converters must have ids distinct from any other manager and are available through the Blueprint Container's getComponentInstance method.

121.4.8   manager

The component XML schema type is the base type of the bean, service, reference-list, and reference elements. All manager sub-types share the following attributes:

- id – The manager and its Metadata are identified by its id as defined in its Component Definition. In general this id is therefore referred to as the *component id*. This is an optional attribute. If it is not defined, a default calculated unique id will be assigned to it for top-level managers. For inlined managers, the id attribute cannot be set, their Metadata must return null. All top level manager ids must be unique in a Blueprint Container.
  The id attribute must be of type ID as defined in XML Schema, see [9] *XML Schema*. The syntax for an id is therefore:

    ```
    id      ::= ID        // See [9] XML Schema #ID
    ```

  Ids generally use camel case, like myComponent, and they are case sensitive. That is, component id madHatter and madhatter are distinct ids. Applications should not use ids starting with the prefix blueprint.
  Ids are not required, if no component id is specified, the Blueprint Container must assign a unique id when it is a configured in a top level element. This calculated id must start with a dot ('.' \u002E).
- activation – Defines the activation mode to be lazy or eager. See *Eager Instantiation* on page 208.
- dependsOn – The list of explicit dependencies that must be activated. See *Explicit Dependencies* on page 213.

The Metadata interface of top level managers will be a sub-interface of ComponentMetadata and is available from the Blueprint Container by its component id.

Figure 121.7   *Inheritance hierarchy for managers*

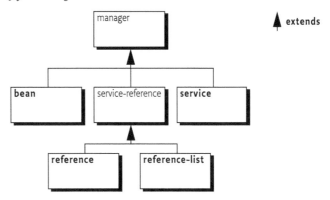

121.4.9 Explicit Dependencies

The dependsOn list contains the ids of the top-level managers the bean explicitly depends on. Unless stated otherwise in the specific manager description, explicit dependencies must be activated before their manager is activated.

For example:

```
<bean id="alice" class="com.acme.MadHatter"
    depends-on="cheshire rabbit queen"/>
```

This example will ask the top level managers cheshire, rabbit, and queen to provide an object before alice is activated. For a discussion about dependencies see *Manager Dependencies* on page 199.

121.4.10 Lazy and Eager

During initialization, all *eager* top level managers are requested to provide a component instance. Applications can use this request as an indication to start providing their intended functionality.

Managers that are *lazy*, that is, not singleton scope, activation is lazy, or inlined, are activated when they are first asked to provide a component instance. Therefore, even lazy managers can activate during initialization when they happen to be a dependency of another manager that activates its dependencies.

Services and service references can also have lazy or eager activation. The eager activation will ensure that all listeners are properly actuated during the corresponding activation. For services, the service object is then also requested at startup.

The following example defines an eager bean by making it a singleton and setting the activation to eager:

```
<bean id="eager" scope="singleton"
      class="com.acme.FooImpl" activation="eager"/>
```

121.4.11 Target

In several places in the Blueprint schema it is necessary to refer to a *target*. A target is a:

- ref – Must reference one of the following managers
- reference – An inlined reference manager
- bean – An inlined bean manager

The target type is normally used for listeners, service objects, and other places where a general application component instance is required.

121.5 Bean Manager

A bean manager provides an arbitrary Java object. It constructs this object from a given class or factory and then configures the object by injecting its *properties* with other component instances or more general object values.

The provided component instance can be a singleton or a new object can be returned on every invocation (prototype), this behavior is defined with the scope attribute, see *Scope* on page 217.

The provided object can optionally be notified when all of its properties have been injected, and when the providing bean manager will be deactivated, see *Life Cycle Callbacks* on page 219.

121.5.1 Bean Component XML

The structure of a bean element is:

```
bean                    ::= ( <argument> | <property> )*
```

Figure 121.8   Bean Structure

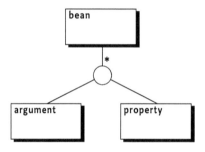

121.5.2 <bean>

The Metadata for a bean manager is represented in the BeanMetadata interface, which extends ComponentMetadata. Table 121.1 on page 214 provides an overview of the related XML definitions and the BeanMetadata interface. The table only provides a summary, the sometimes subtle interactions between the different features are discussed in later sections.

Table 121.1   Bean Manager Features

Attribute or Element	Syntax	Bean Metadata	Description
id	ID	id : String	The id of a top level manager, must be unique in the Blueprint Container. All inlined managers must return null for their id.
activation	lazy | eager	activation : int	Defines if this bean is lazily or eagerly activated. If not explicitly set, the blueprint element's value for the default-activation attributes is used. If this is also not set, the value is eager. See *Lazy and Eager* on page 213.

Table 121.1   *Bean Manager Features*

Attribute or Element	Syntax	Bean Metadata	Description
depends-on	NCName*	dependsOn : List<String>	Explicit list of ids that are the dependencies. These referred managers must be activated before this bean can provide an object. See *Explicit Dependencies* on page 213. This is a whitespace separated list.
class	fqn	className : String	Class name of the object to be provided or the class name for a static factory. See *Construction* on page 217.
scope	singleton | prototype	scope : String	The scope defines the construction strategy for the component instance. The default is singleton except for inlined bean managers, where it is prototype. There is no schema default, so if it is not explicitly set, the Metadata will be null. See *Scope* on page 217.
init-method	method	initMethod : String	The name of a method to invoke when a provided object has been injected with all its properties. If this is not set, it is null. See *Life Cycle Callbacks* on page 219.
destroy-method	method	destroyMethod : String	A name of a method to invoke on the provided objects with singleton scope when the Blueprint Container is destroyed. If this is not set, it is null. See *Life Cycle Callbacks* on page 219.
factory-method	method	factoryMethod : String	The name of the method on a static or component instance factory. See *Construction* on page 217.
factory-ref	NCName	factoryComponent : String	A reference to a manager that acts as the factory. See *Construction* on page 217.
<argument>	Table	arguments : List<BeanArgument>	Defined as sub-elements of the bean element. A BeanArgument object contains the value of an argument in the factory method or constructor. The order of the arguments is declaration order. See *Construction* on page 217.
<property>	Table	properties : List<BeanProperties>	Defined as sub-elements of the bean element. A BeanProperty object provides the property name and injection value. See *Properties* on page 218.

The bean element has the following constraints that are not enforced by the schema but must be enforced by the Blueprint Container:

- The destroyMethod must not be set when the scope is prototype.
- The activation must not be set to eager if the bean also has prototype scope.
- The following combinations of arguments are valid, all other combinations are invalid:
  - className
  - className, factory-method
  - factory-ref, factory-method

121.5.3   <argument>

The argument element holds a value for a constructor or factory method's parameters.

Table 121.2   Bean Argument Features

Attribute or Element	Syntax	Bean Argument	Description
index	int >= 0	index : int	The index of the argument in the constructor or factory-method signature. If this is not set, the Blueprint Container must use the type information to calculate it to match the disambiguation algorithm. The index will be -1 when not explicitly set.
type	fqn	valueType : String	The fully qualified class name of a Java type to match the argument to the signature against.
ref	NCName	value : RefMetadata	A reference to a top level manager that provides the value for the argument.
value	<<type>>	value : ValueMetadata	The Value Metadata based on the value property.
<...>	object	value : Metadata	An inlined value.

The argument element has the following additional constraints:

- Either all arguments have a specified index or none have a specified index.
- If indexes are specified, they must be unique and run from 0..(n-1), where n is the number of arguments.
- The following attributes and elements are mutually exclusive:
  - ref
  - value
  - An inlined object value

121.5.4   <property>

The property element holds the information to inject a bean property with an object value.

Table 121.3   Bean Property Features

Attribute or Element	Syntax	Bean Property	Description
name	method ('.' method)*	name : String	The property name, for example foo. The method name can consist of dot separated method names, indicating nested property access.
ref	NCName	value : RefMetadata	A reference to a top level manager.

Table 121.3   *Bean Property Features*

value	<<type>>	value : ValueMetadata	A Value Metadata where the type is null.
<...>	object	value : Metadata	An inlined object value.

The argument element has the following additional constraints:

- The following attributes/elements are mutually exclusive
  - ref
  - value
  - An inlined object value

121.5.5   Scope

A bean manager has a recipe for the construction and injection of an object value. However, there can be different strategies in constructing its component instance, this strategy is reflected in the scope. The following scopes are architected for this specification:

- singleton – The bean manager only holds a single component instance. This object is created and set when the bean is activated. Subsequent requests must provide the same instance. Singleton is the default scope. It is usually used for core component instances as well as stateless services.
- prototype – The object is created and configured anew each time the bean is requested to provide a component instance, that is, every call to getComponentInstance must result in a new component instance. This is usually the only possible scope for stateful objects. All inlined beans are always prototype scope.

Implementations can provide additional scope types. However, these types must only be allowed when a defining namespace is included in the definitions and is actually used in the definitions to specify the dependency on this feature.

121.5.6   Construction

The Blueprint specification supports a number of ways for a bean manager to construct an object. Each possibility is a combination of the following Metadata properties:

- className – Defines the fully qualified name of a class to construct, or the name of a class with a static factory method. The class must be loadable from the Blueprint bundle loadClass method.
- factoryMethod – A static or instance factory method name that corresponds to a publicly accessible method on the given class or factory manager.
- factoryComponent – The id of a top-level target manager in the Blueprint Container that is an instance factory.

The Bean manager can have a number of BeanArgument objects that specify arguments for the constructor or for the factory class/object method. The matching constructor or method must be publicly accessible. The argument's valueType can be used to disambiguate between multiple signatures of constructors or methods. See *Signature Disambiguation* on page 238.

The value of the argument is always a Metadata object. Such an object can be converted into a general object value, see *Object Values* on page 232.

The construction properties can be used in a rather large number of combinations, however, not all combinations are valid. Table 121.4 shows the different valid combinations. If none of the combinations matches, then the Bean Metadata is erroneous.

In Table 121.4, a variation of the following bean definition is assumed:

```
<bean class="C" factory-method="f" factory-ref="fc">
    <argument value="1"/>
    <argument value="2"/>
</bean>
```

This definition is invalid because it specifies an invalid combination of metadata properties. The only valid combinations are subsets, they are all specified in the following table.

Table 121.4   *Component Attributes and Construction*

className	factory-method	factory-ref	argument	Corresponding Java Code
C				new C
C	f			C.f()
C			1,2	new C(1,2)
C	f		1,2	C.f(1,2)
	f	$fc		$fc.f()
	f	$fc	1,2	$fc.f(1,2)
*	*	*	*	failure

The object created this way will be the provided object of the bean after any properties are injected. If the factoryMethod returns a primitive type, then this primitive must be converted to the corresponding wrapper type before any usage.

121.5.7 Properties

Dependency injection configures a constructed object with the help of the properties, which is a a List of BeanProperty objects. A Bean Property has the following features:

- name – The name of the bean property. This name refers to the set method on the constructed object as specified in the design pattern for beans getters and setters, see [6] *Java Beans Specification*. For example, if the property name is foo, then the public method setFoo(arg) will be used to set the value. There should only be one set method with a single argument for a specific property. If overloaded properties are encountered, the chosen set method is unspecified.
  Nested property names are allowed when setting bean properties, as long as all parts of the path, except the property that is set, result in a non-null value. The parts of the path are separated with a dot ('.' \u002E). For example:

  ```
  <property name="foo.bar.baz" value="42"/>
  ```

  This example gets the foo property, from the constructed object, it then gets the bar property and then sets the baz property on that object with the given value.
- value – The value of the property is always a Metadata object. This Metadata object can be converted to a value object, see *Object Values* on page 232.

After the Metadata object is converted to an object value, it must be injected into the property. If the value object is not directly assignable to the property type (as defined by its only set method and the rules in *Type Compatibility* on page 239), then the Blueprint Container must use the type conversion mechanism to create a new object that matches the desired type, or fail. See *Dependency Injection* on page 238 for more information about dependency injection.

For example, the following bean creates an instance and then injects a three into a the foo property that it gets from the bar property. The string that holds the three is converted to a double:

```
<bean id="foo" class="com.acme.Foo">
  <property name="bar.foo" value="3"/>
</bean>

// Classes
package com.acme;
public class Bar {
   double v;
```

```
      public void setFoo(double v) { this.v = v; }
   }
   public class Foo {
      Bar bar = new Bar();
      public void getBar() { return bar; }
   }

   // Corresponding Java code
   Foo foo = new Foo();
   foo.getBar().setFoo(3.0);
```

121.5.8   Life Cycle Callbacks

The bean element provides two attributes that define the *callback* method names for initialization and destruction. A callback must be implemented as a publicly accessible method without any arguments. The callback method names must exist as void() methods.

The initMethod specifies the name of an initialization method that is called after all properties have been injected. The destroyMethod specifies the name of a destroy method that is called when the Blueprint Container has destroyed a component instance. Only bean managers with singleton scope support the destroyMethod. The destroy callback cannot be used for beans that have prototype scope, the responsibility for destroying those instances lies with the application.

121.5.9   Activation and Deactivation

A singleton bean manager must construct its single object during activation and then callback its initMethod method. Prototype scoped beans are created after activation and also have their initMethod invoked. The destroy method is called during the destruction of all the beans in singleton scope, this happens after deactivation.

A prototype bean manager has no special activities for deactivation.

121.6   Service Manager

The service manager defined by a service element is responsible for registering a service object with the service registry. It must ensure that this service is only registered when it is *enabled.* Where enabled means that all its mandatory service reference managers in its dependencies are satisfied.

121.6.1   <service>

The XML structure of the <service> manager is:

```
service                  ::=   <interfaces>
                               <service-properties>
                               <registration-listener>*
                               target
interfaces               ::=   <value>+
service-properties       ::=   <entry>+
registration-listener ::=   target
```

The service manager has the features outlined in Table 121.5 on page 220. The following additional constraints apply:

- The interface attribute and interfaces element are mutually exclusive.
- If the auto-export attribute is set to anything else but disabled, neither the interface attribute nor the interfaces element must be used.
- The ref attribute and inlined element are mutually exclusive

Table 121.5   *Service Manager Features*

Attribute or Element	Type	Service Metadata	Description
id	ID	id : String	Optional component id of the manager, if it is a top level manager.
activation	lazy | eager	activation : int	Defines if this service is lazily or eagerly initialized. If not explicitly set, the blueprint element's value for the default-activation attributes is used. If this is also not set, the value is eager. See also *Lazy and Eager* on page 213.
depends-on	NCName*	dependsOn : List<String>	Explicit list of ids that are the dependencies. These managers must be activated at the start of the registration phase. See *Explicit Dependencies* on page 213. This is a whitespace separated list.
interface	fqn	interfaces : List<String>	Name of the interface under which this service should be registered. See *Service Interfaces* on page 222.
auto-export	disabled | interfaces | class- hierarchy | all-classes	autoExport : int	Defines the way the class must be analyzed to find the interfaces under which the service must be registered. The schema default is disabled. See *Service Interfaces* on page 222
ranking	int	ranking : int	The service.ranking value. The schema default is 0, which implies no service property. See *Ranking* on page 224.
ref	NCName	value : RefMetadata	Reference to the manager that provides the service object. See *Service Object* on page 223.
<service- properties>	See <map> on page 235.	serviceProperties : List<MapEntry>	The service properties for this service. See *Service Properties* on page 222.
<registration- listener>	See Table 121.6	registrationListeners : List<Registration Listener>	The registration listeners. See *Registration Listener* on page 224.

Table 121.5   *Service Manager Features*

Attribute or Element	Type	Service Metadata	Description

<interfaces>	<value>*	interfaces
		: List<String>
			Names of interfaces under which this service should be registered. Each interface name must be listed as a child value element. This value element has no attributes. For example:
			
			`<interfaces>`
			`  <value>com.acme.Foo</value>`
			`  <value>com.acme.Bar</value>`
			`</interfaces>`
			
			The value element must only hold a string value. See *Service Interfaces* on page 222

<...>	target	value : Target	An inlined target manager that is used for the service object. See *Service Object* on page 223

121.6.2   **<registration-listener>**

The service element can contain zero or more registration-listener elements, that define registration listeners to be notified of service registration and unregistration events. This element has the following structure:

```
registration-listener ::= target*
```

The registration-listener element defines the callback methods for registration and unregistration.

Table 121.6   *Registration Listener Features*

Attribute or Element	Type	Registration Listener	Description
ref	NCName	registrationListener : Target	A reference to a top level manager.
registration-method	method	registrationMethod : String	The name of the method to call after the service has been registered. See *Registration Listener* on page 224.
unregistration-method	method	unregistrationMethod : String	The name of the method to call before the service will be unregistered. See *Registration Listener* on page 224.
<...>	target	registrationListener : Target	An inlined target manager

The additional constraint is:

- The ref attribute and the inlined manager are mutually exclusive.
- Either or both of the registrationMethod and unregistrationMethod must be set.
- For each method name set, there must be at least one method matching the possible prototypes in the registration listener object, see *Registration Listener* on page 224.

121.6.3   **Explicit Dependencies**

A service manager must initialize any explicit dependencies in the start of its registration phase, even before it tracks its enabled state. The presence of explicit dependencies will not activate the service manager.

121.6.4   **Provided Object**

A service manager provides a proxy to a ServiceRegistration object. If this proxy is used when the dependencies are not met, and the service is therefore unregistered, an Illegal State Exception must be thrown. In all other cases, the proxy acts as if it was the ServiceRegistration object associated with the registration of its service object.

The unregister method on the returned object must not be used. If the application code calls unregister then this must result in an Unsupported Operation Exception.

121.6.5   **Service Interfaces**

Each service object is registered under one or more interface names. The list of interface names is provided by interfaces or autoExport.

The autoExport tells the Blueprint Container to calculate the interface(s) from the type of the service object. The autoExport can have the following values:

- disabled – No auto-detection of service interface names is undertaken, the interface names must be found in interfaces. This is the default mode.
- interfaces – The service object will be registered using all of its implemented public Java interface types, including any interfaces implemented by super classes.
- class-hierarchy – The service object will be registered using its actual type and any public super-types up to the Object class (not included).
- all-classes – The service object will be registered using its actual type, all public super-types up to the Object class (not including), as well as all public interfaces implemented by the service object and any of its super classes.

The autoExport requires the actual class object for introspection for all its modes except disabled, which can cause a bundle with a lazy activation policy to activate because a class will be loaded from the Blueprint bundle.

As an example:

```
<bean id="fooImpl"  class="FooImpl"/>

public class FooImpl implements Foo { ... }
```

Then the following service definitions are equivalent:

```
<service id="foo">
   <interfaces>
      <value>com.acme.Foo</value>
   </interface>
</service>
<service id="foo" interface="com.acme.Foo" ref="fooImpl"/>
<service id="foo" auto-export="interfaces" ref="fooImpl"/>
```

121.6.6   **Service Properties**

Each service can optionally be registered with *service properties*. The serviceProperties is a list of MapEntry, see *‹entry›* on page 236. This metadata must be used to create the service properties. Service properties creation can have side effects because they can use component instances. The service properties must therefore be created once before the first time the first time the service is registered.

The service manager adds the following automatic service properties that cannot be overridden. When these properties are explicitly set, they must be ignored.

- osgi.service.blueprint.compname – This will reflect the id of the manager that provides the service object, unless it is inlined. Inlined beans are always anonymous and must not have this property set.
- service.ranking – If the ranking attribute is not zero, this property will be set and hold an Integer object with the given value, see *Ranking* on page 224.

For example, the following definition is followed by equivalent Java code needed to register the service:

```
<service ref="fooImpl" interface="com.acme.Foo">
  <service-properties>
    <entry key="size" value="42"/>
  </service-properties>
</service>

Dictionary d = new Hashtable();
d.put("size", "42");
d.put("osgi.service.blueprint.compname", "fooImpl");
ServiceRegistration sr =
    bundleContext.registerService("com.acme.Foo",
      blueprintContainer.getComponentInstance("fooImpl"),
        d);
```

Service properties should specify the valueType of the entry unless the value to be registered needs to be a String object. The service property types should be one of:

- *Primitives Number* – int, long, float, double, byte, short, char, boolean
- *Scalar* – String, Integer, Long, Float, Double, Byte, Short, Character, Boolean.
- *Array* – An array of either the allowable primitive or scalar types.
- *Collection* – An object implementing the Collection interface that contains scalar types.

See *‹entry›* on page 236 types for information how to create these types.

121.6.7   Service Object

The service manager must not request the Blueprint Container for the service object until it is actually needed because a bundle requests it. The service object is represented in the value. This is a Metadata object that can be used to construct an object value, see *Object Values* on page 232.

For example:

```
<service id="fooService" ref="fooImpl" .../>

<service id="fooService" ... >
    <bean class="com.acme.fooImpl"/>
</service>
```

121.6.8   Scope

A service manager must always register a Service Factory as service object and then dispatch the service requests to the service object. A service manager must obtain a single component instance as service object. This component instance is shared between all bundles. That is, even if the service object comes from a prototype scoped manager, only one instance is ever created per service manager.

If this component instance implements Service Factory, then all incoming service requests are forwarded to this single component instance.

121.6.9   Ranking

When registering a service with the service registry, an optional *service ranking* can be specified that orders service references. The service ranking is registered as the SERVICE_RANKING property defined in the OSGi service layer. When a bundle looks up a service in the service registry, given two or more matching services, then the one with the highest number will be returned. The default ranking value for the OSGi service registry is zero, therefore, this property must not be registered when ranking is zero, which is also the default value.

For example:

```
<service ref="fooImpl" interface="com.acme.FooImpl"
        ranking="900" />
```

This will result in the following service property:

```
service.ranking=new Integer(900)
```

121.6.10   Registration Listener

The registrationListeners represent the objects that need to be called back after the service has been registered and just before it will be unregistered.

The listenerComponent must be a Target object; it is the target for the following callbacks:

- registrationMethod – The name of the notification method that is called after this service has been registered.
- unregistrationMethod – This method is called when this service will be unregistered.

The signatures for the callback methods depend on the scope and if the service object implements the ServiceFactory interface. The different possibilities are outlined in Table 121.7 on page 224.

Table 121.7   *Interaction scopes and types for callback signature.*

Scope	Type	Signature	Comment
singleton	ServiceFactory	void(ServiceFactory,Map)	All service requests are handled by the component instance.
singleton	T	void(super T,Map)	T is assignable from the service object's type.
prototype	ServiceFactory	void(ServiceFactory,Map)	All service requests are handled by the first component instance.
prototype	T	void(,Map)	The first argument must be null because for prototype service objects, the component instance is created when a bundle requests the service. Therefore, at registration time there is no service object available.

If multiple signatures match, then all methods must be called in indeterminate order. At least one method must match.

The service manager must provide the registration listener with the current registration state when the listener is registered. This initial notification must take place before any other callback methods are called on this listener on other threads. That is, if the service is registered at that time, it must call the registration method and otherwise the unregistration method.

The following example shows two registration listeners, one with a referred bean and another one with an inlined bean.

```
<service ref="fooImpl" interface="com.acme.Foo">
  <registration-listener registration-method="reg"
      unregistration-method="unreg">
    <bean class="com.acme.FooListener"/>
  </registration-listener>
</service>

<service ref="fooImpl" interface="com.acme.Foo">
  <registration-listener registration-method="reg"
      unregistration-method="unreg" ref="fooListener"/>
</service>
<bean id="fooListener" class="com.acme.FooListener"/>

package com.acme;
public class FooListener {
  public void reg( Foo foo, Map properties ) { ... }
  public void unreg( Foo foo, Map properties ) { ... }
}
```

The manager that provides the registration listener object is an implicit dependency of the enclosing service manager. However, the registration listener component instance is specifically allowed to use to the service manager though this is technically a cyclic dependency. Therefore, a bean is allowed to be both be injected with a ServiceRegistration object from the service manager as well as being a registered listener to the same service manager.

In the following example, the foo service manager uses manager main, both as a registration listener as well as top-level bean main being injected with reference foo.

```
<service id="foo" interface="com.acme.Foo" ref="main">
  <registration-listener
      registration-method="register" ref="main"/>
</service>

<bean id="main" class="com.acme.Main" init-method="done">
  <property name="foo" ref="foo"/>
</bean>
```

121.6.11 Enabled

A service manager needs a service object that is referred to by the value Metadata property. This value can in its turn depend on other managers transitively. If any of these managers are service reference managers, then they can be satisfied or not. If these service reference managers are marked to be mandatory, then they influence the *enabled* state of the first service manager. Only if all of these mandatory service reference managers in the dependency graph are satisfied, then the first service manager is enabled.

A service manager must have a Service Factory registered with the OSGi service registry after the primary initialization of the Blueprint Container has been done until the Blueprint Container is destroyed while it is enabled. See see *Service Registration* on page 207.

121.6.12   Activation and Deactivation

When a service manager is activated, it must actuate its registration listeners. Each registration listener must be called back during its actuation with the current service registration state as described in the *Registration Listener* on page 224. Normally, this will also request the container for a service object but this can be further delayed in certain circumstances. See *Service Object* on page 223 for more details.

During deactivation, a service manager must disable any registration listeners and release any dependencies it has on these component instances.

121.7   Service Reference Managers

The reference, and reference-list elements are all *service references*. They select a number of services in the service registry. The structure of these elements is as follows:

```
reference        ::= <reference-listener>*
reference-list   ::= <reference-listener>*
```

The inheritance hierarchy for service references is depicted in Figure 121.9 on page 226.

Figure 121.9   *Inheritance hierarchy for service references*

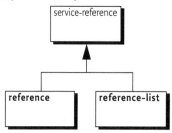

121.7.1   Service Reference

The service reference managers have almost identical Metadata and share most behavior. The only schema differences between a reference manager and a reference-list manager are:

- timeout – A reference manager supports a timeout.
- memberType – The reference-list can define its member-type

The features of the service references are explained in Table 121.8 on page 226.

Table 121.8   *Service Reference Manager Features*

Attribute or Element	Type	ServiceReference-Metadata	Description
id	ID	id : String	The component id of a top level manager
activation	lazy | eager	activation : int	Defines if this service reference is lazily of eagerly initialized. If not explicitly set, the blueprint element's value for the default-activation attributes is used. If this is also not set, the value is eager. See also *Lazy and Eager* on page 213.

Table 121.8   *Service Reference Manager Features*

Attribute or Element	Type	ServiceReference-Metadata	Description
depends-on	NCName*	dependsOn : List<String>	Explicit list of component ids that are the dependencies. These managers must be activated before this service reference's activation. See *Explicit Dependencies* on page 213. This is a whitespace separated List.
availability	mandatory | optional	availability : int	Defines if a service reference is mandatory or optional. The default for the availability attribute is defined by the default-availability attribute in the blueprint element. If the default-availability attribute is not defined, the value is mandatory.
interface	fqn	interface : String	A single name of an interface class. It is allowed to not specify an interface name.
component-name	NCName	componentName : String	Points to another manager in another Blueprint Container registered in the service registry. If set, the component name must be part of the effective filter.
filter	filter	filter : String	The given filter string, can be null.
<reference-listener>	See *<reference-listener>* on page 228	referenceListeners : List<Listener>	The Metadata of the reference listeners

The additional constraints for service references are:

- The interface, if set, must refer to a public interface.

121.7.2   **<reference>**

A reference manager, selecting a single service, has the additional feature explained in Table 121.9 on page 227.

Table 121.9   *Reference Features*

Attribute or Element	Type	Reference Metadata	Description
timeout	long >= 0	timeout : long	The timeout in ms. Zero is indefinite.

An additional constraint on the reference is:

- The timeout must be equal or larger than zero.

121.7.3   **<reference-list>**

A reference-list manager, selecting multiple services, has the additional feature explained in Table 121.10 on page 228.

Table 121.10   *Reference-list Features*

Attribute or Element	Type	Reference List Metadata	Description
member-type	service-object | service-reference	memberType : int	Defines if the members of the list are ServiceReference objects or the proxies to the actual service objects.

121.7.4   ‹reference-listener›

The reference element can notify reference listeners of the service selection changes with the referenceListeners. The reference-listener element has the following structure:

```
reference-listener   ::= target*
```

The reference-listener element defines the callback methods for binding and unbinding a service.

Table 121.11   *Reference Listener Features*

Attribute or Element	Type	Reference Listener	Description
ref	NCName	listenerComponent : Target	A reference to a top level target manager.
bind-method	method	bindMethod : String	The name of the method to call after the service has been bound. See *Reference Listeners* on page 230.
unbind-method	method	unbindMethod : String	The name of the method to call before the service will be unbound. See *Reference Listeners* on page 230.
‹...›	target	listenerComponent : Target	An inlined target manager

The additional constraints are:

- The ref attribute and the inlined manager are mutually exclusive.
- Either or both bindMethod and unbindMethod must be specified.
- At least one specified method must exist with each given method name, see *Reference Listeners* on page 230.

121.7.5   Provided Object For a Reference

The provided object for a service reference manager is a *proxy* backed by a service object from the service registry. Therefore, even though the injected object will remain constant, it can change its reference to a backing service at any time, implying it can only be used with stateful services if reference listeners are used. If use when no suitable backing service is available, it will wait until it times out. See *Service Dynamics* on page 245 for more details. The model is depicted in Figure 121.10.

Figure 121.10   *Constant references with dynamic selection*

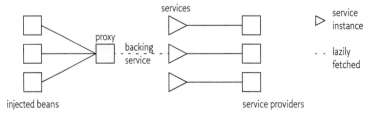

The following example shows how a property can be set to the service object.

```
public class C {
    public void setProxy(T ref) { ... }
}
<reference id="p" interface="T"/>
<bean id="c" class="C">
    <property name="proxy" ref="p"/>
</bean>
```

121.7.6   Provided Object For a Reference-list

The reference-list provided object implements the List interface; this List contains proxies to the backing services. These proxies do not have a timeout. That is, when a proxy from a reference-list is used, it must not wait when the backing service is no longer available but it must immediately throw a Service Unavailable Exception.

Changes to the list are dynamic. When a backing service is unregistered, the corresponding proxy is removed from the list synchronously with the service event. When a new service enters the selection, it is added synchronously with the service event. Proxies to newly discovered services must be added at the end of the list. The structure is depicted in Figure 121.11.

Figure 121.11   *Constant reference to list with dynamic selection*

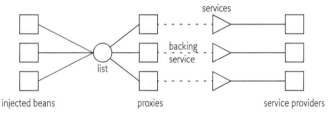

The member type of the list depends on the memberType. If this is set to:

- service-object – Inject a List of service objects, this is the default.
- service-reference – Inject a list of ServiceReference objects

If generics information is available, then it is an error if the generic member type of the target list is not assignable with the memberType. If the member target type is in itself specified with generic arguments, like List<T<U>>, then the assignment must fail because this would require conversion and no conversion can take place for this assignment. For information about generics, see *Generics* on page 243.

121.7.7   Read Only Lists

The list is a read-only view on the actual set of proxies to the service objects. This List object must only support the following methods:

```
contains(Object)
containsAll(Collection)
equals(Object)
get(int)
hashCode()
indexOf(Object)
isEmpty()
iterator()          // no remove method
lastIndexOf(Object)
listIterator()      // not supported
listIterator(int)   // not supported
```

```
size()
subList(int, int)  // same list type as parent
toArray()
toArray(T[])
```

All other methods must throw an Unsupported Operation Exception. The List Iterator is not supported for these lists.

121.7.8   Selection

A service reference must provide a *selection* of services from the service registry. The Blueprint Container must logically use a filter for the selection that is the and (&) of the following assertions:

- The interface, if specified
- If componentName is not null, a filter that asserts osgi.blueprint.compname=$componentName
  This is a convenience function to easily refer to managers in other Blueprint Containers. Registered Blueprint services will automatically get this property set to their blueprint name.
- If filter is not null, the filter

The selection is defined as the set of Service References selected by the given filter.

121.7.9   Availability

A service reference is *satisfied* when one or more services match the selection. The availability is used to specify whether a service reference needs to be satisfied before initialization, see *Grace Period* on page 207, or if it controls the registration state of any service managers that depend on this service reference manager (explicit and implicit), see *Mandatory Dependencies* on page 246. The availability can have the following values:

- mandatory – Mandatory indicates that the service reference needs to be satisfied.
- optional – Optional indicates that the satisfaction of this reference is not relevant for any registered services, or for the grace period.

It is an error to declare a mandatory reference to a service that is registered by the same bundle. Such a definition could cause either deadlock or a timeout.

The fact that Blueprint specification has mandatory service references gives no guarantee that a valid service object is available when the service reference is used, in the dynamic world of OSGi, services can get unregistered at any time.

The following example declares a mandatory service reference for a single service. The usage of the reference can stall a maximum of 5 seconds if no service matches the selection.

```
<reference
    id          ="log"
    interface   ="org.osgi.service.log.LogService"
    availability ="mandatory"
    timeout     ="5000" />
```

121.7.10   Reference Listeners

The referenceListeners are represented as ReferenceListener objects. They define the following callbacks:

- bindMethod – Called after a service is selected by the service reference manager. For a reference manager, this method can be called repeatedly without an intermediate unbind callback. This happens when a service is unregistered but a replacement can be found immediately.
- unbindMethod – Called when the service is no longer used by the service reference manager but before it has been returned to the service registry with the unget method. For a reference manager, no unbind method is called when the service can immediately be replaced with an alternative service when the service goes away.

A reference listener callback can have any of the following signatures:

- `public void(ServiceReference)` – Provide the `ServiceReference` object associated with this service reference. This callback type provides access to the service's properties without actually getting the service.
- `public void( super T)` – Provide the proxy to the service object, where T is on of the types implemented by the service object proxy.
- `public void ( super T,Map)` – Provide the proxy to the service object. T is a type that is assignable from the service object. The `Map` object provides the service properties of the corresponding `ServiceReference` object.

All signatures must be supported regardless of the value of `memberType` that was specified in the reference-list. The service object given to the reference listeners must be the proxy to the service object.

The callbacks must be made synchronously with the corresponding OSGi service event. For reference-list callbacks, the service proxy is guaranteed to be available in the collection before a bind callback is invoked, and to remain in the collection until after an unbind callback has completed.

If a service listener defines multiple overloaded methods for a callback, then every method with a matching signature is invoked in an undefined order.

For example, the following definition will result in calling all the `setLog` methods on a `FooImpl` object:

```
<reference id="log"
      interface="org.osgi.service.log.LogService">
   <reference-listener
      bind-method="setLog">
         <bean class="com.acme.FooImpl"/>
   </reference-listener>
</reference>

public class FooImpl {
    public void setLog(Object o, Map m) { ... }
    public void setLog(LogService l, Map m) { ... }
    public void setLog(ServiceReference ref) { ... }
}
```

The manager that provides the reference listener object is treated as an implicit dependency of the enclosing service reference. This manager is specifically allowed to use to the service reference in a property injection or constructor argument, though this is technically a cyclic dependency. Therefore, a bean must be allowed to both be injected with a reference as well as listening to the bind and unbind callbacks of that same reference.

In the following example, the foo reference manager uses manager main, both as a reference listener as well as manager main being injected with reference foo.

```
<reference id="foo" interface="com.acme.Foo">
   <reference-listener bind-method="setL" ref="main"/>
</reference>
<bean id="main" class="com.acme.Main">
    <property name="r" ref="foo"/>
</bean>
```

121.7.11   Service Proxies

The Blueprint extender must generate proxies for the service reference managers. Reference managers provide proxies that dynamically select a *backing* service, which can change over time. A reference-list provides a list of proxies that have a fixed backing service, these proxies are added and removed from the list. based on the selection, they do not have a time-out.

The backing service for a reference proxy must not be gotten from the OSGi service registry until an actual service object is needed, that is, when an actual method is called on the proxy. If the backing service becomes unregistered, then the proxy must unget the reference to the backing service (if it had gotten it) and get another service object the next time a method on the proxy is called. If a replacement can be found immediately, the reference listener's bind method must be called without calling the unbind method. Other threads that need the same service object must block until the service object has become available or times out.

The proxies must implement all the methods that are defined in the interface. The interface must refer to an interface, not a class. The proxy must only support the methods in the given interface. That is, it must not proxy methods available on the service object that are not available in the given interface. If no interface is defined, the proxy must be implemented as if the interface had no methods defined.

Blueprint bundles must ensure that the proper semantics are maintained for hashCode and equals methods. If these methods are not defined in the interface, then the proxy must use the default semantics of the Object class for equals and hashCode methods.

121.7.12 Activation and Deactivation

Service reference managers are active before activation because they must handle the enable status of service managers.

During activation, a service reference must actuate its listeners and provide these listeners with the initial state of the reference. For a reference, if there is a selected object, the bind method must be called with the proxy object, otherwise the unbind method must be called with a null as proxy object. For a reference-list, the bind method must be called for each member of the list. If the list is empty, the unbind method must be called with a null as proxy object.

During deactivation, the listeners must be disabled.

121.8 Object Values

Top-level managers can use *object values* in different places. These object values are defined with XML elements and attributes. After parsing, they are all converted to sub-interfaces of the Metadata interface, transitively reachable from top-level managers. For example, the following definition creates a bean that is injected with the byte array: byte[] {7,42}:

```
<bean class="com.acme.FooImpl">
  <property name="array">
    <array value-type="byte">
      <value>7</value>
      <value>42</value>
    </array>
  </property>
</bean>
```

This definition provides the configuration data for an *array value*, which is represented by the CollectionMetadata interface. A Metadata object can be used to construct its object value during runtime whenever a new object must be constructed.

In most places where an object value can be used, it can be anything, including objects provided by a managers and even null. However, maps require non-null keys. The object values are therefore split in value and nonNullValue types.

The syntax for object values has the following structure:

```
nonNullValue::=    <ref>
            |      <idref>
```

```
                       |     <value>
                       |     <map>
                       |     <props>
                       |     collection
                       |     manager // see manager on page 212
        value          ::= nonNullValue | <null>
        collection     ::= <list> | <set> | <array>
```

Object values also include inlined managers. The use of an inlined manager for an object value means that manager will provide a value every time the object value is constructed. Each of the object values is created anew and the types are mutable, except for the service references. The use of managers in object values must create an implicit dependency between the top level managers and any transitively reachable manager from their Metadata.

121.8.1   <ref>

The ref element is a reference to a top-level manager in the same Blueprint Container. The ref element has a single attribute component-id.

Table 121.12   *Ref Features*

Attribute	Type	Ref Metadata	Description
component-id	NCName	componentId : String	A reference to a top level manager.

For example, the following definition uses the foo manager to instantiate the service object.

```
<service id="fooService" interface="com.acme.Foo">
  <ref component-id="fooImpl"/>
</service>
<bean id="fooImpl" class="com.acme.FooImpl"/>

public class FooImpl implements Foo { }
```

121.8.2   <idref>

The idref element provides the component id of another manager in the same Blueprint Container. This reference can then be used by the application to look up a manager in the Blueprint Container during runtime. The idref element is a safe way to provide a component id because the Blueprint Container will verify that the component id exists, thereby showing errors early. The idref does not create an implicit dependency on the given manager.

Table 121.13   *IdRef Features*

Attribute	Type	Id Ref Metadata	Description
component-id	NCName	componentId : String	A reference to a top level manager.

The following example provides the foo object with the reference to the database.

```
<bean id="foo" class="com.acme.FooImpl">
  <property name="db">
    <idref component-id="jdbc"/>
  </property>
</bean>

<bean id="jdbc" ... />
```

The following definition is equivalent to except that a non existent component id will not be detected until the foo object access the Blueprint Container. In the previous example this was detected directly after the definitions were parsed.

```
<bean id="foo" class="com.acme.FooImpl">
  <property name="db" value="jdbc"/>
</bean>
<bean id="jdbc" ... />
```

121.8.3 <value>

A value element represents an object that can directly be constructed from a string formed by its text contents.

Table 121.14   Value Features

Attribute, Element	Type	Value Metadata	Description
type	type	type : String	The optional type name to be used in type converting the given string to a target type. This type can commit the conversion to a specific choice. If this type is not set, then it must return null. For the type syntax, see *Syntax for Java types* on page 210.
...	<<type>>	stringValue : String	The string value that must be converted to the target type, if set.

If a value element is used as a member in a list, map, array, or set then the enclosing collection can define a default value for the type attribute of its value elements.

The following example creates a list of two OSGi version objects.

```
<list value-type="org.osgi.framework.Version">
  <value>1.3.4</value>
  <value>5.6.2.v200911121020</value>
</list>
```

The corresponding Java code is:

```
Arrays.asList( new Version("1.3.4"),
  new Version("5.6.2.v200911121020") )
```

121.8.4 <null>

A null element results in a Java null. It has no attributes and no elements. It corresponds to Null Metadata.

121.8.5 <list>, <set>, <array>

Lists, sets, and arrays are referred to as *collections*. List and array are ordered sequences of objects, where equal objects can occur multiple times. A set discards equal objects.

The structure of a collection element is:

```
collection ::= value *
```

Table 121.15   Collection Features

Attribute or Element	Type	Collection Metadata	Description
value-type	type	valueType : String	Optionally set the type for ValueMetadata children.
		collectionClass : Class< List | Set | Object[] >	The actual collection class to be used, derived from the appropriate definition.
‹...›	object*	values : List<Metadata>	The Metadata for the children of the collection

The valueType sets the default for any contained ValueMetadata objects. The result of a collection element is an object that implements the given collection interface or is an Object[]. That is, the resulting object is mutable and can be used by the application. However, type conversion can create a copy of this list.

The following example creates a List of Lists of 2x2 of int values:

```
<list>
    <list value-type="int">
        <value >2</value>
        <value >7</value>
    </list>
    <list value-type="int">
        <value >9</value>
        <value >5</value>
    </list>
</list>
```

The corresponding Java code is:

```
Arrays.asList(
    new int[] {2,7},
    new int[]{9,5},
)
```

121.8.6   ‹map›

A map is a sequence of associations between a *key* and some object., this association is called an *entry*. The structure of a map element is therefore:

```
map        ::=   <entry> *
```

Table 121.16   Map Features

Attribute or Element	Type	Map Metadata	Description
key-type	type	keyType : String	Optional default type for keys. For the syntax see *Syntax for Java types* on page 210.
value-type	type	valueType : String	Optional default type for values. For the syntax see *Syntax for Java types* on page 210.
‹entry›	See ‹entry› on page 236	values : List<MapEntry>	The MapEntry object for the children of the map or properties.

There are no additional constraints.

121.8.7   **<entry>**

The entry element provides an association between a key and a value. The structure of the element is:

```
entry      ::=   <key> object
key        ::=   nonNullValue
```

Table 121.17   Entry Features

Attribute	Type	Map Entry	Description
key	<<type>>	key : NonNullMetadata	Specify the key of the entry.
key-ref	NCName	key : NonNullMetadata	Reference to a top-level manager
<key>	nonNull- Value	key : NonNullMetadata	Contains an inlined value that is never null.
value	<<type>>	value : Metadata	Specify the value directly, this will be a string type.
value-ref	NCName	value : RefMetadata	A reference to a top-level manager
<...>	object	value : Metadata	An inlined manager

Additional constraints:

- key, key-ref attributes and key element are mutually exclusive.
- value, value-ref attributes and value element are mutually exclusive.
- The resulting object of a key must not be a primitive type.

The following example shows the different way an entry can get its key. In this case the value is always a string.

```
<map>
    <entry key="bar"      value="..."/>    // 1
    <entry key-ref="bar" value="..."/>    // 2
    <entry value="...">                    // 3
        <key>
            <value type="org.osgi.framework.Version">
                2.71
            </value>
        </key>
    </entry>
</map>
```

The previous example is equivalent to the following Java code:

```
Map m = new HashMap();
m.put( "bar", "...");
m.put( container.getComponentInstance("bar"), "...");
m.put( new Version("2.71"), "...");
```

The following examples shows the different ways a value of an entry can be defined.

```
<map>
    <entry key="1" value="1"/>
    <entry key="2" value-ref="foo"/>
    <entry key="3">
        <value type="org.osgi.framework.Version">3.14</value>
    </entry>
```

```
</map>
```

The previous code is equivalent to the following Java code.

```
Map m = new HashMap()
m.put("1", "1");
m.put("2", container.getComponentInstance("foo"))
m.put("3", new Version("3.14"));
```

121.8.8   **<props>**

The props element specifies a Properties object. The structure of a props element is as follows:

```
props          ::=      prop *
```

Each prop element is an association between two strings. It defines the following attributes:

- key – A string specifying the property key. This attribute is required.
- value – A string specifying the property value.

The following example initializes the same Properties object in two s ways.

```
<props>
    <prop key="1">one</prop>
    <prop key="2">two</prop>
</props>

<props>
    <prop key="1"    value="one"/>
    <prop key="2"    value="two"/>
</props>
```

This is equivalent to the following Java code:

```
Properties p = new Properties();
p.setProperty( "1", "one");
p.setProperty( "2", "two");
```

121.8.9   **Manager as Value**

Each manager can be the provider of component instances that act as object values. When a manager is used in an object value, then that is the manager asked to provide a component instance. The managers are specified in *manager* on page 212. The simple example is a bean. Any inlined bean can act as an object value. For example:

```
<list>
    <bean class="com.acme.FooImpl"/>
</list>
```

Some managers have side effects when they are instantiated. For example, a service manager will result in a ServiceRegistration object but it will also register a service.

```
<map>
    <entry key="foo">
        <service interface="com.acme.Foo">
            <bean class="com.acme.FooImpl"/>
        </service>
    </entry>
</map>
```

121.9   Dependency Injection

A bean has a recipe for constructing a component instance with a constructor or factory and then providing it with its *properties*. These properties are then injected with *object values*, see *Object Values* on page 232.

The following types of dependencies can be injected:

- *Constructor arguments* – The arguments specify the parameters for a constructor.
- *Static Factory arguments* – The arguments specify the parameters for a static method.
- *Instance Factory arguments* – The arguments specify the parameters for a method on an object provided by another manager.
- *Properties* – The value of the Bean Property specifies the single parameter for the property's set method.

In all the previous cases, the Blueprint Container must find an appropriate method or constructor to inject the dependent objects into the bean. The process of selecting the correct method or constructor is described in the following section, which assumes a Bean Argument as context, where a Bean Property acts as a Bean Argument without an index or type set.

121.9.1   Signature Disambiguation

Constructors, factory methods, and property set methods are described with Metadata. The Blueprint Container must map these descriptions to an actual method or constructor. In practice, there can be multiple methods/constructors that could potentially map to the same description. It is therefore necessary to disambiguate this selection. Both factory methods and constructors have the same concept of *signatures*. A signature consists of an ordered sequence of zero or more types. For methods, only publicly accessible methods with the appropriate name are considered. For constructors, all publicly accessible constructors are considered. The disambiguation process described here is valid for all constructors and methods because the signature concept applies to both of them.

1. Discard any signatures that have the wrong cardinality
2. Find the list of signatures that have *assignable* types for each argument in their corresponding positions. Assignable is defined in *Type Compatibility* on page 239. If a type was specified for an argument, then this type must match the name of the corresponding reified type in the signature exactly.
3. If this result list has one element, then this element is the answer. If this list has more than one element, then the disambiguation fails.
4. Otherwise, find the list of signatures that have *compatible* types for each argument in their corresponding positions. Compatibility is defined in *Type Compatibility* on page 239.
5. If this result list has one element, then this element is the answer. If the list has more than one element, then the disambiguation fails.
6. If the arguments cannot be reordered (the index of the argument is used and is thus not -1, or there are less than two arguments) then the disambiguation fails.
7. Find all signatures that match a re-ordered combination of the arguments. Reordering must begin with the first argument and match this argument against the first *assignable* types in a signature, going from position 0 to n. If the type is assignable from the argument, then it is locked in that position. If the argument has a type, then it must exactly match the name of the selected signature type. The same is done for the subsequent arguments. If all arguments can find an exclusive position in the signature this way, than the signature is added to the result.
8. If the result list contains one signature, then this is the resulting signature. If the list has more than one element, then the disambiguation fails.
9. Repeat step 6, but now look for *compatible* types instead of assignable types.
10. If the result list contains one signature, then this is the resulting signature.
11. Otherwise, the disambiguation fails

An example elucidates how the disambiguation works. Assuming the following definition and classes:

```
<bean ...>
  <argument>
    <bean class="Bar"/>
  </argument>
  <argument>
    <bean class="Foo"/>
  </argument>
<bean>

public class Bar extends Foo {}
public class Foo {}
```

The following bullets provide examples how signatures are matched against the previous definition.

- (Bar,Foo) – The arguments will be in the given order and the orderd match will succeed. This is the normal case.
- (Foo,Bar) – This will not match because in the re-ordered match, the Bar argument (which is a Foo sub-type) is matched against the first argument. The second Foo argument can then no longer find a compatible type because that slot is taken by the Bar instance.
- (Object,Object) – This will be called with (aBar,aFoo).

Multiple constructors on a class can require disambiguation with the arguments type. In the following example, the Multiple class has two constructors that would both match the constructor arguments because a String object can be converted to both a File object and a URL object.

```
public class Multiple {
    public Multiple(URL a);
    public Multiple(File a);
}
```

An attempt to configure a Multiple object without the type will fail, because it is not possible to determine the correct constructor. Therefore, the type should be set to disambiguate this:

```
<bean class="Multiple">
  <argument type="java.net.URL" value="http://www.acme.us"/>
</bean>
```

121.9.2   Type Compatibility

During injection, it is necessary to decide about type *assignability* or type *compatibility* in several places. If generics are present, a type must be *reified* in its class, see *Generics* on page 243. In this specification, the canonical representation for a type is T<P1..Pn>, where n is zero for a non-parameterized type, which is always true in a VM less than Java 5. The ReifiedType class models this kind of type.

If type T or S is primitive, then they are treated as their corresponding wrapper class for deciding assignability and compatibility. Therefore, a type T<P1..Pn> (target) is *assignable* from an object s of type S (source) when the following is true:

- n == 0, and
- T.isAssignableFrom(S)

T<P1..Pn> is *compatible* with an object s of type S when it is assignable or it can be converted using the Blueprint built-in type converter. The convertability must be verified with the canConvert(s, T<P1..Pn>) method. That is, type compatibility is defined as:

- assignable(T<P1..Pn>,S), and
- cs.canConvert(s,T<P1..Pn>) returns true

Where cs is the Blueprint built in type converter that also uses the custom type converters.

121.9.3   Type Conversion

Strings in Blueprint definitions, object values, and component instances must be made compatible with the type expected by an injection target (method or constructor argument, or property) before being injected, which can require *type conversion*. The Blueprint Container supports a number of built-in type conversions, and provides an extension mechanism for configuring additional type converters. Custom type converters have priority over built-in converters.

The goal of the type conversion is to convert a source object s with type S to a target type T<P1..Pn>. The conversion of the Blueprint built-in type converter must take place in the following order:

1 If T<P1..Pn> is assignable from S, which implies n=0, then no conversion is necessary, except that primitives must be converted to their wrapper types.
2 Try all type converters in declaration order with the canConvert(s,T<P1..Pn>) method, exceptions are ignored and logged. The first converter that returns true is considered the converter, its result is obtained by calling convert(s,T<P1..Pn>). Exceptions in this method must be treated as an error.
3 If T is an array, then S must be an array or it must implement Collection, otherwise the conversion fails. Each member of array s must be type converted to the component type of T using the generics information if available, see the getComponentType method on Class. This is a recursive process. The result must be stored in an array of type T.
4 If T implements Collection, then S must be an array or implement Collection, otherwise the conversion fails. If the platform supports generics, the members of object s must be converted to the member type of the collection if this is available from the generics information, or to Object otherwise. The Blueprint Container must create a target collection and add all members of s to this new object in the iteration order of s. The target collection depends on type T:
    •   If T is one of the interfaces listed in *Concrete Types for Interfaces* on page 243, then the target collection must be the corresponding concrete class.
    •   T must represent a public concrete class with an empty publicly accessible constructor, the target collection is then a new instance of T.
    •   Otherwise T represents an interface and the conversion must fail.
5 If T implements Map or extends Dictionary, then S must implement Map or extend Dictionary as well, otherwise the conversion fails. If the platform supports generics, the members of map s must be converted to the key and value type of the target map. This is a recursive process. Without generics, the members are not converted and put as is.
    The target map depends on T:
    •   If T is a public concrete class (not interface) with an empty publicly accessible constructor then the target map must be a new instance of T.
    •   If T is one of the Map interfaces or Dictionary listed in *Concrete Types for Interfaces* on page 243, then the target map must be the corresponding concrete class.
    •   Otherwise, the conversion fails.
6 If T is one of the primitive types (byte, char, short, int, long, float, double, boolean) then treat T as the corresponding wrapper class.
7 If T extends class Number and S extends also class Number then convert the source to a number of type T. If the target type cannot hold the value then the conversion fails. However, precision may be lost if a double or float is converted to one of the integer types.
8 If source type S is not class String, then the conversion fails.
9 The conversion is attempted based on the target type T from the string s. The following target types are supported:
    •   boolean or Boolean – Construct the appropriate boolean type while accepting the following additional values for true and false respectively:
        •   yes, no
        •   on, off
    •   Character – The string s must have a length of 1, this single character is then converted to a Character object.
    •   Locale – The string s is converted to a Locale using the following syntax (no spaces are allowed between terms).

```
locale  ::=  <java language-code> ( '_' country)+
country ::=  <java country-code>
             ('_' <java variant-code>)+
```

- Pattern – Create the Pattern object with Pattern.compile(String).
- Properties – Create a new Properties object and load the properties from the string. The string must follow the format described with the Properties.load method.
- Enum subclass – Convert the string s to the appropriate member of the given enum with the Enum.valueOf method. If the string is not one of the enum values, then the conversion must fail.
- Class – The string s must conform to the syntax in *Syntax for Java types* on page 210. This type must be loaded through the Bundle's loadClass method. The resulting class must match any generic constraints on T. If this fails, the conversion fails.

10 If target type T has a constructor (String), then use this constructor to create an instance with the source string s. This convention caters for many of the built-in Java types such as BigDecimal, BigInteger, File, URL, and so on, as well as for custom types.

If none of the above steps has found a proper conversion than the conversion fails. Failing a conversion must end with throwing an Illegal Argument Exception.

121.9.4 Type Converters

A type converter converts a source type to a target type. The source type for a type converter is not constrained. A type converter must support the following methods:

- canConvert(Object,ReifiedType) – A light weight method that inspects the object and returns true if it can convert it to the given Reified Type, false otherwise. Converters normally can convert a type S to a type T<...>. However, converters can convert to multiple types and the value of the source object can influence the returned type. For example, a converter could convert a string to a type based on its content.
- convert(Object,ReifiedType) – The actual conversion method. This method should not fail if the canConvert method has returned true.

The ReifiedType class provides access to the target class. In a Java 1.4 environment, the ReifiedType object will provide a Class object for conversion and no type arguments. In a Java 5 environment, the ReifiedType object provides access to the reified class as well as the type arguments. Generics and reified types are described in *Generics* on page 243.

Type converters are normal managers with some limitations due to the dependency handling. If they depend on general managers or services then there is a change that cyclic dependencies are created.

Converters must be defined in the type-converters element, see *<type-converters>* on page 212, to be registered as a converter. Component instances of managers in this section must implement the Converter interface. Converters must also only transitively depend on built-in converters. It must be possible to initialize all converters before any of them are used. Type converters should not use the type conversion before all type converters are fully configured.

Converters are ordered within one definition resource but there is no resource ordering, so the overall ordering is not defined, making it a good practice to concentrate all converters in a single XML definition. The definition ordering is used during type conversion. That is, converters are not ordered by their specialization, a converter that is earlier can convert a more general type will override a converter that is later in the list but could have converted to a more specific type.

Converters must always use the type arguments of the given Reified Type, even if they are running on Java 1.4. The default behavior of the Reified Type will automatically work.

The following example demonstrates how a converter can use generics to use an AtomicReference<T> whenever type T is supported. Such a type could be for a property like:

```
public void setInteger( AtomicReference<Integer> atomic );
```

The Atomic Converter uses the generic argument to convert a source object to an Integer and then creates an AtomicReference with this converted object. The definition of the type converter looks like:

```
<type-converters>
  <bean class="AtomicConverter">
    <argument ref="blueprintConverter"/>
  </bean>
</type-converters>
```

The Blueprint converter is injected in the constructor of the AtomicInteger class, in order to allow the conversion of the generic arguments. The Blueprint built-in type converter must not be used before all type converters are registered because a needed type converter might not have been registered yet. This is the reason type converters should not require type conversion in their initialization because the state of this converter is not well defined at this time.

The conversion class looks like:

```
public class AtomicConverter {
  Converter bpc;
  public AtomicConverter(Converter bpc) { this.bpc=bpc; }

  public boolean canConvert(Object s,ReifiedType T) {
    return T.getRawClass() == AtomicReference.class
    && bpc.canConvert(s, T.getActualTypeArgument(0));
  }

  public Object convert( Object s, ReifiedType T )
                                         throws Exception {
    Object obj = bpc.convert(
      s,T.getActualTypeArgument(0) );

    return new AtomicReference<Object>(obj);
  }
}
```

Any injection that now targets an AtomicReference<T> value will automatically be converted into an AtomicReference of the appropriate type because of the example converter. The following definitions test this behavior:

```
public class Foo<T extends Integer> {
  public Foo( AtomicReference<T> v) {}
}

<bean id="foo" class="Foo"> <argument value="6"/> </bean>
```

This definition will create an foo object with the Foo(AtomicReference<T>) constructor. The source type is a string and there is no assignability for an Atomic Reference, so the registered type converters are consulted. The Atomic Converter recognizes that the target T is an AtomicReference class and indicates it can convert. The convert method then uses the generic argument information, which is an Integer object in the example, to convert the string "6" to an Integer object and return the appropriate AtomicReference object.

121.9.5   Built-in Converter

A Blueprint Container must contain an environment manager called blueprintConverter. The related component instance must implement the Converter interface.

The built-in Converter provides access to the provided type converters as well as the built in types. This service provides the type conversion as defined in *Type Conversion* on page 240.

Injecting a reference to the blueprintConverter environment manager into a bean provides access to all the type conversions that the Blueprint Container and registered type converters are able to perform. However, if this converter is injected in a type converter, then by definition, not all custom type converters are yet registered with the built-in converter. Type converters should therefore in general not rely on type conversion during their construction.

121.9.6   Concrete Types for Interfaces

The Blueprint extender can choose an implementation class when it provides an instance during conversion to an interface as well as when it natively provides an object. The actual implementation class can make a noticeable difference in disambiguation, type conversion, and general behavior. Therefore this sections describe the concrete types an implementation must use for specific interfaces if the platform allows this.

Table 121.18   Implementation types for interfaces

	Interface/Abstract class	Implementation class
	Collection	ArrayList
	List	ArrayList
Java 5	Queue	LinkedList
	Set	LinkedHashSet
	SortedSet	TreeSet
	Map	LinkedHashMap
	SortedMap	TreeMap
Java 5	ConcurrentMap	ConcurrentHashMap
	Dictionary	Hashtable

If possible, the instances of these types must preserve the definition ordering.

121.9.7   Generics

Java 5 introduced the concept of *generics*. Before Java 5, a *type*, was simply a class or interface, both represented by the Class object. Generics augment these classes and interfaces with additional *type constraints*. These type constraints are not available on an instance because an instance always references a raw Class. For an instance all generic type constraints are *erased*. That is, a List<Integer> object is indistinguishable from a List<String> object, which are indistinguishable from a List object. Objects always refer to a raw Class object, this is the one returned from the getClass method. This Class object is shared between all instances and can therefore not have the actual type constraints (like String, Integer in the list examples).

When a class is used the compiler captures the type constraints and associates them with the specific use and encodes them in a Type object. For example, a field declaration captures the full generic type information:

```
List<String> strings;
```

A field has a getGenericType method that provides access to a Type object, which is a super interface for all type information in the Java 5 and later runtime. In the previous example, this would be a Parameterized Type that has a raw class of List and a type argument that is the String class. These constraints are reflectively available for:

- A superclass
- Implemented interfaces

- Fields
- For each method or constructor:
  - Return type
  - Exception types
  - Parameter types

Generics influence the type conversion rules because most of the time the Blueprint extender knows the actual Type object for an injection. Therefore, conversion must take place to a type like T<P1..Pn>, where T is a raw Class object and P1..Pn form the available type parameters. For a non-parametrized class and for other VMs than 1.4, n is always zero, that is no type arguments are available. The P arguments are in itself instances of Type. The form T<P1..Pn> is called the *reified* form. It can be constructed by traversing the Type graph and calculating a class that matches the constraints. For example < extends List<T>> defines a *wild card* constraint, that has a List<T> as reified type, where T is a Type Variable defined elsewhere that can have additional constraints. The resulting type must be an instance of List<T>. A reified type will use an object implementing List for such an example because that is the only class that is guaranteed to be compatible. The rules to reify the different Type interfaces are:

- Class – A Class represents unparameterized raw type and is reified into T<>. For example:

  ```
  String string;
  ```

- ParameterizedType – A Parameterized Type defines a raw type and 1..n typed parameters. The raw type of the Parameterized Type is also reified and represents T. The arguments map directly to the arguments of the reified form. An example of a Parameterized Type is:

  ```
  Map<String,Object> map;
  ```

- TypeVariable – Represents a Type Variable. A type variable is listed in a generics type declaration, for example in Map<K,V>, the K and V are the type variables. A type variable is bounded by a number of types because it is possible to declare a bounded type like: <A extends Readable&Closeable>. A Type Variable is reified by taking its first bound in reified form, this is the same as in Java 5 where the first bounds is the erasure type. However, this can fail if multiple bounds are present. An example of a Type Variable is:

  ```
  public <T extends ServiceTracker> void setMap(T st) {}
  ```

  In this example, the parameter st will have a reified type of ServiceTracker.
- WildcardType – A Wildcard Type constrains a type to a set of lower bounds and a set of upper bounds, at least in the reflective API. In the Java 5 and later syntax a Wildcard Type can only specify 0 or one lower and one upper bound, for example <T extends Number> constraints the Type Variable T to at least extend the Number class. A Wildcard Type is reified into its reified upper bound when no lower bound is set, and otherwise it is reified into its reified lower bound. An example of a Wildcard Type is seen in the example of a Type Variable.
- GenericArrayType – A Generic Array Type represents an array. Its component type is reified and then converted to an array. The Reified Type will have the array class as reified class and the type arguments reflect the type arguments of the component type. For example:

  ```
  public void setLists(List<String>[] lists) {}
  ```

  This example will have a Reified Type of List[]<String>.

This specification is written to allow Java 1.4 implementations and clients, the API therefore has no generics. Therefore, the Type class in Java 5 and later cannot be used in the API. However, even if it could use the Type class, using the type classes to create the reified form is non-trivial and error prone. The API therefore provides a concrete class that gives convenient access to the reified form without requiring the usage of the Type class.

The ReifiedType class provides access to the reified form of Class, which is itself and has no type arguments. However, Blueprint extender implementations that recognize Java 5 generics should subclass the ReifiedType class and use this in the conversion process. The subclass can calculate the reified form of any Type subclasses.

121.10 Service Dynamics

The Blueprint Container specification handles the complexities of the dynamic nature of OSGi by *hiding* the dynamic behavior of the OSGi service registry, at least temporarily. This dynamic behavior is caused by service references that select one or more services that can come and go at runtime.

The Blueprint Container must handle the dynamics in the following way:

- *Proxied references* – Service reference managers must provide a proxy implementing the specified interfaces, instead of the actual service object it refers to. The proxy must fetch the real service lazily. For reference managers, when a proxy is used, and no candidate is available, a candidate must be found within a limited time. If no candidate service is available during this time, a Service Unavailable Exception must be thrown. The reference-list manager also maintains proxies but these proxies must throw a Service Unavailable Exception immediately when the proxy is used and the backing service is no longer available.
  When proxied references are used with stateful services, then the application code must register a reference listener to perform the necessary initialization and cleanup when a new backing service is bound.
- *Conditional Service Registrations* – The service manager is responsible for registering a service with the OSGi service registry. A service manager is statically dependent on the transitive set of managers that it depends on. If these static dependencies contain mandatory service references, then the manager's service must not be registered when any of these mandatory service references is unsatisfied, see *Enabled* on page 225.

121.10.1 Damping

When an operation is invoked on an unsatisfied proxy from a reference manager (either optional or mandatory), the invocation must block until either the reference becomes satisfied or a time-out expires (whichever comes first). During this wait, a WAITING event must be broadcast, see *Events* on page 248.

The default timeout for service invocations is 5 minutes. The optional timeout of the reference element specifies an alternate timeout (in milliseconds). If no matching service becomes available within the timeout, then a Service Unavailable Exception must be thrown. A timeout of zero means infinite and a negative timeout is an error.

For example:

```
<reference id="logService"
     interface="org.osgi.service.log.LogService"
     timeout="100000" />

<bean id="bar" class="BarImpl">
  <property name="log" ref="logService"/>
</bean>
```

When this Blueprint Container is instantiated, the reference manager provides a proxy for the Log Service, which gets injected in the log property. If no Log Service is available, then the proxy will have no backing service. If the bar object attempts to log, it will block and if the timeout expires the proxy must throw a Service Unavailable Exception.

If at some later point in time, a Log Service is registered then it becomes satisfied again. If bar now logs a message, the proxy will get the service object again and forward the method invocation to the actual Log Service implementation.

The damping ensures that a mandatory service reference that becomes unsatisfied does not cause the Blueprint Container to be destroyed. Temporary absences of mandatory services are tolerated to allow for administrative operations and continuous operation of as much of the system as possible.

A reference-list manager does not provide damping. It only removes the service proxy from the collection if its service goes away. Using a collection reference manager will never block, it will just have no members if its selection is empty. A timeout attribute is therefore not supported by the reference-list elements. However, the elements are proxied and it is possible that they throw a Service Unavailable Exception when used and the backing service has disappeared. The exceptions for a reference-list proxy will be thrown immediately when the proxy is used.

121.10.2 Iteration

The provided object of a reference-list manager implements the List interface. Depending on the memberType or the optional generics information, it provides a collection that contains the member objects, that is, either proxies to the service object, or ServiceReference objects. These collections are read-only for the receiver, however, their contents can dynamically change due to changes in the selection. The access to these collections with iterators must give a number of guarantees:

- *Safe* – All iterators of reference-list managers must be safe to traverse according to the Iterator interface contract, even while the underlying collection is being modified locally or in another thread. If the hasNext method returns true, the iterator must return a member object on the subsequent next method invocation. If there is no longer a service object available when requested, then a dummy proxy must be returned that throws a Service Unavailable Exception whenever it is used.
- *Visibility* – All the changes made to the collection that affect member objects not yet returned by the iterator must be visible in the iteration. Proxies for new services must be added at the end of the List. Proxies already returned can be affected by changes in the service registry after the iterator has returned them.

After the iterator has returned false for the hasNext method, no more objects can be obtained from it. A List Iterator must not be supported.

121.10.3 Mandatory Dependencies

A service manager can have mandatory service reference managers in its transitive dependencies. Such a service manager must ensure that the service object is registered with the OSGi service registry during the runtime phase when all its mandatory service references that it depends on are satisfied. This called *tracking* the dependency. A service manager is *enabled* when all its mandatory references in its dependencies are satisfied.

This tracking only works for dependencies declared directly in the definitions; dependencies established during runtime by calling the getComponentInstance method are not tracked.

In the following example, service manager S has a transitive dependency on the mandatory reference manager M, which means the Blueprint Container must ensure that the service object provided by bean A is registered when reference manager M is satisfied.

```
<service id="S" ref="A" interface="com.acme.Foo"/>
<bean id="A" class="com.acme.FooImpl">
    <property name="bar" ref="m"/>
```

```
    </bean>
    <reference id="M" interface="com.acme.Bar"
        availability="mandatory"/>
```

However, if the dependency from manager A on manager M is not declared but created through code that manipulates the Blueprint Container then the dependency is not tracked.

121.11 Blueprint Container

The Blueprint Container has a registry where all top-level managers, as well as *environment* managers, are registered by their component id. The Blueprint Container can be injected in application code with the environment blueprintContainer manager. For example:

```
<bean class="com.acme.FooImpl">
    <property name="container" ref="blueprintContainer"/>
</bean>
```

The Blueprint Container allows application code to get objects that are provided by the top-level managers through the getComponentInstance method. However, the Blueprint Container should not be required to get a component instance; the proper way to use Blueprint is to inject them. This declarative approach makes the Blueprint Container aware of any dependencies; one of the primary goals of a dependency injection framework. The Blueprint Container's introspective features are commonly used for management and other non-application purposes.

The Blueprint Container is registered as a service during the runtime phase so that other bundles can use it for these, and other, purposes.

121.11.1 Environment Managers

The Blueprint Container provides a number of *environment managers*. These managers have defined names and provide convenient access to information about the environment. Environment managers cannot be overridden by explicitly defined managers because it is invalid to define a manager with an existing component id. All component ids starting with blueprint are reserved for this specification and future incarnations.

There is no XML definition for environment managers but their Metadata must be provided as ComponentMetadata objects.

The following ids are used for the environment managers:

- blueprintContainer – The Blueprint Container.
- blueprintBundle – A manager that provides the Blueprint bundle's Bundle object.
- blueprintBundleContext – A manager that provides the Blueprint bundle's BundleContext object.
- blueprintConverter – A manager that provides an object implementing the Converter interface. This represents the built-in conversion facility that the Blueprint Container uses to convert objects. See *Built-in Converter* on page 242.

121.11.2 Component Instances

The Blueprint Container provides access to the component instances that the top level managers can provide, as well as their Metadata. The Blueprint Container has the following methods for requesting a component instance and to find out what managers are available:

- getComponentInstance(String) – This method will provide a component instance from the component id. If the manager has not been activated yet, it must atomically activate and ensure its explicit and implicit dependencies are activated transitively.
- getComponentIds() – Returns a set of component ids in this Blueprint Container. These ids must consist of all top level managers (including calculated ids) and environment managers.

121.11.3   Access to Component Metadata

Each of the manager types has specific Component Metadata subtypes associated with it, except Environment managers that use Component Metadata. The Blueprint Container provides access by component id to the Component Metadata of the top level managers. However, managers can also be defined inline, in which case they do not have a component id. Therefore, the Blueprint Container can also enumerate all the managers that are represented by a Metadata sub-interface.

- getComponentMetadata(String) – Answer the Component Metadata sub-type for the given component id. Environment managers will return a ComponentMetadata object, the other managers each have their own specific Metadata type.
- getMetadata(Class) – Answer a collection with the Metadata of the given type, regardless if it is defined as/in a top-level or inlined manager. For example, getMetadata(ServiceMetadata.class) returns all Service Metadata in the Blueprint container. This includes all top level managers as well as any inlined managers. For Environment Managers, this method returns a ComponentMetadata object.

121.11.4   Concurrency

A Blueprint Container must be thread safe. Each method must handle the case when multiple threads access the underlying registry of managers. Activation of managers must be atomic. That is, other threads must be blocked until a manager is completely activated.

The Blueprint Container must handle reentrant calls.

121.12   Events

The Blueprint Container must track all Blueprint Listener services and keep these listeners updated of the progress or failure of all its managed bundles. The Blueprint Listener is kept informed by sending it events synchronously. These events are therefore normally delivered in order but in exceptional cases this can be seen out of order for a listener when new events are initiated synchronously from within a callback. Therefore, Blueprint Listener services should see the event as a notification, where actual work should be processed on another thread.

Blueprint Events must be sent to each registered Blueprint Listener service. This service has the following method:

- blueprintEvent(BlueprintEvent) – Notify the listener of a new Blueprint Event. These events are send synchronously with their cause. That is, all listeners must be notified before the Blueprint Container continues to the next step.

The events must be delivered as BlueprintEvent objects. The event types that they represent, and the data that these objects carry, is further described in *Blueprint Event* on page 248.

A Blueprint Listener services must be given the initial state of all managed bundles before normal processing starts, see *Replay* on page 249.

Blueprint Listener services that throw Exceptions or do not return in a reasonable time as judged by the Blueprint extender implementation, should be logged, if possible, and further ignored.

121.12.1   Blueprint Event

The Blueprint Event supports the following event types:

- CREATING – The Blueprint extender has started creating a Blueprint Container for the bundle.
- GRACE_PERIOD – The Blueprint Container enters the grace period. This event can be repeated multiple times when the list of dependencies changes due to changes in the service registry.
- CREATED – The Blueprint Container is ready. The application is now running.

- WAITING – A service reference is blocking because of unsatisfied mandatory dependencies. This event can happen multiple times in a row.
- DESTROYING – The Blueprint Container is being destroyed because the Blueprint bundle or Blueprint extender has stopped.
- DESTROYED – The Blueprint Container is completely destroyed.
- FAILURE – An error occurred during the creation of the Blueprint Container.

The Blueprint Event provides the following methods:

- getBundle() – The Blueprint bundle
- getCause() – Any occurred exception or null
- getDependencies() – A list of filters that specify the unsatisfied mandatory references.
- getExtenderBundle() – The Blueprint extender bundle.
- getTimestamp() – The time the event occurred
- getType() – The type of the event.
- isReplay() – Indicates if the event is a replay (true) or if it is a new event (false), see *Replay* on page 249.

121.12.2   Replay

The Blueprint Extender must remember the last Blueprint Event for each ready bundle that it manages, see *Initialization Steps* on page 203. During the (synchronous) service registration event of a Blueprint Listener service, the Blueprint extender must inform the Blueprint Listener service about all its managed bundles by sending it the last known event for each bundle the Blueprint extender manages. This initial event is called the *replay* event, and is marked as such.

The replay event must be delivered to the Blueprint Listener service as the first event, before any other event is delivered, during the registration of the Blueprint Listener service. That is, the blueprintEvent method must have returned before the first non-replay event can be delivered and no events must be lost. The replay events must be sent every time a Blueprint Listener service is registered.

The set of managed bundles is defined by bundles that are active and are managed by the Blueprint extender, even if their initialization ended in failure.

The BlueprintEvent object for a replay event must return true for the isReplay() method in this situation, and false in all other situations.

121.12.3   Event Admin Mapping

When the Event Admin service is present, the Blueprint extender must create an Event Admin event for each defined Blueprint Event. This Event Admin event must be asynchronously given to the Event Admin service with the postEvent method.

The topic of the Event Admin event is derived from the Blueprint event type with a fixed prefix. All topics must have the prefix of:

    TOPIC_BLUEPRINT_EVENTS

After this prefix, the name of the Blueprint Event type must be used as the suffix. That is, CREATING, GRACE_PERIOD, etc. For example, org/osgi/service/blueprint/container/GRACE_PERIOD.

For each Blueprint event the following properties must be included:

- TYPE – The type of the Event, see *Blueprint Event* on page 248.
- BUNDLE– (Bundle) The Bundle object of the Blueprint bundle
- BUNDLE_ID – (Long) The id of the Blueprint bundle.
- BUNDLE_SYMBOLICNAME – (String) The Bundle Symbolic Name of the Blueprint bundle.
- BUNDLE_VERSION - (Version) The version of the Blueprint bundle.
- EXTENDER_BUNDLE – (Bundle) the Bundle object of the Blueprint extender bundle.
- EXTENDER_BUNDLE_ID – (Long) The id of the Blueprint extender bundle

- EXTENDER_BUNDLE_SYMBOLICNAME – (String) The Bundle Symbolic Name of the Blueprint extender bundle.
- EXTENDER_BUNDLE_VERSION – (Version) The version of the Blueprint extender bundle
- TIMESTAMP – (Long) The time when the event occurred
- CAUSE – (Throwable) The failure cause, only included for a FAILURE event.
- DEPENDENCIES – (String[]) The filter of an unsatisfied service reference. Can only appear in a GRACE_PERIOD, WAITING or FAILURE event caused by a time-out.
- EVENT – (BlueprintEvent) The BlueprintEvent object that caused this event.

The property names for Blueprint Listener events may be conveniently referenced using the constants defined in the org.osgi.service.event.EventConstants and EventConstants interfaces.

The Event Admin events do not follow the replay model in use for Blueprint Listener services. That is, the Event Admin must only be kept informed about events as they occur.

121.13 Class Loading

The module layer in OSGi provides advanced class loading rules that potentially can cause bundles to live in different class spaces. This means that not all bundles can collaborate because the classes involved in the collaboration can come from different class loaders, which results in confusing Class Cast Exceptions on classes with the same name. It is therefore crucial that the Blueprint Container uses the Bundle Context and the bundle class loader of the Blueprint bundle for all actions that are made on behalf of the Blueprint bundle. Especially, access to the OSGi service registry must use the Bundle Context of the Blueprint bundle. Any dynamic class loading must use the Blueprint bundle's loadClass method. The normal OSGi mechanics will then ensure class space consistency for resolved bundles.

121.13.1 Blueprint Extender and Bundle Compatibility

For many Blueprint bundles, there is no class space compatibility issue. These bundles do not use any Blueprint classes and are therefore by definition compatible with any extender. However, if the Blueprint bundle uses some of the Blueprint packages, it must import these packages. Blueprint Containers must verify that they are *type compatible* with the Blueprint bundle before they attempt to manage it. See *Type Compatibility* on page 251.

121.13.2 XML and Class Loading

The Blueprint definition resources contain textual references to classes. These textual references will be loaded with the class loader of the Blueprint bundle. This implies that all the classes of provided component instances must be either imported or available from the bundle.

The Blueprint specification has the following attributes and elements that can cause imports:

- class
- value-type
- interface
- interfaces
- type
- key-type

All these attributes and elements are defined with the Tclass and Ttype XML Schema type for the Blueprint namespace. The Tclass defines simple class names, and Ttype defines types defined in *Syntax for Java types* on page 210.

121.13.3 Foreign Bundle Context

When using the Blueprint Container in its Blueprint bundle, the types that the managers provide are guaranteed to be compatible with the caller.

When using a Blueprint Container service in another bundle (for example, getting it as a service) then there is no guarantee of type compatibility or even visibility between the versions of the types of the returned managers, and the versions of the types visible to the caller. Care must therefore be taken when casting the return value of the getComponentInstance method to a more specific type.

121.13.4 Converters and Class Loading

A converter is closely coupled to its target class. If the converter comes from another bundle, then the converter bundle must ensure class space consistency between the converter implementation and the target class. This can be achieved by specifying the target class in the uses directive.

For example:

```
Export-Package:
    com.converters.ac;uses:="com.converters.dc"
```

A bundle that references a type converter defined in the Blueprint bundle does not need to export that type. When creating a Blueprint Container, the extender bundle uses the class loader of the Blueprint bundle.

121.13.5 Type Compatibility

Two bundles are type compatible for a given class if they both load the same class object, or if either bundle cannot load the given class.

To mitigate type incompatibility problems, a Blueprint extender must export the org.osgi.service.blueprint package. In the uses: directive, it should list any packages of classes that can be shared between the Blueprint extender and the Blueprint bundle. Blueprint bundles should import this package.

121.13.6 Visibility and Accessibility

The Blueprint Container must load any classes it needs through the Blueprint bundle's loadClass method. If a class can not be loaded, then the initialization fails. Class loading issues are further discussed in *Class Loading* on page 250.

The Blueprint Container must respect the accessibility of the class and any of its members. That is, the Blueprint Container must not use the setAccessibility method. All classes and reflected members must therefore be declared public or be implicitly public like the default constructor.

121.14 Metadata

An important aspect of the Blueprint specification is the so called *metadata* interfaces. These interfaces are used in the Blueprint Container to enable programmatic access to the XML definitions. During the parsing phase the Blueprint Container reads the XML and converts it to an object implementing the appropriate interface.

The XML elements and XML Schema types map to the Metadata interfaces. For example, <bean> maps to BeanMetadata. However, in several cases, the attributes and/or sub-elements in the Metadata interfaces are merged when possible. For example, the interface attribute and interfaces element in the service element are merged in the ServiceMetadata class' getInterfaces() method.

The interfaces are arranged in a comprehensive hierarchy that reflects their usage and constraints. This hierarchy is depicted inFigure 121.12 on page 252.

The hierarchy can roughly be divided in two parts. The first part is the sub-interfaces of the ComponentMetadata interface. These interfaces are defining the configuration data of the top-level and inlined managers. The manager's component instance(s) are injected with values during runtime. The configuration of how to create a specific value is also described with Metadata interfaces.

For example, a Map object is described with configuration information in the MapMetadata inter-face. The hierarchy makes it clear that Component Metadata is also a value that can be injected. Keys in maps or properties can not be null. This is the reason the hierarchy is split at the top into a null value branch and a branch that can only generates non-null values.

The Target interface describes managers that can be used as the target for the reference listener or the registration listener, or a ref.

Figure 121.12   Metadata Interfaces Hierarchy

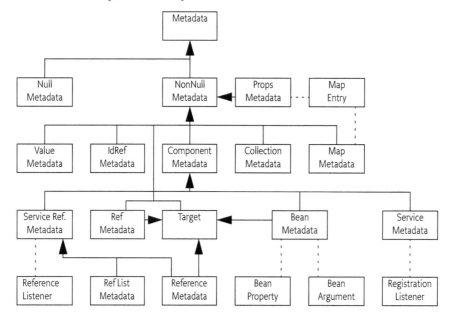

121.15   **Blueprint XML Schema**

The Blueprint schema included in this specification can be found in digital form at [10] *OSGi XML Schemas.* The schema listed here is not annotated, the digital form has annotations.

```
<xml version="1.0" encoding="UTF-8">
<xsd:schema
   xmlns="http://www.osgi.org/xmlns/blueprint/v1.0.0"
   xmlns:xsd="http://www.w3.org/2001/XMLSchema"
   targetNamespace="http://www.osgi.org/xmlns/blueprint/v1.0.0"
   elementFormDefault="qualified"
   attributeFormDefault="unqualified"
   version="1.0.0">
   <xsd:complexType name="Tcomponent" abstract="true">
      <xsd:attribute name="id" type="xsd:ID"/>
      <xsd:attribute name="activation" type="Tactivation"/>
      <xsd:attribute name="depends-on" type="TdependsOn"/>
   </xsd:complexType>
   <xsd:element name="blueprint" type="Tblueprint"/>
   <xsd:complexType name="Tblueprint">
      <xsd:sequence>
         <xsd:element name="description" type="Tdescription" minOccurs="0"/>
         <xsd:element name="type-converters" type="Ttype-converters"
               minOccurs="0" maxOccurs="1"/>
         <xsd:choice minOccurs="0" maxOccurs="unbounded">
            <xsd:element name="service" type="Tservice"/>
            <xsd:element name="reference-list" type="Treference-list"/>
            <xsd:element name="bean" type="Tbean"/>
            <xsd:element name="reference" type="Treference"/>
            <xsd:any namespace="##other" processContents="strict"/>
```

```xml
                    </xsd:choice>
                </xsd:sequence>
                <xsd:attribute name="default-activation" default="eager" type="Tactivation"/>
                <xsd:attribute name="default-timeout" type="Ttimeout" default="300000"/>
                <xsd:attribute name="default-availability" type="Tavailability" default="mandatory"/>
                <xsd:anyAttribute namespace="##other" processContents="strict"/>
            </xsd:complexType>
            <xsd:complexType name="Ttype-converters">
                <xsd:choice minOccurs="0" maxOccurs="unbounded">
                    <xsd:element name="bean" type="Tbean"/>
                    <xsd:element name="reference" type="Treference"/>
                    <xsd:element name="ref" type="Tref"/>
                    <xsd:any namespace="##other" processContents="strict"/>
                </xsd:choice>
            </xsd:complexType>
            <xsd:group name="GtargetComponent">
                <xsd:choice>
                    <xsd:element name="bean" type="Tinlined-bean"/>
                    <xsd:element name="reference" type="Tinlined-reference"/>
                    <xsd:element name="ref" type="Tref"/>
                    <xsd:any namespace="##other" processContents="strict"/>
                </xsd:choice>
            </xsd:group>
            <xsd:group name="GallComponents">
                <xsd:choice>
                    <xsd:element name="service" type="Tinlined-service"/>
                    <xsd:element name="reference-list" type="Tinlined-reference-list"/>
                    <xsd:group ref="GtargetComponent"/>
                </xsd:choice>
            </xsd:group>
            <xsd:group name="GbeanElements">
                <xsd:sequence>
                    <xsd:element name="description" type="Tdescription" minOccurs="0"/>
                    <xsd:choice minOccurs="0" maxOccurs="unbounded">
                        <xsd:element name="argument" type="Targument"/>
                        <xsd:element name="property" type="Tproperty"/>
                        <xsd:any namespace="##other" processContents="strict"/>
                    </xsd:choice>
                </xsd:sequence>
            </xsd:group>
            <xsd:complexType name="Tbean">
                <xsd:complexContent>
                    <xsd:extension base="Tcomponent">
                        <xsd:group ref="GbeanElements"/>
                        <xsd:attribute name="class" type="Tclass"/>
                        <xsd:attribute name="init-method" type="Tmethod"/>
                        <xsd:attribute name="destroy-method" type="Tmethod"/>
                        <xsd:attribute name="factory-method" type="Tmethod"/>
                        <xsd:attribute name="factory-ref" type="Tidref"/>
                        <xsd:attribute name="scope" type="Tscope"/>
                        <xsd:anyAttribute namespace="##other" processContents="strict"/>
                    </xsd:extension>
                </xsd:complexContent>
            </xsd:complexType>
            <xsd:complexType name="Tinlined-bean">
                <xsd:complexContent>
                    <xsd:restriction base="Tbean">
                        <xsd:group ref="GbeanElements"/>
                        <xsd:attribute name="id" use="prohibited"/>
                        <xsd:attribute name="depends-on" type="TdependsOn"/>
                        <xsd:attribute name="activation" use="prohibited" fixed="lazy"/>
                        <xsd:attribute name="class" type="Tclass"/>
                        <xsd:attribute name="init-method" type="Tmethod"/>
                        <xsd:attribute name="destroy-method" use="prohibited"/>
                        <xsd:attribute name="factory-method" type="Tmethod"/>
                        <xsd:attribute name="factory-ref" type="Tidref"/>
                        <xsd:attribute name="scope" use="prohibited" fixed="prototype"/>
                        <xsd:anyAttribute namespace="##other" processContents="strict"/>
                    </xsd:restriction>
                </xsd:complexContent>
            </xsd:complexType>
            <xsd:complexType name="Targument">
                <xsd:sequence>
                    <xsd:element name="description" type="Tdescription" minOccurs="0"/>
                    <xsd:group ref="Gvalue" minOccurs="0"/>
```

```
          </xsd:sequence>
          <xsd:attribute name="index" type="xsd:nonNegativeInteger"/>
          <xsd:attribute name="type" type="Ttype"/>
          <xsd:attribute name="ref" type="Tidref"/>
          <xsd:attribute name="value" type="TstringValue"/>
      </xsd:complexType>
      <xsd:complexType name="Tproperty">
          <xsd:sequence>
              <xsd:element name="description" type="Tdescription" minOccurs="0"/>
              <xsd:group ref="Gvalue" minOccurs="0"/>
          </xsd:sequence>
          <xsd:attribute name="name" type="Tmethod" use="required"/>
          <xsd:attribute name="ref" type="Tidref"/>
          <xsd:attribute name="value" type="TstringValue"/>
      </xsd:complexType>
      <xsd:complexType name="Tkey">
          <xsd:group ref="GnonNullValue"/>
      </xsd:complexType>
      <xsd:complexType name="Treference">
          <xsd:complexContent>
              <xsd:extension base="TserviceReference">
                  <xsd:sequence>
                      <xsd:any namespace="##other"
                              minOccurs="0" maxOccurs="unbounded" processContents="strict"/>
                  </xsd:sequence>
                  <xsd:attribute name="timeout" type="Ttimeout"/>
              </xsd:extension>
          </xsd:complexContent>
      </xsd:complexType>
      <xsd:complexType name="Tinlined-reference">
          <xsd:complexContent>
              <xsd:restriction base="Treference">
                  <xsd:sequence>
                      <xsd:group ref="GserviceReferenceElements"/>
                      <xsd:any namespace="##other"
                              minOccurs="0" maxOccurs="unbounded" processContents="strict"/>
                  </xsd:sequence>
                  <xsd:attribute name="id" use="prohibited"/>
                  <xsd:attribute name="depends-on" type="TdependsOn"/>
                  <xsd:attribute name="activation" use="prohibited" fixed="lazy"/>
                  <xsd:attribute name="interface" type="Tclass"/>
                  <xsd:attribute name="filter" type="xsd:normalizedString"/>
                  <xsd:attribute name="component-name" type="Tidref"/>
                  <xsd:attribute name="availability" type="Tavailability"/>
                  <xsd:attribute name="timeout" type="Ttimeout"/>
                  <xsd:anyAttribute namespace="##other" processContents="strict"/>
              </xsd:restriction>
          </xsd:complexContent>
      </xsd:complexType>
      <xsd:complexType name="Treference-list">
          <xsd:complexContent>
              <xsd:extension base="TserviceReference">
                  <xsd:sequence>
                      <xsd:any namespace="##other"
                              minOccurs="0" maxOccurs="unbounded" processContents="strict"/>
                  </xsd:sequence>
                  <xsd:attribute name="member-type" type="Tservice-use" default="service-object"/>
              </xsd:extension>
          </xsd:complexContent>
      </xsd:complexType>
      <xsd:complexType name="Tinlined-reference-list">
          <xsd:complexContent>
              <xsd:restriction base="Treference-list">
                  <xsd:sequence>
                      <xsd:group ref="GserviceReferenceElements"/>
                      <xsd:any namespace="##other"
                              minOccurs="0" maxOccurs="unbounded" processContents="strict"/>
                  </xsd:sequence>
                  <xsd:attribute name="id" use="prohibited"/>
                  <xsd:attribute name="depends-on" type="TdependsOn"/>
                  <xsd:attribute name="activation" use="prohibited" fixed="lazy"/>
                  <xsd:attribute name="interface" type="Tclass"/>
                  <xsd:attribute name="filter" type="xsd:normalizedString"/>
                  <xsd:attribute name="component-name" type="Tidref"/>
                  <xsd:attribute name="availability" type="Tavailability"/>
```

```
                <xsd:attribute name="member-type" type="Tservice-use" default="service-object"/>
                <xsd:anyAttribute namespace="##other" processContents="strict"/>
            </xsd:restriction>
        </xsd:complexContent>
    </xsd:complexType>
    <xsd:complexType name="TserviceReference">
        <xsd:complexContent>
            <xsd:extension base="Tcomponent">
                <xsd:sequence>
                    <xsd:group ref="GserviceReferenceElements"/>
                </xsd:sequence>
                <xsd:attribute name="interface" type="Tclass"/>
                <xsd:attribute name="filter" type="xsd:normalizedString"/>
                <xsd:attribute name="component-name" type="Tidref"/>
                <xsd:attribute name="availability" type="Tavailability"/>
                <xsd:anyAttribute namespace="##other" processContents="strict"/>
            </xsd:extension>
        </xsd:complexContent>
    </xsd:complexType>
    <xsd:group name="GserviceReferenceElements">
        <xsd:sequence>
            <xsd:element name="description" type="Tdescription" minOccurs="0"/>
            <xsd:element name="reference-listener"
                 type="TreferenceListener" minOccurs="0" maxOccurs="unbounded"/>
        </xsd:sequence>
    </xsd:group>
    <xsd:complexType name="TreferenceListener">
        <xsd:sequence>
            <xsd:group ref="GtargetComponent" minOccurs="0"/>
        </xsd:sequence>
        <xsd:attribute name="ref" type="Tidref"/>
        <xsd:attribute name="bind-method" type="Tmethod"/>
        <xsd:attribute name="unbind-method" type="Tmethod"/>
    </xsd:complexType>
    <xsd:simpleType name="Tactivation">
        <xsd:restriction base="xsd:NMTOKEN">
            <xsd:enumeration value="eager"/>
            <xsd:enumeration value="lazy"/>
        </xsd:restriction>
    </xsd:simpleType>
    <xsd:simpleType name="Tavailability">
        <xsd:restriction base="xsd:NMTOKEN">
            <xsd:enumeration value="mandatory"/>
            <xsd:enumeration value="optional"/>
        </xsd:restriction>
    </xsd:simpleType>
    <xsd:complexType name="Tservice">
        <xsd:complexContent>
            <xsd:extension base="Tcomponent">
                <xsd:sequence>
                    <xsd:group ref="GserviceElements"/>
                </xsd:sequence>
                <xsd:attribute name="interface" type="Tclass"/>
                <xsd:attribute name="ref" type="Tidref"/>
                <xsd:attribute name="auto-export" type="TautoExportModes" default="disabled"/>
                <xsd:attribute name="ranking" type="xsd:int" default="0"/>
                <xsd:anyAttribute namespace="##other" processContents="strict"/>
            </xsd:extension>
        </xsd:complexContent>
    </xsd:complexType>
    <xsd:complexType name="Tinlined-service">
        <xsd:complexContent>
            <xsd:restriction base="Tservice">
                <xsd:sequence>
                    <xsd:group ref="GserviceElements"/>
                </xsd:sequence>
                <xsd:attribute name="id" use="prohibited"/>
                <xsd:attribute name="depends-on" type="TdependsOn"/>
                <xsd:attribute name="activation" use="prohibited" fixed="lazy"/>
                <xsd:attribute name="interface" type="Tclass"/>
                <xsd:attribute name="ref" type="Tidref"/>
                <xsd:attribute name="auto-export" type="TautoExportModes" default="disabled"/>
                <xsd:attribute name="ranking" type="xsd:int" default="0"/>
                <xsd:anyAttribute namespace="##other" processContents="strict"/>
            </xsd:restriction>
```

```
        </xsd:complexContent>
    </xsd:complexType>
    <xsd:group name="GbaseServiceElements">
        <xsd:sequence>
            <xsd:element name="description" type="Tdescription" minOccurs="0"/>
            <xsd:element name="interfaces" type="Tinterfaces" minOccurs="0"/>
            <xsd:element name="service-properties" type="TserviceProperties" minOccurs="0"/>
            <xsd:element name="registration-listener"
                type="TregistrationListener" minOccurs="0" maxOccurs="unbounded"/>
        </xsd:sequence>
    </xsd:group>
    <xsd:group name="GserviceElements">
        <xsd:sequence>
            <xsd:group ref="GbaseServiceElements"/>
            <xsd:group ref="GtargetComponent" minOccurs="0"/>
        </xsd:sequence>
    </xsd:group>
    <xsd:complexType name="TregistrationListener">
        <xsd:sequence>
            <xsd:group ref="GtargetComponent" minOccurs="0"/>
        </xsd:sequence>
        <xsd:attribute name="ref" type="Tidref"/>
        <xsd:attribute name="registration-method" type="Tmethod"/>
        <xsd:attribute name="unregistration-method" type="Tmethod"/>
    </xsd:complexType>
    <xsd:group name="Gvalue">
        <xsd:choice>
            <xsd:group ref="GnonNullValue"/>
            <xsd:element name="null" type="Tnull"/>
        </xsd:choice>
    </xsd:group>
    <xsd:complexType name="Tnull"/>
    <xsd:group name="GnonNullValue">
        <xsd:choice>
            <xsd:group ref="GallComponents"/>
            <xsd:element name="idref" type="Tref"/>
            <xsd:element name="value" type="Tvalue"/>
            <xsd:element name="list" type="Tcollection"/>
            <xsd:element name="set" type="Tcollection"/>
            <xsd:element name="map" type="Tmap"/>
            <xsd:element name="array" type="Tcollection"/>
            <xsd:element name="props" type="Tprops"/>
        </xsd:choice>
    </xsd:group>
    <xsd:complexType name="Tref">
        <xsd:attribute name="component-id" type="Tidref" use="required"/>
    </xsd:complexType>
    <xsd:complexType name="Tvalue" mixed="true">
        <xsd:attribute name="type" type="Ttype"/>
    </xsd:complexType>
    <xsd:complexType name="TtypedCollection">
        <xsd:attribute name="value-type" type="Ttype"/>
    </xsd:complexType>
    <xsd:complexType name="Tcollection">
        <xsd:complexContent>
            <xsd:extension base="TtypedCollection">
                <xsd:group ref="Gvalue" minOccurs="0" maxOccurs="unbounded"/>
            </xsd:extension>
        </xsd:complexContent>
    </xsd:complexType>
    <xsd:complexType name="Tprops">
        <xsd:sequence>
            <xsd:element name="prop" type="Tprop" minOccurs="0" maxOccurs="unbounded"/>
        </xsd:sequence>
    </xsd:complexType>
    <xsd:complexType name="Tprop" mixed="true">
        <xsd:attribute name="key" type="TstringValue" use="required"/>
        <xsd:attribute name="value" type="TstringValue"/>
    </xsd:complexType>
    <xsd:complexType name="Tmap">
        <xsd:complexContent>
            <xsd:extension base="TtypedCollection">
                <xsd:sequence>
                    <xsd:element name="entry" type="TmapEntry" minOccurs="0" maxOccurs="unbounded"/>
                </xsd:sequence>
```

```
                    <xsd:attribute name="key-type" type="Ttype"/>
                </xsd:extension>
            </xsd:complexContent>
        </xsd:complexType>
        <xsd:complexType name="TmapEntry">
            <xsd:sequence>
                <xsd:element name="key" type="Tkey" minOccurs="0"/>
                <xsd:group ref="Gvalue" minOccurs="0"/>
            </xsd:sequence>
            <xsd:attribute name="key" type="TstringValue"/>
            <xsd:attribute name="key-ref" type="Tidref"/>
            <xsd:attribute name="value" type="TstringValue"/>
            <xsd:attribute name="value-ref" type="Tidref"/>
        </xsd:complexType>
        <xsd:complexType name="TserviceProperties">
            <xsd:sequence>
                <xsd:element name="entry"
                    type="TservicePropertyEntry" minOccurs="0" maxOccurs="unbounded"/>
                <xsd:any namespace="##other"
                    processContents="strict" minOccurs="0" maxOccurs="unbounded"/>
            </xsd:sequence>
        </xsd:complexType>
        <xsd:complexType name="TservicePropertyEntry">
            <xsd:sequence>
                <xsd:group ref="Gvalue" minOccurs="0"/>
            </xsd:sequence>
            <xsd:attribute name="key" type="TstringValue" use="required"/>
            <xsd:attribute name="value" type="TstringValue"/>
        </xsd:complexType>
        <xsd:complexType name="Tdescription" mixed="true">
            <xsd:choice minOccurs="0" maxOccurs="unbounded"/>
        </xsd:complexType>
        <xsd:complexType name="Tinterfaces">
            <xsd:choice minOccurs="1" maxOccurs="unbounded">
                <xsd:element name="value" type="TinterfaceValue"/>
            </xsd:choice>
        </xsd:complexType>
        <xsd:simpleType name="TinterfaceValue">
            <xsd:restriction base="Tclass"/>
        </xsd:simpleType>
        <xsd:simpleType name="Tclass">
            <xsd:restriction base="xsd:NCName"/>
        </xsd:simpleType>
        <xsd:simpleType name="Ttype">
            <xsd:restriction base="xsd:token">
                <xsd:pattern value="[\i-[:]][\c-[:]]*(\[\])*"/>
            </xsd:restriction>
        </xsd:simpleType>
        <xsd:simpleType name="Tmethod">
            <xsd:restriction base="xsd:NCName"/>
        </xsd:simpleType>
        <xsd:simpleType name="Tidref">
            <xsd:restriction base="xsd:NCName"/>
        </xsd:simpleType>
        <xsd:simpleType name="TstringValue">
            <xsd:restriction base="xsd:normalizedString"/>
        </xsd:simpleType>
        <xsd:simpleType name="TautoExportModes">
            <xsd:restriction base="xsd:NMTOKEN">
                <xsd:enumeration value="disabled"/>
                <xsd:enumeration value="interfaces"/>
                <xsd:enumeration value="class-hierarchy"/>
                <xsd:enumeration value="all-classes"/>
            </xsd:restriction>
        </xsd:simpleType>
        <xsd:simpleType name="Ttimeout">
            <xsd:restriction base="xsd:unsignedLong"/>
        </xsd:simpleType>
        <xsd:simpleType name="TdependsOn">
            <xsd:restriction>
                <xsd:simpleType>
                    <xsd:list itemType="Tidref"/>
                </xsd:simpleType>
                <xsd:minLength value="1"/>
            </xsd:restriction>
```

```
    </xsd:simpleType>
    <xsd:simpleType name="Tscope">
        <xsd:restriction base="xsd:NMTOKEN">
            <xsd:enumeration value="singleton"/>
            <xsd:enumeration value="prototype"/>
        </xsd:restriction>
    </xsd:simpleType>
    <xsd:simpleType name="Tservice-use">
        <xsd:restriction base="xsd:NMTOKEN">
            <xsd:enumeration value="service-object"/>
            <xsd:enumeration value="service-reference"/>
        </xsd:restriction>
    </xsd:simpleType>
</xsd:schema>
```

121.16   Security

121.16.1   Blueprint Extender

A Blueprint Extender must use the Bundle Context of the Blueprint bundle. This will ensure that much of the resources allocated will be used on behalf of the Blueprint bundle. However, most Java 2 permissions will also verify the stack and this will inevitably include the Blueprint extender's code. Therefore, the Blueprint extender will require the combined set of permissions needed by all Blueprint bundles. It is therefore likely that in practical situations the Blueprint extender requires All Permission.

The Blueprint bundle requires permission for all actions that are done by the Blueprint Container on behalf of this bundle. That is, the Blueprint Container must not give any extra permissions to the Blueprint bundle because it is being extended.

A Blueprint Container must therefore use a doPriviliged block around all actions that execute code on behalf of the Blueprint bundle. This doPrivileged block must use an Access Control Context that represents the permissions of the Blueprint bundle.

For example, if a Blueprint bundle defines the following bean:

```
<bean class="java.lang.System" factory-method="exit">
    <argument value="1"/>
</bean>
```

Then the Blueprint bundle must have the proper permission to exit the system or the Blueprint bundle must fail when the bean is constructed. At the same time, a Blueprint bundle must not be required to have any permission needed by the Blueprint Container to performs its tasks.

A Blueprint Container must never use the setAccessibility method on a returned member. Only publicly accessible members must be used. Using a non-publicly accessible member must initiate failure, resulting in the destruction of the container.

121.16.2   Blueprint Bundle

A Blueprint Bundle must have all the permissions required by its code. There is one additional permission required for the Blueprint Bundle. The Blueprint extender will register a Blueprint Container service on behalf of the Blueprint bundle, and the Blueprint bundle must therefore have:

```
ServicePermission(...BlueprintContainer, [REGISTER])
```

121.17   org.osgi.service.blueprint.container

Blueprint Container Package Version 1.0.

Bundles wishing to use this package must list the package in the Import-Package header of the bundle's manifest. For example:

```
Import-Package: org.osgi.service.blueprint.container; version="[1.0,2.0)"
```

This package defines the primary interface to a Blueprint Container, BlueprintContainer. An instance of this type is available inside a Blueprint Container as an implicitly defined component with the name "blueprintContainer".

This package also declares the supporting exception types, listener, and constants for working with a Blueprint Container.

121.17.1 Summary

- *BlueprintContainer* - A Blueprint Container represents the managed state of a Blueprint bundle.
- *BlueprintEvent* - A Blueprint Event.
- *BlueprintListener* - A BlueprintEvent Listener.
- *ComponentDefinitionException* - A Blueprint exception indicating that a component definition is in error.
- *Converter* - Type converter to convert an object to a target type.
- *EventConstants* - Event property names used in Event Admin events published by a Blueprint Container.
- *NoSuchComponentException* - A Blueprint exception indicating that a component does not exist in a Blueprint Container.
- *ReifiedType* - Provides access to a concrete type and its optional generic type parameters.
- *ServiceUnavailableException* - A Blueprint exception indicating that a service is unavailable.

121.17.2 public interface BlueprintContainer

A Blueprint Container represents the managed state of a Blueprint bundle. A Blueprint Container provides access to all managed components. These are the beans, services, and service references. Only bundles in the ACTIVE state (and also the STARTING state for bundles awaiting lazy activation) can have an associated Blueprint Container. A given Bundle Context has at most one associated Blueprint Container. A Blueprint Container can be obtained by injecting the predefined "blueprintContainer" component id. The Blueprint Container is also registered as a service and its managed components can be queried.

Concurrency Thread-safe

121.17.2.1 public Set<String> getComponentIds( )

- ☐ Returns the set of component ids managed by this Blueprint Container.

Returns An immutable Set of Strings, containing the ids of all of the components managed within this Blueprint Container.

121.17.2.2 public Object getComponentInstance(String id)

id The component id for the requested component instance.

- ☐ Return the component instance for the specified component id. If the component's manager has not yet been activated, calling this operation will atomically activate it. If the component has singleton scope, the activation will cause the component instance to be created and initialized. If the component has prototype scope, then each call to this method will return a new component instance.

Returns A component instance for the component with the specified component id.

Throws NoSuchComponentException – If no component with the specified component id is managed by this Blueprint Container.

121.17.2.3 public ComponentMetadata getComponentMetadata(String id)

id The component id for the requested Component Metadata.

    ❑ Return the Component Metadata object for the component with the specified component id.

Returns The Component Metadata object for the component with the specified component id.

Throws NoSuchComponentException – If no component with the specified component id is managed by this Blueprint Container.

121.17.2.4   **public Collection<T> getMetadata(Class<T> type)**

Type Arguments <T extends ComponentMetadata>

    <T> Type of Component Metadata.

    type The super type or type of the requested Component Metadata objects.

    ❑ Return all ComponentMetadata objects of the specified Component Metadata type. The supported Component Metadata types are ComponentMetadata (which returns the Component Metadata for all defined manager types), BeanMetadata , ServiceReferenceMetadata (which returns both ReferenceMetadata and ReferenceListMetadata objects), and ServiceMetadata. The collection will include all Component Metadata objects of the requested type, including components that are declared inline.

Returns An immutable collection of Component Metadata objects of the specified type.

121.17.3   public class BlueprintEvent

A Blueprint Event.

BlueprintEvent objects are delivered to all registered BlueprintListener services. Blueprint Events must be asynchronously delivered in chronological order with respect to each listener.

In addition, after a Blueprint Listener is registered, the Blueprint extender will synchronously send to this Blueprint Listener the last Blueprint Event for each ready Blueprint bundle managed by this extender. This *replay* of Blueprint Events is designed so that the new Blueprint Listener can be informed of the state of each Blueprint bundle. Blueprint Events sent during this replay will have the isReplay() flag set. The Blueprint extender must ensure that this replay phase does not interfere with new Blueprint Events so that the chronological order of all Blueprint Events received by the Blueprint Listener is preserved. If the last Blueprint Event for a given Blueprint bundle is DESTROYED, the extender must not send it during this replay phase.

A type code is used to identify the type of event. The following event types are defined:

- CREATING
- CREATED
- DESTROYING
- DESTROYED
- FAILURE
- GRACE_PERIOD
- WAITING

In addition to calling the registered BlueprintListener services, the Blueprint extender must also send those events to the Event Admin service, if it is available.

See Also BlueprintListener, EventConstants

Concurrency Immutable

121.17.3.1   **public static final int CREATED = 2**

The Blueprint extender has created a Blueprint Container for the bundle. This event is sent after the Blueprint Container has been registered as a service.

121.17.3.2   **public static final int CREATING = 1**

The Blueprint extender has started creating a Blueprint Container for the bundle.

121.17.3.3 **public static final int DESTROYED = 4**

The Blueprint Container for the bundle has been completely destroyed. This event is sent after the Blueprint Container has been unregistered as a service.

121.17.3.4 **public static final int DESTROYING = 3**

The Blueprint extender has started destroying the Blueprint Container for the bundle.

121.17.3.5 **public static final int FAILURE = 5**

The Blueprint Container creation for the bundle has failed. If this event is sent after a timeout in the Grace Period, the getDependencies() method must return an array of missing mandatory dependencies. The event must also contain the cause of the failure as a Throwable through the getCause() method.

121.17.3.6 **public static final int GRACE_PERIOD = 6**

The Blueprint Container has entered the grace period. The list of missing dependencies must be made available through the getDependencies() method. During the grace period, a GRACE_PERIOD event is sent each time the set of unsatisfied dependencies changes.

121.17.3.7 **public static final int WAITING = 7**

The Blueprint Container is waiting on the availability of a service to satisfy an invocation on a referenced service. The missing dependency must be made available through the getDependencies() method which will return an array containing one filter object as a String.

121.17.3.8 **public BlueprintEvent(int type, Bundle bundle, Bundle extenderBundle)**

type The type of this event.

bundle The Blueprint bundle associated with this event. This parameter must not be null.

extenderBundle The Blueprint extender bundle that is generating this event. This parameter must not be null.

☐ Create a simple BlueprintEvent object.

121.17.3.9 **public BlueprintEvent(int type, Bundle bundle, Bundle extenderBundle, String[] dependencies)**

type The type of this event.

bundle The Blueprint bundle associated with this event. This parameter must not be null.

extenderBundle The Blueprint extender bundle that is generating this event. This parameter must not be null.

dependencies An array of String filters for each dependency associated with this event. Must be a non-empty array for event types GRACE_PERIOD and WAITING. It is optional for event type FAILURE. Must be null for other event types.

☐ Create a BlueprintEvent object associated with a set of dependencies.

121.17.3.10 **public BlueprintEvent(int type, Bundle bundle, Bundle extenderBundle, Throwable cause)**

type The type of this event.

bundle The Blueprint bundle associated with this event. This parameter must not be null.

extenderBundle The Blueprint extender bundle that is generating this event. This parameter must not be null.

cause A Throwable object describing the root cause of the event. May be null.

☐ Create a BlueprintEvent object associated with a failure cause.

121.17.3.11 **public BlueprintEvent(int type, Bundle bundle, Bundle extenderBundle, String[] dependencies,**

Throwable cause)

type   The type of this event.

bundle   The Blueprint bundle associated with this event. This parameter must not be null.

extenderBundle   The Blueprint extender bundle that is generating this event. This parameter must not be null.

dependencies   An array of String filters for each dependency associated with this event. Must be a non-empty array for event types GRACE_PERIOD and WAITING. It is optional for event type FAILURE. Must be null for other event types.

cause   A Throwable object describing the root cause of this event. May be null.

☐   Create a BlueprintEvent object associated with a failure cause and a set of dependencies.

121.17.3.12   public BlueprintEvent(BlueprintEvent event, boolean replay)

event   The original BlueprintEvent to copy. Must not be null.

replay   true if this event should be used as a replay event.

☐   Create a new BlueprintEvent from the specified BlueprintEvent. The timestamp property will be copied from the original event and only the replay property will be overridden with the given value.

121.17.3.13   public Bundle getBundle( )

☐   Return the Blueprint bundle associated with this event.

Returns   The Blueprint bundle associated with this event.

121.17.3.14   public Throwable getCause( )

☐   Return the cause for this FAILURE event.

Returns   The cause of the failure for this event. May be null .

121.17.3.15   public String[] getDependencies( )

☐   Return the filters identifying the missing dependencies that caused this event.

Returns   The filters identifying the missing dependencies that caused this event if the event type is one of WAITING, GRACE_PERIOD or FAILURE or null for the other event types.

121.17.3.16   public Bundle getExtenderBundle( )

☐   Return the Blueprint extender bundle that is generating this event.

Returns   The Blueprint extender bundle that is generating this event.

121.17.3.17   public long getTimestamp( )

☐   Return the time at which this event was created.

Returns   The time at which this event was created.

121.17.3.18   public int getType( )

☐   Return the type of this event.

The type values are:

- CREATING
- CREATED
- DESTROYING
- DESTROYED
- FAILURE
- GRACE_PERIOD
- WAITING

Returns The type of this event.

121.17.3.19   **public boolean isReplay( )**

    ❑ Return whether this event is a replay event.

Returns true if this event is a replay event and false otherwise.

121.17.4   public interface BlueprintListener

A BlueprintEvent Listener.

To receive Blueprint Events, a bundle must register a Blueprint Listener service. After a Blueprint Listener is registered, the Blueprint extender must synchronously send to this Blueprint Listener the last Blueprint Event for each ready Blueprint bundle managed by this extender. This replay of Blueprint Events is designed so that the new Blueprint Listener can be informed of the state of each Blueprint bundle. Blueprint Events sent during this replay will have the isReplay() flag set. The Blueprint extender must ensure that this replay phase does not interfere with new Blueprint Events so that the chronological order of all Blueprint Events received by the Blueprint Listener is preserved. If the last Blueprint Event for a given Blueprint bundle is DESTROYED, the extender must not send it during this replay phase.

See Also BlueprintEvent

Concurrency Thread-safe

121.17.4.1   **public void blueprintEvent(BlueprintEvent event)**

event The BlueprintEvent.

    ❑ Receives notifications of a Blueprint Event. Implementers should quickly process the event and return.

121.17.5   public class ComponentDefinitionException
extends RuntimeException

A Blueprint exception indicating that a component definition is in error. This exception is thrown when a configuration-related error occurs during creation of a Blueprint Container.

121.17.5.1   **public ComponentDefinitionException( )**

    ❑ Creates a Component Definition Exception with no message or exception cause.

121.17.5.2   **public ComponentDefinitionException(String explanation)**

explanation The associated message.

    ❑ Creates a Component Definition Exception with the specified message

121.17.5.3   **public ComponentDefinitionException(String explanation, Throwable cause)**

explanation The associated message.

cause The cause of this exception.

    ❑ Creates a Component Definition Exception with the specified message and exception cause.

121.17.5.4   **public ComponentDefinitionException(Throwable cause)**

cause The cause of this exception.

    ❑ Creates a Component Definition Exception with the exception cause.

121.17.6　　public interface Converter

Type converter to convert an object to a target type.

Concurrency　Thread-safe

121.17.6.1　public boolean canConvert(Object sourceObject, ReifiedType targetType)

sourceObject　The source object s to convert.

targetType　The target type T.

    □　Return if this converter is able to convert the specified object to the specified type.

Returns　true if the conversion is possible, false otherwise.

121.17.6.2　public Object convert(Object sourceObject, ReifiedType targetType) throws Exception

sourceObject　The source object s to convert.

targetType　The target type T.

    □　Convert the specified object to an instance of the specified type.

Returns　An instance with a type that is assignable from targetType's raw class

Throws　Exception – If the conversion cannot succeed. This exception should not be thrown when the can-Convert method has returned true.

121.17.7　　public class EventConstants

Event property names used in Event Admin events published by a Blueprint Container.

Each type of event is sent to a different topic:

org/osgi/service/blueprint/container/ ⟨*event-type*⟩

where ⟨*event-type*⟩ can have the values CREATING, CREATED, DESTROYING, DESTROYED, FAILURE, GRACE_PERIOD, or WAITING.

Such events have the following properties:

- type
- event
- timestamp
- bundle
- bundle.symbolicName
- bundle.id
- bundle.version
- extender.bundle.symbolicName
- extender.bundle.id
- extender.bundle.version
- dependencies
- cause

Concurrency　Immutable

121.17.7.1　public static final String BUNDLE = "bundle"

The Blueprint bundle associated with this event. This property is of type Bundle.

121.17.7.2　public static final String BUNDLE_ID = "bundle.id"

The bundle id of the Blueprint bundle associated with this event. This property is of type Long.

121.17.7.3   **public static final String BUNDLE_SYMBOLICNAME = "bundle.symbolicName"**

The bundle symbolic name of the Blueprint bundle associated with this event. This property is of type String.

121.17.7.4   **public static final String BUNDLE_VERSION = "bundle.version"**

The bundle version of the Blueprint bundle associated with this event. This property is of type Version.

121.17.7.5   **public static final String CAUSE = "cause"**

The cause for a FAILURE event. This property is of type Throwable.

121.17.7.6   **public static final String DEPENDENCIES = "dependencies"**

The filters identifying the missing dependencies that caused this event for a FAILURE, GRACE_PERIOD, or WAITING event. This property type is an array of String.

121.17.7.7   **public static final String EVENT = "event"**

The BlueprintEvent object that caused this event. This property is of type BlueprintEvent.

121.17.7.8   **public static final String EXTENDER_BUNDLE = "extender.bundle"**

The Blueprint extender bundle that is generating this event. This property is of type Bundle.

121.17.7.9   **public static final String EXTENDER_BUNDLE_ID = "extender.bundle.id"**

The bundle id of the Blueprint extender bundle that is generating this event. This property is of type Long.

121.17.7.10   **public static final String EXTENDER_BUNDLE_SYMBOLICNAME = "extender.bundle.symbolicName"**

The bundle symbolic of the Blueprint extender bundle that is generating this event. This property is of type String.

121.17.7.11   **public static final String EXTENDER_BUNDLE_VERSION = "extender.bundle.version"**

The bundle version of the Blueprint extender bundle that is generating this event. This property is of type Version.

121.17.7.12   **public static final String TIMESTAMP = "timestamp"**

The time the event was created. This property is of type Long.

121.17.7.13   **public static final String TOPIC_BLUEPRINT_EVENTS = "org/osgi/service/blueprint/container"**

Topic prefix for all events issued by the Blueprint Container

121.17.7.14   **public static final String TOPIC_CREATED = "org/osgi/service/blueprint/container/CREATED"**

Topic for Blueprint Container CREATED events

121.17.7.15   **public static final String TOPIC_CREATING = "org/osgi/service/blueprint/container/CREATING"**

Topic for Blueprint Container CREATING events

121.17.7.16   **public static final String TOPIC_DESTROYED = "org/osgi/service/blueprint/container/DESTROYED"**

Topic for Blueprint Container DESTROYED events

121.17.7.17   **public static final String TOPIC_DESTROYING = "org/osgi/service/blueprint/container/ DESTROYING"**

Topic for Blueprint Container DESTROYING events

121.17.7.18   **public static final String TOPIC_FAILURE = "org/osgi/service/blueprint/container/FAILURE"**

Topic for Blueprint Container FAILURE events

121.17.7.19   **public static final String TOPIC_GRACE_PERIOD = "org/osgi/service/blueprint/container/ GRACE_PERIOD"**

Topic for Blueprint Container GRACE_PERIOD events

121.17.7.20   **public static final String TOPIC_WAITING = "org/osgi/service/blueprint/container/WAITING"**

Topic for Blueprint Container WAITING events

121.17.7.21   **public static final String TYPE = "type"**

The type of the event that has been issued. This property is of type Integer and can take one of the values defined in BlueprintEvent.

121.17.8   public class NoSuchComponentException extends RuntimeException

A Blueprint exception indicating that a component does not exist in a Blueprint Container. This exception is thrown when an attempt is made to create a component instance or lookup Component Metadata using a component id that does not exist in the Blueprint Container.

121.17.8.1   **public NoSuchComponentException(String msg, String id)**

msg The associated message.

id The id of the non-existent component.

☐ Create a No Such Component Exception for a non-existent component.

121.17.8.2   **public NoSuchComponentException(String id)**

id The id of the non-existent component.

☐ Create a No Such Component Exception for a non-existent component.

121.17.8.3   **public String getComponentId( )**

☐ Returns the id of the non-existent component.

Returns The id of the non-existent component.

121.17.9   public class ReifiedType

Provides access to a concrete type and its optional generic type parameters.

Java 5 and later support generic types. These types consist of a raw class with type parameters. This class models such a Type class but ensures that the type is *reified*. Reification means that the Type graph associated with a Java 5 Type instance is traversed until the type becomes a concrete class. This class is available with the getRawClass() method. The optional type parameters are recursively represented as Reified Types.

In Java 1.4, a class has by definition no type parameters. This class implementation provides the Reified Type for Java 1.4 by making the raw class the Java 1.4 class and using a Reified Type based on the Object class for any requested type parameter.

A Blueprint extender implementations can subclass this class and provide access to the generic type parameter graph for conversion. Such a subclass must *reify* the different Java 5 Type instances into the reified form. That is, a form where the raw Class is available with its optional type parameters as Reified Types.

Concurrency Immutable

121.17.9.1   **public ReifiedType(Class<?> clazz)**

clazz The raw class of the Reified Type.

□ Create a Reified Type for a raw Java class without any generic type parameters. Subclasses can provide the optional generic type parameter information. Without subclassing, this instance has no type parameters.

121.17.9.2   **public ReifiedType getActualTypeArgument(int i)**

i The zero-based index of the requested type parameter.

□ Return a type parameter for this type. The type parameter refers to a parameter in a generic type declaration given by the zero-based index i. For example, in the following example:

```
Map<String, ? extends Metadata>
```

type parameter 0 is String, and type parameter 1 is Metadata.

This implementation returns a Reified Type that has Object as class. Any object is assignable to Object and therefore no conversion is then necessary. This is compatible with versions of Java language prior to Java 5. This method should be overridden by a subclass that provides access to the generic type parameter information for Java 5 and later.

Returns The ReifiedType for the generic type parameter at the specified index.

121.17.9.3   **public Class<?> getRawClass( )**

□ Return the raw class represented by this type. The raw class represents the concrete class that is associated with a type declaration. This class could have been deduced from the generics type parameter graph of the declaration. For example, in the following example:

```
Map<String, ? extends Metadata>
```

The raw class is the Map class.

Returns The raw class represented by this type.

121.17.9.4   **public int size( )**

□ Return the number of type parameters for this type.

This implementation returns 0. This method should be overridden by a subclass that provides access to the generic type parameter information for Java 5 and later.

Returns The number of type parameters for this type.

121.17.10   **public class ServiceUnavailableException**
extends ServiceException

A Blueprint exception indicating that a service is unavailable. This exception is thrown when an invocation is made on a service reference and a backing service is not available.

121.17.10.1   **public ServiceUnavailableException(String message, String filter)**

message The associated message.

filter The filter used for the service lookup.

□ Creates a Service Unavailable Exception with the specified message.

121.17.10.2   **public ServiceUnavailableException(String message, String filter, Throwable cause)**

message The associated message.

filter The filter used for the service lookup.

cause The cause of this exception.

❑ Creates a Service Unavailable Exception with the specified message and exception cause.

121.17.10.3   **public String getFilter( )**

❑ Returns the filter expression that a service would have needed to satisfy in order for the invocation to proceed.

Returns The failing filter.

121.18   org.osgi.service.blueprint.reflect

Blueprint Reflection Package Version 1.0.

Bundles wishing to use this package must list the package in the Import-Package header of the bundle's manifest. For example:

```
Import-Package: org.osgi.service.blueprint.reflect; version="[1.0,2.0)"
```

This package provides a reflection-based view of the configuration information for a Blueprint Container.

121.18.1   Summary

- *BeanArgument* - Metadata for a factory method or constructor argument of a bean.
- *BeanMetadata* - Metadata for a Bean component.
- *BeanProperty* - Metadata for a property to be injected into a bean.
- *CollectionMetadata* - Metadata for a collection based value.
- *ComponentMetadata* - Metadata for managed components.
- *IdRefMetadata* - Metadata for the verified id of another component managed by the Blueprint Container.
- *MapEntry* - Metadata for a map entry.
- *MapMetadata* - Metadata for a Map based value.
- *Metadata* - Top level Metadata type.
- *NonNullMetadata* - Metadata for a value that cannot null.
- *NullMetadata* - Metadata for a value specified to be null via the <null> element.
- *PropsMetadata* - Metadata for a java.util.Properties based value.
- *ReferenceListener* - Metadata for a reference listener interested in the reference bind and unbind events for a service reference.
- *ReferenceListMetadata* - Metadata for a list of service references.
- *ReferenceMetadata* - Metadata for a reference that will bind to a single matching service in the service registry.
- *RefMetadata* - Metadata for a reference to another component managed by the Blueprint Container.
- *RegistrationListener* - Metadata for a registration listener interested in service registration and unregistration events for a service.
- *ServiceMetadata* - Metadata for a service to be registered by the Blueprint Container when enabled.
- *ServiceReferenceMetadata* - Metadata for a reference to an OSGi service.
- *Target* - A common interface for managed components that can be used as a direct target for method calls.

• *ValueMetadata* - Metadata for a simple String value that will be type-converted if necessary before injecting.

121.18.2   public interface BeanArgument

Metadata for a factory method or constructor argument of a bean. The arguments of a bean are obtained from BeanMetadata.getArguments(). This is specified by the argument elements of a bean.

Concurrency Thread-safe

121.18.2.1   public int getIndex( )

☐ Return the zero-based index into the parameter list of the factory method or constructor to be invoked for this argument. This is determined by specifying the index attribute for the bean. If not explicitly set, this will return -1 and the initial ordering is defined by its position in the BeanMetadata.getArguments() list. This is specified by the index attribute.

Returns The zero-based index of the parameter, or -1 if no index is specified.

121.18.2.2   public Metadata getValue( )

☐ Return the Metadata for the argument value. This is specified by the value attribute.

Returns The Metadata for the argument value.

121.18.2.3   public String getValueType( )

☐ Return the name of the value type to match the argument and convert the value into when invoking the constructor or factory method. This is specified by the type attribute.

Returns The name of the value type to convert the value into, or null if no type is specified.

121.18.3   public interface BeanMetadata
extends Target , ComponentMetadata

Metadata for a Bean component.

This is specified by the bean element.

Concurrency Thread-safe

121.18.3.1   public static final String SCOPE_PROTOTYPE = "prototype"

The bean has prototype scope.

See Also getScope ()

121.18.3.2   public static final String SCOPE_SINGLETON = "singleton"

The bean has singleton scope.

See Also getScope ()

121.18.3.3   public List<BeanArgument> getArguments( )

☐ Return the arguments for the factory method or constructor of the bean. This is specified by the child argument elements.

Returns An immutable List of BeanArgument objects for the factory method or constructor of the bean. The List is empty if no arguments are specified for the bean.

121.18.3.4   public String getClassName( )

☐ Return the name of the class specified for the bean. This is specified by the class attribute of the bean definition.

Returns The name of the class specified for the bean. If no class is specified in the bean definition, because the a factory component is used instead, then this method will return null.

121.18.3.5		**public String getDestroyMethod( )**

☐ Return the name of the destroy method specified for the bean. This is specified by the destroy-method attribute of the bean definition.

Returns The name of the destroy method specified for the bean, or null if no destroy method is specified.

121.18.3.6		**public Target getFactoryComponent( )**

☐ Return the Metadata for the factory component on which to invoke the factory method for the bean. This is specified by the factory-ref attribute of the bean.

When a factory method and factory component have been specified for the bean, this method returns the factory component on which to invoke the factory method for the bean. When no factory component has been specified this method will return null. When a factory method has been specified for the bean but a factory component has not been specified, the factory method must be invoked as a static method on the bean's class.

Returns The Metadata for the factory component on which to invoke the factory method for the bean or null if no factory component is specified.

121.18.3.7		**public String getFactoryMethod( )**

☐ Return the name of the factory method for the bean. This is specified by the factory-method attribute of the bean.

Returns The name of the factory method of the bean or null if no factory method is specified for the bean.

121.18.3.8		**public String getInitMethod( )**

☐ Return the name of the init method specified for the bean. This is specified by the init-method attribute of the bean definition.

Returns The name of the init method specified for the bean, or null if no init method is specified.

121.18.3.9		**public List<BeanProperty> getProperties( )**

☐ Return the properties for the bean. This is specified by the child property elements.

Returns An immutable List of BeanProperty objects, with one entry for each property to be injected in the bean. The List is empty if no property injection is specified for the bean.

121.18.3.10		**public String getScope( )**

☐ Return the scope for the bean.

Returns The scope for the bean. Returns null if the scope has not been explicitly specified in the bean definition.

See Also SCOPE_SINGLETON, SCOPE_PROTOTYPE

## 121.18.4		**public interface BeanProperty**

Metadata for a property to be injected into a bean. The properties of a bean are obtained from Bean-Metadata.getProperties(). This is specified by the property elements of a bean. Properties are defined according to the Java Beans conventions.

Concurrency Thread-safe

121.18.4.1		**public String getName( )**

☐ Return the name of the property to be injected. The name follows Java Beans conventions. This is specified by the name attribute.

Returns The name of the property to be injected.

121.18.4.2   **public Metadata getValue( )**

     □   Return the Metadata for the value to be injected into a bean. This is specified by the value attribute or in inlined text.

Returns   The Metadata for the value to be injected into a bean.

121.18.5   public interface CollectionMetadata extends NonNullMetadata

Metadata for a collection based value. Values of the collection are defined by Metadata objects. This Collection Metadata can constrain the values of the collection to a specific type.

Concurrency   Thread-safe

121.18.5.1   **public Class<?> getCollectionClass( )**

     □   Return the type of the collection. The possible types are: array (Object[]), Set, and List. This information is specified in the element name.

Returns   The type of the collection. Object[] is returned to indicate an array.

121.18.5.2   **public List<Metadata> getValues( )**

     □   Return Metadata for the values of the collection.

Returns   A List of Metadata for the values of the collection.

121.18.5.3   **public String getValueType( )**

     □   Return the type specified for the values of the collection. The value-type attribute specified this information.

Returns   The type specified for the values of the collection.

121.18.6   public interface ComponentMetadata extends NonNullMetadata

Metadata for managed components. This is the base type for BeanMetadata, ServiceMetadata and ServiceReferenceMetadata.

Concurrency   Thread-safe

121.18.6.1   **public static final int ACTIVATION_EAGER = 1**

The component's manager must eagerly activate the component.

See Also   getActivation()

121.18.6.2   **public static final int ACTIVATION_LAZY = 2**

The component's manager must lazily activate the component.

See Also   getActivation()

121.18.6.3   **public int getActivation( )**

     □   Return the activation strategy for the component. This is specified by the activation attribute of a component definition. If this is not set, then the default-activation in the blueprint element is used. If that is also not set, then the activation strategy is ACTIVATION_EAGER.

Returns   The activation strategy for the component.

See Also   ACTIVATION_EAGER, ACTIVATION_LAZY

121.18.6.4   **public List<String> getDependsOn( )**

     □   Return the ids of any components listed in a depends-on attribute for the component.

Returns   An immutable List of component ids that are explicitly declared as a dependency, or an empty List if none.

121.18.6.5   **public String getId( )**

□   Return the id of the component.

Returns   The id of the component. The component id can be null if this is an anonymously defined and/or in-lined component.

121.18.7   **public interface IdRefMetadata
extends NonNullMetadata**

Metadata for the verified id of another component managed by the Blueprint Container. The id itself will be injected, not the component to which the id refers. No implicit dependency is created.

Concurrency   Thread-safe

121.18.7.1   **public String getComponentId( )**

□   Return the id of the referenced component. This is specified by the component-id attribute of a component.

Returns   The id of the referenced component.

121.18.8   **public interface MapEntry**

Metadata for a map entry. This type is used by MapMetadata, PropsMetadata and ServiceMetadata.

Concurrency   Thread-safe

121.18.8.1   **public NonNullMetadata getKey( )**

□   Return the Metadata for the key of the map entry. This is specified by the key attribute or element.

Returns   The Metadata for the key of the map entry. This must not be null.

121.18.8.2   **public Metadata getValue( )**

□   Return the Metadata for the value of the map entry. This is specified by the value attribute or element.

Returns   The Metadata for the value of the map entry. This must not be null.

121.18.9   **public interface MapMetadata
extends NonNullMetadata**

Metadata for a Map based value.

This is specified by the map element.

Concurrency   Thread-safe

121.18.9.1   **public List<MapEntry> getEntries( )**

□   Return the entries for the map.

Returns   An immutable List of MapEntry objects for each entry in the map. The List is empty if no entries are specified for the map.

121.18.9.2   **public String getKeyType( )**

□   Return the name of the type of the map keys. This is specified by the key-type attribute of the map.

Returns   The name of the type of the map keys, or null if none is specified.

121.18.9.3   **public String getValueType( )**

□ Return the name of the type of the map values. This is specified by the value-type attribute of the map.

Returns The name of the type of the map values, or null if none is specified.

121.18.10   public interface Metadata

Top level Metadata type. All Metdata types extends this base type.

Concurrency Thread-safe

121.18.11   public interface NonNullMetadata extends Metadata

Metadata for a value that cannot null. All Metadata subtypes extend this type except for NullMetadata.

This Metadata type is used for keys in Maps because they cannot be null.

Concurrency Thread-safe

121.18.12   public interface NullMetadata extends Metadata

Metadata for a value specified to be null via the ‹null› element.

Concurrency Thread-safe

121.18.12.1   **public static final NullMetadata NULL**

Singleton instance of NullMetadata.

121.18.13   public interface PropsMetadata extends NonNullMetadata

Metadata for a java.util.Properties based value.

The MapEntry objects of properties are defined with keys and values of type String.

This is specified by the props element.

Concurrency Thread-safe

121.18.13.1   **public List<MapEntry> getEntries( )**

□ Return the entries for the properties.

Returns An immutable List of MapEntry objects for each entry in the properties. The List is empty if no entries are specified for the properties.

121.18.14   public interface ReferenceListener

Metadata for a reference listener interested in the reference bind and unbind events for a service reference.

Concurrency Thread-safe

121.18.14.1   **public String getBindMethod( )**

□ Return the name of the bind method. The bind method will be invoked when a matching service is bound to the reference. This is specified by the bind-method attribute of the reference listener.

Returns The name of the bind method.

121.18.14.2   **public Target getListenerComponent( )**

       □ Return the Metadata for the component that will receive bind and unbind events. This is specified by the ref attribute or via an inlined component.

Returns The Metadata for the component that will receive bind and unbind events.

121.18.14.3   **public String getUnbindMethod( )**

       □ Return the name of the unbind method. The unbind method will be invoked when a matching service is unbound from the reference. This is specified by the unbind-method attribute of the reference listener.

Returns The name of the unbind method.

121.18.15   public interface ReferenceListMetadata extends ServiceReferenceMetadata

Metadata for a list of service references.

This is specified by the reference-list element.

Concurrency Thread-safe

121.18.15.1   **public static final int USE_SERVICE_OBJECT = 1**

Reference list values must be proxies to the actual service objects.

See Also getMemberType()

121.18.15.2   **public static final int USE_SERVICE_REFERENCE = 2**

Reference list values must be ServiceReference objects.

See Also getMemberType()

121.18.15.3   **public int getMemberType( )**

       □ Return whether the List will contain service object proxies or ServiceReference objects. This is specified by the member-type attribute of the reference list.

Returns Whether the List will contain service object proxies or ServiceReference objects.

See Also USE_SERVICE_OBJECT, USE_SERVICE_REFERENCE

121.18.16   public interface ReferenceMetadata extends Target , ServiceReferenceMetadata

Metadata for a reference that will bind to a single matching service in the service registry.

This is specified by the reference element.

Concurrency Thread-safe

121.18.16.1   **public long getTimeout( )**

       □ Return the timeout for service invocations when a backing service is is unavailable. This is specified by the timeout attribute of the reference.

Returns The timeout, in milliseconds, for service invocations when a backing service is is unavailable.

121.18.17   public interface RefMetadata extends Target , NonNullMetadata

Metadata for a reference to another component managed by the Blueprint Container.

Concurrency Thread-safe

121.18.17.1 **public String getComponentId( )**

❑ Return the id of the referenced component. This is specified by the component-id attribute of a component.

Returns The id of the referenced component.

121.18.18 public interface RegistrationListener

Metadata for a registration listener interested in service registration and unregistration events for a service.

The registration listener is called with the initial state of the service when the registration listener is actuated.

Concurrency Thread-safe

121.18.18.1 **public Target getListenerComponent( )**

❑ Return the Metadata for the component that will receive registration and unregistration events. This is specified by the ref attribute or via an inlined component.

Returns The Metadata for the component that will receive registration and unregistration events.

121.18.18.2 **public String getRegistrationMethod( )**

❑ Return the name of the registration method. The registration method will be invoked when the associated service is registered with the service registry. This is specified by the registration-method attribute of the registration listener.

Returns The name of the registration method.

121.18.18.3 **public String getUnregistrationMethod( )**

❑ Return the name of the unregistration method. The unregistration method will be invoked when the associated service is unregistered from the service registry. This is specified by the unregistration-method attribute of the registration listener.

Returns The name of the unregistration method.

121.18.19 public interface ServiceMetadata
extends ComponentMetadata

Metadata for a service to be registered by the Blueprint Container when enabled.

This is specified by the service element.

Concurrency Thread-safe

121.18.19.1 **public static final int AUTO_EXPORT_ALL_CLASSES = 4**

Advertise all Java classes and interfaces in the component instance type as service interfaces.

See Also getAutoExport()

121.18.19.2 **public static final int AUTO_EXPORT_CLASS_HIERARCHY = 3**

Advertise all Java classes in the hierarchy of the component instance type as service interfaces.

See Also getAutoExport()

121.18.19.3 **public static final int AUTO_EXPORT_DISABLED = 1**

Do not auto-detect types for advertised service interfaces

See Also getAutoExport()

121.18.19.4 **public static final int AUTO_EXPORT_INTERFACES = 2**

Advertise all Java interfaces implemented by the component instance type as service interfaces.

See Also getAutoExport()

121.18.19.5   **public int getAutoExport( )**

☐ Return the auto-export mode for the service. This is specified by the auto-export attribute of the service.

Returns The auto-export mode for the service.

See Also AUTO_EXPORT_DISABLED, AUTO_EXPORT_INTERFACES, AUTO_EXPORT_CLASS_HIERARCHY, AUTO_EXPORT_ALL_CLASSES

121.18.19.6   **public List<String> getInterfaces( )**

☐ Return the type names of the interfaces that the service should be advertised as supporting. This is specified in the interface attribute or child interfaces element of the service.

Returns An immutable List of String for the type names of the interfaces that the service should be advertised as supporting. The List is empty if using auto-export or no interface names are specified for the service.

121.18.19.7   **public int getRanking( )**

☐ Return the ranking value to use when advertising the service. If the ranking value is zero, the service must be registered without a service.ranking service property. This is specified by the ranking attribute of the service.

Returns The ranking value to use when advertising the service.

121.18.19.8   **public Collection<RegistrationListener> getRegistrationListeners( )**

☐ Return the registration listeners to be notified when the service is registered and unregistered with the framework. This is specified by the registration-listener elements of the service.

Returns An immutable Collection of RegistrationListener objects to be notified when the service is registered and unregistered with the framework. The Collection is empty if no registration listeners are specified for the service.

121.18.19.9   **public Target getServiceComponent( )**

☐ Return the Metadata for the component to be exported as a service. This is specified inline or via the ref attribute of the service.

Returns The Metadata for the component to be exported as a service.

121.18.19.10   **public List<MapEntry> getServiceProperties( )**

☐ Return the user declared properties to be advertised with the service. This is specified by the service-properties element of the service.

Returns An immutable List of MapEntry objects for the user declared properties to be advertised with the service. The List is empty if no service properties are specified for the service.

121.18.20   public interface ServiceReferenceMetadata extends ComponentMetadata

Metadata for a reference to an OSGi service. This is the base type for ReferenceListMetadata and ReferenceMetadata.

Concurrency Thread-safe

121.18.20.1   **public static final int AVAILABILITY_MANDATORY = 1**

A matching service is required at all times.

See Also getAvailability()

121.18.20.2   **public static final int AVAILABILITY_OPTIONAL = 2**

A matching service is not required to be present.

See Also getAvailability()

121.18.20.3   **public int getAvailability( )**

❑ Return whether or not a matching service is required at all times. This is specified in the availability attribute of the service reference.

Returns Whether or not a matching service is required at all times.

See Also AVAILABILITY_MANDATORY, AVAILABILITY_OPTIONAL

121.18.20.4   **public String getComponentName( )**

❑ Return the value of the component-name attribute of the service reference. This specifies the id of a component that is registered in the service registry. This will create an automatic filter, appended with the filter if set, to select this component based on its automatic id attribute.

Returns The value of the component-name attribute of the service reference or null if the attribute is not specified.

121.18.20.5   **public String getFilter( )**

❑ Return the filter expression that a matching service must match. This is specified by the filter attribute of the service reference.

Returns The filter expression that a matching service must match or null if a filter is not specified.

121.18.20.6   **public String getInterface( )**

❑ Return the name of the interface type that a matching service must support. This is specified in the interface attribute of the service reference.

Returns The name of the interface type that a matching service must support or null when no interface name is specified.

121.18.20.7   **public Collection<ReferenceListener> getReferenceListeners( )**

❑ Return the reference listeners to receive bind and unbind events. This is specified by the reference-listener elements of the service reference.

Returns An immutable Collection of ReferenceListener objects to receive bind and unbind events. The Collection is empty if no reference listeners are specified for the service reference.

121.18.21   public interface Target
extends NonNullMetadata

A common interface for managed components that can be used as a direct target for method calls. These are bean, reference, and ref, where the ref must refer to a bean or reference component.

See Also BeanMetadata, ReferenceMetadata, RefMetadata

Concurrency Thread-safe

121.18.22   public interface ValueMetadata
extends NonNullMetadata

Metadata for a simple String value that will be type-converted if necessary before injecting.

Concurrency Thread-safe

121.18.22.1   **public String getStringValue( )**

❑ Return the unconverted string representation of the value. This is specified by the value attribute or text part of the value element.

Returns The unconverted string representation of the value.

121.18.22.2   **public String getType( )**

☐ Return the name of the type to which the value should be converted. This is specified by the type attribute.

Returns The name of the type to which the value should be converted or null if no type is specified.

121.19   Changes

- API augmented with generic signatures
- Clarified that step 3 in *Destroy the Blueprint Container* on page 208 is the lowest ranking.
- Table 121.14, "Value Features," on page 234, the type element row, indicated that it returns the collection's value type if available. This is wrong, null must be returned when not set and the collection's value type must be obtained through the appropriate Collection Metadata. The table is updated.
- A service manager can get component instances for its service properties while its explicit dependencies are not yet activated. A service manager must therefore activate its explicit dependencies at the beginning of the service registration phase. This does not have to cause the activation of the service manager itself. This was unclear in the previous version. This change caused a signifcant a rather large number of sections to change.
- Removed mandatory detection of cycles caused by user code.
- The previous specification mandated the creation of service properties for each registration. However, service properties can use arbitrary component instances and this noticeable side effects. Therefore, the specification now mandates the creation of the service properties to happen once before the first registration. See *Service Properties* on page 222.
- Clarified the relationship between Component Metadata and Environment managers. Environment are represented a Component Metadata, all other managers use a sub-class of the ComponentMetadata interface.

121.20   References

[1]   *OSGi Core Specifications*
       http://www.osgi.org/Specifications/HomePage

[2]   *Spring Framework*
       http://www.springsource.org/

[3]   *Spring Dynamic Modules*
       http://www.springsource.org/osgi

[4]   *Guice*
       http://code.google.com/p/google-guice/

[5]   *Picocontainer*
       http://www.picocontainer.org/

[6]   *Java Beans Specification*
       http://java.sun.com/javase/technologies/desktop/javabeans/docs/spec.html

[7]   *XML Namespaces*
       http://www.w3.org/TR/REC-xml-names

[8]   *Properties format*
       http://tiny.cc/uu2Js

[9]   *XML Schema*
       http://www.w3.org/XML/Schema

[10]   *OSGi XML Schemas*
        http://www.osgi.org/Release4/XMLSchemas

122   Remote Service Admin Service Specification

Version 1.0

122.1   Introduction

The OSGi core framework specifies a model where bundles can use distributed services, see [1] *OSGi Core Specifications.* The basic model for OSGi remote services is that a bundle can register services that are *exported* to a communication *Endpoint* and use services that are *imported* from a communication Endpoint. However, the remote services chapter does not explain *what* services are exported and/or imported; it leaves such decisions to the distribution provider. The distribution provider therefore performs multiple roles and cannot be leveraged by other bundles in scenarios that the distribution provider had not foreseen.

The primary role of the distribution provider is purely mechanical; it creates Endpoints and registers service proxies and enables their communication. The second role is about the policies around the desired topology. The third role is discovery. To establish a specific topology it is necessary to find out about exported services in other frameworks.

This specification therefore defines an API for the distribution provider and discovery of services in a network. A management agent can use this API to provide an actual distribution policy. This management agent, called the Topology Manager, can control the export and import of services delegating the intrinsic knowledge of the low level details of communication protocols, proxying of services, and discovering services in the network to services defined in this specification.

This specification is an extension of the Remote Service chapter, see chapter13 on page 7. Though some aspects are repeated in this specification, a full understanding of the Remote Services chapter is required for full understanding of this document.

122.1.1   Essentials

- *Simple* – Make it as simple as possible for a Topology Manager to implement distribution policies.
- *Dynamic* – Discover available Endpoints dynamically, for example through a discovery protocol like [4] *Service Location Protocol (SLP)* or [5] *JGroups.*
- *Inform* – Provide a mechanism to inform other parties about created and removed Endpoints.
- *Configuration* – Allow bundles to describe Endpoints as a bundle resource that are provided to the Distribution Provider.
- *Selective* – Not all parties are interested in all services. Endpoint registries must be able to express the scope of services they are interested in.
- *Multiple* – Allow the collaboration of multiple Topology Managers, Remote Service Admin services, and Discovery Providers.
- *Dynamic* – Allow the dynamic discovery of Endpoints.
- *Federated* –Enable a global view of all available services in a distributed environment.

122.1.2   Entities

- *Remote Service Admin* – An implementation of this specification provides the mechanisms to import and export services through a set of configuration types. The Remote Service Admin service is a passive Distribution Provider, not taking any action to export or import itself.
- *Topology Manager* – The Topology Manager provides the policy for importing and exporting services through the Remote Service Admin service.

- *Endpoint* – An Endpoint is a communications access mechanism to a service in another framework, a (web) service, another process, or a queue or topic destination, etc., requiring some protocol for communications.
- *Endpoint Description* – A properties based description of an Endpoint. Endpoint Descriptions can be exchanged between different frameworks to create connections to each other's services. Endpoint Descriptions can also be created to Endpoints not originating in an OSGi Framework.
- *Endpoint Description Provider* – A party that can inform others about the existence of Endpoints.
- *Endpoint Listener* – A listener service that receives updates of Endpoints that match its scope. This Endpoint Listener is used symmetrically to implement a federated registry. The Topology Manager can use it to notify interested parties about created and removed Endpoints, as well as to receive notifications from other parties, potentially remote, about their available Endpoints.
- *Remote Service Admin Listener* – A listener service that is informed of all the primitive actions that the Remote Service Admin performs like importing and exporting as well as errors.
- *Endpoint Configuration Extender* – A bundle that can detect configuration data describing an Endpoint Description in a bundle resource, using the extender pattern.
- *Discovery* – An Endpoint Listener that detects the Endpoint Descriptions through some discovery protocol.
- *Cluster* – A group of computing systems that closely work together, usually in a fast network.

Figure 122.1   Remote Service Admin Entities

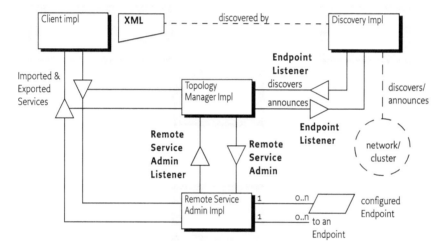

122.1.3   Synopsis

Topology Managers are responsible for the distribution policies of a service platform. To implement a policy, a Topology Manager must be aware of the environment, for this reason, it can register:

- Service listeners to detect services that can be exported according to the Remote Services chapter.
- Listener and Find Hook services to detect bundles that have an interest in specific services that potentially could be imported.
- A Remote Service Admin Listener service to detect the activity of other Topology Managers.
- An Endpoint Listener service to detect Endpoints that are made available through discovery protocols, configuration data, or other means.

Using this information, the manager implements a topology using the Remote Service Admin service. A Topology Manager that wants to export a service can create an *Export Registration* by providing one or more Remote Service Admin services a Service Reference plus a Map with the required properties. A Remote Service Admin service then creates a number of Endpoints based on the available configuration types and returns a collection of ExportRegistration objects. A collection is returned because a single service can be exported to multiple Endpoints depending on the available configuration type properties.

Each Export Registration is specific for the caller and represents an existing or newly created Endpoint. The Export Registration associates the exported Service Reference with an *Endpoint Description*. If there are problems with the export operation, the Remote Service Admin service reports these on the Export Registration objects. That is, not all the returned Export Registrations have to be valid.

An Endpoint Description is a property based description of an Endpoint. Some of these properties are defined in this specification, other properties are defined by configuration types. These configuration types must follow the same rules as the configuration types defined in the Remote Services chapter. Remote Service Admin services that support the configuration types in the Endpoint Description can import a service from that Endpoint solely based on that Endpoint Description.

In similar vein, the Topology Manager can import a service from a remote system by creating an Import Registration out of an Endpoint Description. The Remote Service Admin service then registers a service that is a proxy for the remote Endpoint and returns an ImportRegistration object. If there are problems with the import, the Remote Service Admin service that cannot be detected early, then the Remote Service Admin service reports these on the returned ImportRegistration object.

For introspection, the Remote Service Admin can list its current set of Import and Export References so that a Topology Manager can get the current state. The Remote Service Admin service also informs all Topology Managers and observers of the creation, deletion, and errors of Import and Export Registrations through the Remote Service Admin Listener service. Interested parties like the Topology Manager can register such a service and will be called back with the initial state as well as any subsequent changes.

An important aspect of the Topology Manager is the distributed nature of the scenarios it plays an orchestrating role in. A Topology Manager needs to be aware of Endpoints in the network, not just the ones provided by Remote Service Admin services in its local framework. The Endpoint Listener service is specified for this purpose. This service is provided for both directions, symmetrically. That is, it is used by the Topology Manager to inform any observers about the existence of Endpoints that are locally available, as well as for parties that represent a discovery mechanism. For example Endpoints available on other systems, Endpoint Descriptions embedded in resources in bundles, or Endpoint Descriptions that are available in some other form.

Endpoint Listener services are not always interested in the complete set of available Endpoints because this set can potentially be very large. For example, if a remote registry like [6] *UDDI* is used then the number of Endpoints can run into the thousands or more. An Endpoint Listener service can therefore scope the set of Endpoints with an OSGi LDAP style filter. Parties that can provide information about Endpoints must only notify Endpoint Listener services when the Endpoint Description falls within the scope of the Endpoint Listener service. Parties that use some discovery mechanism can use the scope to trigger directed searches across the network.

122.2   Actors

The OSGi Remote Services specification is about the distribution of services. The core specification does not outline the details of how the distribution provider knows the desired topology, this policy aspect is left up to implementations. In many situations, this is a desirable architecture because it provides freedom of implementation to the distribution provider. However, such an architecture does not enable a separation of the mechanisms and *policy*. Therefore, this Remote Service Admin specification provides an architecture that enables a separate bundle from the distribution provider to define the topology. It splits the responsibility of the Remote Service specification in a number of *roles*. These roles can all have different implementations but they can collaborate through the services defined in this specification. These roles are:

- *Topology Managers* – Topology Managers are the (anonymous) players that implement the policies for distributing services; they are closely aligned with the concept of an OSGi *management agent.* It is expected that Topology Managers will be developed for scenarios like import/export all applicable services, configuration based imports- and exports, and scenarios like fail-over, load-balancing, as well as standards like domain managers for the [7] *Service Component Architecture (SCA).*
- *Remote Service Admin* – The Remote Service Admin service provides the basic mechanism to import and export services. This service is policy free; it will not distribute services without explicitly being told so. A service platform can host multiple Remote Service Admin services that, for example, support different configuration types.
- *Discovery* – To implement a distribution policy, a Topology Manager must be aware of what Endpoints are available. This specification provides an abstraction of a *federated Endpoint registry.* This registry can be used to both publish as well as consume Endpoints from many different sources. The federated registry is defined for local services but is intended to be used with standard and proprietary service discovery protocols. The federated registry is implemented with the Endpoint Listener service.

These roles are depicted in Figure 122.2 on page 284.

Figure 122.2   *Roles*

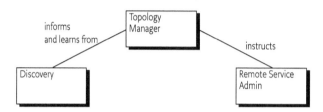

122.3   **Topology Managers**

Distributed processing has become mainstream because of the massive scale required for Internet applications. Only with distributed architectures is it possible to scale systems to *Internet size* with hundreds of millions of users. To allow a system to scale, servers are grouped in clusters where they can work in unison or geographically dispersed in even larger configurations. The distribution of the work-load is crucial for the amount of scalability provided by an architecture and often has domain specific dispatching techniques. For example, the hash of a user id can be used to select the correct profile database server. In this fast moving world it is very unlikely that a single architecture or distribution policy would be sufficient to satisfy many users. It is therefore that this specification separates the *how* from the *what.* The complex mechanics of importing and exporting services are managed by a Remote Service Admin service (the how) while the different policies are implemented by Topology Managers (the what). This separation of concerns enables the development of Topology Managers that can run on many different systems, providing high user functionality. For example, a Topology Manager could implement a fail-over policy where some strategic services are redirected when their connections fail. Other Topology Managers could use a discovery protocol like SLP to find out about other systems in a cluster and automatically configure the cluster.

The key value of this architecture is demonstrated by the example of an *SCA domain controller.* An SCA domain controller receives a description of a domain (a set of systems and modules) and must ensure that the proper connections are made between the participating SCA modules. By splitting the roles, an SCA domain manager can be developed that can run on any compatible Remote Service Admin service implementation.

122.3.1 Multiple Topology Managers

There is no restriction on the number of Topology Managers, nor is there a restriction on the number of Remote Service Admin service implementations. It is up to the deployer of the service platform to select the appropriate set of these service implementations. It is the responsibility of the Topology Managers to listen to the Remote Service Admin Listener and track Endpoints created and deleted by other Topology Managers and act appropriately.

122.3.2 Example Use Cases

122.3.2.1 Promiscuous Policy

A *cluster* is a set of machines that are connected in a network. The simplest policy for a Topology Manager is to share exported services in such a cluster. Such a policy is very easy to implement with the Remote Services Admin service. In the most basic form, this Topology Manager would use some multicast protocol to communicate with its peers. These peers would exchange EndpointDescription objects of exported services. Each Topology Manager would then import any exported service.

This scenario can be improved by separating the promiscuous policy from the discovery. Instead of embedding the multicast protocol, a Topology manager could use the Endpoint Listener service. This service allows the discovery of remote services. At the same time, the Topology Manager could tell all other Endpoint Listener services about the services it has created, allowing them to be used by others in the network.

Splitting the Topology Manager and discovery in two bundles allows different implementations of the discovery bundle, for example, to use different protocols.

122.3.2.2 Fail Over

A more elaborate scheme is a *fail-over policy*. In such a policy a service can be replaced by a service from another machine. There are many ways to implement such a policy, an simple example strategy is provided here for illustration.

A Fail-Over Topology Manager is given a list of stateless services that require fail-over, for example through the *Configuration Admin Service Specification* on page 45. The Fail-Over Manager tracks the systems in the its cluster that provide such services. This tracking can use an embedded protocol or it can be based on the Endpoint Listener service model.

In the Fail-Over policy, the fail-over manager only imports a single service and then tracks the error status of the imported service through the Remote Service Admin Listener service. If it detects the service is becoming unavailable, it closes the corresponding Import Registration and imports a service from an alternative system instead. In Figure 122.3 *Fail Over Scenario in a cluster*, there are 4 systems in a cluster. The topology/fail-over manager ensures that there is always one of the services in system A, B, or C available in D.

Figure 122.3   *Fail Over Scenario in a cluster*

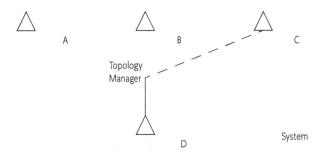

There are many possible variations on this scenario. The managers could exchange load information, allowing the service switch to be influenced by the load of the target systems. The important aspect is that the Topology Manager can ignore the complex details of discovery protocols, communication protocols, and service proxying and instead focus on the topology.

122.4 Endpoint Description

An *Endpoint* is a point of rendezvous of distribution providers. It is created by an exporting distribution provider or some other party, and is used by importing distribution providers to create a connection. An *Endpoint Description* describes an Endpoint in such a way that an importing Remote Service Admin service can create this connection if it recognizes the *configuration type* that is used for that Endpoint. The configuration type consists of a name and a set of properties associated with that name.

The core concept of the Endpoint Description is a Map of properties. The structure of this map is the same as service properties, and the defined properties are closely aligned with the properties of an imported service. An EndpointDescription object must only consist of the data types that are supported for service properties. This makes the property map serializable with many different mechanisms. The EndpointDescription class provides a convenient way to access the properties in a type safe way.

An Endpoint Description has case insensitive keys, just like the Service Reference's properties.

The properties map must contain all the prescribed service properties of the exported service after intents have been processed, as if the service was registered as an imported service. That is, the map must not contain any properties that start with service.exported.* but it must contain the service.imported.* variation of these properties. The Endpoint Description must reflect the imported service properties because this simplifies the use of filters from the service hooks. Filters applied to the Endpoint Description can then be the same filters as applied by a bundle to select an imported service from the service registry.

The properties that can be used in an Endpoint Description are listed in Table 122.1 on page 286. The RemoteConstants class contains the constants for all of these property names.

Table 122.1   *Endpoint Properties*

Endpoint Property Name	Type	Description
service.exported.*		Must not be set
service.imported	*	Must always be set to some value. See *SERVICE_IMPORTED* on page 314.
objectClass	String[]	Must be set to the value of service.exported.interfaces, of the exported service after expanding any wildcards. Though this property will be overridden by the framework for the corresponding service registration, it must be set in the Endpoint Description to simplify the filter matching. These interface names are available with the getInterfaces() method.
service.intents	String+	Intents implemented by the exporting distribution provider and, if applicable, the exported service itself. Any qualified intents must have their expanded form present. These expanded intents are available with the getIntents() method. See *SERVICE_INTENTS* on page 314.

Endpoint Property Name	Type	Description
endpoint.service.id	Long	The service id of the exported service. Can be absent or 0 if the corresponding Endpoint is not for an OSGi service. The remote service id is available as getServiceId(). See also *ENDPOINT_SERVICE_ID* on page 313.
endpoint.framework.uuid	String	A universally unique id identifying the instance of the exporting framework. Can be absent if the corresponding Endpoint is not for an OSGi service. See *Framework UUID* on page 289. The remote framework UUID is available with the getFrameworkUUID() method. See also *ENDPOINT_FRAMEWORK_UUID* on page 312.
endpoint.id	String	The Id for this Endpoint, can never be null. This information is available with the getId(). See *Endpoint Id* on page 288 and also *ENDPOINT_ID* on page 312.
endpoint.package. version.<package-name>	String	The Java package version for the embedded <package>. For example, the property endpoint.package.version.com.acme=1.3 describes the version for the com.acme package. The version for a package can be obtained with the getPackageVersion(String). The version does not have to be set, if not set, the value must be assumed to be 0.
service.imported.configs	String+	The configuration types that can be used to implement the corresponding Endpoint. This property maps to the corresponding property in the Remote Services chapter. This property can be obtained with the getConfigurationTypes() method. The Export Registration has all the possible configuration types, where the Import Registration reports the configuration type actually used. *SERVICE_IMPORTED_CONFIGS* on page 314.
<config>.*	*	Where <config> is one of the configuration type names listed in service.imported.configs. The content of these properties must be valid for creating a connection to the Endpoint in another framework. That is, any locally readable URLs from bundles must be converted in such a form that they can be read by the importing framework. How this is done is configuration type specific.
*	*	All remaining public service properties must be present (that is, not starting with dot ('.' \u002e)). If the values can not be marshalled by the Distribution Provider then they must be ignored.

The EndpointDescription class has a number of constructors that make it convenient to instantiate it for different purposes:

- `EndpointDescription(Map)` – Instantiate the Endpoint Description from a Map object.
- `EndpointDescription(ServiceReference,Map)` – Instantiate an Endpoint Description based on a Service Reference and a Map. The base properties of this Endpoint Description are the Service Reference properties but the properties in the given Map must override any of their case variants in the Service Reference. This allows the construction of an Endpoint Description from an exportable service while still allowing overrides of specific properties by the Topology Manager.

The Endpoint Description must use the allowed properties as given in Table 122.1 on page 286. The Endpoint Description must automatically skip any `service.exported.*` properties.

The Endpoint Description provides the following methods to access the properties in a more convenient way:

- `getInterfaces()` – Answers a list of Java interface names. These are the interfaces under which the services must be registered. These interface names can also be found at the `objectClass` property. A service can only be imported when there is at least one Java interface name available.
- `getConfigurationTypes()` – Answer the configuration types that are used for exporting this Endpoint. The configuration types are associated with a number of properties.
- `getId()` – Returns an Id uniquely identifying an Endpoint. The syntax of this Id should be defined in the specification for the associated configuration type. Two Endpoint Descriptions with the same Id describe the same Endpoint.
- `getFrameworkUUID()` – Get a Universally Unique Identifier (UUID) for the framework instance that has created the Endpoint, *Framework UUID* on page 289.
- `getServiceId()` – Get the service id for the framework instance that has created the Endpoint. If there is no service on the remote side the value must be 0.
- `getPackageVersion(String)` – Get the version for the given package.
- `getIntents()` – Get the list of specified intents.
- `getProperties()` – Get all the properties.

Two Endpoint Descriptions are deemed equal when their Endpoint Id is equal. The Endpoint Id is a mandatory property of an Endpoint Description, it is further described at *Endpoint Id* on page 288. The hash code is therefore also based on the Endpoint Id.

122.4.1 Validity

A valid Endpoint Description must at least satisfy the following assertions:

- It must have a non-null Id that uniquely identifies the Endpoint
- It must at least have one Java interface name
- It must at least have one configuration type set
- Any version for the packages must have a valid version syntax.

122.4.2 Mutability

An `EndpointDescription` object is immutable and with all final fields. It can be freely used between different threads.

122.4.3 Endpoint Id

An Endpoint Id is an opaque unique identifier for an Endpoint. There is no syntax defined for this string except that whitespace at the beginning and ending must be ignored. The actual syntax for this Endpoint Id must be defined by the actual configuration type.

Two Endpoint Descriptions are deemed identical when their Endpoint Id is equal. The Endpoint Ids must be compared as string compares with leading and trailing spaces removed. The Endpoint Description class must use the String class' hash Code from the Endpoint Id as its own `hashCode`.

122.4.4   Framework UUID

Each framework registers its services with a service id that is only unique for that specific framework. The OSGi framework is not a singleton, making it possible that a single VM process holds multiple OSGi frameworks. Therefore, to identify an OSGi service uniquely it is necessary to identify the framework that has registered it. This identifier is a *Universally Unique IDentifier* (UUID) that is set for each framework. This UUID is contained in the following framework property:

```
org.osgi.framework.uuid
```

If an Endpoint Description has no associated OSGi service then the UUID of that Endpoint Description must not be set and its service id must be 0.

The deployer should ensure that this property is set properly before the framework is started as either a framework property in the launch, a system property, or the use of a framework implementation that automatically sets this property. If no such property is set, a Remote Service Admin must:

1   Start a synchronized block on the class literal String object org.osgi.framework.uuid. This can be done like:

```
synchronized("org.osgi.framework.uuid"){ … }
```

2   Check if the framework UUID is set in the Framework properties, if so, use this one and exit the synchronized block.
3   Create a new UUID.
4   Set the UUID property in the System properties.
5   leave the synchronized block.

These steps ensure that the same UUID is consistently used for all exported services. The Remote Service Admin implementation must have the proper permissions to read and write the System properties if the UUID is not set.

The framework UUID must be constructed according to the java.util.UUID class in the form returned from its toString method.

A local Endpoint Description will have its framework UUID set to the local framework. This makes it straightforward to filter for Endpoint Descriptions that are describing local Endpoints or that describe remote Endpoints. For example, a manager can take the filter from a listener and ensure that it is only getting remote Endpoint Descriptions:

```
(&
  (!
    (service.remote.framework.uuid
       =72dc5fd9-5f8f-4f8f-9821-9ebb433a5b72)
  )
  (objectClass=org.osgi.service.log.LogService)
)
```

Where 72dc5fd9-5f8f-4f8f-9821-9ebb433a5b72 is the UUID of the local framework. A discovery bundle can register the following filter in its scope to receive all locally generated Endpoints:

```
(service.remote.framework.uuid
       =72dc5fd9-5f8f-4f8f-9821-9ebb433a5b72)
```

122.4.5   Resource Containment

Configuration types can, and usually do, use URLs to point to local resources describing in detail the Endpoint parameters for specific protocols. However, the purpose of an Endpoint Description is to describe an Endpoint to a remote system. This implies that there is some marshalling process that will transfer the Endpoint Description to another process. This other process is unlikely to be able to access resource URLs. Local bundle resource URLs are only usable in the framework that originates them but even HTTP based URLs can easily run into problems due to firewalls or lack of routing.

Therefore, the properties for a configuration type should be stored in such a way that the receiving process can access them. One way to achieve this is to contain the configuration properties completely in the Endpoint Description and ensure they only use the basic data types that the remote services chapter in the core requires every Distribution Provider to support.

The Endpoint Description XML format provides an xml element that is specifically added to make it easy to embed XML based configuration documents. The XML Schema is defined in *Endpoint Description Extender Format* on page 300.

122.5   Remote Service Admin

The Remote Service Admin service abstracts the core functionality of a distribution provider: exporting a service to an Endpoint and importing services from an Endpoint. However, in contrast with the distribution provider of the Remote Services specification, the Remote Service Admin service must be told explicitly what services to import and export.

122.5.1   Exporting

An exportable service can be exported with the exportService(ServiceReference,Map) method. This method creates a number of Endpoints by inspecting the merged properties from the Service Reference and the given Map. Any property in the Map overrides the Service Reference properties, regardless of case. That is, if the map contains a key then it will override any case variant of this key in the Service Reference. However, if the Map contains the objectClass or service.id property key in any case variant, then these properties must not override the Service Reference's value.

The Remote Service Admin service must interpret the merged properties according to the Remote Services chapter. This means that it must look at the following properties (as defined in chapter 13 on page 7):

- service.exported.configs – (String+) A list of configuration types that should be used to export this service. Each configuration type represents the configuration parameters for an Endpoint. A Remote Service Admin service should create an Endpoint for each configuration type that it supports and ignore the types it does not recognize. If this property is not set, then the Remote Service Admin implementation must choose a convenient configuration type that then must be reported on the Endpoint Description with the service.imported.configs associated with the returned Export Registration.
- service.exported.intents – (String+) A list of intents that the Remote Service Admin service must implement to distribute the given service.
- service.exported.intents.extra – (String+) This property is merged with the service.exported.intents property.
- service.exported.interfaces – (String+) This property must be set; it marks this service for export and defines the interfaces. The list members must all be contained in the types listed in the objectClass service property from the Service Reference. The single value of an asterisk ('*', \u002A) indicates all interfaces in the registration's objectClass property and ignore the classes. Being able to set this property outside the Service Reference implies that the Topology Manager can export any registered service, also services not specifically marked to be exported.
- service.intents – (String+) A list of intents that this service has implemented.

A Topology Manager cannot remove properties, null is invalid as a property value.

The Remote Service Admin returns a collection of ExportRegistration objects. This collection must contain an entry for each configuration type the Remote Service Admin has recognized. Unrecognized configuration types must be ignored. However, it is possible that this list contains *invalid registrations*, see *Invalid Registrations* on page 294.

If a Service was already exported then the Remote Service Admin must still return a new ExportRegistration object that is linked with the earlier registrations. That is, an Endpoint can be shared between multiple Export Registrations. The Remote Service Admin service must ensure that the corresponding Endpoint remains available as long as there is at least one open Export Registration for that Endpoint.

For each successful creation of an export registration, the Remote Service Admin service must publish an EXPORT_REGISTRATION event, see *Events* on page 299. This event must be emitted, even if the Endpoint already existed and is thus shared with another Export Registration. If the creation of an Endpoint runs into an error, an EXPORT_ERROR event must be emitted.

Each valid Export Registration corresponds to an Endpoint for the given service. This Endpoint must remain active until all of the Export Registrations are closed that share this Endpoint.

The Endpoint can now be published so that other processes or systems can import this Endpoint. To aid with this import, the Export Registration has a getExportReference() method that returns an ExportReference object. This reference provides the following information:

- getExportedEndpoint() – This is the associated Endpoint Description. This Endpoint Description is a properties based description of an Endpoint. The property keys and their semantics are outlined in *Endpoint Description* on page 286. It can be used to inform other systems of the availability of an Endpoint.
- getExportedService() – The Service Reference to the exported service.

Both methods must return null when the associated Export Registration is closed.

A Distribution Provider that recognizes the configuration type in an Endpoint can create a connection to an Endpoint on other systems as long as firewalls and networks permit. The Endpoint Description can therefore be communicated to other systems to announce the availability of an Endpoint. The Topology Manager can optionally announce the availability of an Endpoint to the Endpoint Listener services, see *Discovery* on page 295. The decision to announce the availability of an Endpoint is one of the policies that is provided by a specific Topology Manager.

The Export Registrations remain open until:

- Explicitly closed by the Topology Manager, or
- The Remote Service Admin service is no longer used by the Topology Manager that created the Export Registration.

If the Remote Service Admin service can no longer maintain the corresponding Endpoint due to failures than these should be reported through the events. However, the registrations should remain open until explicitly closed by the Topology Manager.

See *Registration Life Cycle* on page 293 for more information.

The Export Registrations are not permanent; persistence is in the realm of the Topology Manager.

122.5.2   Importing

To import a service, a Topology Manager must have an Endpoint Description that describes the Endpoint the imported service should connect to. With this Endpoint Description, a Remote Service Admin service can then import the corresponding Endpoint. A Topology Manager can obtain these Endpoint Descriptions through internal configuration; it can use the discovery model enabled by the Endpoint Listener service, see *Discovery* on page 295, or some alternate means.

A service can be imported with the Remote Service Admin importService(EndpointDescription) method. This method takes an Endpoint Description and picks one of the embedded configuration types to establish a connection with the corresponding Endpoint to create a local service proxy. This proxy can then be mapped to either a remote OSGi service or an alternative, for example a web service. In certain cases the service proxy can be lazy, only verifying the reachability of the Endpoint when it is actually invoked for the first time. This implies that a service proxy can block when invoked until the proper communication setup has taken place.

If the Remote Service Admin service does not recognize any of the configuration types then it must return null. If there are multiple configuration types recognized then the Remote Service Admin is free to select any one of the recognized types.

If an Endpoint was already imported as a service proxy, then the Remote Service Admin service must return a new Import Registration that is associated with the existing service proxy/Endpoint combination. The Remote Service Admin service must ensure that the imported service proxy remains available as long as there is at least one open Import Registration that refers to it and the corresponding remote Endpoint is still valid.

The Remote Service Admin service must ensure that service properties are according to the Remote Services chapter for an imported service. This means that it must register the following properties:

- service.imported – (*) Must be set to any value.
- service.imported.configs – (String+) The configuration information used to import this service. Any associated properties for this configuration types must be properly mapped to the importing system. For example, a URL in these properties must point to a valid resource when used in the importing framework, see *Resource Containment* on page 290. Multiple configuration types can be listed if they are synonyms for exactly the same Endpoint that is used to export this service.
- service.intents – (String+) The Remote Service Admin must set this property to convey the combined intents of:
  - The exporting service, and
  - The intents that the exporting distribution provider adds, and
  - The intents that the importing distribution provider adds.
- Any additional properties listed in the Endpoint Description that should not be excluded. See *Endpoint Description* on page 286 for more details about the properties in the Endpoint Description.

A Remote Service Admin service must strictly follow the rules for importing a service as outlined in the Remote Services chapter.

The Remote Service Admin must return an ImportRegistration object or null. Even if an Import Registration is returned, it can still be an *invalid registration*, see *Invalid Registrations* on page 294 if the setup of the connection failed asynchronously. The Import Registration must always be a new object. Each valid Import Registration corresponds to a proxy service, potentially shared, that was created for the given Endpoint. The issues around proxying are described in *Proxying* on page 294.

For each successful creation of an import registration, the Remote Service Admin service must publish an IMPORT_REGISTRATION event, if there is an error it must publish an IMPORT_ERROR, see *Events* on page 299.

For more information see *Registration Life Cycle* on page 293.

The Import Registration provides access to an ImportReference object with the getImportReference(). This object has the following methods:

- getImportedEndpoint() – Provides the Endpoint Description for this imported service.
- getImportedService() – Provides the Service Reference for the service proxy.

The Import Registration will remain open as long as:

- The corresponding remote Endpoint remains available, and
- The Remote Service Admin service is still in use by the Topology Manager that created the Import Registration.

That is, the Import Registrations are not permanent, any persistence is in the realm of the Topology Manager. See *Registration Life Cycle* on page 293 for more details.

122.5.3 Reflection

The Remote Service Admin service provides the following methods to get the list of the current exported and imported services:

- `getExportedServices()` – List the Export References for services that are exported by this Remote Service Admin service as directed by any of the Topology Managers.
- `getImportedEndpoints()` – List the Import References for services that have been imported by this Remote Service Admin service as directed by any of the Topology Managers.

122.5.4 Registration Life Cycle

The registration life cycle of imported and exported services is non-trivial because:

- Multiple Export Registrations can use to the same Endpoint.
- Multiple Import Registrations can use to the same service proxy

For example, Topology Manager A could create an Export Registration for service S to Endpoint E. Topology Manager B could attempt to create exactly the same Endpoint E for service S. However, an Endpoint occupies a unique address and it is often not possible to create multiple Endpoints for the same address. A Remote Service Admin service must therefore detect the case that multiple registrations share the same Endpoint between Topology Manager A's registration and B's registration. However, if Topology Manager B now closes its Export Registration then Topology Manager A still assumes the availability of the Endpoint. This scenario is depicted in Figure 122.4 on page 293. A similar example can be made for an Import Registration. In that case the same service proxy can be shared between multiple Import Registrations.

Figure 122.4　　*Sharing Endpoints and proxies*

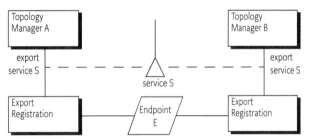

To simplify the implementation of Topology Managers, the Remote Service Admin must make this sharing of Endpoints and proxies between different registrations transparent. Both the Import and Export Registrations must be unique objects for every registration call. That is, even if the same Topology Manager creates a registration for the same Endpoint/proxy then it must still receive a new registration. Though reference counting of the close operations could be used to detect when an Endpoint or proxy can be cleared, it would require that the Topology Manager exactly matches the close calls with the creation of the registrations. However, it is very hard to ensure that the close method is only called once in certain error and cleanup scenarios. The Remote Service Admin must therefore return unique objects for all registrations and manage the cleanup of proxies and Endpoints internally, even if the close method is called multiple times on a registration.

A Remote Service Admin service must use a Service Factory for its service object to maintain separation between Topology Managers. All registrations obtained through a Remote Service Admin service are life cycle bound to the Topology Manager that created it. That is, if a Topology Manager ungets its Remote Service Admin service, all registrations obtained through this service must automatically be closed. This model ensures that all registrations are properly closed if either the Remote Service Admin or the Topology Manager stops because in both cases the framework performs the unget automatically.

122.5.5   Invalid Registrations

The Remote Service Admin service is explicitly allowed to return *invalid* Import and Export Registrations. First, in a communications stack it can take time to discover that there are issues, allowing the registration to return before it has completed can potentially save time. Second, it allows the Topology Manager to discover problems with the configuration information. Without the invalid Export Registrations, the Topology Manager would have to scan the log or associate the Remote Service Admin Events with a specific import/export method call, something that can be difficult to do.

If the registration is invalid, the getException() method must return a Throwable object. If the registration has initialized correctly, this method will return null. The getExportReference() and getImportReference() methods must throw an Illegal State Exception when the registration is invalid. A Remote Service Admin service is allowed to block for a reasonable amount of time when any of these methods is called, including the getException method, to finish initialization.

An invalid registration can be considered as never having been opened, it is therefore not necessary to close it; however, closing an invalid or closed registration must be a dummy operation and never throw an Exception. However, a failed registration must generate a corresponding error event.

122.5.6   Proxying

It is the responsibility of the Remote Service Admin service to properly proxy an imported service. This specification does not mandate the technique used to proxy an Endpoint as a service in the service platform. The OSGi Remote Services specification allows a distribution provider to limit what it can proxy.

One of the primary aspects of a proxy is to ensure class space consistency between the exporting bundle and importing bundles. This can require the generation of a proxy-per-bundle to match the proper class spaces. It is the responsibility of the Remote Service Admin to ensure that no Class Cast Exceptions occur.

A common technique to achieve maximum class space compatibility is to use a Service Factory. A Service Factory provides the calling bundle when it first gets the service, making it straightforward to verify the package version of the interface that the calling bundle uses. Knowing the bundle that requests the service allows the creation of specialized proxies for each bundle. The interface class(es) for the proxy can then be loaded directly from the bundle, ensuring class compatibility. Interfaces should be loadable by the bundle otherwise that bundle can not use the interface in its code. If an interface cannot be loaded then it can be skipped. A dedicated class loader can then be created that has visibility to all these interfaces and is used to define the proxy class. This design ensures proper visibility and consistency. Implementations can optimize this model by sharing compatible class loaders between bundles.

The proxy will have to call arbitrary methods on arbitrary services. This has a large number of security implications, see *Security* on page 304.

122.6   Discovery

The topology of the distributed system is decided by the Topology Manager. However, in a distributed environment, the Topology Manager needs to *discover* Endpoints in other frameworks. There is a very large number of ways how a Topology Manager could learn about other Endpoints, ranging from static configuration, a centralized administration, all the way to fully dynamic discovery protocols like the Service Location Protocol (SLP) or JGroups. To support the required flexibility, this specification defines an *Endpoint Listener* service that allows the dissemination of Endpoint information. This service provides a symmetric solution because the problem is symmetric: it is used by a Topology Manager to announce changes in its local topology as well as find out about other Endpoint Descriptions. Where those other Endpoint Descriptions come from can vary widely. This design is depicted in Figure 122.5 on page 295.

Figure 122.5   *Topology Information Dissemination Examples*

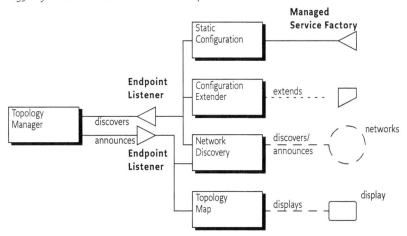

The design of the Endpoint Listener allows a federated registry of Endpoint Descriptions. Any party that is interested in Endpoint Descriptions should register an Endpoint Listener service. This will signal that it is interested in topology information to any *Endpoint Description Providers*. Each Endpoint Listener service must be registered with a service property that holds a set of filter strings to indicate the *scope* of its interest. These filters must match an Endpoint Description before the corresponding Endpoint Listener service is notified of the availability of an Endpoint Description. Scoping is intended to limit the delivery of unnecessary Endpoint Descriptions as well as signal the need for specific Endpoints.

A Topology Manager has knowledge of its local Endpoints and is likely to be only interested in remote Endpoints. It can therefore set the scope to only match remote Endpoint Descriptions. See *Framework UUID* on page 289 for how to limit the scope to local or remote Endpoints. At the same time, a Topology manager should inform any locally registered Endpoint Listener services with Endpoints that it has created or deleted.

This architecture allows many different use cases. For example, a bundle could display a map of the topology by registering an Endpoint Listener with a scope for local Endpoints. Another example is the use of SLP to announce local Endpoints to a network and to discover remote Endpoints from other parties on this network.

An instance of this design is shown in Figure 122.6 on page 296. In this figure, there are 3 frameworks that collaborate through some discovery bundle. The Top framework has created an Endpoint and decides to notify all Endpoint Listeners registered in this framework that are scoped to this new Endpoint. Local bundle D has set its scope to all Endpoint Descriptions that originate from its local framework, it therefore receives the Endpoint Description from T. Bundle D then sends the Endpoint Description to all its peers on the network.

In the Quark framework, the manager bundle T has expressed an interest by setting its scope to a filter that matches the Endpoint Description from the Top framework. When the bundle D on the Quark framework receives the Endpoint Description from bundle D on the Top framework, it matches it against all local Endpoint Listener's scope. In this case, the local manager bundle T matches and is given the Endpoint Description. The manager then uses the Remote Service Admin service to import the exported service described by the given Endpoint Description.

Figure 122.6   *Endpoint Discovery Architecture. T=Topology Manager, D=Discovery*

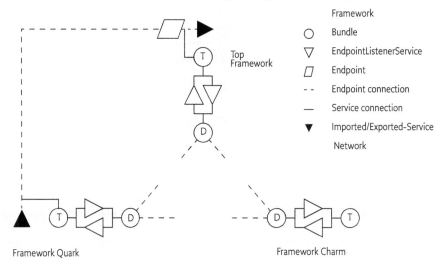

The previous description is just one of the possible usages of the Endpoint Listener. For example, the discovery bundles could communicate the scopes to their peers. These peers could then register an Endpoint Listener per peer, minimizing the network traffic because Endpoint Descriptions do not have to be broadcast to all peers.

Another alternative usage is described in *Endpoint Description Extender Format* on page 300. In this chapter the extender pattern is used to retrieve Endpoint Descriptions from resources in locally active bundles.

122.6.1   Scope and Filters

An Endpoint Listener service is registered with the ENDPOINT_LISTENER_SCOPE service property. This property, which is String+, must be set and must contain at least one filter. If there is not at least one filter, then that Endpoint Listener must not receive any Endpoint Descriptions.

Each filter in the scope is applied against the properties of the Endpoint Description until one succeeds. Only if one succeeds is the Endpoint informed about the existence of an Endpoint.

The Endpoint Description is designed to reflect the properties of the imported service, there is therefore a correspondence with the filters that are used by bundles that are listening for service registrations. The purpose of this design is to match the filter available through Listener Hook services, see *On Demand* on page 298.

However, the purpose of the filters is more generic than just this use case. It can also be used to specify the interest in local Endpoints or remote Endpoints. For example, Topology Managers are only interested in remote Endpoints while discoverers are only interested in local Endpoints. It is easy to discriminate between local and remote by filtering on the endpoint.framework.uuid property. Endpoint Descriptions contain the Universally Unique ID (UUID) of the originating framework.This UUID must be available from the local framework as well. See *Framework UUID* on page 289.

122.6.2   Endpoint Listener Interface

The EndpointListener interface has the following methods:

- endpointAdded(EndpointDescription,String) – Notify the Endpoint Listener of a new Endpoint Description. The second parameter is the filter that matched the Endpoint Description. Registering the same Endpoint multiple times counts as a single registration.
- endpointRemoved(EndpointDescription,String) – Notify the Endpoint Listener that the provided Endpoint Description is no longer available.

These methods must only be called if the Endpoint Listener service has a filter in its scope that matches the Endpoint Description properties. The reason for the filter string in the methods is to simplify and speed up matching an Endpoint Description to the cause of interest. For example, if the Listener Hook is used to do on demand import of services, then the filter can be associated with the Listener Info of the hook, see *On Demand* on page 298. If multiple filters in the scope match the Endpoint Description than the first filter in the scope must be passed.

The Endpoint Listener interface is *idempotent*. Endpoint Description Providers must inform an Endpoint Listener service that is registered of all their matching Endpoints. The only way to find out about all available Endpoints is to register an Endpoint Listener that is then informed by all available Endpoint Description Providers of their known Endpoint Descriptions that match their scope.

122.6.3   Endpoint Listener Implementations

An Endpoint Listener service tracks the known Endpoints in its given scope. There are potentially a large number of bundles involved in creating this federated registry of Endpoints. To ensure that no Endpoint Descriptions are orphaned or unnecessarily missed, an Endpoint Listener implementation must follow the following rules:

- *Registration* – An Endpoint Listener service is called with an endpointAdded(EndpointDescription,String) method for all known Endpoint Descriptions that the bundles in the local framework are aware of.
- *Tracking providers* – An Endpoint Listener must track the bundles that provide it with Endpoint Descriptions. If a bundle that provided Endpoint Descriptions is stopped, all Endpoint Descriptions that were provided by that bundle must be removed. This can be implemented straightforwardly with a Service Factory.
- *Scope modification* – An Endpoint Listener is allowed to modify the set of filters in its scope through a service property modification. This modification must result in new and/or existing Endpoint Descriptions to be added, however, existing Endpoints that are no longer in scope are not required to be explicitly removed by the their sources. It is the responsibility for the Endpoint Listener to remove these orphaned Endpoint Description from its view.

Endpoint Descriptions can be added from different sources and providers of Endpoint Descriptions often use asynchronous and potentially unreliable communications. An implementation must therefore handle the addition of multiple equal Endpoint Descriptions from different sources as well as from the same source. Implementations must not count the number of registrations, a remove operation of an Endpoint Description is final for each source. That is, if source A added Endpoint Description e, then it can only be removed by source A. However, if source A added e multiple times, then it only needs to be removed once. Removals of Endpoint Descriptions that have not been added (or were removed before) should be ignored.

The discovery of Endpoints is a fundamentally indeterministic process and implementations of Endpoint Listener services should realize that there are no guarantees that an added Endpoint Description is always describing a valid Endpoint.

122.6.4 Endpoint Description Providers

The Endpoint Listener service is based on an asynchronous, unreliable, best effort model because there are few guarantees in a distributed world. It is the task of an Endpoint Description Provider, for example a discovery bundle, to keep the Endpoint Listener services up to date of any Endpoint Descriptions the provider is aware of and that match the tracked service's scope.

If an Endpoint Listener service is registered, a provider must add all matching Endpoint Descriptions that it is aware of and match the tracked Endpoint Listener's scope. This can be done during registration or asynchronously later. For example, it is possible to use the filters in the scope to request remote systems for any Endpoint Descriptions that match those filters. For expediency reasons, the service registration event should not be delayed until those results return; it is therefore applicable to add these Endpoint Descriptions later when the returns from the remote systems finally arrive.

A tracked Endpoint Listener is allowed to modify its scope by setting new properties on its Service Registration. An Endpoint Description provider must process the new scope and add any newly matching Endpoint Descriptions. It is not necessary to remove any Endpoint Descriptions that were added before but no longer match the new scope. Removing those orphaned descriptions is the responsibility of the Endpoint Listener implementation.

It is not necessary to remove any registered Endpoint Descriptions when the Endpoint Listener is unregistered; also here it is the responsibility of the Endpoint Listener to do the proper cleanup.

122.6.5 On Demand

A common distribution policy is to import services that are being listened for by local bundles. For example, when a bundle opens a Service Tracker on the Log Service, a Topology Manager could be notified and attempt to find a Log Service in the local cluster and then import this service in the local Service Registry.

The OSGi framework provides service hooks for exactly this purpose. A Topology Manager can register a Listener Hook service and receive the information about bundles that have specified an interests in specific services.

For example, a bundle creates the following Service Tracker:

```
ServiceTracker st = new ServiceTracker(context,
    LogService.class.getName() );
st.open();
```

This Service Tracker will register a Service Listener with the OSGi framework. This will cause the framework to add a ListenerInfo to any Listener Hook services. The getFilter method on a ListenerInfo object provides a filter that is directly applicable for the Endpoint Listener's scope. In the previous example, this would be the filter:

```
(objectClass=org.osgi.service.log.LogService)
```

A Topology Manager could verify if this listener is satisfied. That is, if it has at least one service. If no such service could be found, it could then add this filter to its Endpoint Listener's scope to detect remote implementations of this service. If such an Endpoint is detected, it could then request the import of this service through the Remote Service Admin service.

122.7   Events

The Remote Service Admin service must synchronously inform any Remote Service Admin Listener services of events as they happen. Client of the events should return quickly and not perform any but trivial processing in the same thread.

The following event types are defined:

- EXPORT_ERROR – An exported service has run into an unrecoverable error, although the Export Registration has not been closed yet. The event carries the Export Registration as well as the Exception that caused the problem, if present.
- EXPORT_REGISTRATION – The Remote Service Admin has registered a new Export Registration.
- EXPORT_UNREGISTRATION – An Export Registration has been closed, the service is no longer exported and the Endpoint is no longer active when this was the last registration for that service/ Endpoint combination.
- EXPORT_WARNING – An exported service is experiencing problems but the Endpoint is still available.
- IMPORT_ERROR – An imported service has run into a fatal error and has been shut down. The Import Registration should be closed by the Topology Manager that created them.
- IMPORT_REGISTRATION – A new Import Registration was created for a potentially existing service/Endpoint combination.
- IMPORT_UNREGISTRATION – An Import Registration was closed, removing the proxy if this was the last registration.
- IMPORT_WARNING – An imported service is experiencing problems but can continue to function.

The following properties are available on the event:

- getType() – The type of the event.
- getException() – Any exception, if present.
- getExportReference() – An export reference, if applicable.
- getImportReference() – An import reference, if applicable.
- getSource() – The source of the event, the Remote Service Admin service.

122.7.1   Event Admin Mapping

All Remote Service Admin events must be posted, which is asynchronously, to the Event Admin service, if present, under the following topic:

```
org/osgi/service/remoteserviceadmin/<type>
```

Where <type> represents the type of the event, for example IMPORT_ERROR.

The Event Admin event must have the following properties:

- bundle – (Bundle) The Remote Service Admin bundle
- bundle.id – (Long) The id of the Remote Service Admin bundle.
- bundle.symbolicname – (String) The Bundle Symbolic Name of the Remote Service Admin bundle.version – (Version) The version of the Remote Service Admin bundle.
- bundle.signer – (String[]) Signer of the Remote Service Admin bundle
- cause – The exception, if present.
- endpoint.service.id – (Long) Remote service id, if present
- endpoint.framework.uuid – (String) Remote service's Framework UUID, if present
- endpoint.id – (String) The id of the Endpoint, if present
- objectClass – (String[]) The interface names, if present
- service.imported.configs – (String+) The configuration types of the imported services, if present
- timestamp – (Long) The time when the event occurred
- event – (RemoteServiceAdminEvent) The RemoteServiceAdminEvent object that caused this event.

122.8 Endpoint Description Extender Format

The Endpoint Description Extender format is a possibility to deliver Endpoint Descriptions in bundles. This section defines an XML schema and how to locate XML definition resources that use this schema to define Endpoint Descriptions. The definition resource is a simple property based model that can define the same information as the properties on an imported service. If a bundle with the description is *ready* (ACTIVE or lazy activation and in the STARTING state), then this static description can be disseminated through the Endpoint Listeners that have specified an interest in this description. If the bundle is stopped, the corresponding Endpoints must be removed.

XML documents containing remote service descriptions must be specified by the Remote-Service header in the manifest. The structure of the Remote Service header is:

    Remote-Service ::= header // Core 3.2.4

The value of the header is a comma separated list of paths. A path is:

- A directory if it ends with a slash ('/'). A directory is scanned for *.xml files.
- A path with wildcards. Such a path can use the wildcards in its last component, as defined in the findEntries method.
- A complete path, not having wildcards not ending in a slash ('/').

The Remote-Service header has no architected directives or attributes, unrecognized attributes and directives must be ignored.

A Remote-Service manifest header specified in a fragment must be ignored. However, XML documents referenced by a bundle's Remote-Service manifest header can be contained in attached fragments. The required behavior for this is implemented in the findEntries method.

The extender must process each XML document specified in this header. If an XML document specified by the header cannot be located in the bundle and its attached fragments, the extender must log an error message with the Log Service, if present, and continue.

For example:

    Remote-Service: lib/, remote/osgi/*.dsc, cnf/google.xml

This matches all resources in the lib directory matching *.xml, all resources in the /remote/osgi directory that end with .dsc, as well as the google.xml resource in the cnf directory.

The namespace of these XML resources must be:

    http://www.osgi.org/xmlns/rsa/v1.0.0

This namespace describes a set of Endpoint Descriptions, where each Endpoint Description can provide a set of properties. The structure of this schema is:

    endpoint-descriptions ::= <endpoint-description>*
    endpoint-description   ::= <property>*
    property   ::= (<array> | <list> | <set> | <xml>)?
    array   ::= <value> *
    list   ::= <value> *
    set   ::= <value> *
    xml   ::= <*> *

This structure is depicted in Figure 122.7 on page 301.

Figure 122.7   *Endpoint Description XML Structure*

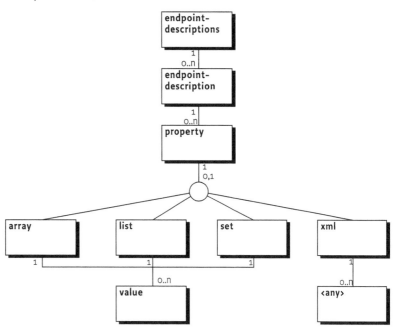

The property element has the attributes listed in table 122.3.

Table 122.2   *Property Attributes*

Attribute	Type	Description
name	String	The required name of the property. The type maps to the XML Schema xsd:string type.
value-type	String | long | Long | double | Double | float | Float | int | Integer | byte | Byte | char | Character | boolean | Boolean | short | Short	The optional type name of the property, the default is String. Any value in the value attribute or the value element when collections are used must be converted to the corresponding Java types. If the primitive form, for example byte, is specified for non-array types, then the value must be silently converted to the corresponding wrapper type.
value	String	The value. Must be converted to the specified type if this is not the String type. The value attribute must not be used when the property element has a child element.

A property can have an array, list, set, or xml child element. If a child element is present then it is an error if the value attribute is defined. It is also an error of there is no child element and no value attribute.

The array, list, or set are *multi-valued*. That is, they contain 0 or more value elements. A value element contains text (a string) that must be converted to the given value-type or if not specified, left as is. Conversion must *trim* the leading and trailing white space characters as defined in the Character.isWhitespace method. No trimming must be done for strings. An array of primitive integers like int[] {1,42,97} can be encoded as follows:

```
<property name="integers" value-type="int">
    <array>
        <value> 1</value>
        <value>42</value>
        <value>97</value>
    </array>
</property>
```

The xml element is used to convey XML from other namespaces, it is allowed to contain one foreign Xml root element, with any number of children, that will act as the root element of an XML document. This root element will be included in the corresponding property as a string. The XML element must be a valid XML document but not contain the XML processing instructions, the part between the <? and ?>. The value-type of the property must be String or not set when an xml element is used, using another type is invalid.

The xml element can be used to embed configuration information, making the Endpoint Description self contained. For example, the *SCA Configuration Type Specification* on page 431 uses this xml element to provide an embedded SCA Configuration Document in a String object.

The following is an example of an endpoint-descriptions resource.

```
<?xml version="1.0" encoding="UTF-8"?>
<endpoint-descriptions
    xmlns="http://www.osgi.org/xmlns/rsa/v1.0.0">
    <endpoint-description>
        <property name="service.intents">
            <list>
                <value>SOAP</value>
                <value>HTTP</value>
            </list>
        </property>
        <property name="endpoint.id" value="http://ws.acme.com:9000/hello"/>
        <property name="objectClass" value="com.acme.Foo"/>
        <property name="endpoint.package.version.com.acme" value="4.2"/>
        <property name="service.imported.configs" value="com.acme"/>
        <property name="com.acme.ws.xml">
            <xml>
                <config xmlns="http://acme.com/defs">
                    <port>1029</port>
                    <host>www.acme.com</host>
                </config>
            </xml>
        </property>
    </endpoint-description>
</endpoint-descriptions>
```

Besides being in a separate resource, the static configuration as described here could also be part of a larger XML file. In that case the parser must ignore elements not part of the http://www.osgi.org/xmlns/rsa/v1.0.0 namespace schema.

122.8.1   XML Schema

This name space of the schema is:

http://www.osgi.org/xmlns/rsa/v1.0.0

```
<schema
  xmlns              ="http://www.w3.org/2001/XMLSchema"
  xmlns:rsa          ="http://www.osgi.org/xmlns/rsa/v1.0.0"
  targetNamespace    ="http://www.osgi.org/xmlns/rsa/v1.0.0"
  elementFormDefault ="qualified" version="1.0.0">

  <element name="endpoint-descriptions" type="rsa:Tendpoint-descriptions"/>
  <complexType name="Tendpoint-descriptions">
    <sequence>
      <element name="endpoint-description" type="rsa:Tendpoint-description" minOccurs="1" maxOccurs="unbounded"/>
      <any namespace="##other" minOccurs="0" maxOccurs="unbounded" processContents="lax"/>
    </sequence>
    <anyAttribute/>
  </complexType>

  <complexType name="Tendpoint-description">
    <sequence>
      <element name="property" type="rsa:Tproperty" minOccurs="1" maxOccurs="unbounded"/>
      <any namespace="##other" minOccurs="0" maxOccurs="unbounded" processContents="lax"/>
    </sequence>
    <anyAttribute/>
  </complexType>

  <complexType name="Tproperty" mixed="true">
    <sequence>
      <choice minOccurs="0" maxOccurs="1">
        <element name="array" type="rsa:Tmulti-value"/>
        <element name="list" type="rsa:Tmulti-value"/>
        <element name="set" type="rsa:Tmulti-value"/>
        <element name="xml" type="rsa:Txml"/>
      </choice>
      <any namespace="##other" minOccurs="0" maxOccurs="unbounded" processContents="lax"/>
    </sequence>
    <attribute name="name" type="string" use="required"/>
    <attribute name="value" type="string" use="optional"/>
    <attribute name="value-type" type="rsa:Tvalue-types" default="String" use="optional"/>
    <anyAttribute/>
  </complexType>

  <complexType name="Tmulti-value">
    <sequence>
      <element name="value" minOccurs="0" maxOccurs="unbounded" type="rsa:Tvalue"/>
      <any namespace="##other" minOccurs="0" maxOccurs="unbounded" processContents="lax"/>
    </sequence>
    <anyAttribute/>
  </complexType>

  <complexType name="Tvalue" mixed="true">
    <sequence>
      <element name="xml" minOccurs="0" maxOccurs="1" type="rsa:Txml"/>
      <any namespace="##other" minOccurs="0" maxOccurs="unbounded" processContents="lax"/>
    </sequence>
    <anyAttribute/>
  </complexType>

  <simpleType name="Tvalue-types">
    <restriction base="string">
      <enumeration value="String"/>
      <enumeration value="long"/>
      <enumeration value="Long"/>
      <enumeration value="double"/>
      <enumeration value="Double"/>
      <enumeration value="float"/>
      <enumeration value="Float"/>
      <enumeration value="int"/>
      <enumeration value="Integer"/>
      <enumeration value="byte"/>
      <enumeration value="Byte"/>
      <enumeration value="char"/>
```

```
        <enumeration value="Character"/>
        <enumeration value="boolean"/>
        <enumeration value="Boolean"/>
        <enumeration value="short"/>
        <enumeration value="Short"/>
    </restriction>
</simpleType>

<complexType name="Txml">
    <sequence>
        <any namespace="##other" minOccurs="1" maxOccurs="1" processContents="lax"/>
    </sequence>
    <anyAttribute/>
</complexType>

<attribute name="must-understand" type="boolean" default="false"/>
</schema>
```

122.9   Security

From a security point of view distribution is a significant threat. A Distribution Provider requires very significant capabilities to be able to proxy services. In many situations it will be required to grant the distribution provider All Permission. It is therefore highly recommended that Distribution Providers use trusted links and ensure that it is not possible to attack a system through the Remote Services Admin service and used discovery protocols.

122.9.1   Import and Export Registrations

Import and Export Registrations are *capabilities*. That is, they can only be obtained when the caller has the proper permissions but once obtained they are no longer checked. The caller should therefore be careful to share those objects with other bundles. Export and Import References are free to share.

122.9.2   Framework UUID Runtime Permission

The Remote Service Admin bundle can have the need for reading and writing the System property or the Framework UUID when this is not set by the deployer, the launcher, or the framework. This requires the following permission:

```
PropertyPermission[
    "org.osgi.framework.uuid", "read,write"]
```

122.9.3   Endpoint Permission

The Remote Service Admin implementation requires a large set of permissions because it must be able to distribute potentially any service. Giving these extensive capabilities to all Topology Managers would make it harder to developer general Topology Managers that implements specific scenarios. For this reason, this specification provides an Endpoint Permission.

When an Endpoint Permission must be verified, it must be created with an Endpoint Description as argument, like:

```
sm.checkPermission( new EndpointPermission(anEndpoint, localUUID, READ));
```

The standard name and action constructor is used to define a permission. The name argument is a filter expression. The filter for an Endpoint Permission is applied to the properties of an Endpoint Description. The localUUID must map to the UUID of the framework of the caller of this constructor, see *Framework UUID* on page 289. This localUUID is used to allow a the permissions to use the <<LOCAL>> magic name in the permission filter to refer to the local framework.

The filter expression can use the following magic value:

- <<LOCAL>> – This value represents the framework UUID of the framework that this bundle belongs to. The following example restricts the visibility to descriptions of local Endpoints:

```
            ALLOW {
             ...EndpointPermission
                 "(endpoint.framework.uuid=<<LOCAL>>)"
                 "READ" }
```

An Endpoint Permission that has the actions listed in Table 122.3 on page 305.

Table 122.3   Endpoint Permission Actions

Action	Methods	Description
IMPORT	importService(EndpointDescription)	Import an Endpoint
EXPORT	exportService(ServiceReference,Map)	Export a service
READ	getExportedServices() getImportedEndpoints() remoteAdminEvent(RemoteServiceAdminEvent)	See the presence of distributed services. The IMPORT and EXPORT action imply READ. Distribution of events to the Remote Service Admin Listener. The Remote Service Admin must verify that the listener's bundle has the proper permission. No events should be delivered that are not implied.

122.10　org.osgi.service.remoteserviceadmin

Remote Service Admin Package Version 1.0.

Bundles wishing to use this package must list the package in the Import-Package header of the bundle's manifest. For example:

```
Import-Package: org.osgi.service.remoteserviceadmin; version="[1.0,2.0)"
```

122.10.1　Summary

- *EndpointDescription* - A description of an endpoint that provides sufficient information for a compatible distribution provider to create a connection to this endpoint An Endpoint Description is easy to transfer between different systems because it is property based where the property keys are strings and the values are simple types.
- *EndpointListener* - A white board service that represents a listener for endpoints.
- *EndpointPermission* - A bundle's authority to export, import or read an Endpoint.
- *ExportReference* - An Export Reference associates a service with a local endpoint.
- *ExportRegistration* - An Export Registration associates a service to a local endpoint.
- *ImportReference* - An Import Reference associates an active proxy service to a remote endpoint.
- *ImportRegistration* - An Import Registration associates an active proxy service to a remote endpoint.
- *RemoteConstants* - Provide the definition of the constants used in the Remote Service Admin specification.
- *RemoteServiceAdmin* - A Remote Service Admin manages the import and export of services.
- *RemoteServiceAdminEvent* - Provides the event information for a Remote Service Admin event.
- *RemoteServiceAdminListener* - A RemoteServiceAdminEvent listener is notified synchronously of any export or import registrations and unregistrations.

122.10.2   public class EndpointDescription

A description of an endpoint that provides sufficient information for a compatible distribution provider to create a connection to this endpoint An Endpoint Description is easy to transfer between different systems because it is property based where the property keys are strings and the values are simple types. This allows it to be used as a communications device to convey available endpoint information to nodes in a network. An Endpoint Description reflects the perspective of an *importer*. That is, the property keys have been chosen to match filters that are created by client bundles that need a service. Therefore the map must not contain any service.exported.* property and must contain the corresponding service.imported.* ones. The service.intents property must contain the intents provided by the service itself combined with the intents added by the exporting distribution provider. Qualified intents appear fully expanded on this property.

Concurrency Immutable

122.10.2.1   public EndpointDescription(Map<String,Object> properties)

properties The map from which to create the Endpoint Description. The keys in the map must be type String and, since the keys are case insensitive, there must be no duplicates with case variation.

☐ Create an Endpoint Description from a Map.

The endpoint.id, service.imported.configs and objectClass properties must be set.

Throws IllegalArgumentException – When the properties are not proper for an Endpoint Description.

122.10.2.2   public EndpointDescription(ServiceReference reference, Map<String,Object> properties)

reference A service reference that can be exported.

properties Map of properties. This argument can be null. The keys in the map must be type String and, since the keys are case insensitive, there must be no duplicates with case variation.

☐ Create an Endpoint Description based on a Service Reference and a Map of properties. The properties in the map take precedence over the properties in the Service Reference.

This method will automatically set the endpoint.framework.uuid and endpoint.service.id properties based on the specified Service Reference as well as the service.imported property if they are not specified as properties.

The endpoint.id, service.imported.configs and objectClass properties must be set.

Throws IllegalArgumentException – When the properties are not proper for an Endpoint Description

122.10.2.3   public boolean equals(Object other)

other The EndpointDescription object to be compared.

☐ Compares this EndpointDescription object to another object.

An Endpoint Description is considered to be **equal to** another Endpoint Description if their ids are equal.

Returns true if object is a EndpointDescription and is equal to this object; false otherwise.

122.10.2.4   public List<String> getConfigurationTypes( )

☐ Returns the configuration types. A distribution provider exports a service with an endpoint. This endpoint uses some kind of communications protocol with a set of configuration parameters. There are many different types but each endpoint is configured by only one configuration type. However, a distribution provider can be aware of different configuration types and provide synonyms to increase the change a receiving distribution provider can create a connection to this endpoint. This value of the configuration types is stored in the RemoteConstants.SERVICE_IMPORTED_CONFIGS service property.

Returns An unmodifiable list of the configuration types used for the associated endpoint and optionally synonyms.

122.10.2.5   public String getFrameworkUUID( )

☐ Return the framework UUID for the remote service, if present. The value of the remote framework uuid is stored in the RemoteConstants.ENDPOINT_FRAMEWORK_UUID endpoint property.

Returns Remote Framework UUID, or null if this endpoint is not associated with an OSGi framework having a framework uuid.

122.10.2.6   public String getId( )

☐ Returns the endpoint's id. The id is an opaque id for an endpoint. No two different endpoints must have the same id. Two Endpoint Descriptions with the same id must represent the same endpoint. The value of the id is stored in the RemoteConstants.ENDPOINT_ID property.

Returns The id of the endpoint, never null. The returned value has leading and trailing whitespace removed.

122.10.2.7   public List<String> getIntents( )

☐ Return the list of intents implemented by this endpoint. The intents are based on the service.intents on an imported service, except for any intents that are additionally provided by the importing distribution provider. All qualified intents must have been expanded. This value of the intents is stored in the RemoteConstants.SERVICE_INTENTS service property.

Returns An unmodifiable list of expanded intents that are provided by this endpoint.

122.10.2.8   public List<String> getInterfaces( )

☐ Provide the list of interfaces implemented by the exported service. The value of the interfaces is derived from the objectClass property.

Returns An unmodifiable list of Java interface names implemented by this endpoint.

122.10.2.9   public Version getPackageVersion(String packageName)

packageName The name of the package for which a version is requested.

☐ Provide the version of the given package name. The version is encoded by prefixing the given package name with endpoint.package.version., and then using this as an endpoint property key. For example:

    endpoint. package. version. com. acme

The value of this property is in String format and will be converted to a Version object by this method.

Returns The version of the specified package or Version.emptyVersion if the package has no version in this Endpoint Description.

Throws IllegalArgumentException – If the version property value is not String.

122.10.2.10   public Map<String,Object> getProperties( )

☐ Returns all endpoint properties.

Returns An unmodifiable map referring to the properties of this Endpoint Description.

122.10.2.11   public long getServiceId( )

☐ Returns the service id for the service exported through this endpoint. This is the service id under which the framework has registered the service. This field together with the Framework UUID is a globally unique id for a service. The value of the remote service id is stored in the RemoteConstants.ENDPOINT_SERVICE_ID endpoint property.

Returns Service id of a service or 0 if this Endpoint Description does not relate to an OSGi service.

122.10.2.12   **public int hashCode( )**

☐   Returns a hash code value for the object.

Returns   An integer which is a hash code value for this object.

122.10.2.13   **public boolean isSameService(EndpointDescription other)**

other   The Endpoint Description to look at

☐   Answers if this Endpoint Description refers to the same service instance as the given Endpoint Description. Two Endpoint Descriptions point to the same service if they have the same id or their framework UUIDs and remote service ids are equal.

Returns   True if this endpoint description points to the same service as the other

122.10.2.14   **public boolean matches(String filter)**

filter   The filter to test.

☐   Tests the properties of this EndpointDescription against the given filter using a case insensitive match.

Returns   true If the properties of this EndpointDescription match the filter, false otherwise.

Throws   IllegalArgumentException – If filter contains an invalid filter string that cannot be parsed.

122.10.2.15   **public String toString( )**

☐   Returns the string representation of this EndpointDescription.

Returns   String form of this EndpointDescription.

122.10.3   **public interface EndpointListener**

A white board service that represents a listener for endpoints. An Endpoint Listener represents a participant in the distributed model that is interested in Endpoint Descriptions. This white board service can be used in many different scenarios. However, the primary use case is to allow a remote manager to be informed of Endpoint Descriptions available in the network and inform the network about available Endpoint Descriptions. Both the network bundle and the manager bundle register an Endpoint Listener service. The manager informs the network bundle about Endpoints that it creates. The network bundles then uses a protocol like SLP to announce these local end-points to the network. If the network bundle discovers a new Endpoint through its discovery protocol, then it sends an Endpoint Description to all the Endpoint Listener services that are registered (except its own) that have specified an interest in that endpoint. Endpoint Listener services can express their *scope* with the service property ENDPOINT_LISTENER_SCOPE. This service property is a list of filters. An Endpoint Description should only be given to a Endpoint Listener when there is at least one filter that matches the Endpoint Description properties. This filter model is quite flexible. For example, a discovery bundle is only interested in locally originating Endpoint Descriptions. The following filter ensure that it only sees local endpoints.

        (org.osgi.framework.uuid=72dc5fd9-5f8f-4f8f-9821-9ebb433a5b72)

In the same vein, a manager that is only interested in remote Endpoint Descriptions can use a filter like:

        (!(org.osgi.framework.uuid=72dc5fd9-5f8f-4f8f-9821-9ebb433a5b72))

Where in both cases, the given UUID is the UUID of the local framework that can be found in the Framework properties. The Endpoint Listener's scope maps very well to the service hooks. A manager can just register all filters found from the Listener Hook as its scope. This will automatically provide it with all known endpoints that match the given scope, without having to inspect the filter string. In general, when an Endpoint Description is discovered, it should be dispatched to all registered Endpoint Listener services. If a new Endpoint Listener is registered, it should be informed about all currently known Endpoints that match its scope. If a getter of the Endpoint Listener service is unregistered, then all its registered Endpoint Description objects must be removed. The Endpoint Listener models a *best effort* approach. Participating bundles should do their utmost to keep the listeners up to date, but implementers should realize that many endpoints come through unreliable discovery processes.

Concurrency Thread-safe

122.10.3.1   **public static final String ENDPOINT_LISTENER_SCOPE = "endpoint.listener.scope"**

Specifies the interest of this listener with filters. This listener is only interested in Endpoint Descriptions where its properties match the given filter. The type of this property must be String+.

122.10.3.2   **public void endpointAdded(EndpointDescription endpoint, String matchedFilter)**

endpoint The Endpoint Description to be published

matchedFilter The filter from the ENDPOINT_LISTENER_SCOPE that matched the endpoint, must not be null.

☐ Register an endpoint with this listener. If the endpoint matches one of the filters registered with the ENDPOINT_LISTENER_SCOPE service property then this filter should be given as the matchedFilter parameter. When this service is first registered or it is modified, it should receive all known endpoints matching the filter.

122.10.3.3   **public void endpointRemoved(EndpointDescription endpoint, String matchedFilter)**

endpoint The Endpoint Description that is no longer valid.

matchedFilter The filter from the ENDPOINT_LISTENER_SCOPE that matched the endpoint, must not be null.

☐ Remove the registration of an endpoint. If an endpoint that was registered with the endpointAdded(EndpointDescription, String) method is no longer available then this method should be called. This will remove the endpoint from the listener. It is not necessary to remove endpoints when the service is unregistered or modified in such a way that not all endpoints match the interest filter anymore.

122.10.4   **public final class EndpointPermission
extends Permission**

A bundle's authority to export, import or read an Endpoint.

- The export action allows a bundle to export a service as an Endpoint.
- The import action allows a bundle to import a service from an Endpoint.
- The read action allows a bundle to read references to an Endpoint.

Permission to read an Endpoint is required in order to detect events regarding an Endpoint. Untrusted bundles should not be able to detect the presence of certain Endpoints unless they have the appropriate EndpointPermission to read the specific service.

Concurrency Thread-safe

122.10.4.1   **public static final String EXPORT = "export"**

The action string export. The export action implies the read action.

122.10.4.2   **public static final String IMPORT = "import"**

The action string import. The import action implies the read action.

122.10.4.3   **public static final String READ = "read"**

The action string read.

122.10.4.4   **public EndpointPermission(String filterString, String actions)**

filterString   The filter string or "∗" to match all endpoints.

actions   The actions read, import, or export.

❑   Create a new EndpointPermission with the specified filter.

The filter will be evaluated against the endpoint properties of a requested EndpointPermission.

There are three possible actions: read, import and export. The read action allows the owner of this permission to see the presence of distributed services. The import action allows the owner of this permission to import an endpoint. The export action allows the owner of this permission to export a service.

Throws   IllegalArgumentException – If the filter has an invalid syntax or the actions are not valid.

122.10.4.5   **public EndpointPermission(EndpointDescription endpoint, String localFrameworkUUID, String actions)**

endpoint   The requested endpoint.

*localFrameworkUUID*The UUID of the local framework. This is used to support matching the endpoint.framework.uuid endpoint property to the <<LOCAL>> value in the filter expression.

actions   The actions read, import, or export.

❑   Creates a new requested EndpointPermission object to be used by code that must perform checkPermission. EndpointPermission objects created with this constructor cannot be added to an EndpointPermission permission collection.

Throws   IllegalArgumentException – If the endpoint is null or the actions are not valid.

122.10.4.6   **public boolean equals(Object obj)**

obj   The object to test for equality.

❑   Determines the equality of two EndpointPermission objects. Checks that specified object has the same name, actions and endpoint as this EndpointPermission.

Returns   true If obj is a EndpointPermission, and has the same name, actions and endpoint as this EndpointPermission object; false otherwise.

122.10.4.7   **public String getActions( )**

❑   Returns the canonical string representation of the actions. Always returns present actions in the following canonical order: read, import, export.

Returns   The canonical string representation of the actions.

122.10.4.8   **public int hashCode( )**

❑   Returns the hash code value for this object.

Returns   Hash code value for this object.

122.10.4.9   **public boolean implies(Permission p)**

p   The target permission to check.

❑   Determines if a EndpointPermission object "implies" the specified permission.

Returns   true if the specified permission is implied by this object; false otherwise.

122.10.4.10   **public PermissionCollection newPermissionCollection( )**

❑   Returns a new PermissionCollection object for storing EndpointPermission objects.

Returns   A new PermissionCollection object suitable for storing EndpointPermission objects.

122.10.5 **public interface ExportReference**

An Export Reference associates a service with a local endpoint. The Export Reference can be used to reference an exported service. When the service is no longer exported, all methods must return null.

Concurrency Thread-safe

122.10.5.1 **public EndpointDescription getExportedEndpoint( )**

☐ Return the Endpoint Description for the local endpoint.

Returns The Endpoint Description for the local endpoint. Must be null when the service is no longer exported.

122.10.5.2 **public ServiceReference getExportedService( )**

☐ Return the service being exported.

Returns The service being exported. Must be null when the service is no longer exported.

122.10.6 **public interface ExportRegistration**

An Export Registration associates a service to a local endpoint. The Export Registration can be used to delete the endpoint associated with an this registration. It is created with the RemoteServiceAdmin.exportService(ServiceReference,Map) method. When this Export Registration has been closed, all methods must return null.

Concurrency Thread-safe

122.10.6.1 **public void close( )**

☐ Delete the local endpoint and disconnect any remote distribution providers. After this method returns, all methods must return null. This method has no effect when this registration has already been closed or is being closed.

122.10.6.2 **public Throwable getException( )**

☐ Return the exception for any error during the export process. If the Remote Service Admin for some reasons is unable to properly initialize this registration, then it must return an exception from this method. If no error occurred, this method must return null. The error must be set before this Export Registration is returned. Asynchronously occurring errors must be reported to the log.

Returns The exception that occurred during the initialization of this registration or null if no exception occurred.

122.10.6.3 **public ExportReference getExportReference( )**

☐ Return the Export Reference for the exported service.

Returns The Export Reference for this registration.

Throws IllegalStateException – When this registration was not properly initialized. See getException().

122.10.7 **public interface ImportReference**

An Import Reference associates an active proxy service to a remote endpoint. The Import Reference can be used to reference an imported service. When the service is no longer imported, all methods must return null.

Concurrency Thread-safe

122.10.7.1 **public EndpointDescription getImportedEndpoint( )**

☐ Return the Endpoint Description for the remote endpoint.

Returns The Endpoint Description for the remote endpoint. Must be null when the service is no longer imported.

122.10.7.2   **public ServiceReference getImportedService( )**

❑ Return the Service Reference for the proxy for the endpoint.

Returns   The Service Reference to the proxy for the endpoint. Must be null when the service is no longer imported.

122.10.8   public interface ImportRegistration

An Import Registration associates an active proxy service to a remote endpoint. The Import Registration can be used to delete the proxy associated with an endpoint. It is created with the RemoteServiceAdmin.importService(EndpointDescription) method. When this Import Registration has been closed, all methods must return null.

Concurrency   Thread-safe

122.10.8.1   **public void close( )**

❑ Close this Import Registration. This must close the connection to the endpoint and unregister the proxy. After this method returns, all other methods must return null. This method has no effect when this registration has already been closed or is being closed.

122.10.8.2   **public Throwable getException( )**

❑ Return the exception for any error during the import process. If the Remote Service Admin for some reasons is unable to properly initialize this registration, then it must return an exception from this method. If no error occurred, this method must return null. The error must be set before this Import Registration is returned. Asynchronously occurring errors must be reported to the log.

Returns   The exception that occurred during the initialization of this registration or null if no exception occurred.

122.10.8.3   **public ImportReference getImportReference( )**

❑ Return the Import Reference for the imported service.

Returns   The Import Reference for this registration.

Throws   IllegalStateException – When this registration was not properly initialized. See getException().

122.10.9   public class RemoteConstants

Provide the definition of the constants used in the Remote Service Admin specification.

Concurrency   Immutable

122.10.9.1   **public static final String ENDPOINT_FRAMEWORK_UUID = "endpoint.framework.uuid"**

Endpoint property identifying the universally unique id of the exporting framework. Can be absent if the corresponding endpoint is not for an OSGi service.

The value of this property must be of type String.

122.10.9.2   **public static final String ENDPOINT_ID = "endpoint.id"**

Endpoint property identifying the id for this endpoint. This service property must always be set.

The value of this property must be of type String.

122.10.9.3   **public static final String ENDPOINT_PACKAGE_VERSION_ = "endpoint.package.version."**

Prefix for an endpoint property identifying the interface Java package version for an interface. For example, the property endpoint.package.version.com.acme=1.3 describes the version of the package for the com.acme.Foo interface. This endpoint property for an interface package does not have to be set. If not set, the value must be assumed to be 0.

Since endpoint properties are stored in a case insensitive map, case variants of a package name are folded together.

The value of properties having this prefix must be of type String.

122.10.9.4 **public static final String ENDPOINT_SERVICE_ID = "endpoint.service.id"**

Endpoint property identifying the service id of the exported service. Can be absent or 0 if the corresponding endpoint is not for an OSGi service.

The value of this property must be of type Long.

122.10.9.5 **public static final String REMOTE_CONFIGS_SUPPORTED = "remote.configs.supported"**

Service property identifying the configuration types supported by a distribution provider. Registered by the distribution provider on one of its services to indicate the supported configuration types.

The value of this property must be of type String, String[], or Collection<String>.

122.10.9.6 **public static final String REMOTE_INTENTS_SUPPORTED = "remote.intents.supported"**

Service property identifying the intents supported by a distribution provider. Registered by the distribution provider on one of its services to indicate the vocabulary of implemented intents.

The value of this property must be of type String, String[], or Collection<String>.

122.10.9.7 **public static final String SERVICE_EXPORTED_CONFIGS = "service.exported.configs"**

Service property identifying the configuration types that should be used to export the service. Each configuration type represents the configuration parameters for an endpoint. A distribution provider should create an endpoint for each configuration type that it supports.

This property may be supplied in the propertiesDictionary object passed to the BundleContext.registerService method. The value of this property must be of type String, String[], or Collection<String>.

122.10.9.8 **public static final String SERVICE_EXPORTED_INTENTS = "service.exported.intents"**

Service property identifying the intents that the distribution provider must implement to distribute the service. Intents listed in this property are reserved for intents that are critical for the code to function correctly, for example, ordering of messages. These intents should not be configurable.

This property may be supplied in the propertiesDictionary object passed to the BundleContext.registerService method. The value of this property must be of type String, String[], or Collection<String>.

122.10.9.9 **public static final String SERVICE_EXPORTED_INTENTS_EXTRA = "service.exported.intents.extra"**

Service property identifying the extra intents that the distribution provider must implement to distribute the service. This property is merged with the service.exported.intents property before the distribution provider interprets the listed intents; it has therefore the same semantics but the property should be configurable so the administrator can choose the intents based on the topology. Bundles should therefore make this property configurable, for example through the Configuration Admin service.

This property may be supplied in the propertiesDictionary object passed to the BundleContext.registerService method. The value of this property must be of type String, String[], or Collection<String>.

122.10.9.10   **public static final String SERVICE_EXPORTED_INTERFACES = "service.exported.interfaces"**

Service property marking the service for export. It defines the interfaces under which this service can be exported. This list must be a subset of the types under which the service was registered. The single value of an asterisk ("*", \u002A) indicates all the interface types under which the service was registered excluding the non-interface types. It is strongly recommended to only export interface types and not concrete classes due to the complexity of creating proxies for some type of concrete classes.

This property may be supplied in the propertiesDictionary object passed to the BundleContext.registerService method. The value of this property must be of type String, String[], or Collection<String>.

122.10.9.11   **public static final String SERVICE_IMPORTED = "service.imported"**

Service property identifying the service as imported. This service property must be set by a distribution provider to any value when it registers the endpoint proxy as an imported service. A bundle can use this property to filter out imported services.

The value of this property may be of any type.

122.10.9.12   **public static final String SERVICE_IMPORTED_CONFIGS = "service.imported.configs"**

Service property identifying the configuration types used to import the service. Any associated properties for this configuration types must be properly mapped to the importing system. For example, a URL in these properties must point to a valid resource when used in the importing framework. If multiple configuration types are listed in this property, then they must be synonyms for exactly the same remote endpoint that is used to export this service.

The value of this property must be of type String, String[], or Collection<String>.

See Also   SERVICE_EXPORTED_CONFIGS

122.10.9.13   **public static final String SERVICE_INTENTS = "service.intents"**

Service property identifying the intents that this service implement. This property has a dual purpose:

- A bundle can use this service property to notify the distribution provider that these intents are already implemented by the exported service object.
- A distribution provider must use this property to convey the combined intents of: The exporting service, and, the intents that the exporting distribution provider adds, and the intents that the importing distribution provider adds.

To export a service, a distribution provider must expand any qualified intents. Both the exporting and importing distribution providers must recognize all intents before a service can be distributed.

The value of this property must be of type String, String[], or Collection<String>.

122.10.10   **public interface RemoteServiceAdmin**

A Remote Service Admin manages the import and export of services. A Distribution Provider can expose a control interface. This interface allows a Topology Manager to control the export and import of services. The API allows a Topology Manager to export a service, to import a service, and find out about the current imports and exports.

Concurrency   Thread-safe

122.10.10.1   **public Collection<ExportRegistration> exportService(ServiceReference reference, Map<String, Object> properties)**

reference   The Service Reference to export.

properties The properties to create a local Endpoint that can be implemented by this Remote Service Admin. If this is null, the Endpoint will be determined by the properties on the service. The properties are the same as given for an exported service. They override any properties in the specified Service Reference (case insensitive). The properties objectClass and service.id, in any case variant, are ignored. Those properties in the Service Reference cannot be overridden. This parameter can be null, this should be treated as an empty map.

❑ Export a service to a given Endpoint. The Remote Service Admin must create an Endpoint from the given description that can be used by other Distribution Providers to connect to this Remote Service Admin and use the exported service. The property keys of a Service Reference are case insensitive while the property keys of the specified properties map are case sensitive. A property key in the specified properties map must therefore override any case variant property key in the properties of the specified Service Reference.

If the caller does not have the appropriate EndpointPermission[endpoint,EXPORT] for an Endpoint, and the Java Runtime Environment supports permissions, then the getException method on the corresponding returned ExportRegistration will return a SecurityException.

Returns A Collection of ExportRegistrations for the specified Service Reference and properties. Multiple Export Registrations may be returned because a single service can be exported to multiple Endpoints depending on the available configuration type properties. The result is never null but may be empty if this Remove Service Admin does not recognize any of the configuration types.

Throws IllegalArgumentException – If any of the properties has a value that is not syntactically correct or if the service properties and the overlaid properties do not contain a RemoteConstants.SERVICE_EXPORTED_INTERFACES entry.

UnsupportedOperationException – If any of the intents expressed through the properties is not supported by the distribution provider.

122.10.10.2   public Collection<ExportReference> getExportedServices( )

❑ Return the currently active Export References.

If the caller does not have the appropriate EndpointPermission[endpoint,READ] for an Endpoint, and the Java Runtime Environment supports permissions, then returned collection will not contain a reference to the exported Endpoint.

Returns A Collection of ExportReferences that are currently active.

122.10.10.3   public Collection<ImportReference> getImportedEndpoints( )

❑ Return the currently active Import References.

If the caller does not have the appropriate EndpointPermission[endpoint,READ] for an Endpoint, and the Java Runtime Environment supports permissions, then returned collection will not contain a reference to the imported Endpoint.

Returns A Collection of ImportReferences that are currently active.

122.10.10.4   public ImportRegistration importService(EndpointDescription endpoint)

endpoint The Endpoint Description to be used for import.

❑ Import a service from an Endpoint. The Remote Service Admin must use the given Endpoint to create a proxy. This method can return null if the service could not be imported.

Returns An Import Registration that combines the Endpoint Description and the Service Reference or null if the Endpoint could not be imported.

Throws SecurityException – If the caller does not have the appropriate EndpointPermission[endpoint, IMPORT] for the Endpoint, and the Java Runtime Environment supports permissions.

122.10.11   **public class RemoteServiceAdminEvent**

Provides the event information for a Remote Service Admin event.

Concurrency   Immutable

122.10.11.1   **public static final int EXPORT_ERROR = 6**

A fatal exporting error occurred. The Export Registration has been closed.

122.10.11.2   **public static final int EXPORT_REGISTRATION = 2**

Add an export registration. The Remote Service Admin will call this method when it exports a service. When this service is registered, the Remote Service Admin must notify the listener of all existing Export Registrations.

122.10.11.3   **public static final int EXPORT_UNREGISTRATION = 3**

Remove an export registration. The Remote Service Admin will call this method when it removes the export of a service.

122.10.11.4   **public static final int EXPORT_WARNING = 7**

A problematic situation occurred, the export is still active.

122.10.11.5   **public static final int IMPORT_ERROR = 5**

A fatal importing error occurred. The Import Registration has been closed.

122.10.11.6   **public static final int IMPORT_REGISTRATION = 1**

Add an import registration. The Remote Service Admin will call this method when it imports a service. When this service is registered, the Remote Service Admin must notify the listener of all existing Import Registrations.

122.10.11.7   **public static final int IMPORT_UNREGISTRATION = 4**

Remove an import registration. The Remote Service Admin will call this method when it removes the import of a service.

122.10.11.8   **public static final int IMPORT_WARNING = 8**

A problematic situation occurred, the import is still active.

122.10.11.9   **public RemoteServiceAdminEvent(int type, Bundle source, ExportReference exportReference, Throwable exception)**

type   The event type.

source   The source bundle, must not be null.

exportReference   The exportReference, can not be null.

exception   Any exceptions encountered, can be null.

❑   Create a Remote Service Admin Event for an export notification.

122.10.11.10   **public RemoteServiceAdminEvent(int type, Bundle source, ImportReference importReference, Throwable exception)**

type   The event type.

source   The source bundle, must not be null.

importReference   The importReference, can not be null.

exception Any exceptions encountered, can be null.

☐ Create a Remote Service Admin Event for an import notification.

122.10.11.11   **public Throwable getException( )**

☐ Return the exception for this event.

Returns The exception or null.

122.10.11.12   **public ExportReference getExportReference( )**

☐ Return the Export Reference for this event.

Returns The Export Reference or null.

122.10.11.13   **public ImportReference getImportReference( )**

☐ Return the Import Reference for this event.

Returns The Import Reference or null.

122.10.11.14   **public Bundle getSource( )**

☐ Return the bundle source of this event.

Returns The bundle source of this event.

122.10.11.15   **public int getType( )**

☐ Return the type of this event.

Returns The type of this event.

122.10.12   **public interface RemoteServiceAdminListener**

A RemoteServiceAdminEvent listener is notified synchronously of any export or import registrations and unregistrations.

If the Java Runtime Environment supports permissions, then filtering is done. RemoteServiceAdminEvent objects are only delivered to the listener if the bundle which defines the listener object's class has the appropriate EndpointPermission[endpoint,READ] for the endpoint referenced by the event.

See Also RemoteServiceAdminEvent

Concurrency Thread-safe

122.10.12.1   **public void remoteAdminEvent(RemoteServiceAdminEvent event)**

event The RemoteServiceAdminEvent object.

☐ Receive notification of any export or import registrations and unregistrations as well as errors and warnings.

122.11   References

[1] *OSGi Core Specifications*
http://www.osgi.org/Specifications/HomePage

[2] *OSGi Service Property Namespace*
http://www.osgi.org/Specifications/ServicePropertyNamespace

[3] *UUIDs*
http://en.wikipedia.org/wiki/Universally_Unique_Identifier

[4]   *Service Location Protocol (SLP)*
        http://en.wikipedia.org/wiki/Service_Location_Protocol

[5]   *JGroups*
        http://www.jgroups.org/

[6]   *UDDI*
        http://en.wikipedia.org/wiki/Universal_Description_Discovery_and_Integration

[7]   *Service Component Architecture (SCA)*
        http://www.osoa.org/display/Main/Home

123   JTA Transaction Services Specification

Version 1.0

123.1   Introduction

Transactions are the key abstraction to provide reliability with large scale distributed systems and are a primary component of enterprise systems. This specification provides an OSGi service based design for the Java Transaction Architecture (JTA) Specification, which describes the standard transaction model for Java applications. Providing the JTA specification as a service based model enables the use of independent implementations. This JTA Transaction Services Specification provides a managed model, where an Application Container (such as the Java EE EJB container) manages the transaction and the enlistment of resources, and an unmanaged model, where each application is responsible for these tasks itself.

This specification provides a brief overview of JTA and then the use of it through 3 transaction services: User Transaction, Transaction Manager, and Transaction Synchronization.

This specification is based on [1] *Java Transaction API Specification 1.1*.

123.1.1   Essentials

- *Portability* – It is important that applications are easy to port from other environments that support JTA.
- *Pluggability* – Allow different vendors to provide implementations of this specification.
- *JTA Compatible* – Support full JTA 1.1 Specification

123.1.2   Entities

- *JTA Provider* – Implementation of this specification. It is responsible, on request from a Transaction Originator, for starting and ending transactions and coordinating the work of Resource Managers that become involved in each Transaction. This entity provides the User Transaction service, Transaction Manager service, and the Transaction Synchronization Registry service.
- *Transaction* – An atomic unit of work that is associated with a thread of execution.
- *Transaction Originator* – An Application or its Container, that directs the JTA Provider to begin and end Transactions.
- *User Transaction* – A service used by a Transaction Originator for beginning and ending transactions.
- *Transaction Manager* – A service used by a Transaction Originator for managing both transaction demarcation and enlistment of Durable Resources or Volatile Resources.
- *Transaction Synchronization Registry* – A service for enlistment of Volatile Resources for getting notifications before and after ending Transactions.
- *Application Bundle* – An entity that initiates work that executes under a Transaction.
- *Container* – An entity that is distinct from the Application and which provides a managed environment for Applications. Unmanaged environments do not distinguish between the Application and Container entities.
- *Resource Manager* – Provides the transactional resources whose work is externally coordinated by a JTA Provider. Examples of Resource Managers include databases, Java Message Service providers and enterprise information systems.

- *Durable Resource* – A resource whose work is made durable when the Transaction is successfully committed. Durable Resources can be enlisted with a Transaction to ensure that work is performed within the scope of the Transaction and to participate in the outcome of a Transaction. Durable Resource enlistment is the responsibility of the Application Bundle or its Container. Durable Resources implement the javax.transaction.xa.XAResource interface
- *Volatile Resource* – Resources that are associated with a Transaction but are no longer needed after the Transaction, for example transaction-scoped caches. Volatile Resources are registered with the JTA Provider to receive notifications before and after the outcome of the Transaction. Volatile Resources implement the javax.transaction.Synchronization interface
- *Transaction Services* – The triplet of the User Transaction, Transaction Manager, and Transaction Synchronization Registry services registered by the JTA Provider.

Figure 123.1   *Transaction Service Specification Entities*

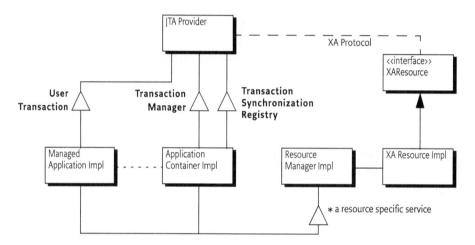

123.1.3   Dependencies

This specification is based on the following packages:

    javax.transaction
    javax.transaction.xa

These packages must be exported as version 1.1.

123.1.4   Synopsis

The JTA Provider register the Transaction Services:

- *User Transaction* – Offers transaction demarcation capabilities to an Application bundle.
- *Transaction Manager* – Offers transaction demarcation and further transaction management capabilities to an Application Bundle or an Application Container.
- *Transaction Synchronization Registry* – Offers a callback registration service for volatile transactional participants wishing to be notified of the completion of the transaction.

A JTA Provider must register these services when it is started. A JTA Provider may put restrictions on which bundles can use these services. For example, in a Java EE environment, the JTA Provider does not expose the TransactionManager interface to applications. An OSGi environment which supports the Java EE specifications will typically provide access to the Transaction Manager service only to Java EE Containers.

A typical example of the use of a transaction is for transferring money from one bank account to another. Two Durable Resources are involved, one provided by the database from which the money is to be withdrawn and another provided by the database to which the money will be deposited. An Application Bundle acting as the Transaction Originator gets the User Transaction service and uses it to begin a transaction. This transaction is associated with the current thread (implicitly) by the JTA Provider. On the same thread of execution, the Application Bundle connects to the database from which the money is to be withdrawn and updates the balance in the source account by the amount to be debited.

The database is a resource manager whose connections have associated XA Resources; the first time a connection is used within the scope of a new transaction the Application Bundle, or a Container, obtains the XA Resource associated with the connection and enlists it with the JTA Provider through the Transaction Manager service. On the same thread of execution, the Application Bundle connects to the second database and updates the balance in the target account by the amount to be credited. An XA Resource for the second connection is enlisted with the Transaction Manager service as well by the Application Bundle or a Container.

Now that the money has been transferred the Transaction Originator requests a commit of the Transaction (on the same thread of execution) via the User Transaction Service, causing the JTA Provider to initiate the two-phase commit process with the two Resource Managers through the enlisted XA Resources. The transaction is then atomically committed or rolled back.

123.2 JTA Overview

A transaction is a unit of work in which interactions with multiple participants can be coordinated by a third party such that the final outcome of these interactions has well-defined transactional semantics. A variety of well-known transaction models exist with specific characteristics; the transactions described in this specification provide *Atomic Consistent Isolated and Durable* (ACID) semantics as defined in [2] *XA+ Specification* whereby all the participants in a transaction are coordinated to an *atomic* outcome in which the work of all the participants is either completely committed or completely rolled back.

The [2] *XA+ Specification* defines a *Distributed Transaction Processing* (DTP) software architecture for transactional work that is distributed across multiple Resource Managers and coordinated externally by a Transaction Manager using the two-phase commit XA protocol. The DTP architecture defines the roles of the *Transaction Manager* and *Resource Manager*; this specification uses the term *JTA Provider* rather than *Transaction Manager* to distinguish it from the *Transaction Manager service*. Note that Distributed Transaction Processing does not imply distribution of transactions across multiple frameworks or JVMs.

The [1] *Java Transaction API Specification 1.1* defines the Java interfaces required for the management of transactions on the enterprise Java platform.

123.2.1 Global and Local Transactions

A transaction may be a *local transaction* or a *global transaction*. A local transaction is a unit of work that is local to a single Resource Manager and may succeed or fail independently of the work of other Resource Managers. A global transaction, sometimes referred to as a distributed transaction, is a unit of work that may encompass multiple Resource Managers and is coordinated by a JTA Provider external to the Resource Manager(s) as described in the DTP architecture. The term *transaction* in this specification always refers to a global transaction.

The JTA Provider is responsible for servicing requests from a Transaction Originator to create and complete transactions, it manages the state of each transaction it creates, the association of each transaction with the thread of execution, and the coordination of any Resource Managers that become involved in the global transaction. The JTA Provider ensures that each transaction is associated with, at most, one application thread at a time and provides the means to move that association from one thread to another as needed.

The model for resource commit coordination is the *two phase commit* XA protocol, with Resource Managers being directed by the JTA Provider. The first time an Application accesses a Resource Manager within the scope of a new global transaction, the Application, or its Container, obtains an XA Resource from the Resource Manager and *enlists* this XA Resource with the JTA Provider.

At the end of a transaction, the Transaction Originator must decide whether to initiate a *commit* or *rollback* request for all the changes made within the scope of the Transaction. The Transaction Originator requests that the JTA Provider completes the transaction. The JTA Provider then negotiates with each enlisted Resource Manager to reach a coordinated outcome. A failure in the transaction at any point before the second phase of two-phase commit results in the transaction being rolled back.

XA is a *presumed abort* protocol and implementations of XA-compliant JTA Providers and Resource Managers can be highly optimized to perform no logging of transactional state until a commit decision is required. A Resource Manager durably records its prepare decision, and a JTA Provider durably records any commit decision it makes. Failures between a decision on the outcome of a transaction and the enactment of that outcome are handled during *transaction recovery* to ensure the atomic outcome of the transaction.

123.2.2   Durable Resource

Durable Resources are provided by Resource Managers and must implement the XAResource interface described in the [1] *Java Transaction API Specification 1.1*. An XAResource object is enlisted with a transaction to ensure that the work of the Resource Manager is associated with the correct transaction and to participate in the two-phase commit process. The XAResource interface is driven by the JTA Provider during the completion of the transaction and is used to direct the Resource Manager to commit or rollback any changes made under the corresponding transaction.

123.2.3   Volatile Resource

Volatile resources are components that do not participate in the two phase commit but are called immediately prior to and after the two phase commit. They implement the [1] *Java Transaction API Specification 1.1* Synchronization interface. If a request is made to commit a transaction then the volatile participants have the opportunity to perform some *before completion* processing such as flushing cached updates to persistent storage. Failures during the *before completion* processing must cause the transaction to rollback. In both the commit and rollback cases the volatile resources are called after two phase commit to perform *after completion* processing. *After completion* procession cannot affect the outcome of the transaction.

123.2.4   Threading

As noted above in *Global and Local Transactions* on page 321, a global transaction must not be associated with more than one application thread at a time but can be moved over time from one application thread to another. In some environments Applications run in containers which restrict the ability of the Application component to explicitly manage the transaction-thread association by restricting access to the Transaction Manager. For example, Java EE application servers provide web and EJB Containers for application components and, while the Containers themselves can explicitly manage transaction-thread associations, these containers do not allow the Applications to do so. Applications running in these containers are required to complete any transactions they start on that same application thread. In general, Applications that run inside a Container must follow the rules defined by that Container. For further details of the considerations specific to Java EE containers, see the section *Transactions and Threads* in [4] *Java Platform, Enterprise Edition (Java EE) Specification, v5*.

123.3   Application

An *Application* is a bundle that may use transactions, either as a Transaction Originator or as a bundle that is called as part of an existing transaction. A Transaction Originator Application bundle starts a transaction and end it with a commit or rollback using the User Transaction or Transaction Manager service.

A Transaction Originator Application bundle may not make use of Resource Managers itself but may simply provide transaction demarcation and then call other bundles which do use Resource Managers. In such a case the Transaction Originator Application bundle requires only the use of the User Transaction service for transaction demarcation. The called bundles may use the Transaction Manager service if they use Resource Managers.

Application Bundles that use Resource Managers have to know the enlistment strategy for the Resource Managers they use. There are two possibilities:

- *Application Bundle Enlistment* – The Application Bundle must enlist the Resource Managers itself. For each Resource Manager it uses it must enlist that Resource Manager with the Transaction Manager.
- *Container-Managed Enlistment* – An Application runs in a container, such as a Java EE Container, which manages the Resource Manager enlistment on behalf of the Application.

These scenarios are explained in the following sections.

123.3.1   No Enlistment

A Transaction Originator Application bundle that uses no Resource Managers itself but starts a Transaction before calling another bundle may use the *User Transaction* service to control the Transaction demarcation.

For example, an Application can use the User Transaction service to begin a global transaction:

```
UserTransaction ut = getUserTransaction();
ut.begin();
```

The User Transaction service associates a transaction with the current thread until that transaction is completed via:

```
UserTransaction ut = getUserTransaction();
ut.commit();
```

Or the equivalent rollback method. The getUserTransaction method implementation (not shown) can get the User Transaction service directly from the service registry or from an injected field.

123.3.2   Application Bundle Enlistment

An Application Bundle is responsible for enlisting Resource Managers itself. That is, it must enlist Resource Manager it uses with the *Transaction Manager* service. The Transaction Manager service is an implementation of the JTA TransactionManager interface, registered by the JTA Provider.

For example, an Application Bundle can get an XADataSource object from a Data Source Factory service. Such a Data Source object can provide an XAConnection object that then can provide an XAResource object. XAResource objects can then be enlisted with the Transaction Manager service.

For example:

```
TransactionManager    tm;
XADataSource          left;
XADataSource          right;

void acid() throws Exception {
    tm.begin();
```

```
Transaction transaction = tm.getTransaction();
try {
  XAConnection left = this.left.getXAConnection();
  XAConnection right = this.right.getXAConnection();
  transaction.enlistResource( left.getXAResource() );
  transaction.enlistResource( right.getXAResource() );
  doWork(left.getConnection(), right.getConnection());
  tm.commit();
} catch( Throwable t ) {
  tm.rollback();
  throw t; } }
// ...
void setTransactionManager( TransactionManager tm ) { this.tm = tm; }
void setDataSourceFactory( DataSourceFactory dsf ) {
  left = dsf.createXADataSource( getLeftProperties() );
  right = dsf.createXADataSource( getRightProperties() );
}
```

In the previous example, the Transaction Manager service could have been injected with a component model like Declarative Services:

```
<reference interface="javax.transaction.TransactionManager"
  bind="setTransactionManager"/>
<reference name="dsf" interface="org.osgi.service.jdbc.DataSourceFactory"
  bind="setDataSourceFactory"/>
```

For example, it is possible to provide a Data Source service that provides automatic enlistment of the Connection as an XA Resource when one of its getConnection methods is called inside a transaction. The following code contains a Declarative Service component that implement this design. The component references a Transaction Manager service and a Data Source Factory service and provides a Data Source service that proxies an XA Data Source. Applications depend on the Data Source service, assuming that the Data Source service automatically enlists the connections it uses inside a transaction. See for an overview Figure 123.2 on page 324.

Figure 123.2   *Data Source Proxy*

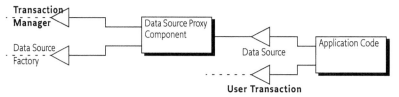

This general purpose Data Source Proxy component can be fully configured by the Configuration Admin service to instantiate this component for each needed database connection. The Declarative Services service properties can be used to select a Data Source Factory for the required database driver (using the target), as well as provide the configuration properties for the creation of an XA Data Source. That is, such a component could be part of a support library.

The code for such an Application component could start like:

```
public class DataSourceProxy implements DataSource {
  Properties             properties= new Properties();
  TransactionManager     tm;
  XADataSource           xads;
```

The activate method is called when the component's dependencies are met, that is, there is a Transaction Manager service as well as a matching Data Source Factory service. In this method, the properties of the component are copied to a Properties object to be compatible with the Data Source Factory factory methods.

```
void activate(ComponentContext c) {
  // copy the properties set by the Config Admin into properties
  ...
}
```

The relevant methods in the Data Source Proxy component are the getConnection methods. The contract for this proxy component is that it enlists the XA Data Connection's XA Resource when it is called inside a transaction. This enlistment is done in the private enlist method.

```
public Connection getConnection() throws SQLException {
  XAConnection connection = xads.getXAConnection();
  return enlist(connection); }

public Connection getConnection(String username, String password)
    throws SQLException {
  XAConnection connection = xads.getXAConnection(username,password);
  return enlist(connection); }
```

The enlist method checks if there currently is a transaction active. If not, it ignores the enlistment, the connection will then not be connection to the transaction. If there is a current transaction, it enlists the corresponding XA Resource.

```
private Connection enlist(XAConnection connection) throws SQLException {
  try {
    Transaction transaction = tm.getTransaction();
    if (transaction != null)
      transaction.enlistResource( connection.getXAResource());
  } catch (Exception e) {
    SQLException sqle=
      new SQLException("Failed to enlist");
    sqle.initCause(e);
    throw sqle;
  }
  return connection.getConnection();
}
```

What remains are a number of boilerplate methods that forward to the XA Data Source or set the dependencies.

```
void setTransactionManager(TransactionManager tm) { this.tm = tm;}
void setDataSourceFactory(DataSourceFactory dsf) throws Exception {
  xads = dsf.createXADataSource(properties);}
public PrintWriter getLogWriter()
  throws SQLException { return xads.getLogWriter(); }

public int getLoginTimeout()
  throws SQLException { return xads.getLoginTimeout();}

public void setLogWriter(PrintWriter out)
  throws SQLException { xads.setLogWriter(out); }

public void setLoginTimeout(int seconds)
  throws SQLException { xads.setLoginTimeout(seconds);}
```

This is a fully coded example, it only lacks the configuration definitions for the Configuration Admin service.

This example Data Source proxy component makes it possible for an Application to depend on a Data Source service. The connections the Application uses from this Data Source are automatically transactional as long as there is a current transaction when the service is called. However, this approach only works when all bundles in the service platform follow the same enlistment strategy because this specification does not provide a common enlistment strategy.

123.3.3 Container Managed Enlistment

The Application Container is responsible for enlisting Resource Managers used by the Application. For example, the Java EE Web and EJB Containers have a well defined model for managing resources within a transaction. If an Application runs inside a Java EE Container then it is the responsibility of the Java EE Container to handle the resource enlistment, the actual rules are beyond this specification.

A Transaction Originator Application bundle running inside a Container which manages any Resource Managers enlistment may use the User Transaction service for transaction demarcation, assuming this service is made available by the Container.

When a Java EE Container runs inside an OSGi Service Platform then it must ensure that any services seen by its contained Applications are the same Transaction services as other bundles on that service platform.

123.4 Resource Managers

Resource Managers perform work that needs to be committed or rolled back in a transaction. To participate in a transaction, a Resource Manager must have an XA Resource enlisted with the current transaction. This specification does not define how OSGi service implementations should be enlisted. This can be done by a Java EE Container, the Applications themselves, or through some other unspecified means.

123.5 The JTA Provider

The JTA Provider is the entity that provides the transaction services:

- *User Transaction* – A service that implements the JTA UserTransaction interface.
- *Transaction Manager* – A service that implements the JTA TransactionManager interface.
- *Transaction Synchronization Registry* – A service that implements the JTA TransactionSynchronizationRegistry interface.

There can be at most one JTA Provider in an OSGi framework and this JTA Provider must ensure that at most one transaction is associated with an application thread at any moment in time. All JTA Provider's transaction services must map to the same underlying JTA implementation. All JTA services should only be registered once.

123.5.1 User Transaction

The User Transaction service may be used by an Application bundle, acting as the Transaction Originator, to demarcate transaction boundaries when the bundle has no need to perform resource enlistement.

123.5.2   Transaction Manager

The Transaction Manager service offers transaction demarcation and further transaction management capabilities, such as Durable and Volatile resource enlistment, to an Application bundle or Application Container.

123.5.3   Transaction Synchronization Service

The Transaction Synchronization Registry service may be used by an Application bundle or a Container. The service provides for the registration of Volatile Resources that implement the JTA Synchronization interface.

For example:

```
private class MyVolatile implements Synchronization {...}
TransactionSynchronizationRegistry tsr = ...; // may be injected
tsr.registerInterposedSynchronization(new MyVolatile());
```

123.6   Life Cycle

123.6.1   JTA Provider

The life cycle of the transaction services and bundles that make up the JTA Provider must be dealt with appropriately such that implementations always ensure the atomic nature of transactions. When the JTA Provider is stopped and its services are unregistered, the JTA Provider must make sure that all active transactions are dealt with appropriately. A JTA Provider can decide to rollback all active transactions or it can decide to keep track of existing active transactions and allow them to continue to their normal conclusion but not allow any new transactions to be created. Any failures caused by executing code outside their life cycle can be dealt with as general failures. From a transactional consistency point of view, stopping the bundle(s) that implement the JTA Provider while transactional work is in-flight, is no different from a failure of the framework hosting the JTA Provider. In either case transaction recovery is initiated by the JTA Provider after it has re-started.

There are well-defined XA semantics between a JTA Provider and Resource Managers in the event of a failure of either at any point in a transaction. If a Resource Manager bundle is stopped while it is involved in-flight transactions then the JTA Provider should exhibit the same external behavior it does in the event of a communication failure with the Resource Manager. For example a JTA Provider will respond to an XAER_RMFAIL response resulting from calling the XAResource commit method by retrying the commit. The mechanism used by the JTA Provider to determine when to retry the commit is a detail of the implementation.

123.6.2   Application Bundles

Applications can act in the role of the Transaction Originator. There is no guarantee that an Application that starts a transaction will always be available to complete the transaction since the client can fail independently of the JTA Provider. A failure of the Application Bundle to complete, in a timely fashion, a transaction it originated must finally result in the JTA Provider rolling back the transaction.

123.6.3   Error Handling

This specification does not define a specific error handling strategy. Exceptions and errors that occur during transaction processing can result in the transaction being marked *rollback-only* by the container or framework in which an Application runs or may be left for the Application to handle. An Application which receives an error or an exception while running under a transaction can choose to mark the transaction rollback-only.

123.7   Security

This specification relies on the security model of JTA.

123.8   References

[1]   *Java Transaction API Specification 1.1*
       http://java.sun.com/javaee/technologies/jta/index.jsp

[2]   *XA+ Specification*
       Version 2, The Open Group, ISBN: 1-85912-046-6

[3]   *Transaction Processing*
       J. Gray and A. Reuter. Morgan Kaufmann Publishers, ISBN 1.55860-190-2

[4]   *Java Platform, Enterprise Edition (Java EE) Specification, v5*
       http://jcp.org/en/jsr/detail?id=244

124 JMX™ Management Model Specification

Version 1.0

124.1 Introduction

The Java Management Extensions (JMX) is the standard API specification for providing a management interface to Java SE and Java EE applications. The JMX specification defines the design patterns, APIs, services and architecture for application management, network management and monitoring in the Java programming language. The need to administer, monitor and manage a container is today recognized as a prerequisite in the enterprise software domain.

While OSGi defines a rich API for controlling all aspects of the framework, this API is not suitable for direct usage in the JMX framework because it was not designed to be remoted. This specification provides an interface adaptation of the existing OSGi framework, which can be used to expose an OSGi Framework manipulation API to any JMX compliant implementation. Interfaces and system semantics for a monitoring system are specified for exposing the underlying artifacts of the OSGi framework such as services and bundles. Additionally, the management of a number of core and compendium services have been standardized in this document.

Finally, a standardized JMX object naming standard is proposed so that management objects are uniformly named across implementations such that any JMX compliant system can find, manipulate and interact with the framework and artifacts that it manages.

This specification requires version 1.2 or later of JMX, which imply the use of Java 5.

124.1.1 Essentials

- *Life Cycle* – Must allow support of full life cycle management of bundles.
- *Batch* – Support batch oriented operations to minimize the influence of network capacity and latency.
- *Compatible* – This specification must work naturally with JMX.
- *Efficient* –Minimize the number of registered objects to not overload the MBean Server and communication channels.
- *Open MBean* – Support the Open MBean layer of JMX instead of using domain specific objects.
- *Core* – Supports all the Framework's operations.
- *Core Services* – Support the framework services if registered. Conditional Permission Admin is not supported.

124.1.2 Entities

- *MBean* – A Managed Bean. The core concept of JMX to manage an entity.
- *MBean Server* – The MBean Server is the access point for registering MBeans.
- *Manager* – The entity that implements the MBeans and registers them with the registered MBean servers.
- *Object Name* – A name for an MBean registered with an MBean Server.
- *Bundle State MBean* – Provides central access to the state of a bundle in a framework. It provides both a general MBean interface as well as an Open Type description.
- *Framework MBean* – Represents the general framework's state and can be used to manage the life cycle of bundles.

- *Service State MBean* – Provides access to the service information in the service registry. It provides both a general MBean interface as well as an Open Type description.
- *Configuration Admin MBean* – Can be used to manipulate a Configuration Admin service.
- *Permission Admin MBean* – Provides access to the Permission Admin service.
- *Provisioning Service MBean* – Provides access to the Provisioning Service.
- *User Admin MBean* – Provides access to the User Admin service.
- *Item* – A helper class to create Open Types. This class is intended to make the Javadoc easier to navigate and keep definitions close together. This is otherwise hard to do with Open Type. This class has no utility for management applications.
- *Open Type* – A JMX metadata standard to describe MBeans.
- *Remote Manager* – The entity accessing a MBean Server remotely.
- *JConsole* – The default Java Remote Manager.

Figure 124.1   *MBeans*

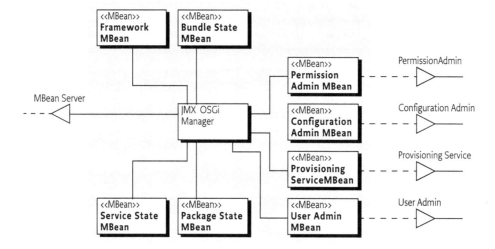

124.1.3   Synopsis

This specification plays a part in both the OSGi framework as well as in a remote manager.

A JMX OSGi manager bundle obtains one or more MBean servers that are registered as services. The JMX OSGi manager then registers all its managed beans: Framework MBean, Bundle State MBean, Package State MBean, and the Service State MBean under their JMX object names. If a number of optional services are registered, then the JMX OSGi bundle must also register a corresponding MBean with the MBean server for each of the services that it can obtain.

A remote manager can access an MBean Server running in a (remote) VM. The remote manager can then discover any MBeans. These MBeans can be manipulated as dynamic types or as specific types as outlined in this specification.

124.2   JMX Overview

JMX is a specification which defines how arbitrary remote communication protocols and mechanisms can be adapted to interact with the underlying management APIs exposed by JMX compliant implementations. JMX is not a remote communication standard, the actual protocols can vary. The JMX architecture is composed of three levels:

- *Instrumentation* – The managed resources of the system are instrumented using *managed beans* (a.k.a. MBeans) which expose their management interfaces through a JMX agent for remote management and monitoring.
- *Agent* – The JMX agent layer is mainly represented by the MBean server. This is the *managed object* server where the MBeans are registered. The JMX agent includes a set of functions for manipulating the registered MBeans, which directly expose and control the underlying resources, and then make them available to remote managers.
- *Remote Manager* – The remote management layer provides the specification for the actual remote communication protocol adapters and defines standard *connectors* which make the JMX agent accessible to remote managers outside of the Java process that hosts the agent.

The JMX Architecture is depicted in Figure 124.2.

Figure 124.2   JMX Architecture

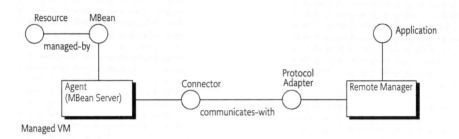

124.2.1   Connectors and Adapters

Connectors are used to connect an agent with a remote JMX-enabled managers. This form of communication involves a connector in the JMX agent and a connector client in the management application. Protocol adapters provide a management view of the JMX agent through a given protocol.

Remote managers that connect to a protocol adapter are usually specific to the given protocol. Remote Managers can be generic consoles (such as JConsole; see *Using JConsole to Monitor Applications* on page 373), or domain-specific monitoring applications. External applications can interact with the MBeans through the use of JMX connectors and protocol adapters.

124.2.2   Object Name

All managed objects in JMX are referenced via JMX *Object Names*. Object Names are strings which can be resolved within the context of a JMX MBean Server in order. An Object Name consists of two parts:

```
ObjectName ::= domain ':' properties
properties ::= property ( ',' property )*
```

To avoid collisions between MBeans supplied by different vendors, a recommended convention is to begin the domain name with the reverse DNS name of the organization that specifies the MBeans, followed by a period and a string whose interpretation is determined by that organization.

MBeans specified by the OSGi Alliance would have domains that start with osgi.

124.2.3   MBeans

Any object can be registered with an MBean Server and manipulated remotely over an *MBean Server Connection*. An MBean Server Connection can represent the a local MBean Server or a remote MBean Server. An MBean is always identified by an *Object Name*. The Object Name identifies a remote MBean uniquely within a specific MBean Server Connection.

Standard manipulations of a remote MBean are done through *attributes* and *operations*, which are similar to properties and methods for Java beans. Not all methods on the implementation class can be used, the registering party must specifically provide access to the methods that can be called remotely. The registrar can define the exposed operations with the following mechanisms:

* *Design Pattern* – Let the registered object implement an *MBean interface* that has the fully qualified name of the implementation class suffixed with MBean. The MBean server will then limit access to attributes and properties defined in the MBean interface. For example, the com.acme.Resource class should implement the com.acme.ResourceMBean interface. The com.acme.ResourceMBean interface would define the properties and operations.
* *Dynamic MBean* – Register a Dynamic MBean, which handles the access to the operations and attributes programmatically. The JMX specification provides the DynamicMBean interface for this purpose. If the MBean registered with an MBean Server implements this interface, then the MBean Server must get the MBean's metadata through the DynamicMBean interface instead of using reflection. Therefore, Dynamic MBeans can provide more rich metadata that describes their operations and attributes.
* *Standard MBean* – Register a Standard MBean. A standard MBean works the same as the previous bullet but does not require the implementation class name to map to the MBean interface name.

Attributes map to properties on the registered MBean interface and operations allow the invocation of an arbitrary method on the remote MBean with arbitrary parameters. The following code example shows how to get a the size property of a remote MBean in this way:

```
void drop( MBeanServerConnection mbs, ObjectName objectName) {
  Integer sizeI = (Integer)
     mbs.getAttribute(objectName, "Size");
  int size = sizeI.intValue();
  if (size > desiredSize) {
    mbs.invoke(objectName,"dropOldest",
      new Integer[] {new Integer(size - desiredSize)},
      new String[] {"int"});
  }
}
```

In release 1.2 the JMX specification introduced the *MBean Server Invocation Handler* to simplify the manipulation of the remote MBeans by creating a *proxy* for an *MBean interface* that implements all the relevant methods. An MBean interface defines the methods and properties for an MBean. The proxy has a reference to an *MBean Server Connection*, it can therefore automate the invocation of the appropriate methods from the MBean interface. Therefore, by using an MBean interface, it is possible to simplify the remote manager:

```
MBeanServer mbs = ...;
CacheControlMBean cacheControl = (CacheControlMBean)
 MbeanServerInvocationHandler.newProxyInstance(
   mbs, objectName, CacheControlMBean.class, false);

int size = cacheControl.getSize();
if (size > desiredSize)
  cacheControl.dropOldest(size - desiredSize);
```

The creation of the proxy is somewhat verbose, but once it is available, the MBean can be accessed like a local object. The proxy is much easier to use and read, and much less error-prone, than accessing the MBean Server method through invoking operations and getting attributes.

The MBean interface can also ensure a certain amount of type safety. The MBean implementation can implement the MBean interface and the remote manager uses the proxy implementing this interface. However, neither is required. The MBean can directly implement the methods without implementing the interface and the remote manager can directly manipulate the attributes and invocations.

The key advantage is therefore the documentation of the management interface. Using an MBean interface, this can be done very concisely and it allows the usage of standard tools for Java source code and Javadoc.

124.2.4 Open Types

The distributed nature of remote management poses a number of problems for exchanging general objects.

- *Versioning* – All participating parties require access to the same version of the object's class.
- *Serialization* – Not all objects are easy to serialize.
- *Size* – Arbitrary objects can transitively link to large amounts of data.
- *Descriptive* – Classes provide little or no support for editing.
- *Limited* – Classes are Java specific, making it harder to interact with non-Java environments.

An alternative is to limit the management types to be exchanged to small, well defined set. Open MBeans limit the used data types to small number of types called the *basic types*. These types are supported by all JMX 1.2 and later implementations. This basic set of types contains:

- *Primitives* – boolean, byte, char, short, int, long, float, double.
- *Primitive Arrays* – boolean[], byte[], char[], short[], int[], long[], float[], double[].
- *Wrappers* – Boolean, Byte, Character, Short, Integer, Long, Float, Double.
- *Scalars* – String, BigDecimal, BigInteger, Date, ObjectName.
- *Complex* – CompositeData, TabularData, and complex arrays.
- *Return* – Void, operation return only.

The Complex types are unique to JMX, they are used to provide access to complex data (like objects) without using classes. The complex types are *self describing*. The metadata associated with these complex types allow a remote manager to discover the structure and automatically construct a (graphic) user interface for these complex objects.

Open MBeans must be Dynamic MBeans when registered. Furthermore, they must provide Open MBean variations of the Info objects that describe the operations and attributes.

124.3 OSGi JMX Management

The OSGi JMX Management model is based on Open MBeans, see *Open Types* on page 333. This specification declares a number of MBeans for the core Framework, some of the core services, and a number of compendium services. Though Open MBeans are based on Dynamic MBeans, this specification uses the traditional MBean interface to define the management interaction patterns. The implementer of this specification must register an implementation of these interfaces as a Dynamic MBean. An implementation should provide the additional Open MBeans Info objects for the operations and attributes.

This specification defines the following Open MBeans:

- *Core Framework* – FrameworkMBean, BundleStateMBean, ServiceStateMBean, and PackageStateMBean.
- *Core Services* – PermissionAdminMBean. The Conditional Permission Admin is not included in this specification.
- *Compendium Services* – ConfigurationAdminMBean, UserAdminMBean, ProvisioningServiceMbean

124.3.1   ## Naming

The MBean interfaces have been named after the service they manage. That is the ConfigurationAdminMBean interface manages the Configuration Admin service, which is modelled with the ConfigurationAdmin interface.

Package names are constructed from taking the corresponding resource package and inserting jmx. after org.osgi. For example

org.osgi.framework	org.osgi.jmx.framework
org.osgi.service.cm	org.osgi.jmx.service.cm

It is not possible to use the MBean interface design pattern because the MBean interfaces are in OSGi packages. The design pattern requires the fully qualified name of the implementation suffixed with MBean to match the MBean interface name. This would require that the implementation class resides in an OSGi package, which would extend these packages.

However, the StandardMBean class allows the association of one of the OSGi MBean interfaces with an arbitrary class.

124.3.2   ## Object Naming

Object Names for OSGi managed MBeans must follow the following structure:

```
object-name   ::= ( core | compendium ) ',version=' version
core          ::= 'osgi.core:' framework-type
compendium    ::= 'osgi.compendium:' service-type
framework-type::= ( 'type=' token ) | service-type
service-type  ::= 'service=' token
```

There are the following additional constraints:

- *Spaces* – Spaces between any of the terminals are not permitted.
- *Version* – The version must be limited to a major and minor version part. The given version must identify the package of the corresponding resource. For example, if the Configuration Admin service is on version 1.3.2.200910101250, then the version in the Object Name must be 1.3.
- *Service* – The service-type should use the package name of the corresponding service. For example, for Configuration Admin this would be service=cm. In Figure 124.3 the object names are demonstrated in JConsole.

Figure 124.3   *JConsole demonstrating the Object Naming hierarchy*

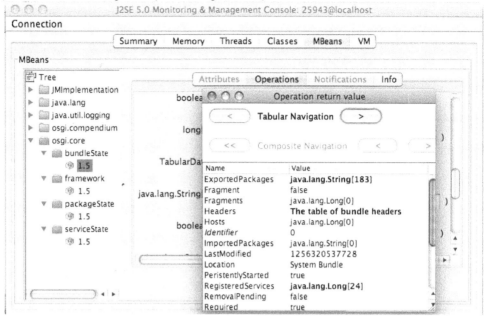

The actual object names are defined in the MBean interfaces. For example, the Object Name for the Configuration Admin MBean is:

```
osgi.compendium:service=cm,version=1.3
```

In this specification, all management interfaces are specified to return opaque Strings or longs rather than Object Names so that the MBean interfaces contain no JMX specific artifacts and can be used with a variety of remote access protocols such as SNMP, etc. Non JMX use of these APIs can use these Strings as their own opaque identifiers without any change to the interfaces themselves.

124.3.3   The MBean Server

An implementation of this specification must find all MBean Servers services that has access to. It should then register all MBeans with each server found in the service registry.

A compliant implementation must register all the framework's MBeans: FrameworkMBean, BundleStateMBean, ServiceStateMBean, and PakageStateMBean. The registration of the compendium services is optional. However, if they are registered they must implement the behavior as defined in this specification.

124.3.4   Registrations

The OSGi MBeans are designed to minimize the notifications. That is, the objects model a command interface to access the required information. Their registration is not intended to signify anything else than the start of the manager bundle and the availability of the underlying resource.

Implementations must always register only one of each of the Framework MBean types (Framework MBean, Service State MBean, Bundle State MBean, and Package State MBean). All other MBean types depend on the registered services they manage. Each service requires its unique MBean. If no corresponding service is present, then no MBean should be registered. Modified events must be ignored. If a manager supports a specific OSGi MBean for a compendium service then it must register an MBean for each instance of that service.

124.4   MBeans

This specification defines MBean interfaces listed in Table 124.1 on page 336 The Object Name specified in this table is broken into a number of lines for readability, however, newlines and whitespace is not allowed in the Object Name.

Table 124.1   MBeans

MBean	Object Name	Description
FrameworkMBean	osgi.core: type=framework, version=1.5	Provides access to bundle life cycle methods of the framework including batch install and update operations. See *FrameworkMBean* on page 352.
BundleStateMBean	osgi.core: type=bundleState version=1.5	Provides detailed access to the state of one bundle and aggregated state of a group of bundles. See *BundleStateMBean* on page 344.
ServiceStateMBean	osgi.core: type=serviceState version=1.5	Provides detailed access to the state of one service and aggregated state of a group of services. *ServiceStateMBean* on page 359
PackageStateMBean	osgi.core: type=packageState, version=1.5	Provides detailed access to the state of one package and aggregated state of a group of packages. See *PackageStateMBean* on page 358.
PermissionAdminMBean	osgi.core: service=permissionadmin, version=1.2	Based on the Permission Admin service. See *PermissionAdminMBean* on page 365.
ConfigurationAdminMBean	osgi.compendium: service=cm, version=1.3	Manages a Configuration Admin service. See *ConfigurationAdminMBean* on page 362.
ProvisioningServiceMBean	osgi.compendium: service=provisioning, version=1.2	Manages a Provisioning Service. See *ProvisioningServiceMBean* on page 366.
UserAdminMBean	osgi.compendium: service=useradmin, version=1.1	Manages a User Admin service. See *UserAdminMBean* on page 367

124.5   Open Types

The specification of the MBeans are using the Composite Data and Tabular Data in several places. These Open Types are typed with Composite Type and Tabular Type. This section documents the different instances of these types that are used in this specification.

124.5.1   BATCH_ACTION_RESULT and BATCH_INSTALL_RESULT

A number of methods in the FrameworkMBean interface operate on multiple bundles. Each of these bundles can succeed or fail. All these operations fail after the first bundle has failed and then return a Composite Data that is typed by the BATCH_ACTION_RESULT_TYPE or BATCH_INSTALL_RESULT_TYPE. The only difference between these results is that the action results identify the bundles by their id and the install result identifies the result by the location.

The BATCH_ACTION_RESULT_TYPE and BATCH_INSTALL_RESULT_TYPE have the following fields:

- BUNDLE_IN_ERROR – (Long or String) The id or location of the bundle that generated the error, if any. For an install result, this field returns a location, for an action result the field is the id of the bundle. This field is absent if the install or action succeeded.
- COMPLETED – (Long[] or String[]) The ids/locations of the bundles that completed successfully before an error was found. For an install result, this field returns a location, for an action result the field is the id of the bundle. The COMPLETED field is not included after a successful operation as it would be redundant information. After a successful operation all of the bundles have been successfully completed.
- ERROR – (String) The error message of the operation and any additional information an implementation wants to convey.
- REMAINING – (Long[] or String[]) The id/locations of the bundles that were not processed because a prior bundle generated an error. For an install result, this field returns a location, for an action result the field is the id of the bundle. If no error occurred, this field is absent.
- SUCCESS – (Boolean) Is true if the operation succeed and false if it failed.

See *BATCH_ACTION_RESULT_TYPE* on page 352 and *BATCH_INSTALL_RESULT_TYPE* on page 352.

124.5.2   BUNDLE

A BUNDLE_TYPE Composite Type consists of the following fields:

- EXPORTED_PACKAGES – (String[]) A list of exported package names.
- FRAGMENT – (Boolean) Is true when the bundle is a fragment.
- FRAGMENTS – (Long[]) The list of ids of hosted fragment bundles.
- HEADERS – (TabularData) The manifest headers in a Tabular Data object typed by HEADERS_TYPE. This table contains the raw data; Any OSGi headers are not parsed in directives and attributes, the table consists of the header name (KEY) and the header value (VALUE).
- HOSTS – (Long[]) If this is a fragment only, in that case it contains the hosts of this fragment.
- IDENTIFIER – (Long) Bundle id.
- IMPORTED_PACKAGES – (String[]) The names of the imported packages.
- LAST_MODIFIED – (Long) The last modified time.
- LOCATION – (String) The location string.
- PERSISTENTLY_STARTED – (Boolean) True if this bundle is persistently started.
- REGISTERED_SERVICES – (Long[]) A list of service ids that are registered by this bundle.
- REMOVAL_PENDING – (Boolean) True if the bundle has its removal pending after update or uninstall as defined by the Package Admin service.
- REQUIRED – (Boolean) True if this bundle is required as defined by the Package Admin service.
- REQUIRED_BUNDLES – (Long[]) A list of bundle ids that are required by this bundle.
- REQUIRING_BUNDLES – (Long[]) A list of bundle ids that this bundle requires.
- START_LEVEL – (Integer) The bundle's start level.
- STATE – (String) The bundle's state. One of:
  - INSTALLED
  - RESOLVED
  - STARTING
  - ACTIVE
  - STOPPING
  - UNINSTALLED

- UNKNOWN
- SERVICES_IN_USE – (Long[]) List of service ids in use by this bundle.
- SYMBOLIC_NAME – (String) The Bundle Symbolic Name.
- VERSION – (String) The version of the bundle.

See for detailed information the *BUNDLE_TYPE* on page 344.

124.5.3   HEADER

A HEADER_TYPE Composite Type provides the manifest headers of a bundle. A HEADER_TYPE is used in the HEADERS_TYPE, which represents the type for a Tabular Data. The type consists of the following items:

- KEY – (String) The manifest header name.
- VALUE – (String) The manifest header value

See *HEADER_TYPE* on page 345.

124.5.4   SERVICE

A SERVICE_TYPE Composite Type provides the properties of a service. A SERVICE_TYPE is used in the SERVICES_TYPE, which represents the type for a Tabular Data. The type consists of the following items:

- BUNDLE_IDENTIFIER – (Long) The identifier of the bundle that owns this service.
- IDENTIFIER – (Long) The service id.
- OBJECT_CLASS – (String[]) The objectClass property of a service
- PROPERTIES – (TabularData) The service properties.
- USING_BUNDLES – (Long[]) The ids of the bundles using this service.

See *SERVICE_TYPE* on page 361.

124.5.5   PACKAGE

A PACKAGE_TYPE Composite Type provides the properties of a service. A PACKAGE_TYPE is used in the PACKAGES_TYPE, which represents the type for a Tabular Data. The type consists of the following items:

- EXPORTING_BUNDLES – (Long) The identifier of the bundle that exports the package.
- IMPORTING_BUNDLES – (Long) The ids of the bundles importing the package.
- NAME – (String) The name of the package.
- REMOVAL_PENDING – (Boolean) True if the package is pending removal because the corresponding bundle is updated or uninstalled.
- VERSION – (String) The version of the package.

See *PACKAGE_TYPE* on page 358.

124.5.6   PROPERTY

A PROPERTY_TYPE Composite Type provides the properties of a service. A PROPERTY_TYPE is used in the PROPERTIES_TYPE, which represents the type for a Tabular Data. The type consists of the following items:

- KEY – (String) The name of the property
- VALUE – (String) The value of the property. Values that contain white space (see Character.isWhitespace()), quote characters (both single quote ("'" \u0027) and double quote ('"' \u0022)), or backslashes ('\' \u005C), must be quoted. A string can be quoted with single or double quotes, any of the previously mentioned characters must be escaped with a backslash ('\' \u005C). Values must be trimmed of whitespace before usage.
- TYPE – (String) The type of the property value. The type must follow the following syntax:

```
type     ::= scalar | vector | array
vector   ::= 'Vector of ' scalar
array    ::= 'Array of ' (scalar | primitive)
scalar   ::=    'String'   | 'BigInteger' | 'BigDecimal'
              | 'Byte'     | 'Character'  | 'Short'
              | 'Integer'  | 'Long'       | 'Float'
              | 'Double'
primitive::=    'byte'     | 'char'       | 'short'
              | 'int'      | 'long'       | 'float'
              | 'double
```

This encoding does not support arrays in vectors or arrays. Arrays and vectors can only contain scalars. Null is not an allowed value. For example, the encoding of a byte array like byte[] {1,2,3,5,7} would look like:

```
type:    'Array of byte'
value:   '1,2,3,4,5'
```

Quoting can be used as follows:

```
type:    Array of String
value:   'abc', 'def', '\'quoted\'', "'quoted'", "\\"
```

The PROPERTY_TYPE and PROPERTIES_TYPE are defined in the JmxConstants class because they are shared between different MBeans, see *PROPERTIES_TYPE* on page 343.

124.6   Item

The MBean interfaces do not only define the Java interface, they also define the Open Types. These types are defined with the Item class in this specification to simplify the definitions; the Item class has no role in a management application. The Item class is used to allow the items used in Composite Types to be encoded in the interface. This is not possible with the standard Open Types because they use exceptions and use parallel arrays. For example, the following code defines a static Open Type without the Item class:

```
static CompositeType HEADER;
static {
  try {
    HEADER = new CompositeType( "HEADER" "This is a header",
    new String[] {"KEY", "VALUE"},
    new String[] {"A key for a header", "A value for a header" },
    new OpenType[] { SimpleType.STRING, SimpleType.STRING } );
  catch(OpenDataException e) {
    ...
  }
}
```

This code can be replaced with the Item class:

```
static Item KEY = new Item("KEY", "A key for header", SimpleType.STRING );
static Item VALUE = new Item("VALUE", "A value for header", SimpleType.STRING );
static CompositeType HEADER = Item.composite( "HEADER", "This is a header",
  KEY, VALUE );
```

The Item class also provides a number of convenience methods to construct the different Open Types. However, the intention is to simplify the specification definitions, not as an aid in management operations.

124.7   Security

Exposing any system remotely opens up a, potentially, devastating security hole in a system. Remote entities should establish their identity and the management system should be able to control the access these entities have over the management system. JMX seamlessly inter operates with the Java Authentication and Authorization Service (JAAS) and Java 2 platform Standard Edition (Java SE) Security Architecture.

The JMX OSGi manager must have access to the services it manages and the operations it invokes. It is likely that this bundle requires All Permission because it needs to invoke operations on the Conditional Permission Admin. It is strongly advised that implementations limit the set of available permissions based on authenticating the remote manager.

124.8   org.osgi.jmx

OSGi JMX Package Version 1.0.

Bundles wishing to use this package must list the package in the Import-Package header of the bundle's manifest. For example:

```
Import-Package: org.osgi.jmx; version="[1.0,2.0)"
```

124.8.1   Summary

- *Item* - The item class enables the definition of open types in the appropriate interfaces.
- *JmxConstants* - Constants for OSGi JMX Specification.

124.8.2   public class Item

The item class enables the definition of open types in the appropriate interfaces. This class contains a number of methods that make it possible to create open types for CompositeType, TabularType, and ArrayType. The normal creation throws a checked exception, making it impossible to use them in a static initializer. The constructors are also not very suitable for static construction. An Item instance describes an item in a Composite Type. It groups the triplet of name, description, and Open Type. These Item instances allows the definitions of an item to stay together.

Concurrency Immutable

124.8.2.1   public Item(String name, String description, OpenType type, String ... restrictions)

name The name of the item.

description The description of the item.

type The Open Type of this item.

restrictions Ignored, contains list of restrictions

☐ Create a triple of name, description, and type. This triplet is used in the creation of a Composite Type.

124.8.2.2   public static ArrayType arrayType(int dim, OpenType elementType)

dim The dimension

elementType The element type

☐ Return a new Array Type.

Returns A new Array Type

124.8.2.3   public static CompositeType compositeType(String name, String description, Item ... items)

name The name of the Tabular Type.

description	The description of the Tabular Type.
items	The items that describe the composite type.

☐ Create a Composite Type

Returns	a new Composite Type
Throws	RuntimeException – when the Tabular Type throws an OpenDataException

124.8.2.4 **public static CompositeType extend(CompositeType parent, String name, String description, Item ... items)**

parent	The parent type, can be null
name	The name of the type
description	The description of the type
items	The items that should be added/override to the parent type

☐ Extend a Composite Type by adding new items. Items can override items in the parent type.

Returns	A new Composite Type that extends the parent type
Throws	RuntimeException – when an OpenDataException is thrown

124.8.2.5 **public static TabularType tabularType(String name, String description, CompositeType rowType, String ... index)**

name	The name of the Tabular Type.
description	The description of the Tabular Type.
rowType	The Open Type for a row
index	The names of the items that form the index .

☐ Create a Tabular Type.

Returns	A new Tabular Type composed from the parameters.
Throws	RuntimeException – when the Tabular Type throws an OpenDataException

124.8.3 public class JmxConstants

Constants for OSGi JMX Specification. Additionally, this class contains a number of utility types that are used in different places in the specification. These are LONG_ARRAY_TYPE, STRING_ARRAY_TYPE, and PROPERTIES_TYPE.

Concurrency	Immutable

124.8.3.1 **public static final String ARRAY_OF = "Array of "**

For an encoded array we need to start with ARRAY_OF. This must be followed by one of the names in SCALAR.

124.8.3.2 **public static final String BIGDECIMAL = "BigDecimal"**

Value for PROPERTY_TYPE value in the case of java.math.BigDecimal

124.8.3.3 **public static final String BIGINTEGER = "BigInteger"**

Value for PROPERTY_TYPE value in the case of java.math.BigInteger

124.8.3.4 **public static final String BOOLEAN = "Boolean"**

Value for PROPERTY_TYPE value in the case of java.lang.Boolean

124.8.3.5   **public static final String BYTE = "Byte"**

Value for PROPERTY_TYPE value in the case of java.lang.Byte

124.8.3.6   **public static final String CHARACTER = "Character"**

Value for PROPERTY_TYPE value in the case of java.lang.Character

124.8.3.7   **public static final String DOUBLE = "Double"**

Value for PROPERTY_TYPE value in the case of java.lang.Double

124.8.3.8   **public static final String FLOAT = "Float"**

Value for PROPERTY_TYPE value in the case of java.lang.Float

124.8.3.9   **public static final String INTEGER = "Integer"**

Value for PROPERTY_TYPE value in the case of java.lang.Integer

124.8.3.10   **public static final String KEY = "Key"**

The key KEY.

124.8.3.11   **public static final Item KEY_ITEM**

The key of a property. The key is KEY and the type is SimpleType.STRING.

124.8.3.12   **public static final String LONG = "Long"**

Value for PROPERTY_TYPE value in the case of java.lang.Long

124.8.3.13   **public static final ArrayType LONG_ARRAY_TYPE**

The MBean Open type for an array of longs

124.8.3.14   **public static final String OSGI_COMPENDIUM = "osgi.compendium"**

The domain name of the selected OSGi compendium MBeans

124.8.3.15   **public static final String OSGI_CORE = "osgi.core"**

The domain name of the core OSGi MBeans

124.8.3.16   **public static final String P_BOOLEAN = "boolean"**

Value for PROPERTY_TYPE value in the case of the boolean primitive type.

124.8.3.17   **public static final String P_BYTE = "byte"**

Value for PROPERTY_TYPE value in the case of the byte primitive type.

124.8.3.18   **public static final String P_CHAR = "char"**

Value for PROPERTY_TYPE value in the case of the char primitive type.

124.8.3.19   **public static final String P_DOUBLE = "double"**

Value for PROPERTY_TYPE value in the case of the double primitive type.

124.8.3.20   **public static final String P_FLOAT = "float"**

Value for PROPERTY_TYPE value in the case of the float primitive type.

124.8.3.21   **public static final String P_INT = "int"**

Value for PROPERTY_TYPE value in the case of the int primitive type.

124.8.3.22   **public static final String P_LONG = "long"**

Value for PROPERTY_TYPE value in the case of the long primitive type.

124.8.3.23   **public static final String P_SHORT = "short"**

Value for PROPERTY_TYPE value in the case of the short primitive type.

124.8.3.24   **public static final TabularType PROPERTIES_TYPE**

Describes a map with properties. The row type is PROPERTY_TYPE. The index is defined to the KEY of the property.

124.8.3.25   **public static final CompositeType PROPERTY_TYPE**

A Composite Type describing a a single property. A property consists of the following items KEY_ITEM, VALUE_ITEM, and TYPE_ITEM.

124.8.3.26   **public static final List<String> SCALAR**

A set of all scalars that can be used in the TYPE property of a PROPERTIES_TYPE. This contains the following names:

- BIGDECIMAL
- BIGINTEGER
- BOOLEAN
- BYTE
- CHARACTER
- DOUBLE
- FLOAT
- INTEGER
- LONG
- SHORT
- STRING
- P_BYTE
- P_CHAR
- P_DOUBLE
- P_FLOAT
- P_INT
- P_LONG
- P_SHORT

124.8.3.27   **public static final String SHORT = "Short"**

Value for PROPERTY_TYPE value in the case of java.lang.Short

124.8.3.28   **public static final String STRING = "String"**

Value for PROPERTY_TYPE value in the case of java.lang.String

124.8.3.29   **public static final ArrayType STRING_ARRAY_TYPE**

The MBean Open type for an array of strings

124.8.3.30   **public static final String TYPE = "Type"**

The key TYPE.

124.8.3.31   **public static final Item TYPE_ITEM**

The type of the property. The key is TYPE and the type is SimpleType.STRING. This string must follow the following syntax: TYPE ::= ('Array of '│'Vector of ')? SCALAR

124.8.3.32   **public static final String VALUE = "Value"**

The key VALUE.

124.8.3.33   **public static final Item VALUE_ITEM**

The value of a property. The key is VALUE and the type is SimpleType.STRING. A value will be encoded by the string given in TYPE. The syntax for this type is given in TYPE_ITEM.

124.8.3.34   **public static final String VECTOR_OF = "Vector of "**

For an encoded vector we need to start with ARRAY_OF. This must be followed by one of the names in SCALAR.

124.9   **org.osgi.jmx.framework**

OSGi JMX Framework Package Version 1.5.

Bundles wishing to use this package must list the package in the Import-Package header of the bundle's manifest. For example:

```
Import-Package: org.osgi.jmx.framework; version="[1.5,2.0)"
```

124.9.1   Summary

- *BundleStateMBean* - This MBean represents the Bundle state of the framework.
- *FrameworkMBean* - The FrameworkMbean provides mechanisms to exert control over the framework.
- *PackageStateMBean* - This MBean provides information about the package state of the framework.
- *ServiceStateMBean* - This MBean represents the Service state of the framework.

124.9.2   public interface BundleStateMBean

This MBean represents the Bundle state of the framework. This MBean also emits events that clients can use to get notified of the changes in the bundle state of the framework.

Concurrency Thread-safe

124.9.2.1   **public static final String ACTIVE = "ACTIVE"**

Constant ACTIVE for the STATE

124.9.2.2   **public static final CompositeType BUNDLE_EVENT_TYPE**

The Composite Type that represents a bundle event. This composite consists of:

- IDENTIFIER
- LOCATION
- SYMBOLIC_NAME
- EVENT

124.9.2.3   **public static final CompositeType BUNDLE_TYPE**

The Composite Type that represents a bundle. This composite consist of:

- EXPORTED_PACKAGES

- FRAGMENT
- FRAGMENTS
- HEADERS
- HOSTS
- IDENTIFIER
- IMPORTED_PACKAGES
- LAST_MODIFIED
- LOCATION
- PERSISTENTLY_STARTED
- REGISTERED_SERVICES
- REMOVAL_PENDING
- REQUIRED
- REQUIRED_BUNDLES
- REQUIRING_BUNDLES
- START_LEVEL
- STATE
- SERVICES_IN_USE
- SYMBOLIC_NAME
- VERSION

It is used by BUNDLES_TYPE.

124.9.2.4   **public static final TabularType BUNDLES_TYPE**

The Tabular Type for a list of bundles. The row type is BUNDLE_TYPE.

124.9.2.5   **public static final String EVENT = "BundleEvent"**

The key EVENT, used in EVENT_ITEM.

124.9.2.6   **public static final Item EVENT_ITEM**

The item containing the event type. The key is EVENT and the type is SimpleType.INTEGER

124.9.2.7   **public static final String EXPORTED_PACKAGES = "ExportedPackages"**

The key EXPORTED_PACKAGES, used in EXPORTED_PACKAGES_ITEM.

124.9.2.8   **public static final Item EXPORTED_PACKAGES_ITEM**

The item containing the exported package names in BUNDLE_TYPE .The key is EXPORTED_PACKAGES and the the type is JmxConstants.STRING_ARRAY_TYPE.

124.9.2.9   **public static final String FRAGMENT = "Fragment"**

The key FRAGMENT, used in FRAGMENT_ITEM.

124.9.2.10   **public static final Item FRAGMENT_ITEM**

The item containing the fragment status in BUNDLE_TYPE. The key is FRAGMENT and the the type is SimpleType.BOOLEAN.

124.9.2.11   **public static final String FRAGMENTS = "Fragments"**

The key FRAGMENTS, used in FRAGMENTS_ITEM.

124.9.2.12   **public static final Item FRAGMENTS_ITEM**

The item containing the list of fragments the bundle is host to in BUNDLE_TYPE. The key is FRAGMENTS and the type is JmxConstants.LONG_ARRAY_TYPE.

124.9.2.13   **public static final CompositeType HEADER_TYPE**

The Composite Type describing an entry in bundle headers. It consists of KEY_ITEM and VALUE_ITEM.

124.9.2.14   **public static final String HEADERS = "Headers"**

The key HEADERS, used in HEADERS_ITEM.

124.9.2.15   **public static final Item HEADERS_ITEM**

The item containing the bundle headers in BUNDLE_TYPE. The key is HEADERS and the the type is HEADERS_TYPE.

124.9.2.16   **public static final TabularType HEADERS_TYPE**

The Tabular Type describing the type of the Tabular Data value that is returned from getHeaders(long) method. The primary item is KEY_ITEM.

124.9.2.17   **public static final String HOSTS = "Hosts"**

The key HOSTS, used in HOSTS_ITEM.

124.9.2.18   **public static final Item HOSTS_ITEM**

The item containing the bundle identifiers representing the hosts in BUNDLE_TYPE. The key is HOSTS and the type is JmxConstants.LONG_ARRAY_TYPE

124.9.2.19   **public static final String IDENTIFIER = "Identifier"**

The key IDENTIFIER, used in IDENTIFIER_ITEM.

124.9.2.20   **public static final Item IDENTIFIER_ITEM**

The item containing the bundle identifier in BUNDLE_TYPE. The key is IDENTIFIER and the the type is SimpleType.LONG.

124.9.2.21   **public static final String IMPORTED_PACKAGES = "ImportedPackages"**

The key IMPORTED_PACKAGES, used in EXPORTED_PACKAGES_ITEM.

124.9.2.22   **public static final Item IMPORTED_PACKAGES_ITEM**

The item containing the imported package names in BUNDLE_TYPE .The key is IMPORTED_PACKAGES and the the type is JmxConstants.STRING_ARRAY_TYPE.

124.9.2.23   **public static final String INSTALLED = "INSTALLED"**

Constant INSTALLED for the STATE

124.9.2.24   **public static final String KEY = "Key"**

The key KEY, used in KEY_ITEM.

124.9.2.25   **public static final Item KEY_ITEM**

The item describing the key of a bundle header entry. The key is KEY and the type is SimpleType.STRING.

124.9.2.26   **public static final String LAST_MODIFIED = "LastModified"**

The key LAST_MODIFIED, used in LAST_MODIFIED_ITEM.

124.9.2.27   **public static final Item LAST_MODIFIED_ITEM**

The item containing the last modified time in the BUNDLE_TYPE. The key is LAST_MODIFIED and the the type is SimpleType.LONG.

124.9.2.28   **public static final String LOCATION = "Location"**

The key LOCATION, used in LOCATION_ITEM.

124.9.2.29   **public static final Item LOCATION_ITEM**

The item containing the bundle location in BUNDLE_TYPE. The key is LOCATION and the the type is SimpleType.STRING.

124.9.2.30   **public static final String OBJECTNAME = "osgi.core:type=bundleState,version=1.5"**

The Object Name for a Bundle State MBean.

124.9.2.31   **public static final String PERSISTENTLY_STARTED = "PeristentlyStarted"**

The key PERSISTENTLY_STARTED, used in PERSISTENTLY_STARTED_ITEM.

124.9.2.32   **public static final Item PERSISTENTLY_STARTED_ITEM**

The item containing the indication of persistently started in BUNDLE_TYPE. The key is PERSISTENTLY_STARTED and the the type is SimpleType.BOOLEAN.

124.9.2.33   **public static final String REGISTERED_SERVICES = "RegisteredServices"**

The key REGISTERED_SERVICES, used in REGISTERED_SERVICES_ITEM.

124.9.2.34   **public static final Item REGISTERED_SERVICES_ITEM**

The item containing the registered services of the bundle in BUNDLE_TYPE. The key is REGISTERED_SERVICES and the the type is JmxConstants.LONG_ARRAY_TYPE.

124.9.2.35   **public static final String REMOVAL_PENDING = "RemovalPending"**

The key REMOVAL_PENDING, used in REMOVAL_PENDING_ITEM.

124.9.2.36   **public static final Item REMOVAL_PENDING_ITEM**

The item containing the indication of removal pending in BUNDLE_TYPE. The key is REMOVAL_PENDING and the type is SimpleType.BOOLEAN.

124.9.2.37   **public static final String REQUIRED = "Required"**

The key REQUIRED, used in REQUIRED_ITEM.

124.9.2.38   **public static final String REQUIRED_BUNDLES = "RequiredBundles"**

The key REQUIRED_BUNDLES, used in REQUIRED_BUNDLES_ITEM.

124.9.2.39   **public static final Item REQUIRED_BUNDLES_ITEM**

The item containing the required bundles in BUNDLE_TYPE. The key is REQUIRED_BUNDLES and the type is JmxConstants.LONG_ARRAY_TYPE

124.9.2.40   **public static final Item REQUIRED_ITEM**

The item containing the required status in BUNDLE_TYPE. The key is REQUIRED and the the type is SimpleType.BOOLEAN.

124.9.2.41   **public static final String REQUIRING_BUNDLES = "RequiringBundles"**

The key REQUIRING_BUNDLES, used in REQUIRING_BUNDLES_ITEM.

124.9.2.42   **public static final Item REQUIRING_BUNDLES_ITEM**

The item containing the bundles requiring this bundle in BUNDLE_TYPE. The key is
REQUIRING_BUNDLES and the type is JmxConstants.LONG_ARRAY_TYPE

124.9.2.43   **public static final String RESOLVED = "RESOLVED"**

Constant RESOLVED for the STATE

124.9.2.44   **public static final String SERVICES_IN_USE = "ServicesInUse"**

The key SERVICES_IN_USE, used in SERVICES_IN_USE_ITEM.

124.9.2.45   **public static final Item SERVICES_IN_USE_ITEM**

The item containing the services in use by this bundle in BUNDLE_TYPE. The key is
SERVICES_IN_USE and the the type is JmxConstants.LONG_ARRAY_TYPE.

124.9.2.46   **public static final String START_LEVEL = "StartLevel"**

The key START_LEVEL, used in START_LEVEL_ITEM.

124.9.2.47   **public static final Item START_LEVEL_ITEM**

The item containing the start level in BUNDLE_TYPE. The key is START_LEVEL and the the type is
SimpleType.INTEGER.

124.9.2.48   **public static final String STARTING = "STARTING"**

Constant STARTING for the STATE

124.9.2.49   **public static final String STATE = "State"**

The key STATE, used in STATE_ITEM.

124.9.2.50   **public static final Item STATE_ITEM**

The item containing the bundle state in BUNDLE_TYPE. The key is STATE and the the type is Simple-
Type.STRING. The returned values must be one of the following strings:

- INSTALLED
- RESOLVED
- STARTING
- ACTIVE
- STOPPING
- UNINSTALLED
- UNKNOWN

124.9.2.51   **public static final String STOPPING = "STOPPING"**

Constant STOPPING for the STATE

124.9.2.52   **public static final String SYMBOLIC_NAME = "SymbolicName"**

The key SYMBOLIC_NAME, used in SYMBOLIC_NAME_ITEM.

124.9.2.53   **public static final Item SYMBOLIC_NAME_ITEM**

The item containing the symbolic name in BUNDLE_TYPE. The key is SYMBOLIC_NAME and the the
type is SimpleType.STRING.

124.9.2.54   **public static final String UNINSTALLED = "UNINSTALLED"**

Constant UNINSTALLED for the STATE

124.9.2.55   **public static final String UNKNOWN = "UNKNOWN"**

Constant UNKNOWN for the STATE

124.9.2.56   **public static final String VALUE = "Value"**

The key VALUE, used in VALUE_ITEM.

124.9.2.57   **public static final Item VALUE_ITEM**

The item describing the value of a bundle header entry. The key is VALUE and the type is Simple-Type.STRING.

124.9.2.58   **public static final String VERSION = "Version"**

The key VERSION, used in VERSION_ITEM.

124.9.2.59   **public static final Item VERSION_ITEM**

The item containing the symbolic name in BUNDLE_TYPE. The key is SYMBOLIC_NAME and the the type is SimpleType.STRING.

124.9.2.60   **public String[] getExportedPackages(long bundleId) throws IOException**

bundleId

    ☐ Answer the list of exported packages for this bundle.

Returns the array of package names, combined with their version in the format ‹packageName;version›

Throws IOException – if the operation fails

IllegalArgumentException – if the bundle indicated does not exist

124.9.2.61   **public long[] getFragments(long bundleId) throws IOException**

bundleId

    ☐ Answer the list of the bundle ids of the fragments associated with this bundle

Returns the array of bundle identifiers

Throws IOException – if the operation fails

IllegalArgumentException – if the bundle indicated does not exist

124.9.2.62   **public TabularData getHeaders(long bundleId) throws IOException**

bundleId the unique identifier of the bundle

    ☐ Answer the headers for the bundle uniquely identified by the bundle id. The Tabular Data is typed by the HEADERS_TYPE.

Returns the table of associated header key and values

Throws IOException – if the operation fails

IllegalArgumentException – if the bundle indicated does not exist

124.9.2.63   **public long[] getHosts(long fragment) throws IOException**

fragment the bundle id of the fragment

    ☐ Answer the list of bundle ids of the bundles which host a fragment

Returns the array of bundle identifiers

Throws IOException – if the operation fails

IllegalArgumentException – if the bundle indicated does not exist

124.9.2.64   **public String[] getImportedPackages(long bundleId) throws IOException**

bundleId the bundle identifier

❑ Answer the array of the packages imported by this bundle

Returns the array of package names, combined with their version in the format ⟨packageName;version⟩

Throws IOException – if the operation fails

IllegalArgumentException – if the bundle indicated does not exist

124.9.2.65   **public long getLastModified(long bundleId) throws IOException**

bundleId the unique identifier of a bundle

❑ Answer the last modified time of a bundle

Returns the last modified time

Throws IOException – if the operation fails

IllegalArgumentException – if the bundle indicated does not exist

124.9.2.66   **public String getLocation(long bundleId) throws IOException**

bundleId the identifier of the bundle

❑ Answer the location of the bundle.

Returns The location string of this bundle

Throws IOException – if the operation fails

IllegalArgumentException – if the bundle indicated does not exist

124.9.2.67   **public long[] getRegisteredServices(long bundleId) throws IOException**

bundleId the bundle identifier

❑ Answer the list of service identifiers representing the services this bundle exports

Returns the list of service identifiers

Throws IOException – if the operation fails

IllegalArgumentException – if the bundle indicated does not exist

124.9.2.68   **public long[] getRequiredBundles(long bundleIdentifier) throws IOException**

bundleIdentifier the bundle identifier

❑ Answer the list of identifiers of the bundles this bundle depends upon

Returns the list of bundle identifiers

Throws IOException – if the operation fails

IllegalArgumentException – if the bundle indicated does not exist

124.9.2.69   **public long[] getRequiringBundles(long bundleIdentifier) throws IOException**

bundleIdentifier the bundle identifier

❑ Answer the list of identifiers of the bundles which require this bundle

Returns the list of bundle identifiers

Throws IOException – if the operation fails

IllegalArgumentException – if the bundle indicated does not exist

124.9.2.70 **public long[] getServicesInUse(long bundleIdentifier) throws IOException**

bundleIdentifier the bundle identifier

❑ Answer the list of service identifiers which refer to the the services this bundle is using

Returns the list of service identifiers

Throws IOException – if the operation fails

IllegalArgumentException – if the bundle indicated does not exist

124.9.2.71 **public int getStartLevel(long bundleId) throws IOException**

bundleId the identifier of the bundle

❑ Answer the start level of the bundle

Returns the start level

Throws IOException – if the operation fails

IllegalArgumentException – if the bundle indicated does not exist

124.9.2.72 **public String getState(long bundleId) throws IOException**

bundleId the identifier of the bundle

❑ Answer the symbolic name of the state of the bundle

Returns the string name of the bundle state

Throws IOException – if the operation fails

IllegalArgumentException – if the bundle indicated does not exist

124.9.2.73 **public String getSymbolicName(long bundleId) throws IOException**

bundleId the identifier of the bundle

❑ Answer the symbolic name of the bundle

Returns the symbolic name

Throws IOException – if the operation fails

IllegalArgumentException – if the bundle indicated does not exist

124.9.2.74 **public String getVersion(long bundleId) throws IOException**

bundleId the identifier of the bundle

❑ Answer the location of the bundle.

Returns The location string of this bundle

Throws IOException – if the operation fails

IllegalArgumentException – if the bundle indicated does not exist

124.9.2.75 **public boolean isFragment(long bundleId) throws IOException**

bundleId the identifier of the bundle

❑ Answer whether the bundle is a fragment or not

Returns true if the bundle is a fragment

Throws IOException – if the operation fails

IllegalArgumentException – if the bundle indicated does not exist

124.9.2.76 **public boolean isPersistentlyStarted(long bundleId) throws IOException**

bundleId the identifier of the bundle

      □ Answer if the bundle is persistently started when its start level is reached

Returns true if the bundle is persistently started

Throws IOException – if the operation fails

      IllegalArgumentException – if the bundle indicated does not exist

124.9.2.77   **public boolean isRemovalPending(long bundleId) throws IOException**

bundleId the identifier of the bundle

      □ Answer true if the bundle is pending removal

Returns true if the bundle is pending removal

Throws IOException – if the operation fails

      IllegalArgumentException – if the bundle indicated does not exist

124.9.2.78   **public boolean isRequired(long bundleId) throws IOException**

bundleId the identifier of the bundle

      □ Answer true if the bundle is required by another bundle

Returns true if the bundle is required by another bundle

Throws IOException – if the operation fails

      IllegalArgumentException – if the bundle indicated does not exist

124.9.2.79   **public TabularData listBundles( ) throws IOException**

      □ Answer the bundle state of the system in tabular form. Each row of the returned table represents a single bundle. The Tabular Data consists of Composite Data that is type by BUNDLES_TYPE.

Returns the tabular representation of the bundle state

Throws IOException –

124.9.3   public interface FrameworkMBean

The FrameworkMbean provides mechanisms to exert control over the framework. For many operations, it provides a batch mechanism to avoid excessive message passing when interacting remotely.

Concurrency Thread-safe

124.9.3.1   **public static final CompositeType BATCH_ACTION_RESULT_TYPE**

The Composite Type for a batch action result. refreshBundle(long) and refreshBundles(long[]). Notice that a batch action result returns uses an id for the BUNDLE_IN_ERROR while the BATCH_INSTALL_RESULT_TYPE uses a location. This Composite Type consists of the following items:

- BUNDLE_IN_ERROR_ID_ITEM
- COMPLETED_ITEM
- ERROR_ITEM
- REMAINING_ID_ITEM
- SUCCESS_ITEM

124.9.3.2   **public static final CompositeType BATCH_INSTALL_RESULT_TYPE**

The Composite Type which represents the result of a batch install operation. It is used in installBundles(String[]) and installBundlesFromURL(String[], String[]). This Composite Type consists of the following items:

- BUNDLE_IN_ERROR_LOCATION_ITEM
- COMPLETED_ITEM

- ERROR_ITEM
- P
- SUCCESS_ITEM

124.9.3.3 **public static final String BUNDLE_IN_ERROR = "BundleInError"**

The key for BUNDLE_IN_ERROR. This key is used with two different items: BUNDLE_IN_ERROR_ID_ITEM and BUNDLE_IN_ERROR_LOCATION_ITEM that each have a different type for this key. It is used in BATCH_ACTION_RESULT_TYPE and BATCH_INSTALL_RESULT_TYPE.

124.9.3.4 **public static final Item BUNDLE_IN_ERROR_ID_ITEM**

The item containing the bundle which caused the error during the batch operation. This item describes the bundle in error as an id. The key is BUNDLE_IN_ERROR and the type is SimpleType.LONG. It is used in BATCH_ACTION_RESULT_TYPE.

See Also for the item that has a location for the bundle in error.

124.9.3.5 **public static final Item BUNDLE_IN_ERROR_LOCATION_ITEM**

The item containing the bundle which caused the error during the batch operation. This item describes the bundle in error as a location. The key is BUNDLE_IN_ERROR and the type is SimpleType.LONG. It is used in BATCH_INSTALL_RESULT_TYPE.

See Also for the item that has a location for the bundle in error.

124.9.3.6 **public static final String COMPLETED = "Completed"**

The key COMPLETED, used in COMPLETED_ITEM.

124.9.3.7 **public static final Item COMPLETED_ITEM**

The item containing the list of bundles completing the batch operation. The key is COMPLETED and the type is JmxConstants.LONG_ARRAY_TYPE. It is used in BATCH_ACTION_RESULT_TYPE and BATCH_INSTALL_RESULT_TYPE.

124.9.3.8 **public static final String ERROR = "Error"**

The key ERROR, used in ERROR_ITEM.

124.9.3.9 **public static final Item ERROR_ITEM**

The item containing the error message of the batch operation. The key is ERROR and the type is SimpleType.STRING. It is used in BATCH_ACTION_RESULT_TYPE and BATCH_INSTALL_RESULT_TYPE.

124.9.3.10 **public static final String OBJECTNAME = "osgi.core:type=framework,version=1.5"**

The fully qualified object name of this mbean.

124.9.3.11 **public static final String REMAINING = "Remaining"**

The key REMAINING, used in REMAINING_ID_ITEM and REMAINING_LOCATION_ITEM.

124.9.3.12 **public static final Item REMAINING_ID_ITEM**

The item containing the list of remaining bundles unprocessed by the failing batch operation. The key is REMAINING and the type is JmxConstants.LONG_ARRAY_TYPE. It is used in BATCH_ACTION_RESULT_TYPE and BATCH_INSTALL_RESULT_TYPE.

124.9.3.13 **public static final Item REMAINING_LOCATION_ITEM**

The item containing the list of remaining bundles unprocessed by the failing batch operation. The key is REMAINING and the type is JmxConstants.STRING_ARRAY_TYPE. It is used in BATCH_ACTION_RESULT_TYPE and BATCH_INSTALL_RESULT_TYPE.

124.9.3.14   **public static final String SUCCESS = "Success"**

The SUCCESS, used in SUCCESS_ITEM.

124.9.3.15   **public static final Item SUCCESS_ITEM**

The item that indicates if this operation was successful. The key is SUCCESS and the type is Simple-Type.BOOLEAN. It is used in BATCH_ACTION_RESULT_TYPE and BATCH_INSTALL_RESULT_TYPE.

124.9.3.16   **public int getFrameworkStartLevel( ) throws IOException**

□   Retrieve the framework start level

Returns   the framework start level

Throws   IOException – if the operation failed

124.9.3.17   **public int getInitialBundleStartLevel( ) throws IOException**

□   Answer the initial start level assigned to a bundle when it is first started

Returns   the start level

Throws   IOException – if the operation failed

124.9.3.18   **public long installBundle(String location) throws IOException**

location   the location of the bundle to install

□   Install the bundle indicated by the bundleLocations

Returns   the bundle id the installed bundle

Throws   IOException – if the operation does not succeed

124.9.3.19   **public long installBundleFromURL(String location, String url) throws IOException**

location   the location to assign to the bundle

url   the URL which will supply the bytes for the bundle

□   Install the bundle indicated by the bundleLocations

Returns   the bundle id the installed bundle

Throws   IOException – if the operation does not succeed

124.9.3.20   **public CompositeData installBundles(String[] locations) throws IOException**

locations   the array of locations of the bundles to install

□   Batch install the bundles indicated by the list of bundleLocationUrls

Returns   the resulting state from executing the operation

Throws   IOException – if the operation does not succeed

See Also   for the precise specification of the CompositeData type representing the returned result.

124.9.3.21   **public CompositeData installBundlesFromURL(String[] locations, String[] urls) throws IOException**

locations   the array of locations to assign to the installed bundles

urls   the array of urls which supply the bundle bytes

□   Batch install the bundles indicated by the list of bundleLocationUrls

Returns   the resulting state from executing the operation

Throws   IOException – if the operation does not succeed

See Also BatchBundleResult for the precise specification of the CompositeData type representing the returned result.

124.9.3.22   **public void refreshBundle(long bundleIdentifier) throws IOException**

bundleIdentifier the bundle identifier

❏ Force the update, replacement or removal of the packages identified by the specified bundle.

Throws IOException – if the operation failed

124.9.3.23   **public void refreshBundles(long[] bundleIdentifiers) throws IOException**

bundleIdentifiers the array of bundle identifiers

❏ Force the update, replacement or removal of the packages identified by the list of bundles.

Throws IOException – if the operation failed

124.9.3.24   **public boolean resolveBundle(long bundleIdentifier) throws IOException**

bundleIdentifier the bundle identifier

❏ Resolve the bundle indicated by the unique symbolic name and version

Returns true if the bundle was resolved, false otherwise

Throws IOException – if the operation does not succeed

IllegalArgumentException – if the bundle indicated does not exist

124.9.3.25   **public boolean resolveBundles(long[] bundleIdentifiers) throws IOException**

bundleIdentifiers = the identifiers of the bundles to resolve

❏ Batch resolve the bundles indicated by the list of bundle identifiers

Returns true if the bundles were resolved, false otherwise

Throws IOException – if the operation does not succeed

124.9.3.26   **public void restartFramework( ) throws IOException**

❏ Restart the framework by updating the system bundle

Throws IOException – if the operation failed

124.9.3.27   **public void setBundleStartLevel(long bundleIdentifier, int newlevel) throws IOException**

bundleIdentifier the bundle identifier

newlevel the new start level for the bundle

❏ Set the start level for the bundle identifier

Throws IOException – if the operation failed

124.9.3.28   **public CompositeData setBundleStartLevels(long[] bundleIdentifiers, int[] newlevels) throws IOException**

bundleIdentifiers the array of bundle identifiers

newlevels the array of new start level for the bundles

❏ Set the start levels for the list of bundles.

Returns the resulting state from executing the operation

Throws IOException – if the operation failed

See Also for the precise specification of the CompositeData type representing the returned result.

124.9.3.29   **public void setFrameworkStartLevel(int newlevel) throws IOException**

newlevel   the new start level

☐   Set the start level for the framework

Throws   IOException – if the operation failed

124.9.3.30   **public void setInitialBundleStartLevel(int newlevel) throws IOException**

newlevel   the new start level

☐   Set the initial start level assigned to a bundle when it is first started

Throws   IOException – if the operation failed

124.9.3.31   **public void shutdownFramework( ) throws IOException**

☐   Shutdown the framework by stopping the system bundle

Throws   IOException – if the operation failed

124.9.3.32   **public void startBundle(long bundleIdentifier) throws IOException**

bundleIdentifier   the bundle identifier

☐   Start the bundle indicated by the bundle identifier

Throws   IOException – if the operation does not succeed

IllegalArgumentException – if the bundle indicated does not exist

124.9.3.33   **public CompositeData startBundles(long[] bundleIdentifiers) throws IOException**

bundleIdentifiers   the array of bundle identifiers

☐   Batch start the bundles indicated by the list of bundle identifier

Returns   the resulting state from executing the operation

Throws   IOException – if the operation does not succeed

See Also   for the precise specification of the CompositeData type representing the returned result.

124.9.3.34   **public void stopBundle(long bundleIdentifier) throws IOException**

bundleIdentifier   the bundle identifier

☐   Stop the bundle indicated by the bundle identifier

Throws   IOException – if the operation does not succeed

IllegalArgumentException – if the bundle indicated does not exist

124.9.3.35   **public CompositeData stopBundles(long[] bundleIdentifiers) throws IOException**

bundleIdentifiers   the array of bundle identifiers

☐   Batch stop the bundles indicated by the list of bundle identifier

Returns   the resulting state from executing the operation

Throws   IOException – if the operation does not succeed

See Also   for the precise specification of the CompositeData type representing the returned result.

124.9.3.36   **public void uninstallBundle(long bundleIdentifier) throws IOException**

bundleIdentifier   the bundle identifier

☐   Uninstall the bundle indicated by the bundle identifier

Throws   IOException – if the operation does not succeed

IllegalArgumentException – if the bundle indicated does not exist

124.9.3.37   **public CompositeData uninstallBundles(long[] bundleIdentifiers) throws IOException**

bundleIdentifiers   the array of bundle identifiers

☐ Batch uninstall the bundles indicated by the list of bundle identifiers

Returns   the resulting state from executing the operation

Throws   IOException – if the operation does not succeed

See Also   for the precise specification of the CompositeData type representing the returned result.

124.9.3.38   **public void updateBundle(long bundleIdentifier) throws IOException**

bundleIdentifier   the bundle identifier

☐ Update the bundle indicated by the bundle identifier

Throws   IOException – if the operation does not succeed

IllegalArgumentException – if the bundle indicated does not exist

124.9.3.39   **public void updateBundleFromURL(long bundleIdentifier, String url) throws IOException**

bundleIdentifier   the bundle identifier

url   the URL to use to update the bundle

☐ Update the bundle identified by the bundle identifier

Throws   IOException – if the operation does not succeed

IllegalArgumentException – if the bundle indicated does not exist

124.9.3.40   **public CompositeData updateBundles(long[] bundleIdentifiers) throws IOException**

bundleIdentifiers   the array of bundle identifiers

☐ Batch update the bundles indicated by the list of bundle identifier.

Returns   the resulting state from executing the operation

Throws   IOException – if the operation does not succeed

See Also   for the precise specification of the CompositeData type representing the returned result.

124.9.3.41   **public CompositeData updateBundlesFromURL(long[] bundleIdentifiers, String[] urls) throws IOException**

bundleIdentifiers   the array of bundle identifiers

urls   the array of URLs to use to update the bundles

☐ Update the bundle uniquely identified by the bundle symbolic name and version using the contents of the supplied urls.

Returns   the resulting state from executing the operation

Throws   IOException – if the operation does not succeed

IllegalArgumentException – if the bundle indicated does not exist

See Also   for the precise specification of the CompositeData type representing the returned result.

124.9.3.42   **public void updateFramework( ) throws IOException**

       □ Update the framework by updating the system bundle.

Throws IOException – if the operation failed

124.9.4   public interface PackageStateMBean

This MBean provides information about the package state of the framework.

Concurrency Thread-safe

124.9.4.1   **public static final String EXPORTING_BUNDLES = "ExportingBundles"**

The key EXPORTING_BUNDLE, used in EXPORTING_BUNDLES_ITEM.

124.9.4.2   **public static final Item EXPORTING_BUNDLES_ITEM**

The item containing the bundle identifier in PACKAGE_TYPE. The key is EXPORTING_BUNDLES and the type is JmxConstants.LONG_ARRAY_TYPE.

124.9.4.3   **public static final String IMPORTING_BUNDLES = "ImportingBundles"**

The key IMPORTING_BUNDLES, used in IMPORTING_BUNDLES_ITEM.

124.9.4.4   **public static final Item IMPORTING_BUNDLES_ITEM**

The item containing the bundle identifier in PACKAGE_TYPE. The key is IMPORTING_BUNDLES and the type is JmxConstants.LONG_ARRAY_TYPE.

124.9.4.5   **public static final String NAME = "Name"**

The key NAME, used in NAME_ITEM.

124.9.4.6   **public static final Item NAME_ITEM**

The item containing the name of the package in PACKAGE_TYPE. The key is NAME and the type is SimpleType.LONG.

124.9.4.7   **public static final String OBJECTNAME = "osgi.core:type=packageState,version=1.5"**

The fully qualified object name of this MBean.

124.9.4.8   **public static final CompositeType PACKAGE_TYPE**

The Composite Type for a CompositeData representing a package. This type consists of:

- EXPORTING_BUNDLES_ITEM
- IMPORTING_BUNDLES_ITEM
- NAME_ITEM
- REMOVAL_PENDING_ITEM
- VERSION_ITEM

The key is defined as NAME and EXPORTING_BUNDLES

124.9.4.9   **public static final TabularType PACKAGES_TYPE**

The Tabular Type used in listPackages(). They key is NAME, VERSION, and EXPORTING_BUNDLES.

124.9.4.10   **public static final String REMOVAL_PENDING = "RemovalPending"**

The name of the item containing the pending removal status of the package in the CompositeData. Used

124.9.4.11   **public static final Item REMOVAL_PENDING_ITEM**

The item representing the removal pending status of a package. The key is REMOVAL_PENDING and the type is SimpleType.BOOLEAN.

124.9.4.12   **public static final String VERSION = "Version"**

The name of the item containing the package version in the CompositeData. Used in VERSION_ITEM.

124.9.4.13   **public static final Item VERSION_ITEM**

The item containing the version of the package in PACKAGE_TYPE. The key is VERSION and the type is SimpleType.STRING.

124.9.4.14   **public long[] getExportingBundles(String packageName, String version) throws IOException**

packageName - the package name

version - the version of the package

□ Answer the identifier of the bundle exporting the package

Returns the bundle identifiers exporting such a package

Throws IOException – if the operation fails

IllegalArgumentException – if the package indicated does not exist

124.9.4.15   **public long[] getImportingBundles(String packageName, String version, long exportingBundle) throws IOException**

packageName The package name

version The version of the package

exportingBundle The exporting bundle for the given package

□ Answer the list of identifiers of the bundles importing the package

Returns the list of bundle identifiers

Throws IOException – if the operation fails

IllegalArgumentException – if the package indicated does not exist

124.9.4.16   **public boolean isRemovalPending(String packageName, String version, long exportingBundle) throws IOException**

packageName The package name

version The version of the package

exportingBundle The bundle exporting the package

□ Answer if this package is exported by a bundle which has been updated or uninstalled

Returns true if this package is being exported by a bundle that has been updated or uninstalled.

Throws IOException – if the operation fails

IllegalArgumentException – if the package indicated does not exist

124.9.4.17   **public TabularData listPackages( ) throws IOException**

□ Answer the package state of the system in tabular form The Tabular Data is typed by PACKAGES_TYPE, which has PACKAGE_TYPE as its Composite Type.

Returns the tabular representation of the package state

Throws IOException – When fails

124.9.5   public interface ServiceStateMBean

This MBean represents the Service state of the framework. This MBean also emits events that clients can use to get notified of the changes in the service state of the framework.

Concurrency Thread-safe

124.9.5.1   **public static final String BUNDLE_IDENTIFIER = "BundleIdentifier"**

The key BUNDLE_IDENTIFIER, used in BUNDLE_IDENTIFIER_ITEM.

124.9.5.2   **public static final Item BUNDLE_IDENTIFIER_ITEM**

The item containing the bundle identifier in SERVICE_TYPE. The key is BUNDLE_IDENTIFIER and the type is SimpleType.LONG .

124.9.5.3   **public static final String BUNDLE_LOCATION = "BundleLocation"**

The key BUNDLE_LOCATION, used in SERVICE_EVENT_TYPE.

124.9.5.4   **public static final Item BUNDLE_LOCATION_ITEM**

The item containing the bundle location in EVENT_ITEM. The key is BUNDLE_LOCATION and the the type is SimpleType.STRING .

124.9.5.5   **public static final String BUNDLE_SYMBOLIC_NAME = "BundleSymbolicName"**

The key BUNDLE_SYMBOLIC_NAME, used in SERVICE_EVENT_TYPE.

124.9.5.6   **public static final Item BUNDLE_SYMBOLIC_NAME_ITEM**

The item containing the symbolic name in EVENT. The key is BUNDLE_SYMBOLIC_NAME and the the type is SimpleType.STRING.

124.9.5.7   **public static final String EVENT = "ServiceEvent"**

The key EVENT, used in EVENT_ITEM.

124.9.5.8   **public static final Item EVENT_ITEM**

The item containing the event type. The key is EVENT and the type is SimpleType.INTEGER

124.9.5.9   **public static final String IDENTIFIER = "Identifier"**

The key IDENTIFIER, used IDENTIFIER_ITEM.

124.9.5.10   **public static final Item IDENTIFIER_ITEM**

The item containing the service identifier in SERVICE_TYPE. The key is IDENTIFIER and the type is SimpleType.LONG.

124.9.5.11   **public static final String OBJECT_CLASS = "objectClass"**

The key OBJECT_CLASS, used OBJECT_CLASS_ITEM.

124.9.5.12   **public static final Item OBJECT_CLASS_ITEM**

The item containing the interfaces of the service in SERVICE_TYPE. The key is OBJECT_CLASS and the type is JmxConstants.STRING_ARRAY_TYPE.

124.9.5.13   **public static final String OBJECTNAME = "osgi.core:type=serviceState,version=1.5"**

The fully qualified object name of this mbean.

124.9.5.14   **public static final String PROPERTIES = "Properties"**

The key PROPERTIES, used in PROPERTIES_ITEM.

124.9.5.15   **public static final Item PROPERTIES_ITEM**

The item containing service properties. The key is PROPERTIES and the type is JmxConstants.PROPERTIES_TYPE.

124.9.5.16   **public static final CompositeType SERVICE_EVENT_TYPE**

The Composite Type that represents a service event. This composite consists of:

- IDENTIFIER
- OBJECT_CLASS
- BUNDLE_LOCATION
- BUNDLE_SYMBOLIC_NAME
- EVENT

124.9.5.17   **public static final CompositeType SERVICE_TYPE**

The Composite Type for a CompositeData representing a service. This type consists of:

- BUNDLE_IDENTIFIER
- IDENTIFIER
- OBJECT_CLASS
- PROPERTIES
- USING_BUNDLES

124.9.5.18   **public static final TabularType SERVICES_TYPE**

The Tabular Type for a Service table. The rows consists of SERVICE_TYPE Composite Data and the index is IDENTIFIER .

124.9.5.19   **public static final String USING_BUNDLES = "UsingBundles"**

The key USING_BUNDLES, used in USING_BUNDLES_ITEM.

124.9.5.20   **public static final Item USING_BUNDLES_ITEM**

The item containing the bundles using the service in SERVICE_TYPE. The key is USING_BUNDLES and the type is JmxConstants.LONG_ARRAY_TYPE.

124.9.5.21   **public long getBundleIdentifier(long serviceId) throws IOException**

serviceId   the identifier of the service

☐ Answer the bundle identifier of the bundle which registered the service

Returns   the identifier for the bundle

Throws   IOException – if the operation fails

IllegalArgumentException – if the service indicated does not exist

124.9.5.22   **public String[] getObjectClass(long serviceId) throws IOException**

serviceId   the identifier of the service

☐ Answer the list of interfaces that this service implements

Returns   the list of interfaces

Throws   IOException – if the operation fails

IllegalArgumentException – if the service indicated does not exist

124.9.5.23   **public TabularData getProperties(long serviceId) throws IOException**

serviceId the identifier of the service

    ☐ Answer the map of properties associated with this service

Returns the table of properties. These include the standard mandatory service.id and objectClass properties as defined in the org.osgi.framework.Constants interface

Throws IOException – if the operation fails

    IllegalArgumentException – if the service indicated does not exist

See Also for the details of the TabularType

124.9.5.24   **public long[] getUsingBundles(long serviceId) throws IOException**

serviceId the identifier of the service

    ☐ Answer the list of identifiers of the bundles that use the service

Returns the list of bundle identifiers

Throws IOException – if the operation fails

    IllegalArgumentException – if the service indicated does not exist

124.9.5.25   **public TabularData listServices( ) throws IOException**

    ☐ Answer the service state of the system in tabular form.

Returns the tabular representation of the service state

Throws IOException – If the operation fails

    IllegalArgumentException – if the service indicated does not exist

See Also for the details of the TabularType

124.10   org.osgi.jmx.service.cm

OSGi JMX CM Package Version 1.3.

Bundles wishing to use this package must list the package in the Import-Package header of the bundle's manifest. For example:

```
Import-Package: org.osgi.jmx.service.cm; version="[1.3,2.0)"
```

124.10.1   **public interface ConfigurationAdminMBean**

This MBean provides the management interface to the OSGi Configuration Administration Service.

Concurrency Thread-safe

124.10.1.1   **public static final String OBJECTNAME = "osgi.compendium:service=cm,version=1.3"**

The object name for this mbean.

124.10.1.2   **public String createFactoryConfiguration(String factoryPid) throws IOException**

factoryPid the persistent id of the factory

    ☐ Create a new configuration instance for the supplied persistent id of the factory, answering the PID of the created configuration

Returns the PID of the created configuration

Throws   IOException – if the operation failed

124.10.1.3   **public String createFactoryConfigurationForLocation(String factoryPid, String location) throws IOException**

factoryPid   the persistent id of the factory

location   the bundle location

❑   Create a factory configuration for the supplied persistent id of the factory and the bundle location bound to bind the created configuration to, answering the PID of the created configuration

Returns   the pid of the created configuation

Throws   IOException – if the operation failed

124.10.1.4   **public void delete(String pid) throws IOException**

pid   the persistent identifier of the configuration

❑   Delete the configuration

Throws   IOException – if the operation fails

124.10.1.5   **public void deleteConfigurations(String filter) throws IOException**

filter   the string representation of the org.osgi.framework.Filter

❑   Delete the configurations matching the filter specification.

Throws   IOException – if the operation failed

IllegalArgumentException – if the filter is invalid

124.10.1.6   **public void deleteForLocation(String pid, String location) throws IOException**

pid   the persistent identifier of the configuration

location   the bundle location

❑   Delete the configuration

Throws   IOException – if the operation fails

124.10.1.7   **public String getBundleLocation(String pid) throws IOException**

pid   the persistent identifier of the configuration

❑   Answer the bundle location the configuration is bound to

Returns   the bundle location

Throws   IOException – if the operation fails

124.10.1.8   **public String[][] getConfigurations(String filter) throws IOException**

filter   the string representation of the org.osgi.framework.Filter

❑   Answer the list of PID/Location pairs of the configurations managed by this service

Returns   the list of configuration PID/Location pairs

Throws   IOException – if the operation failed

IllegalArgumentException – if the filter is invalid

124.10.1.9   **public String getFactoryPid(String pid) throws IOException**

pid   the persistent identifier of the configuration

❑   Answer the factory PID if the configuration is a factory configuration, null otherwise.

Returns   the factory PID

     Throws IOException – if the operation fails

124.10.1.10   **public String getFactoryPidForLocation(String pid, String location) throws IOException**

     pid the persistent identifier of the configuration

     location the bundle location

     ☐ Answer the factory PID if the configuration is a factory configuration, null otherwise.

     Returns the factory PID

     Throws IOException – if the operation fails

124.10.1.11   **public TabularData getProperties(String pid) throws IOException**

     pid the persistent identifier of the configuration

     ☐ Answer the contents of the configuration

     Returns the table of contents

     Throws IOException – if the operation fails

     See Also for the details of the TabularType

124.10.1.12   **public TabularData getPropertiesForLocation(String pid, String location) throws IOException**

     pid the persistent identifier of the configuration

     location the bundle location

     ☐ Answer the contents of the configuration

     Returns the table of contents

     Throws IOException – if the operation fails

     See Also for the details of the TabularType

124.10.1.13   **public void setBundleLocation(String pid, String location) throws IOException**

     pid the persistent identifier of the configuration

     location the bundle location

     ☐ Set the bundle location the configuration is bound to

     Throws IOException – if the operation fails

124.10.1.14   **public void update(String pid, TabularData properties) throws IOException**

     pid the persistent identifier of the configuration

     properties the table of properties

     ☐ Update the configuration with the supplied properties For each property entry, the following row is supplied

     Throws IOException – if the operation fails

     See Also for the details of the TabularType

124.10.1.15   **public void updateForLocation(String pid, String location, TabularData properties) throws IOException**

     pid the persistent identifier of the configuration

     location the bundle location

     properties the table of properties

     ☐ Update the configuration with the supplied properties For each property entry, the following row is supplied

Throws IOException – if the operation fails

See Also for the details of the TabularType

124.11   org.osgi.jmx.service.permissionadmin

OSGi JMX Permission Admin Package Admin Package Version 1.2.

Bundles wishing to use this package must list the package in the Import-Package header of the bundle's manifest. For example:

Import-Package: org.osgi.jmx.service.permission; version="[1.2,2.0)"

124.11.1   public interface PermissionAdminMBean

This MBean represents the OSGi Permission Manager Service

Concurrency Thread-safe

124.11.1.1   public static final String OBJECTNAME = "osgi.core:service=permissionadmin,version=1.2"

Permission Admin MBean object name.

124.11.1.2   public String[] getPermissions(String location) throws IOException

location location identifying the bundle

☐ Answer the list of encoded permissions of the bundle specified by the bundle location

Returns the array of String encoded permissions

Throws IOException – if the operation fails

124.11.1.3   public String[] listDefaultPermissions( ) throws IOException

☐ Answer the list of encoded permissions representing the default permissions assigned to bundle locations that have no assigned permissions

Returns the array of String encoded permissions

Throws IOException – if the operation fails

124.11.1.4   public String[] listLocations( ) throws IOException

☐ Answer the bundle locations that have permissions assigned to them

Returns the bundle locations

Throws IOException – if the operation fails

124.11.1.5   public void setDefaultPermissions(String[] encodedPermissions) throws IOException

encodedPermissions the string encoded permissions

☐ Set the default permissions assigned to bundle locations that have no assigned permissions

Throws IOException – if the operation fails

124.11.1.6   public void setPermissions(String location, String[] encodedPermissions) throws IOException

location the location of the bundle

encodedPermissions the string encoded permissions to set

☐ Set the permissions on the bundle specified by the bundle location

Throws IOException – if the operation fails

124.12 org.osgi.jmx.service.provisioning

OSGi JMX Initial Provisioning Package Version 1.2.

Bundles wishing to use this package must list the package in the Import-Package header of the bundle's manifest. For example:

```
Import-Package: org.osgi.jmx.service.provisioning; version="[1.2,2.0)"
```

124.12.1 public interface ProvisioningServiceMBean

This MBean represents the management interface to the OSGi Initial Provisioning Service

Concurrency Thread-safe

124.12.1.1 public static final String OBJECTNAME = "osgi.compendium:service=provisioning,version=1.2"

Provisioning MBean object name.

124.12.1.2 public void addInformation(TabularData info) throws IOException

info the set of Provisioning Information key/value pairs to add to the Provisioning Information dictionary. Any keys are values that are of an invalid type will be silently ignored.

☐ Adds the key/value pairs contained in info to the Provisioning Information dictionary. This method causes the PROVISIONING_UPDATE_COUNT to be incremented.

Throws IOException – if the operation fails

See Also for details of the Tabular Data

124.12.1.3 public void addInformationFromZip(String zipURL) throws IOException

zipURL the String form of the URL that will be resolved into a ZipInputStream which will be used to add key/value pairs to the Provisioning Information dictionary and install and start bundles. If a ZipEntry does not have an Extra field that corresponds to one of the four defined MIME types (MIME_STRING, MIME_BYTE_ARRAY, MIME_BUNDLE, and MIME_BUNDLE_URL) in will be silently ignored.

☐ Processes the ZipInputStream contents of the provided zipURL and extracts information to add to the Provisioning Information dictionary, as well as, install/update and start bundles. This method causes the PROVISIONING_UPDATE_COUNT to be incremented.

Throws IOException – if an error occurs while processing the ZipInputStream of the URL. No additions will be made to the Provisioning Information dictionary and no bundles must be started or installed.

124.12.1.4 public TabularData listInformation( ) throws IOException

☐ Returns a table representing the Provisioning Information Dictionary.

Returns The table representing the manager dictionary.

Throws IOException – if the operation fails

See Also for details of the Tabular Data

124.12.1.5 public void setInformation(TabularData info) throws IOException

info the new set of Provisioning Information key/value pairs. Any keys are values that are of an invalid type will be silently ignored.

☐ Replaces the Provisioning Information dictionary with the entries of the supplied table. This method causes the PROVISIONING_UPDATE_COUNT to be incremented.

Throws IOException – if the operation fails

See Also for details of the Tabular Data

124.13   org.osgi.jmx.service.useradmin

OSGi JMX User Admin Package Version 1.1.

Bundles wishing to use this package must list the package in the Import-Package header of the bundle's manifest. For example:

```
Import-Package: org.osgi.jmx.service.useradmin; version="[1.1,2.0)"
```

124.13.1   public interface UserAdminMBean

This MBean provides the management interface to the OSGi User Manager Service

Concurrency Thread-safe

124.13.1.1   public static final CompositeType AUTORIZATION_TYPE

The Composite Type for an Authorization object. It consists of the NAME_ITEM and TYPE_ITEM items.

124.13.1.2   public static final String CREDENTIALS = "Credentials"

The CREDENTIALS key, used in CREDENTIALS_ITEM.

124.13.1.3   public static final Item CREDENTIALS_ITEM

The item containing the credentials of a user. The key is CREDENTIALS and the type is JmxConstants.PROPERTIES_TYPE .

124.13.1.4   public static final CompositeType GROUP_TYPE

The Composite Type for a Group. It extends USER_TYPE and adds MEMBERS_ITEM, and REQUIRED_MEMBERS_ITEM. This type extends the USER_TYPE. It adds:

- MEMBERS
- REQUIRED_MEMBERS

124.13.1.5   public static final String MEMBERS = "Members"

The MEMBERS key, used in MEMBERS_ITEM.

124.13.1.6   public static final Item MEMBERS_ITEM

The item containing the members of a group. The key is MEMBERS and the type is JmxConstants.STRING_ARRAY_TYPE. It is used in GROUP_TYPE.

124.13.1.7   public static final String NAME = "Name"

The key NAME, used in NAME_ITEM.

124.13.1.8   public static final Item NAME_ITEM

The item for the user name for an authorization object. The key is NAME and the type is SimpleType.STRING.

124.13.1.9   public static final String OBJECTNAME = "osgi.compendium:service=useradmin,version=1.1"

User Admin MBean object name.

124.13.1.10   **public static final String PROPERTIES = "Properties"**

The PROPERTIES key, used in PROPERTIES_ITEM.

124.13.1.11   **public static final Item PROPERTIES_ITEM**

The item containing the properties of a Role. The key is PROPERTIES and the type is JmxConstants.PROPERTIES_TYPE.

124.13.1.12   **public static final String REQUIRED_MEMBERS = "RequiredMembers"**

The REQUIRED_MEMBERS key, used in REQUIRED_MEMBERS_ITEM.

124.13.1.13   **public static final Item REQUIRED_MEMBERS_ITEM**

The item containing the required members of a group. The key is REQUIRED_MEMBERS and the type is JmxConstants.STRING_ARRAY_TYPE. It is used in GROUP_TYPE .

124.13.1.14   **public static final CompositeType ROLE_TYPE**

The Composite Type for a Role. It contains the following items:

- NAME
- TYPE
- PROPERTIES

124.13.1.15   **public static final String ROLES = "Roles"**

The key ROLES, used in ROLES_ITEM.

124.13.1.16   **public static final Item ROLES_ITEM**

The item containing the roles for this authorization object. The key is ROLES. and the type is JmxConstants.STRING_ARRAY_TYPE.

124.13.1.17   **public static final String TYPE = "Type"**

The Role TYPE key, used in TYPE_ITEM.

124.13.1.18   **public static final Item TYPE_ITEM**

The item containing the type of the roles encapsulated by this authorization object. The key is TYPE and the type is SimpleType.INTEGER.

124.13.1.19   **public static final CompositeType USER_TYPE**

A Composite Type for a User. A User contains its Role description and adds the credentials. It extends ROLE_TYPE and adds CREDENTIALS_ITEM. This type extends the ROLE_TYPE. It adds:

- CREDENTIALS

124.13.1.20   **public void addCredential(String key, byte[] value, String username) throws IOException**

key   The key of the credential to add

value   The value of the credential to add

username   The name of the user that gets the credential.

☐   Add credentials to a user, associated with the supplied key

Throws   IOException – if the operation fails

IllegalArgumentException – if the user name is not a User

124.13.1.21   **public void addCredentialString(String key, String value, String username) throws IOException**

key The key of the credential to add

value The value of the credential to add

username The name of the user that gets the credential.

 ☐ Add credentials to a user, associated with the supplied key

Throws IOException – if the operation fails

    IllegalArgumentException – if the username is not a User

124.13.1.22   **public boolean addMember(String groupname, String rolename) throws IOException**

groupname The group name that receives the rolename as member.

rolename The rolename (User or Group) that must be added.

 ☐ Add a member to the group.

Returns true if the role was added to the group

Throws IOException – if the operation fails

124.13.1.23   **public void addProperty(String key, byte[] value, String rolename) throws IOException**

key The added property key

value The added byte[] property value

rolename The role name that receives the property

 ☐ Add or update a property on a role.

Throws IOException – if the operation fails

124.13.1.24   **public void addPropertyString(String key, String value, String rolename) throws IOException**

key The key of the property to add

value The value of the property to add (String)

rolename The role name

 ☐ Add or update a property on a role

Throws IOException – if the operation fails

124.13.1.25   **public boolean addRequiredMember(String groupname, String rolename) throws IOException**

groupname The group name that is addded

rolename The role that

 ☐ Add a required member to the group

Returns true if the role was added to the group

Throws IOException – if the operation fails

124.13.1.26   **public void createGroup(String name) throws IOException**

name Name of the group to create

 ☐ Create a Group

Throws IOException – if the operation fails

124.13.1.27   **public void createRole(String name) throws IOException**

name of the role to create

 ☐ Create a Role

Throws IOException – if the operation fails

124.13.1.28   **public void createUser(String name) throws IOException**

    name Name of the user to create

      ❑ Create a User

Throws IOException – if the operation fails

124.13.1.29   **public CompositeData getAuthorization(String user) throws IOException**

    user The user name

      ❑ Answer the authorization for the user name. The Composite Data is typed by AUTORIZATION_TYPE.

Returns the Authorization typed by AUTORIZATION_TYPE.

Throws IOException – if the operation fails

      IllegalArgumentException – if the user name is not a User

124.13.1.30   **public TabularData getCredentials(String username) throws IOException**

    username The user name

      ❑ Answer the credentials associated with a user. The returned Tabular Data is typed by JmxConstants.PROPERTIES_TYPE.

Returns the credentials associated with the user, see JmxConstants.PROPERTIES_TYPE

Throws IOException – if the operation fails

      IllegalArgumentException – if the user name is not a User

124.13.1.31   **public CompositeData getGroup(String groupname) throws IOException**

    groupname The group name

      ❑ Answer the Group associated with the group name. The returned Composite Data is typed by GROUP_TYPE

Returns the Group, see GROUP_TYPE

Throws IOException – if the operation fails

      IllegalArgumentException – if the group name is not a Group

124.13.1.32   **public String[] getGroups(String filter) throws IOException**

    filter The filter to apply

      ❑ Answer the list of group names

Returns The list of group names

Throws IOException – if the operation fails

124.13.1.33   **public String[] getImpliedRoles(String username) throws IOException**

    username The name of the user that has the implied roles

      ❑ Answer the list of implied roles for a user

Returns The list of role names

Throws IOException – if the operation fails

      IllegalArgumentException – if the username is not a User

124.13.1.34   **public String[] getMembers(String groupname) throws IOException**

    groupname The name of the group to get the members from

       ❏ Answer the the user names which are members of the group

Returns The list of user names

Throws IOException – if the operation fails

        IllegalArgumentException – if the groupname is not a group

124.13.1.35   **public TabularData getProperties(String rolename) throws IOException**

rolename The name of the role to get properties from

       ❏ Answer the properties associated with a role. The returned Tabular Data is typed by JmxConstants.PROPERTIES_TYPE.

Returns the properties associated with the role, see JmxConstants.PROPERTIES_TYPE

Throws IOException – if the operation fails

124.13.1.36   **public String[] getRequiredMembers(String groupname) throws IOException**

groupname The name of the group to get the required members from

       ❏ Answer the list of user names which are required members of this group

Returns The list of user names

Throws IOException – if the operation fails

        IllegalArgumentException – if the group name is not a group

124.13.1.37   **public CompositeData getRole(String name) throws IOException**

name The name of the role to get the data from

       ❏ Answer the role associated with a name. The returned Composite Data is typed by ROLE_TYPE.

Returns the Role, see ROLE_TYPE

Throws IOException – if the operation fails

124.13.1.38   **public String[] getRoles(String filter) throws IOException**

filter The string representation of the org.osgi.framework.Filter that is used to filter the roles by applying to the properties, if null all roles are returned.

       ❏ Answer the list of role names which match the supplied filter

Returns The list the role names

Throws IOException – if the operation fails

124.13.1.39   **public CompositeData getUser(String username) throws IOException**

username The name of the requested user

       ❏ Answer the User associated with the user name. The returned Composite Data is typed by USER_TYPE.

Returns The User, see USER_TYPE

Throws IOException – if the operation fails

        IllegalArgumentException – if the username is not a User

124.13.1.40   **public String[] getUsers(String filter) throws IOException**

filter The filter to apply

       ❏ Answer the list of user names in the User Admin database

Returns The list of user names

Throws IOException – if the operation fails

124.13.1.41 **public String getUserWithProperty(String key, String value) throws IOException**

key The key to compare

value The value to compare

☐ Answer the user name with the given property key-value pair from the User Admin service database.

Returns The User

Throws IOException – if the operation fails

124.13.1.42 **public String[] listGroups( ) throws IOException**

☐ Answer the list of group names

Returns The list of group names

Throws IOException – if the operation fails

124.13.1.43 **public String[] listRoles( ) throws IOException**

☐ Answer the list of role names in the User Admin database

Returns The list of role names

Throws IOException – if the operation fails

124.13.1.44 **public String[] listUsers( ) throws IOException**

☐ Answer the list of user names in the User Admin database

Returns The list of user names

Throws IOException – if the operation fails

124.13.1.45 **public void removeCredential(String key, String username) throws IOException**

key The key of the credential to remove

username The name of the user for which the credential must be removed

☐ Remove the credential associated with the given user

Throws IOException – if the operation fails

IllegalArgumentException – if the username is not a User

124.13.1.46 **public boolean removeGroup(String name) throws IOException**

name

☐ Remove the Group associated with the name

Returns true if the remove succeeded

Throws IOException – if the operation fails

124.13.1.47 **public boolean removeMember(String groupname, String rolename) throws IOException**

groupname The group name

rolename

☐ Remove a role from the group

Returns true if the role was removed from the group

Throws IOException – if the operation fails

IllegalArgumentException – if the groupname is not a Group

124.13.1.48 **public void removeProperty(String key, String rolename) throws IOException**

key

rolename

  □ Remove a property from a role

 Throws IOException – if the operation fails

124.13.1.49 **public boolean removeRole(String name) throws IOException**

 name

  □ Remove the Role associated with the name

 Returns true if the remove succeeded

 Throws IOException – if the operation fails

124.13.1.50 **public boolean removeUser(String name) throws IOException**

 name

  □ Remove the User associated with the name

 Returns true if the remove succeeded

 Throws IOException – if the operation fails

124.14 References

[1] *OSGi Core Specifications*
   http://www.osgi.org/Specifications/HomePage

[2] *JMX*
   http://en.wikipedia.org/wiki/JMX

[3] *Java Management Extensions (JMX) Technology Overview*
   http://java.sun.com/j2se/1.5.0/docs/guide/jmx/overview/JMXoverviewTOC.html

[4] *JSR 3: Java Management Extensions (JMX) Specification*
   http://www.jcp.org/en/jsr/detailid=3

[5] *JSR 255: Java Management Extensions (JMX) Specification, version 2.0*
   http://www.jcp.org/en/jsr/detailid=255

[6] *JSR 160: JavaTM Management Extensions (JMX) Remote API*
   http://www.jcp.org/en/jsr/detailid=160

[7] *JSR 262: Web Services Connector for Java Management Extensions (JMX) Agents*
   http://www.jcp.org/en/jsr/detailid=262

[8] *JavaTM Management Extensions (JMXTM)API Specification*
   http://java.sun.com/j2se/1.5.0/docs/guide/jmx/spec.html

[9] *Using JConsole to Monitor Applications*
   http://java.sun.com/developer/technicalArticles/J2SE/jconsole.html

125   JDBC™ Service Specification

Version 1.0

125.1   Introduction

The Java Database Connectivity (JDBC) standard provides an API for applications to interact with relational database systems from different vendors. To abstract over concrete database systems and vendor specific characteristics, the JDBC specification provides various classes and Service Provider Interfaces (SPI) that can be used for database interaction. Implementations are database specific and provided by the corresponding driver. This specification defines how OSGi-aware JDBC drivers can provide access to their implementations. Applications can rely on this mechanism to transparently access drivers and to stay independent from driver specific classes. Additionally, this mechanism helps to use common OSGi practices and to avoid class loading problems.

This specification uses a number of packages that are defined in Java SE 1.4 or later.

125.1.1   Essentials

- *Registration* – Provide a mechanism for JDBC driver announcements.
- *Lookup* – Inspect available database drivers and provide means for driver access.
- *Services* – Uses a service model for getting the driver objects.
- *Compatible* – Minimize the amount of work needed to support this specification for existing drivers.

125.1.2   Entities

- *Relational Database Management Systems* – (RDBMS) An external database system.
- *Database Driver* – JDBC-compliant database driver that is delivered in a bundle.
- *Data Source Factory* – Provides one of the different Data Sources that gives access to a database driver.
- *Application* – The application that wants to access a relational database system.

Figure 125.1   *JDBC Class/Service Overview*

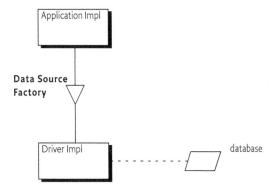

125.1.3   Dependencies

The classes and interfaces used in this specification come from the following packages:

```
javax.sql
```

java.sql

These packages have no associated version. It is assumed they come from the runtime environment. This specification is based on Java SE 1.4 or later.

125.1.4 Synopsis

A JDBC *Database Driver* is the software that maps the JDBC specification to a specific implementation of a relational database. For OSGi, JDBC drivers are delivered as driver bundles. A driver bundle registers a Data Source Factory service when it is ACTIVE. Service properties are used to specify the database driver name, version, etc. The Data Source Factory service provides methods to create DataSource, ConnectionPoolDataSource, XADataSource, or Driver objects. These objects are then used by an application to interact with the relational database system in the standard way.

The application can query the service registry for available Data Source Factory services. It can select particular drivers by filtering on the service properties. This service based model is easy to use with dependency injection frameworks like Blueprint or Declarative Services.

125.2 Database Driver

A Database Driver provides the connection between an *Application* and a particular database. A single OSGi Framework can contain several Database Drivers simultaneously. To make itself available to Applications, a Database Driver must register a Data Source Factory service. Applications must be able to find the appropriate Database Driver. The Database Driver must therefore register the Data Source Factory service with the following service properties:

- OSGI_JDBC_DRIVER_CLASS – (String) The required name of the driver implementation class. This property is the primary key to find a driver's Data Source Factory. It is not required that there is an actual class with this name.
- OSGI_JDBC_DRIVER_NAME – (String) The optional driver name. This property is informational.
- OSGI_JDBC_DRIVER_VERSION – (String) The driver version. The version is not required to be an OSGi version, it should be treated as an opaque string. This version is likely not related to the package of the implementation class or its bundle.

The previous properties are vendor-specific and are meant to further describe the Database Driver to the Application.

Each Data Source Factory service must relate to a single Database Driver. The Database Driver implementation bundle does not necessarily need to be the registrar of the Data Source Factory service. Any bundle can provide the Data Source Factory service and delegate to the appropriate driver specific implementation classes. However, as JDBC driver implementations evolve to include built-in support for OSGi they can provide the Data Source Factory service themselves. This implies that the same driver can be registered multiple times.

125.2.1 Life Cycle

A Data Source Factory service should be registered while its Driver Bundle is in the ACTIVE state or when it has a lazy activation policy and is in the STARTING state.

What happens to the objects created by the Data Source Factory service, and the objects they created, is undefined in this specifications. Database Drivers are not mandated to track the proper life cycle of these objects.

125.2.2   Package Dependencies

A Database Driver must import the javax.sql package. The java.sql package that contains the Driver and SQLException interface is automatically imported because it starts with java.. Both packages are contained in the JRE since Java SE 1.4. These packages are not normally versioned with OSGi version numbers. Bundles using the Data Source Factory must therefore ensure they get the proper imports, which is usually from the JRE. Due to the lack of specified metadata, the deployer is responsible for ensuring this.

125.3   Applications

125.3.1   Selecting the Data Source Factory Service

Applications can query the OSGi service registry for available Database Drivers by getting a list of Data Source Factory services. Normally, the application needs access to specific drivers that match their needed relational database type. The service properties can be used to find the desired Database Driver. This model is well supported by dependency injection frameworks like Blueprint or Declarative Services. However, it can of course also be used with the basic service methods. The following code shows how a Service Tracker can be used to get a Database Driver called ACME DB.

```
Filter filter = context.createFilter(
  "(&(objectClass=" +
    DataSourceFactory.class.getName() +
  ")(" +
    DataSourceFactory.OSGI_JDBC_DRIVER_CLASS + "=com.acme.db.Driver))");

ServiceTracker tracker = new ServiceTracker(context, filter, null);
tracker.open();

DataSourceFactory dsf = (DataSourceFactory) tracker.getService();
```

125.3.2   Using Database Drivers

The Data Source Factory service can be used to obtain instances for the following JDBC related types:

- javax.sql.DataSource
- javax.sql.ConnectionPoolDataSource
- javax.sql.XADataSource
- java.sql.Driver

Which type of Connection provider that is actually required depends on the Application and the use case. For each type, the Data Source Factory service provides a method that returns the corresponding instance. Each method takes a Properties object as a parameter to pass a configuration to the Database Driver implementation. The configuration is driver-specific and can be used to specify the URL for the database and user credentials. Common property names for these configuration properties are also defined in the DataSourceFactory interface.

A Data Source Factory is not required to implement all of the factory methods. If an implementation does not support a particular type then it must throw a SQL Exception. This specification does not provide a mechanism to depend on a Data Source Factory service that implements a particular factory method.

The following code shows how a DataSource object could be created.

```
Properties props = new Properties();
props.put(DataSourceFactory.JDBC_URL, "jdbc:acme:ACME DB");
props.put(DataSourceFactory.JDBC_USER, "foo");
props.put(DataSourceFactory.JDBC_PASSWORD, "secret");
```

```
DataSource dataSource = dsf.createDataSource(props);
```

The DataSourceFactory interface has several static fields that represent common property keys for the Properties instance. General properties are:

- JDBC_DATABASE_NAME
- JDBC_DATASOURCE_NAME
- JDBC_DESCRIPTION
- JDBC_NETWORK_PROTOCOL
- JDBC_PASSWORD
- JDBC_PORT_NUMBER
- JDBC_ROLE_NAME
- JDBC_SERVER_NAME
- JDBC_USER
- JDBC_URL

The following additional property keys are provided for applications that want to create a ConnectionPoolDataSource object or a XAPoolDataSource object:

- JDBC_INITIAL_POOL_SIZE
- JDBC_MAX_IDLE_TIME
- JDBC_MAX_POOL_SIZE
- JDBC_MAX_STATEMENTS
- JDBC_MIN_POOL_SIZE
- JDBC_PROPERTY_CYCLE

Which property keys and values are supported depends on the driver implementation. Drivers can support additional custom configuration properties.

125.4 Security

This specification depends on the JDBC specification for security.

125.5 org.osgi.service.jdbc

JDBC Service Package Version 1.0.

Bundles wishing to use this package must list the package in the Import-Package header of the bundle's manifest. For example:

```
Import-Package: org.osgi.service.jdbc; version="[1.0,2.0)"
```

125.5.1 public interface DataSourceFactory

A factory for JDBC connection factories. There are 3 preferred connection factories for getting JDBC connections: javax.sql.DataSource, javax.sql.ConnectionPoolDataSource, and javax.sql.XADataSource. DataSource providers should implement this interface and register it as an OSGi service with the JDBC driver class name in the OSGI_JDBC_DRIVER_CLASS property.

Concurrency Thread-safe

125.5.1.1 public static final String JDBC_DATABASE_NAME = "databaseName"

The "databaseName" property that DataSource clients should supply a value for when calling create-DataSource(Properties).

125.5.1.2 **public static final String JDBC_DATASOURCE_NAME = "dataSourceName"**

The "dataSourceName" property that DataSource clients should supply a value for when calling createDataSource(Properties).

125.5.1.3 **public static final String JDBC_DESCRIPTION = "description"**

The "description" property that DataSource clients should supply a value for when calling createDataSource(Properties).

125.5.1.4 **public static final String JDBC_INITIAL_POOL_SIZE = "initialPoolSize"**

The "initialPoolSize" property that ConnectionPoolDataSource and XADataSource clients should supply a value for when calling createConnectionPoolDataSource(Properties) or createXADataSource(Properties).

125.5.1.5 **public static final String JDBC_MAX_IDLE_TIME = "maxIdleTime"**

The "maxIdleTime" property that ConnectionPoolDataSource and XADataSource clients should supply a value for when calling createConnectionPoolDataSource(Properties) or createXADataSource(Properties).

125.5.1.6 **public static final String JDBC_MAX_POOL_SIZE = "maxPoolSize"**

The "maxPoolSize" property that ConnectionPoolDataSource and XADataSource clients should supply a value for when calling createConnectionPoolDataSource(Properties) or createXADataSource(Properties).

125.5.1.7 **public static final String JDBC_MAX_STATEMENTS = "maxStatements"**

The "maxStatements" property that ConnectionPoolDataSource and XADataSource clients should supply a value for when calling createConnectionPoolDataSource(Properties) or createXADataSource(Properties).

125.5.1.8 **public static final String JDBC_MIN_POOL_SIZE = "minPoolSize"**

The "minPoolSize" property that ConnectionPoolDataSource and XADataSource clients should supply a value for when calling createConnectionPoolDataSource(Properties) or createXADataSource(Properties).

125.5.1.9 **public static final String JDBC_NETWORK_PROTOCOL = "networkProtocol"**

The "networkProtocol" property that DataSource clients should supply a value for when calling createDataSource(Properties).

125.5.1.10 **public static final String JDBC_PASSWORD = "password"**

The "password" property that DataSource clients should supply a value for when calling createDataSource(Properties).

125.5.1.11 **public static final String JDBC_PORT_NUMBER = "portNumber"**

The "portNumber" property that DataSource clients should supply a value for when calling createDataSource(Properties).

125.5.1.12 **public static final String JDBC_PROPERTY_CYCLE = "propertyCycle"**

The "propertyCycle" property that ConnectionPoolDataSource and XADataSource clients should supply a value for when calling createConnectionPoolDataSource(Properties) or createXADataSource(Properties).

125.5.1.13   **public static final String JDBC_ROLE_NAME = "roleName"**

The "roleName" property that DataSource clients should supply a value for when calling create-DataSource(Properties).

125.5.1.14   **public static final String JDBC_SERVER_NAME = "serverName"**

The "serverName" property that DataSource clients should supply a value for when calling create-DataSource(Properties).

125.5.1.15   **public static final String JDBC_URL = "url"**

The "url" property that DataSource clients should supply a value for when calling createData-Source(Properties).

125.5.1.16   **public static final String JDBC_USER = "user"**

The "user" property that DataSource clients should supply a value for when calling createData-Source(Properties).

125.5.1.17   **public static final String OSGI_JDBC_DRIVER_CLASS = "osgi.jdbc.driver.class"**

Service property used by a JDBC driver to declare the driver class when registering a JDBC Data-SourceFactory service. Clients may filter or test this property to determine if the driver is suitable, or the desired one.

125.5.1.18   **public static final String OSGI_JDBC_DRIVER_NAME = "osgi.jdbc.driver.name"**

Service property used by a JDBC driver to declare the driver name when registering a JDBC Data-SourceFactory service. Clients may filter or test this property to determine if the driver is suitable, or the desired one.

125.5.1.19   **public static final String OSGI_JDBC_DRIVER_VERSION = "osgi.jdbc.driver.version"**

Service property used by a JDBC driver to declare the driver version when registering a JDBC Data-SourceFactory service. Clients may filter or test this property to determine if the driver is suitable, or the desired one.

125.5.1.20   **public ConnectionPoolDataSource createConnectionPoolDataSource(Properties props) throws SQLException**

props   The properties used to configure the ConnectionPoolDataSource. null indicates no properties. If the property cannot be set on the ConnectionPoolDataSource being created then a SQLException must be thrown.

□   Create a new ConnectionPoolDataSource using the given properties.

Returns   A configured ConnectionPoolDataSource.

Throws   SQLException – If the ConnectionPoolDataSource cannot be created.

125.5.1.21   **public DataSource createDataSource(Properties props) throws SQLException**

props   The properties used to configure the DataSource . null indicates no properties. If the property cannot be set on the DataSource being created then a SQLException must be thrown.

□   Create a new DataSource using the given properties.

Returns   A configured DataSource.

Throws   SQLException – If the DataSource cannot be created.

125.5.1.22   **public Driver createDriver(Properties props) throws SQLException**

props   The properties used to configure the Driver. null indicates no properties. If the property cannot be set on the Driver being created then a SQLException must be thrown.

☐   Create a new Driver using the given properties.

Returns   A configured Driver.

Throws   SQLException – If the Driver cannot be created.

125.5.1.23   **public XADataSource createXADataSource(Properties props) throws SQLException**

props   The properties used to configure the XADataSource. null indicates no properties. If the property cannot be set on the XADataSource being created then a SQLException must be thrown.

☐   Create a new XADataSource using the given properties.

Returns   A configured XADataSource.

Throws   SQLException – If the XADataSource cannot be created.

125.6   References

[1]   *OSGi Core Specifications*
      http://www.osgi.org/Specifications/HomePage

[2]   *Java SE 1.4*
      http://java.sun.com/products/archive/j2se-eol.html

126   JNDI Services Specification

Version 1.0

126.1   Introduction

Naming and directory services have long been useful tools in the building of software systems. The ability to use a programming interface to publish and consume objects can provide many benefits to any system. The Java Naming and Directory Interface (JNDI) is a registry technology in Java applications, both in the Java SE and Java EE space. JNDI provides a vendor-neutral set of APIs that allow clients to interact with a naming service from different vendors.

The JNDI as used in the Java SE environment relies on the class loading model provided by the JDK to find providers. By default, it attempts to load the JNDI provider class using the Thread Context Class Loader. In an OSGi environment, this type of Context creation is not desirable since it relies on the JNDI provider classes being visible to the JNDI client, or require it to set the Context Class Loader; in both cases breaking modularity. For modularity reasons, it is important that clients are not required to express a dependency on the implementation of services they use.

This specification will define how JNDI can be utilized from within an OSGi framework. The specification consists of three key parts:

- *OSGi Service Model* – How clients interact with JNDI when running inside an OSGi Framework.
- *JNDI Provider Model* – How JNDI providers can advertise their existence so they are available to OSGi and traditional clients.
- *Traditional Model* – How traditional JNDI applications and providers can continue to work in an OSGi Framework without needing to be rewritten when certain precautions are taken.

126.1.1   Essentials

- *Naming Service* – Provide an integration model for JNDI API clients and providers.
- *Flexible* – Provide a standard mechanism for publishing and locating JNDI providers.
- *Compatibility* – Support the traditional JNDI programming model used by Java SE and Java EE clients.
- *Service Based* – Provide a service model that clients and providers can use to leverage JNDI facilities.
- *Migration* – Provide a mechanism to access OSGi services from a JNDI context.

126.1.2   Entities

- *JNDI Implementation* – The Implementer of the JNDI Context Manager, JNDI Provider Admin, and setter of the JNDI static singletons.
- *JNDI Client* – Any code running within an OSGi bundle that needs to use JNDI.
- *JNDI Context Manager* – A service that allows clients to obtain Contexts via a service.
- *JNDI Provider Admin* – A service that allows the conversion of objects for providers.
- *JNDI Provider* – Provides a Context implementation.
- *Context* – A Context abstracts a namespace. Implementations are provided by JNDI providers and the Contexts are used by JNDI clients. The corresponding interface is javax.naming.Context.
- *Dir Context* – A sub-type of Context that provides mechanisms for examining and updating the attributes of an object in a directory structure, and for performing searches in an hierarchical naming systems like LDAP. The corresponding interface is javax.naming.directory.DirContext.
- *Initial Context Factory* – A factory for creating instances of Context objects. This factory is used to integrate new JNDI Providers. In general, a single Initial Context Factory constructs Context

objects for a single provider implementation. The corresponding interface is
javax.naming.spi.InitialContextFactory.

- *Initial Context Factory Builder* – A factory for InitialContextFactory objects. A single Initial Context Factory Builder can construct InitialContextFactory objects for different types of Contexts. The interface is javax.naming.spi.InitialContextFactoryBuilder.
- *Object Factory* – Used in conversion of objects. The corresponding interface is javax.naming.spi.ObjectFactory.
- *Dir Object Factory* – An Object Factory that takes attribute information for object conversion. The corresponding interface is javax.naming.spi.DirObjectFactory.
- *Object Factory Builder* – A factory for ObjectFactory objects. A single Object Factory Builder can construct ObjectFactory instances for different types of conversions. The corresponding interface is javax.naming.spi.ObjectFactoryBuilder.
- *Reference* – A description of an object that can be turned into an object through an Object Factory. The associated Referenceable interface implemented on an object indicates that it can provide a Reference object.

Figure 126.1   *JNDI Service Specification Service Entities*

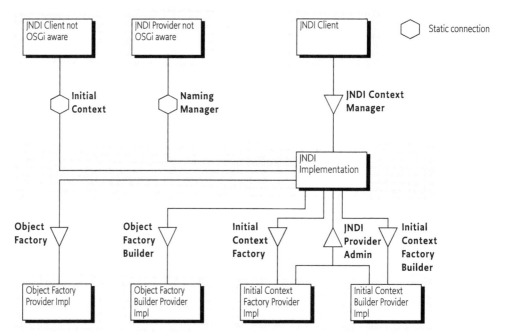

126.1.3   Dependencies

The classes and interfaces used in this specification come from the following packages:

    javax.naming
    javax.naming.spi
    javax.naming.directory

These packages have no associated version. It is assumed they come from the runtime environment. This specification is based on Java SE 1.4 or later.

126.1.4   Synopsis

A client bundle wishing to make use of JNDI in order to access JNDI Providers such as LDAP or DNS in OSGi should not use the Naming Manager but instead use the JNDI Context Manager service. This service can be asked for a Context based on environment properties. The environment properties are based on an optional argument in the newInitialContext method, the Java System properties, and an optional resource in the caller's bundle.

These environment properties can specify an implementation class name for a factory that can create a Context object. If such a class name is specified, then it is searched for in the service registry. If such a service is found, then that service is used to create a new Context, which is subsequently returned. If no class name is specified, the service registry is searched for Initial Context Factory services. These services are tried in ranking order to see if they can create an appropriate Context, the first one that can create a Context is then used.

If no class name is specified, all Initial Context Factory Builder services are tried to see if they can create a Context, the first non-null result is used. If no Context can be found, a No Initial Context Exception is thrown. Otherwise, the JNDI Context Manager service returns an initial Context that uses the just created Context from a provider as the backing service. This initial Context delegates all operations to this backing Context, except operations that use a name that can be interpreted as a URL, that is, the name contains a colon. URL operations are delegated a URL Context that is associated with the used scheme. URL Contexts are found through the general object conversion facility provided by the JNDI Provider Admin service.

The JNDI Provider Admin service provides a general object conversion facility that can be extended with Object Factory and Object Factory Builder services that are traditionally provided through the Naming Manager getObjectInstance method. A specific case for this conversion is the use of Reference objects. Reference objects can be used to store objects persistently in a Context implementation. Reference objects must be converted to their corresponding object when retrieved from a Context.

During the client's use of a Context it is possible that its provider's service is unregistered. In this case the JNDI Context Manager must release the backing Context. If the initial Context is used and no backing Context is available, the JNDI Context Manager must re-create a new Context, if possible. Otherwise a Naming Exception is thrown. If subsequently a proper new backing Context can be created, the initial Context must start operating again.

The JNDI Context Manager service must track the life cycle of a calling bundle and ensure that any returned Context objects are closed and returned objects are properly cleaned up when the bundle is closed or the JNDI Context Manager service is unget.

When the client bundle is stopped, any returned initial Context objects are closed and discarded. If the Initial Context Factory, or Initial Context Factory Builder, service that created the initial Context goes away then the JNDI Context Manager service releases the Context backing the initial Context and attempts to create a replacement Context.

Clients and JNDI Context providers that are unaware of OSGi use static methods to connect to the JRE JNDI implementation. The InitialContext class provides access to a Context from a provider and providers use the static NamingManager methods to do object conversion and find URL Contexts. This traditional model is not aware of OSGi and can therefore only be used reliably if the consequences of this lack of OSGi awareness are managed.

126.2   JNDI Overview

The Java Naming and Directory Interface (JNDI) provides an abstraction for name spaces that is included in Java SE. This section describes the basic concepts of JNDI as provided in Java SE. These concepts are later used in the service model provided by this specification.

126.2.1   Context and Dir Context

The *[2] Java Naming and Directory Interface* (JNDI) defines an API for *namespaces*. These namespaces are abstracted with the Context interface. Namespaces that support *attributes*, such as a namespace as the Lightweight Directory Access Protocol (LDAP), are represented by the DirContext class, which extends the Context class. If applicable, a Context object can be cast to a DirContext object. The distinction is not relevant for this specification, except in places where it is especially mentioned.

The Context interface models a set of name-to-object *bindings* within a namespace. These bindings can be looked-up, created, and updated through the Context interface. The Context interface can be used for federated, flat, or hierarchical namespaces.

126.2.2   Initial Context

Obtaining a Context for a specific namespace, for example DNS, is handled through the InitialContext class. Creating an instance of this class will cause the JRE to find a *backing* Context. The Initial Context is only a facade for the backing Context. The facade context provides URL based lookups.

The backing Context is created by a *JNDI Provider*. How this backing Context is created is an elaborate process using class loading techniques or a provisioning mechanism involving *builders*, see 126.2.6 *Naming Manager Singletons* for more information about the builder provisioning mechanism.

If there is no Initial Context Factory Builder set, the class name of a class implementing the InitialContextFactory interface is specified as a property in the *environment*. The environment is a Hashtable object that is constructed from different sources and then merged with System properties and a resource in the calling bundle, see *Environment* on page 387. In a standard Java SE JNDI, the given class name is then used to construct an InitialContextFactory object and this object is then used to create the backing Context. This process is depicted in Figure 126.2 on page 386.

Figure 126.2   *Initial Context and Backing Context*

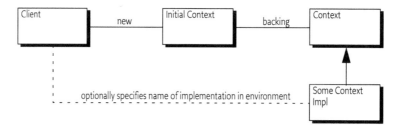

126.2.3   URL Context Factory

The InitialContext class implements the Context interface. It can therefore delegate all the Context interface methods to the backing Context object. However, it provides a special URL lookup behavior for names that are formed like URLs, that is, names that contain a colon (':') character. This behavior is called a *URL lookup*.

URL lookups are not delegated to the backing Context but are instead first tried via a *URL Context* based lookup on the given scheme, like:

    myscheme: foo

For example a lookup using acme:foo/javax.sql.DataSource results in a URL Context being used, rather than the backing Context.

JNDI uses class loading techniques to search for an ObjectFactory class that can be used to create this URL Context. The Naming Manager provides a static method getURLContext for this purpose. If such a URL Context is found, it is used with the requested operation and uses the full URL. If no such URL Context can be found, the backing Context is asked to perform the operation with the given name.

The URL lookup behavior is only done when the backing Context was created by the JNDI implementation in the JRE. If the backing Context had been created through the singleton provisioning mechanism, then no URL lookup is done for names that have a colon. The URL lookup responsibility is then left to the backing Context implementation.

126.2.4　Object and Reference Conversion

The NamingManager class provides a way to create objects from a *description* with the getObjectInstance method. In general, it will iterate over a number of ObjectFactory objects and ask each one of them to provide the requested object. The first non-null result indicates success. These ObjectFactory objects are created from an environment property.

A special case for the description argument in the getObjectInstance method is the *Reference*. A Reference is a description of an object that can be stored persistently. It can be re-created into an actual object through the static getObjectInstance method of the NamingManager class. The Reference object describes the actual ObjectFactory implementing class that must be used to create the object.

This default behavior is completely replaced with the Object Factory Builder singleton by getting the to be used ObjectFactory object directly from the set singleton Object Factory Builder.

126.2.5　Environment

JNDI clients need a way to set the configuration properties to select the proper JNDI Provider. For example, a JNDI Provider might require an identity and a password in order to access the service. This type of configuration is referred to as the *environment* of a Context. The environment is a set of properties. Common property names can be found in [4] *JNDI Standard Property Names*. The set of properties is build from the following sources (in priority order, that is later entries are shadowed by earlier entries):

1　Properties set in the environment Hashtable object given in the constructor argument (if any) of the InitialContext class.
2　Properties from the Java System Properties
3　Properties found in $JAVA_HOME/lib/jndi.properties

There are some special rules around the handling of specific properties.

126.2.6　Naming Manager Singletons

The default behavior of the JRE implementation of JNDI can be extended in a standardized way. The NamingManager class has two static singletons that allow JNDI Providers outside the JRE to provide InitialContextFactory and ObjectFactory objects. These singletons are set with the following static methods on the NamingManager class:

- setObjectFactoryBuilder(ObjectFactoryBuilder) – A hook to provide ObjectFactory objects.
- setInitialContextFactoryBuilder(InitialContextFactoryBuilder) – A hook to provide InitialContextFactory objects. This hook is consulted to create a Context object that will be associated with an InitialContext object the client creates.

These JNDI Provider hooks are *singletons* and must be set *before* any application code creates an InitialContext object or any objects are converted. If these singletons are not set, the JNDI implementation in the JRE will provide a default behavior that is based on searching through classes defined in an environment property.

Both singletons can only be set once. A second attempt to set these singletons results in an Illegal State Exception being thrown.

126.2.7   Built-In JNDI Providers

The Java Runtime Environment (JRE) defines the following default providers:

- *LDAP* – Lightweight Directory Access Protocol (LDAP) service provider
- *COS* – Corba Object Service (COS) naming service provider
- *RMI* – Remote Method Invocation (RMI) Registry service provider
- *DNS* – Domain Name System (DNS) service provider

Although these are the default JNDI Service Providers, the JNDI architecture provides a number of mechanisms to plug-in new types of providers.

126.3   JNDI Context Manager Service

The JNDI Context Manager service allows clients to obtain a Context using the OSGi service model. By obtaining a JNDI Context Manager service, a client can get a Context object so that it can interact with the available JNDI Providers. This service replaces the approach where the creation of a new InitialContext object provided the client with access to an InitialContext object that was backed by a JNDI Provider's Context.

The JNDIContextManager interface defines the following methods for obtaining Context objects:

- newInitialContext() – Obtain a Context object using the default environment properties.
- newInitialContext(Map) – Get a Context object using the default environment properties merged with the given properties.
- newInitialDirContext() – Get a DirContext object using a default environment properties.
- newInitialDirContext(Map) –Get a DirContext object using the default environment properties merged with the given properties.

The JNDI Context Manager service returns Context objects that implement the same behavior as the InitialContext class; the returned Context object does not actually extend the InitialContext class, its only guarantee is that it implements the Context interface.

This Context object is a facade for the context that is created by the JNDI Provider. This JNDI Provider's Context is called the *backing Context*. This is similar to the behavior of the InitialContext class. However, in this specification, the facade can change or loose the backing Context due to the dynamics of the OSGi service platform.

The returned facade must also provides URL lookups, just like an Initial Context. However, the URL Context lookup must be based on Object Factory services with a service property that defines the scheme.

The environment properties used to create the backing Context are constructed in a similar way as the environment properties of the Java SE JNDI, see *Environment and Bundles* on page 388.

The following sections define in detail how a JNDI Provider Context must be created and managed.

126.3.1   Environment and Bundles

The Java SE JNDI looks for a file in $JAVAHOME/lib/jndi.properties, see *Environment* on page 387. A JNDI Implementation must not use this information but it must use a resource in the bundle that uses the JNDI Context Manager service. The order is therefore:

1 Properties set in the environment Hashtable object given in the constructor argument (if any) of the InitialContext class.
2 Properties from the Java System Properties
3 A properties resource from the bundle that uses the service called /jndi.properties.

The following four properties do not overwrite other properties but are merged:

- java.naming.factory.object

- java.naming.factory.state
- java.naming.factory.control
- java.naming.factory.url.pkgs

These property values are considered lists and the ultimate value used by the JNDI Providers is taken by merging the values found in each stage into a single colon separated list. For more information see [4] *JNDI Standard Property Names*.

The environment consists of the merged properties. This environment is then passed to the Initial Context Factory Builder for the creation of an Initial Context Factory.

126.3.2   Context Creation

When a client calls one of the newInitialContext (or newInitialDirContext) methods, the JNDI Context Manager service must construct an object that implements the Context interface based on the environment properties. All factory methods in the InitialContextFactory and InitialContextFactoryBuilder classes take a Hashtable object with the environment as an argument, see *Environment and Bundles* on page 388.

The caller normally provides a specific property in the environment that specifies the class name of a provider class. This property is named:

java.naming.factory.initial

The algorithm to find the provider of the requested Context can differ depending on the presence or absence of the java.naming.factory.initial property in the environment.

In the following sections the cases for presence or absence of the java.naming.factory.initial property are described. Several steps in these algorithm iterate over a set of available services. This iteration must always take place in service *ranking order*. Service ranking order is achieved by sorting on ascending service.ranking service property and then descending service.id property.

Exception handling in the following steps is as follows:

- If an Exception is thrown by an Initial Context Factory Builder service, then this Exception must be logged but further ignored.
- Exceptions thrown by the InitialContextFactory objects when creating a Context must be thrown to the caller.

126.3.2.1   Implementation Class Present in Environment

If the implementation class is specified, a JNDI Provider is searched in the service registry with the following steps, which stop when a backing Context can be created:

1 Find a service in ranking order that has a name matching the given implementation class name as well as the InitialContextFactory class name. The searching must take place through the Bundle Context of the requesting bundle but must not require that the requesting bundle imports the package of the implementation class. If such a matching Initial Context Factory service is found, it must be used to construct the Context object that will act as the backing Context.
2 Get all the Initial Context Factory Builder services. For each such service, in ranking order:
    - Ask the Initial Context Factory Builder service to create a new InitialContextFactory object. If this is null then continue with the next service.
    - Create the Context with the found Initial Context Factory and return it.
3 If no backing Context could be found using these steps, then the JNDI Context Manager service must throw a No Initial Context Exception.

126.3.2.2   No Implementation Class Specified

If the environment does not contain a value for the java.naming.factory.initial property then the following steps must be used to find a backing Context object.

1 Get all the Initial Context Factory Builder services. For each such service, in ranking order, do:

- Ask the Initial Context Factory Builder service to create a new InitialContextFactory object. If this is null, then continue with the next service.
- Create the backing Context object with the found Initial Context Factory service and return it.
2 Get all the Initial Context Factory services. For each such service, in ranking order, do:
  - Ask the Initial Context Factory service to create a new Context object. If this is null then continue with the next service otherwise create a new Context with the created Context as the backing Context.
3 If no Context has been found, an initial Context is returned without any backing. This returned initial Context can then only be used to perform URL based lookups.

126.3.3   Rebinding

A JNDI Provider can be added or removed to the service registry at any time because it is an OSGi service; OSGi services are by their nature dynamic. When a JNDI Provider unregisters an Initial Context Factory that was used to create a backing service then the JNDI Context Manager service must remove the association between any returned Contexts and their now invalid backing Contexts.

The JNDI Context Manager service must try to find a replacement whenever it is accessed and no backing Context is available. However, if no such replacement can be found the called function must result in throwing a No Initial Context Exception.

126.3.4   Life Cycle and Dynamism

When a client has finished with a Context object, then the client must close this Context object by calling the close method. When a Context object is closed, the resources held by the JNDI Implementation on the client's behalf for that Context must all be released. Releasing these resources must not affect other, independent, Context objects returned to the same client.

If a client ungets the JNDI Context Manager service, all the Context objects returned through that service instance must automatically be closed by the JNDI Context Manager. When the JNDI Context Manager service is unregistered, the JNDI Context Manager must automatically close all Contexts held.

For more information about life cycle issues, see also *Life Cycle Mismatch* on page 397.

126.4   JNDI Provider Admin service

JNDI provides a general object conversion service, see *Object and Reference Conversion* on page 387. For this specification, the responsibility of the static method on the NamingManager getObjectInstance is replaced with the JNDI Provider Admin service. The JNDIProviderAdmin interface provides the following methods that can be used to convert a description object to an object:

- getObjectInstance(Object,javax.naming.Name,javax.naming.Context,Map) – Used by Context implementations to convert a description object to another object.
- getObjectInstance(Object,javax.naming.Name,javax.naming.Context,Map, javax.naming.directory.Attributes) – Used by a Dir Context implementations to convert a description object to another object.

In either case, the first argument is an object, called the *description*. JNDI allows a number of different Java types here. When either method is called, the following algorithm is followed to find a matching Object Factory to find/create the requested object. This algorithm is identical for both methods, except that the call that takes the Attributes argument consults Dir Object Factory services first and then Object Factory services while the method without the Attributes parameter only consults Object Factory services.

1 If the description object is an instance of Referenceable, then get the corresponding Reference object and use this as the description object.
2 If the description object is not a Reference object then goto step 5.

3   If a factory class name is specified, the JNDI Provider Admin service uses its own Bundle Context to search for a service registered under the Reference's factory class name. If a matching Object Factory is found then it is used to create the object from the Reference object and the algorithm stops here.

4   If no factory class name is specified, iterate over all the Reference object's StringRefAddrs objects with the address type of URL. For each matching address type, use the value to find a matching URL Context, see *URL Context Provider* on page 393, and use it to recreate the object. See the Naming Manager for details. If an object is created then it is returned and the algorithm stops here.

5   Iterate over the Object Factory Builder services in ranking order. Attempt to use each such service to create an ObjectFactory or DirObjectFactory instance. If this succeeds (non null) then use this ObjectFactory or DirObjectFactory instance to recreate the object. If successful, the algorithm stops here.

6   If the description was a Reference and without a factory class name specified, or if the description was not of type Reference, then attempt to convert the object with each Object Factory service (or Dir Object Factory service for directories) service in ranking order until a non-null value is returned.

7   If no ObjectFactory implementations can be located to resolve the given description object, the description object is returned.

If an Exception occurs during the use of an Object Factory Builder service then this exception should be logged but must be ignored. If, however, an Exception occurs during the calling of a found ObjectFactory or DirObjecFactory object then this Exception must be re-thrown to the caller of the JNDI Provider Admin service.

126.5   JNDI Providers

JNDI Providers can be registered by registering an appropriate service. These services are consulted by the JNDI Implementation for creating a Context as well as creating/finding/converting general objects.

126.5.1   Initial Context Factory Builder Provider

An Initial Context Factory Builder provider is asked to provide an Initial Context Factory when no implementation class is specified or no such implementation can be found. An Initial Context Factory Builder service can be used by containers for other bundles to control the initial Context their applications receive.

An Initial Context Factory Builder provider must register an Initial Context Factory Builder service. The service.ranking property defines the iteration ordering of multiple Initial Context Factory Builder services. Implementations must be careful to correctly provide defaults.

For example, a container could use a thread local variable to mark the stack for a specific application. The implementation of the Initial Context Factory Builder can then detect specific calls from this application. To make the next code example work, an instance must be registered as an Initial Context Factory Builder service.

```
public class Container implements InitialContextFactoryBuilder {
    ThreadLocal<Application> apps;

    void startApp(final Application app) {
        Thread appThread = new Thread(app.getName()) {
            public void run() {
                apps.set(app);
                    app.run();
    }}}
```

```
      public InitialContextFactory
        createInitialContextFactory( Hashtable<?,?> ht ){
        final Application app = apps.get();
        if ( app == null )
          return null;

        return new InitialContextFactory() {
            public Context getInitialContext( Hashtable<?,?> env) {
              return app.getContext(env);
          }
        };
    } }
```

126.5.2 Initial Context Factory Provider

An Initial Context Factory provides Contexts of a specific type. For example, those contexts allow communications with an LDAP server. An Initial Context Factory Provider must register the its Initial Context Factory service under the following names:

- *Implementation Class* – An Initial Context Factory provider must register a service under the name of the implementation class. This allows the JNDI Context Manager to find implementations specified in the environment properties.
- *Initial Context Factory* – As a general Initial Context Factory. If registered as such, it can be consulted for a default Initial Context. Implementations must be careful to only return a Context when the environment properties are appropriate. See *No Implementation Class Specified* on page 389

An Initial Context Factory service can create both DirContext as well as Context objects.

For example, SUN JREs for Java SE provide an implementation of a Context that can answer DNS questions. The name of the implementation class is a well known constant. The following class can be used with Declarative Services to provide a lazy implementation of a DNS Context:

```
public class DNSProvider implements InitialContextFactory {
    public Context createInitialContextFactory( Hashtable<?,?> env ) throws
        NamingException {
        try {
          Class<InitialContextFactory> cf = (Class<InitialContextFactory>)
              l.loadClass("com.sun.jndi.dns.DnsContextFactory" );
          InitialContextFactory icf = cf.newInstance();
          return icf.createInitialContextFactory(env);
        } catch( Throwable t ) {
          return null;
        }
    }
}
```

126.5.3 Object Factory Builder Provider

An Object Factory Builder provider must register an Object Factory Builder service. Such a service can be used to provide ObjectFactory and/or DirObjectFactory objects. An Object Factory Builder service is requested for such an object when no specific converter can be found. This service can be leveraged by bundles that act as a container for other bundles to control the object conversion for their subjects.

126.5.4 Object Factory Provider

An Object Factory provider can participate in the conversion of objects. It must register a service under the following names:

- *Implementation Class* – A service registered under its implementation class can be leveraged by a description that is a Reference object. Such an object can contain the name of the factory class. The implementation class can implement the DirObjectFactory interface or the ObjectFactory interface.
- *Object Factory* – The ObjectFactory interface is necessary to ensure class space consistency.
- *Dir Object Factory* – If the Object Factory provider can accept the additional Attributes argument in the getObjectInstance method of the JNDI Provider Admin service than it must also register as a Dir Object Factory service.

126.5.5   URL Context Provider

A *URL Context Factory* is a special type of an Object Factory service. A URL Context Factory must be registered as an Object Factory service with the following service property:

- osgi.jndi.url.scheme – The URL scheme associated with this URL Context, for example acme. The scheme must not contain the colon (':').

A URL Context is used for URL based operations on an initial Context. For example, a lookup to acme:foo/javax.sql.DataSource must not use the provider based lookup mechanism of the backing Context but instead causes a lookup for the requested URL Context. A URL Context also provides a secondary mechanism for restoring Reference objects.

When an initial Context returned by the JNDI Context Manager service is given a URL based operation, it searches in the service registry for an Object Factory service that is published with the URL scheme property that matches the scheme used from the lookup request.

It then calls the getInstance method on the Object Factory service with the following parameters:

- *Object* – Should be either a String, String[], or null.
- *Name* – must be null
- *Context* – must be null
- *Hashtable* – The environment properties.

Calling the getInstance method must return a Context object. This context is then used to perform the lookup.

The life cycle of the Object Factory used to create the URL Context is tied to the JNDI context that was used to perform the URL based JNDI operation. By the time JNDI context is closed any ObjectFactory objects held to process the URL lookups must be released (unget).

126.5.6   JRE Context Providers

The Java Runtime Environment (JRE) defines a number default naming providers., see *Built-In JNDI Providers* on page 388. These naming providers are not OSGi aware, but are commonly used and are provided by the JRE. These naming providers rely on the NamingManager class for object conversion and finding URL Contexts.

The JRE default providers are made available by the JNDI Implementation. This JNDI Implementation must register a *built-in* Initial Context Factory Builder service that is capable of loading any InitialContextFactory classes of the JRE providers.

When this built-in Initial Context Factory Builder is called to create an InitialContextFactory object it must look in the environment properties that were given as an argument and extract the java.naming.factory.initial property; this property contains the name of the class of a provider. The built-in Initial Context Factory Builder then must use the bootstrap class loader to load the given InitialContextFactory class and creates a new instance with the no arguments constructor and return it. If this fails, it must return null. This mechanism will allow loading of any built-in providers.

This built-in Initial Context Factory Builder service must be registered with no service.ranking property. This will give it the default ranking and allows other providers to override the default.

126.6   OSGi URL Scheme

A URL scheme is available that allows JNDI based applications to access services in the service regis-try, see *Services and State* on page 395 about restrictions on these services. The URL scheme is specified as follows:

```
service   ::= 'osgi:service/' interface  ( '/' filter )?
interface ::= <jndi-service-name> | fqn
```

No spaces are allowed between the terms.

This OSGi URL scheme can be used to perform a lookup of a single matching service using the inter-face name and filter. The URL Context must use the *owning bundle* to perform the service queries. The owning bundle is the bundle that requested the initial Context from the JNDI Context Manager ser-vice or received its Context through the InitialContext class. The returned objects must not be incom-patible with the class space of the owning bundle.

The lookup for a URL with the osgi: scheme and service path returns the service with highest service.ranking and the lowest service.id. This scheme only allows a single service to be found. Mul-tiple services can be obtained with the osgi: scheme and servicelist path:

```
servicelist ::= 'osgi:servicelist/' ( interface ( '/' filter )? )?
```

If this osgi:servicelist scheme is used from a lookup method then a Context object is returned instead of a service object. Calling the listBindings method will produce a NamingEnumeration object that provides Binding objects. A Binding object contains the name, class of the service, and the service object. The bound object is the service object contained in the given Context.

When the Context class list method is called, the Naming Enumeration object provides a NameClassPair object. This NameClassPair object will include the name and class of each service in the Context. The list method can be useful in cases where a client wishes to iterate over the available services without actually getting them. If the service itself is required, then listBindings method should be used.

If multiple services matched the criteria listed in the URL, there would be more than one service available in the Context, and the corresponding Naming Enumeration would contain the same num-ber of services.

If multiple services match, a call to listBindings on this Context would return a list of bindings whose name are a string with the service.id number, for example:

```
1283
```

Thus the following lookup is valid:

```
osgi:servicelist/javax.sql.DataSource/(&(db=mydb)(version=3.1))
```

A service can provide a *JNDI service name* if it provides the following service property:

- osgi.jndi.service.name – An alternative name that the service can be looked up by when the osgi: URL scheme is used.

If a service is published with a JNDI service name then the service matches any URL that has this ser-vice name in the place of interface. For example, if the JNDI service name is foo, then the following URL selects this service:

```
osgi:service/foo
```

Using a JNDI service name that can be interpreted as an interface name must be avoided, if this hap-pens the result is undefined.

A JNDI client can also obtain the Bundle Context of the owning bundle by using the osgi: scheme namespace with the framework/bundleContext name. The following URL must return the Bundle Context of the owning bundle:

```
osgi:framework/bundleContext
```

After the NamingEnumeration object has been used it must be closed by the client. Implementations must then unget any gotten services or perform other cleanup.

126.6.1   Service Proxies

The OSGi URL Context handles the complexities by hiding the dynamic nature of OSGi. The OSGi URL Context must handle the dynamics by *proxying* the service objects. This proxy must implement the interface given in the URL. If the JNDI service name instead of a class name is used, then all interfaces under which the service is registered must be implemented. If an interface is not compatible with the owning bundle's class space then it must not be implemented on the proxy, it must then be ignored. If this results in no implemented interfaces then an Illegal Argument Exception must be thrown.

Interfaces can always be proxied but classes are much harder. For this reason, an implementation is free to throw an Illegal Argument Exception when a class is used in the URL or in one of the registration names.

Getting the actual service object can be delayed until the proxy is actually used to call a method. If a method is called and the actual service has been unregistered, then the OSGi URL Context must attempt to rebind it to another service that matches the criteria given in the URL the next time it is called. When no alternative service is available, a Service Exception with the UNREGISTERED type code must be thrown. Services obtained with the osgi: URL scheme must therefore be stateless because the rebinding to alternative services is not visible to the caller; there are no listeners defined for this rebinding, see *Services and State* on page 395.

If the reference was looked up using osgi:servicelist then proxies must still be used, however, these proxies must not rebind when their underlying service is unregistered. Instead, they must throw a Service Exception with the UNREGISTERED type whenever the proxy is used and the proxied service is no longer available.

126.6.2   Services and State

A service obtained through a URL Context lookup is proxied. During the usage of this service, the JNDI Implementation can be forced to transparently rebind this service to another instance. The JNDI specification is largely intended for portability. For this reason, it has no mechanism architected to receive notifications about this rebinding. The client code is therefore unable to handle the dynamics.

The consequence of this model is that stateful services require extra care because applications cannot rely on the fact that they always communicate with the same service. Virtually all OSGi specified services have state.

126.7   Traditional Client Model

A JNDI Implementation must at startup register the InitialContextFactoryBuilder object and the ObjectFactoryBuilder object with the NamingManager class. As described in *JNDI Overview* on page 385, the JNDI code in the JRE will then delegate all Context related requests to the JNDI Implementation. Setting these singletons allows code that is not aware of the OSGi service platform to use Context implementations from JNDI Providers registered with the OSGi service registry and that are managed as bundles. The JNDI Implementation therefore acts as a broker to the service registry for OSGi unaware code.

This brokering role can only be played when the JNDI Implementation can set the singletons as specified in *Naming Manager Singletons* on page 387. If the JNDI Implementation cannot set these singletons then it should log an error with the Log Service, if available. It can then not perform the following sections.

126.7.1   New Initial Context

The client typically requests a Context using the following code:

```
Hashtable env = new Hashtable();
env.put(Context.INITIAL_CONTEXT_FACTORY, "com.sun.jndi.ldap.LdapCtxFactory");
InitialContext ctx = new InitialContext(env);
```

The created InitialContext object is a facade for the real Context that is requested by the caller. It provides the bootstrapping mechanism for JNDI Provider plugability. In order to obtain the provider's Context, the InitialContext class makes a call to the static getContext method on the NamingManager class. The JNDI code in the JRE then delegates any request for an initial Context object to the JNDI Implementation through the registered InitialContextFactoryBuilder singleton. The JNDI Implementation then determines the Bundle Context of the caller as described in *Caller's Bundle Context* on page 396. If no such Bundle Context can be found, a No Initial Context Exception is thrown to the caller. This Bundle Context must be from an ACTIVE bundle.

This Bundle Context is then used to get the JNDI Context Manager service. This service is then used as described in *Context Creation* on page 389 to get an initial Context. This initial Context is then used in the InitialContext object as the *default initial context*. In this specification this is normally called the backing context. An InitialContext object constructed through an Initial Context Factory Builder will not use the URL lookup mechanism, it must delegate all operations to the its backing context. A Context obtained through the JNDI Context Manager provides the URL lookup behavior instead.

126.7.2   Static Conversion

JNDI provides a general object conversion facility that is used by the URL Context and the process of restoring an object from a Reference object, see *Object and Reference Conversion* on page 387. A JNDI Implementation must take over this conversion by setting the static Object Factory Builder singleton, see *Naming Manager Singletons* on page 387. Non-OSGi aware Context implementations will use the NamingManager static getObjectInstance method for object conversion. This method then delegates to the set singleton Object Factory Builder to obtain an ObjectFactory object that understands how to convert the given description to an object. The JNDI Implementation must return an Object Factory that understands the OSGi service registry. If the getObjectInstance method is called on this object it must use the same rules as defined for the JNDI Provider Admin service getObjectInstance(Object, javax.naming.Name,javax.naming.Context,Map) method, see *JNDI Provider Admin service* on page 390. The Bundle Context that must be used with respect to this service is the caller's Bundle Context, see *Caller's Bundle Context* on page 396. If the Bundle Context is not found, the description object must be returned. The calling bundle must not be required to import the org.osgi.service.jndi package.

126.7.3   Caller's Bundle Context

The following mechanisms are used to determine the callers Bundle Context:

1   Look in the JNDI environment properties for a property called

```
osgi.service.jndi.bundleContext
```

If a value for this property exists then use it as the Bundle Context. If the Bundle Context has been found stop.
2   Obtain the Thread Context Class Loader; if it, or an ancestor class loader, implements the BundleReference interface, call its getBundle method to get the client's Bundle; then call getBundleContext on the Bundle object to get the client's Bundle Context. If the Bundle Context has been found stop.
3   Walk the call stack until the invoker is found. The invoker can be the caller of the InitialContext class constructor or the NamingManager or DirectoryManager getObjectInstance methods.
  •   Get the class loader of the caller and see if it, or an ancestor, implements the BundleReference interface.

- If a Class Loader implementing the BundleReference interface is found call the getBundle method to get the clients Bundle; then call the getBundleContext method on the Bundle to get the clients Bundle Context.
- If the Bundle Context has been found stop, else continue with the next stack frame.

126.7.4 Life Cycle Mismatch

The use of static access to the JNDI mechanisms, NamingManager and InitialContext class methods, in the traditional client programming model produces several problems with regard to the OSGi life cycle. The primary problem being that there is no dependency management in place when static methods are used. These problems do not exist for the JNDI Context Manager service. Therefore, OSGi applications are strongly encouraged to use the JNDI Context Manager service.

The traditional programming model approach relies on two JVM singletons in the Naming Manager, see *Naming Manager Singletons* on page 387. The JNDI Implementation bundle must set both singletons before it registers its JNDI Context Manager service and JNDI Provider Admin service. However, in OSGi there is no defined start ordering, primarily because bundles can be updated at any moment in time and will at such time not be available to provide their function anyway. For this reason, OSGi bundles express their dependencies with services.

The lack of start ordering means that a bundle could create an InitialContext object before the JNDI Implementation has had the chance to set the static Initial Context Factory Builder singleton. This means that the JNDI implementation inside the JRE will provide its default behavior and likely have to throw an exception. A similar exception is thrown for the Object Factory Builder singleton.

There is a also a (small) possibility that a client will call new InitialContext() after the singletons have been set, but before the JNDI Context Manager and JNDI Provider Admin services have been registered. This specification requires that these services are set after the singletons are set. In this race condition the JNDI Implementation should throw a No Initial Context Exception, explaining that the JNDI services are not available yet.

126.8 Security

126.8.1 JNDI Implementation

A JNDI Implementation may wish to assert that the user of the provider has some relevant Java 2 security permission. Since the JNDI implementation is an intermediary between the JNDI client and provider this means that the JNDI implementation needs to have any permissions required to access any JNDI Provider. As a result the JNDI implementation needs All Permission. This will result in the JNDI clients permissions being checked to see if it has the relevant permission to access the JNDI Provider.

The JNDI Implementation must make any invocation to access these services in a doPriviledged check. A JNDI client must therefore not be required to have the following permissions, which are needed by a JNDI Implementation:

```
ServicePermission    ..ObjectFactory                   REGISTER,GET
ServicePermission    ..DirObjectFactory                REGISTER,GET
ServicePermission    ..ObjectFactoryBuilder            REGISTER,GET
ServicePermission    ..InitialContextFactory           REGISTER,GET
ServicePermission    ..InitialContextFactoryBuilder    REGISTER,GET
ServicePermission    ..JNDIProviderAdmin               REGISTER,GET
```

The JNDI Implementation bundle must have the appropriate permissions to install the InitialContextFactoryBuilder and ObjectFactoryBuilder instances using the appropriate methods on the NamingManager class. This requires the following permission:

```
RuntimePermission                                       "setFactory"
```

126.8.2   JNDI Clients

A JNDI client using the JNDI Context Manager service must have the following permissions:

```
ServicePermission  ..JNDIContextManager              GET
```

Obtaining a reference to a JNDI Context Manager service should be considered a privileged operation and should be guarded by permissions.

126.8.3   OSGi URL namespace

A JNDI client must not be able to obtain services or a Bundle Contexts that the client bundle would not be able to get via the core OSGi API. To allow a client to use the osgi namespace to get a service the bundle must have the corresponding Service Permission. When using the osgi namespace to obtain the Bundle Context the client bundle must have Admin Permission for the Bundle Context. These permissions must be enforced by the osgi URL namespace handler.

126.9   org.osgi.service.jndi

JNDI Package Version 1.0.

Bundles wishing to use this package must list the package in the Import-Package header of the bundle's manifest. For example:

```
Import-Package: org.osgi.service.jndi; version="[1.0,2.0)"
```

126.9.1   Summary

- *JNDIConstants* - Constants for the JNDI implementation.
- *JNDIContextManager* - This interface defines the OSGi service interface for the JNDIContextManager.
- *JNDIProviderAdmin* - This interface defines the OSGi service interface for the JNDIProviderAdmin service.

126.9.2   public class JNDIConstants

Constants for the JNDI implementation.

Concurrency Immutable

126.9.2.1   public static final String BUNDLE_CONTEXT = "osgi.service.jndi.bundleContext"

This JNDI environment property can be used by a JNDI client to indicate the caller's BundleContext. This property can be set and passed to an InitialContext constructor. This property is only useful in the "traditional" mode of JNDI.

126.9.2.2   public static final String JNDI_SERVICENAME = "osgi.jndi.service.name"

This service property is set on an OSGi service to provide a name that can be used to locate the service other than the service interface name.

126.9.2.3   public static final String JNDI_URLSCHEME = "osgi.jndi.url.scheme"

This service property is set by JNDI Providers that publish URL Context Factories as OSGi Services. The value of this property should be the URL scheme that is supported by the published service.

126.9.3   public interface JNDIContextManager

This interface defines the OSGi service interface for the JNDIContextManager. This service provides the ability to create new JNDI Context instances without relying on the InitialContext constructor.

Concurrency Thread-safe

126.9.3.1   **public Context newInitialContext( ) throws NamingException**

     □ Creates a new JNDI initial context with the default JNDI environment properties.

Returns an instance of javax.naming.Context

Throws NamingException – upon any error that occurs during context creation

126.9.3.2   **public Context newInitialContext(Map environment) throws NamingException**

environment JNDI environment properties specified by caller

     □ Creates a new JNDI initial context with the specified JNDI environment properties.

Returns an instance of javax.naming.Context

Throws NamingException – upon any error that occurs during context creation

126.9.3.3   **public DirContext newInitialDirContext( ) throws NamingException**

     □ Creates a new initial DirContext with the default JNDI environment properties.

Returns an instance of javax.naming.directory.DirContext

Throws NamingException – upon any error that occurs during context creation

126.9.3.4   **public DirContext newInitialDirContext(Map environment) throws NamingException**

environment JNDI environment properties specified by the caller

     □ Creates a new initial DirContext with the specified JNDI environment properties.

Returns an instance of javax.naming.directory.DirContext

Throws NamingException – upon any error that occurs during context creation

126.9.4   public interface JNDIProviderAdmin

This interface defines the OSGi service interface for the JNDIProviderAdmin service. This service provides the ability to resolve JNDI References in a dynamic fashion that does not require calls to NamingManager.getObjectInstance(). The methods of this service provide similar reference resolution, but rely on the OSGi Service Registry in order to find ObjectFactory instances that can convert a Reference to an Object. This service will typically be used by OSGi-aware JNDI Service Providers.

Concurrency Thread-safe

126.9.4.1   **public Object getObjectInstance(Object refInfo, Name name, Context context, Map environment) throws Exception**

refInfo Reference info

name the JNDI name associated with this reference

context the JNDI context associated with this reference

environment the JNDI environment associated with this JNDI context

     □ Resolve the object from the given reference.

Returns an Object based on the reference passed in, or the original reference object if the reference could not be resolved.

Throws Exception – in the event that an error occurs while attempting to resolve the JNDI reference.

126.9.4.2   **public Object getObjectInstance(Object refInfo, Name name, Context context, Map environment, Attributes attributes) throws Exception**

refInfo Reference info

name the JNDI name associated with this reference

context the JNDI context associated with this reference

environment the JNDI environment associated with this JNDI context

attributes the naming attributes to use when resolving this object

☐ Resolve the object from the given reference.

Returns an Object based on the reference passed in, or the original reference object if the reference could not be resolved.

Throws `Exception` – in the event that an error occurs while attempting to resolve the JNDI reference.

126.10   References

[1]   *OSGi Core Specifications*
http://www.osgi.org/Specifications/HomePage

[2]   *Java Naming and Directory Interface*
http://java.sun.com/javase/6/docs/technotes/guides/jndi/index.html

[3]   *Java Naming and Directory Interface Tutorial from Sun Microsystems*
http://java.sun.com/products/jndi/tutorial/index.html

[4]   *JNDI Standard Property Names*
http://java.sun.com/j2se/1.5.0/docs/api/javax/naming/Context.html

127   JPA Service Specification

Version 1.0

127.1   Introduction

The Java Persistence API (JPA) is a specification that sets a standard for persistently storing objects in enterprise and non-enterprise Java based environments. JPA provides an Object Relational Mapping (ORM) model that is configured through persistence descriptors. This Java Persistence Service specification defines how persistence units can be published in an OSGi service platform, how client bundles can find these persistence units, how database drivers are found with the OSGi JDBC Specification, as well as how JPA providers can be made available within an OSGi framework.

Applications can be managed or they can be unmanaged. Managed applications run inside a Java EE Container and unmanaged applications run in a Java SE environment. The managed case requires a provider interface that can be used by the container, while in the unmanaged case the JPA provider is responsible for supporting the client directly. This specification is about the unmanaged model of JPA except in the areas where the managed model is explicitly mentioned. Additionally, multiple concurrent providers for the unmanaged case are not supported.

This JPA Specification supports both [2] *JPA 1.0* and [3] *JPA 2.0*.

127.1.1   Essentials

- *Dependencies* – There must be a way for persistence clients, if they so require, to manage their dependencies on a compatible persistence unit.
- *Compatibility* – The Persistence Unit service must be able to function in non-managed mode according to existing standards and interfaces outlined in the JPA specification.
- *Modularity* – Persistent classes and their accompanying configuration can exist in a separate bundle from the client that is operating on them using the Persistence Unit service.
- *JDBC* – Leverage the OSGi JDBC Specification for access to the database.

127.1.2   Entities

- *JPA* – The Java Persistence API, [2] *JPA 1.0* and [3] *JPA 2.0*.
- *JPA Provider* – An implementation of JPA, providing the Persistence Provider and JPA Services to Java EE Containers and Client Bundles.
- *Interface Bundle* – A bundle containing the interfaces and classes in the javax.persistence namespace (and its sub-namespaces) that are defined by the JPA specification.
- *Persistence Bundle* – A bundle that includes, a Meta-Persistence header, one or more Persistence Descriptor resources, and the entity classes specified by the Persistence Units in those resources.
- *Client Bundle* – The bundle that uses the Persistence Bundle to retrieve and store objects.
- *Persistence Descriptor* – A resource describing one or more Persistence Units.
- *Persistence Unit* – A named configuration for the object-relational mappings and database access as defined in a Persistence Descriptor.
- *Entity Manager* – The interface that provides the control point of retrieving and persisting objects in a relational database based on a single Persistence Unit for a single session.
- *Entity Manager Factory* – A service that can create Entity Managers based on a Persistence Unit for different sessions.
- *Entity Manager Factory Builder* – A service that can build an Entity Manager Factory for a specific Persistence Unit with extra configuration parameters.
- *Managed Client* – A Client Bundle that is managed by a Container

- *Static Client* – A Client that uses the static factory methods in the Persistence class instead of services.
- *Static Persistence* – The actor that enables the use of the Persistence class static factory methods to obtain an Entity Manager Factory.
- *JDBC Provider* – The bundle providing a Data Source Factory service.

Figure 127.1   JPA Service overview

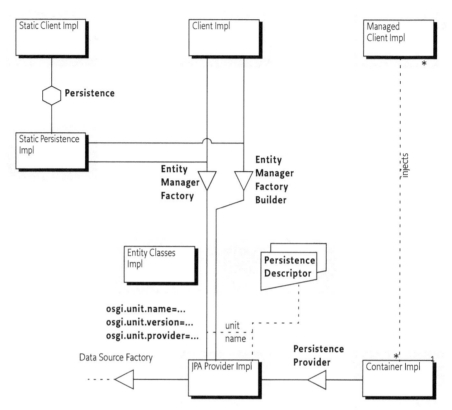

127.1.3   Dependencies

This specification is based on JPA 1.0 and JPA 2.0. JPA 2.0 is backward compatible with JPA 1.0. For this reason, the versions of the packages follow the OSGi recommended version policy with the addition of a special JPA marker that annotates the specification version for JPA. All JPA Packages must also have an attribute called jpa that specifies the JPA version. The purpose of this attribute is to make it clear what JPA version belongs to this package.

Table 127.1   Dependency versions

JPA	Packages	Export Version	Client Import Range	Provider Imp. Range
JPA 1.0	javax.persistence	1.0	[1.0,2.0)	[1.0,1.1)
	javax.persistence.spi	1.0	[1.0,2.0)	[1.0,1.1)
JPA 2.0	javax.persistence	1.1	[1.1,2.0)	[1.1,1.2)
	javax.persistence.spi	1.1	[1.1,2.0)	[1.1,1.2)

For example, JPA should have an export declaration like:

```
Export-Package: javax.persistence; version=1.1; jpa=2.0, ...
```

Synopsis

A JPA Provider tracks Persistence Bundles; a Persistence Bundle contains a Meta-Persistence manifest header. This manifest header enumerates the Persistence Descriptor resources in the Persistence Bundle. Each resource's XML schema is defined by the JPA 1.0 or JPA 2.0 specification. The JPA Provider reads the resource accordingly and extracts the information for one or more Persistence Units. For each found Persistence Unit, the JPA Provider registers an Entity Manager Factory Builder service. If the database is defined in the Persistence Unit, then the JPA Provider registers an Entity Manager Factory service during the availability of the corresponding Data Source Factory.

The identification of these services is handled through a number of service properties. The Entity Manager Factory service is named by the standard JPA interface, the Builder version is OSGi specific; it is used when the Client Bundle needs to create an Entity Manager Factory based on configuration properties.

A Client Bundle that wants to persist or retrieve its entity classes depends on an Entity Manager Factory (Builder) service that corresponds to a Persistence Unit that lists the entity classes. If such a service is available, the client can use this service to get an Entity Manager, allowing the client to retrieve and persist objects as long as the originating Entity Manager Factory (Builder) service is registered.

In a non-OSGi environment, it is customary to get an Entity Manager Factory through the Persistence class. This Persistence class provides a number of static methods that give access to any locally available JPA providers. This approach is not recommended in an OSGi environment due to class loading and start ordering issues. However, OSGi environments can support access through this static factory with a Static Persistence bundle.

127.2   JPA Overview

Java Persistence API (JPA) is a specification that is part of [4] *Java EE 5*. This OSGi Specification is based on [2] *JPA 1.0* and [3] *JPA 2.0*. This section provides an overview of JPA as specified in the JCP. The purpose of this section is to introduce the concepts behind JPA and define the terminology that will be used in the remainder of the chapter.

The purpose of JPA is to simplify access to relational databases for applications on the object-oriented Java platform. JPA provides support for storing and retrieving objects in a relational database. The JPA specification defines in detail how objects are mapped to tables and columns under the full control of the application. The core classes involved are depicted in Figure 127.2.

Figure 127.2   *JPA Client View*

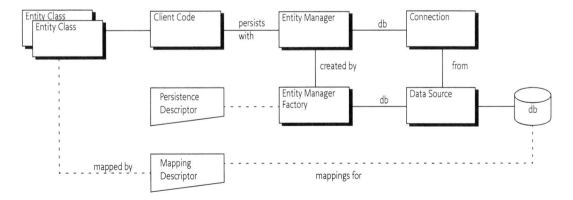

The JPA specifications define a number of concepts that are defined in this section for the purpose of this OSGi specification. However, the full syntax and semantics are defined in the JPA specifications.

127.2.1   Persistence

Classes that are stored and retrieved through JPA are called the *entity classes*. In this specification, the concept of entity classes includes the *embeddable* classes, which are classes that do not have any persistent identity, and mapped superclasses that allow mappings, but are not themselves persistent. Entity classes are not required to implement any interface or extend a specific superclass, they are Plain Old Java Objects (POJOs). It is the responsibility of the *JPA Provider* to connect to a database and map the store and retrieve operations of the entity classes to their tables and columns. For performance reasons, the entity classes are sometimes *enhanced.* This enhancement can take place during build time, deploy time, or during class loading time. Some enhancements use byte code weaving, some enhancements are based on sub-classing.

The JPA Provider cannot automatically perform its persistence tasks; it requires configuration information. This configuration information is stored in the *Persistence Descriptor.* A Persistence Descriptor is an XML file according of one of the two following namespaces:

```
http://java.sun.com/xml/ns/persistence/persistence_1_0.xsd
http://java.sun.com/xml/ns/persistence/persistence_2_0.xsd
```

The JPA standard Persistence Descriptor must be stored in META-INF/persistence.xml. It is usually in the same class path entry (like a JAR or directory) as the entity classes.

The JPA Provider parses the Persistence Descriptor and extracts one or more *Persistence Units.* A Persistence Unit includes the following aspects:

*   *Name* – Every Persistence Unit must have a name to identify it to clients. For example: Accounting.
*   *Provider Selection* – Restriction to a specific JPA Provider, usually because there are dependencies in the application code on provider specific functionality.
*   *JDBC Driver Selection* – Selects the JDBC driver, the principal and the credentials for selecting and accessing a relational database. See 127.2.4 *JDBC Access in JPA.*
*   *Properties* – Standard and JPA Provider specific properties.

The object-relational mappings are stored in special mapping resources or are specified in annotations.

A Persistence Unit can be *complete* or *incomplete.* A complete Persistence Unit identifies the database driver that is needed for the Persistence Unit, though it does not have to contain the credentials. An incomplete Persistence Unit lacks this information.

The relations between the class path, its entries, the entity classes, the Persistence Descriptor and the Persistence Unit is depicted in Figure 127.3 on page 404.

Figure 127.3   *JPA Configuration*

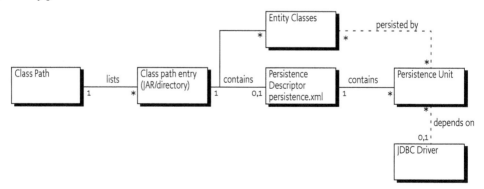

JPA recognizes the concept of a *persistence root*. The persistence root is the root of the JAR (or directory) on the class path that contains the META-INF/persistence.xml resource.

127.2.2 JPA Provider

The JPA specifications provide support for multiple JPA Providers in the same application. An Application selects a JPA Provider through the Persistence class, using static factory methods. One of these methods accepts a map with *configuration properties*. Configuration properties can override information specified in a Persistence Unit or these properties add new information to the Persistence Unit.

The default implementation of the Persistence class discovers providers through the Java EE services model, this model requires a text resource in the class path entry called:

    META-INF/services/javax.persistence.PersistenceProvider

This text resource contains the name of the JPA Provider implementation class.

The Persistence class createEntityManagerFactory method provides the JPA Provider with the name of a Persistence Unit. The JPA Provider must then scan the class path for any META-INF/persistence.xml entries, these are the available Persistence Descriptors. It then extracts the Persistence Units to find the requested Persistence Unit. If no such Persistence Unit can be found, or the JPA Provider is restricted from servicing this Persistence Unit, then null is returned. The Persistence class will then continue to try the next found or registered JPA Provider.

A Persistence Unit can restrict JPA Providers by specifying a *JPA Provider class*, this introduces a *provider dependency*. The specified JPA Provider class must implement the PersistenceProvider interface. This *implementation class name* must be available from the JPA Provider's documentation. JPA Providers that do not own the specified JPA Provider class must ignore such a Persistence Unit.

Otherwise, if the Persistence Unit is not restricted, the JPA Provider is *assigned* to this Persistence Unit; it must be ready to provide an EntityManagerFactory object when the application requests one.

The JPA Provider uses the Persistence Unit, together with any additional configuration properties, to construct an *Entity Manager Factory*. The application then uses this Entity Manager Factory to construct an *Entity Manager*, optionally providing additional configuration properties. The Entity Manager then provides the operations for the application to store and retrieve entity classes from the database.

The additional configuration properties provided with the creation of the Entity Manager Factory or the Entity Manager are often used to specify the database driver and the credentials. This allows the Persistence Unit to be specified without committing to a specific database, leaving the choice to the application at runtime.

The relations between the application, Entity Manager, Entity Manager Factory and the JPA Provider are depicted in Figure 127.4 on page 406.

Figure 127.4   *JPA Dynamic Model*

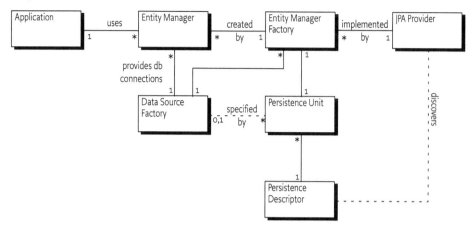

127.2.3   Managed and Unmanaged

The JPA specifications make a distinction between a *managed* and an *unmanaged* mode. In the managed mode the presence of a Java EE Container is assumed. Such a container provides many services for its contained applications like transaction handling, dependency injection, etc. One of these aspects can be the interface to the relational database. The JPA specifications therefore have defined a special method for Java EE Containers to manage the persistence aspects of their Managed Clients. This method is the createContainerEntityManagerFactory method on the PersistenceProvider interface. This method is purely intended for Java EE Containers and should not be used in other environments.

The other method on the PersistenceProvider interface is intended to be used by the Persistence class static factory methods. The Persistence class searches for an appropriate JPA Provider by asking all available JPA Providers to create an Entity Manager Factory based on configuration properties. The first JPA Provider that is capable of providing an Entity Manager Factory wins. The use of these static factory methods is called the *unmanaged mode*. It requires a JPA Provider to scan the class path to find the assigned Persistence Units.

127.2.4   JDBC Access in JPA

A Persistence Unit is configured to work with a relational database. JPA Providers communicate with a relational database through compliant JDBC database drivers. The database and driver parameters are specified in the Persistence Unit or configured during Entity Manager Factory or Entity Manager creation with the configuration properties. The configuration properties for selecting a database in non-managed mode were proprietary in JPA 1.0 but have been standardized in version 2.0 of JPA:

- javax.persistence.jdbc.driver – Fully-qualified name of the driver class
- javax.persistence.jdbc.url – Driver-specific URL to indicate database information
- javax.persistence.jdbc.user – User name to use when obtaining connections
- javax.persistence.jdbc.password – Password to use when obtaining connections

127.3   Bundles with Persistence

The primary goal of this specification is to simplify the programming model for bundles that need persistence. In this specification there are two application roles:

- *Persistence Bundle* – A Persistence Bundle contains the entity classes and one or more Persistence Descriptors, each providing one or more Persistence Units.

• *Client Bundle* –A Client Bundle contains the code that manipulates the entity classes and uses an Entity Manager to store and retrieve these entity classes with a relational database. The Client Bundle obtains the required Entity Manager(s) via a service based model.

These roles can be combined in a single bundle.

127.3.1 Services

A JPA Provider uses Persistence Units to provide Client Bundles with a configured *Entity Manager Factory* service and/or an *Entity Manager Factory Builder* service for each assigned Persistence Unit:

• *Entity Manager Factory service* – Provides an EntityManagerFactory object that depends on a complete Persistence Unit. That is, it is associated with a registered Data Source Factory service.
• *Entity Manager Factory Builder service* – The Entity Manager Factory Builder service provides the capability of creating an EntityManagerFactory object with additional configuration properties.

These services are collectively called the *JPA Services*. Entity Managers obtained from such JPA Services can only be used to operate on entity classes associated with their corresponding Persistence Unit.

127.3.2 Persistence Bundle

A *Persistence Bundle* is a bundle that specifies the Meta-Persistence header, see *Meta Persistence Header* on page 409. This header refers to one or more Persistence Descriptors in the Persistence Bundle. Commonly, this is the META-INF/persistence.xml resource. This location is the standard for non-OSGi environments, however an OSGi bundle can also use other locations as well as multiple resources.

For example, the contents of a simple Persistence Bundle with a single Person entity class could look like:

```
META-INF/
META-INF/MANIFEST.MF
OSGI-INF/address.xml
com/acme/Person.class
```

The corresponding manifest would then look like:

```
Manifest-Version: 1.0
Bundle-ManifestVersion: 2
Meta-Persistence: OSGI-INF/address.xml
Bundle-SymbolicName: com.acme.simple.persistence
Bundle-Version: 3.2.4.200912231004
```

A Persistence Bundle is a normal bundle; it must follow all the rules of OSGi and can use all OSGi constructs like Bundle-Classpath, fragment bundles, import packages, export packages, etc. However, there is one limitation: any entity classes must originate in the bundle's JAR, it cannot come from a fragment. This requirement is necessary to simplify enhancing entity classes.

127.3.3 Client Bundles

A Client Bundle uses the entity classes from a Persistence Bundle to provide its required functionality. To store and retrieve these entity classes a Client Bundle requires an Entity Manager that is configured for the corresponding Persistence Unit.

An Entity Manager is intended to be used by a single session, it is not thread safe. Therefore, a client needs an Entity Manager Factory to create an Entity Manager. In an OSGi environment, there are multiple routes to obtain an Entity Manager Factory.

A JPA Provider must register an Entity Manager Factory service for each assigned Persistence Unit that is *complete.* Complete means that it is a configured Persistence Unit, including the reference to the relational database. The Entity Manager Factory service is therefore bound to a Data Source Factory service and Client Bundles should not attempt to rebind the Data Source Factory with the configuration properties of the createEntityManager(Map) method. See *Rebinding* on page 413 for the consequences. If the Data Source Factory must be bound by the Client Bundle then the Client Bundle should use the *Custom Configured Entity Manager* on page 408.

The Entity Manager Factory service must be registered with the service properties as defined in *Service Registrations* on page 411. These are:

- osgi.unit.name – (String) The name of the Persistence Unit
- osgi.unit.version – (String) The version of the associated Persistence Bundle
- osgi.unit.provider – (String) The implementation class name of the JPA Provider

The life cycle of the Entity Manager Factory service is bound to the Persistence Bundle, the JPA Provider, and the selected Data Source Factory service.

A Client Bundle that wants to use an Entity Manager Factory service should therefore use an appropriate filter to select the Entity Manager Factory service that corresponds to its required Persistence Unit. For example, the following snippet uses Declarative Services, see *Declarative Services Specification* on page 141, to statically depend on such a service:

```
<reference name="accounting"
    target="(&(osgi.unit.name=Accounting)(osgi.unit.version=3.2.*))"
    interface="javax.persistence.EntityManagerFactory"/>
```

127.3.4   Custom Configured Entity Manager

If a Client Bundle needs to provide configuration properties for the creation of an Entity Manager Factory it should use the *Entity Manager Factory Builder* service. This can for example be used to provide the database selection properties when the Persistence Unit is incomplete or if the database selection needs to be overridden.

The Entity Manager Factory Builder service's life cycle must not depend on the availability of any Data Source Factory, even if a JDBC driver class name is specified in the Persistence Descriptor. The Entity Manager Factory Builder service is registered with the same service properties as the corresponding Entity Factory service, see *Service Registrations* on page 411.

The following method is defined on the EntityManagerFactoryBuilder interface:

- createEntityManagerFactory(Map) – Returns a custom configured EntityManagerFactory instance for the Persistence Unit associated with the service. Accepts a map with the configuration properties to be applied during Entity Manager Factory creation. The method must return a proper Entity Manager Factory or throw an Exception.

The createEntityManagerFactory method allows standard and vendor-specific properties to be passed in and applied to the Entity Manager Factory being created. However, some properties cannot be honored by the aforementioned method. For example, the javax.persistence.provider JPA property, as a means to specify a specific JPA Provider at runtime, cannot be supported because the JPA Provider has already been decided; it is the JPA Provider that registered the Entity Manager Factory Builder service. A JPA Provider should throw an Exception if it recognizes the property but it cannot use the property when specified through the builder. Unrecognized properties must be ignored.

Once an Entity Manager Factory is created the specified Data Source becomes associated with the Entity Manager Factory. It is therefore not possible to re-associate an Entity Manager Factory with another Data Source by providing different properties. A JPA Provider must throw an Exception when an attempt is made to re-specify the database properties. See *Rebinding* on page 413 for further information.

As an example, a sample snippet of a client that wants to operate on a persistence unit named Accounting and pass in the JDBC user name and password properties is:

```
ServiceReference[] refs = context.getServiceReferences(
   EntityManagerFactoryBuilder.class.getName(),
   "(osgi.unit.name=Accounting)");
if ( refs != null ) {
   EntityManagerFactoryBuilder emfBuilder =
      (EntityManagerFactoryBuilder) context.getService(refs[0]);
   if ( emfBuilder != null ) {
     Map<String,Object> props = new HashMap<String,Object>();
     props.put("javax.persistence.jdbc.user", userString);
     props.put("javax.persistence.jdbc.password", passwordString);
     EntityManagerFactory emf = emfBuilder.createEntityManagerFactory(props);
     EntityManager em = emf.createEntityManager();
     ...
}
```

The example does not handle the dynamic dependencies on the associated Data Source Factory service.

127.4   Extending a Persistence Bundle

A Persistence Bundle is identified by its Meta-Persistence manifest header that references a number of Persistence Descriptor resources. Persistence bundles must be detected by a JPA Provider. The JPA Provider must parse any Persistence Descriptors in these bundles and detect the assigned Persistence Units. For each assigned Persistence Unit, the JPA Provider must register an Entity Manager Factory Builder service when the Persistence Bundle is ready, see *Ready Phase* on page 411.

For complete and assigned Persistence Units, the JPA Provider must find the required Data Source Factory service based on the driver name. When the Persistence Bundle is ready and the selected Data Source Factory is available, the JPA Provider must have an Entity Manager Factory service registered that is linked to that Data Source Factory.

When the Persistence Bundle is stopped (or the JPA Provider stops), the JPA Provider must close all connections and cleanup any resources associated with the Persistence Bundle.

This process is outlined in detail in the following sections.

127.4.1   Class Space Consistency

A JPA Provider must ignore Persistence Bundles that are in another class space for the javax.persistence.* packages. Such a JPA Provider cannot create JPA Services that would be visible and usable by the Client Bundles.

127.4.2   Meta Persistence Header

A *Persistence Bundle* is a bundle that contains the Meta-Persistence header. If this header is not present, then this specification does not apply and a JPA Provider should ignore the corresponding bundle.

The persistence root of a Persistence Unit is the root of the Persistence Bundle's JAR

The Meta-Persistence header has a syntax of:

```
Meta-Persistence ::= ( jar-path ( ',' jar-path )* )?
jar-path         ::= path ( '!/' spath )?
spath            ::= path       // must not start with slash ('/')
```

The header may include zero or more comma-separated jar-paths, each a path to a Persistence Descriptor resource in the bundle. Paths may optionally be prefixed with the slash ('/') character. The JPA Provider must always include the META-INF/persistence.xml first if it is not one of the listed paths. Wildcards in directories are not supported. The META-INF/persistence.xml is therefore the default location for an empty header.

For example:

```
Meta-Persistence: META-INF/jpa.xml, persistence/jpa.xml
```

The previous example will instruct the JPA Provider to process the META-INF/persistence.xml resource first, even though it is not explicitly listed. The JPA Provider must then subsequently process META-INF/jpa.xml and the persistence/jpa.xml resources.

The paths in the Meta-Persistence header must be used with the Bundle.getEntry() method, or a mechanism with similar semantics, to obtain the corresponding resource. The getEntry method does not force the bundle to resolve when still unresolved; resolving might interfere with the efficiency of any required entity class enhancements. However, the use of the getEntry method implies that fragment bundles cannot be used to contain Persistence Descriptors nor entity classes.

Paths in the Meta-Persistence header can reference JAR files that are nested in the bundle by using the !/jar: URL syntax to separate the JAR file from the path within the JAR, for example:

```
Meta-Persistence: embedded.jar!/META-INF/persistence.xml
```

This example refers to a resource in the embedded.jar resource, located in the META-INF directory of embedded.jar.

The !/ splits the jar-path in a prefix and a suffix:

- *Prefix* – The prefix is a path to a JAR resource in the bundle.
- *Suffix* – The suffix is a path to a resource in the JAR identified by the prefix.

For example:

```
embedded.jar!/META-INF/persistence.xml
prefix:     embedded.jar
suffix:     META-INF/persistence.xml
```

It is not required that all listed or implied resources are present in the bundle's JAR. For example, it is valid that the default META-INF/persistence.xml resource is absent. However, if no Persistence Units are found at all then the absence of any Persistence Unit is regarded as an error that should be logged. In this case, the Persistence Bundle is further ignored.

127.4.3　Processing

A JPA Provider can detect a Persistence Bundle as early as its installation time. This early detection allows the JPA Provider to validate the Persistence Bundle as well as prepare any mechanisms to enhance the classes for better performance. However, this process can also be delayed until the bundle is started.

The JPA Provider must validate the Persistence Bundle. A valid Persistence Bundle must:

- Have no parsing errors of the Persistence Descriptors
- Validate all Persistence Descriptors against their schemas
- Have at least one assigned Persistence Unit
- Have all entity classes mentioned in the assigned Persistence Units on the Persistence Bundle's JAR.

A Persistence Bundle that uses multiple providers for its Persistence Units could become incompatible with future versions of this specification.

If any validation fails, then this is an error and should be logged. Such a bundle is ignored completely even if it also contains valid assigned Persistence Units. Only a bundle update can recover from this state.

Persistence Units can restrict JPA Providers by specifying a provider dependency. JPA Providers that do not own this JPA Provider implementation class must ignore such a Persistence Unit completely. Otherwise, if the JPA Provider can service a Persistence Unit, it assigns itself to this Persistence Unit.

If after the processing of all Persistence Descriptors, the JPA Provider has no assigned Persistence Units, then the JPA Provider must further ignore the Persistence Bundle.

127.4.4   Ready Phase

A Persistence Bundle is *ready* when its state is ACTIVE or, when a lazy activation policy is used, STARTING. A JPA Provider must track the ready state of Persistence Bundles that contain assigned Persistence Units.

While a Persistence Bundle is ready, the JPA Provider must have, for each assigned Persistence Unit, an Entity Manager Factory Builder service registered to allow Client Bundles to create new EntityManagerFactory objects. The JPA Provider must also register an Entity Manager Factory for each assigned and complete Persistence Unit that has its corresponding Data Source available in the service registry.

The service registration process is asynchronous with the Persistence Bundle start because a JPA Provider could start after a Persistence Bundle became ready.

127.4.5   Service Registrations

The JPA Services must be registered through the Bundle Context of the corresponding Persistence Bundle to ensure proper class space consistency checks by the OSGi Framework.

JPA Services are always related to an assigned Persistence Unit. To identify this Persistence Unit and the assigned JPA Provider, each JPA Service must have the following service properties:

- osgi.unit.name – (String) The name of the Persistence Unit. This property corresponds to the name attribute of the persistence-unit element in the Persistence Descriptor. It is used by Client Bundles as the primary filter criterion to obtain a JPA Service for a required Persistence Unit. There can be multiple JPA Services registered under the same osgi.unit.name, each representing a different version of the Persistence Unit.
- osgi.unit.version – (String) The version of the Persistence Bundle, as specified in Bundle-Version header, that provides the corresponding Persistence Unit. Client Bundles can filter their required JPA Services based on a particular Persistence Unit version.
- osgi.unit.provider – (String) The JPA Provider implementation class name that registered the service. The osgi.unit.provider property allows Client Bundles to know the JPA Provider that is servicing the Persistence Unit. Client Bundles should be careful when filtering on this property, however, since the JPA Provider that is assigned a Persistence Unit may not be known by the Client Bundle ahead of time. If there is a JPA Provider dependency, it is better to specify this dependency in the Persistence Unit because other JPA Providers are then not allowed to assign such a Persistence Unit and will therefore not register a service.

127.4.6   Registering the Entity Manager Factory Builder Service

Once the Persistence Bundle is ready, a JPA Provider must register an Entity Manager Factory Builder service for each assigned Persistence Unit from that Persistence Bundle.

The Entity Manager Factory Builder service must be registered with the service properties listed in *Service Registrations* on page 411. The Entity Manager Factory Builder service is registered under the org.osgi.service.jpa.EntityManagerFactoryBuilder name. This interface is using the JPA packages and is therefore bound to one of the two supported versions, see *Dependencies* on page 402.

The Entity Manager Factory Builder service enables the creation of a parameterized version of an Entity Factory Manager by allowing the caller to specify configuration properties. This approach is necessary if, for example, the Persistence Unit is not complete.

127.4.7 Registering the Entity Manager Factory

A complete Persistence Unit is configured with a specific relational database driver, see *JDBC Access in JPA* on page 406. A JPA Provider must have an Entity Manager Factory service registered for each assigned and complete Persistence Unit when:

- The originating Persistence Bundle is ready, and
- A *matching* Data Source Factory service is available. Matching a Data Source Factory service to a Persistence Unit is discussed in *Database Access* on page 413.

A JPA Provider must track the life cycle of the matching Data Source Factory service; while this service is unavailable the Entity Manager Factory service must also be unavailable. Any active Entity Managers created by the Entity Manager Factory service become invalid to use at that time.

The Entity Manager Factory service must be registered with the same service properties as described for the Entity Manager Factory Builder service, see *Service Registrations* on page 411. It should be registered under the following name:

```
javax.persistence.EntityManagerFactory
```

The EntityManagerFactory interface is from the JPA packages and is therefore bound to one of the two supported versions, see *Dependencies* on page 402.

An Entity Manager Factory is bound to a Data Source Factory service because its assigned Persistence Unit was complete. However, a Client Bundle could still provide JDBC configuration properties for the createEntityManager(Map) method. This not always possible, see *Rebinding* on page 413.

127.4.8 Stopping

If a Persistence Bundle is being stopped, then the JPA Provider must ensure that any resources allocated on behalf of the Persistence Bundle are cleaned up and all open connections are closed. This cleanup must happen synchronously with the STOPPING event. Any Exceptions being thrown while cleaning up should be logged but must not stop any further clean up.

If the JPA Provider is being stopped, the JPA Provider must unregister all JPA Services that it registered through the Persistence Bundles and clean up as if those bundles were stopped.

127.5 JPA Provider

JPA Providers supply the implementation of the JPA Services and the Persistence Provider service. It is the responsibility of a JPA Provider to store and retrieve the entity classes from a relational database. It is the responsibility of the JPA Provider to register a Persistence Provider and start tracking Persistence Bundles, see *Extending a Persistence Bundle* on page 409.

127.5.1 Managed Model

A JPA Provider that supports running in managed mode should register a specific service for the Java EE Containers: the Persistence Provider service. The interface is the standard JPA PersistenceProvider interface. See *Dependencies* on page 402 for the issues around the multiple versions that this specification supports.

The service must be registered with the following service property:

- javax.persistence.provider – The JPA Provider implementation class name, a documented name for all JPA Providers.

The Persistence Provider service enables a Java EE Container to find a particular JPA Provider. This service is intended for containers only, not for Client Bundles because there are implicit assumptions in the JPA Providers about the Java EE environment. A Java EE Container must obey the life cycle of the Persistence Provider service. If this service is unregistered then it must close all connections and clean up the corresponding resources.

127.5.2   Database Access

A Persistence Unit is configured to work with a relational database. JPA Providers must communicate with a relational database through a compliant JDBC database driver. The database and driver parameters are specified with properties in the Persistence Unit or the configuration properties when a Entity Manager Factory Builder is used to build an Entity Manager Factory. All JPA Providers, regardless of version, in an OSGi environment must support the following properties for database access:

- javax.persistence.jdbc.driver – Fully-qualified name of the driver class.
- javax.persistence.jdbc.url – Driver-specific URL to indicate database information
- javax.persistence.jdbc.user – User name to use when obtaining connections
- javax.persistence.jdbc.password – Password to use when obtaining connections

There are severe limitations in specifying these properties after the Entity Manager Factory is created for the first time, see *Rebinding* on page 413.

127.5.3   Data Source Factory Service Matching

Providers must use the javax.persistence.jdbc.driver property, as defined in *JDBC Access in JPA* on page 406, to obtain a Data Source Factory service. The Data Source Factory is specified in *JDBC™ Service Specification* on page 375. The javax.persistence.jdbc.driver property must be matched with the value of the Data Source Factory service property named osgi.jdbc.driver.class.

The Data Source Factory service is registered with the osgi.jdbc.driver.class service property that holds the class name of the driver. This property must match the javax.persistence.jdbc.driver service property of the Persistence Unit.

For example, if the Persistence Unit specifies the com.acme.db.Driver database driver in the javax.persistence.jdbc.driver property (or in the Persistence Descriptor property element), then the following filter would select an appropriate Data Source Factory:

```
(&(objectClass=org.osgi.service.jdbc.DataSourceFactory)
  (osgi.jdbc.driver.class=com.acme.db.Driver))
```

Once the Data Source Factory is obtained, the JPA Provider must obtain a DataSource object. This Data Source object must then be used for all relational database access.

In [2] *JPA 1.0* the JPA JDBC properties were not standardized. JPA Providers typically defined a set of JDBC properties, similar to those defined in JPA 2.0, to configure JDBC driver access. JPA 1.0 JPA Providers must look up the Data Source Factory service first using the JPA 2.0 JDBC properties. If these properties are not defined then they should fall back to their proprietary driver properties.

127.5.4   Rebinding

In this specification, the Entity Manager Factory service is only registered when the Persistence Unit is complete and a matching Data Source Factory service is available. However, the API of the Entity Manager Factory allows the creation of an Entity Manager with configuration properties. Those configuration properties could contain the JDBC properties to bind to another Data Source Factory service than it had already selected.

This case must not be supported by a JPA Provider, an Illegal Argument Exception must be thrown. If such a case would be supported then the life cycle of the Entity Manager Factory service would still be bound to the first Data Source Factory. There would be no way for the JPA Provider to signal to the Client Bundle that the returned Entity Manager is no longer valid because the rebound Data Source Factory was unregistered.

Therefore, after an Entity Manager Factory has been created, a JPA Provider must verify that the new properties are compatible with the properties of the already created Entity Manager Factory. If no, then an Exception must be thrown. If they are compatible, then an instance of the previous Entity Manager Factory should be returned.

127.5.5 Enhancing Entity Classes

JPA Providers may choose to implement the JPA specifications using various implementation approaches and techniques. This promotes innovation in the area, but also opens the door to limitations and constraints arising due to implementation choices. For example, there are JPA Providers that perform byte code weaving during the entity class loading. Dynamic byte code weaving requires that the entity classes are not loaded until the JPA Provider is first able to intercept the loading of the entity class and be given an opportunity to do its weaving. It also implies that the Persistence Bundle and any other bundles that import packages from that bundle must be refreshed if the JPA Provider needs to be changed.

This is necessary because the JPA Services are registered against the Bundle Contexts of the Persistence Bundles and not the Bundle Context of the JPA Providers. Client Bundles must then unget the service to unbind themselves from the uninstalled JPA Provider. However, since most JPA Providers perform some kind of weaving or class transformation on the entity classes, the Persistence Bundle will likely need to be refreshed. This will cause the Client Bundles to be refreshed also because they depend on the packages of the entity classes.

127.5.6 Class Loading

JPA Providers cannot have package dependencies on entity classes in Persistence Bundles because they cannot know at install time what Persistence Bundles they will be servicing. However, when a JPA Provider is servicing a Persistence Bundle, it must be able to load classes and resources from that Persistence Bundle according to the OSGi bundle rules. To do this class loading it must obtain a class loader that has the same visibility as the Persistence Bundle's bundle class loader. This will also allow it to load and manage metadata for the entity classes and resources for that Persistence Bundle's assigned Persistence Units. These resources and entity classes must reside directly in the Persistence Bundle, they must be accessed using the getEntry method. Entity classes and resources must not reside in fragments.

127.5.7 Validation

There is not yet an OSGi service specification defined for validation providers. If validation is required, the validation implementation will need to be included with the JPA Provider bundle.

127.6 Static Access

Non-managed client usage of JPA has traditionally been achieved through the Persistence class. Invoking a static method on the Persistence class is a dependency on the returned JPA Provider that cannot be managed by the OSGi framework.

However, such an unmanaged dependency is supported in this specification by the Static Persistence bundle. This bundle provides backwards compatibility for programs that use existing JPA access patterns. However, usage of this static model requires that the deployer ensures that the actors needed are in place at the appropriate times by controlling the life cycles of all participating bundles. The normal OSGi safe-guards and dependency handling do not work in the case of static access.

A Static Persistence Bundle must provide static access from the Persistence class to the JPA Services.

127.6.1 Access

There are two methods on the Persistence class:

- createEntityManagerFactory(String)
- createEntityManagerFactory(String,Map)

Both methods take the name of a Persistence Unit. The last method also takes a map that contains extra configuration properties. To support the usage of the static methods on the Persistence class, the implementation of the Persistence.createEntityManagerFactory method family must do a lookup of one of the JPA Services associated with the selected Persistence Unit.

If no configuration properties are specified, the Static Persistence Bundle must look for an Entity Manager Factory service with the osgi.unit.name property set to the given name. The default service should be used because no selector for a version is provided. If no such service is available, null must be returned. Provisioning of multiple versioned Persistence Units is not supported. Deployers should ensure only a single version of a Persistence Unit with the same name is present in an OSGi framework at any moment in time.

Otherwise, if configuration properties are provided, the Static Access implementation must look for an Entity Manager Factory Builder service with the osgi.unit.name property set to the given Persistence Unit name. If no such service exists, null must be returned. Otherwise, the default service must be used to create an Entity Manager Factory with the given configuration properties. The result must be returned to the caller.

For service lookups, the Static Persistence Bundle must use its own Bundle Context, it must not attempt to use the Bundle Context of the caller. All exceptions should be passed to the caller.

The class space of the Entity Manager Factory and the class space of the client cannot be enforced to be consistent by the framework because it is the Persistence class that is doing the lookup of the service, and not the actual calling Client Bundle that will be using the Entity Manager Factory. The framework cannot make the connection and therefore cannot enforce that the class spaces correspond. Deployers should therefore ensure that the involved class spaces are correctly wired.

127.7   Security

The security for this specification is based on the JPA specification.

127.8   org.osgi.service.jpa

JPA Package Version 1.0.

Bundles wishing to use this package must list the package in the Import-Package header of the bundle's manifest. For example:

```
Import-Package: org.osgi.service.jpa; version="[1.0,2.0)"
```

127.8.1   public interface EntityManagerFactoryBuilder

This service interface offers JPA clients the ability to create instances of EntityManagerFactory for a given named persistence unit. A service instance will be created for each named persistence unit and can be filtered by comparing the value of the osgi.unit.name property containing the persistence unit name.   This service is used specifically when the caller wants to pass in factory-scoped properties as arguments. If no properties are being used in the creation of the EntityManagerFactory then the basic EntityManagerFactory service should be used.

127.8.1.1   public static final String JPA_UNIT_NAME = "osgi.unit.name"

The name of the persistence unit.

127.8.1.2   **public static final String JPA_UNIT_PROVIDER = "osgi.unit.provider"**

The class name of the provider that registered the service and implements the JPA javax.persistence.PersistenceProvider interface.

127.8.1.3   **public static final String JPA_UNIT_VERSION = "osgi.unit.version"**

The version of the persistence unit bundle.

127.8.1.4   **public EntityManagerFactory createEntityManagerFactory(Map<String,Object> props)**

props   Properties to be used, in addition to those in the persistence descriptor, for configuring the EntityManagerFactory for the persistence unit.

☐ Return an EntityManagerFactory instance configured according to the properties defined in the corresponding persistence descriptor, as well as the properties passed into the method.

Returns   An EntityManagerFactory for the persistence unit associated with this service. Must not be null.

127.9   References

[1]   *OSGi Core Specifications*
http://www.osgi.org/Specifications/HomePage

[2]   *JPA 1.0*
http://jcp.org/en/jsr/summary?id=220

[3]   *JPA 2.0*
http://jcp.org/en/jsr/summary?id=317

[4]   *Java EE 5*
http://java.sun.com/javaee/technologies/javaee5.jsp

128   Web Applications Specification

Version 1.0

128.1   Introduction

The Java EE Servlet model has provided the backbone of web based applications written in Java. Given the popularity of the Servlet model, it is desirable to provide a seamless experience for deploying existing and new web applications to Servlet containers operating on the OSGi service platform. Previously, the Http Service in the catalogue of OSGi compendium services was the only model specified in OSGi to support the Servlet programming model. However, the Http Service, as defined in that specification, is focused on the run time, as well as manual construction of the servlet context, and thus does not actually support the standard Servlet packaging and deployment model based on the Web Application Archive, or WAR format.

This specification defines the Web Application Bundle, which is a bundle that performs the same role as the WAR in Java EE. A WAB uses the OSGi life cycle and class/resource loading rules instead of the standard Java EE environment. WABs are normal bundles and can leverage the full set of features of the OSGi Service Platform.

Web applications can also be installed as traditional WARs through a manifest rewriting process. During the install, a WAR is transformed into a WAB. This specification was based on ideas developed in *PAX Web Extender* on page 429.

This Web Application Specification provides support for web applications written to the Servlet 2.5 specification, or later. Given that Java Server Pages, or JSPs, are an integral part of the Java EE web application framework, this specification also supports the JSP 2.1 specification or greater if present. This specification details how a web application packaged as a WAR may be installed into an OSGi Service Platform, as well as how this application may interact with, and obtain, OSGi services.

128.1.1   Essentials

- *Extender* – Enable the configuration of components inside a bundle based on configuration data provided by the bundle developer.
- *Services* – Enable the use of OSGi services within a Web Application.
- *Deployment* – Define a mechanism to deploy Web Applications, both OSGi aware and non OSGi aware, in the OSGi environment.
- *WAR File Support* – Transparently enhance the contents of a WAR's manifest during installation to add any headers necessary to deploy a WAR as an OSGi bundle.

128.1.2   Entities

- *Web Container* – The implementation of this specification. Consists of a Web Extender, a Web URL Handler and a Servlet and Java Server Pages Web Runtime environment.
- *Web Application* – A program that has web accessible content. A Web Application is defined by *Java EE Web Applications on page 429*.
- *Web Application Archive (WAR)* – The Java EE standard resource format layout of a JAR file that contains a deployable Web Application.
- *Web Application Bundle* – A Web Application deployed as an OSGi bundle, also called a WAB.
- *WAB* – The acronym for a Web Application Bundle.
- *Web Extender* – An extender bundle that deploys the Web Application Bundle to the Web Runtime based on the Web Application Bundle's state.

- *Web URL Handler* – A URL handler which transforms a Web Application Archive (WAR) to conform to the OSGi specifications during installation by installing the WAR through a special URL so that it becomes a Web Application Bundle.
- *Web Runtime* – A Java Server Pages and Servlet environment, receiving the web requests and translating them to servlet calls, either from Web Application servlets or other classes.
- *Web Component* – A Servlet or Java Server Page (JSP).
- *Servlet* – An object implementing the Servlet interface; this is for the request handler model in the Servlet Specification.
- *Servlet Context* – The model representing the Web Application in the Servlet Specification.
- *Java Server Page (JSP)* – A declarative, template based model for generating content through Servlets that is optionally supported by the Web Runtime.
- *Context Path* – The URI path prefix of any content accessible in a Web Application.

Figure 128.1   *Web Container Entities*

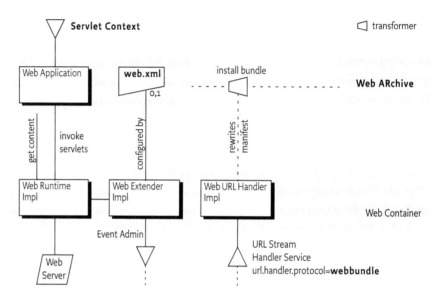

128.1.3   Dependencies

The package dependencies for the clients of this specification are listed in Table 128.1.

Table 128.1   *Dependency versions*

Packages	Export Version	Client Import Range
javax.servlet	2.5	[2.5,3.0)
javax.servlet.http	2.5	[2.5,3.0)
javax.servlet.jsp.el	2.1	[2.1,3.0)
javax.servlet.jsp.jstl.core	1.2	[1.2,2.0)
javax.servlet.jsp.jstl.fmt	1.2	[1.2,2.0)
javax.servlet.jsp.jstl.sql	1.2	[1.2,2.0)
javax.servlet.jsp.jstl.tlv	1.2	[1.2,2.0)
javax.servlet.jsp.resources	2.1	[2.1,3.0)
javax.servlet.jsp.tagext	2.1	[2.1,3.0)
javax.servlet.jsp	2.1	[2.1,3.0)

JSP is optional for the Web Runtime.

Synopsis

The Web Application Specification is composed of a number of cooperating parts, which are implemented by a *Web Container*. A Web Container consists of:

- *Web Extender* – Responsible for deploying Web Application Bundles (WAB) to a Web Runtime,
- *Web Runtime* – Provides support for Servlet and optionally for JSPs, and
- *Web URL Handler* – Provides on-the-fly enhancements of non-OSGi aware Web ARchives (WAR) so that they can be installed as a WAB.

WABs are standard OSGi bundles with additional headers in the manifest that serve as deployment instructions to the Web Extender. WABs can also contain the Java EE defined web.xml descriptor in the WEB-INF/ directory. When the Web Extender detects that a WAB is ready the Web Extender deploys the WAB to the Web Runtime using information contained in the web.xml descriptor and the appropriate manifest headers. The Bundle Context of the WAB is made available as a Servlet Context attribute. From that point, the Web Runtime will use the information in the WAB to serve content to any requests. Both dynamic as well as static content can be provided.

The Web URL Handler allows the deployment of an unmodified WAR as a WAB into the OSGi framework. This Web URL Handler provides a URL stream handler with the webbundle: scheme. Installing a WAR with this scheme allows the Web URL Handler to interpose itself as a filter on the input stream of the contents of the WAR, transforming the contents of the WAR into a WAB. The Web URL Handler rewrites the manifest by adding necessary headers to turn the WAR into a valid WAB. Additional headers can be added to the manifest that serve as instructions to the Web Extender.

After a WAB has been deployed to the Web Runtime, the Web Application can interact with the OSGi framework via the provided Bundle Context. The Servlet Context associated with this WAB follows the same life cycle as the WAB. That is, when the underlying Web Application Bundle is started, the Web Application is deployed to the Web Runtime. When the underlying Web Application Bundle is stopped because of a failure or other reason, the Web Application is undeployed from the Web Runtime.

128.2   Web Container

A Web Container is the implementation of this specification. It consists of the following parts:

- *Web Extender* – Detects Web Application Bundles (WAB) and tracks their life cycle. Ready WABs are deployed to the Web Runtime.
- *Web Runtime* – A runtime environment for a Web Application that supports the [4] *Servlet 2.5 specification* and [5] *JSP 2.1 specification* or later. The Web Runtime receives web requests and calls the appropriate methods on servlets. Servlets can be implemented by classes or Java Server Pages.
- *Web URL Handler* – A URL stream handler providing the webbundle: scheme. This scheme can be used to install WARs in an OSGi Service Platform. The Web URL Handler will then automatically add the required OSGi manifest headers.

The extender, runtime, and handler can all be implemented in the same or different bundles and use unspecified mechanisms to communicate. This specification uses the defined names of the sub-parts as the actor; the term Web Container is the general name for this collection of actors.

128.3   Web Application Bundle

Bundles are the deployment and management entities under OSGi. A *Web Application Bundle* (WAB) is deployed as an OSGi bundle in an OSGi framework, where each WAB provides a single *Web Application*. A Web Application can make use of the [4] *Servlet 2.5 specification* and [5] *JSP 2.1 specification* programming models, or later, to provide content for the web.

A WAB is defined as a normal OSGi bundle that contains web accessible content, both static and dynamic. There are no restrictions on bundles. A Web Application can be packaged as a WAB during application development, or it can be transparently created at bundle install time from a standard Web Application aRchive (WAR) via transformation by the Web URL Handler, see *Web URL Handler* on page 424.

A WAB is a valid OSGi bundle and as such must fully describe its dependencies and exports (if any). As Web Applications are modularized further into multiple bundles (and not deployed as WAR files only) it is possible that a WAB can have dependencies on other bundles.

A WAB may be installed into the framework using the BundleContext.installBundle methods. Once installed, a WAB's life cycle is managed just like any other bundle in the framework. This life cycle is tracked by the Web Extender who will then deploy the Web Application to the Web Runtime when the WAB is ready and will undeploy it when the WAB is no longer ready. This state is depicted in Figure 128.2.

Figure 128.2   *State diagram Web Application*

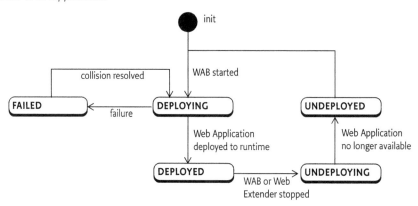

128.3.1   WAB Definition

A WAB is differentiated from non Web Application bundles through the specification of the additional manifest header:

    Web-ContextPath ::= path

The Web-ContextPath header specifies the value of the *Context Path* of the Web Application. All web accessible content of the Web Application is available on the web server relative to this Context Path. For example, if the context path is /sales, then the URL would be something like: http://www.acme.com/sales. The Context Path must always begin with a forward slash ('/').

The Web Extender must not recognize a bundle as a Web Application unless the Web-ContextPath header is present in its manifest and the header value is a valid path for the bundle.

A WAB can optionally contain a web.xml resource to specify additional configuration. This web.xml must be found with the Bundle findEntries method at the path:

    WEB-INF/web.xml

The findEntries method includes fragments, allowing the web.xml to be provided by a fragment. The Web Extender must fully support a web.xml descriptor that specifies Servlets, Filters, or Listeners whose classes are required by the WAB.

128.3.2   Starting the Web Application Bundle

A WAB's Web Application must be *deployed* while the WAB is *ready*. Deployed means that the Web Application is available for web requests. Once deployed, a WAB can serve its web content on the given Context Path. Ready is when the WAB:

- Is in the ACTIVE state, or
- Has a lazy activation policy and is in the STARTING state.

The Web Extender should ensure that serving static content from the WAB does not activate the WAB when it has a lazy activation policy.

To deploy the WAB, the Web Extender must initiate the deploying of the Web Application into a Web Runtime. This is outlined in the following steps:

1   Wait for the WAB to become ready. The following steps can take place asynchronously with the starting of the WAB.
2   Post an org/osgi/service/web/DEPLOYING event. See *Events* on page 426.
3   Validate that the Web-ContextPath manifest header does not match the Context Path of any other currently deployed web application. If the Context Path value is already in use by another Web Application, then the Web Application must not be deployed, and the deployment fails, see *Failure* on page 421. The Web Extender should log the collision. If the prior Web Application with the same Context Path is undeployed later, this Web Application should be considered as a candidate, see *Stopping the Web Application Bundle* on page 423.
4   The Web Runtime processes deployment information by processing the web.xml descriptor, if present. The Web Container must perform the necessary initialization of Web Components in the WAB as described in the [4] *Servlet 2.5 specification*. This involves the following sub-steps in the given order:
   - Create a Servlet Context for the Web Application.
   - Instantiate configured Servlet event listeners.
   - Instantiate configured application filter instances etc.

   The Web Runtime is required to complete instantiation of listeners prior to the start of execution of the first request into the Web Application by the Web Runtime. Attribute changes to the Servlet Context and Http Session objects can occur concurrently. The Servlet Container is not required to synchronize the resulting notifications to attribute listener classes. Listener classes that maintain state are responsible for the integrity of the data and should handle this case explicitly.

   If event listeners or filters are used in the web.xml, then the Web Runtime will load the corresponding classes from the bundle activating the bundle if it was lazily started. Such a configuration will therefore not act lazily.
5   Publish the Servlet Context as a service with identifying service properties, see *Publishing the Servlet Context* on page 421.
6   Post an org/osgi/service/web/DEPLOYED event to indicate that the web application is now available. See *Events* on page 426.

If at any moment before the org/osgi/service/web/DEPLOYED event is published the deployment of the WAB fails, then the WAB deployment fails, see *Failure* on page 421.

128.3.3   Failure

Any validation failures must prevent the Web Application from being accessible via HTTP, and must result in a org/osgi/service/web/FAILED event being posted. See *Events* on page 426. The situation after the failure must be as if the WAB was never deployed.

128.3.4   Publishing the Servlet Context

To help management agents with tracking the state of Web Applications, the Web Extender must register the Servlet Context of the WAB as a service, using the Bundle Context of the WAB. The Servlet Context service must be registered with the service properties listed in Table 128.2.

Table 128.2   *Servlet Context Service Properties*

Property Name	Type	Description
osgi.web.symbolicname	String	The symbolic name for the Web Application Bundle
osgi.web.version	String	The version of the Web Application Bundle. If no Bundle-Version is specified in the manifest then this property must not be set.
osgi.web.contextpath	String	The Context Path from which the WAB's content will be served.

128.3.5   Static Content

A deployed WAB provides content on requests from the web. For certain access paths, this can serve content from the resources of the web application: this is called *static content*. A Web Runtime must use the Servlet Context resource access methods to service static content, the resource loading strategy for these methods is based on the findEntries method, see *Resource Lookup* on page 428. For confidentiality reasons, a Web Runtime must not return any static content for paths that start with one of the following prefixes:

```
WEB-INF/
OSGI-INF/
META-INF/
OSGI-OPT/
```

These *protected directories* are intended to shield code content used for dynamic content generation from accidentally being served over the web, which is a potential attack route. In the servlet specification, the WEB-INF/ directory in the WAR is protected in such a way. However, this protection is not complete. A dependent JAR can actually be placed outside the WEB-INF directory that can then be served as static content. The same is true for a WAB. Though the protected directories must never be served over the web, there are no other checks required to verify that no content can be served that is also available from the Bundle class path.

It is the responsibility of the author of the WAB to ensure that confidential information remains confidential by placing it in one of the protected directories. WAB bundles should be constructed in such a way that they do not accidentally expose code or confidential information. The simplest way to achieve this is to follow the WAR model where code is placed in the WEB-INF/classes directory and this directory is placed on the Bundle's class path as the first entry. For example:

```
Bundle-ClassPath: WEB-INF/classes, WEB-INF/lib/acme.jar
```

128.3.6   Dynamic Content

Dynamic content is content that uses code to generate the content, for example a servlet. This code must be loaded from the bundle with the Bundle loadClass method, following all the Bundle class path rules.

Unlike a WAR, a WAB is not constrained to package classes and code resources in the WEB-INF/classes/ directory or dependent JARs in WEB-INF/lib/ only. These entries can be packaged in any way that's valid for an OSGi bundle as long as such directories and JARs are part of bundle class path as set with the Bundle-ClassPath header and any attached fragments. JARs that are specified in the Bundle-ClassPath header are treated like JARs in the WEB-INF/lib/ directory of the Servlet specification. Similarly, any directory that is part of the Bundle-ClassPath header is treated like WEB-INF/classes/ directory of the Servlet specification.

Like WARs, code content that is placed outside the protected directories can be served up to clients as static content.

128.3.7   Content Serving Example

This example consists of a WAB with the following contents:

```
acme.jar:
   Bundle-ClassPath: WEB-INF/classes, LIB/bar.jar
   Web-ContextPath: /acme

   WEB-INF/lib/foo.jar
   LIB/bar.jar
   index.html
   favicon.ico
```

The content of the embedded JARs foo.jar and bar.jar is:

```
foo.jar:                        bar.jar:
   META-INF/foo.tld                META-INF/bar.tld
   foo/FooTag.class                bar/BarTag.class
```

Assuming there are no special rules in place then the following lists specifies the result of a number of web requests for static content:

```
/acme/index.html          acme.wab:index.html
/acme/favicon.ico         acme.wab:favicon.ico
/acme/WEB-INF/lib/foo.jar not found because protected directory
/acme/LIB/bar.jar         acme.wab:LIB/bar.jar  (code, but not not protected)
```

In this example, the tag classes in bar.jar must be found (if JSP is supported) but the tag classes in foo.jar must not because foo.jar is not part of the bundle class path.

128.3.8   Stopping the Web Application Bundle

A web application is stopped by stopping the corresponding WAB. In response to a WAB STOPPING event, the Web Extender must *undeploy* the corresponding Web Application from the Servlet Container and clean up any resources. This undeploying must occur synchronously with the WAB's stopping event. This will involve the following steps:

1   An org/osgi/service/web/UNDEPLOYING event is posted to signal that a Web Application will be removed. See *Events* on page 426.
2   Unregister the corresponding Servlet Context service
3   The Web Runtime must stop serving content from the Web Application.
4   The Web Runtime must clean up any Web Application specific resources as per servlet 2.5 specification.
5   Emit an org/osgi/service/web/UNDEPLOYED event. See *Events* on page 426.
6   It is possible that there are one or more *colliding* WABs because they had the same Context Path as this stopped WAB. If such colliding WABs exists then the Web Extender must attempt to deploy the colliding WAB with the lowest bundle id.

Any failure during undeploying should be logged but must not stop the cleaning up of resources and notification of (other) listeners as well as handling any collisions.

128.3.9   Uninstalling the Web Application Bundle

A web application can be uninstalled by uninstalling the corresponding WAB. The WAB will be uninstalled from the OSGi framework.

128.3.10   Stopping of the Web Extender

When the Web Extender is stopped all deployed WABs are undeployed as described in *Stopping the Web Application Bundle* on page 423. Although the WAB is undeployed it remains in the ACTIVE state. When the Web Extender leaves the STOPPING state all WABs will have been undeployed.

128.4   Web URL Handler

The Web URL Handler acts as a filter on the Input Stream of an install operation. It receives the WAB or WAR and it then generates a JAR that conforms to the WAB specification by rewriting the manifest resource. This process is depicted in Figure 128.3 *Web URL Handler*.

Figure 128.3   *Web URL Handler*

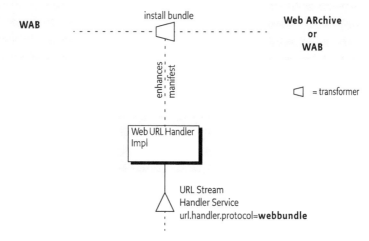

When the Web Container bundle is installed it must provide the webbundle: scheme to the URL class. The Web URL Handler has two primary responsibilities:

- *WAB* – If the source is already a bundle then only the Web-ContextPath can be set or overwritten.
- *WAR* – If the source is a WAR (that is, it must not contain any OSGi defined headers) then convert the WAR into a WAB.

The Web URL Handler can take parameters from the query arguments of the install URL, see 128.4.3 *URL Parameters*.

The URL handler must validate query parameters, and ensure that the manifest rewriting results in valid OSGi headers. Any validation failures must result in Bundle Exception being thrown and the bundle install must fail.

Once a WAB is generated and installed, its life cycle is managed just like any other bundle in the framework.

128.4.1   URL Scheme

The Web URL Handler's scheme is defined to be:

```
scheme      ::= 'webbundle:" embedded '?' web-params
embedded    ::= <embedded URL according to RFC 1738>
web-params ::= ( web-param ( '&' web-param )* )?
web-param  ::= <key> '=' <value>
```

The web-param <key> and <value> as well as the <embedded url> must follow [7] *Uniform Resource Locators, RFC 1738* for their escaping and character set rules. A Web URL must further follow all the rules of a URL. Whitespaces are not allowed between terms.

An example for a webbundle: URL:

```
webbundle:http://www.acme.com:8021/sales.war?
```

Any URL scheme understood by the framework can be embedded, such as an http:, or file: URL. Some forms of embedded URL also contain URL query parameters and this must be supported. The embedded URL most be encoded as a standard URL. That is, the control characters like colon (':'), slash ('/'), percent ('%'), and ampersand ('?') must not be encoded. Thus the value returned from the getPath method may contain a query part. Any implementation must take care to preserve both the query parameters for the embedded URL, and for the complete webbundle: URL. A question mark must always follow the embedded URL to simplify this processing. The following example shows an HTTP URL with some query parameters:

webbundle:http://www.acme.com/sales?id=123?Bundle-SymoblicName=com.example

128.4.2   URL Parsing

The URL object for a webbundle: URL must return the following values for the given methods:

- getProtocol – webbundle
- getPath – The complete embedded URL
- getQuery – The parameters for processing of the manifest.

For the following example:

webbundle:http://acme.com/repo?war=example.war?Bundle-SymoblicName=com.example

The aforementioned methods must return:

- getProtocol –webbundle
- getPath –http://acme.com/repo?war=example.war
- getQuery –Bundle-SymoblicName=com.example

128.4.3   URL Parameters

All the parameters in the webbundle: URL are optional except for the Web-ContextPath parameter. The parameter names are case insensitive, but their values must be treated as case sensitive. Table 128.3 describes the parameters that must be supported by any webbundle: URL Stream handler. A Web URL Handler is allowed to support additional parameters.

Table 128.3   *Web bundle URL Parameters*

Parameter Name	Description
Bundle-SymbolicName	The desired symbolic name for the resulting WAB.
Bundle-Version	The version of the resulting WAB. The value of this parameter must follow the OSGi versioning syntax.
Bundle-ManifestVersion	The desired bundle manifest version. Currently, the only valid value for this parameter is 2.
Import-Package	A list of packages that the war file depends on.
Web-ContextPath	The Context Path from which the Servlet Container should serve content from the resulting WAB. This is the only valid parameter when the input JAR is already a bundle. This parameter must be specified.

128.4.4   WAB Modification

The Web URL Handler can set or modify the Web-ContextPath of a WAB if the input source is already a bundle. It must be considered as a bundle when any of the OSGi defined headers listed in Table 128.3 is present in the bundle.

For WAB Modification, the Web URL Handler must only support the Web-ContextPath parameter and it must not modify any existing headers other than the Web-ContextPath. Any other parameter given must result in a Bundle Exception.

128.4.5   WAR Manifest Processing

The Web URL Handler is designed to support the transparent deployment of Java EE Web ARchives (WAR). Such WARs are ignorant of the requirements of the underlying OSGi service platform that hosts the Web Runtime. These WARs are not proper OSGi bundles because they do not contain the necessary metadata in the manifest. For example, a WAR without a Bundle-ManifestVersion, Import-Package, and other headers cannot operate in an OSGi service platform.

The Web URL Handler implementation copies the contents of the embedded URL to the output and rewrites the manifest headers based on the given parameters. The result must be a WAB.

Any parameters specified must be treated as manifest headers for the web. The following manifest headers must be set to the following values if not specified:

- Bundle-ManifestVersion – Must be set to 2.
- Bundle-SymbolicName – Generated in an implementation specific way.
- Bundle-ClassPath – Must consist of:
    - WEB-INF/classes/
    - All JARs from the WEB-INF/lib directory in the WAR. The order of these embedded JARs is unspecified.
    - If these JARs declare dependencies in their manifest on other JARs in the bundle, then these jars must also be appended to the Bundle-ClassPath header. The process of detecting JAR dependencies must be performed recursively as indicated in the Servlet Specification.
- Web-ContextPath – The Web-ContextPath must be specified as a parameter. This Context Path should start with a leading slash ('/'). The Web URL handler must add the preceding slash it if it is not present.

The Web URL Handler is responsible for managing the import dependencies of the WAR. Implementations are free to handle the import dependencies in an implementation defined way. They can augment the Import-Package header with byte-code analysis information, add a fixed set of clauses, and/or use the Dynamic-ImportPackage header as last resort.

Any other manifest headers defined as a parameter or WAR manifest header not described in this section must be copied to the WAB manifest by the Web URL Handler. Such an header must not be modified.

128.4.6   Signed WAR files

When a signed WAR file is installed using the Web URL Handler, then the manifest rewriting process invalidates the signatures in the bundle. The OSGi specification requires fully signed bundles for security reasons, security resources in partially signed bundles are ignored.

If the use of the signing metadata is required, the WAR must be converted to a WAB during development and then signed. In this case, the Web URL Handler cannot be used. If the Web URL Handler is presented with a signed WAR, the manifest name sections that contain the resource's check sums must be stripped out by the URL stream handler. Any signer files (*.SF and their corresponding DSA/RSA signature files) must also be removed.

128.5   Events

The Web Extender must track all WABs in the OSGi service platform in which the Web Extender is installed. The Web Extender must post Event Admin events, which is asynchronous, at crucial points in its processing. The topic of the event must be one of the following values:

- org/osgi/service/web/DEPLOYING – The Web Extender has accepted a WAB and started the process of deploying a Web Application.
- org/osgi/service/web/DEPLOYED – The Web Extender has finished deploying a Web Application, and the Web Application is now available for web requests on its Context Path.

- org/osgi/service/web/UNDEPLOYING – The web extender started undeploying the Web Application in response to its corresponding WAB being stopped or the Web Extender is stopped.
- org/osgi/service/web/UNDEPLOYED – The Web Extender has undeployed the Web Application. The application is no longer available for web requests.
- org/osgi/service/web/FAILED – The Web Extender has failed to deploy the Web Application, this event can be fired after the DEPLOYING event has fired and indicates that no DEPLOYED event will be fired.

For each event topic above, the following properties must be published:

- bundle.symbolicName – (String) The bundle symbolic name of the WAB.
- bundle.id – (Long) The bundle id of the WAB.
- bundle – (Bundle) The Bundle object of the WAB.
- bundle.version – (Version) The version of the WAB.
- context.path – (String) The Context Path of the Web Application.
- timestamp – (Long) The time when the event occurred
- extender.bundle – (Bundle) The Bundle object of the Web Extender Bundle
- extender.bundle.id – (Long) The id of the Web Extender Bundle.
- extender.bundle.symbolicName – (String) The symbolic name of the Web Extender Bundle.
- extender.bundle.version – (Version) The version of the Web Extender Bundle.

In addition, the org/osgi/service/web/FAILED event must also have the following property:

- exception – (Throwable) If an exception caused the failure, an exception detailing the error that occurred during the deployment of the WAB.
- collision – (String) If a name collision occurred, the Web-ContextPath that had a collision
- collision.bundles – (Long) If a name collision occurred, a list of bundle ids that all have the same value for the Web-ContextPath manifest header.

128.6 Interacting with the OSGi Environment

128.6.1 Bundle Context Access

In order to properly integrate in an OSGi environment, a Web Application can access the OSGi service registry for publishing its services, accessing services provided by other bundles, and listening to bundle and service events to track the life cycle of these artifacts. This requires access to the Bundle Context of the WAB.

The Web Extender must make the Bundle Context of the corresponding WAB available to the Web Application via the Servlet Context osgi-bundlecontext attribute. A Servlet can obtain a Bundle Context as follows:

```
BundleContext ctxt = (BundleContext)
    servletContext.getAttribute("osgi-bundlecontext");
```

128.6.2 Other Component Models

Web Applications sometimes need to inter-operate with services provided by other component models, such as a Declarative Services or Blueprint. Per the Servlet specification, the Servlet Container owns the life cycle of a Servlet; the life cycle of the Servlet must be subordinate to the life cycle of the Servlet Context, which is only dependent on the life cycle of the WAB. Interactions between different bundles are facilitated by the OSGi service registry. This interaction can be managed in several ways:

- A Servlet can obtain a Bundle Context from the Servlet Context for performing service registry operations.
- Via the JNDI Specification and the osgi:service JNDI namespace. The OSGi JNDI specification describes how OSGi services can be made available via the JNDI URL Context. It defines an

osgi:service namespace and leverages URL Context factories to facilitate JNDI integration with the OSGi service registry.

Per this specification, it is not possible to make the Servlet life cycle dependent on the availability of specific services. Any synchronization and service dependency management must therefore be done by the Web Application itself.

128.6.3 Resource Lookup

The getResource and getResourceAsStream methods of the ServletContext interface are used to access resources in the web application. For a WAB, these resources must be found according to the findEntries method, this method includes fragments. For the getResource and getResourceAsStream method, if multiple resources are found, then the first one must be used.

The getResourcePaths method must map to the Bundle getEntryPaths method, its return type is a Set and can not handle multiples. However, the paths from the getEntryPaths method are relative while the methods of the getResourcePaths must be absolute.

For example, assume the following manifest for a bundle:

```
Bundle-ClassPath: localized, WEB-INF
...
```

This WAB has an attached fragment acme-de.jar with the following content:

```
META-INF/MANIFEST.MF
localized/logo.png
```

The getResource method for localized/logo.png uses the findEntries method to find a resource in the directory /localized and the resource logo.png. Assuming the host bundle has no localized/ directory, the Web Runtime must serve the logo.png resource from the acme-de.jar.

128.6.4 Resource Injection and Annotations

The Web Application web.xml descriptor can specify the metadata-complete attribute on the web-app element. This attribute defines whether the web.xml descriptor is *complete*, or whether the classes in the bundle should be examined for deployment annotations. If the metadata-complete attribute is set to true, the Web Runtime must ignore any servlet annotations present in the class files of the Web Application. Otherwise, if the metadata-complete attribute is not specified, or is set to false, the container should process the class files of the Web Application for annotations, if supported.

A WAB can make use of the annotations defined by [8] *JSR 250 Common Annotations for the Java Platform* if supported by the Web Extender. Such a WAB must import the packages the annotations are contained in. A Web Extender that does not support the use of JSR 250 annotations must not process a WAB that imports the annotations package.

128.6.5 JavaServer Pages Support

Java Server Pages (JSP) is a rendering technology for template based web page construction. This specification supports [5] *JSP 2.1 specification* if available with the Web Runtime. The servlet element in a web.xml descriptor is used to describe both types of Web Components. JSP components are defined implicitly in the web.xml descriptor through the use of an implicit .jsp extension mapping, or explicitly through the use of a jsp-group element.

128.6.6 **Compilation**

A Web Runtime compiles a JSP page into a Servlet, either during the deployment phase, or at the time of request processing, and dispatches the request to an instance of such a dynamically created class. Often times, the compilation task is delegated to a separate JSP compiler that will be responsible for identifying the necessary tag libraries, and generating the corresponding Servlet. The container then proceeds to load the dynamically generated class, creates an instance and dispatches the servlet request to that instance.

Supporting in-line compilation of a JSP inside a bundle will require that the Web Runtime maintains a private area where it can store such compiled classes. The Web Runtime can leverage its private bundle storage area. The Web Runtime can construct a special class loader to load generated JSP classes such that classes from the bundle class path are visible to newly compiled JSP classes.

The JSP specification does not describe how JSP pages are dynamically compiled or reloaded. Various Web Runtime implementations handle the aspects in proprietary ways. This specification does not bring forward any explicit requirements for supporting dynamic aspects of JSP pages.

128.7 Security

The security aspects of this specification are defined by the *Servlet 2.5 specification* on page 429.

128.8 References

[1] *OSGi Core Specifications*
http://www.osgi.org/Specifications/HomePage

[2] *Jave Enterprise Edition Release 5*
http://java.sun.com/javaee/technologies/javaee5.jsp
Java 1.5.0 Packages

[3] *Java EE Web Applications*
http://java.sun.com/javaee/technologies/webapps/

[4] *Servlet 2.5 specification*
http://jcp.org/aboutJava/communityprocess/mrel/jsr154/index.html

[5] *JSP 2.1 specification*
http://jcp.org/aboutJava/communityprocess/final/jsr245/index.html

[6] *PAX Web Extender*
http://wiki.ops4j.org/display/ops4j/Pax+Web+Extender

[7] *Uniform Resource Locators, RFC 1738*
http://www.ietf.org/rfc/rfc1738.txt

[8] *JSR 250 Common Annotations for the Java Platform*
http://jcp.org/aboutJava/communityprocess/pfd/jsr250/index.html

129 SCA Configuration Type Specification

Version 1.0

129.1 Introduction

The [3] *Service Component Architecture (SCA)* provides an assembly model for distributed applications and systems using a service oriented architecture. The components that are assembled can be written in different technologies for example Java EE, BPEL, C++, and scripting languages. They can execute on different machines, and can communicate through different protocols and technologies. For example SOAP/HTTP as well as JMS and JCA. SCA enables the precise configuration of the communications between its components allowing the configuration to be deployed to different SCA runtimes without change. SCA enables inter-operability when used with interoperable protocols, such as HTTP.

The OSGi Remote Services model, which is based on the chapter about *Remote Services* on page 7, describes how to distribute OSGi services in general. The Remote Services specification provides an extendable model for configuration types, enabling the use of a wide array of technologies. This SCA Configuration Type Specification defines such a configuration type. It provides a mapping of the SCA distribution configuration to the OSGi Remote Services model, as well as the Remote Service Admin Endpoint Description, thus enabling OSGi runtimes to be configured for portability and inter-operability.

This specification is based on the [4] *SCA Assembly specification v1.1 CD03* and [5] *SCA Policy Framework specification v1.1 CD02.*

129.1.1 Essentials

- *Portable* – Allow an exported or imported service to be configured once for Distribution Providers from different origins.
- *Interoperable* – Allow two Distribution Providers to be configured such that they can communicate with each other. This is achieved through the use of an interoperable Binding.
- *Extensible* – Allow the configuration to be extended in new ways, for example, adding new *Bindings Intents* and *Policy Sets.*
- *Compatible* – Compatible with the SCA standards.

129.1.2 Entities

- *Distribution Provider* – An implementation of the communications stack that distributes services according to the chapter about *Remote Services* on page 7.
- *SCA Distribution Provider* – A Distribution Provider that supports the SCA configuration type.
- *Web Service* – A communications stack to provide services available over HTTP, typically used to refer to a service using the SOAP/HTTP protocol.
- *Communications Stack* – The software that enables the communication between different systems.
- *Binding Type* – An XML schema type that defines the configuration details of an Endpoint. Different Binding Types are needed for different protocols and require different configuration details.
- *Binding* – An XML element of a particular Binding Type detailing an actual Endpoint.
- *Intent* – An abstract policy requirement on the interaction between a service provider and a service client. For example the confidentiality Intent could be implemented by encrypting the communications between the provider and the client.

- *Policy Set* – An implementation of an Intent, optionally restricted to a specific Binding Type. A Policy Set is expressed in a language such as [7] *WS-Policy specification*. For example, a Policy Set might configure Triple-DES encryption as the implementation for the confidentiality Intent when applied to the sca:binding.ws (web service) Binding Type.
- *SCA Configuration Bundle* – A bundle containing Intents, Policy Sets, and Bindings in one or more of its resources.
- *SCA Configuration Extender* – A bundle that can detect SCA configuration data in an SCA Configuration Bundle using the extender pattern.
- *SCA Configuration Document* – An XML document containing SCA Configuration.
- *Endpoint* – An Endpoint is a communications access mechanism to a service in another framework, a (web) service, another process, a queue or topic destination, etc., requiring some protocol for communications.
- *Endpoint Description* – A description of an Endpoint, defined in *Endpoint Description* on page 286.

Figure 129.1   *Class and Service overview*

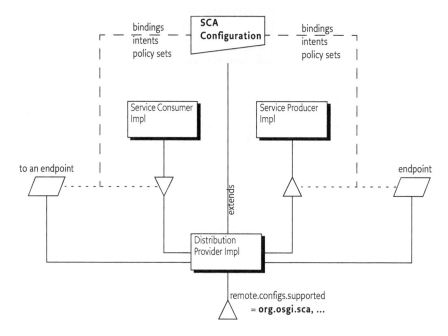

129.1.3   Synopsis

Endpoints are created using metadata descriptions, the SCA Configuration, that are typed by the SCA specifications. This configuration defines the Bindings and policy information used to configure an exported Endpoint or describe the Endpoint to an importing framework. SCA Configurations can be installed into a framework through an *SCA Configuration Bundle*. An SCA Configuration Bundle is a bundle containing one or more SCA Configuration Documents. The Distribution Provider manages an internal registry based on these SCA Configurations. The internal registry is representing a view on the SCA domain; clusters of computers can potentially share this internal registry. However, the life cycle of the information in this registry is tied to the life cycle of the bundle that provides the SCA Configuration.

A Distribution Provider is responsible for managing remote services; remote services can be exported and imported. For exporting a service, an Endpoint can be created when the following criteria are met on an active service:

- *Ready* – A service is registered and satisfies the rules necessary for it to be considered available for exporting.

- *Configured* – The configuration the service refers to in its properties, both directly and indirectly, is available, correct, and complete.

The satisfaction of these criteria can change over time, for example, due to new SCA Configuration Bundles becoming ready, being uninstalled, services being registered, services being unregistered, or having their configuration changed. The Distribution Provider is responsible for tracking all such changes and managing the Endpoint life cycle of an exported service accordingly.

A Remote Service Admin service can also import Endpoints that are configured with the SCA Configuration Type. An SCA Distribution Provider must be able to import such a service.

129.2 SCA Overview

The Service Component Architecture (SCA) is a programming model for assembling applications and systems using a *service oriented architecture*. The specifications for SCA are developed at [2] *OASIS*. The core SCA specification is the [4] *SCA Assembly specification v1.1 CD03* that defines how components of different implementation technologies, such as Java EE, BPEL, and scripting languages, can be assembled and deployed.

129.2.1 Bindings and Binding Types

To assist the deployment, the assembly contains XML descriptions of the required topology. An important aspect of this description is the *Binding*. A Binding provides the details of an Endpoint. Bindings can be attached to SCA services or SCA references (dependencies) of the assembled components in order to enable communications. For example, an RMI Binding would need the server and port number of an RMI Registry.

Binding details vary significantly per protocol. This is the reason that the SCA model recognizes *Binding Types*. A Binding Type is defined as an XML Schema type in an XML namespace. Such a type must be substitutable for the sca:binding element. Vendors can also define Binding Types that are not specified by SCA. For example, a Binding Type for RMI authored by the ACME company could look like:

```
<?xml version="1.0" encoding="UTF-8"?>
<schema xmlns="http://www.w3.org/2001/XMLSchema"
    xmlns:sca="http://www.osoa.org/xmlns/sca/1.0"
    xmlns:acme="http://acme.com/defs" >
    targetNamespace="http://acme.com/defs">

    <element name="binding.rmi" type="RMIBinding"
        substitutionGroup="sca:binding"/>

    <complexType name="RMIBinding">
      <complexContent>
        <extension base="sca:Binding">
          <attribute name="host" type="string" use="required"/>
          <attribute name="port" type="string" use="optional"/>
        </extension>
      </complexContent>
    </complexType>
</schema>
```

The details for a Binding are therefore configured in an element of a specific Binding Type. The Binding Type sca:binding.ws is quite common; this type defines the configuration for a web service. Therefore, an sca:binding.ws element details the particulars for a concrete web services Binding.

A set of standard Binding Types are specified in SCA for web services, JMS, EJB, and JCA. All these bindings are optional for implementations of SCA. Any Binding Type must be supported by the runtime on which an assembly is deployed.

Though Bindings provide the primary details of a Communication Stack, there are usually many options for a particular service to define. SCA specifies a *Policy Framework* that allows constraints, capabilities and quality requirements to be described for such a service.

129.2.2 Policy Framework

The SCA policy framework is defined with *Intents* and *Policy Sets*.

Intents give a name to abstract concepts such as integrity and confidentiality. The indirection of Intents allows the authors of services to specify their abstract communications requirements and not be concerned how these requirements are actually implemented. These Intents must then be satisfied by the deployer with a specific *implementation*. For example, a service author could have specified the confidentiality Intent which is then provided by the deployer by ensuring that the communications are encrypted with the Blowfish encryption algorithm, using a 442 bits key.

Intents can be suffixed with a dot ('.' \u002E) and a *qualifier* to create a *qualified Intent*. For example, integrity.message qualifies the integrity Intent.

Qualifiers have only one level and there must always be one qualifier that is the *default qualifier*. A service author that requires an Intent can be satisfied by a Distribution Provider that provides that Intent or any of its qualified forms. That is, requiring the SOAP Intent on an exported service is satisfied by the SOAP.v1_2 qualified Intent of a Distribution Provider. Providing a qualified Intent implies all the semantics of its unqualified Intent. Requiring a qualified Intent can only be satisfied with that specific qualified Intent. Each Intent can mark one qualified Intent as its default, if only one qualified Intent is specified then this is the default. The default qualified Intent is used to resolve a choice when no other information is available. For example, the SOAP intent could mark the v1_2 qualifier as default. In such a case, a Distribution Provider must use the SOAP.v1_2 qualified Intent, even though an exported service only required the SOAP Intent.

Intents can also be grouped in *profile Intent*s.

A Binding Type can state Intents that it inherently provides. For example, a web service Binding inherently provides the SOAP Intent. An instance of a Binding Type, a *Binding*, can configure requirements for additional Intents. This allows the Binding to configure-in additional aspects of the communications that were not inherently provided by the Binding Type, or the Intents required by the service. For example, a Binding could add the confidentiality Intent.

The *implementation* of an Intent is provided by a *Policy Set*. A Policy Set uses a policy language to define this implementation. A Policy Set can apply to all Binding Types or it can apply to a specific Binding Type. For example, an SCA service could be configured with the SCA web services Binding (binding.ws element) and the confidentiality Intent. A Policy Set that matches the tuple (confidentiality, binding.ws) then defines that the implementation is the Triple-DES encryption algorithm.

SCA provides a mechanism to define Policy Sets using standard policy languages, such as the [7] *WS-Policy specification*.

In order for a service to be correctly configured, the relationships between Intents, Bindings and Policy Sets must be consistent. For example, a Policy Set could state that it provides the confidentiality Intent and applies to the binding.ws Binding. However, if the Intent does not also state it applies to the web service Binding then the relationships do not match and the configuration is invalid or incomplete.

129.2.3 Relationships

Intents and Policy Sets are configured in the intent and policySet elements as well as the elements and attributes defined by the Binding Types. Figure 129.2 shows these elements and XML Schema Type from the SCA Policy Framework that are applicable to this specification. The relationships between these elements and types are described in Table 129.1 on page 435. The relationships in Figure 129.2 and Table 129.1 are named after their corresponding element or attribute in the SCA Schema.

Figure 129.2   *Policy Framework Model*

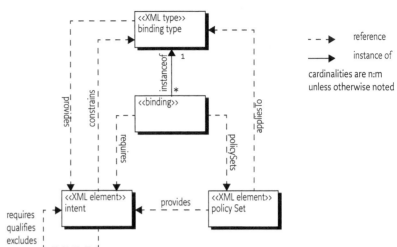

An overview of the policy framework elements and relationships is given below, and an example provided in the sections that describe each of the entities. See *sca-config Element* on page 441, *policySet Element* on page 444, and *intent Element* on page 442.

Table 129.1   *Policy Framework Relationships*

From	Relationship	To	Description
Binding Type	provides	Intent	Binding Types can provide (either always, or optionally) Intents. Such Intents do not require additional Policy Set configuration. For example, the web service Binding always provides the SOAP Intent and can optionally provide the SOAP.v1_1 or SOAP.v1_2 Intents.
Binding	requires	Intent	A Binding can be configured to require additional Intents that were not expressed on the services that refer to it.
	policySets	Policy Set	A Binding can refer directly to Policy Sets, short-cutting the need to define an Intent.
Intent	constrains	Binding Type	An Intent can constrain a Binding Type. This makes the Intent only applicable for Bindings of the given type.
	requires	Intent	An Intent can require another Intent. This mechanism enables the creation of *profile Intents*. A profile Intent is an Intent defined in terms of other Intents. For example, a communicationProtection Intent could be defined as the combination of the confidentiality and integrity Intents.

Table 129.1   *Policy Framework Relationships*

	qualifies	Intent	A qualified Intent is an Intent that provides further qualification of another Intent. For example the Intent SOAP.v1_2 qualifies SOAP further by constraining it to a specific version of the SOAP protocol.
	excludes	Intent	An Intent can exclude another Intent. Exclusion of an Intent states that the two cannot be used together; such Intents are mutually exclusive.
Policy Set	provides	Intent	A Policy Set can provide concrete configuration for Intents. For example, a Policy Set could define a specific encryption algorithm to use for the confidentiality Intent.
	appliesTo	Binding Type	A Policy Set can apply to a Binding Type or all types of Binding. Applying to a Binding Type means it is valid to configure the Policy Set on Bindings of that Binding Type. Configuration can either be done indirectly through the use of an Intent that the Policy Set provides, or directly by referring to the Policy Set by name in the Binding configuration.

129.3   SCA Configuration Bundles

An OSGi Distribution Provider that supports SCA configuration types must track *SCA Configuration Bundles*. These are bundles that are marked to have *SCA Configuration Documents*, this detection is explained in *Detection of SCA Configuration Bundles* on page 437. If such an SCA Configuration Bundle is found, then its resources are parsed as SCA Configuration Documents and, when found to be correct, their configuration placed in an *internal registry*. This internal registry contains the defined Bindings, Intents, and Policy Sets indexed by their names. The Intents, Policy Sets, and Bindings are then available for bundles that want to export or import services. If the SCA Configuration Bundle is stopped, the internal registry must be purged from any of the information that was derived from the bundle's resources.

For example, if an SCA Configuration Bundle defines the acme:FooRMI Binding together with the acme:protected Intent, then the following service properties could be used to export a service:

```
service.exported.configs= org.osgi.sca
org.osgi.sca.bindings   = FooRMI
service.exported.intents= protected
```

129.3.1   Naming

Service properties can export a service with a qualified name or the short name for Bindings and Intents. These names have the following structure:

```
name ::= NCName | QName
```

Both QName and NCName are defined by [8] *XML Schema*. The structure for a QName is:

```
QName ::= '{' <namespace> '}' NCName
```

Spaces are not allowed in a name.

For example, a new Intent named protected, defined in an SCA Configuration Resource and a targetNamespace of http://acme.com, would be identifiable through the qualified name:

```
{http://acme.com}protected
```

There is no specific support for versioning. A name defined in a namespace must be treated as identical if it appears in multiple documents. Namespaces can implement versioning by suffixing the namespace with a version number.

129.3.2 Internal Registry

The Distribution Provider must maintain an internal registry that contains the following types:

- *Intent Vocabulary* – The vocabulary of the Intents. These Intents must become available on the Distribution Provider's remote.intents.supported service property once they are available in the internal registry and have an appropriate implementation.
- *Policy Set Dictionary* – A dictionary of Policy Sets. These Policy Sets define the implementations of the Intents.
- *Binding Dictionary* – Maps the defined Bindings. These Bindings must be of Binding Types that are supported by the Distribution Provider. Adding new Binding Types is out of scope for this specification.

The internal registry must maintain the items by their qualified name but it must be possible to find entries with short names. There is no requirement that the internal registry is internally consistent nor *complete* (see *Complete* on page 448) at all times. Duplicate qualified names for the same type are, however, never allowed. It is legal to refer to names that have not been defined, however, such referrers cannot be used in configuration types until they are complete.

The Internal SCA Registry should, at any moment in time, only contain the error-free definitions of ready SCA Configuration Bundles. Due to the asynchronous nature of processing the definitions, it is likely that some time lag will happen, users of this specification must take this lag into account.

129.3.3 Detection of SCA Configuration Bundles

A bundle is an *SCA Configuration Bundle* if its manifest contains an SCA-Configuration header and it has one or more SCA Configuration Documents. The structure of an SCA Configuration Document is defined in *SCA Configuration Document* on page 440. A Distribution Provider is responsible for obtaining and releasing configurations based on the bundle life cycle of SCA Configuration Bundles.

The SCA-Configuration header has the following syntax:

```
SCA-Configuration ::= header
                      // Core 3.2.4 Common Header Syntax
```

If the header is present, but no value is provided, then its default value is:

```
OSGI-INF/sca-config/*.xml
```

This specification does not define any attributes or directives for this header, implementations of this specification must ignore unrecognized attributes and directives. Implementations can provide proprietary parameters that should be registered with the OSGi Alliance to prevent name collisions. The non-localized version of the SCA-Configuration header must be used.

The last component of each path in the SCA-Configuration clauses may use wildcards so that the Bundle findEntries method can be used to locate the SCA Configuration resource within the bundle and its fragments. The findEndtries method must always be used in the non-recursive mode. Valid paths in the header have one of the following forms:

- *Absolute path* – The path to a resource in the fragment or directory, this resource must exist. For example cnf/start.xml.

- *Directory* – The path to directory in a fragment or the bundle's JAR; the path must end in a slash ('/'). The pattern used in the findEntries method must then be *.xml. The directory is allowed to be empty.
- *Pattern* – The last component of the path specifies a resource name with optional wildcards. The part before is the path of a directory in the bundle or one of its fragments. These two parts specify the parameter to the findEntries method. It is allowed to have no matching resources. An example of a pattern is: cnf/*.xml.

If the SCA-Configuration header is not present, then the bundle must not be searched for SCA Configuration Documents. An SCA-Configuration manifest header specified in a fragment must be ignored by the Distribution Provider.

If no SCA Configuration Documents can be found, then the SCA Configuration Bundle is ignored for the purpose of SCA Configuration data. SCA Configuration Documents referenced by an SCA-Configuration manifest header, or its default, may be contained in attached fragments; this is the normal mode for the findEntries method.

For example, the following header will read the resources /bindings/acme.xml, policy/security.xml, and all resources whose path ends in .xml in the /other bundle directory:

```
SCA-Configuration: bindings/acme.xml, policy/security.xml, other/*.xml
```

129.3.4　Parsing

The Distribution Provider must parse the specified SCA Configuration Documents and place the found definitions in the internal registry. Parsing fails if:

- The XML is not well formed.
- An SCA Configuration Document does not validate against its schema.
- The contained elements do not meet one or more of their constraints as defined in this specification.
- Any error occurs.

A *failure* invalidates all SCA configuration for the entire SCA Configuration Bundle. Failures should be logged if a Log Service is present. The Distribution Provider must cease processing of the SCA Configuration Bundle and discard any configuration information it has already processed. That is, either all information from an SCA Configuration Bundle is in the internal registry or none.

129.3.5　Activation of New SCA Configuration

When a new SCA Configuration Bundle is detected, a Distribution Provider must:

1　Wait until the configuration bundle is *ready*. A configuration bundle is ready when it is in the ACTIVE state. In the case where the configuration bundle has a lazy activation policy, ready must also include the STARTING state.
2　Verify that the bundle is an SCA Configuration Bundle, see *Detection of SCA Configuration Bundles* on page 437.
3　Parse the SCA Configuration Documents as defined in *SCA Configuration Document* on page 440.
4　Validate the new Intent, Policy Set and Binding definitions against the current internal registry. Multiple Intent definitions with the same qualified name are not permitted, just as Bindings and Policy Sets must have unique qualified names within the internal SCA registry. Duplications (same qualified name) are treated as a failure.
5　Process any additional Distribution Provider specific configuration. If the Distribution Provider encounters any configuration that it does not understand and the must-understand attribute is set to true, then this is a failure. The must-understand attribute is an OSGi specific extension.
6　Add new Intents to the Distribution Providers's vocabulary. See *intent Element* on page 442 for the rules on when Intents should be added to the Distribution Provider's vocabulary.
7　Add new Policy Sets to the internal SCA registry Policy Set dictionary.
8　Add any new Bindings to the internal SCA registry Binding dictionary.

9   Perform any service export or import changes resulting from the updates to the Distribution Provider's internal registry. This can result in new Endpoints being created, existing Endpoints being modified, or new proxies to remote services being registered. See *Registering a Service for Export* on page 449 and *Getting an Imported Service* on page 449.

The previous steps can happen in parallel for different bundles.

129.3.6   Deactivation of an SCA Configuration

When an SCA Configuration Bundle is stopped then the Distribution Provider must:

1   Remove the bundle's Intents, Policy Sets and Bindings from the internal registry.
2   Remove any additional configuration that the bundle contributed.
3   Update the remote.supported.configs service property with the currently complete Intents.
4   Remove any Endpoints for exported services that are now no longer fully configured. See *Registering a Service for Export* on page 449, for the steps used to determine when an Endpoint is fully configured for an exported service.
5   Remove any proxies for imported services that were configured information from the SCA Configuration Bundle.

129.3.7   Example SCA Configuration

The following example shows an extract of an SCA Configuration that contributes a number of Bindings. The first Binding describes a web service Endpoint of the type binding.ws and the next Binding configuration describes the vendor specific acme configuration for an RMI Endpoint. Such a vendor specific Binding Type can only be used when the Distribution Provider has built-in supports for this hypothetical type.

```
<sca:binding.ws
    name      ="FooWS"
    uri       ="http://acme.com/Foo" requires="sca:SOAP.v1_2"
/>
<acme:binding.rmi
    name      ="FooRMI"
    host      ="acme.com"
    port      ="8099"
    serviceName="Foo"
/>
```

The service property values used to reference both Bindings from the previous example SCA configuration look as follows:

```
service.exported.configs= org.osgi.sca
org.osgi.sca.bindings   = [FooWS,{http://acme.com/defs}FooRMI]
```

The relationships of this example between these Binding Types, Bindings, service and Endpoints are illustrated in Figure 129.3.

Figure 129.3   *Example SCA Configuration Schema*

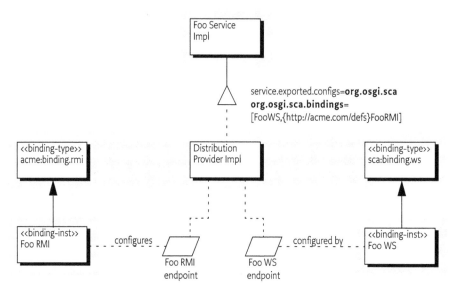

A Distribution Provider that supports one or more Binding Types like sca:binding.ws or
acme:binding.rmi must uses the rules described in *Registering a Service for Export* on page 449 to
decide whether or not to create an Endpoint for any services that reference the Bindings. A Binding
can be referred to either through its NCName or QName, see *Naming* on page 436. In the previous
example, The FooWS Binding value is using a short NCName, the {http://acme.com/defs}FooRMI
Binding uses the longer QName. The QName form is more verbose but reduces the risk of name
clashes. A Distribution Provider must support matching both forms.

If an NCName can be matched against multiple bindings then this is considered an error. Such an
error should be logged if a Log Service is available. This error does not affect the use of other bindings
listed in the org.osgi.sca.bindings property.

129.4   **SCA Configuration Document**

An SCA Configuration Document defines the Bindings, Policy Sets and Intents for exporting and
importing OSGi services. It is an XML document that is typed by the schema defined in *XML Schema*
on page 451.

129.4.1   **XML**

In the following sections, the XML is explained using the normal regular expression based syntax
notation used for headers. There is, however, one addition to the normal usage specific to XML, and
that is the use of the angled brackets (<>). A term enclosed in angled brackets, indicates the use of an
actual element, similar to a literal. Without the angled brackets it is the definition of a term that is
expanded later to a one or more other terms or elements. For example:

```
people    ::= <person> *
person    ::= <child>* address
address   ::= <fr> | <us> | <nl>
```

This example uses <person> as a literal for the person element and address as a term that is defined
later. The following XML is an instance of the previous example definition:

```
<people>
  <person id="mieke">
```

```
        <child name="mischa"/>
        <child name="thomas"/>
        <fr zip="34160"/>
    </person>
</people>
```

Attributes are described in tables or in text. The following sections are a normative description of the semantics of the schema. However, the structure information is illustrative. The actual XML Schema is defined in *XML Schema* on page 451.

The reason many attributes that refer to other elements are typed with xsd:string and not QName or NCName is done to align the schema with its source, the SCA Schema. In SCA, these attributes can contain XPath expressions and must therefore be strings. This specifications only supports QName and NCName though.

A number of attributes contain *XPath expressions*. The expressions are ran against a virtual XML tree that has an top element with an undefined name and contains all the binding elements of the internal registry. For example, the XPath expression //sca:binding.ws is guaranteed to select all web service bindings in the internal registry.

The @ sign is used to indicate an XML attribute. An XML type for an attribute can be suffixed with a plus sign ('+'). This indicates a list of whitespace separated elements.

129.4.2   sca-config Element

An SCA Configuration Document root element is the sca-config element. The schema structure is depicted in Figure 129.4; it is summarized as follows:

```
sca-config ::= ( <intent> | <policySet> | <<binding>> )*
```

The intent, and policySet elements (and their child nodes) are defined in the SCA specification. However, the actual Binding Instances are defined in elements from the SCA or other namespaces. This distinction is indicated by using it as an element with double angled brackets: <<binding>>. The actual Binding Type XML schema must be supported by the Distribution Provider.

Figure 129.4   *SCA Configuration Schema*

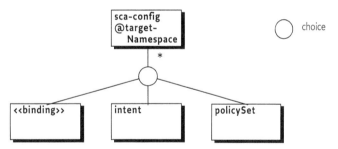

129.4.3   Default Example Definitions

In the following sections, the sca-config element and its namespace definitions are omitted for brevity. However, the use of the prefixes is consistent. Further, it is assumed that the target namespace of the example is the ACME company's namespace. All examples therefore are assumed to be contained in the following XML fragment:

```
<?xml version="1.0" encoding="UTF-8"?>
<scact:sca-config
    targetNamespace  ="http://acme.com/defs"
    xmlns:scact      ="http://www.osgi.org/xmlns/scact/v1.0.0"
    xmlns:sca        ="http://docs.oasis-open.org/ns/opencsa/sca/200912"
```

```
xmlns:acme        ="http://acme.com/defs">
<!-- example goes here -->
</scact:sca-config>
```

There are many types used in this specification that are defined in the XML Schema specification. These types are prefixes with the xsd prefix which stands for:

```
http://www.w3.org/2001/XMLSchema
```

129.4.4   intent Element

The intent element defines an Intent. Its structure is:

```
intent ::= <qualifier> *
```

Intents contributed in an intent element must become part of the Distribution Provider's Intent vocabulary once they are complete, see *Complete* on page 448. This includes the Intent name itself as well as all its defined qualified variations. These Intent names must include the NCName form, allowing the occurrence of duplicates.

The Distribution Provider is responsible for ensuring its Intent vocabulary reflects the Intents it is configured to support. For example, if an SCA Configuration Bundle with a Policy Set that provides the confidentiality Intent is uninstalled, and there are no other implementations of that Intent available, then it must be removed from the Distribution Provider's Intent vocabulary. Intents can apply to specific binding types only. It is therefore possible that an Intent is part of a Distribution Provider's vocabulary but is not available for a specific Binding Instance.

The details of how Intents are defined is described in the[5] *SCA Policy Framework specification v1.1 CD02*. This OSGi Specification only uses the constrains attribute for all, or specific Binding Types, such as the Binding Type sca:binding.ws. A Distribution Provider can choose to support other constrains attribute values. If a Distribution Provider encounters a value it does not understand then it must not use any of the information defined in the offending SCA Configuration Bundle.

An intent element can have a number of *qualifiers*. This allows the specification of qualified Intents The qualifier element is explained in *qualifier Element* on page 444. The intent element structure is illustrated in Figure 129.5.

Figure 129.5   *intent Element*

The attributes and sub-elements of the intent element are described in table Table 129.2 on page 442.

Table 129.2   *Intent Attributes*

Attribute	Type	Description
name	NCName	The name of the Intent being defined.

Table 129.2	*Intent Attributes*		
	constrains	QName+ (optional)	In SCA, intent elements can apply to many specific SCA artifacts. In this specification an intent element can either constrain a specific Binding Type, for example acme:binding.rmi, or all Binding Types: sca:binding. The sca:binding type is the substitution type of all Binding Type. This attribute must be used with a whitespace separated list.
			If the constrains attribute is omitted then it is assumed that the use of the intent element is unrestricted.
	requires	QName+ (optional)	An intent element can require other intent elements. The requires attribute enables the creation of profile Intents. This attribute must be used with a whitespace separated list.
	excludes	QName+ (optional)	A list of Intents that are incompatible with this Intent. It is an error to register a service with incompatible Intents; a Distribution Provider must not distribute such a service. This attribute must be used with a whitespace separated list.
	mutuallyExclusive	xsd:boolean (optional)	true signifies that the qualified Intents defined in children elements are mutually exclusive and must not be used together. If false or not set then any of the defined qualified Intents can be used together.
	intentType	sca:Interaction | sca:Implementation (optional)	SCA allows Intents to configure the Distribution Providers as well as any *interaction policies*. OSGi only uses interaction Intents (the default) and therefore this element can be omitted. A Distribution Provider that does not recognize Implementation Intents must fail if such an Implement Intent is specified. Implementation Intents must not become part of the Distribution Provider's vocabulary.
	description	xsd:string (optional)	A human readable text description of the Intent.

The following example shows how a Distribution Provider is configured with a new Intent called acme:protection. This new Intent definition states that it constrains the sca:binding.ws Binding Type. The protection Intent is in the acme namespace because of the targetNamespace attribute set for all examples, see *Default Example Definitions* on page 441. The XML for this example XML fragment looks like:

```
<sca:intent
    name       ="protection"
    constrains ="sca:binding.ws"
/>
```

This example could also have stated it applied to all Bindings by omitting the constrains attribute or specifying sca:binding in the constrains attribute. Figure 129.6 shows an illustration of the acme:protection Intent's relationship with sca:binding.ws.

Figure 129.6   *The acme:protection Intent*

129.4.5 qualifier Element

The qualifier element allows an intent element to have qualifiers. An intent element can contain any number of qualifier elements, each qualifier element specifies a suffix for the parent Intent. These qualifiers are used to make an Intent more specific. For example, the qualified Intent confidentiality.message would be have an intent@name of confidentiality and a qualifier with the name set to message. One, and only one, of the qualifier elements must be set to be the default qualifier. If only one qualifier element is defined then this is the default by definition.

Table 129.3 on page 444 is the description of the qualifier element. See *Remote Services* on page 7 for the definition of qualified Intents.

Table 129.3   *qualifier Element*

Attribute	Type	Description
name	NCName	The name of the qualifier. For example, transport for the qualified Intent confidentiality.transport.
default	xsd:boolean (optional)	true if this qualifier is the default, false if not. The default for the default attribute is false. One qualifer element must set the default attribute to true. If there is only one qualifier than it is by default the default and does not have to be explicitly set. In this case, if it is explicitly set to false then this is invalid.
description	xsd:string (optional)	A human readable text description of the qualified Intent.

129.4.6 policySet Element

A policySet element defines how Intents are implemented. The structure of the policySet element is:

```
policySet  ::= (<policySetReference> | <intentMap> | policy )*
policy     ::= << policy defined in some policy language >>
```

The Policy Sets provide a place to insert policy using various policy languages. They allow multiple entries, but the ways in which those are combined are defined by the policy language being used. For example, WS-Policy allows these to be additive or alternatives.

A policySetReference element contains a reference to another policySet element, see 129.4.7 *policy-SetReference Element*. A policySetReference element enables policySet elements to be defined in terms of other policySet elements.

An intentMap sub-element is used to define the implementation for a qualified Intent. See [5] *SCA Policy Framework specification v1.1 CD02* for more details. See also *intentMap Element* on page 446.

Figure 129.7 illustrates the schema for policySet elements.

Figure 129.7   *policySet element*

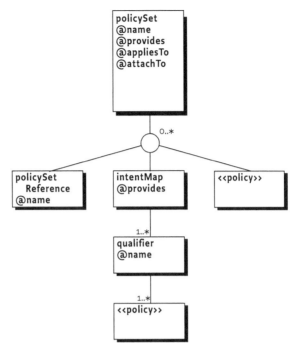

The attributes of the policySet element are described in Table 129.4.

Table 129.4   *policySet Element*

Attribute	Type	Description
name	NCName	The name of the Policy Set. This name can be used to refer to the Policy Set from a Binding. The name must be combined with the targetNamespace of the sca-configelement to give the QName for the Policy Set.
provides	QName+ (optional)	A list of QName values (whitespace separated) declaring the Intents the Policy Set provides (implements).
appliesTo	xsd:string	Identifies what Bindings the Policy Set applies to. Can be either a specific Binding (e.g. acme:binding.rmi) or all Binding Types (sca:binding). This attribute is an XPath expression in SCA.
attachTo	xsd:string (optional)	Not used. If a value is specified and a Distribution Provider does not understand attachTo then it must not use the SCA Configuration Bundle.

The following example shows the contribution of a Policy Set. In this example, the policySet element describes the particular encryption options to be used to implement the acme:protection Intent on the web service binding binding.ws. Each time a service with this Intent is exported to an Endpoint using binding.ws, then this is the encryption policy the Distribution Provider must use.

```
service.exported.configs= org.osgi.sca
org.osgi.sca.bindings   = FooWS
service.intents         = {http://acme.com/defs}protection
```

The policySet element is defined using [7] *WS-Policy specification.* The Policy Set is named acme:Encrypted; it provides the acme:protection Intent, and applies it to the sca:binding.ws Binding Type only.

```
<sca:binding.ws name="FooWS" ... />
<sca:intent
   name       ="protection"
   constrains ="sca:binding.ws"
/>
<sca:policySet
   name       ="Encrypted"
   provides   ="acme:protection"
   appliesTo  ="sca:binding.ws"
   xmlns:wsp  ="http://schemas.xmlsoap.org/ws/2004/09/policy"
   xmlns:sp   ="http://schemas.xmlsoap.org/ws/2005/07/securitypolicy">
   <wsp:Policy>
      <wsp:ExactlyOne>
         <sp:Basic256Rsa15 />
         <sp:TripleDesRsa15 />
      </wsp:ExactlyOne>
   </wsp:Policy>
</sca:policySet>
```

These relationships are illustrated in figure Figure 129.8.

Figure 129.8   *acme:Encrypted policySet*

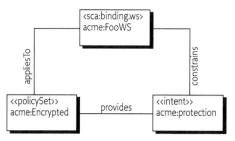

129.4.7   policySetReference Element

A reference to another Policy Set to enable policySet elements to be defined in terms of other Policy Sets. Table 129.5 defines the attribute in a policySetReference element.

Table 129.5   *policySetReference Element*

Attribute	Type	Description
name	QName	A QName identifying a policySet element being referenced. See *policySet Element* on page 444.

129.4.8   intentMap Element

An intentMap element is used to provide additional policy information of a qualifier. An intentMap element has the following structure:

```
intentMap  ::= <qualifier>*
qualifier  ::= policy ( policy ) *
```

See Table 129.6 for the intentMap element's attribute.

See [5] *SCA Policy Framework specification v1.1 CD02* for more details.

The qualifier sub-element intentMap has an attributes as defined in Table 129.7

Table 129.6	*intentMap Element*		
Attribute	**Type**	**Description**	
provides	QName	Identifying the Intent whose qualifiers are configured by this intentMap. The Intent must also be listed in the provides attribute of the containing policySet. For example, confidentiality, and the qualifiers configured by the intentMap element, could be message and transport.	

Table 129.7	*qualifier Element*		
Member	**Type**	**Description**	
name	xsd:string	The name of the intent qualifier to which the policy applies.	

The following example shows a Policy Set that implements the confidentiality Intent with two qualifiers transport and message.

```
<sca:policySet
    xmlns:wsp="http://schemas.xmlsoap.org/ws/2004/09/policy"

    name="SecureMessaging"
    provides="confidentiality"
    appliesTo="//binding.ws">

    <sca:intentMap provides="confidentiality" >
        <sca:qualifier name="transport">
            <wsp:PolicyAttachment ... />
        </sca:qualifier>
        <sca:qualifier name="message">
            <wsp:PolicyAttachment ... />
        </sca:qualifier>
    </sca:intentMap>
</sca:policySet>
```

129.5　Exporting and Importing Services

129.5.1　Service Configuration Properties

The following properties are used to convey SCA configuration information from the service importers and exporters to the Distribution Provider. Some rows define property values for properties defined in the Remote Services specification, other rows are properties whose names follow conventions defined in the Remote Services specification but whose specific values are defined in this specification, these are put in bold. Because these properties define an additional level of detail on the properties specified in Remote Services chapter, any Remote Service properties must be supported in conjunction with those defined here.

Table 129.8	*Configuration Properties*		
Service Property Name	**Type**	**Description**	
remote.configs.supported	String+	For the SCA configuration type, this property must include the value org.osgi.sca	
remote.intents.supported	String+	All supported Intents in their unqualified as well as their qualified form.	

Table 129.8	*Configuration Properties*		
	service.exported.configs	String+	A list of configuration types that should be used to export the service. For the SCA configuration type, this property must include the value org.osgi.sca.
	service.imported.configs	String+	For the SCA configuration type, this property must include the value org.osgi.sca.
	org.osgi.sca.binding	String+	Each value is an XML Schema NCName or QName identifying an individual Binding. Each Binding defines the configuration for an Endpoint. These names refer to the internal registry or the scoped configuration. See *Internal Registry* on page 437 and *Scoped Configurations* on page 448.
	org.osgi.sca.binding.types	String+	Registered by a Distribution Provider to indicate the Binding Types supported. The Binding Types must be listed with their NCName as well as their QName. See *Dependencies* on page 450.
	org.osgi.sca.config.url	String+ (optional)	A URL to an SCA Configuration Document with a scoped configuration, see *Scoped Configurations* on page 448. The URL must be accessible from the importing framework. If the org.osgi.sca.config.xml property is also present, then this property must be ignored.
	org.osgi.sca.config.xml	String (optional)	An SCA Configuration Document that provides a scoped configuration, see *Scoped Configurations* on page 448.

129.5.2   Complete

Services can only be imported and exported when their SCA Configuration information is *complete*. This information is complete when all necessary named Bindings, Policy Sets, and Intents can be found in the internal registry or when scoped, in the scoped configuration.

Complete is dynamic because the life cycles of the donating SCA Configuration Bundles are dynamic and starting and stopping bundles can cause changes in the internal registry. It is therefore possible that the completeness of an exported service or imported Endpoint changes over time. The Distribution Provider must ensure that the configuration of exports and imports is complete when they are active. If the configuration becomes incomplete, then the Distribution Provider must do a rebinding based the new configuration situation.

129.5.3   Scoped Configurations

The org.osgi.sca.configs.url or org.osgi.sca.configs.xml service properties can provide *scoped* SCA Configuration. Scoped configuration is additional SCA Configuration over and above the configuration in the internal registry.

This scoped configuration has the following additional rules:

- Scoped configuration can only contain bindings. It can not contain Policy Set or Intent definitions.
- Scoped Configurations must never be stored in the internal registry, the configuration only applies to the corresponding service.

The scoped bindings can refer to the internal registry, it can contain more definitions than required, and it can use the same names for Bindings but not for Intents, and Policy Sets that reside in the internal registry.

If a named Bindings exists in the internal registry and the scoped configuration, then the scoped information takes priority for the corresponding service.

References from the internal registry must not have access to the scoped configuration, even if they were referred to from a scoped configuration or a service property. For example, a Binding found in the internal registry must not have access to an Intent or Policy Set defined in the scoped configuration.

129.5.4 Registering a Service for Export

The rules covering the registration of a service for export are described in the Remote Service chapter. The SCA Configuration Type adds the following conditions that must be met:

- The service property service.exported.configs must contain the value org.osgi.sca.
- The Distribution Provider's internal registry, or a scoped configuration, contains complete definitions for all of the Bindings referred to the service property org.osgi.sca.bindings. Bindings can be referred to by either their NCName or QName.
- All Intents and/or Policy Sets listed in a supported Binding's requires or policySets attributes are part of the Distribution Provider's internal registry or, if scoped, in the optional scoped configuration.
- All Intents must be implemented by the selected Binding Type or in an available and applicable Policy Set.
- The Endpoint must implement at least all of the Intents listed in the service.exported.intents, service.exported.intents.extra service properties. The Endpoint must also implement the Intents and Policy Sets listed in the requires and policySets attributes of the used Binding.

For example, if a service were registered with the following property:

```
service.exported.intents.extra=integrity
```

And is then configured with a Binding with the attribute requires like:

```
<acme:binding.rmi requires="confidentiality" ... />
```

Then the Endpoint must implement both the integrity and confidentiality Intents.

A Distribution Provider must create an Endpoint for each of the Bindings it supports, including any constraints on Intents and Policy Sets; these Bindings must be alternatives. Synonyms are allowed within the SCA configuration type and are handled in the same way as synonyms from multiple configuration types.

129.5.5 Getting an Imported Service

The Remote Services specification defines the properties which must be treated as special when the Endpoint for an exported service is imported as an OSGi service in another framework. An imported service configured with the SCA Configuration Type must also have the following properties:

- service.imported.configs – Contains the configuration types that can be used to import this service. This must include the org.osgi.sca value. Any other types included must be synonymous and therefore refer to exactly the same Endpoint as the org.osgi.sca configuration.
- org.osgi.sca.bindings – Names Bindings from the internal registry for a specific Endpoint. If multiple Bindings are listed in this property then they must be synonyms for the same Endpoint. The named bindings can refer to the internal registry or the scoped bindings.
- A Distribution Provider can optionally list the scoped configuration for this service with the org.osgi.sca.configs.url or org.osgi.configs.xml service properties, see *Scoped Configurations* on page 448.

129.5.6   Dependencies

A bundle that uses the SCA Configuration Type has an implicit dependency on the Distribution Provider to support that type. To make this dependency explicit, the Distribution Provider must register a service with the following property and value

```
remote.configs.supported=org.osgi.sca
```

A Distribution Provider must also list other configuration types it supports in addition to org.osgi.sca, the type of this property is String+.

A bundle that uses a specific Binding Type also has an implicit dependency on a Distribution Provider that supports this type. To make this dependency explicit, the Distribution Provider must register a service property with the name:

```
org.osgi.sca.binding.types
```

The value must be set to the list of Binding Types supported by the Distribution Provider. This property is of type String+. This property must list both the NCName and the QName for each Binding Types it supports.

For example

```
org.osgi.sca.binding.types = [binding.ws, «
    {http://docs.oasis-open.org/ns/opencsa/sca/200912}binding.ws, «
    binding.rmi, «
    {http://acme.com/defs}binding.rmi]
```

129.6   SCA and Remote Service Admin

The *Remote Service Admin Service Specification* on page 281 provides an API for the Distribution Provider; it enables a topology manager to import and export services. A discovery mechanism is also provided to discover *Endpoint Descriptions* through different protocols. Endpoint Descriptions are property based and provide the details for a specific Endpoint. Using these properties it must be possible to create a connection to the corresponding Endpoint and import a service, if the used configuration type is recognized. The Endpoint Description properties are typically set by the Remote Service Admin that created the Endpoint and describe the Endpoint details to importers of that Endpoint.

The Endpoint Description is therefore extensible for different configuration types. This section describes the mapping of the SCA Configuration Type into the Endpoint Description. This mapping must be used by any Remote Service Admin that supports the SCA Configuration Type. The properties and values specified here are in addition to those defined in the Remote Service Admin Service Specification.

129.6.1   Configuration

An Endpoint Description is moved between systems and can therefore not refer to an internal registry. However, the SCA Configuration Type allows scoped configurations, see, see *Scoped Configurations* on page 448. Scoped configurations allow the Endpoint Description to describe all the necessary Bindings, Policy Sets, and Intents.

Scoped configuration can be provided through:

- org.osgi.sca.configs.url – A URL to an SCA Configuration Document. This URL must be accessible by an importing framework.
- org.osgi.sca.configs.xml – Embedded XML contained in the property. The embedded XML is supported with the String data type for properties and using an xml element to define it.

When a Remote Service Admin service creates an Endpoint Description it must ensure that at least a complete SCA Configuration for that Endpoint is included in that Endpoint Description as either a URL or embedded XML.

A Remote Service Admin must recognize the scoped configuration in the properties used to create an Import Registration or an Export Registration.

129.6.2   Example Endpoint Description

The following example shows how a remote Foo service is described using the Endpoint Description XML format, including the SCA configuration type configuration. In this example, the embedded form is chosen.

```
<?xml version="1.0" encoding="UTF-8"?>
<rsa:endpoint-descriptions
   xmlns:rsa="http://www.osgi.org/xmlns/rsa/v1.0.0"
   xmlns:xsi="http://www.w3.org/2001/XMLSchema-instance">
   <endpoint-description>
      <property name ="objectClass"                value ="com.acme.Foo" />
      <property name ="service.intents"            value ="confidentiality" />
      <property name ="service.imported.configs"   value="org.osgi.sca" />
      <property name ="org.osgi.sca.bindings" type="String">
         <array>
            <value>FooWS</value>
            <value>{http://acme.com/defs}FooRMI</value>
         </array>
      </property>
      <property name    ="org.osgi.sca.config.xml" type="String">
      <xml>
         <scact:sca-config targetNamespace="http://acme.com/defintions"
            xmlns:scact      ="http://www.osgi.org/xmlns/scact/v1.0.0"
            xmlns:sca        ="http://docs.oasis-open.org/ns/opencsa/sca/200912"
            xmlns:acme       ="http://acme.com/defintions">
            <sca:binding.ws name="FooWS"
               uri="http://acme.com/Foo" requires="sca:soap.v1_2" />
            <acme:binding.rmi name="FooRMI"
               host="acme.com" port="8099" serviceName="Foo" />
            <sca:intent>
               ...
            </sca:intent>
            <sca:policySet>
               ...
            </sca:policySet>
         </scact:sca-config>
      </xml>
      </property>
   </endpoint-description>
</rsa:endpoint-descriptions>
```

129.7   XML Schema

Below is the full XML schema for the SCA Configuration Documents used by the SCA Configuration Type. The namespace for this XML Schema is:

```
http://www.osgi.org/xmlns/scact/v1.0.0
```

```
<schema
```

```
xmlns                   ="http://www.w3.org/2001/XMLSchema"
xmlns:sca               ="http://docs.oasis-open.org/ns/opencsa/sca/200912"
xmlns:scact             ="http://www.osgi.org/xmlns/scact/v1.0.0"
targetNamespace         ="http://www.osgi.org/xmlns/scact/v1.0.0"
version                 ="1.0.0"
elementFormDefault      ="qualified">

<import
    namespace="http://docs.oasis-open.org/ns/opencsa/sca/200912"
    schemaLocation="http://docs.oasis-open.org/opencsa/sca-assembly/sca-policy-1.1-cd02.xsd"/>

<import
    namespace="http://docs.oasis-open.org/ns/opencsa/sca/200912"
    schemaLocation="http://docs.oasis-open.org/opencsa/sca-assembly/sca-core-1.1-cd03.xsd"/>

<element name="sca-config" type="scact:Tsca-config" />

<complexType name="Tsca-config">
  <choice minOccurs="0" maxOccurs="unbounded">
    <element ref="sca:binding" />
    <element ref="sca:intent" />
    <element ref="sca:policySet" />
  </choice>
  <attribute name="targetNamespace" type="anyURI" use="required" />
</complexType>

<attribute name="must-understand" type="boolean" default="false"/>
</schema>
```

129.8 Security

There are no extra security rules for this specification.

129.9 References

[1] *OSGi Core Specifications*
     http://www.osgi.org/Specifications/Download

[2] *OASIS*
     http://www.oasis-open.org

[3] *Service Component Architecture (SCA)*
     http://www.oasis-opencsa.org/

[4] *SCA Assembly specification v1.1 CD03*
     http://docs.oasis-open.org/opencsa/sca-assembly/sca-assembly-1.1-spec.pdf

[5] *SCA Policy Framework specification v1.1 CD02*
     http://docs.oasis-open.org/opencsa/sca-policy/sca-policy-1.1-spec-cd02.pdf
     http://www.oasis-open.org/committees/sca-policy/

[6] *SCA Bindings specifications*
     http://www.oasis-open.org/committees/sca-bindings/

[7] *WS-Policy specification*
     http://www.w3.org/Submission/WS-Policy/

[8] *XML Schema*
     http://www.w3.org/XML/Schema

701   **Tracker Specification**

Version 1.4

701.1   Introduction

The Framework provides a powerful and very dynamic programming environment: Bundles are installed, started, stopped, updated, and uninstalled without shutting down the Framework. Dependencies between bundles are monitored by the Framework, but bundles *must* cooperate in handling these dependencies correctly. Two important *dynamic* aspects of the Framework are the service registry and the set of installed bundles.

Bundle developers must be careful not to use service objects that have been unregistered and are therefore stale. The dynamic nature of the Framework service registry makes it necessary to track the service objects as they are registered and unregistered to prevent problems. It is easy to overlook race conditions or boundary conditions that will lead to random errors. Similar problems exist when tracking the set of installed bundles and their state.

This specification defines two utility classes, ServiceTracker and BundleTracker, that make tracking services and bundles easier. A ServiceTracker class can be customized by implementing the ServiceTrackerCustomizer interface or by sub-classing the ServiceTracker class. Similarly, a BundleTracker class can be customized by sub-classing or implementing the BundleTrackerCustomizer interface.

These utility classes significantly reduce the complexity of tracking services in the service registry and the set of installed bundles.

701.1.1   Essentials

- *Simplify* – Simplify the tracking of services or bundles.
- *Customizable* – Allow a default implementation to be customized so that bundle developers can start simply and later extend the implementation to meet their needs.
- *Small* – Every Framework implementation should have this utility implemented. It should therefore be very small because some Framework implementations target minimal OSGi Service Platforms.
- *Services* – Track a set of services, optionally filtered, or track a single service.
- *Bundles* – Track bundles based on their state.
- *Cleanup* – Properly clean up when tracking is no longer necessary

701.1.2   Operation

The fundamental tasks of a tracker are:

- To create an initial list of *targets* (service or bundle).
- To listen to the appropriate events so that the targets are properly tracked.
- To allow the client to customize the tracking process through programmatic selection of the services/bundles to be tracked, as well as to perform client code when a service/bundle is added or removed.

A ServiceTracker object is populated with a set of services that match given search criteria, and then listens to ServiceEvent objects which correspond to those services. A Bundle Tracker is populated with the set of installed bundles and then listens to BundleEvent objects to notify the customizer of changes in the state of the bundles.

701.1.3   Entities

Figure 701.1   *Class diagram of org.osgi.util.tracker*

701.2   Tracking

The OSGi Framework is a dynamic multi-threaded environment. In such an environments callbacks can occur on different threads at the same time. This dynamism causes many complexities. One of the surprisingly hard aspects of this environment is to reliably track services and bundles (called *targets* from now on).

The complexity is caused by the fact that the BundleListener and ServiceListener interfaces are only providing access to the *changed* state, not to the existing state when the listener is registered. This leaves the programmer with the problem to merge the set of existing targets with the changes to the state as signified by the events, without unwantedly duplicating a target or missing a remove event that would leave a target in the tracked map while it is in reality gone. These problems are caused by the multi-threaded nature of an OSGi service platform.

The problem is illustrated with the following (quite popular) code:

```
// Bad Example! Do not do this!
Bundle[] bundles = context.getBundles();
for ( Bundle bundle : bundles ) {
    map.put(bundle.getLocation(), bundle );
}

context.addBundleListener( new BundleListener() {
    public void bundleChanged(BundleEvent event) {
        Bundle bundle = event.getBundle();
        switch(event.getType()) {
        case BundleEvent.INSTALLED:
            map.put(bundle.getLocation(), bundle );
            break;

        case BundleEvent.UNINSTALLED:
            map.remove(bundle.getLocation());
            break;

        default:
            // ignore
        }
    }
}
```

```
});
```

Assume the code runs the first part, getting the existing targets. If during this time a targets state changes, for example bundle is installed or uninstalled, then the event is missed and the map will miss a bundle or it will contain a bundle that is already gone. An easy solution seems to be to first register the listener and then get the existing targets. This solves the earlier problem but will be introduce other problems. In this case, an uninstall event can occur before the bundle has been discovered.

Proper locking can alleviate the problem but it turns out that this easily create solutions that are very prone to deadlocks. Solving this tracking problem is surprisingly hard. For this reason, the OSGi specifications contain a *bundle tracker* and a *service tracker* that are properly implemented. These classes significantly reduce the complexity of the dynamics in an OSGi Service Platform.

701.2.1 Usage

Trackers can be used with the following patterns:

- *As-is* – Each tracker can be used without further customizing. A tracker actively tracks a map of targets and this map can be consulted with a number of methods when the information is needed. This is especially useful for the Service Tracker because it provides convenience methods to wait for services to arrive.
- *Callback object* – Each tracker provides a call back interface that can be implemented by the client code.
- *Sub-classing* – The trackers are designed to be sub-classed. Sub-classes have access to the bundle context and only have to override the callback methods they need.

701.2.2 General API

A tracker hides the mechanisms in the way the targets are stored and evented. From a high level, a tracker maintains a *map* of targets to *wrapper* objects. The wrapper object can be defined by the client, though the Bundle Tracker uses the Bundle object and the Service Tracker uses the service object as default wrapper. The tracker notifies the client of any changes in the state of the target.

A tracker must be constructed with a Bundle Context. This context is used to register listeners and obtain the initial list of targets during the call to the open method. At the end of the life of a tracker it must be closed to release any remaining objects. It is advised to properly close all trackers in the bundle activator's stop method.

A tracker provides a uniform callback interface, which has 3 different methods.

- *Adding* – Provide a new object, obtained from the store or from an event and return the wrapper or a related object. The adding method can decide not to track the target by returning a null object. When null is returned, no modified or remove methods are further called. However, it is possible that the adding method is called again for the same target.
- *Modified* –The target is modified. For example, the service properties have changed or the bundle has changed state. This callback provides a mechanism for the client to update its internal structures. The callback provides the wrapper object.
- *Removing* – The target is no longer tracked. This callback is provided the wrapper object returned from the adding method. This allows for simplified cleanup if the client maintains state about the target.

Each tracker is associated with a callback interface, which it implements itself. That is, a Service Tracker implements the ServiceTrackerCustomizer interface. By implementing this customizer, the tracker can also be sub-classed, this can be quite useful in many cases. Sub-classing can override only one or two of the methods instead of having to implement all methods. When overriding the callback methods, it must be ensured that the wrapper object is treated accordingly to the base implementation in all methods. For example, the Service Tracker's default implementation for the adding method checks out the service and therefore the remove method must unget this same service. Changing the wrapper object type to something else can therefore clash with the default implementations.

Trackers can provide all the objects that are tracked, return the mapped wrapper from the target, and deliver the number of tracked targets.

701.2.3 Tracking Count

The tracker also maintains a count that is updated each time that an object is added, modified, or removed, that is any change to the implied map. This tracking count makes it straightforward to verify that a tracker has changed; just store the tracking count and compare it later to see if it has changed.

701.2.4 Multi Threading

The dynamic environment of OSGi requires that tracker are thread safe. However, the tracker closely interacts with the client through a callback interface. The tracker implementation must provide the following guarantees:

- The tracker code calling a callback must not hold any locks

Clients must be aware that their callbacks are reentrant though the tracker implementations guarantee that the add/modified/remove methods can only called in this order for a specific target. A tracker must not call these methods out of order.

701.2.5 Synchronous

Trackers use *synchronous* listeners; the callbacks are called on the same thread as that of the initiating event. Care should be taken to not linger in the callback and perform non-trivial work. Callbacks should return immediately and move substantial work to other threads.

701.3 Service Tracker Class

The purpose of a Service Tracker is to track *service references*, that is, the target is the ServiceReference object. The ServiceTracker interface defines three constructors to create ServiceTracker objects, each providing different search criteria:

- ServiceTracker(BundleContext,String,ServiceTrackerCustomizer) – This constructor takes a service interface name as the search criterion. The ServiceTracker object must then track all services that are registered under the specified service interface name.
- ServiceTracker(BundleContext,Filter,ServiceTrackerCustomizer) – This constructor uses a Filter object to specify the services to be tracked. The ServiceTracker must then track all services that match the specified filter.
- ServiceTracker(BundleContext,ServiceReference,ServiceTrackerCustomizer) – This constructor takes a ServiceReference object as the search criterion. The ServiceTracker must then track only the service that corresponds to the specified ServiceReference. Using this constructor, no more than one service must ever be tracked, because a ServiceReference refers to a specific service.

Each of the ServiceTracker constructors takes a BundleContext object as a parameter. This BundleContext object must be used by a ServiceTracker object to track, get, and unget services.

A new ServiceTracker object must not begin tracking services until its open method is called. There are 2 versions of the open method:

- open() – This method is identical to open(false). It is provided for backward compatibility reasons.

- open(boolean) – The tracker must start tracking the services as were specified in its constructor. If the boolean parameter is true, it must track all services, regardless if they are compatible with the bundle that created the Service Tracker or not. See Section 5.9 "Multiple Version Export Considerations" for a description of the compatibility issues when multiple variations of the same package can exist. If the parameter is false, the Service Tracker must only track compatible versions.

701.3.1 Using a Service Tracker

Once a ServiceTracker object is opened, it begins tracking services immediately. A number of methods are available to the bundle developer to monitor the services that are being tracked, including the ones that are in the service registry at that time. The ServiceTracker class defines these methods:

- getService() – Returns one of the services being tracked or null if there are no active services being tracked.
- getServices() – Returns an array of all the tracked services. The number of tracked services is returned by the size method.
- getServiceReference() – Returns a ServiceReference object for one of the services being tracked. The service object for this service may be returned by calling the ServiceTracker object's getService() method.
- getServiceReferences() – Returns a list of the ServiceReference objects for services being tracked. The service object for a specific tracked service may be returned by calling the ServiceTracker object's getService(ServiceReference) method.
- waitForService(long) – Allows the caller to wait until at least one instance of a service is tracked or until the time-out expires. If the time-out is zero, the caller must wait until at least one instance of a service is tracked. waitForService must not used within the BundleActivator methods, as these methods are expected to complete in a short period of time. A Framework could wait for the start method to complete before starting the bundle that registers the service for which the caller is waiting, creating a deadlock situation.
- remove(ServiceReference) – This method may be used to remove a specific service from being tracked by the ServiceTracker object, causing removedService to be called for that service.
- close() – This method must remove all services being tracked by the ServiceTracker object, causing removedService to be called for all tracked services.
- getTrackingCount() – A Service Tracker can have services added, modified, or removed at any moment in time. The getTrackingCount method is intended to efficiently detect changes in a Service Tracker. Every time the Service Tracker is changed, it must increase the tracking count.

701.3.2 Customizing the Service Tracker class

The behavior of the ServiceTracker class can be customized either by providing a ServiceTrackerCustomizer object, implementing the desired behavior when the ServiceTracker object is constructed, or by sub-classing the ServiceTracker class and overriding the ServiceTrackerCustomizer methods.

The ServiceTrackerCustomizer interface defines these methods:

- addingService(ServiceReference) – Called whenever a service is being added to the ServiceTracker object.
- modifiedService(ServiceReference,Object) – Called whenever a tracked service is modified.
- removedService(ServiceReference,Object) – Called whenever a tracked service is removed from the ServiceTracker object.

When a service is being added to the ServiceTracker object or when a tracked service is modified or removed from the ServiceTracker object, it must call addingService, modifiedService, or removedService, respectively, on the ServiceTrackerCustomizer object (if specified when the ServiceTracker object was created); otherwise it must call these methods on itself.

A bundle developer may customize the action when a service is tracked. Another reason for customizing the ServiceTracker class is to programmatically select which services are tracked. A filter may not sufficiently specify the services that the bundle developer is interested in tracking. By implementing addingService, the bundle developer can use additional runtime information to determine if the service should be tracked. If null is returned by the addingService method, the service must not be tracked.

Finally, the bundle developer can return a specialized object from addingService that differs from the service object. This specialized object could contain the service object and any associated information. This returned object is then tracked instead of the service object. When the removedService method is called, the object that is passed along with the ServiceReference object is the one that was returned from the earlier call to the addingService method.

701.3.3   Customizing Example

An example of customizing the action taken when a service is tracked might be registering a Servlet object with each Http Service that is tracked. This customization could be done by sub-classing the ServiceTracker class and overriding the addingService and removedService methods as follows:

```
public Object addingService( ServiceReference reference) {
    Object obj = context.getService(reference);
    HttpService svc = (HttpService)obj;
    // Register the Servlet using svc
    ...
    return svc;
}
public void removedService( ServiceReference reference,
    Object obj ){
    HttpService svc = (HttpService)obj;
    // Unregister the Servlet using svc
    ...
    context.ungetService(reference);
}
```

701.4   Bundle Tracker

The purpose of the Bundle Tracker is to simplify tracking bundles. A popular example where bundles need to be tracked is the *extender* pattern. An extender uses information in other bundles to provide its function. For example, a Declarative Services implementation reads the component XML file from the bundle to learn of the presence of any components in that bundle.

There are, however, other places where it is necessary to track bundles. The Bundle Tracker significantly simplifies this task.

701.4.1   Bundle States

The state diagram of a Bundle is significantly more complex than that of a service. However, the interface is simpler because there is only a need to specify for which states the bundle tracker should track a service.

Bundle states are defined as a bit in an integer, allowing the specifications of multiple states by setting multiple bits. The Bundle Tracker therefore uses a *bit mask* to specify which states are of interest. For example, if a client is interested in active and resolved bundles, it is possible to specify the Bundle ACTIVE | RESOLVED | STARTING states in the mask.

The Bundle Tracker tracks bundles whose state matches the mask. That is, when a bundle is not tracked it adds that bundle to the tracked map when its state matches the mask. If the bundle reaches a new state that is not listed in the mask, the bundle will be removed from the tracked map. If the state changes but the bundle should still be tracked, then the bundle is considered to be modified.

701.4.2 Constructor

The BundleTracker interface defines the following constructors to create BundleTracker objects:

- BundleTracker(BundleContext,int,BundleTrackerCustomizer) – Create a Bundle Tracker that tracks the bundles which state is listed in the mask. The customizer may be null, in that case the callbacks can be implemented in a subclass.

A new BundleTracker object must not begin tracking services until its open method is called.

- open() – Start tracking the bundles, callbacks can occur before this method is called.

701.4.3 Using a Bundle Tracker

Once a BundleTracker object is opened, it begins tracking bundles immediately. A number of methods are available to the bundle developer to monitor the bundles that are being tracked. The BundleTracker class defines the following methods:

- getBundles() – Returns an array of all the tracked bundles.
- getObject(Bundle) – Returns the wrapper object that was returned from the addingBundle method.
- remove(Bundle) – Removes the bundle from the tracked bundles. The removedBundle method is called when the bundle is not in the tracked map.
- size() – Returns the number of bundles being tracked.
- getTrackingCount() – A Bundle Tracker can have bundles added, modified, or removed at any moment in time. The getTrackingCount method is intended to efficiently detect changes in a Bundle Tracker. Every time the Bundle Tracker is changed, it must increase the tracking count.

701.4.4 Customizing the Bundle Tracker class

The behavior of the BundleTracker class can be customized either by providing a BundleTrackerCustomizer object when the BundleTracker object is constructed, or by sub-classing the BundleTracker class and overriding the BundleTrackerCustomizer methods on the BundleTracker class.

The BundleTrackerCustomizer interface defines these methods:

- addingBundle(Bundle,BundleEvent) – Called whenever a bundle is being added to the BundleTracker object. This method should return a wrapper object, which can be the Bundle object itself. If null is returned, the Bundle must not be further tracked.
- modifiedBundle(Bundle,BundleEvent,Object) – Called whenever a tracked bundle is modified. The object that is passed is the object returned from the addingBundle method, the wrapper object.
- removedBundle(Bundle,BundleEvent,Object) – Called whenever a tracked bundle is removed from the BundleTracker object. The passed object is the wrapper returned from the addingBundle method.

The BundleEvent object in the previous methods can be null.

When a bundle is being added the OSGi Framework, or when a tracked bundle is modified or uninstalled from the OSGi Framework, the Bundle Tracker must call addingBundle, modifiedBundle, or removedBundle, respectively, on the BundleTrackerCustomizer object (if specified when the BundleTracker object was created); otherwise it must call these methods on itself, allowing them to be overridden in a subclass.

The bundle developer can return a specialized object from addingBundle that differs from the Bundle object. This wrapper object could contain the Bundle object and any associated client specific information. This returned object is then used as the wrapper instead of the Bundle object. When the removedBundle method is called, the wrapper is passed as an argument.

701.4.5 Extender Model

The Bundle Tracker allows the implementation of extenders with surprisingly little effort. The following example checks a manifest header (Http-Mapper) in all active bundles to see if the bundle has resources that need to be mapped to the HTTP service. This extender enables bundles that have no code, just content.

This example is implemented with a BundleTrackerCustomizer implementation, though sub-classing the BundleTracker class is slightly simpler because the open/close methods would be inherited, the tracker field is not necessary and it is not necessary to provide a dummy implementation of modifiedBundle method. However, the Service Tracker example already showed how to use inheritance.

The Extender class must implement the customizer and declare fields for the Http Service and a Bundle Tracker.

```
public class Extender implements BundleTrackerCustomizer {
    final HttpService     http;
    final BundleTracker   tracker;
```

It is necessary to parse the Http-Mapper header. Regular expression allow this to be done very concise.

```
final static Pattern HTTPMAPPER=
    Pattern.compile(
      "\\s*([-/\\w.]+)\\s*=\\s*([-/\\w.]+)\\s*");
```

The Bundle Tracker requires a specialized constructor. This example only works for *active* bundles. This implies that a bundle only provides contents when it is started, enabling an administrator to control the availability.

```
Extender(BundleContext context, HttpService http) {
    tracker = new BundleTracker(
      context,Bundle.ACTIVE, this );
    this.http = http;
}
```

The following method implements the callback from the Bundle Tracker when a new bundle is discovered. In this method a specialized HttpContext object is created that knows how to retrieve its resources from the bundle that was just discovered. This context is registered with the Http Service. If no header is found null is returned so that non-participating bundles are no longer tracked.

```
public Object addingBundle(Bundle bundle,
    BundleEvent event) {
    String header = bundle.getHeaders()
      .get("Http-Mapper") + "";
    Matcher match = HTTPMAPPER.matcher(header);
    if (match.matches()) {
      try {
        ExtenderContext wrapper =
          new ExtenderContext(bundle, match.group(1));
        http.registerResources(
          match.group(1), // alias
```

```
                match.group(2), // resource path
                wrapper          // the http context
              );
              return wrapper;
          } catch (NamespaceException nspe) {
              // error is handled in the fall through
          }
      }
      System.err.println(
        "Invalid header for Http-Mapper: " + header);
      return null;
  }
```

The modifiedBundle method does not have to be implemented because this example is not interested in state changes because the only state of interest is the ACTIVE state. Therefore, the remaining method left to implement is the removedBundle method. If the wrapper object is non-null then we need to unregister the alias to prevent collisions in the http namespace when the bundle is reinstalled or updated.

```
public void removedBundle(
    Bundle bundle, BundleEvent event,
    Object object) {
        ExtenderContext wrapper = (ExtenderContext) object;
        http.unregister(wrapper.alias);
}
```

The remaining methods would be unnecessary if the Extender class had extended the BundleTracker class. The BundleTrackerCustomizer interface requires a dummy implementation of the modifiedBundle method:

```
public void modifiedBundle(
    Bundle bundle, BundleEvent event, Object object) {
    // Nothing to do
}
```

It is usually not a good idea to start a tracker in a constructor because opening a service tracker will immediately cause a number of callbacks for the existing bundles. If the Extender class was subclassed, then this could call back the uninitialized sub class methods. It is therefore better to separate the initialization from the opening. There is therefore a need for an open and close method.

```
    public void close() {
        tracker.close();
    }
    public void open() {
        tracker.open();
    }
}
```

The previous example uses an HttpContext subclass that can retrieve resources from the target bundle:

```
public class ExtenderContext implements HttpContext {
    final Bundle    bundle;
    final String    alias;

    ExtenderContext(Bundle bundle, String alias) {
        this.bundle = bundle;
        this.alias = alias;
    }
```

```
      public boolean handleSecurity(
         HttpServletRequest rq, HttpServletResponse rsp) {
         return true;
      }
      public String getMimeType(String name) {
         return null;
      }
      public URL getResource(String name) {
         return bundle.getResource(name);
      }
   }
```

701.5 Security

A tracker contains a BundleContext instance variable that is accessible to the methods in a subclass. A BundleContext object should never be given to other bundles because it is a *capability*. The framework makes allocations based on the bundle context with respect to security and resource management.

The tracker implementations do not have a method to get the BundleContext object, however, subclasses should be careful not to provide such a method if the tracker is given to other bundles.

The services that are being tracked are available via a ServiceTracker. These services are dependent on the BundleContext as well. It is therefore necessary to do a careful security analysis when ServiceTracker objects are given to other bundles. The same counts for the Bundle Tracker. It is strongly advised to not pass trackers to other bundles.

701.5.1 Synchronous Bundle Listener

The Bundle Tracker uses the synchronous bundle listener because it is impossible to provide some of the guarantees the Bundle Tracker provides without handling the events synchronously. Synchronous events can block the complete system, therefore Synchronous Bundle Listeners require AdminPermission[*,LISTENER]. The wildcard * can be replaced with a specifier for the bundles that should be visible to the Bundle Tracker. See *Admin Permission* on page 118 for more information.

Code that calls the open and close methods of Bundle Trackers must therefore have the appropriate Admin Permission.

701.6 org.osgi.util.tracker

Tracker Package Version 1.4.

Bundles wishing to use this package must list the package in the Import-Package header of the bundle's manifest. For example:

```
Import-Package: org.osgi.util.tracker; version="[1.4,2.0)"
```

701.6.1 Summary

- *BundleTracker* - The BundleTracker class simplifies tracking bundles much like the ServiceTracker simplifies tracking services.
- *BundleTrackerCustomizer* - The BundleTrackerCustomizer interface allows a BundleTracker to customize the Bundles that are tracked.
- *ServiceTracker* - The ServiceTracker class simplifies using services from the Framework's service registry.

- *ServiceTrackerCustomizer* - The ServiceTrackerCustomizer interface allows a ServiceTracker to customize the service objects that are tracked.

701.6.2   public class BundleTracker
implements BundleTrackerCustomizer

The BundleTracker class simplifies tracking bundles much like the ServiceTracker simplifies tracking services.

A BundleTracker is constructed with state criteria and a BundleTrackerCustomizer object. A BundleTracker can use the BundleTrackerCustomizer to select which bundles are tracked and to create a customized object to be tracked with the bundle. The BundleTracker can then be opened to begin tracking all bundles whose state matches the specified state criteria.

The getBundles method can be called to get the Bundle objects of the bundles being tracked. The getObject method can be called to get the customized object for a tracked bundle.

The BundleTracker class is thread-safe. It does not call a BundleTrackerCustomizer while holding any locks. BundleTrackerCustomizer implementations must also be thread-safe.

Since 1.4

Concurrency Thread-safe

701.6.2.1   protected final BundleContext context

The Bundle Context used by this BundleTracker.

701.6.2.2   public BundleTracker(BundleContext context, int stateMask, BundleTrackerCustomizer customizer)

context The BundleContext against which the tracking is done.

stateMask The bit mask of the ORing of the bundle states to be tracked.

customizer The customizer object to call when bundles are added, modified, or removed in this BundleTracker. If customizer is null, then this BundleTracker will be used as the BundleTrackerCustomizer and this BundleTracker will call the BundleTrackerCustomizer methods on itself.

☐ Create a BundleTracker for bundles whose state is present in the specified state mask.

Bundles whose state is present on the specified state mask will be tracked by this BundleTracker.

See Also Bundle.getState()

701.6.2.3   public Object addingBundle(Bundle bundle, BundleEvent event)

bundle The Bundle being added to this BundleTracker object.

event The bundle event which caused this customizer method to be called or null if there is no bundle event associated with the call to this method.

☐ Default implementation of the BundleTrackerCustomizer.addingBundle method.

This method is only called when this BundleTracker has been constructed with a null BundleTrackerCustomizer argument.

This implementation simply returns the specified Bundle.

This method can be overridden in a subclass to customize the object to be tracked for the bundle being added.

Returns The specified bundle.

See Also BundleTrackerCustomizer.addingBundle(Bundle, BundleEvent)

701.6.2.4　　**public void close( )**

　　　□　Close this BundleTracker.

　　　This method should be called when this BundleTracker should end the tracking of bundles.

　　　This implementation calls getBundles() to get the list of tracked bundles to remove.

701.6.2.5　　**public Bundle[] getBundles( )**

　　　□　Return an array of Bundles for all bundles being tracked by this BundleTracker.

　Returns　An array of Bundles or null if no bundles are being tracked.

701.6.2.6　　**public Object getObject(Bundle bundle)**

　bundle　The Bundle being tracked.

　　　□　Returns the customized object for the specified Bundle if the specified bundle is being tracked by this BundleTracker.

　Returns　The customized object for the specified Bundle or null if the specified Bundle is not being tracked.

701.6.2.7　　**public int getTrackingCount( )**

　　　□　Returns the tracking count for this BundleTracker. The tracking count is initialized to 0 when this BundleTracker is opened. Every time a bundle is added, modified or removed from this BundleTracker the tracking count is incremented.

　　　The tracking count can be used to determine if this BundleTracker has added, modified or removed a bundle by comparing a tracking count value previously collected with the current tracking count value. If the value has not changed, then no bundle has been added, modified or removed from this BundleTracker since the previous tracking count was collected.

　Returns　The tracking count for this BundleTracker or -1 if this BundleTracker is not open.

701.6.2.8　　**public void modifiedBundle(Bundle bundle, BundleEvent event, Object object)**

　bundle　The Bundle whose state has been modified.

　event　The bundle event which caused this customizer method to be called or null if there is no bundle event associated with the call to this method.

　object　The customized object for the specified Bundle.

　　　□　Default implementation of the BundleTrackerCustomizer.modifiedBundle method.

　　　This method is only called when this BundleTracker has been constructed with a null BundleTrackerCustomizer argument.

　　　This implementation does nothing.

　See Also　BundleTrackerCustomizer.modifiedBundle(Bundle, BundleEvent, Object)

701.6.2.9　　**public void open( )**

　　　□　Open this BundleTracker and begin tracking bundles.

　　　Bundle which match the state criteria specified when this BundleTracker was created are now tracked by this BundleTracker.

　Throws　IllegalStateException – If the BundleContext with which this BundleTracker was created is no longer valid.

　　　SecurityException – If the caller and this class do not have the appropriate AdminPermission[context bundle,LISTENER], and the Java Runtime Environment supports permissions.

701.6.2.10   **public void remove(Bundle bundle)**

bundle The Bundle to be removed.

□ Remove a bundle from this BundleTracker. The specified bundle will be removed from this BundleTracker . If the specified bundle was being tracked then the BundleTrackerCustomizer.removedBundle method will be called for that bundle.

701.6.2.11   **public void removedBundle(Bundle bundle, BundleEvent event, Object object)**

bundle The Bundle being removed.

event The bundle event which caused this customizer method to be called or null if there is no bundle event associated with the call to this method.

object The customized object for the specified bundle.

□ Default implementation of the BundleTrackerCustomizer.removedBundle method.

This method is only called when this BundleTracker has been constructed with a null BundleTrackerCustomizer argument.

This implementation does nothing.

See Also BundleTrackerCustomizer. removedBundle(Bundle, BundleEvent, Object)

701.6.2.12   **public int size( )**

□ Return the number of bundles being tracked by this BundleTracker.

Returns The number of bundles being tracked.

701.6.3   public interface BundleTrackerCustomizer

The BundleTrackerCustomizer interface allows a BundleTracker to customize the Bundles that are tracked. A BundleTrackerCustomizer is called when a bundle is being added to a BundleTracker. The BundleTrackerCustomizer can then return an object for the tracked bundle. A BundleTrackerCustomizer is also called when a tracked bundle is modified or has been removed from a BundleTracker.

The methods in this interface may be called as the result of a BundleEvent being received by a BundleTracker. Since BundleEvents are received synchronously by the BundleTracker, it is highly recommended that implementations of these methods do not alter bundle states while being synchronized on any object.

The BundleTracker class is thread-safe. It does not call a BundleTrackerCustomizer while holding any locks. BundleTrackerCustomizer implementations must also be thread-safe.

Since 1.4

Concurrency Thread-safe

701.6.3.1   **public Object addingBundle(Bundle bundle, BundleEvent event)**

bundle The Bundle being added to the BundleTracker.

event The bundle event which caused this customizer method to be called or null if there is no bundle event associated with the call to this method.

□ A bundle is being added to the BundleTracker.

This method is called before a bundle which matched the search parameters of the BundleTracker is added to the BundleTracker. This method should return the object to be tracked for the specified Bundle. The returned object is stored in the BundleTracker and is available from the getObject method.

Returns The object to be tracked for the specified Bundle object or null if the specified Bundle object should not be tracked.

701.6.3.2   **public void modifiedBundle(Bundle bundle, BundleEvent event, Object object)**

bundle The Bundle whose state has been modified.

event The bundle event which caused this customizer method to be called or null if there is no bundle event associated with the call to this method.

object The tracked object for the specified bundle.

☐ A bundle tracked by the BundleTracker has been modified.

This method is called when a bundle being tracked by the BundleTracker has had its state modified.

701.6.3.3   **public void removedBundle(Bundle bundle, BundleEvent event, Object object)**

bundle The Bundle that has been removed.

event The bundle event which caused this customizer method to be called or null if there is no bundle event associated with the call to this method.

object The tracked object for the specified bundle.

☐ A bundle tracked by the BundleTracker has been removed.

This method is called after a bundle is no longer being tracked by the BundleTracker.

701.6.4   public class ServiceTracker
implements ServiceTrackerCustomizer

The ServiceTracker class simplifies using services from the Framework's service registry.

A ServiceTracker object is constructed with search criteria and a ServiceTrackerCustomizer object. A ServiceTracker can use a ServiceTrackerCustomizer to customize the service objects to be tracked. The ServiceTracker can then be opened to begin tracking all services in the Framework's service registry that match the specified search criteria. The ServiceTracker correctly handles all of the details of listening to ServiceEvents and getting and ungetting services.

The getServiceReferences method can be called to get references to the services being tracked. The getService and getServices methods can be called to get the service objects for the tracked service.

The ServiceTracker class is thread-safe. It does not call a ServiceTrackerCustomizer while holding any locks. ServiceTrackerCustomizer implementations must also be thread-safe.

Concurrency Thread-safe

701.6.4.1   **protected final BundleContext context**

The Bundle Context used by this ServiceTracker.

701.6.4.2   **protected final Filter filter**

The Filter used by this ServiceTracker which specifies the search criteria for the services to track.

Since 1.1

701.6.4.3   **public ServiceTracker(BundleContext context, ServiceReference reference,**
ServiceTrackerCustomizer customizer)

context The BundleContext against which the tracking is done.

reference The ServiceReference for the service to be tracked.

customizer The customizer object to call when services are added, modified, or removed in this ServiceTracker. If customizer is null, then this ServiceTracker will be used as the ServiceTrackerCustomizer and this ServiceTracker will call the ServiceTrackerCustomizer methods on itself.

☐ Create a ServiceTracker on the specified ServiceReference.

The service referenced by the specified ServiceReference will be tracked by this ServiceTracker.

701.6.4.4 **public ServiceTracker(BundleContext context, String clazz, ServiceTrackerCustomizer customizer)**

context The BundleContext against which the tracking is done.

clazz The class name of the services to be tracked.

customizer The customizer object to call when services are added, modified, or removed in this ServiceTracker. If customizer is null, then this ServiceTracker will be used as the ServiceTrackerCustomizer and this ServiceTracker will call the ServiceTrackerCustomizer methods on itself.

☐ Create a ServiceTracker on the specified class name.

Services registered under the specified class name will be tracked by this ServiceTracker.

701.6.4.5 **public ServiceTracker(BundleContext context, Filter filter, ServiceTrackerCustomizer customizer)**

context The BundleContext against which the tracking is done.

filter The Filter to select the services to be tracked.

customizer The customizer object to call when services are added, modified, or removed in this ServiceTracker. If customizer is null, then this ServiceTracker will be used as the ServiceTrackerCustomizer and this ServiceTracker will call the ServiceTrackerCustomizer methods on itself.

☐ Create a ServiceTracker on the specified Filter object.

Services which match the specified Filter object will be tracked by this ServiceTracker.

Since 1.1

701.6.4.6 **public Object addingService(ServiceReference reference)**

reference The reference to the service being added to this ServiceTracker.

☐ Default implementation of the ServiceTrackerCustomizer.addingService method.

This method is only called when this ServiceTracker has been constructed with a null ServiceTrackerCustomizer argument.

This implementation returns the result of calling getService on the BundleContext with which this ServiceTracker was created passing the specified ServiceReference.

This method can be overridden in a subclass to customize the service object to be tracked for the service being added. In that case, take care not to rely on the default implementation of removedService to unget the service.

Returns The service object to be tracked for the service added to this ServiceTracker.

See Also ServiceTrackerCustomizer.addingService(ServiceReference)

701.6.4.7 **public void close( )**

☐ Close this ServiceTracker.

This method should be called when this ServiceTracker should end the tracking of services.

This implementation calls getServiceReferences() to get the list of tracked services to remove.

701.6.4.8	**public Object getService(ServiceReference reference)**

reference	The reference to the desired service.

□	Returns the service object for the specified ServiceReference if the specified referenced service is being tracked by this ServiceTracker.

Returns	A service object or null if the service referenced by the specified ServiceReference is not being tracked.

701.6.4.9	**public Object getService( )**

□	Returns a service object for one of the services being tracked by this ServiceTracker.

If any services are being tracked, this implementation returns the result of calling getService(getServiceReference()).

Returns	A service object or null if no services are being tracked.

701.6.4.10	**public ServiceReference getServiceReference( )**

□	Returns a ServiceReference for one of the services being tracked by this ServiceTracker.

If multiple services are being tracked, the service with the highest ranking (as specified in its service.ranking property) is returned. If there is a tie in ranking, the service with the lowest service ID (as specified in its service.id property); that is, the service that was registered first is returned. This is the same algorithm used by BundleContext.getServiceReference.

This implementation calls getServiceReferences() to get the list of references for the tracked services.

Returns	A ServiceReference or null if no services are being tracked.

Since	1.1

701.6.4.11	**public ServiceReference[] getServiceReferences( )**

□	Return an array of ServiceReferences for all services being tracked by this ServiceTracker.

Returns	Array of ServiceReferences or null if no services are being tracked.

701.6.4.12	**public Object[] getServices( )**

□	Return an array of service objects for all services being tracked by this ServiceTracker.

This implementation calls getServiceReferences() to get the list of references for the tracked services and then calls getService(ServiceReference) for each reference to get the tracked service object.

Returns	An array of service objects or null if no services are being tracked.

701.6.4.13	**public int getTrackingCount( )**

□	Returns the tracking count for this ServiceTracker. The tracking count is initialized to 0 when this ServiceTracker is opened. Every time a service is added, modified or removed from this ServiceTracker, the tracking count is incremented.

The tracking count can be used to determine if this ServiceTracker has added, modified or removed a service by comparing a tracking count value previously collected with the current tracking count value. If the value has not changed, then no service has been added, modified or removed from this ServiceTracker since the previous tracking count was collected.

Returns	The tracking count for this ServiceTracker or -1 if this ServiceTracker is not open.

Since	1.2

701.6.4.14	**public void modifiedService(ServiceReference reference, Object service)**

reference	The reference to modified service.

service	The service object for the modified service.

□ Default implementation of the ServiceTrackerCustomizer.modifiedService method.

This method is only called when this ServiceTracker has been constructed with a null ServiceTrackerCustomizer argument.

This implementation does nothing.

See Also ServiceTrackerCustomizer.modifiedService(ServiceReference, Object)

701.6.4.15   **public void open( )**

□ Open this ServiceTracker and begin tracking services.

This implementation calls open(false).

Throws IllegalStateException – If the BundleContext with which this ServiceTracker was created is no longer valid.

See Also open(boolean)

701.6.4.16   **public void open(boolean trackAllServices)**

trackAllServices If true, then this ServiceTracker will track all matching services regardless of class loader accessibility. If false, then this ServiceTracker will only track matching services which are class loader accessible to the bundle whose BundleContext is used by this ServiceTracker.

□ Open this ServiceTracker and begin tracking services.

Services which match the search criteria specified when this ServiceTracker was created are now tracked by this ServiceTracker.

Throws IllegalStateException – If the BundleContext with which this ServiceTracker was created is no longer valid.

Since 1.3

701.6.4.17   **public void remove(ServiceReference reference)**

reference The reference to the service to be removed.

□ Remove a service from this ServiceTracker. The specified service will be removed from this ServiceTracker. If the specified service was being tracked then the ServiceTrackerCustomizer.removedService method will be called for that service.

701.6.4.18   **public void removedService(ServiceReference reference, Object service)**

reference The reference to removed service.

service The service object for the removed service.

□ Default implementation of the ServiceTrackerCustomizer.removedService method.

This method is only called when this ServiceTracker has been constructed with a null ServiceTrackerCustomizer argument.

This implementation calls ungetService, on the BundleContext with which this ServiceTracker was created, passing the specified ServiceReference.

This method can be overridden in a subclass. If the default implementation of addingService method was used, this method must unget the service.

See Also ServiceTrackerCustomizer.removedService(ServiceReference, Object)

701.6.4.19   **public int size( )**

□ Return the number of services being tracked by this ServiceTracker.

Returns The number of services being tracked.

701.6.4.20   **public Object waitForService(long timeout) throws InterruptedException**

timeout The time interval in milliseconds to wait. If zero, the method will wait indefinitely.

☐ Wait for at least one service to be tracked by this ServiceTracker. This method will also return when this ServiceTracker is closed.

It is strongly recommended that waitForService is not used during the calling of the BundleActivator methods. BundleActivator methods are expected to complete in a short period of time.

This implementation calls getService() to determine if a service is being tracked.

Returns Returns the result of getService().

Throws InterruptedException – If another thread has interrupted the current thread.

IllegalArgumentException – If the value of timeout is negative.

701.6.5   public interface ServiceTrackerCustomizer

The ServiceTrackerCustomizer interface allows a ServiceTracker to customize the service objects that are tracked. A ServiceTrackerCustomizer is called when a service is being added to a ServiceTracker. The ServiceTrackerCustomizer can then return an object for the tracked service. A ServiceTrackerCustomizer is also called when a tracked service is modified or has been removed from a ServiceTracker.

The methods in this interface may be called as the result of a ServiceEvent being received by a ServiceTracker. Since ServiceEvents are synchronously delivered by the Framework, it is highly recommended that implementations of these methods do not register (BundleContext.registerService), modify (ServiceRegistration.setProperties) or unregister (ServiceRegistration.unregister) a service while being synchronized on any object.

The ServiceTracker class is thread-safe. It does not call a ServiceTrackerCustomizer while holding any locks. ServiceTrackerCustomizer implementations must also be thread-safe.

Concurrency Thread-safe

701.6.5.1   **public Object addingService(ServiceReference reference)**

reference The reference to the service being added to the ServiceTracker.

☐ A service is being added to the ServiceTracker.

This method is called before a service which matched the search parameters of the ServiceTracker is added to the ServiceTracker. This method should return the service object to be tracked for the specified ServiceReference. The returned service object is stored in the ServiceTracker and is available from the getService and getServices methods.

Returns The service object to be tracked for the specified referenced service or null if the specified referenced service should not be tracked.

701.6.5.2   **public void modifiedService(ServiceReference reference, Object service)**

reference The reference to the service that has been modified.

service The service object for the specified referenced service.

☐ A service tracked by the ServiceTracker has been modified.

This method is called when a service being tracked by the ServiceTracker has had it properties modified.

701.6.5.3   **public void removedService(ServiceReference reference, Object service)**

reference The reference to the service that has been removed.

service The service object for the specified referenced service.

❑ A service tracked by the ServiceTracker has been removed.

This method is called after a service is no longer being tracked by the ServiceTracker.

702 **XML Parser Service Specification**

Version 1.0

702.1 Introduction

The Extensible Markup Language (XML) has become a popular method of describing data. As more bundles use XML to describe their data, a common XML Parser becomes necessary in an embedded environment in order to reduce the need for space. Not all XML Parsers are equivalent in function, however, and not all bundles have the same requirements on an XML parser.

This problem was addressed in the Java API for XML Processing, see [4] *JAXP* for Java 2 Standard Edition and Enterprise Edition. This specification addresses how the classes defined in JAXP can be used in an OSGi Service Platform. It defines how:

- Implementations of XML parsers can become available to other bundles
- Bundles can find a suitable parser
- A standard parser in a JAR can be transformed to a bundle

702.1.1 Essentials

- *Standards* – Leverage existing standards in Java based XML parsing: JAXP, SAX and DOM
- *Unmodified JAXP code* – Run unmodified JAXP code
- *Simple* – It should be easy to provide a SAX or DOM parser as well as easy to find a matching parser
- *Multiple* – It should be possible to have multiple implementations of parsers available
- *Extendable* – It is likely that parsers will be extended in the future with more functionality

702.1.2 Entities

- *XMLParserActivator* – A utility class that registers a parser factory from declarative information in the Manifest file.
- *SAXParserFactory* – A class that can create an instance of a SAXParser class.
- *DocumentBuilderFactory* – A class that can create an instance of a DocumentBuilder class.
- *SAXParser* – A parser, instantiated by a SaxParserFactory object, that parses according to the SAX specifications.
- *DocumentBuilder* – A parser, instantiated by a DocumentBuilderFactory, that parses according to the DOM specifications.

Figure 702.1   *XML Parsing diagram*

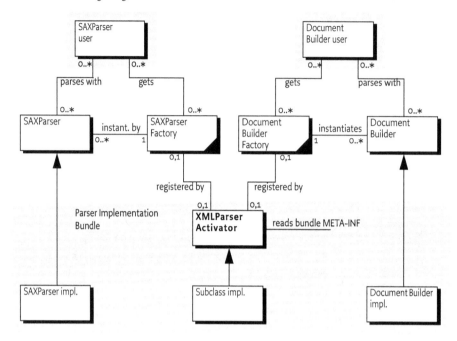

702.1.3   Operations

A bundle containing a SAX or DOM parser is started. This bundle registers a SAXParserFactory and/or a DocumentBuilderFactory service object with the Framework. Service registration properties describe the features of the parsers to other bundles. A bundle that needs an XML parser will get a SAXParserFactory or DocumentBuilderFactory service object from the Framework service registry. This object is then used to instantiate the requested parsers according to their specifications.

702.2   JAXP

XML has become very popular in the last few years because it allows the interchange of complex information between different parties. Though only a single XML standard exists, there are multiple APIs to XML parsers, primarily of two types:

- The Simple API for XML (SAX1 and SAX2)
- Based on the Document Object Model (DOM 1 and 2)

Both standards, however, define an abstract API that can be implemented by different vendors.

A given XML Parser implementation may support either or both of these parser types by implementing the org.w3c.dom and/or org.xml.sax packages. In addition, parsers have characteristics such as whether they are validating or non-validating parsers and whether or not they are name-space aware.

An application which uses a specific XML Parser must code to that specific parser and become coupled to that specific implementation. If the parser has implemented [4] *JAXP*, however, the application developer can code against SAX or DOM and let the runtime environment decide which parser implementation is used.

JAXP uses the concept of a *factory*. A factory object is an object that abstracts the creation of another object. JAXP defines a DocumentBuilderFactory and a SAXParserFactory class for this purpose.

JAXP is implemented in the javax.xml.parsers package and provides an abstraction layer between an application and a specific XML Parser implementation. Using JAXP, applications can choose to use any JAXP compliant parser without changing any code, simply by changing a System property which specifies the SAX- and DOM factory class names.

In JAXP, the default factory is obtained with a static method in the SAXParserFactory or DocumentBuilderFactory class. This method will inspect the associated System property and create a new instance of that class.

702.3 XML Parser service

The current specification of JAXP has the limitation that only one of each type of parser factories can be registered. This specification specifies how multiple SAXParserFactory objects and DocumentBuilderFactory objects can be made available to bundles simultaneously.

Providers of parsers should register a JAXP factory object with the OSGi service registry under the factory class name. Service properties are used to describe whether the parser:

- Is validating
- Is name-space aware
- Has additional features

With this functionality, bundles can query the OSGi service registry for parsers supporting the specific functionality that they require.

702.4 Properties

Parsers must be registered with a number of properties that qualify the service. In this specification, the following properties are specified:

- PARSER_NAMESPACEAWARE – The registered parser is aware of name-spaces. Name-spaces allow an XML document to consist of independently developed DTDs. In an XML document, they are recognized by the xmlns attribute and names prefixed with an abbreviated name-space identifier, like: <xsl:if ...>. The type is a Boolean object that must be true when the parser supports name-spaces. All other values, or the absence of the property, indicate that the parser does not implement name-spaces.
- PARSER_VALIDATING – The registered parser can read the DTD and can validate the XML accordingly. The type is a Boolean object that must true when the parser is validating. All other values, or the absence of the property, indicate that the parser does not validate.

702.5 Getting a Parser Factory

Getting a parser factory requires a bundle to get the appropriate factory from the service registry. In a simple case in which a non-validating, non-name-space aware parser would suffice, it is best to use getServiceReference(String).

```
DocumentBuilder getParser(BundleContext context)
    throws Exception {
    ServiceReference ref = context.getServiceReference(
        DocumentBuilderFactory.class.getName() );
    if ( ref == null )
        return null;
    DocumentBuilderFactory factory =
        (DocumentBuilderFactory) context.getService(ref);
    return factory.newDocumentBuilder();
}
```

In a more demanding case, the filtered version allows the bundle to select a parser that is validating and name-space aware:

```
SAXParser getParser(BundleContext context)
   throws Exception {
   ServiceReference refs[] = context.getServiceReferences(
      SAXParserFactory.class.getName(),
        "(&(parser.namespaceAware=true)"
    + "(parser.validating=true))" );
   if ( refs == null )
      return null;
   SAXParserFactory factory =
      (SAXParserFactory) context.getService(refs[0]);
   return factory.newSAXParser();
}
```

702.6   Adapting a JAXP Parser to OSGi

If an XML Parser supports JAXP, then it can be converted to an OSGi aware bundle by adding a BundleActivator class which registers an XML Parser Service. The utility org.osgi.util.xml.XMLParserActivator class provides this function and can be added (copied, not referenced) to any XML Parser bundle, or it can be extended and customized if desired.

702.6.1   JAR Based Services

Its functionality is based on the definition of the [5] *JAR File specification, services directory*. This specification defines a concept for service providers. A JAR file can contain an implementation of an abstractly defined service. The class (or classes) implementing the service are designated from a file in the META-INF/services directory. The name of this file is the same as the abstract service class.

The content of the UTF-8 encoded file is a list of class names separated by new lines. White space is ignored and the number sign ('#' or \u0023) is the comment character.

JAXP uses this service provider mechanism. It is therefore likely that vendors will place these service files in the META-INF/services directory.

702.6.2   XMLParserActivator

To support this mechanism, the XML Parser service provides a utility class that should be normally delivered with the OSGi Service Platform implementation. This class is a Bundle Activator and must start when the bundle is started. This class is copied into the parser bundle, and *not* imported.

The start method of the utility BundleActivator class will look in the META-INF/services service provider directory for the files javax.xml.parsers.SAXParserFactory (SAXFACTORYNAME) or javax.xml.parsers.DocumentBuilderFactory (DOMFACTORYNAME). The full path name is specified in the constants SAXCLASSFILE and DOMCLASSFILE respectively.

If either of these files exist, the utility BundleActivator class will parse the contents according to the specification. A service provider file can contain multiple class names. Each name is read and a new instance is created. The following example shows the possible content of such a file:

```
# ACME example SAXParserFactory file
com.acme.saxparser.SAXParserFast          # Fast
com.acme.saxparser.SAXParserValidating  # Validates
```

Both the javax.xml.parsers.SAXParserFactory and the javax.xml.parsers.DocumentBuilderFactory provide methods that describe the features of the parsers they can create. The XMLParserActivator activator will use these methods to set the values of the properties, as defined in *Properties* on page 475, that describe the instances.

702.6.3   Adapting an Existing JAXP Compatible Parser

To incorporate this bundle activator into a XML Parser Bundle, do the following:

- If SAX parsing is supported, create a /META-INF/services/javax.xml.parsers.SAXParserFactory resource file containing the class names of the SAXParserFactory classes.
- If DOM parsing is supported, create a /META-INF/services/javax.xml.parsers.DocumentBuilderFactory file containing the fully qualified class names of the DocumentBuilderFactory classes.
- Create manifest file which imports the packages org.w3c.dom, org.xml.sax, and javax.xml.parsers.
- Add a Bundle-Activator header to the manifest pointing to the XMLParserActivator, the sub-class that was created, or a fully custom one.
- If the parsers support attributes, properties, or features that should be registered as properties so they can be searched, extend the XMLParserActivator class and override setSAXProperties(javax.xml.parsers.SAXParserFactory,Hashtable) and setDOMProperties(javax.xml.parsers.DocumentBuilderFactory,Hashtable).
- Ensure that custom properties are put into the Hashtable object. JAXP does not provide a way for XMLParserActivator to query the parser to find out what properties were added.
- Bundles that extend the XMLParserActivator class must call the original methods via super to correctly initialize the XML Parser Service properties.
- Compile this class into the bundle.
- Install the new XML Parser Service bundle.
- Ensure that the org.osgi.util.xml.XMLParserActivator class is contained in the bundle.

702.7   Usage of JAXP

A single bundle should export the JAXP, SAX, and DOM APIs. The version of contained packages must be appropriately labeled. JAXP 1.1 or later is required which references SAX 2 and DOM 2. See [4] *JAXP* for the exact version dependencies.

This specification is related to related packages as defined in the JAXP 1.1 document. Table 702.1 contains the expected minimum versions.

Table 702.1   JAXP 1.1 minimum package versions

Package	Minimum Version
javax.xml.parsers	1.1
org.xml.sax	2.0
org.xml.sax.helpers	2.0
org.xsml.sax.ext	1.0
org.w3c.dom	2.0

The Xerces project from the Apache group, [6] *Xerces 2 Java Parser*, contains a number libraries that implement the necessary APIs. These libraries can be wrapped in a bundle to provide the relevant packages.

702.8   Security

A centralized XML parser is likely to see sensitive information from other bundles. Provisioning an XML parser should therefore be limited to trusted bundles. This security can be achieved by providing ServicePermission[javax.xml.parsers.DocumentBuilderFactory | javax.xml.parsers.SAXFactory, REGISTER] to only trusted bundles.

Using an XML parser is a common function, and ServicePermission[javax.xml.parsers.DOMParserFactory | javax.xml.parsers.SAXFactory, GET] should not be restricted.

The XML parser bundle will need FilePermission[<<ALL FILES>>,READ] for parsing of files because it is not known beforehand where those files will be located. This requirement further implies that the XML parser is a system bundle that must be fully trusted.

702.9   org.osgi.util.xml

XML Parser Package Version 1.0.

Bundles wishing to use this package must list the package in the Import-Package header of the bundle's manifest. For example:

```
Import-Package: org.osgi.util.xml; version="[1.0,2.0)"
```

702.9.1   **public class XMLParserActivator**
implements BundleActivator , ServiceFactory

A BundleActivator class that allows any JAXP compliant XML Parser to register itself as an OSGi parser service. Multiple JAXP compliant parsers can concurrently register by using this BundleActivator class. Bundles who wish to use an XML parser can then use the framework's service registry to locate available XML Parsers with the desired characteristics such as validating and namespace-aware.

The services that this bundle activator enables a bundle to provide are:

- javax.xml.parsers.SAXParserFactory(SAXFACTORYNAME)
- javax.xml.parsers.DocumentBuilderFactory(DOMFACTORYNAME)

The algorithm to find the implementations of the abstract parsers is derived from the JAR file specifications, specifically the Services API.

An XMLParserActivator assumes that it can find the class file names of the factory classes in the following files:

- /META-INF/services/javax.xml.parsers.SAXParserFactory is a file contained in a jar available to the runtime which contains the implementation class name(s) of the SAXParserFactory.
- /META-INF/services/javax.xml.parsers.DocumentBuilderFactory is a file contained in a jar available to the runtime which contains the implementation class name(s) of the DocumentBuilderFactory

If either of the files does not exist, XMLParserActivator assumes that the parser does not support that parser type.

XMLParserActivator attempts to instantiate both the SAXParserFactory and the DocumentBuilderFactory. It registers each factory with the framework along with service properties:

- PARSER_VALIDATING- indicates if this factory supports validating parsers. It's value is a Boolean.
- PARSER_NAMESPACEAWARE- indicates if this factory supports namespace aware parsers It's value is a Boolean.

Individual parser implementations may have additional features, properties, or attributes which could be used to select a parser with a filter. These can be added by extending this class and overriding the setSAXProperties and setDOMProperties methods.

Concurrency   Thread-safe

702.9.1.1   **public static final String DOMCLASSFILE = "/META-INF/services/ javax.xml.parsers.DocumentBuilderFactory"**

Fully qualified path name of DOM Parser Factory Class Name file

702.9.1.2   **public static final String DOMFACTORYNAME = "javax.xml.parsers.DocumentBuilderFactory"**

Filename containing the DOM Parser Factory Class name. Also used as the basis for the SERVICE_PID registration property.

702.9.1.3   **public static final String PARSER_NAMESPACEAWARE = "parser.namespaceAware"**

Service property specifying if factory is configured to support namespace aware parsers. The value is of type Boolean.

702.9.1.4   **public static final String PARSER_VALIDATING = "parser.validating"**

Service property specifying if factory is configured to support validating parsers. The value is of type Boolean.

702.9.1.5   **public static final String SAXCLASSFILE = "/META-INF/services/ javax.xml.parsers.SAXParserFactory"**

Fully qualified path name of SAX Parser Factory Class Name file

702.9.1.6   **public static final String SAXFACTORYNAME = "javax.xml.parsers.SAXParserFactory"**

Filename containing the SAX Parser Factory Class name. Also used as the basis for the SERVICE_PID registration property.

702.9.1.7   **public XMLParserActivator( )**

702.9.1.8   **public Object getService(Bundle bundle, ServiceRegistration registration)**

bundle   The bundle using the service.

registration   The ServiceRegistration object for the service.

☐   Creates a new XML Parser Factory object.

A unique XML Parser Factory object is returned for each call to this method.

The returned XML Parser Factory object will be configured for validating and namespace aware support as specified in the service properties of the specified ServiceRegistration object. This method can be overridden to configure additional features in the returned XML Parser Factory object.

Returns   A new, configured XML Parser Factory object or null if a configuration error was encountered

702.9.1.9   **public void setDOMProperties(DocumentBuilderFactory factory, Hashtable props)**

factory   - the DocumentBuilderFactory object

props   - Hashtable of service properties.

☐   Set the customizable DOM Parser Service Properties.

This method attempts to instantiate a validating parser and a namespace aware parser to determine if the parser can support those features. The appropriate properties are then set in the specified props object.

This method can be overridden to add additional DOM2 features and properties. If you want to be able to filter searches of the OSGi service registry, this method must put a key, value pair into the properties object for each feature or property. For example, properties.put("http://www.acme.com/features/foo", Boolean.TRUE);

702.9.1.10   **public void setSAXProperties(SAXParserFactory factory, Hashtable properties)**

factory - the SAXParserFactory object

properties - the properties object for the service

☐ Set the customizable SAX Parser Service Properties.

This method attempts to instantiate a validating parser and a namespace aware parser to determine if the parser can support those features. The appropriate properties are then set in the specified properties object.

This method can be overridden to add additional SAX2 features and properties. If you want to be able to filter searches of the OSGi service registry, this method must put a key, value pair into the properties object for each feature or property. For example, properties.put("http://www.acme.com/features/foo", Boolean.TRUE);

702.9.1.11   **public void start(BundleContext context) throws Exception**

context The execution context of the bundle being started.

☐ Called when this bundle is started so the Framework can perform the bundle-specific activities necessary to start this bundle. This method can be used to register services or to allocate any resources that this bundle needs.

This method must complete and return to its caller in a timely manner.

This method attempts to register a SAX and DOM parser with the Framework's service registry.

Throws Exception– If this method throws an exception, this bundle is marked as stopped and the Framework will remove this bundle's listeners, unregister all services registered by this bundle, and release all services used by this bundle.

702.9.1.12   **public void stop(BundleContext context) throws Exception**

context The execution context of the bundle being stopped.

☐ This method has nothing to do as all active service registrations will automatically get unregistered when the bundle stops.

Throws Exception– If this method throws an exception, the bundle is still marked as stopped, and the Framework will remove the bundle's listeners, unregister all services registered by the bundle, and release all services used by the bundle.

702.9.1.13   **public void ungetService(Bundle bundle, ServiceRegistration registration, Object service)**

bundle The bundle releasing the service.

registration The ServiceRegistration object for the service.

service The XML Parser Factory object returned by a previous call to the getService method.

☐ Releases a XML Parser Factory object.

702.10   References

[1]   *XML*
http://www.w3.org/XML

[2]   *SAX*
       http://www.saxproject.org/

[3]   *DOM Java Language Binding*
       http://www.w3.org/TR/REC-DOM-Level-1/java-language-binding.html

[4]   *JAXP*
       http://java.sun.com/xml/jaxp

[5]   *JAR File specification, services directory*
       http://java.sun.com/j2se/1.4/docs/guide/jar/jar.html

[6]   *Xerces 2 Java Parser*
       http://xml.apache.org/xerces2-j

End Of Document